WITHDRAWN

Chamber Music

Chamber Music

An International Guide to Works and Their Instrumentation

VICTOR RANGEL-RIBEIRO AND ROBERT MARKEL

Computer Program Designed and Developed by Glenn H. Babakian

Facts On File
New York • Oxford

Chamber Music: An International Guide to Works and Their Instrumentation

Facts On File, Inc.
460 Park Avenue South
New York NY 10016

Library of Congress Cataloging-in-Publication Data
Rangel-Ribeiro, Victor.
Chamber music : an international guide to works and their instrumentation / Victor Rangel-Ribeiro.
p. cm.
Includes index.
ISBN 0-8160-2296-8
1. Chamber music—Bibliography. I. Title.
ML 128.C4R3 1993
016.785'0026—dc20 92-43442

A British CIP catalogue record for this book is available from the British Library.

Facts On File books are available at special discounts when purchased in bulk quantities for businesses, associations, institutions or sales promotions. Please call our Special Sales Department in New York at 212-683-2244 or 800/322-8755.

Text design by Ron Monteleone
Jacket design by Victore Design Works
Composition by ComCom
Manufacturing by the Maple-Vail Book Manufacturing Group

Printed in the United States of America

10 9 8 7 6 5 4 3 2 1

This book is printed on acid-free paper.

To lovers of Chamber Music
around the world and to those who
make it possible.

CONTENTS

ACKNOWLEDGMENTS

A special bravo to Glenn Babakian, who constantly improvised computer solutions to the musical questions we threw at him. Our thanks also to Eva Ribeiro Murray; to Jerome Kitzke of the American Music Center; and to the staff at the Music Division, New York Public Library of the Performing Arts at Lincoln Center, all of whom greatly helped in our research.

We would also like to offer a round of applause to our Facts On File editor, Phil Saltz, who conducted us with a steady beat and a first-rate musician's eye on the details.

Research for this book has been made possible by the sponsorship of the New York Foundation for the Arts, with funding provided by the Josephine Bay Paul and C. Michael Paul Foundation, Inc.

PREFACE

This book is an answer to a question that has increasingly plagued musicians in our time: Given the variety of instruments now in use, where does one turn for a full list of chamber music works written for one's own instrument? Publishers' catalogues are of little help, since each house lists only its own publications, and (in the United States at least) often only the "best-sellers." While a few specialized catalogues for some instruments do exist, they ignore the vast bulk of the repertoire. Until now, there has not been any single book that filled the void.

In planning *Chamber Music: An International Guide to Works and Their Instrumentation*, we decided to present as broad a sweep of the repertoire as possible, from its beginnings in the pre-Baroque era right down to music written in 1992. *Chamber Music* is therefore both comprehensive and up to date.

It is also innovative in ways that make good sense. For example, to get a general idea of the types of combinations Beethoven wrote for—string trios and quartets, piano trios, and works for winds—one need merely turn to Part III. In that section, our Master Index, we list all composers alphabetically. Find Beethoven, run your finger horizontally along that line, and you'll see what *types* of chamber music he wrote. To get *detailed* information on his output, however, check the listings under Beethoven in Part II. There you will find the information you need: opus numbers, keys, dates of composition or publication, instrumentation, and whether the works have been published by a single publisher or by several. The same holds true for any other composer. No need to flip pages back and forth as you peck and hunt through trios, quartets, quintets, etc., for strings, for winds, and for combinations of the two, with or without keyboard and sundry other instruments.

Setting the Limits

Our listings cover the sweep of the chamber music repertoire as it has developed over the past 450 years—the sweep of it, but not all of it. To have included every composition that was published in all that time would have defeated our purpose, which was to produce a handy reference work of value to the composers and performers of today.

In setting the limits, we decided to focus on music for three or more instruments, ignoring the duo and solo repertoire. The upper limit, originally set at 14 instruments, began to creep upward, as we discovered that many contemporary composers were writing works for larger ensembles. So the limit now stands at 20, and is holding firm.

We narrowed the field further by stipulating that the music be for ensembles of diverse instruments. For example, a work for two violins and viola would qualify, but not one for three violins or three violas.

In dealing with Renaissance and Baroque music, however, we have listed works calling for three viols or three gambas or three recorders, since these instruments come in different sizes and constitute a family grouping.

Time, we found, had been working in our favor, as over the centuries it separated the wheat from the chaff: The less durable composers and their works had been first neglected in the concert hall, and then dropped from their publishers' lists. Even with the most famous, time took its toll. Hence, while Bach, Beethoven, and Mozart held pride of place in every major catalogue, until recently not all their works were available to the general public or to the average performer. Not, that is, until the youthful or less-favored compositions began to be valued for the light they shed on the master and his musical development.

Going Beyond the Catalogue Listings

Could current catalogue listings then be our criteria as to which works would be included and which excluded? Not entirely, but they could provide a basis. So we combed the listings in more than a hundred catalogues, and came up with close to 8,000 chamber works. Then we checked this list against three major reference works—*Cobbett's Cyclopedic Survey of Chamber Music* (2d ed., London: Oxford University Press, 3 vols., 1963); *Baker's Biographical Dictionary of Musicians*, ed. Nicolas Slonimsky (7th ed., New York: Schirmer Books, 1984), and the *New Grove's Dictionary of Music and Musicians* (London: Macmillan; Washington, D.C.: Grove's Dictionaries of Music, 1980).

As a first step, we looked at minor composers from the past whose works were no longer being listed in current catalogues, and reinstated those of historic significance. Focusing now on composers of major stature, we added works that, for one reason or another, had been omitted from the trade catalogues now in use, listing the last known publisher that we could find.

With 20th-century composers, we found that if a publishing house has a miniature score for sale, chances are that it has the set of performance parts as well, either for sale or for rental. We also found that materials available for sale one year may be withdrawn and placed on rental the next.

1800 as Turning Point

By the end of the 18th century, several favored instruments had already become obsolete—for example, the recorder, the harpsichord, and the gamba—and new instruments, such as the clarinet, were already much in use. So we decided to treat the end of the 18th century as a turning point. There was a second reason for this decision. We show the instruments in a grid. To have listed Renaissance, Baroque, and modern instruments on the same grid would have made it almost impossible to read.

For easier reference, therefore, we have divided the vast chamber music output of the past—some 8,000 compositions are represented here—into two sections. Part I consists of works written by composers who lived out the bulk of their lives in the 18th century or earlier; Part II consists largely of works written from 1800 on.

About the Composers, and Where They Fall

We say "largely" because we have not separated pre-1800 works by Beethoven from those he composed after that date, nor did we split the works of other composers of his time. Instead, some hard decisions had to be made. Although Beethoven's life neatly straddles both the 18th and 19th centuries, his major works fall in the latter period, and even his earlier compositions are forward-looking.

Beethoven's works, therefore, belong in Part II. Joseph Haydn, on the other hand, although he lived until 1809, is essentially an 18th-century composer, and that's where you'll find him, in Part I, along with his brother Michael and a certain Wolfgang Amadeus. A lesser-known Wolfgang Amadeus Mozart, born in 1791, can be found in Part II.

The Bach family posed a very special problem. Good Sebastian and his legitimate progeny, of course, fitted neatly in Part I, where their works are strongly represented. But where does one put the renegade son P.D.Q.? The fact that he lived his entire life backward (1807–1742?) would put him in Part I, but he earned a proud place in Part II because his posthumous output continues undiminished to this day. Long may his ghost continue to write.

Some composers who have been listed in Part I (notably Mozart) have also managed to get themselves listed in Part II. That has happened when their compositions have been transcribed or rearranged by other hands for instruments that are more characteristic of our own time (for example, for brass instruments, including tuba).

About the Continuo as a Single Entity, and Baroque Music in General

In counting the number of instruments called for in a Baroque composition, we have counted the basso continuo as one. For this reason, Baroque duo sonatas are not included in our volume, although in reality they are performed by three players.

Nor is the gamba listed separately when it is merely performing its role in the continuo. We list it in its own column, however, whenever the composer has assigned it an independent role to play.

About Baroque Concerti and Concerti Grossi

Instrumental ensembles varied in size in the Baroque period, and many of the works that have come down to us can be performed either by large or by small chamber ensembles. To many, a small-scale *Messiah* would be unthinkable because of the size of the forces Handel himself brought together for his performances, and also because of the grandeur of the work. On the other hand, while Handel scored some of his *concerti grossi* for large orchestral forces, others within the same opus number were designed to be played by smaller groups. We have included the latter in our listings.

Contemporary records indicate that J.S. Bach performed some of his Brandenburg concerti—notably numbers 4 and 5—with the handful of musicians he had at his disposal at that time. We have included those two but omitted the others in the Brandenburg set that obviously require a much larger ensemble.

As for Bach's concerti for solo instruments and orchestra, they could all have been included, notably those for one or two violins and for one or more harpsichords. They have the intimacy inherent in all chamber music, and would benefit from being performed with a reduced body of strings. The same can be said, with somewhat less conviction, of the concerti by Antonio Vivaldi. We refrained from including these works, however, preferring to leave so personal a decision to the performers.

About Quartet, Quatuor, Quartetto, and Other Mysteries

The listings in *Chamber Music* have been culed from well over 100 catalogues published in a variety of European languages; and while two violinists, a viola player, and a cellist may be a Frenchman's *quatuor,* to an Italian they are a *quartetto.* With contemporary composers, we have retained the term used by their publisher of record. Because of the international nature of publishing today, this sometimes leads to two or more terms, at least one of them foreign, being used to describe the same type of ensemble. Thus Marc Neikrug, American composer, has had a *Streichquartett* published by Bärenreiter in Germany and a string quartet (his second) published by Boosey and Hawkes in the United States.

With composers from an earlier period, such as Beethoven, the problem is different. Their works are in the public doman, and the very same piece of music may be available from publishers in half-a-dozen countries. In such cases we have described them by their generic English names—as string quartets, or quintets, or whatever.

Occasionally you may come across an entry for Composer X that lists his Quartet No. 5, but not numbers 1–4. What happened to them is one of the mysteries we set out to solve. Extensive talks with composers, publishers, and agents revealed the following probable reasons:

1. Quartets 1–4 are languishing in manuscript, the publisher having deemed them unworthy of publication;
2. They were published but withdrawn, having been deemed unworthy by the composer;
3. They were published, but stillborn, having been deemed unworthy by the public.

Take your pick. Whatever the demerits of the other works, however, Quartet No. 5 stands as a monument to X's genius.

Descriptive Titles: To Der or Die

Beneath each composer's name the titles of his compositions are arranged alphabetically. While we have retained definite as well as indefinite articles—*a, an, the* in English; *der, die, das* in German, etc.—these have been ignored in alphabetization. Thus, under Throgmorton, Loretta, her "Get a Life!" will precede "A Song for Morpheus," but follow "The Easy Thing to Do."

*About Our So-Flexible Composers****

Lastly a word about some 20th-century works where the composer has set down the notes to be played, or jotted down a general set of directions, but has left the precise choice of instruments to the performers. How to fit into our precise grid a work that could be performed by any one of several hundred combinations? We've taken the easy way out and marked such works with a triple asterisk: ***.

When you see a title followed by three asterisks, remember—you get to decide which instruments will play.

Victor Rangel-Ribeiro
Robert Markel
New York

HOW TO USE THIS DIRECTORY TO FIND MUSIC FOR YOUR INSTRUMENT

Parts I and II

The reason why computers are able to track down data so quickly is their ability to latch on to a relevant bit of information and hunt for it, ignoring anything else that may crop up. *Chamber Music* makes your own search for music easier, in similar fashion, by letting you focus on your own favorite instrument and follow where it leads.

1. To find music for your particular instrument, first locate it on the grid at the top of each page. Once you have found it, run your finger down the page, and you will quickly be able to determine how many works there are, who wrote them, and (if this information is available) in what year, in what key, and their approximate performance time.

2. If the instrument you play is so unusual that it does not appear on the grid itself, check that part of each listing that tells whether any unusual instruments are called for. If they are, read the comment that appears immediately below the listing; it will tell you which unusual instruments are being used and what substitutions may be made.

3. When the title of a composition is followed by three asterisks—***—it means that either the composer has left the choice of instruments to the performer, or that the instrumentation has not been specified in the catalogue.

4. Year: Wherever possible we have given the year in which a composition was completed. Where this was not available we have provided the year of first publication.

5. Duration: Not all contemporary composers specify the desired performance time of their works; we have provided timings where they have been available.

6. Numbers in any column tell how many instruments of that particular type are called for in the score. For example, "11" in the violin column means a total of 11 violins all told. However, the same is not true in the percussion section (see number 7 below).

7. A lone percussionist may play several instruments in the course of a piece. (In fact, a work exists that calls on one performer to play 99 of them.) A number in the percussion column will tell how many percussionists are actually needed, irrespective of the number of instruments they will be called on to play.

8. Wind instruments: Flutes of all sizes are grouped together in a single column, as are clarinets, saxophones, and bassoons. A number in a column, such as "2," means that two instruments are being used. If no comment follows the listing, then the instruments are standard (i.e., B-flat clarinets, alto saxophones). If, however, one or both instruments should not be standard, that would be noted in a comment (for example, clarinet in C; bass clarinet; tenor sax; contrabassoon).

9. Voice: When a composition calls for just one voice, and that voice is specified, we use the following codes to identify it:

S = Soprano	M = Mezzo
T = Tenor	B = Baritone
H = High	L = Low
F = Female	N = Narrator

If a score calls for a bass, male, or medium voice, we use the figure "1" in the voice column and specify the type of voice in a comment.

A "1" or any other number in the voice column not followed by a comment means that the composer has specified the number of voices, but not their type.

10. Publishers are shown in abbreviated form, usually by the first five letters of their name. For example: Breit stands for Breitkopf and Hartel; Boose for Boosey and Hawkes. A key to all such abbreviations and a complete list of publishers may be found beginning on page 269.

Note: Composers are listed alphabetically in Part I, which includes the Renaissance, Baroque, and Classical periods, as well as in Part II, which comes down to our own time. A few "early" composers are also listed in Part II, with such of their works as have been transcribed for modern instruments.

Part III

Part III is our master index. Here, all the composers who appear in Parts I and II appear in a consolidated alphabetical index running vertically down the left-hand side of the page. Horizontally listed across the top of the page you will find the various types of chamber music: trios, quartets, quintets, etc. for strings, for winds, for brass, or for keyboard in combination with any of these.

One can use the index two ways. To find out which composers wrote specifically for, say, string quintets, find the heading for string quintets at the top of the first page in Part III and run your finger down that column, page after page. To find out whether Chopin wrote any string quintets, find Chopin in the left-hand column, then run your finger horizontally across the page till you come to the string quintet column. If that column is blank, he wrote none.

PART I

Composers to the Time of Haydn and Mozart

	Year Composed or Published	Key	Duration	Viols	Early Winds	Violin	Viola	Cello	Double Bass	Barytone	Gamba	Basso continuo	Harpsichord	Piano	Organ	Guitar/Lute	Harp	Recorder	Piccolo	Flute	Oboe	English Horn	Clarinet	Bassoon/Contrabassoon	Horn	Trumpet	Trombone	Percussion	Voice	Unusual Instruments	Publisher
ABEL, KARL F. (1723–1787)																															
Quartet		G				1	1	1												1											BScho
Quartet		G				1	1	1												1											BScho
Quartet, Op 12 No. 2		A				1	1	1												1											VarPb
ADSON, JOHN (?–1640)																															
Courtly Masquing Ayres																		6													MusRa
AICHINGER, GREGOR (1564–1628)																															
Canzon		C										1														2					Bosse
Ricercar primi toni						2	1	1																							Bosse
Ricercar primi toni (brass)																										2	2				Bosse
ALBICASTRO, HENRICUS (1661–1738)																															
Cantata: Coelestes angelici chori																															
Voice: Soprano or tenor						2	1	1				1																	1		Amade
Sonata No. 3						2						1																			Viewe
Triosonata, Op 8						2						1																			Bären
ALBINONI, TOMASO (1671–1750)																															
12 Triosonatas ("Balletti"), Op 3						2						1																			Kunze
Balletti e sonate a tre, Op 8 Nos. 1-2						2		1				1																			Kunze
Balletto e sonata a tre						2		1				1																			Press
Sonata, Op 2 No. 1		G				2	2	1	1			1																			Kunze
Sonata, Op 2 No. 2						2	2	1	1			1																			Kunze
Sonata a tre (sonata seconda)						2		1				1																			Press
Sonata a tre, Op 1 No. 3		A				2						1																			Nagel
Sonata a tre, Op 1 No. 6		a				2		1					1																		Dobli
Sonata da camera a tre, Op 8 No. 4b		B♭				2						1																			VarPb
Sonata da chiesa a tre, Op 8 No. 4a		g				2						1																			VarPb
ALBRECHTSBERGER, JOHANN G. (1736–1809)																															
2 Fugues						2	1	1																							Amade
Adagio e fuga						2	2	1																							Dobli
Adagio e fuga							2	2																							Dobli
Adagio e fuga		A♭				2	2	1																							Dobli
Adagio e fuga (for double quartet)		C				4	2	2																							Dobli
Adagio e fuga		D				2	1	1																							Dobli
Adagio e fuga		F				3	1	1																							Dobli
Divertimento		A				2	1	1																							Dobli
Divertimento (with bass)		D				2			1																						Amade
Divertimento a tre							1	1	1																						Dobli
Divertimento a tre *Unus Instr:* Violino piccolo		F				2	1																							1	Dobli
Partita		D							1	1										1											Amade
Sonata 1		c				1	1	1																							Dobli
Sonata 2		E♭				1	1	1																							Dobli
String Quartet		G				2	1	1																							Dobli
Trio		G				2		1																							Dobli
Trio 1		C				1	1	1																							Dobli
Trio 2		A				1	1	1																							Dobli
Trio 3		F				1	1	1																							Dobli
ANTES, JOHN (1740–1811)																															
3 Trios, Op 3						2		1																							Boose
ARIOSTI, ATTILIO (1666–1729)																															
La rosa						2						1																	H		DeutV
BACH, C. P. E. (1714–1788)																															
6 Sonatas																				2			2	1	2						MusRa

	Year Composed or Published	Key	Duration	Viols	Early Winds	Violin	Viola	Cello	Double Bass	Barytone	Gamba	Basso continuo	Harpsichord	Piano	Organ	Guitar/Lute	Harp	Recorder	Piccolo	Flute	Oboe	English Horn	Clarinet	Bassoon/Contrabassoon	Horn	Trumpet	Trombone	Percussion	Voice	Unusual Instruments	Publisher
BACH, C. P. E. *(continued)*																															
6 Trios	1778					1		1						1																	Bären
Quartet, Wq 93		a					1	1						1						1											Bären
Quartet, Wq 94		B♭					1	1						1						1											Bären
Quartet, Wq 95		G					1	1						1						1											Bären
Sonata, Wq 90 No.3		C				1		1						1																	Bären
Sonatina		C				2	1	1						1						2											BoteB
Sonatina, Wq 108		E♭				2	1	1					1							2											Bären
Trio		G				2		1						1																	Breit
Trio, Wq 161		B♭				1						1								1											Peter
BACH, J. C. (1732–1795)																															
Sonata		D				1	1					1								1											Bären
BACH, JOHANN C. (1735–1782)																															
6 Easy Trios, Op 4						2		1																							Noetz
Flute Quartet		A				1	1	1												1											MusRa
Flute Quartet		C				1	1	1												1											MusRa
Flute Quartet		D				1	1	1												1											MusRa
Flute Quartet, Op 8 No. 1		C				1	1	1												1											VarPb
Notturno						2						1																			Kunze
Oboe Quartet						1	1	1													1										Kunze
Quartet		C				1	1	1					1																		BScho
Quartet, Op 8 No. 2		E♭				2	1	1																							SudDM
Quartet, Op 8 No. 3		E♭				1	1	1												1											Bären
Quartet, Op 8 No. 5		G				1	1	1												1											Bären
Quartet, Op 19 No. 1							1	1												2											MusRa
Quartet, Op 19 No. 3						1	1	1												1											MusRa
Quartet, Op 20 No. 2		D					1	1												2											Bären
Quintet		D				1		1					1							1	1										Bären
Quintet		F				1	1	1					1								1										BScho
Quintet, Op 11 No. 1		C				1	1					1								1	1										MusRa
Quintet, Op 11 No. 2		G				1	1					1								1	1										MusRa
Quintet, Op 11 No. 3		F				1	1					1								1	1										MusRa
Quintet, Op 11 No. 5		A				1	1					1								1	1										MusRa
Quintet, Op 11 No. 6						1	1					1								1	1										Bären
Sextet		C				1		1				1									1				2						MusRa
Sinfonie																										3	3				Bären
Sonata		F				1		1												1											Moeck
Sonata No. 1		F				1		1					1																		Dobli
Sonata No. 2		G				1		1					1																		Dobli
Sonata No. 3		D				1		1					1																		Dobli
Sonata No. 4		C				1		1					1																		Dobli
Sonata No. 5		A				1		1					1																		Dobli
Sonata No. 6		E♭				1		1					1																		Dobli
Trio		B♭				2	1																								VarPb
Trio (with flute and b.c.)		B♭				1						1								1											SudDM
Trio		C						1												2											Amade
Trio		D				2	1																								VarPb
Trio		E♭				2	1																								VarPb
Trio		G										1								2											SudDM
Trio, Op 15 No. 1		C				1		1					1																		Dobli
Trio, Op 15 No. 2		A				1		1					1																		Dobli
Triosonata		B♭				1								1						1											Hug
BACH, JOHANN S. (1685–1750)																															
10 Canons from The Musical Offering, BWV 1079	1747					1		1					1							1											Dobli
14 Canons, BWV 1087						2							2																		Bären

	Year Composed or Published	Key	Duration	Viols	Early Winds	Violin	Viola	Cello	Double Bass	Barytone	Gamba	Basso continuo	Harpsichord	Piano	Organ	Guitar/Lute	Harp	Recorder	Piccolo	Flute	Oboe	English Horn	Clarinet	Bassoon/Contrabassoon	Horn	Trumpet	Trombone	Percussion	Voice	Unusual Instruments	Publisher
BACH, JOHANN S. *(continued)*																															
15 Terzetti						2		1																							Inter
Adagio (from Goldberg Variations)						1	1	1																							Hinri
Air		D				1										3															Dobli
Art of the Fugue, BWV 1080	1750					2	1	1																							VarPb
Bereite dich, Zion *Unus Instr:* Oboe d'amore						1						1																	A	1	Bären
Betrachte meine Seel' *Voice:* Bass						2										1													1		Dobli
Brandenburg Concerto No. 1, BWV 1046	1721	F				3	1	1				1									3			1	2						VarPb
Brandenburg Concerto No. 2, BWV 1047	1721	F				3	1		1			1								1	1				1						VarPb
Brandenburg Concerto No. 3, BWV 1048	1721	G				3	3	3				1																			VarPb
Brandenburg Concerto No. 4, BWV 1049	1721	G				3	1	1	1			1						2													VarPb
Brandenburg Concerto No. 5, BWV 1050	1721	D				2	1	1	1				1							1											VarPb
Brandenburg Concerto No. 6, BWV 1051	1721	B♭					2	1			2	1																			VarPb
Canonic Trio, BWV 1040	1716	F				1						1									1										McGMa
Complete Arias and Sinfonias (Vol. 1-5) *Voices:* Soprano/alto												1									1								1		MusRa
Complete Arias and Sinfonias (Vol. 6)												1									1								A		MusRa
Complete Arias and Sinfonias (Vol. 7)												1									1								A		MusRa
Complete Arias and Sinfonias (Vol. 8)												1									1								T		MusRa
Complete Arias and Sinfonias (Vol. 9) *Voices:* Tenor/bass												1									1								1		MusRa
Complete Arias and Sinfonias (Vol. 10)												1									1								B		MusRa
Contrapunctus VIII (Art of the Fugue)						1	1	1																							Peter
Contrapunctus XIII (Art of the Fugue)						1	1	1																							Peter
Duets from the Cantatas (Vol. 1) *Voices:* Soprano and alto									1			1			1														2		Hug
Duets from the Cantatas (Vol. 2) *Voices:* Soprano and alto. *Unus Instr:* Oboe d'amore						2	1	1				1	1							1	1								2	1	Hug
Duets from the Cantatas (Vol. 3) *Voices:* Soprano and alto. *Unus Instr:* Oboe d'amore						2	1	1				1			1						1								2	1	Hug
Seufzer, Tränen, BWV 21	1714											1									1								S		Bären
Sheep Can Safely Graze, BWV 208	1716											1						2											S		Bären
Sonate, BWV 1037	1720	C				2						1																			Foeti
Triosonata *Comment:* Oboe d'amore may substitute for one violin		b				2						1																			Hug
Triosonata, BWV 1038	1720	G				1						1								1											Bären
Triosonata, BWV 1039	1720	G										1								2											Var Pb
Village Music (from Peasant Cantata)																1		3													Noetz
Virga Jesse Floruit, BWV 243a *Voices:* Soprano and bass	1723											1																	2		Bären
Wedding Cantata, BWV 216 *Voices:* Soprano and alto	1728							1					1							2	1								2		VarPb

	Year Composed or Published	Key	Duration	Viols	Early Winds	Violin	Viola	Cello	Double Bass	Barytone	Gamba	Basso continuo	Harpsichord	Piano	Organ	Guitar/Lute	Harp	Recorder	Piccolo	Flute	Oboe	English Horn	Clarinet	Bassoon/Contrabassoon	Horn	Trumpet	Trombone	Percussion	Voice	Unusual Instruments	Publisher
BACH, JOHANN S. *(continued)*																															
Weichet nur (Wedding Cantata), BWV 202	1730					2	1					1									1								S		Bären
BACH, WILHELM F. (1710–1784)																															
Trio No. 1, S 12/48		D										1								2											Breit
Trio No. 2, S 12/47		D										1								2											Breit
Trio No. 3, S 12/50		B♭				1						1								1											Breit
Trio No. 4, S 12/49		a											1							2											Breit
BARGAGNI, O (?–?)																															
Canzon ("La Monteverde")																										2	2				MusRa
BÄRMANN, HEINRICH (1784–1847)																															
Clarinet Quintet, Op 23 No. 3		E♭				2	1	1															1								MusRa
BARTOLINI, ORINDIO (1580–1640)																															
Canzon 30																										4	4				MusRa
Doppelchörige Canzonen (with works by Gabrieli) *Comment:* May also be played by brass instruments	1608			8																											Noetz
BASSANI, GIOVANNI B. (1647–1716)																															
Sonata a tre, Op 5 No. 9		C				2		1					1																		Dobli
BEECKE, IGNAZ VON (1733–1803)																															
Quintett						1	1	1												1	1										SudDM
Streichquartett 6		G				2	1	1																							Bären
BEER, JOHANN (1655–1700)																															
Concerto a 4						2						1													2						Hug
BENDA, JIRI A. (1722–1795)																															
Triosonata		E				2								1																	MABoh
Triosonata		E				2								1																	MABoh
BERNHARD, CHRISTOPH (1627–1692)																															
Aus der Tiefen (Out of the Depths)						2						1																	S		Bären
Fürchtet euch nicht (Fear not)						2						1												1					S		Bären
Jauchzet dem Herrn (Praise the Lord)						2						1																	S		Bären
BERNIER, NICOLAS (1664–1734)																															
Le café						1						1																	S		Bären
BERTALI, ANTONIO (1605–1669)																															
6 Sonatas												1														2	3				MusRa
Sonata a tre, No. 1		d				2						1															1				MusRa
Sonata a tre, No. 3		a				2						1												1							MusRa
BESOZZI, ALESSANDRO (1702–1793)																															
6 Trios						1		1													1										Kunze
Sonata a tre, Op 7 No. 6																					2			1							McGMa
BIBER, HEINRICH (1644–1704)																															
Nisi Dominus (Psalm 127) *Voice:* Bass						1						1																	1		DeutV
Sonata a tre		C				2						1															1				MusRa
Sonata a 7	1668	C										1														6		1			VarPb
Sonata No. 1		C				2						1														2					MusRa
Sonata No. 4		C				1						1														1					MusRa
Sonata No. 10		F				1						1														1					MusRa

	Year Composed or Published	Key	Duration	Viols	Early Winds	Violin	Viola	Cello	Double Bass	Barytone	Gamba	Basso continuo	Harpsichord	Piano	Organ	Guitar/Lute	Harp	Recorder	Piccolo	Flute	Oboe	English Horn	Clarinet	Bassoon/Contrabassoon	Horn	Trumpet	Trombone	Percussion	Voice	Unusual Instruments	Publisher
BIBER, HEINRICH *(continued)*																															
Sonata No. 12		C				2						1														2					MusRa
Sonata Sancti Polycarpi		C										1														8		1			MusRa
BIECHTELER, MATTHIAS S. (1668–1743)																															
5 Sonatas						2						1																			Amade
BOCCHERINI, LUIGI (1743–1805)																															
2 Trios (Terzetti)						2		1																							Mercu
3 Trios, Op 38						1	1	1																							Inter
6 Trios, Op 6						2		1																							Amade
6 Trios, Op 9						2		1																							Inter
6 Trios, Op 14						1	1	1																							Zanib
6 Trios, Op 35						2		1																							BScho
6 Trios, Op 47						1	1	1																							Amade
Divertimento, Op 2 No. 3		A				2		1																							Leuck
Flute Quintet, Op 21 No. 1		D				2	1	1												1											MusRa
Flute Quintet, Op 21 No. 5		G				2	1	1												1											MusRa
Flute Quintet, Op 21 No. 6		E♭				2	1	1												1											MusRa
Quintet (with flute and oboe)		C				1	1	1												1	1										MusRa
String Quartet, Op 6 No. 1						2	1	1																							Ricor
String Quartet, Op 6 No. 2						2	1	1																							Ricor
String Quartet, Op 6 No. 3						2	1	1																							Ricor
String Quartet, Op 6 No. 4						2	1	1																							Ricor
String Quartet, Op 6 No. 5						2	1	1																							Ricor
String Quartet, Op 6 No. 6		A				2	1	1																							VarPb
String Quartet, Op 8 No. 5		D				2	1	1																							Peter
String Quartet, Op 10 No. 1						2	1	1																							Ricor
String Quartet, Op 10 No. 2		d				2	1	1																							Peter
String Quartet, Op 10 No. 6		E				2	1	1																							Peter
String Quartet, Op 27 No. 2		g				2	1	1																							Peter
String Quartet, Op 27 No. 3						2	1	1																							Ricor
String Quartet, Op 32 No. 4		A				2	1	1																							Peter
String Quartet, Op 33 No. 5		g				2	1	1																							Peter
String Quartet, Op 33 No. 6		A				2	1	1																							VarPb
String Quartet, Op 39 No. 1		C				2	1	1																							Peter
String Quartet, Op 58 No. 1						2	1	1																							Ricor
String Quartet, Op 58 No. 2						2	1	1																							Ricor
String Quartet, Op 58 No. 3						2	1	1																							Ricor
String Quartet, Op 58 No. 4						2	1	1																							Ricor
String Quartet, Op 58 No. 5						2	1	1																							Ricor
String Quartet, Op 58 No. 6						2	1	1																							Ricor
String Quintet (with 2 cellos), Op 13 No. 5		E				2	1	2																							Ricor
String Quintet (with 2 cellos), Op 20 No. 4		d				2	1	2																							Ricor
String Quintet (with 2 cellos), Op 37 No. 1		C				2	1	2																							Ricor
String Quintet (with 2 cellos), Op 37 No. 2		D				2	1	2																							Ricor
String Quintet (with 2 cellos), Op 47 No. 1						2	1	2																							Ricor
String Quintet (with 2 cellos), Op 47 No. 2		E♭				2	1	2																							Ricor
String Quintet (with 2 violas), Op 60 No. 1		C				2	2	1																							Dobli
String Quintet (with 2 violas), Op 60 No. 2		B♭				2	2	1																							Dobli

	Year Composed or Published	Key	Duration	Viols	Early Winds	Violin	Viola	Cello	Double Bass	Barytone	Gamba	Basso continuo	Harpsichord	Piano	Organ	Guitar/Lute	Harp	Recorder	Piccolo	Flute	Oboe	English Horn	Clarinet	Bassoon/Contrabassoon	Horn	Trumpet	Trombone	Percussion	Voice	Unusual Instruments	Publisher
BOCCHERINI, LUIGI *(continued)*																															
String Quintet (with 2 violas), Op 60 No. 3		A				2	2	1																							Dobli
String Quintet (with 2 violas), Op 60 No. 5		G				2	2	1																							Dobli
String Quintet (with 2 violas), Op 60 No. 6						2	2	1																							Dobli
String Quintet (with 2 violas), Op 62 No. 1		C				2	2	1																							Dobli
String Quintet (with 2 violas), Op 62 No. 2		E♭				2	2	1																							Dobli
String Quintet (with 2 violas), Op 62 No. 3		F				2	2	1																							Dobli
String Quintet (with 2 violas), Op 62 No. 4		B♭				2	2	1																							Dobli
String Quintet (with 2 violas), Op 62 No. 5		D				2	2	1																							Dobli
String Quintet (with 2 violas), Op 62 No. 6		E				2	2	1																							Dobli
Trio (Terzetto), Op 54 No. 3						2		1																							Inter
BODINUS, SEBASTIAN (1700–1753)																															
Sonata a quattro		D				1						1								1					1						Foeti
BOISMORTIER, JOSEPH B. (1689–1755)																															
Sonata, Op 34 No. 1		g										1								3											Bären
Sonata, Op 37 No. 2		e									1	1								1											Bären
Triosonata, Op 37 No. 5		a										1								1				1							MusRa
BONPORTI, FRANCESCO A. (1672–1749)																															
Sonata a tre, Op 4 No. 2	1696	b				2						1																			Dobli
BRADE, WILLIAM (1560–1630)																															
Newe ausserlesene Paduanen . . .	1614			6																											Noetz
Newe . . . Branden, Intraden . . . (Vol. II) *Unus Instr:* 2 Cornettos																											3			2	MusRa
Newe . . . Branden, Intraden . . . (Vol. III) *Unus Instr:* 2 Cornettos																											3			2	MusRa
Newe lustige Volten, Couranten . . .	1621			5																											Noetz
Newe . . . Paduanen, Galliarden . . . *Comment:* May also be played by recorders or string or wind quintet	1609			5																											Noetz
BRESCIANELLO, GIOVANNI A. (1690–1757)																															
Concerto a tre no. 5		A				2		1																							Bären
Concerto a tre no. 6		b				2		1																							Bären
BRUNETTI, GAETANO (1744–1798)																															
Quintet No. 4		D				2	1	1																1							MusRa
BUNS, BENEDICTUS (1642–1716)																															
Triosonata, Op 8 No. 3		d				2						1																			Bären
BUONAMENTE, GIOVANNI B. (1600–1642)																															
Canzon a 5 *Unus Instr:* 2 Cornettos																											3			2	MusRa
BUXTEHUDE, DIETRICH (1637–1707)																															
Dein edles Herz *Voices:* Soprano, alto, tenor, bass						2	2		1			1																	4		Merse

	Year Composed or Published	Key	Duration	Viols	Early Winds	Violin	Viola	Cello	Double Bass	Barytone	Gamba	Basso continuo	Harpsichord	Piano	Organ	Guitar/Lute	Harp	Recorder	Piccolo	Flute	Oboe	English Horn	Clarinet	Bassoon/Contrabassoon	Horn	Trumpet	Trombone	Percussion	Voice	Unusual Instruments	Publisher
BUXTEHUDE, DIETRICH *(continued)*																															
Ecce nunc benedicite domino *Voices:* Alto, 2 tenors, bass						2	1	1				1																	4		Merse
Entreisst euch, meine Sinnen						2						1																	S		Merse
Herr, auf dich traue ich (Solokantate 2)						2						1																	S		Bären
Herr, nun lässt du deinen Diener						2						1																	T		Bären
Jesu, meinens Lebens Leben *Voices:* Soprano, alto, tenor, bass						2	2		1			1								1									4		Merse
Jubilate Domino (Solokantate 7)											1	1																	A		Bären
Klaglied *Comment:* Violins may replace violas							2					1																	S		Merse
Laudate Dominum (Solokantate 9)						2			1			1																	S		Bären
Lobet, Christen, euren Heiland *Voices:* 2 sopranos, bass						2						1																	3		Bären
Mein Herz ist bereit (Solokantate 8) *Voice:* Bass						3		1				1																	1		Bären
Mit Fried und Freud ich fahr dahin *Voices:* Soprano, bass						2	1	1				1																	2		Merse
O fröhliche Stunden, o herrliche Zeit *Voices:* 2 sopranos, alto, bass						2	2		1			1																	4		Merse
O Gottes Stadt (Solokantate 4)						2	1	1				1																	S		Bären
Sicut Moses (Solokantate 3)						2						1																	S		Bären
Singet dem Herrn (Solokantate 1)						1						1																	S		Bären
Triosonate,		d				1		1				1																			Foeti
Was mich auf dieser Welt betrübt						2						1																	S		Merse
CALDARA, ANTONIO (1670–1736)																															
Sinfonia						2	1	1				1														1					Amade
Sonata a quattro no. 3		B♭				2	1					1																			BScho
Sonata a quattro no. 4		b				2	1					1																			BScho
Sonata a tre, Op 1 No. 1	1693	F				2						1																			BScho
Sonata a tre, Op 1 No. 5	1693	e				2						1																			VarPb
Sonata a tre, Op 1 No. 9	1693	b				2		1				1																			Dobli
Sonata da camera, Op 2 No. 3		D				2						1																			Dobli
CAMBINI, GIUSEPPE M. (1746–1825)																															
Trio, Op 45 No. 6																				1	1			1							MusRa
CANNABICH, CHRISTIAN (1731–1798)																															
Oboe Quartet No. 2		B♭				1	1	1													1										Dobli
Recueil des airs du ballet "Orphee"						1	1	1						1																	Kunze
CAPRICORNUS, SAMUEL (1628–1665)																															
Der gerechten Seelen *Voices:* Soprano, alto, tenor, bass						2	2					1																	4		Bären
CAVACCIO, GIOVANNI (1556–1626)																															
Canzona ("La Fina")																										2	2				MusRa
Canzona ("La Foresta")																										2	2				MusRa
CAZZATI, MAURIZIO (1620–1677)																															
Capriccio a tre ("Guastavilani"), Op 50 No. 29		A				2		1					1																		Dobli
CESARE, GIOVANNI M. (1590–1667)																															
Canzona ("La Bavara")													1														4				MusRa

	Year Composed or Published	Key	Duration	Viols	Early Winds	Violin	Viola	Cello	Double Bass	Barytone	Gamba	Basso continuo	Harpsichord	Piano	Organ	Guitar/Lute	Harp	Recorder	Piccolo	Flute	Oboe	English Horn	Clarinet	Bassoon/Contrabassoon	Horn	Trumpet	Trombone	Percussion	Voice	Unusual Instruments	Publisher
CHARPENTIER, MARC-ANTOINE (1645–1704)																															
Magnificat						2						1																			Foeti
Pie Jesu						2						1																			Foeti
Prelude du Te Deum (arr. Thilde)																										3	3				Billa
CHILESE, BASTIAN (?–?)																															
Canzona 31																										4	4				MusRa
Canzona 32																										4	4				MusRa
CIMA, GIOVANNI P. (1570–?)																															
Sonata *Unus Instr:* Zinke		d										1															1			1	Dobli
CLERAMBOULT, LOUIS N. (1676–1749)																															
Sonata magnifique						2						1																			Amade
Sonata prima						2						1																			Amade
COLISTA, LELIO (1629–1680)																															
Sonata a tre		F				2		1					1																		Dobli
Sonata a tre		G				2		1					1																		Dobli
Sonata terza		D				2		1					1																		Dobli
Triosonata		A				2		1				1																			Bären
COPERARIO, GIOVANNI (1575–1626)																															
Fantasia a tre *Comment:* May be played by string trio				3																											Stain
CORBETT, W (?–?)																															
Sonata		C										1								2											Bären
Sonata, Op 1 No. 12		C						1							1						1					1					MusRa
CORELLI, ARCANGELO (1653–1713)																															
12 Triosonatas da camera, Op 2						2						1																			Bären
12 Triosonatas da chiesa, Op 1						2						1																			VarPb
12 Triosonatas da chiesa, Op 3						2						1																			VarPb
12 Triosonatas da chiesa, Op 4						2						1																			Bären
Sonata						2						1														1					MusRa
Sonata (La follia), Op 5 No. 12						2	1	1																							Caris
Sonata a tre, Op 4 No. 3		C														1		2													Dobli
Sonata a tre, Op 4 No. 5		c														1		2													VarPb
Sonata da camera a tre, Op 2 No. 2						2										1															Dobli
CORRETTE, MICHEL (1709–1795)																															
Concerto comique ("Le mirliton"), Op 8 No. 1		B♭										1								3											Amade
Concerto comique ("Margoton"), Op 8 No. 3		C										1						3													Amade
Concerto Noel allemande						3						1																			Amade
Concerto Noel suisse						2						1								1											Amade
COUPERIN, FRANÇOIS (1668–1733)																															
4e Concert						1						1																			Oisea
9e Concert ("Ritratto dell'amore")		G				1						1																			VarPb
Concerts royaux (I-IV)	1710	d									1	1								2											MusRa
Les gouts reunis (Vol. III)				3							1																				MusRa
Les nations: La française		e				2						1																			Oisea
Les nations: La piemontaise		g				2						1																			Oisea
Les nations: L'espagnole		c				2						1																			Oisea
Les nations: L'imperiale		d				2						1																			Oisea
Le Parnasse, ou l'apothéose de Corelli						2						1																			Oisea

	Year Composed or Published	Key	Duration	Viols	Early Winds	Violin	Viola	Cello	Double Bass	Barytone	Gamba	Basso continuo	Harpsichord	Piano	Organ	Guitar/Lute	Harp	Recorder	Piccolo	Flute	Oboe	English Horn	Clarinet	Bassoon/Contrabassoon	Horn	Trumpet	Trombone	Percussion	Voice	Unusual Instruments	Publisher
COUPERIN, FRANÇOIS *(continued)*																															
Pieces en concert (solo violoncello)						2	1	2																							Leduc
Quatuor						2		1						1																	Duran
La Steinkerque (arr. Petit)		B♭																		1	1		1	1	1	2	1				Billa
Trio						2								1																	Duran
Trio						1		1						1																	Duran
Triosonata ("La superbe")	1693	A				2						1																			Hug
DALL'ABACO, EVARISTO F. (1675–1742)																															
Triosonata		C				2						1																			BScho
Triosonata, Op 3 No. 2		F				2						1																			Viewe
D'ANDRIEU, JEAN F. (1684–1740)																															
Sonata a tre, Op 1 No. 6		e				2		1					1																		Dobli
DE FESCH, WILLEM (1687–1757)																															
Triosonata, Op 12 No. 1												1								2											Bären
Triosonata, Op 12 No. 2												1								2											Bären
Triosonata, Op 12 No. 3												1								2											Bären
DELALANDE, MICHEL (1657–1726)																															
Concert de trompette pour les fêtes								1				1									2					1		1			MusRa
Fanfare (arr. Petit)																									1	2	1				Billa
Noëls en trio						2		2	1				1					2			2										Billa
DEVIENNE, FRANÇOIS (1759–1803)																															
6 Trios																							2	1							Kunze
6 Trios (Vol. 1, Nos. 1-3)							1	1												1											Amade
6 Trios (Vol. 2, Nos. 4-6)							1	1												1											Amade
Bassoon Quartet, Op 73 No. 1		C				1	1	1																1							MusRa
Bassoon Quartet, Op 73 No. 2		F				1	1	1																1							MusRa
Bassoon Quartet, Op 73 No. 3		g				1	1	1																1							MusRa
Bassoon Sonata, Op 24 No. 5		C										1												1							MusRa
Flute Quartet, Op 11 No. 1		G				1	1	1												1											MusRa
Flute Trio						1		1												1											Kneus
Quatuor, Op 73 No. 1						1	1	1																							Billa
Sonata		C						1					1							1											Kunze
Sonata, Op 24 No. 3		F										1												1							MusRa
Trio		B♭																		1			1	1							Kunze
Trio		G																		1			1	1							Kunze
Trio, Op 61 No. 1		C																		1			1	1							Kunze
Trio, Op 61 No. 2		F																		1			1	1							Kunze
Trio, Op 61 No. 5		B♭																		1			1	1							MusRa
Trio, Op 61 No. 6		d																		1			1	1							MusRa
DITTERSDORF, KARL D. VON (1739–1799)																															
Bläser-Partita																										2	2				Bären
Divertimento						1	1	1																							Inter
DRUSCHETZKY, GEORG (1745–1819)																															
Bläser-Partita																										2	2				Bären
Partita		E♭																					2	2	2						Kneus
Partita No. 1		B♭																			2		2	2	2						Dobli
Partita No. 2		B♭																			2		2	2	2						Dobli
Partita No. 3		E♭																			2		2	2	2						Dobli
Partita No. 4		E♭																			2		2	2	2						Dobli

	Year Composed or Published	Key	Duration	Viols	Early Winds	Violin	Viola	Cello	Double Bass	Barytone	Gamba	Basso continuo	Harpsichord	Piano	Organ	Guitar/Lute	Harp	Recorder	Piccolo	Flute	Oboe	English Horn	Clarinet	Bassoon/Contrabassoon	Horn	Trumpet	Trombone	Percussion	Voice	Unusual Instruments	Publisher
DRUSCHETZKY, GEORG *(continued)*																															
Partita No. 5		E♭																			2		2	2	2						Dobli
Partita No. 6		E♭																			2		2	2	2						Dobli
EGENOLF, CHRISTIAN (1502–1555)																															
Gassenhawerlin und Reutterliedlin *Comment:* May be played by string quartet	1535			4																											Noetz
ELER, J (?–?)																															
Trio, Op 9 No. 1		F																		1			1	1							MusRa
ERLEBACH, PHILIPP H. (1657–1714)																															
Sonata No. 3		A				1					1	1																			Bären
FARINA, CARLO (1600–1640)																															
Capriccio stravagante	1627		18			1	2	1	1				1																		AMP
FASCH, JOHANN F. (1688–1758)																															
Sonata		B♭				1						1						1			1										Bären
Sonata		D				1						1								1				1							Bären
Sonata *Comment:* Harpsichord ad libitum		F																			2			2							Merse
Triosonata						1						1								1											Kunze
FERRABOSCO, ALFONSO (1575–1628)																															
2 In nomines						3	1	1																							Noetz
5 Fantasies						2	1	1																							Noetz
6 Pavanes						3	1	1																							Noetz
FINGER, GOTTFRIED (1660–?)																															
Sonata		C				1						1									1					1					MusRa
Sonata		C										1									1					1					MusRa
FISCHER, JOHANN K. (1670–1746)																															
French Dances						2						1																			McGMa
Suite No. 5		G				2	2					1																			Bären
Suite No. 6		F				2	2					1																			Bären
Tafelmusik																		3													Dobli
Tafelmusik *Comment:* Harpsichord ad libitum						2	1	1																							Bären
FONTANA, GIOVANNI B. (?–1630)																															
Sonata a tre						2						1																			Dobli
Sonata decima						1						1												1							Dobli
Sonata duodecima						1						1												1							Dobli
Sonata nona						1						1												1							Dobli
Sonata settima a tre *Comment:* Guitar may replace harpsichord						2						1																			Dobli
FÖRSTER, EMANUEL A. (1748–1823)																															
String Quartet, Op 21 No. 1		C				2	1	1																							Dobli
FÖRSTER, KASPAR (1617–1673)																															
Sonata a 7												1									2			1							MusRa
FRANCK, JOHANN W. (1644–1710)																															
Weil, Jesu, ich in meinem Sinn						2		1	1			1																	A		Merse
FRANCK, MELCHIOR (1579–1639)																															
Pièce instrumentale (arr. Petit)																									1	2	1				Billa

	Year Composed or Published	Key	Duration	Viols	Early Winds	Violin	Viola	Cello	Double Bass	Barytone	Gamba	Basso continuo	Harpsichord	Piano	Organ	Guitar/Lute	Harp	Recorder	Piccolo	Flute	Oboe	English Horn	Clarinet	Bassoon/Contrabassoon	Horn	Trumpet	Trombone	Percussion	Voice	Unusual Instruments	Publisher
FRESCOBALDI, GIROLAMO (1583–1643)																															
Canzona a 8 (arr. Cerha)																				2	2			2	2						Dobli
Canzonas *Comment:* May be played by double brass choir	1608			8																											Noetz
Canzon 13																										2	2				MusRa
Canzon 21																										2	3				MusRa
Caprice sur le chant du coucou (arr. Petit)																									1	2	1				Billa
FUX, JOHANN J. (1660–1741)																															
Partita		F				2						1																			Bären
Partita		G				2						1																			Bären
Partita a tre, K 322		g				2						1																			Dobli
Sinfonia												1								1	1										Foeti
Sinfonia a tre, K 330		D				2						1																			Dobli
Sonata da chiesa		d				2						1																			Viewe
Sonata pastorale a tre, K 397		F				2						1																			Dobli
GABRIELI, ANDREA (1510–1586)																															
5 Ricercare in Four Parts *Comment:* May be played by brass choir																		4													MusRa
Canzona (arr. Petit)																									1	2	1				Billa
Ricercare del duodecimo tuono																										2	2				MusRa
Ricercare del sesto tuono																										2	2				MusRa
GABRIELI, DOMENICO (1659–1690)																															
Balletto a tre, Op 1 No. 9						2						1																			Dobli
GABRIELI, GIOVANNI (1557–1612)																															
Canzona a 7	1615			7																											Noetz
Canzona a 12	1615					6	3	3																							Noetz
Canzonas 1 and 2																										2	2				MusRa
Canzonas 3 and 4																										2	2				MusRa
Canzonas 27 and 28																									2	4	4				MusRa
Canzone e sonata 1615: Canzon 1																										2	3				MusRa
Canzone e sonata 1615: Canzon 2																										3	3				MusRa
Canzone e sonata 1615: Canzon 3																										2	4				MusRa
Canzone e sonata 1615: Canzon 4																										4	2				MusRa
Canzone e sonata 1615: Canzon 5																										4	3				MusRa
Canzone e sonata 1615: Canzon 6																										4	3				MusRa
Canzone e sonata 1615: Canzon 7																										4	3				MusRa
Canzone e sonata 1615: Canzon 8																										3	5				MusRa
Canzone e sonata 1615: Canzon 9																										3	5				MusRa
Canzone e sonata 1615: Canzon 10																										4	4				MusRa
Canzone e sonata 1615: Canzon 11																										4	4				MusRa
Canzone e sonata 1615: Canzon 12																										2	6				MusRa
Canzone e sonata 1615: Canzon 13																										4	4				MusRa
Canzone e sonata 1615: Canzon 14																										6	4				MusRa
Canzone e sonata 1615: Canzon 15																										4	6				MusRa
Canzone e sonata 1615: Canzon 16																										6	6				MusRa
Canzone e sonata 1615: Canzon 17																										6	6				MusRa
Canzone e sonata 1615: Canzon 18																										4	10				MusRa
Canzone e sonata 1615: Canzon 19																										3	12				MusRa
Canzone e sonata 1615: Canzon 20																										5	12				MusRa
Doppelchörige Canzonen	1608			8																											Noetz
Symph. sacrae No. 1: Canzon primi toni	1597																									4	4				MusRa

	Year Composed or Published	Key	Duration	Viols	Early Winds	Violin	Viola	Cello	Double Bass	Barytone	Gamba	Basso continuo	Harpsichord	Piano	Organ	Guitar/Lute	Harp	Recorder	Piccolo	Flute	Oboe	English Horn	Clarinet	Bassoon/Contrabassoon	Horn	Trumpet	Trombone	Percussion	Voice	Unusual Instruments	Publisher
GABRIELI, GIOVANNI *(continued)*																															
Symph. sacrae No. 2: Canzon septimi toni	1597																									4	4				MusRa
Symph. sacrae No. 3: Canzon septimi toni	1597																									4	4				MusRa
Symph. sacrae No. 4: Canzon noni toni	1597																									4	4				MusRa
Symph. sacrae No. 5: Canzon duodecimi toni																										4	4				MusRa
Symph. sacrae No. 6: Sonata pian e forte	1597																									2	6				MusRa
Symph. sacrae No. 7: Canzon primi toni	1597																									7	3				MusRa
Symph. sacrae No. 8: Canzon duodecimi toni (1)	1597																									6	4				MusRa
Symph. sacrae No. 9: Canzon duodecimi toni (2)	1597																									6	4				MusRa
Symph. sacrae No. 10: Canzon 12 toni (3)	1597																									5	5				MusRa
Symph. sacrae No. 11: Canzon 12 toni (4)	1597																									6	4				MusRa
Symph. sacrae No. 12: Canzon in echo	1597														2											6	4				MusRa
Symph. sacrae No. 13: Canzon sept. oct.	1597																									6	6				MusRa
Symph. sacrae No. 14: Canzon noni toni	1597																									6	6				MusRa
Symph. sacrae No. 15: Sonata octavi toni	1597																									2	12				MusRa
Symph. sacrae No. 16: Canzon quarti toni	1597																									3	12				MusRa
GASSMANN, FLORIAN L. (1729–1774)																															
6 Trios *Comment:* The trios are available separately						2	1																								Kistn
Divertimento a tre		C				2						1																			Dobli
Trio (arr. Janetsky)		D																					1	1	1						Kunze
GEMINIANI, FRANCESCO (1687–1762)																															
Sonate		A				2						1																			Foeti
GERVAISE, CLAUDE (1540–1560)																															
Bransles, 6 (arr. Petit)																									1	2	1				Billa
Partitas and Dances																									1	2	1				Kunze
GIBBONS, ORLANDO (1583–1625)																															
Fantasias, 6				6																											Faber
Fantasias, 9						2		1																							Stain
GIORDANI, TOMMASO (1730–1806)																															
Sonata, Op 30 No. 3		B♭				1	1						1																		Kunze
GLETLE, JOHANN M. (1626–1683)																															
Justus germinabit *Voice:* Soprano or tenor						2						1																	1		Bären
Popule meus *Voice:* Soprano or tenor							2					1																	1		Bären
Salve Regina *Voices:* Alto, tenor, bass												1																	3		Bären
Tota pulchra es *Voices:* Alto and tenor												1																	2		Bären

	Year Composed or Published	Key	Duration	Viols	Early Winds	Violin	Viola	Cello	Double Bass	Barytone	Gamba	Basso continuo	Harpsichord	Piano	Organ	Guitar/Lute	Harp	Recorder	Piccolo	Flute	Oboe	English Horn	Clarinet	Bassoon/Contrabassoon	Horn	Trumpet	Trombone	Percussion	Voice	Unusual Instruments	Publisher
GLETLE, JOHANN M. *(continued)*																															
Veni, sancte spiritus *Voice:* Soprano or tenor						2						1																	1		Bären
GLUCK, CHRISTOPH W. (1714–1787)																															
Marche religieuse d'Alceste (arr. Petit)																									1	2	1				Billa
Triosonata No. 1		C				2						1																			Bären
Triosonata No. 2		g				2						1																			Bären
Triosonata No. 3		A				2						1																			Bären
Triosonata No. 4		B♭				2						1																			Bären
Triosonata No. 5		E♭				2						1																			Bären
Triosonata No. 6		F				2						1																			Bären
Triosonata No. 7		E				2						1																			Bären
Triosonata No. 8		F				2						1																			Bären
GRAUN, CARL H. (1704–1759)																															
Trio No. 1 *Unus Instr:* Oboe d'amore. May be replaced by clarinet		D																			1			1	1					1	McGMa
Trio No. 2 *Unus Instr:* Oboe d'amore		E																			1			1	1					1	McGMa
GRAUN, JOHANN G. (1703–1771)																															
Sonata		C										1								2											Amade
Sonata		E♭										1								2											Bären
Sonata		F						1				1								1											Bären
Sonata a tre		B♭				1	1					1																			Amade
GRAUPNER, CHRISTOPH (1683–1760)																															
Jesu, führe meine Seele *Voice:* Bass						1						1																	1		Merse
Sonata		G				2	1	1																							Bären
Trio												1										1		1							Kunze
Trio *Unus Instr:* Chalumeau		C										1												1						1	Kunze
GRILLO, GIOVANNI B. (?–1622)																															
Canzona quarta																										4	4				MusRa
GUAMI, GIOSEFFO (1540–1612)																															
Canzon ("La Guamina")																										2	2				MusRa
Canzon 6																										2	2				Bären
Canzonas 24 and 25																										4	4				MusRa
GUSSAGO, CESARIO (?–?)																															
Doppelchörige canzona	1608			8																											Noetz
HAFFNER, WALTHER (?–?)																															
Christ ist erstanden															1											2	2				Merse
HALTENBERGER, BERNHARD (1748–1780)																															
Quartet						1	1													1					1						Kunze
HAMMERSCHMIDT, ANDREAS (1611–1675)																															
Es danken dir, Gott, die Völker *Voice:* Tenor or soprano						2						1																	1		Bären
Gelobet seist du, Jesu Christ												1														2	4		T		Bären
Nun lob, mein Seel, den Herren												1														2	4		S		Bären
HÄNDEL, GEORG F. (1685–1759)																															
2 Arias																					2			1	2						MusRa
2 Songs (from "Neun deutsche Arien")						1		1								1													S		Dobli

	Year Composed or Published	Key	Duration	Viols	Early Winds	Violin	Viola	Cello	Double Bass	Barytone	Gamba	Basso continuo	Harpsichord	Piano	Organ	Guitar/Lute	Harp	Recorder	Piccolo	Flute	Oboe	English Horn	Clarinet	Bassoon/Contrabassoon	Horn	Trumpet	Trombone	Percussion	Voice	Unusual Instruments	Publisher
HÄNDEL, GEORG F. *(continued)*																															
7 Triosonatas, Op 5						2						1																			VarPb
12 Original Triostücke												1						2													Bären
Cantata ("La terra è liberata") *Voices:* ("Soprano and bass")						2	1	1				1								1	2								2		Bären
Cantata ("Nel dolce dell' oblio")																1		1											S		Dobli
Concerto		D				2		1								1															Dobli
Grave and Allegro												1						2													BScho
Italian Cantata ("Cuopre tal volta") *Voice:* Bass						2						1																	1		Bären
Italian Cantata ("Dalla guerra amorosa"), HWV 102 *Voice:* Bass												1																	1		Bären
Italian Cantata ("Tra le fiamme")						2					1	1								2	1			1					S		Bären
Neun deutsche Arien, HWV 202-10						1						1																	S		Bären
Rigaudon, Bourree, and March																					2			1				1			MusRa
Royal Fireworks Music (arr. Reichelt)																		4										1			Dobli
Sonata		F				1						1						1													BScho
Sonata, Op 2 No. 1		c				1						1								1											Breit
Sonata, Op 2 No. 7		g				2								1																	Peter
Sonata a tre, Op 2 No. 1		c				1										1		1													Dobli
Sonata No. 1		c				1						1						1													BScho
Suite (arr. Guignard)								2										2													Amade
Tag für Tag sei Lob und Dank						2									1																Merse
Triosonata		B♭				1						1									1										Bären
Triosonata		F										1						2													Faber
Triosonata, Op 2 No. 8						2						1																			VarPb
Water Music (arr. Reichelt)													1					4													Dobli
HANFF, JOHANN N. (1665–1711)																															
Ich will den Herrn loben allezeit						1						1																	S		Bären
Wohlauf, mein Herz *Voices:* Alto and tenor						2						1												1					2		Merse
HASSE, JOHANN A. (1699–1783)																															
Sonata a tre, Op 3 No. 6		D				2						1																			Dobli
Triosonata		C				2						1																			Harmo
Triosonata		C				1										1		1													Dobli
HASSLER, HANS L. (1564–1612)																															
Intradas from "The Pleasure Garden"						3	2	1																							Bären
Intraden und Canzonen																										3	3				Merse
HAYDN, JOSEF (1732–1809)																															
Cassation, Hob II:6	1764	C				1		1								1															Dobli
Divertimento		A				1	1	1																							Kunze
Divertimento, Hob II:14	1761	C																					2		2						Dobli
Divertimento, Hob XI:34	1776	F				1		1								1															Dobli
Divertimento (Baryton Trio), Hob XI:89	1769	G				2		1																							Noetz
Divertimento (Baryton Trio), Hob XI:90	1769	C				2		1																							Noetz
Divertimento (Baryton Trio), Hob XI:91	1769	D				2		1																							Noetz
Divertimento a sei (Mann und Weib), Hob II:11	1765	C				2	1	1	1											1	1										Dobli
Divertimento a tre, Hob IV:5		E♭				1		1																	1						Dobli
Divertimento I, Hob IV:6	1784	D				1		1												1											Dobli
Divertimento II, Hob IV:7	1784	G				1		1												1											Dobli

	Year Composed or Published	Key	Duration	Viols	Early Winds	Violin	Viola	Cello	Double Bass	Barytone	Gamba	Basso continuo	Harpsichord	Piano	Organ	Guitar/Lute	Harp	Recorder	Piccolo	Flute	Oboe	English Horn	Clarinet	Bassoon/Contrabassoon	Horn	Trumpet	Trombone	Percussion	Voice	Unusual Instruments	Publisher
HAYDN, JOSEF *(continued)*																															
Divertimento III, Hob IV:8	1784	C				1		1												1											Dobli
Divertimento IV, Hob IV:9	1784	G				1		1												1											Dobli
Divertimento V, Hob IV:10	1784	A				1		1												1											Dobli
Divertimento VI, Hob IV:11	1784	D				1		1												1											Dobli
Divertimento No. 1		B♭																		1	1		1	1	1						Press
Divertimento No. 1, Hob II:15	1760	F																			2			2	2						Dobli
Divertimento No. 2, Hob II:23	1765	F																			2			2	2						Dobli
Divertimento No. 3, Hob II:7	1765	C																			2			2	2						Dobli
Divertimento No. 5, Hob II:D18	1765	D																			2			2	2						Dobli
Divertimento No. 6, Hob II:3	1766	G																			2			2	2						Dobli
Divertimento No. 7, Hob deest		G																			2			2	2						Dobli
Divertimento No. 8, Hob deest		D																			2			2	2						Dobli
Easy Trios, 12						2	1																								Inter
Eisenstädter Trios, 5, Hob VC7	1766					2		1																							Breit
German Dances, 12, Hob IX Anh	1792					2		1																							VarPb
Hungarian National March, Hob VIII:4 *Unus Instr:* Contrabassoon		E♭																			2		2	3	2	1		1		1	Dobli
Lira Concerto No. 1, Hob VIIh:1	1786	C												1				2													Dobli
Lira Concerto No. 2, Hob VIIh:2	1787	G												1				2													Dobli
Lira Concerto No. 3, Hob VIIh:3	1787	G												1				2													Dobli
Lira Concerto No. 4, Hob VIIh:4	1786													1				2													Dobli
Lira Concerto No. 5, Hob VIIh:5	1787	F												1				2													Dobli
London Trios, 3						2		1																							Peter
London Trio No. 1 (alt. inst.)	1792							1												2											Harmo
March, Hob VIII:7 *Unus Instr:* Contrabassoon	1792	E♭																			2		2	3	2	1		1		1	Dobli
March for the KK Infantry Regiment, Hb VIII:D1																				1	2		2	3	2	2					Dobli
March for the Prince of Wales, Hob VII:3 *Unus Instr:* Contrabassoon		E♭																			2			3	2	1		1		1	Dobli
March for the Prince of Wales (arr. Gabler)																				1	1		1	1	1						Dobli
March No. 1 for the Derbyshire Cavalry, Hob VIII:1 *Unus Instr:* Contrabassoon	1795	E♭																			2		2	3	2	1		1		1	Dobli
March No. 2 for the Derbyshire Cavalry, Hob VIII:2 *Unus Instr:* Contrabassoon	1795	C																			2		2	3	2	1		1		1	Dobli
Marche Regimento de Marshall, Hob 0 *Unus Instr:* Contrabassoon		G																			2		2	3	2	1		1		1	Dobli
Marcia, Hob VIII:6	1793	E♭																			2		2	3	2	1		1			Dobli
Musical Clock Pieces (arr. Biedermann-Weber)																		3													Dobli
Musical Clock Pieces (arr. Schaller)																		3													Dobli
Notturno No. 1 (arr. Trötzmüller), Hob II:25	1790	C												1				2													Dobli
Notturno No. 2, Hob II:26	1790	F												1				2													Dobli
Notturno No. 3, Hob II:32	1790	C												1				2													Dobli
Notturno No. 4, Hob II:31	1790	C												1				2													Dobli
Notturno No. 5, Hob II:29	1790	C												1				2													Dobli
Notturno No. 6, Hob II:30	1790	G												1				2													Dobli
Notturno No. 7, Hob II:28	1790	F												1				2													Dobli
Notturno No. 8, Hob II:27	1790	G												1				2													Dobli
Octet *Unus Instr:* 2 Basset horns		F																			2		2	2						2	Forbe
Pieces, 9 (arr. Korda)																		3													Dobli
Quartet, No Hob No.		C				1	1	1												1											Hug

	Year Composed or Published	Key	Duration	Viols	Early Winds	Violin	Viola	Cello	Double Bass	Barytone	Gamba	Basso continuo	Harpsichord	Piano	Organ	Guitar/Lute	Harp	Recorder	Piccolo	Flute	Oboe	English Horn	Clarinet	Bassoon/Contrabassoon	Horn	Trumpet	Trombone	Percussion	Voice	Unusual Instruments	Publisher
HAYDN, JOSEF *(continued)*																															
Quartet (Op. 2 No. 2, arr. Scheit), Hob III: 8	1765	D				1	1	1								1															Dobli
Quartet (Op. 5 No. 4), Hob II:4	1765	G				1	1									1				1											VarPb
Romance (from Lira Concerto No. 3), Hob VIIh:3		C						1								2		3													Dobli
Scherzando No. 1, Hob II:33	1760					2						1									2				2						Dobli
Scherzando No. 2, Hob II:34	1760					2						1									2				2						Dobli
Scherzando No. 3, Hob II:35	1760					2						1									2				2						Dobli
Scherzando No. 4, Hob II:36	1760					2						1									2				2						Dobli
Scherzando No. 5, Hob II:37	1760					2						1									2				2						Dobli
Scherzando No. 6, Hob II:38	1760					2						1									2				2						Dobli
Serenade (Passing one bow around)						2	1	1																							Press
String Quartet (Op. 0), Hob II:6		E♭				2	1	1																							Dobli
String Quartet (Op. 3 No. 5), Hob II:17		F				2	1	1																							VarPb
String Quartet (Op. 1 No. 1), Hob III:1	1762	B♭				2	1	1																							VarPb
String Quartet (Op. 1 No. 2), Hob III:2	1762	E♭				2	1	1																							VarPb
String Quartet (Op. 1 No. 3), Hob III:3	1762	D				2	1	1																							VarPb
String Quartet (Op. 1 No. 4), Hob III:4	1764	G				2	1	1																							VarPb
String Quartet (Op. 1 No. 6), Hob III:6	1762	C				2	1	1																							VarPb
String Quartet (Op. 2 No. 1), Hob III:7	1763	A				2	1	1																							VarPb
String Quartet (Op. 2 No. 2), Hob III:8	1765	E				2	1	1																							VarPb
String Quartet (Op. 2 No. 4), Hob III:10	1762	F				2	1	1																							VarPb
String Quartet (Op. 2 No. 6), Hob III:12	1762	B♭				2	1	1																							VarPb
String Quartet (Op. 9 No. 1), Hob III:19	1771	C				2	1	1																							VarPb
String Quartet (Op. 9 No. 2), Hob III:20	1771	E♭				2	1	1																							VarPb
String Quartet (Op. 9 No. 3), Hob III:21	1771	G				2	1	1																							VarPb
String Quartet (Op. 9 No. 4), Hob III:22	1771	d				2	1	1																							VarPb
String Quartet (Op. 9 No. 5), Hob III:23	1771	B♭				2	1	1																							VarPb
String Quartet (Op. 9 No. 6), Hob III:24	1771	A				2	1	1																							VarPb
String Quartet (Op. 17 No. 1), Hob III:25	1771	E				2	1	1																							VarPb
String Quartet (Op. 17 No. 2), Hob III:26	1771	F				2	1	1																							VarPb
String Quartet (Op. 17 No. 3), Hob III:27	1771	E♭				2	1	1																							VarPb
String Quartet (Op. 17 No. 4), Hob III:28	1771	c				2	1	1																							VarPb
String Quartet (Op. 17 No. 5), Hob III:29	1771	G				2	1	1																							VarPb
String Quartet (Op. 17 No. 6), Hob III:30	1771	D				2	1	1																							VarPb

	Year Composed or Published	Key	Duration	Viols	Early Winds	Violin	Viola	Cello	Double Bass	Barytone	Gamba	Basso continuo	Harpsichord	Piano	Organ	Guitar/Lute	Harp	Recorder	Piccolo	Flute	Oboe	English Horn	Clarinet	Bassoon/Contrabassoon	Horn	Trumpet	Trombone	Percussion	Voice	Unusual Instruments	Publisher
HAYDN, JOSEF *(continued)*																															
String Quartet (Op. 20 No. 1), Hob III:31	1772	E♭				2	1	1																							VarPb
String Quartet (Op. 20 No. 2), Hob III:32	1772	C				2	1	1																							VarPb
String Quartet (Op. 20 No. 3), Hob III:33	1772	g				2	1	1																							VarPb
String Quartet (Op. 20 No. 4), Hob III:34	1772	D				2	1	1																							VarPb
String Quartet (Op. 20 No. 5), Hob III:35	1772	f				2	1	1																							VarPb
String Quartet (Op. 20 No. 6), Hob III:36	1772	A				2	1	1																							VarPb
String Quartet (Op. 33 No. 1), Hob III:37	1781	b				2	1	1																							VarPb
String Quartet (Op. 33 No. 2), Hob III:38	1781	E♭				2	1	1																							VarPb
String Quartet (Op. 33 No. 3), Hob III:39	1781	C				2	1	1																							VarPb
String Quartet (Op. 33 No. 4), Hob III:40	1781	B♭				2	1	1																							VarPb
String Quartet (Op. 33 No. 5), Hob III:41	1781	G				2	1	1																							VarPb
String Quartet (Op. 33 No. 6), Hob III:42	1781	D				2	1	1																							VarPb
String Quartet (Op. 42), Hob III:43	1785	d				2	1	1																							VarPb
String Quartet (Op. 50 No. 1), Hob III:44	1787	B♭				2	1	1																							VarPb
String Quartet (Op. 50 No. 2), Hob III:45	1787	C				2	1	1																							VarPb
String Quartet (Op. 50 No. 3), Hob III:46	1787	E♭				2	1	1																							VarPb
String Quartet (Op. 50 No. 4), Hob III:47	1787	f♯				2	1	1																							VarPb
String Quartet (Op. 50 No. 5), Hob III:48	1787	F				2	1	1																							VarPb
String Quartet (Op. 50 No. 6), Hob III:49	1787	D				2	1	1																							VarPb
String Quartet (Op. 54 No. 1), Hob III:58	1788	G				2	1	1																							VarPb
String Quartet (Op. 54 No. 2), Hob III:57	1788	C				2	1	1																							VarPb
String Quartet (Op. 54 No. 3), Hob III:59	1788	E				2	1	1																							VarPb
String Quartet (Op. 55 No. 1), Hob III:60	1788	A				2	1	1																							VarPb
String Quartet (Op. 55 No. 2), Hob III:61	1788	f				2	1	1																							VarPb
String Quartet (Op. 55 No. 3), Hob III:62	1788	B♭				2	1	1																							VarPb
String Quartet (Op. 64 No. 5), Hob III:63	1790	D				2	1	1																							VarPb
String Quartet (Op. 64 No. 6), Hob III:64	1790	E♭				2	1	1																							VarPb
String Quartet (Op. 64 No. 1), Hob III:65	1790	C				2	1	1																							VarPb
String Quartet (Op. 64 No. 2), Hob III:68	1790	b				2	1	1																							VarPb

	Year Composed or Published	Key	Duration	Viols	Early Winds	Violin	Viola	Cello	Double Bass	Barytone	Gamba	Basso continuo	Harpsichord	Piano	Organ	Guitar/Lute	Harp	Recorder	Piccolo	Flute	Oboe	English Horn	Clarinet	Bassoon/Contrabassoon	Horn	Trumpet	Trombone	Percussion	Voice	Unusual Instruments	Publisher
HAYDN, JOSEF *(continued)*																															
String Quartet (Op. 64 No. 3), Hob III:67	1790	B♭				2	1	1																							VarPb
String Quartet (Op. 64 No. 4), Hob III:66	1790	G				2	1	1																							VarPb
String Quartet (Op. 71 No. 1), Hob III:69	1793	B♭				2	1	1																							VarPb
String Quartet (Op. 71 No. 2), Hob III:70	1793	D				2	1	1																							VarPb
String Quartet (Op. 71 No. 3), Hob III:71	1793	E♭				2	1	1																							VarPb
String Quartet (Op. 74 No. 1), Hob III:72	1793	C				2	1	1																							VarPb
String Quartet (Op. 74 No. 2), Hob III:73	1793	F				2	1	1																							VarPb
String Quartet (Op. 74 No. 3), Hob III:74	1793	g				2	1	1																							VarPb
String Quartet (Op. 76 No. 1), Hob III:75	1797	G				2	1	1																							VarPb
String Quartet (Op. 76 No. 2), Hob III:76	1797	d				2	1	1																							VarPb
String Quartet (Op. 76 No. 3), Hob III:77	1797	C				2	1	1																							VarPb
String Quartet (Op. 76 No. 4), Hob III:78	1797	B♭				2	1	1																							VarPb
String Quartet (Op. 76 No. 5), Hob III:79	1797	D				2	1	1																							VarPb
String Quartet (Op. 76 No. 6), Hob III:80	1797	E♭				2	1	1																							VarPb
String Quartet (Op. 77 No. 1), Hob III:81	1799	G				2	1	1																							VarPb
String Quartet (Op. 77 No. 2), Hob III:82	1799	F				2	1	1																							VarPb
String Quartet (Op. 103), Hob III:83	1803	B♭				2	1	1																							VarPb
String Trio No. 1, Hob V:1	1767	E				2		1																							Dobli
String Trio No. 2, Hob V:2	1767	F				2		1																							Dobli
String Trio No. 3, Hob V:3	1767	b				2		1																							Dobli
String Trio No. 4, Hob V:4	1767	E♭				2		1																							Dobli
String Trio No. 6, Hob V:6	1765	E♭				2		1																							Dobli
String Trio No. 7, Hob V:7	1765	A				2		1																							Dobli
String Trio No. 8, Hob V:8	1765	B♭				2		1																							Dobli
String Trio No. 10, Hob V:10	1767	F				2		1																							Dobli
String Trio No. 11, Hob V:12	1767	E				2		1																							Dobli
String Trio No. 12, Hob V:13	1765	B♭				2		1																							Dobli
String Trio No. 13, Hob V:14	1765	b				2		1																							Dobli
String Trio No. 14, Hob V:15	1762	D				2		1																							Dobli
String Trio No. 15, Hob V:16	1766	D				2		1																							Dobli
String Trio No. 16, Hob V:17	1766	E♭				2		1																							Dobli
String Trio No. 17, Hob V:18	1765	B♭				2		1																							Dobli
String Trio No. 18, Hob V:19	1765	E				2		1																							Dobli
String Trio No. 19, Hob V:20	1766	G				2		1																							Dobli
String Trio No. 20, Hob V:D3	1938	D				2		1																							Dobli
String Trio No. 21, Hob V:G1	1964	G				2		1																							Dobli
String Trio No. 22, Hob V:21	1765	D				2		1																							Dobli
String Trio No. 23, Hob V:11	1765	E♭				2		1																							Dobli
String Trio No. 24, Hob V:D1	1955	D				2		1																							Dobli
String Trio No. 25, Hob V:C3	1955	C				2		1																							Dobli

	Year Composed or Published	Key	Duration	Viols	Early Winds	Violin	Viola	Cello	Double Bass	Barytone	Gamba	Basso continuo	Harpsichord	Piano	Organ	Guitar/Lute	Harp	Recorder	Piccolo	Flute	Oboe	English Horn	Clarinet	Bassoon/Contrabassoon	Horn	Trumpet	Trombone	Percussion	Voice	Unusual Instruments	Publisher
HAYDN, JOSEF *(continued)*																															
String Trio No. 26, Hob V:G4	1955	G				2		1																							Dobli
String Trio No. 27, Hob V:B1	1955	B♭				2		1																							Dobli
String Trio No. 28, Hob V:F1	1931	F				2		1																							Dobli
String Trio No. 29, Hob V:C4	1938	C				2		1																							Dobli
String Trio No. 30, Hob V:C5	1938	C				2		1																							Dobli
String Trio No. 31, Hob V:C2	1955	C				2		1																							Dobli
String Trio No. 32, Hob V:C1	1955	C				2		1																							VarPb
String Trio No. 33, Hob V:G3	1955	G				2		1																							Dobli
String Trio No. 34, Hob V:A2	1964	A				2		1																							Dobli
Trio (arr. Staeps)		G																3													Dobli
Trio No. 1, Hob XV:37	1766	F				1		1						1																	Dobli
Trio No. 2, Hob XV:C1	1766	C				1		1						1																	Dobli
Trio No. 3, Hob XIV:6	1767	G				1		1						1																	Dobli
Trio No. 4, Hob XV:39	1767	F				1		1						1																	Dobli
Trio No. 5, Hob XV:1	1766	g				1		1						1																	VarPb
Trio No. 6, Hob XV:40	1760	F				1		1						1																	Dobli
Trio No. 7, Hob XV:41	1767	G				1		1						1																	Dobli
Trio No. 10, Hob XV:35	1771	A				1		1						1																	VarPb
Trio No. 11, Hob XV:34	1771	E				1		1						1																	Dobli
Trio No. 12, Hob XV:36	1774	E♭				1		1						1																	Dobli
Trio No. 13, Hob XV:38	1769	B♭				1		1						1																	Dobli
Trio No. 14, Hob XV:11	1789	f				1		1						1																	Dobli
Trio No. 15, Hob deest		D				1		1						1																	Dobli
Trio No. 16, Hob XIV:C1	1772	C				1		1						1																	Dobli
Trio No. 17, Hob XV:2	1771	F				1		1						1																	VarPb
Trio No. 18, Hob XV:5	1784	G				1		1						1																	VarPb
Trio No. 19, Hob XV:6	1784	F				1		1						1																	VarPb
Trio No. 20, Hob XV:7	1785	D				1		1						1																	VarPb
Trio No. 21, Hob XV:8	1785	A				1		1						1																	VarPb
Trio No. 22, Hob XV:9	1785	A				1		1						1																	VarPb
Trio No. 23, Hob XV:10	1785	E♭				1		1						1																	VarPb
Trio No. 24, Hob XV:11	1789	E♭				1		1						1																	VarPb
Trio No. 25, Hob XV:12	1789	e				1		1						1																	VarPb
Trio No. 26, Hob XV:13	1789	c				1		1						1																	VarPb
Trio No. 27, Hob XV:14	1790	A♭				1		1						1																	VarPb
Trio No. 28, Hob XV:16	1790	D				1		1						1																	Dobli
Trio No. 29, Hob XV:15	1790	G						1						1						1											VarPb
Trio No. 30, Hob XV:17	1790	F						1						1						1											VarPb
Trio No. 31, Hob XV:32	1794	G				1		1						1																	Dobli
Trio No. 32, Hob XV:18	1794	A				1		1						1																	VarPb
Trio No. 33, Hob XV:19	1794	g				1		1						1																	VarPb
Trio No. 34, Hob XV:20	1794	B♭				1		1						1																	VarPb
Trio No. 35, Hob XV:21	1795	C				1		1						1																	VarPb
Trio No. 36, Hob XV:22	1795	E♭				1		1						1																	VarPb
Trio No. 37, Hob XV:23	1795	d				1		1						1																	VarPb
Trio No. 38, Hob XV:24	1795	D				1		1						1																	VarPb
Trio No. 39, Hob XV:25	1795	G				1		1						1																	VarPb
Trio No. 40, Hob XV:26	1794	f♯				1		1						1																	VarPb
Trio No. 41, Hob XV:31	1795	e♭				1		1						1																	VarPb
Trio No. 42, Hob XV:30	1797	E♭				1		1						1																	VarPb
Trio No. 43, Hob XV:27	1797	E♭				1		1						1																	VarPb
Trio No. 44, Hob XV:28	1797	E				1		1						1																	VarPb
Trio No. 45, Hob XV:29	1797	E♭				1		1						1																	VarPb
Trios, 6						2		1																							BScho
Wiener Hofball-Menuette						2		1																							BScho

	Year Composed or Published	Key	Duration	Viols	Early Winds	Violin	Viola	Cello	Double Bass	Barytone	Gamba	Basso continuo	Harpsichord	Piano	Organ	Guitar/Lute	Harp	Recorder	Piccolo	Flute	Oboe	English Horn	Clarinet	Bassoon/Contrabassoon	Horn	Trumpet	Trombone	Percussion	Voice	Unusual Instruments	Publisher
HAYDN, MICHAEL (1737–1806)																															
Andantino		g				2	1	1																							Dobli
Divertimento, Hob IV:D3	1771	D					1		1																1						Dobli
Divertimento, Perger 92	1774	B♭				1	1		1												1			1							Dobli
Divertimento, Perger 94	1785	G				1	1		1											1					1						Dobli
Divertimento, Perger 95	1786	D																			2			2	2						Dobli
Divertimento, Perger 96	1790	G					1		1												1			1	2						Dobli
Divertimento, Perger 98	1772	C				1			1												1										Dobli
Notturno, Perger deest		E♭				2	1		1																2						Dobli
Notturno, Perger 106	1772	F				2	1		1																2						Dobli
Quartet, Perger deest		F				1	1	1												1											Dobli
Quartet, Perger 115	1795	C				1		1	1													1									Dobli
Romance (from Mozart Horn Con., K447), Perger deest		A♭				2	1	1																							Dobli
String Quartet		A				2	1	1																							Kunze
String Quartet, Perger 121	1780	A				2	1	1																							Dobli
String Quartet, Perger 125	1780	B♭				2	1	1																							Dobli
String Quartet No. 1, Perger 124	1777	B♭				2	1	1																							Dobli
String Quartet No. 2, Perger 118	1781	E♭				2	1	1																							Dobli
String Quartet No. 3, Perger 122	1796	A				2	1	1																							Dobli
String Quartet No. 4, Perger 120	1783	g				2	1	1																							Dobli
String Quartet No. 5, Perger 119	1783	F				2	1	1																							Dobli
String Quartet No. 6, Perger 116	1781	C				2	1	1																							Dobli
HEINICHEN, JOHANN D. (1683–1729)																															
Nisi Dominus (Psalm 127)												1									1								S		DeutV
Sonata a tre		c									1	1									1										Dobli
HILTON, JOHN (1599–1657)																															
Preludio and 5 Fantasies						2	1																								Noetz
HINGESTON, JOHN (?–1688)																															
Fantasia												1														2	1				MusRa
HÖCKH, C (?–?)																															
Partita seconda a tre		B♭				2		1					1																		Dobli
HOFFMANN, LEOPOLD (1738–1793)																															
Divertimento a tre		C				2						1																			Dobli
HOTTETERRE, JACQUES (1674–1762)																															
Ballet Suite, "Rustic Wedding"																1		3													Dobli
Trio Sonatas, Op 3 Nos. 1-3												1						2													MusRa
Trio Sonatas, Op 3 Nos. 4-6												1						2													MusRa
JACCHINI, GIUSEPPE (1670–1727)																															
Sonata		B♭													1											2					Merse
JENKINS, JOHN (1592–1678)																															
4 Fantasies						2	1	1																							Noetz
Consort Music				4																											Faber
Consort Music				6																											Faber
JOMMELLI, NICCOLÒ (1714–1774)																															
Triosonata		C				2						1																			Kunze
Triosonata		D				2						1																			Kunze
Triosonata		G				2						1																			Kunze
KAUFFMANN, GEORG F. (1679–1735)																															
Chorale Prelude																					1		1	1							McGMa
KLEINKNECHT, JACOB F. (1722–1794)																															
Sonata		c										1								1	1										DeutV

	Year Composed or Published	Key	Duration	Viols	Early Winds	Violin	Viola	Cello	Double Bass	Barytone	Gamba	Basso continuo	Harpsichord	Piano	Organ	Guitar/Lute	Harp	Recorder	Piccolo	Flute	Oboe	English Horn	Clarinet	Bassoon/Contrabassoon	Horn	Trumpet	Trombone	Percussion	Voice	Unusual Instruments	Publisher
KRIEGER, JOHANN P. (1649–1725)																															
Sing, Oh My Spirit												1									2										McGMa
Triosonata		e				2						1																			Foeti
LAWES, WILLIAM (1602–1645)																															
Consort Sets				6																											Faber
Consort Sets				5																											Faber
Consort Suite		C				3	1	2																							Noetz
Consort Suite		C				2	2	1																							Noetz
LECLAIR, JEAN-MARIE (1697–1764)																															
Concerto		D				2	1					1								1											Foeti
Concerto, Op 7 No. 4		F				3	1					1																			Foeti
Première recreation de musique, Op 6						2						1																			Bären
Triosonata		D						1				1								1											Foeti
Triosonata		F				2						1																			Foeti
LEGRENZI, GIOVANNI (1626–1690)																															
Sonata ("La Comara")						2						1																			Foeti
Sonata a tre ("La Bentivoglia")		B♭				2						1																			Dobli
Sonata a tre ("La Bernarda"), Op 4 No. 1		d				2						1																			Dobli
Triosonata ("La Raspona")		G				2						1																			Bären
LINIKE, JOHANN G. (?–1737)																															
Sonata a 5						1						1								1	1					1					MusRa
LOCATELLI, PIETRO (1695–1764)																															
Sonata a tre		e				2						1																			Harmo
Sonate		g				2						1																			Foeti
LOCKE, MATTHEW (1630–1677)																															
6 Suites						2		1																							Noetz
Broken Consort (Suites 1-3)						2		1																							Noetz
Broken Consort (Suites 4-6)						2		1																							Noetz
LOEILLET, JEAN-BAPT. (1680–1730)																															
Quintet		b										1						2		2											Bären
Sonata, Op 1 No. 1		F										1						1			1										VarPb
Sonata, Op 1 No. 2		G										1									2										MusRa
Sonata, Op 1 No. 3		g										1						1			1										MusRa
Sonata, Op 1 No. 4		D										1								2											MusRa
Sonata, Op 1 No. 5		c										1						1			1										MusRa
Sonata, Op 1 No. 6		e										1						2													MusRa
Sonata, Op 2 No. 1		B♭										1									2										MusRa
Sonata, Op 2 No. 2		F										1						1			1										VarPb
Sonata, Op 2 No. 3		A										1									2										MusRa
Sonata, Op 2 No. 4		d										1						1			1										VarPb
Sonata, Op 2 No. 5		g										1									2										MusRa
Sonata, Op 2 No. 6		c										1						1			1										VarPb
Sonata, Op 2 No. 7		E										1									2										MusRa
Sonata, Op 2 No. 8		b										1								2											MusRa
Sonata, Op 2 No. 9		g										1									2										MusRa
Sonata, Op 2 No. 10		e										1								2											MusRa
Sonata, Op 2 No. 11		d										1									2										MusRa
Sonata, Op 2 No. 12		G										1								2											VarPb
LOTTI, ANTONIO (1667–1740)																															
Trio		A										1								1	1										Sikor

	Year Composed or Published	Key	Duration	Viols	Early Winds	Violin	Viola	Cello	Double Bass	Barytone	Gamba	Basso continuo	Harpsichord	Piano	Organ	Guitar/Lute	Harp	Recorder	Piccolo	Flute	Oboe	English Horn	Clarinet	Bassoon/Contrabassoon	Horn	Trumpet	Trombone	Percussion	Voice	Unusual Instruments	Publisher
LOUIS FERDINAND, (PRINCE) (1772–1806)																															
Octet, Op 10							2	2						1									1		2						MusRa
LULLY, JEAN-BAPT. (1632–1687)																															
Le carousel	1686																				2	1		1		3	1	1			MusRa
French Dances						2						1																			McGMa
LUZZASCHI, LUZZASCHO (1545–1607)																															
Canzon 10																										2	2				MusRa
MARENZIO, LUCA (1553–1599)																															
2 Madrigal Fantasias (arr.)	1635					2	1	1	1																						Noetz
MARINI, BIAGIO (1587–1665)																															
Sonata		C				2						1																			Bären
MASCHERA, FIORENZO (1540–1584)																															
Canzon ("Al S. Pompeo Coradello")																										2	2				MusRa
Canzona ("La Maggia")																										2	2				MusRa
MAZZAFERRATA, GIOVANNI B. (?–1691)																															
Sonata a tre, Op 5 No. 6		F				2		1				1																			Dobli
Sonate		D				2		1				1																			Foeti
MERULO, CLAUDIO (1533–1604)																															
Canzon No. 5																										2	2				MusRa
Canzonas 18, 23, 36																										2	2				MusRa
MICA, JAN A. (1746–1811)																															
Quartet		C				1	1	1													1										Dobli
String Quartet No. 2		C				2	1	1																							MABoh
MICO, RICHARD (?–1665)																															
Madrigal Fantasia (arr.)	1635					2	1	1	1																						Noetz
MOLTER, JOHANN M. (1695–1765)																															
Concerto a quattro no. 1, MWV VIII 5																					2			1		1					MusRa
Concerto a quattro no. 2, MWV VIII 6																					2			1		1					MusRa
Concerto a quattro no. 3, MWV VIII 7																					2			1		1					MusRa
Sinfonia concertante, MWV VIII 1																					2			1	2	1					MusRa
Sinfonia concertante, MWV VIII 2																					2			1	2	1					MusRa
MONN, GEORG M. (1717–1750)																															
Triopartita No. 2		g				2		1					1																		Dobli
Triopartita No. 7		D				2		1					1																		Dobli
MONTEVERDI, CLAUDIO (1567–1643)																															
Ballo ("Moveto al mio bel suon")						2		1					1																		Faber
Madrigal Fantasias (arr.)	1635					2	1	1	1																						Noetz
Scherzi musicali, Vol. 1 *Voices:* 2 Sopranos and bass						2						1																	3		Bären
Scherzi musicali, Vol. 2						2						1																			Bären
MOZART, LEOPOLD (1719–1787)																															
Divertimento		G				1		1												1											Amade
Frog Parthia		C				1		1	1																						Dobli
Sinfonia burlesca							2	2	1																						Dobli
Sonata a tre, Op 1 No. 4		G				2		1					1																		Dobli
MOZART, WOLFGANG A. (1756–1791)																															
Abduction from the Seraglio (for 8 Winds) *Comment:* This is an 18th-century arrangement	1782																				2	2		2	2						Bären

	Year Composed or Published	Key	Duration	Viols	Early Winds	Violin	Viola	Cello	Double Bass	Barytone	Gamba	Basso continuo	Harpsichord	Piano	Organ	Guitar/Lute	Harp	Recorder	Piccolo	Flute	Oboe	English Horn	Clarinet	Bassoon/Contrabassoon	Horn	Trumpet	Trombone	Percussion	Voice	Unusual Instruments	Publisher
MOZART, WOLFGANG A. *(continued)*																															
Adagio, K 580a	1789																					1		1	2						Kneus
Adagio, K 580a *Unus Instr:* 3 Basset horns	1789	F																					1							3	Kunze
Adagio for Winds, K 484c *Unus Instr:* 3 Basset horns	1785																						2							3	MusRa
Allegretto		B♭				2	1	1																							Kunze
Andante für eine Walze (arr. Beyer)						1	1													2											Kunze
Aria ("Non piu di fiori") *Unus Instr:* Basset horn														1																1	MusRa
Canon																					1		1	1							McGMa
Canonic Adagio, K 484d *Unus Instr:* 2 Basset horns																								1						2	MusRa
La clemenza di Tito (for 8 winds) (arr. Triebensee) *Comment:* In 2 volumes	1791																				2		2	2	2						MusRa
Contradances, 6, K 462	1784					2		1																							VarPb
Cosi fan tutte (for 8 Winds) (arr. Wendt)	1790																				2		2	2	2						MusRa
Divertimento (for 10 winds), K 166	1773	E♭																			2	2	2	2	2						MusRa
Divertimento (for 8 Winds), K Anh 226		E♭																			2		2	2	2						VarPb
Divertimento (for String Trio), K 563	1788	E♭				1	1	1																							VarPb
Divertimento for Winds, K Anh 229 *Comment:* May be played by 3 basset horns	1783																						2	1							Harmo
Divertimento No. 1, K Anh 229	1783	B♭				2		1																							B Scho
Divertimento No. 2, K Anh 229	1783	B♭				2		1																							Breit
Divertimento No. 3, K Anh 229	1783	C				2	1																								Breit
Divertimenti Nos. 4 and 5, K Anh 229	1783																						2	1							MusRa
Divertimento No. 6 (for Winds), K 188	1776	C																		2	2		2			2		1			Harmo
Divertimento No. 6, K Anh 229	1783																						2	1							MusRa
Don Giovanni (for 8 Winds) (arr. Triebensee) *Comment:* In 2 volumes	1787																				2		2	2	2						MusRA
Easy String Trios, 3						2		1																							Inter
Fantasie (arr. Beyer), K 594/608	1790					2	2	1																							Kunze
Flute Quartet, K 285	1777	D				1	1	1												1											VarPb
Flute Quartet, K 285a	1778	G				1	1	1												1											VarPb
Flute Quartet, K 285b	1778	C				1	1	1												1											VarPb
Flute Quartet, K 298	1778	A				1	1	1												1											VarPb
Galimathias musicum, K 32	1766					2	1		1				1								2			1	2						VarPb
Kirchensonaten, Vol. 1	1767					2		1							1																Bären
Kirchensonaten, Vol. 2	1775					2		1							1																Bären
Kirchensonaten, Vol. 5	1780					2		1							1											2					Bären
Eine kleine Nachtmusik, K 525 *Comment:* Also available as string quintet, with bass	1787	G				2	1	1																							VarPb
Ländler, 6, K 606	1791					2		1																							Breit
The Magic Flute (for 8 Winds) (arr. Heidenreich) *Comment:* In 2 volumes																					2		2	2	2						MusRa
March of Janissaries (from "Abduction")	1782																			2			2	2	2	1					Bären

	Year Composed or Published	Key	Duration	Viols	Early Winds	Violin	Viola	Cello	Double Bass	Barytone	Gamba	Basso continuo	Harpsichord	Piano	Organ	Guitar/Lute	Harp	Recorder	Piccolo	Flute	Oboe	English Horn	Clarinet	Bassoon/Contrabassoon	Horn	Trumpet	Trombone	Percussion	Voice	Unusual Instruments	Publisher
MOZART, WOLFGANG A. *(continued)*																															
Marriage of Figaro (for 8 Winds) (arr. Wendt) *Comment:* In 2 volumes																					2		2	2	2						MusRa
Menuette, 6 (trans.), K 61h	1769					2		1																							Hug
Minuets, 12						2		1																							B Scho
Minuets with Trios, 7, K 65A	1768					2		1																							OBV
Minuets with Trios, 8 (trans.), K 585	1789					2		1																							OBV
Ein musikalischer Spass, K 522	1787	F				2	1	1																	2						Liena
Oboe Quartet, K 370	1781	F				1	1	1													1										VarPb
Piano Quartet, K 478	1785	g				1	1	1						1																	VarPb
Piano Quartet, K 493		E♭				1	1	1						1																	VarPb
Piano Trio, K 254		B♭				1		1						1																	VarPb
Piano Trio, K 496		G				1		1						1																	VarPb
Piano Trio, Op 498 *Comment:* Clarinet may replace violin		E♭				1		1						1																	VarPb
Piano Trio, K 502		B♭				1		1						1																	VarPb
Piano Trio, K 542		E				1		1						1																	VarPb
Piano Trio, K 548		C				1		1						1																	VarPb
Piano Trio, K 564		G				1		1						1																	VarPb
Quintet for Clarinet and Strings, K 581	1789	A				2	1	1															1								VarPb
Quintet for Horn and Strings, K 407	1782	E♭				1	2	1																	1						VarPb
Quintet for Piano and Winds, K 452	1784	E♭												1							1		1	1	1						VarPb
Quintet Movement, K 580b	1789	F				1	1	1															1		1						Kunze
Rondo (completed by Beyer), K 464a	1785	A				2	1	1																							Kunze
Serenade, K 361 *Unus Instr:* 2 Basset horns	1781	B♭																			2		2	2	4					2	MusRa
Serenade, K 375	1782	E♭																			2		2	2	2						MusRa
Serenade, K 388	1782	c																			2		2	2	2						MusRa
Sonatas, 6, K 10-15	1764					1		1						1																	Bären
String Quartet, K 80	1774	G				2	1	1																							VarPb
String Quartet, K 155	1772	D				2	1	1																							VarPb
String Quartet, K 156	1772	G				2	1	1																							VarPb
String Quartet, K 157	1773	C				2	1	1																							VarPb
String Quartet, K 158	1773	F				2	1	1																							VarPb
String Quartet, K 159	1773	B♭				2	1	1																							VarPb
String Quartet, K 160	1773	E♭				2	1	1																							VarPb
String Quartet, K 168	1773	F				2	1	1																							VarPb
String Quartet, K 169	1773	A				2	1	1																							VarPb
String Quartet, K 170	1773	C				2	1	1																							VarPb
String Quartet, K 171	1773	E♭				2	1	1																							VarPb
String Quartet, K 172	1773	B♭				2	1	1																							VarPb
String Quartet, K 173	1773	d				2	1	1																							VarPb
String Quartet, K 387	1782	G				2	1	1																							VarPb
String Quartet, K 421	1783	d				2	1	1																							VarPb
String Quartet, K 428	1783	E♭				2	1	1																							VarPb
String Quartet, K 458	1784	B♭				2	1	1																							VarPb
String Quartet, K 464	1785	A				2	1	1																							VarPb
String Quartet, K 465	1785	C				2	1	1																							VarPb
String Quartet, K 499	1786	D				2	1	1																							VarPb
String Quartet, K 575	1789	D				2	1	1																							VarPb
String Quartet, K 589	1790	B♭				2	1	1																							VarPb

	Year Composed or Published	Key	Duration	Viols	Early Winds	Violin	Viola	Cello	Double Bass	Barytone	Gamba	Basso continuo	Harpsichord	Piano	Organ	Guitar/Lute	Harp	Recorder	Piccolo	Flute	Oboe	English Horn	Clarinet	Bassoon/Contrabassoon	Horn	Trumpet	Trombone	Percussion	Voice	Unusual Instruments	Publisher
MOZART, WOLFGANG A. *(continued)*																															
String Quartet, K 590	1790	F				2	1	1																							VarPb
String Quintet, K 174	1773	B♭				2	2	1																							VarPb
String Quintet, K 406	1787	c				2	2	1																							VarPb
String Quintet, K 515	1787	C				2	2	1																							VarPb
String Quintet, K 516	1787	g				2	2	1																							VarPb
String Quintet, K 593	1790	D				2	2	1																							VarPb
String Quintet, K 614	1791	E♭				2	2	1																							VarPb
String Quintet Movement, K Anh 79	1787	a				2	2	1																							Amade
String Quintet Movement, K Anh 80	1787	B♭				2	2	1																							Amade
String Trio, K 266	1777	B♭				2		1																							VarPb
String Trio Movement, K Anh 66	1788	G				1	1	1																							Amade
Trio ("Kegelstatt"), K 498	1786	E♭					1							1									1								Liena
Variations on a Theme of Gluck (arr. Druschetzky), K 455	1784																						2	2	2						Kneus
MUFFAT, GEORG (1653–1704)																															
Suite No. 1 (from "Blumenbüschlein")		D				2	1	1				1																			Bären
Suite No. 2		g				2	1	1				1																			Bären
MUFFAT, GOTTLIEB (1690–1770)																															
Sonata pastorale a tre		D				2		1					1																		Dobli
MYSLIVECEK, JOSEF (1737–1781)																															
3 String Quintets						2	2	1																							MABoh
3 Wind Octets																					2		2	2	2						MABoh
Sonata		B♭				1		1												1											Kunze
NAUMANN, JOHANN G. (1741–1801)																															
Trio		E♭				2		1																							Sikor
NEUBAUER, FRANZ C. (1760–1785)																															
Trio								1												2											Kunze
PACHELBEL, JOHANN (1653–1704)																															
Canon						3						1																			Amade
Musicalische Ergötzung, Partia 3		E♭				2						1																			Bären
Musicalische Ergötzung, Partia 4		e				2						1																			Bären
Musicalische Ergötzung, Partia 5		C				2						1																			Bären
Musicalische Ergötzung, Partia 6		B♭				2						1																			Bären
PAISIELLO, GIOVANNI (1740–1816)																															
6 Divertimenti						2	1	1																							Kunze
Quartet		G				1	1	1												1											Kunze
PALLAVICINI, CARLO (?–1688)																															
Madrigal Fantasia (arr.)	1635					2	1	1	1																						Noetz
PEPUSCH, JOHANN C. (1667–1752)																															
Concerto, Op 8 No. 1		F										1						2		2											VarPb
Concerto, Op 8 No. 2		G										1								2	2										VarPb
Concerto, Op 8 No. 3		B♭				2						1									2										VarPb
Concerto, Op 8 No. 4												1						2		2											VarPb
Concerto, Op 8 No. 5												1						2		2											VarPB
Concerto, Op 8 No. 6												1						2		2											VarPb
Triosonata						1						1								1											Kunze
Triosonata		d					1					1								1											Bären

	Year Composed or Published	Key	Duration	Viols	Early Winds	Violin	Viola	Cello	Double Bass	Barytone	Gamba	Basso continuo	Harpsichord	Piano	Organ	Guitar/Lute	Harp	Recorder	Piccolo	Flute	Oboe	English Horn	Clarinet	Bassoon/Contrabassoon	Horn	Trumpet	Trombone	Percussion	Voice	Unusual Instruments	Publisher
PERGOLESI, GIOVANNI B. (1710–1736)																															
Sonata a tre, Op 1 No. 4		d				2		1					1																		Dobli
Triosonate		g				2						1																			Foeti
PERRONI, GIOVANNI (1688–1748)																															
Concerto a tre		F				2										1															Dobli
PEZ, JOHANN C. (1664–1716)																															
Sonata a cuatro						2	1					1																			Leuck
Triosonata		C														1		2													Dobli
PEZEL, JOHANN C. (1639–1694)																															
5-Part Brass Music (Vol. 1, Nos. 1-25)																										2	3				MusRa
5-Part Brass Music (Vol. 2, Nos. 26-50)																										2	3				MusRa
5-Part Brass Music (Vol. 3, Nos. 51-76)																										2	3				MusRa
Bicinia 75 *Comment:* High trumpet												1												1		1					MusRa
Hora Decima (Vol. 1, Nos. 1-20)																										2	3				MusRa
Hora Decima (Vol. 2, Sonatas 21-40)																										2	3				MusRa
Sonatinas 61, 62, 65, 66												1														2					MusRa
Sonatinas 63, 64, 67, 68												1														2					MusRa
Sonatinas 69, 70, 72, 73 *Comment:* High trumpet												1														2					MusRa
Sonatinas 71, 74 *Comment:* High trumpet												1														2					MusRa
Triosonata		D				1						1								1											Kunze
PEZELIUS, JOHANN (1639–1694)																															
2 Sonatinen		B♭										1														2					Merse
PHALESE, PIERRE (1510–1573)																															
Antwerpener Tanzbuch (Vol. 1)	1583				4																										MusRa
Antwerpener Tanzbuch (Vol. 2)	1583				4																										Noetz
Loewener Tanzbuch (Vol. 1)	1571				4																										Noetz
Loewener Tanzbuch (Vol. 2)	1571				4																										Noetz
PICHL, WENZL (1741–1805)																															
String Quartet		A				2	1	1																							Kunze
PLATTI, GIOVANNI (1697–1763)																															
Triosonata		G										1								1	1										MusRa
POGLIETTI, ALESSANDRO (?–1683)																															
Sonata a tre												1								1				1		1					MusRa
POHLE, DAVID (1624–1695)																															
12 Liebesgesänge *Voices:* 2 Mezzo-sopranos						2						1																	2		Bären
PORPORA, NICOLA A. (1686–1768)																															
Sinfonia da camera a tre, Op 2 No. 6		B♭				2		1					1																		Dobli
PORTER, WALTER (1595–1659)																															
Since All Things Love						2						1																			McGMa
PRAETORIUS, MICHAEL (1571–1621)																															
Frantzösische Döntze (Vols. 1-3)	1612				4																										Noetz
PUGNANI, GAETANO (1731–1798)																															
Sonata a tre, Op 1 No. 3		C				2		1					1																		Dobli
PURCELL, DANIEL (1660–1717)																															
Sonata		F										1						2													Bären

	Year Composed or Published	Key	Duration	Viols	Early Winds	Violin	Viola	Cello	Double Bass	Barytone	Gamba	Basso continuo	Harpsichord	Piano	Organ	Guitar/Lute	Harp	Recorder	Piccolo	Flute	Oboe	English Horn	Clarinet	Bassoon/Contrabassoon	Horn	Trumpet	Trombone	Percussion	Voice	Unusual Instruments	Publisher
PURCELL, HENRY (1659–1695)																															
3-Part Sonata No. 1		g				2		1					1																		Dobli
3-Part Sonata No. 2		B♭				2		1					1																		Dobli
3-Part Sonata No. 3		d				2		1					1																		Dobli
3-Part Sonata No. 4		F				2		1					1																		Dobli
3-Part Sonata No. 5		a				2		1					1																		Dobli
3-Part Sonata No. 6		C				2		1					1																		Dobli
3-Part Sonata No. 7		e				2		1					1																		Dobli
3-Part Sonata No. 8		G				2		1					1																		Dobli
3-Part Sonata No. 9		c				2		1					1																		Dobli
3-Part Sonata No. 10		A				2		1					1																		Dobli
3-Part Sonata No. 11		f				2		1					1																		Dobli
3-Part Sonata No. 12		D				2		1					1																		Dobli
Chaconne												1						3													Amade
How Pleasant Is the Flowery Plain *Voices:* Soprano and tenor												1						2											2		Bären
Sonata		B♭																								3	2				Merse
When Night Her Purple Veil						2						1																	B		Faber
QUANTZ, JOHANN J. (1697–1773)																															
Triosonata		B♭										1								2											Bären
Triosonata		C										1						1		1											Bären
Triosonata		C										1						1		1											Bären
Triosonata		D										1								2											Foeti
Triosonata		E♭				2						1								1											Bären
Triosonata		G										1								2											Bären
Triosonata		c										1								1	1										MusRa
Triosonata		e										1								2											Bären
RAMEAU, JEAN P. (1683–1764)																															
Acante et Cephise (airs de ballet)																				1	1		1	1	1						Leduc
Arias from Operas and Ballets												1								1											MusRa
Le berger fidèle						2						1																	T		DeutV
Concerts (6) en sextuor						3	1		2																						Duran
Pièces de clavecin en concert						1					1		1																		Bären
Pièces de clavecin en concert						1		1						1																	Duran
Pièces de clavecin en concert						2								1																	Duran
Pièces de clavecin en concert								1						1						1											Duran
Symphonies et danses (arr. Oubradous)																				1	1		1	1	1						Leduc
REICHA, JOSEPH (1746–1795)																															
Sonata a tre						2		1																							Amade
REICHARD, JOHANN G. (1710–1782)																															
Weinachts-Weissagung						2	1					1																			DeutV
REINHART, FRANZ (?–?)																															
Sonata						2						1														1					Amade
RICCIO, TEODORO (1540–1595)																															
Jubilent omnes						1						1								1				1					H		Bären
RICCIOTTI, CARLO (1681–1756)																															
Concertino No. 2		G				4	1	1				1																			Bären
Concertino No. 3		A				4	1	1				1																			Bären
Concertino No. 4		f				4	1	1				1																			Bären
RICHTER, FRANZ X. (1709–1789)																															
Divertimenti						2	1	1																							MABoh
RIGEL, ANTON (1745–1807)																															
Trio		F				1		1												1											Hug

	Year Composed or Published	Key	Duration	Viols	Early Winds	Violin	Viola	Cello	Double Bass	Barytone	Gamba	Basso continuo	Harpsichord	Piano	Organ	Guitar/Lute	Harp	Recorder	Piccolo	Flute	Oboe	English Horn	Clarinet	Bassoon/Contrabassoon	Horn	Trumpet	Trombone	Percussion	Voice	Unusual Instruments	Publisher
ROSENMÜLLER, JOHANN (1620–1684)																															
Lieber Herre Gott									1		2	1																	S		Bären
ROSETTI, FRANTISEK A. (1746–1792)																															
Notturno		D				1	1	1												1					2						MABoh
Parthia No. 3		D																			2		2	1	2						Kneus
Partita		B♭																			1		2	1	2						Kunze
Partita *Unus Instr:* Contrabassoon		F																			3			2	2					1	Kunze
Quintet for Winds		E♭																		1	1	1	1	1							Kneus
String Quartets, Op 6 Nos. 1-6						2	1	1																							Kunze
ROSIER, CARL (1640–1725)																															
Triosonata		c										1								2											Bären
Triosonata		d										1								2											Bären
RÖSLER, FRANZ A. (1746–1792) See Rosetti, Frantisek Antonio																															
ROSSI, SALOMONE (1587–1628)																															
Sonata ("La moderna")		d				2						1																			Bären
RUGGIERI, GIOVANNI M. (1690–1720)																															
Sonata da chiesa, Op 3 No. 1 *Comment:* Also available with guitar replacing basso continuo		e				2						1																			Dobli
Sonata da chiesa, Op 3 No. 2 *Comment:* Also available with guitar replacing basso continuo		b				2						1																			Dobli
Sonata da chiesa, Op 3 No. 3 *Comment:* Also available with guitar replacing basso continuo		B♭				2						1																			Dobli
Sonata da chiesa, Op 3 No. 4 *Comment:* Also available with guitar replacing basso continuo		F				2						1																			Dobli
Sonata da chiesa, Op 3 No. 5 *Comment:* Also available with guitar replacing basso continuo		g				2						1																			Dobli
Sonata da chiesa, Op 3 No. 6 *Comment:* Also available with guitar replacing basso continuo		A				2						1																			Dobli
Sonata da chiesa, Op 3 No. 7 *Comment:* Also available with guitar replacing basso continuo		a				2						1																			Dobli
Sonata da chiesa, Op 3 No. 8 *Comment:* Also available with guitar replacing basso continuo		G				2						1																			Dobli
Sonata da chiesa, Op 3 No. 9 *Comment:* Also available with guitar replacing basso continuo		d				2						1																			Dobli
Sonata da chiesa, Op 3 No. 10 *Comment:* Also available with guitar replacing basso continuo		D				2						1																			Dobli
SAMMARTINI, GIOVANNI B. (1701–1775)																															
Sonata		D				2							1							1											Noetz
SCARLATTI, ALESSANDRO (1660–1725)																															
Ariette						2		1				1																			Foeti
Correa nel seno amato						2						1																	S		Bären

	Year Composed or Published	Key	Duration	Viols	Early Winds	Violin	Viola	Cello	Double Bass	Barytone	Gamba	Basso continuo	Harpsichord	Piano	Organ	Guitar/Lute	Harp	Recorder	Piccolo	Flute	Oboe	English Horn	Clarinet	Bassoon/Contrabassoon	Horn	Trumpet	Trombone	Percussion	Voice	Unusual Instruments	Publisher
SCHEIDT, SAMUEL (1587–1654)																															
2 Symphonien												1														2	1				Merse
SCHEIN, JOHANN H. (1586–1630)																															
3 Choralkonzerte *Voices:* 2 Sopranos and tenor												1																	3		Bären
Intrada and paduana																										2	2				Press
Suites, 3 (from "Banchetto musicale")						2	2	1																							Bären
SCHELLE, JOHANN (1648–1701)																															
6 Kantaten *Voice:* Bass						2						1																	1		Bären
SCHICKHARDT, JOHANN C. (1680–1762)																															
3 Sonatas											1		1					1			2										Liena
6 Triosonatas												1						2													Bären
Concerto No. 1		C										1						4													Bären
Concerto No. 2		d										1						4													Bären
Concerto No. 3		G										1						4													Bären
Concerto No. 4		F										1						4													Bären
Concerto No. 5		e										1						4													Bären
Concerto No. 6		c										1						4													Bären
Sonata		B♭									1		1					1			1										Liena
Sonata, Op 22 No. 1		F										1						2			1										MusRa
Sonata, Op 22 No. 2		D										1						2			1										MusRa
Sonata, Op 22 No. 3		c										1						2			1										MusRa
Sonata, Op 22 No. 4		G										1						2			1										MusRa
Sonata, Op 22 No. 5		d										1						2			1										MusRa
Sonata, Op 22 No. 6		a										1						2			1										MusRa
Triosonata		F				1										1		1													Dobli
Triosonata		G										1												2							MusRa
SCHILDT, MELCHIOR (1592–1667)																															
Ach mein herzliebes Jesulein						2						1												1					S		Bären
SCHMELZER, JOHANN H. (1623–1680)																															
Sonata ("La carioletta") *Unus Instr:* Cornetto						1						1												1			1			1	MusRa
Sonata a cinque *Unus Instr:* High trumpet						2					1	1												1						1	MusRa
Sonata a tre						1						1														1	1				MusRa
Sonata a tre						1						1												1			1				MusRa
SCHMIKERER, JOSEF A. (1660–1700)																															
Suite No. 1		F				3						1																			Bären
Suite No. 2		d				3						1																			Bären
SCHOP, JOHANN (1590–1667)																															
Jauchzet dem Herren, alle Welt												1																			Merse
SCHÜRMANN, GEORG C. (1672–1751)																															
Arien												1						1						1					H		Bären
SCHÜTZ, HEINRICH (1585–1672)																															
3 Schöne Dinge seind (Sym Sac II:25), SWV 365 *Voices:* 2 Tenors and bass						2						1																	3		VarPb
Adjuro vos (Sym Sac I:8), SWV 264 *Voice:* 2 Tenors												1										2							2		VarPb
Anima mea liquefacta est (Sym Sac I:7), SWV 263 *Voice:* 2 Tenors												1										2							2		VarPb

	Year Composed or Published	Key	Duration	Viols	Early Winds	Violin	Viola	Cello	Double Bass	Barytone	Gamba	Basso continuo	Harpsichord	Piano	Organ	Guitar/Lute	Harp	Recorder	Piccolo	Flute	Oboe	English Horn	Clarinet	Bassoon/Contrabassoon	Horn	Trumpet	Trombone	Percussion	Voice	Unusual Instruments	Publisher
SCHÜTZ, HEINRICH *(continued)*																															
Attendite, popule meus (Sym Sac I:14), SWV 270 *Voice:* Bass												1															4		1		VarPb
Benedicam dominum (Sym Sac I:11), SWV 267 *Voices:* Soprano, tenor, and bass												1																	3	Z	VarPb
Buccinate in neomenia (Sym Sac I:19), SWV 275 *Voices:* 2 Tenors and bass. *Unus Instr:* 2 Zinks												1												1					3	2	VarPb
Cantabo domino (Sym Sac I:4), SWV 260						2						1																	T		VarPb
Domine, labia mea aperies (Sym Sac I:15), SWV 271 *Voices:* Soprano and tenor												1												1			1		2	Z	VarPb
Es steh Gott auf (Sym Sac II:16), SWV 356						2						1																	S		VarPb
Exquisivi dominum (Sym Sac I:12), SWV 268 *Voices:* Soprano, tenor, and bass												1																	3	Z	VarPb
Exultavit cor meum (Sym Sac I:2), SWV 258 *Voice:* Soprano or tenor						2						1																	1		VarPb
Frohlocket mit Händen (Sym Sac II:9), SWV 349 *Voice:* Tenor						2						1																	T		VarPb
Gib unsern Fürsten (Sym Sac II:15), SWV 355 *Voice:* Soprano or tenor						2						1																	1		VarPb
Der Herr ist mein Licht (Sym Sac II:19), SWV 359						2						1																	T		VarPb
Herr, neige deine Himmel (Sym Sac II:21), SWV 361 *Voice:* Bass						2						1																	1		VarPb
Herr, unser Herrscher (Sym Sac II:3), SWV 343						2						1																	S		VarPb
Herzlich lieb hab ich (Sym Sac II:8), SWV 348						2						1																	A		VarPb
Hütet euch (Sym Sac II:11), SWV 351 *Voice:* Bass						2						1																	1		VarPb
In lectulo per noctes (Sym Sac I:16), SWV 272 *Voices:* Soprano and alto												1												3					2		VarPb
In te, domine, speravi (Sym Sac I:3), SWV 259						1						1												1					A		VarPb
Invenerunt me custodes (Sym Sac I:17), SWV 273 *Voices:* Soprano and alto												1												3					2		VarPb
Iss dein Brot (Sym Sac II:18), SWV 358 *Voices:* Soprano and bass						2						1																	2		VarPb
Jubilate Deo (Sym Sac I:6), SWV 262 *Voice:* Bass												1						2											1		VarPb
Jubilate Deo (Sym Sac I:20), SWV 276 *Voices:* 2 Tenors and bass. *Unus Instr:* 2 Zinks												1												1					3	2	VarPb
Lobet den Herrn (Sym Sac II:10), SWV 350						2						1																	T		VarPb
Lobet den Herrn (Sym Sac II:23), SWV 363 *Voices:* Alto, tenor, bass						2						1																	3		VarPb
Mein Herz ist bereit (Sym Sac II:1), SWV 341 *Voice:* Soprano or tenor						2						1																	1		VarPb
O quam tu pulchra es (Sym Sac I:9), SWV 265 *Voices:* Tenor and baritone						2						1																	2		VarPb
Paratum cor meum (Sym Sac I:1), SWV 257 *Voice:* Soprano or tenor						2						1																	1		VarPb

	Year Composed or Published	Key	Duration	Viols	Early Winds	Violin	Viola	Cello	Double Bass	Barytone	Gamba	Basso continuo	Harpsichord	Piano	Organ	Guitar/Lute	Harp	Recorder	Piccolo	Flute	Oboe	English Horn	Clarinet	Bassoon/Contrabassoon	Horn	Trumpet	Trombone	Percussion	Voice	Unusual Instruments	Publisher
SCHÜTZ, HEINRICH *(continued)*																															
Singet dem Herrn (Sym Sac II:2), SWV 342 *Voice:* Soprano or tenor						2						1																	1		VarPb
Die so ihr (Sym Sac II:24), SWV 364 *Voices:* Alto, tenor, and bass						2						1																	3		VarPb
Veni de Libano (Sym Sac I:10), SWV 266 *Voices:* Tenor and baritone						2						1																	2		VarPb
Veni, dilecte mi (Sym Sac I:18), SWV 274 *Voices:* 2 Sopranos and tenor												1															3		3		Bären
Venite ad me (Sym Sac I:5), SWV 261						2						1																	T		Bären
Verleih uns Frieden (Sym Sac II:14), SWV 354 *Voice:* Soprano or tenor						2						1																	1		Bären
Von aufgang der Sonnen (Sym Sac II:22), SWV 362 *Voice:* Bass						2						1																	1		Bären
Von Gott will ich (Sym Sac II:26), SWV 366 *Voices:* 2 Sopranos and bass						2						1																	3		Bären
Wie ein Rubin (Sym Sac II:17), SWV 357 *Voices:* Soprano and alto						2						1																	2		Bären
Zweierlei bitte ich (Sym Sac II:20), SWV 360						2						1																	T		Bären
SIMONETTI, GIOVANNI P. (?–?)																															
Concerto, Op 4		d				2	1					1						1													Amade
Concerto, Op 10 No. 1							1					1						1													Amade
Sonata a tre, Op 5 No. 3		g										1						2													Amade
Sonata a tre, Op 10 No. 2							1					1						1													Amade
Sonatas, Op 2 Nos.1-6												1						2													Amade
SIMPSON, THOMAS (1582–1626)																															
Opus Newer Paduanen, Intraden (2 vols.), Nos. 1-22 *Unus Instr:* 3 Cornetti	1617																										2			3	MusRa
Taffel Consort	1621			4																											Noetz
SPEER, DANIEL G. (1636–1707)																															
Sonata		C										1															4				MusRa
Sonata and Gigue						2						1															1				MusRa
Sonatas, 2		C										1														2	3				MusRa
Sonatas, 2		C										1														1	3				MusRa
Sonatas, 6 ("Musikalisch Türkenspiegel")																										2	3				MusRa
SPERGER, JOHANN M. (1750–1812)																															
Cassation		D					1		1																2						Dobli
Cassation		E♭					1		1																2						Dobli
Cassation		G				1	1		1																2						Dobli
Divertimento		D					1	1												1											Amade
Quartet		D					1	1	1											1											Dobli
STAMITZ, CARL (1746–1801)																															
Quartet, Op 8 No. 1		D				1	1	1												1											Bären
Quartet, Op 8 No. 3		F				1	1	1													1										MusRa
Quartet, Op 8 No. 4		E♭				1	1	1													1										MusRa
Quartet, Op 19 No. 1		E♭				1	1	1															1								VarPb
Quartet, Op 19 No. 2		B♭				1	1	1															1								VarPb
Quartet, Op 19 No. 3		E♭				1	1	1															1								MusRa
Quartet, Op 19 No. 5		B♭				1	1	1																1							VarPb

	Year Composed or Published	Key	Duration	Viols	Early Winds	Violin	Viola	Cello	Double Bass	Barytone	Gamba	Basso continuo	Harpsichord	Piano	Organ	Guitar/Lute	Harp	Recorder	Piccolo	Flute	Oboe	English Horn	Clarinet	Bassoon/Contrabassoon	Horn	Trumpet	Trombone	Percussion	Voice	Unusual Instruments	Publisher
STAMITZ, CARL *(continued)*																															
Quartet, Op 19 No. 6		F				1	1	1																1							VarPb
Trio		E♭				1		1																	1						Dobli
Trio No. 6		G						1												2											VarPb
STANLEY, JOHN (1713–1786)																															
6 Voluntaries															1											2					MusRa
STOLTZENBERG, CHRISTOPH (1690–1764)																															
Kantate ("Kommt her zu miralle") *Voices:* Soprano, alto, and tenor						2						1																	3		Bosse
STÖLZEL, GOTTFRIED H. (1690–1749)																															
Aus der Tiefe rufe ich, Herr, zu dir						2	1	1				1																			Merse
Triosonata No. 1		D				2						1																			Harmo
STRUTIUS, THOMAS (1621–1678)																															
Resonet in laudibus *Voices:* 2 Sopranos and bass						2						1																	3		Bären
SÜSSMAYR, FRANZ X. (1766–1803)																															
Quintet		D				1	1	1												1	1										Dobli
TANTZ, LUDWIG (?–1790)																															
3 Trios, Op 3						1		1						1																	DeutV
TARTINI, GIUSEPPE (1692–1770)																															
6 Sonaten						2						1																			Caris
Sonata a tre, Op 8 No. 6		D				2		1					1																		Dobli
TELEMANN, GEORG P. (1681–1767)																															
Ach Herr, strafe mich nicht (Psalm 6)						2						1																	A		DeutV
Alles redet jetzt und singet *Voices:* Soprano and bass. *Unus Instr:* Bassett horn						2	1	1	1			1								2	1								2	1	Bären
Concerto		G				2						1						1													Amade
Concerto a cinque		D										1									2			1	2						Kunze
Concerto a tre		F											1					1							1						Noetz
Corellisierende Sonaten						2						1																			Bären
Gesegnet ist die Zuversicht *Voices:* Tenor and bass						2						1						2											2		Bären
Gott will Mensch und sterblich werden						1						1																	H		Bären
Ha ha! wo will wi hüt noch danzen						1						1																	S		DeutV
Der harmonische Gottesdienst, Nos. 1-72						1						1																	H		Bären
Hemmet den Eifer, verbannet die Rache												1						1											H		Bären
Die Hoffnung ist mein Leben *Voice:* Bass						1						1																	1		Bären
Ihr Völker, hört *Voice:* Medium												1								1									1		Bären
Jauchzet, ihr Christen						1						1																	H		Bären
Kanarien-Vogel Kantate *Voice:* Medium						2	1					1																	1		Bären
Kleine Kantate von Wald und Au												1								1									S		Bären
Paris Quartet (Concerto secondo)		D				1					1	1								1											Bären
Paris Quartet 3 (Sonata prima)		A				1					1	1								1											Bären
Paris Quartet 4 (Sonata seconda)		g				1					1	1								1											Bären
Paris Quartet 5 (Premiere suite)		e				1					1	1								1											Bären

	Year Composed or Published	Key	Duration	Viols	Early Winds	Violin	Viola	Cello	Double Bass	Barytone	Gamba	Basso continuo	Harpsichord	Piano	Organ	Guitar/Lute	Harp	Recorder	Piccolo	Flute	Oboe	English Horn	Clarinet	Bassoon/Contrabassoon	Horn	Trumpet	Trombone	Percussion	Voice	Unusual Instruments	Publisher
TELEMANN, GEORG P. *(continued)*																															
Paris Quartet 6 (Deuxieme suite)		b				1					1	1								1											Bären
Pyrmonter Kurwoche (Scherzi melodichi)						1	1					1																			Bären
Quartet		G				1						1							1	1											Bären
Quartet		d										1						1		2											Bären
Quartet No. 1 (of 6 Quartets or Trios)		D						2												2											Bären
Quartet No. 2 (of 6 Quartets or Trios)		e						2												2											Bären
Quartet No. 3 (of 6 Quartets or Trios)		A						2												2											Bären
Quartet No. 4 (of 6 Quartets or Trios)		G						2												2											Bären
Quartet No. 5 (of 6 Quartets or Trios)		a						2												2											Bären
Quartet No. 6 (of 6 Quartets or Trios)		E						2												2											Bären
Quartett		A				1	1					1								1											Foeti
Six Concertos *Comment:* The instruments are used in various combinations						1		1				1								1											Bären
Sonata		D				1						1								1											Bären
Sonata		D				1	1					1								1											Foeti
Sonata		F										1						1			1										Bären
Sonata		G				1						1									1										Bären
Sonata		G				1						1								1											Bären
Sonata		b				1		1				1								1											Bären
Sonata		c										1						1			1										Bären
Sonata		e										1								1	1										Bären
Sonata		f				2	2	1					1																		Bären
Sonata		g					1					1								1											Bären
Sonata a tre		f				1						1						1													Amade
Sonatina		e				1						1									1										Bären
Suite		B♭				1						1								1											Bären
Suite		E				1						1								1											Bären
Suite		a				1						1								1											Bären
Suite		b				1						1								1											Bären
Suite		d				1						1								1											Bären
Süsse Hoffnung						2	1	1				1																	T		Bären
Tirsis am Scheidewege						2	1					1						1													Bären
Trio										1		1								1											Kunze
Trio		E♭				2						1																			Bären
Triosonata (from "Der getreue Musikmeister")		A										1								2											Amade
Triosonata		B♭				1						1									1										Bären
Triosonata		B♭										1	1					1													Bären
Triosonata		C										1						2													Bären
Triosonata		D										1								2											Merse
Triosonata		F										1						1			1										Merse
Triosonata		F				1						1						1													Amade
Triosonata		F										1						2													Amade
Triosonata		a				1						1						1													Amade
Triosonata		a										1						1			1										Amade
Triosonata		c										1									2										Amade
Triosonata		e										1						1			1										Bären

	Year Composed or Published	Key	Duration	Viols	Early Winds	Violin	Viola	Cello	Double Bass	Barytone	Gamba	Basso continuo	Harpsichord	Piano	Organ	Guitar/Lute	Harp	Recorder	Piccolo	Flute	Oboe	English Horn	Clarinet	Bassoon/Contrabassoon	Horn	Trumpet	Trombone	Percussion	Voice	Unusual Instruments	Publisher
TELEMANN, GEORG P. *(continued)*																															
Triosonata No. 56		g				1						1									1										Amade
Triosonata No. 63		g				1						1						1													Amade
Triosonata No. 72		b				1	1					1																			Amade
Triosonate		g				1						1									1										Foeti
Der Weiberorden						2						1																	S		DeutV
TOMASINI, LUIGI (1741–1808)																															
Quartetto, Op 8 No. 1						2	1	1																							Zanib
TOMKINS, THOMAS (1572–1656)																															
2 Fantasias a tre						2		1																							BScho
6 Fantasies						2		1																							Noetz
In Nomine a tre (Fantasia on Gloria tibi)						2		1																							Hinri
TORELLI, GIUSEPPE (1658–1709)																															
Sinfonia a tre, Op 5 No. 1		a				2		1					1																		Dobli
Sinfonia a tre, Op 5 No. 3		C				2		1					1																		Dobli
Sinfonia a tre, Op 5 No. 5		g				2		1					1																		Dobli
Sinfonia a tre, Op 5 No. 7		A				2		1					1																		Dobli
Sinfonia a tre, Op 5 No. 9		D				2		1					1																		Dobli
Sinfonia a tre, Op 5 No. 11		e				2		1					1																		Dobli
Sonata a cinque, No. 1						1	1	1				1														1					Dobli
Sonata a cinque, No. 7						1	1	1				1														1					Dobli
TRABACI, GIOVANNI M. (1575–1647)																															
Gaillarde																									1	2	1				Billa
TUMA, FRANTISEK I. (1704–1774)																															
Partita a tre		A				2		1					1																		Dobli
TUNDER, FRANZ (1614–1667)																															
Wachet auf						2	1	1				1																	S		Bären
UCCELLINI, MARCO (1603–1680)																															
Sinfonia a tre, Op 9 No. 7		D				2		1					1																		Dobli
VALENTINE, ROBERT (1680–1735)																															
Sonata		c										1						2													Bären
VANHAL, JOHANN B. (1739–1813)																															
3 Trios, Op 20						1		1															1								Kunze
Divertimento		C																			2			1	2						Kunze
Quartet						1	1	1															1								Kunze
VECCHI, ORAZIO (1550–1605)																															
Madrigal Fantasia (arr.)	1635					2	1	1	1																						Noetz
VEJVANOVSKY, PAVEL J. (1640–1693)																															
Intrada		B♭													1											2					Merse
Intrada		C				2	1	1	1			1														2					Merse
Sonata vespertina		B♭													1											2					Merse
VERACINI, ANTONIO (1659–1733)																															
Sonata a tre, Op 1 No. 1		D				2						1																			Hug
Sonata a tre, Op 1 No. 7						2						1																			Hug
Triosonata, Op 1 No. 10						2						1																			Hug
VIADANA, LODOVICO (1560–1627)																															
Sinfonia ("La bergamasca")																										4	4				MusRa
Sinfonia ("La padovana")																										4	4				MusRa

	Year Composed or Published	Key	Duration	Viols	Early Winds	Violin	Viola	Cello	Double Bass	Barytone	Gamba	Basso continuo	Harpsichord	Piano	Organ	Guitar/Lute	Harp	Recorder	Piccolo	Flute	Oboe	English Horn	Clarinet	Bassoon/Contrabassoon	Horn	Trumpet	Trombone	Percussion	Voice	Unusual Instruments	Publisher
VIERDANCK, JOHANN (1605–1646)																															
Ich verkündige euch grosse Freude *Voices:* 2 Sopranos						2						1																	2		Bären
Mein Herz ist bereit *Voices:* 2 Sopranos						2						1																	2		Bären
Siehe, wie fein							2					1																	S		Bären
VIOTTI, GIOVANNI B. (1755–1824)																															
3 Trios, Op 18						2		1																							Amade
Quartet, Op 22 No. 1		B♭				2	1	1												1											MusRa
Trio, Op 19 No. 1		B♭				2		1																							Noetz
VITALI, GIOVANNI B. (1632–1692)																															
Altra sorte di passamezzo, Op 7 No. 2						2						1																			Amade
Capriccio primo sopra 12 figure, Op 7 No. 4						2						1																			Amade
Capriccio secondo, Op 7 No. 5						2						1																			Amade
Ciaconna, Op 7 No. 3						2						1																			Amade
Passagallo primo, Op 7 No. 6						2						1																			Amade
Passagallo secondo, Op 7 No. 7						2						1																			Amade
Passagallo terzo, Op 7 No. 8						2						1																			Amade
Sonata a tre, Op 2 No. 6		d				2		1					1																		Dobli
Varie partite del passamezzo, Op 7 No. 1						2						1																			Amade
VIVALDI, ANTONIO (1678–1741)																															
All' ombra di sospetto												1								1									H		DeutV
Concerto, F XII:4		g										1						1			1			1							VarPb
Concerto, F XII:6		g				1						1								1	1			1							VarPb
Concerto, F XII:7		D										1						1						1							VarPb
Concerto, F XII:8		g				1						1								1				1							VarPb
Concerto, F XII:9		D				1						1								1	1			1							VarPb
Concerto, F XII:13		G				1						1						1			1			1							VarPb
Concerto, F XII:20		g				1						1						1			1			1							VarPb
Concerto, F XII:24		C				1						1								1	1			1							VarPb
Concerto, F XII:25		D				1						1							1		1			1							VarPb
Concerto, F XII:26		F				1						1								1	1			1							VarPb
Concerto, F XII:29		D				1						1						1			1			1							VarPb
Concerto, F XII:30		C				2						1						1			1										VarPb
Concerto, F XII:42						1						1								1				1							VarPb
Concerto, F XII:43							1					1								1											VarPb
Concerto, RV 101		G				1						1						1			1			1							VarPb
In turbato mare irato						2	1	1				1																	S		DeutV
Sonata a tre, F XIII:45		B♭				2		1					1																		VarPb
Sonata a tre, F XIII:46		g				2		1					1																		VarPb
Trio, RV 86		a										1						1						1							VarPb
Triosonata, F XVI:1		c				1		1				1																			Ricor
Triosonata, F XVI:2		E♭				2	1					1																			Ricor
Triosonata, F XVI:4		g				1						1				1															VarPb
Triosonata, F XVI:8 *Unus Instr:* Musette or vieille (may be replaced by oboe or violin)		A						1				1																		1	Ricor
Triosonata, RV 81		g										1									2										VarPb
VOGEL, JOHANN C. (1758–1788)																															
Quartet, Op 5 No. 1		F				1	1	1																1							MusRa
VRANICKY, PAVEL (1756–1808)																															
String Quartet, Op 15 No. 3		B♭				2	1	1																							MABoh

	Year Composed or Published	Key	Duration	Viols	Early Winds	Violin	Viola	Cello	Double Bass	Barytone	Gamba	Basso continuo	Harpsichord	Piano	Organ	Guitar/Lute	Harp	Recorder	Piccolo	Flute	Oboe	English Horn	Clarinet	Bassoon/Contrabassoon	Horn	Trumpet	Trombone	Percussion	Voice	Unusual Instruments	Publisher
WAGENSEIL, GEORG C. (1715–1777)																															
Konzert		G				2		1									1														DeutV
Parthia		C																			2	2		2	2						Kunze
Sonata, WV 508		B♭				1						1											1								Dobli
Sonata a tre, Op 1 No. 3		B♭				2		1					1																		Dobli
Sonata No. 1, WV 445:1		D						3	1																						Dobli
Sonata No. 2, WV 445:2		F						3	1																						Dobli
Sonata No. 3 (Suite de pièces), WV 445:3		C						3	1																						Dobli
Sonata No. 4, WV 445:4		A						3	1																						Dobli
Sonata No. 5, WV 445:5		B♭						3	1																						Dobli
Sonata No. 6, WV 445:6		G						3	1																						Dobli
WANHAL, JOHANN B. (1739–1813)																															
15 Easy Trios						2		1																							Augen
Quartet		F				1	1	1															1								MusRa
Quartets, Op 7 Nos. 1,2						1	1	1													1										MusRa
Quartet, Op 7 No. 4						1	1	1													1										MusRa
Quartet, Op 7 No. 5						1	1	1													1										MusRa
Quartet, Op 7 No. 6						1	1	1													1										MusRa
WECKMANN, MATTHIAS (1621–1674)																															
Sonata a quattro						1						1									1			1			1				MusRa
WEILAND, JULIUS J. (?–1663)																															
Amor Jesu (Cantata)						1					1	1																	H		Bären
WENDLING, JEAN B. (1723–1797)																															
Trio		G				1		1												1											Kunze
WENTH, J (1745–1801)																															
Divertimento		B♭																			2	1									Kneus
Petite serenade concertante																					2	1									Kneus
Quartetto concertante																					1	1	1	1							Kneus
Variations on a Theme of Paisiello																					2	1									Kneus
WERNER, GREGOR J. (1693–1766)																															
Concerto a quattro		A				2						1								1											Dobli
Concerto a tre		G				1						1								1											Dobli
Sonatina		B♭				2		1					1																		Dobli
Sonatina		D				2		1					1																		Dobli
Sonatina (Kovacs)		F				2		1					1																		Dobli
Sonatina (Mezo)		F				2		1					1																		Dobli
Sonatina		G				2		1					1																		Dobli
Sonatina (Gompas)		g				2		1					1																		Dobli
Sonatina (Mezo)		g				2		1					1																		Dobli
Symphonia 1/Sonata 1						2		1					1																		Dobli
Symphonia 2/Sonata 2						2		1					1																		Dobli
Symphonia 3/Sonata 3						2		1					1																		Dobli
Symphonia 4/Sonata 4						2		1					1																		Dobli
Symphonia 5/Sonata 5						2		1					1																		Dobli
Symphonia 6/Sonata 6						2		1					1																		Dobli
WIDMANN, ERASMUS (1572–1634)																															
Canzones, Intradas	1618					4		1																							Noetz
WILLIAMS, WILLIAM (?–1701)																															
Sonata		a										1						2													Bären
WITT, CHRISTIAN F. (1660–1716)																															
Suite		F										1						3													Bären

	Year Composed or Published	Key	Duration	Viols	Early Winds	Violin	Viola	Cello	Double Bass	Barytone	Gamba	Basso continuo	Harpsichord	Piano	Organ	Guitar/Lute	Harp	Recorder	Piccolo	Flute	Oboe	English Horn	Clarinet	Bassoon/Contrabassoon	Horn	Trumpet	Trombone	Percussion	Voice	Unusual Instruments	Publisher
ZACH, JOHANN (1699–1773)																															
2 Sinfonias		G				2						1																			Bären
Sonata a tre stromenti						2		1																							MABoh
ZACHOW, FRIEDRICH W. (1663–1712)																															
2 Pieces						2		1																							Viewe
ZELENKA, JAN D. (1679–1745)																															
Laudate pueri (Psalm 113)						2	1					1														1			T		Merse
Sonata No. 1		F										1									2			1							Bären
Sonata No. 2		g										1									2			1							Bären
Sonata No. 3						1						1									1										Bären
Sonata No. 3		B♭										1									2			1							Bären
Sonata No. 4		g										1									2			1							Bären
Sonata No. 5		F										1									2			1							Bären
Sonata No. 6		c										1									2			1							Bären

PART II

Composers from Beethoven to Our Own Time

	Year Composed or Published	Key	Duration	Violin	Viola	Cello	Double Bass	Gamba	Piano	Harpsicord	Organ	Guitar	Harp	Recorder	Flute/Piccolo	Oboe	English Horn	Clarinet/Bass Clarinet	Bassoon/Contrabassoon	Saxophone	French Horn	Trumpet	Trombone	Bass Trombone	Tuba	Baritone	Percussion	Voice	Electronic Tape	Unusual Instruments	Publisher
ABBADO, MARCELLO (1926–)																															
Riverberazioni									1						1	1			1												Ricor
ABENDROTH, WALTER (1896–1973)																															
Streichquartett, Op 33	1955		18	2	1	1																									Sikor
Streichtrio, Op 38	1965			1	1	1																									Simro
ABRAHAMSEN, HANS (1952–)																															
Aria	1979		5			1							1		1												1	S			Hanse
Fantasy Pieces	1969		7			1			1						1						1										Hanse
Geduldspiel	1980		6	1	1	1			1						1	1		1			1	1									Hanse
Herbst (Autumn)	1970		10			1						1			1													T			Hanse
Landscapes (Wind Quintet No. 1)	1972		8											1	1	1		1		1											Hanse
Lied in Fall *Comment:* Oboe doubles on English horn	1988		10	2	1	1	1		1						1	1	1	1	1		1	1	1				1				Hanse
Märchenbilder	1985		14	2	1	1	1		1						1	1		1	1		1	1	1				1				Hanse
Piano Pieces (3) by Carl Nielsen	1990		10	2	1	1	1								1	1		1	1		1										Hanse
Preludes 1-10 (String Quartet No. 1)	1973		20	2	1	1																									Hanse
Round and In Between	1972		9																		1	2	2								Hanse
Songs of Denmark	1974		7		1				1						1			1									1	S			Hanse
String Quartet No. 2				2	1	1																									Hanse
Walden (Wind Quintet No. 2)															1	1		1	1		1										Hanse
Winternacht *Unus Instr:* Cornet	1976		13	1		1			1						1			1			1	1								1	Hanse
Winternacht (alt. vers.)	1987		13	1		1			1			1			1			1									1				Hanse
ACKER, DIETER (1940–)																															
Attitudes																		2	2		2										Breit
Cantus duriusculus																					1	2	1		1						Breit
Glossen (Trio No. 2)	1968					1			1									1													BoteB
Glossen (Trio No. 2, alt. inst.)	1968					1				1					1																BoteB
Stigmata (Trio No. 3)				1		1			1																						Breit
Streichquartett 3 (Cantus lugubris)				2	1	1																									Breit
Texturae II	1972		21	4	2	2	1		1						1		1	1	1		1						2				Breit
ADAM, ADOLPHE (1803–1856)																															
Bravura Var. (Theme by Mozart)									1						1													1			Liena
ADAMS, JOHN (1947–)																															
Shaker Loops	1982		28	3	1	2	1																								AMP
ADDISON, JOHN (1920–)																															
Serenade															1	1		1	1		1										Oxfor
ADLER, SAMUEL (1928–)																															
Aeolus, God of the Winds	1977		14	1		1			1									1													Schir
Intrada	1967														1	1		1	1		1										Oxfor
Introit and Toccatina											1											2									RKing
Music for 11															2	1		2	1								5				Oxfor
Piano Trio	1964			1		1			1																						Oxfor
String Quartet No. 7	1981		19	2	1	1																									Schir
Triolet					1								1		1																Peter
ADOLPHE, BRUCE (1955–)																															
Ballade for Piano	1986		12	1		1			1						1			1													AmCom
Dream Dance	1985		9	1		1			1									1													AmCom
Trio	1986		17		1	1			1																						AmCom
Troika	1986		10	1		1												1													AmCom
ADOLPHUS, MILTON (1913–)																															
Elegy, Op 81	1947		12	1	1	1												1			1										AmCom
Septet, Op 39a	1935		14	3	2	1										1															AmCom
Tribach	1957		6						1						1			1													AmCom
ADOMIAN, LAN (1905–1979)																															
5 A.M.						1									1				1			1									Schir

	Year Composed or Published	Key	Duration	Violin	Viola	Cello	Double Bass	Gamba	Piano	Harpsicord	Organ	Guitar	Harp	Recorder	Flute/Piccolo	Oboe	English Horn	Clarinet/Bass Clarinet	Bassoon/Contrabassoon	Saxophone	French Horn	Trumpet	Trombone	Bass Trombone	Tuba	Baritone	Percussion	Voice	Electronic Tape	Unusual Instruments	Publisher
ADOMIAN, LAN *(continued)*																															
Auschwitz (for voice and instruments)	1970		11	1			1											1	1			1	1				1	B			Schir
Fin de verano			6												1	1		1	1		1										Schir
Incursions *Unus Instr:* Celesta			9						1																		5			1	Schir
AESCHBACHER, WALTHER (1901–1969)																															
Concertino, Op 42				1		1									1																Amade
Concertino, Op 42 (Päuler)				2		1																									Amade
Nocturne (Quintet), Op 14				2	1	1															1										Amade
Suite, Op 48																					4	2	2		1		1				Amade
Trio (arr. Päuler)				2										1																	Amade
Trio, Op 21				1	1	1																									Amade
AITKEN, HUGH (1924–)																															
Cantata No. 1 (Elizabethan texts)	1958			1	1	1										1												T			Oxfor
Cantata No. 2 (Rilke poems)					1	1	1								1	1												T			Oxfor
Cantata No. 3					1											1												T			Oxfor
Cantata No. 4						1	1								1	1												S			Oxfor
Short Suite for Strings	1954			2	1	1																									Oxfor
AITKEN, ROBERT (1939–)																															
Keybar	1973		17				2								1			1					1				1		1		Salab
Shadows, Part II (Lalita) *Unus Instr:* Vibraphone, marimba	1973		12			3							2		1												2			2	Salab
ALAIN, JEHAN (1911–1940)																															
Andante con variazioni et scherzo	1990														1	1		1	1		1										Leduc
Inventions à 3 voix	1989														1	1		1													Leduc
ALBERT, STEPHEN (1941–1992)																															
To Wake the Dead *Unus Instr:* Harmonium	1977		28	1					1		1				1			1										S		1	Schir
Treestone *Voices:* Soprano and tenor	1984		45	2	2	1			1				1		1			1			1	1					1	2			Schir
ALBIN, ROGER (1920–)																															
Inchoatif, Incidente et Confluence			22	2	1	1				1					1			1													Ridea
ALBINONI, TOMASO (1671–1750)																															
Sonata "Saint Mark" (arr. Hickman)																					1	2	1		1						Press
Suite (arr. Thilde)		A																			1	2	1		1						Billa
ALBRECHTSBERGER, ANTON (?–)																															
Divertimento		C			1	1	1																								Amade
Divertimento		F		1		1	1																								Amade
ALBRIGHT, WILLIAM (1944–)																															
Enigma Syncopations			15				1				1				1												1				Peter
Quintet			20	2	1	1												1													Peter
Seven Deadly Sins *Comment:* Narrator optional	1974		24	2	1	1			1						1			1										N			Peter
ALFANO, FRANCO (1875–1954)																															
Concerto				1		1			1																						Suvin
Quartetto III		G		2	1	1																									Suvin
Quintetto		a		2	1	1			1																						Suvin
ALKAN, CHARLES V. (1813–1888)																															
Trio, Op 30 No. 1		g		1		1			1																						Billa
ALLANBROOK, DOUGLAS (1921–)																															
Quintet				1	1	1										1		1													Boose
ALTMANN, EDO (?–)																															
Tanz-Suite (after 18th C. dance book)							1								1	1		2	2		2										Hofme

	Year Composed or Published	Key	Duration	Violin	Viola	Cello	Double Bass	Gamba	Piano	Harpsicord	Organ	Guitar	Harp	Recorder	Flute/Piccolo	Oboe	English Horn	Clarinet/Bass Clarinet	Bassoon/Contrabassoon	Saxophone	French Horn	Trumpet	Trombone	Bass Trombone	Tuba	Baritone	Percussion	Voice	Electronic Tape	Unusual Instruments	Publisher
ALWYN, WILLIAM (1905–)																															
Fanfare for a Joyous Occasion	1948																				4	3	3		1		3				Oxfor
AMBROSIUS, HERMANN (1897–)																															
Suite in Alten Stil *Comment:* Oboes ad lib. Viola may replace 1 violin	1944			3		1	1									2															Curti
AMELLER, ANDRE (1912–)																															
Arlequinade																					1	2	1		1						Leduc
Épigraphe																							3		1						Leduc
Fanfares pour tous les temps																					2	4	4		1						Leduc
Largamente																						2	2		1						Leduc
AMES, WILLIAM (1901–1987)																															
Clarinet Quintet	1937		30	2	1	1												1													AmCom
Composition for 10 Instruments	1962		20	2	2	1									1	1		1	1		1										AmCom
Concertante	1980		15	2	2	1										1															AmCom
Dream Vault	1980		20								1										4	4	4				2				AmCom
Emanation	1970		15		1				1						1																AmCom
Henry IV (Incidental Music)	1962		20													1											5				AmCom
House Celebration Piece	1972		9			1			1						1																AmCom
Oboe Quartet	1958		16	1	1	1										1															AmCom
Oboe Sextet	1939		25	2	2	1										1															AmCom
Ode	1950		10			1							1		1																AmCom
Outdoor Suite	1980		10			1									1	1		1													AmCom
Piano Quartet	1949		29	1	1	1			1																						AmCom
Preamble	1955		4												1						1						6				AmCom
Quintet	1935		30	2	1	1			1																						AmCom
Quintet No. 2	1959		21	2	1	1			1																						AmCom
Septet	1977		25	2	1	1			1						1	1															AmCom
Trio	1953		15		1	1			1																						AmCom
Trio (for Oboe and Strings)	1980		15	1		1										1															AmCom
Trio (for Winds and Cello)	1958		17			1									1	1															AmCom
Trio with Harpsichord	1980		15							1					1	1															AmCom
Waltz in 6 Parts	1960		3	1	1	1	1								1	1		1	1												AmCom
AMFITEATROV, DANIELE (1901–1983)																															
Trio				1		1			1																						Suvin
AMON, JOHANN A. (1763–1825)																															
Quartett (solo viola), Op 18 No. 3				1	2	1																									Kunze
Quintett, Op 19 No. 3				1	2	1									1																Kunze
AMRAM, DAVID (1930–)																															
After the Fall (Incidental Music)	1963			1	1		1		1						1					1	1						1				Peter
Conversations	1987		20	1	1	1			1						1																Peter
Dirge and Variations	1962		14	1		1			1																						Peter
Discussions	1961		10			1			1						1												2				Peter
En memoria de Chano Pozo	1988						1					1									1	2	1		1		1				Peter
Fanfare and Processional	1966		6																		2	2	1								Peter
Far Rockaway: Incidental Music	1971					1			1																		1				Peter
Landscapes	1976		10																								4				Peter
Native American Portraits	1976		12	1					1																		1				Peter
Peer Gynt	1959			1	3										1	1		1	1		1						2				Peter
Portraits	1974		10	1	1	1			1																						Peter
Quintet for Winds	1968		19												1	1		1	1		1										Peter
String Quartet	1961		20	2	1	1																									Peter
Summernight's Dream (Incidental Music)	1962		20	1		1			1							1			1			1					1				Peter
Three Songs for America. Texts: John F. and Robert Kennedy, Martin Luther King	1969		9	2	2	1									1	1		1	1		1							B			Peter

	Year Composed or Published	Key	Duration	Violin	Viola	Cello	Double Bass	Gamba	Piano	Harpsicord	Organ	Guitar	Harp	Recorder	Flute/Piccolo	Oboe	English Horn	Clarinet/Bass Clarinet	Bassoon/Contrabassoon	Saxophone	French Horn	Trumpet	Trombone	Bass Trombone	Tuba	Baritone	Percussion	Voice	Electronic Tape	Unusual Instruments	Publisher
AMRAM, DAVID *(continued)*																															
Trio	1958		14																1	1	1										Peter
AMY, GILBERT (1936–)																															
Après . . . “d'un desastre obscur” *Unus Instr:* Piccolo, gongs. Bass clarinet, horn, harp ad libitum	1976		9	1		1			1				1		1			2			1						2	M		3	Unive
Echos XIII *Unus Instr:* Piccolo, bass clarinet	1976		14	1	1	1	1		1				1		2			2	1		1		1							2	Unive
ANCELIN, PIERRE (1934–)																															
Tres leys per ventadour																						2	2		1						Billa
ANDERSON, BETH (1950–)																															
Little Trio	1983		4		1							1			1																AmCom
Network *Comment:* Amplification needed	1982		6						1											4											AmCom
Revel	1984		8	1			1		1									1		1		1	1				1				AmCom
Trio: Dream	1980		10			1			1						1																AmCom
Trio: Dream (alt. inst.)	1980		10			1			1									1													AmCom
Trio: Dream (alt. vers.)	1980		10		1	1			1																						AmCom
ANDERSON, THOMAS J. (1928–)																															
Bagatelles (5)	1963		10	1						1						1															AmCom
Intervals, Set II	1970		3												1	1		2						1	1		2				AmCom
Intervals, Set III *Comment:* Conductor needed. *Unus Instr:* Celesta	1970		5	2		2											1	2	3								1			1	AmCom
Intervals, Set IV	1970		4										1		1	1		1					1								AmCom
Intervals, Set V	1970		5				2		1						1					2		3	1				1				AmCom
Intervals, Set VI	1970		3		3																4						1				AmCom
Transitions, a Fantasy	1971		14	1	1	1			1						1			1	1		1	1	1								AmCom
ANDREAE, VOLKMAR (1879–1962)																															
Quartet, Op 43				1	1	1									1																Amade
ANDRÈS, DANIEL (?–)																															
Quatuor pour cuivres																						2	2								Billa
ANDRIESSEN, HENDRICK (1892–1981)																															
Serenade				2		1																									Harmo
ANDRIEU, MIHAIL G. (?–)																															
Octet, Op 8				2	2	1												2			1										ESPLA
ANGERER, PAUL (1927–)																															
Bläserquintett															1	1		1	1		1										Dobli
Chanson Gaillarde	1963					1				1						1															Dobli
Chanson Gaillarde (alt. inst.)	1963			1					1										1												Dobli
Cogitatio for 9 Solo Instruments	1964			1	1	1	1								1	1		1	1		1										Dobli
Concertante Quartett	1951				1	1										1					1										Dobli
Conférence entre deux violoncelles						2			1																						Dobli
Ei, du feiner Reiter (Variations)				2	1	1																									Dobli
Invocatio	1954			1		1			1																						Dobli
Konzert										1				2																	Dobli
Konzert	1946		23		1					1						1	1		2			1									Unive
Konzert für zwei Blockflöten				2	2	1								2							2										Dobli
Musica articolata (for 13 winds)															2	2		3	2		2	1	1								Dobli
Musica trifida														3																	Dobli
Quartett								1				1		1													1				Dobli
Quinta Tön für Bläser	1946		15												1	1		1	1		1	2	1								Unive
Serenata				1	1														1		1										Dobli

	Year Composed or Published	Key	Duration	Violin	Viola	Cello	Double Bass	Gamba	Piano	Harpsicord	Organ	Guitar	Harp	Recorder	Flute/Piccolo	Oboe	English Horn	Clarinet/Bass Clarinet	Bassoon/Contrabassoon	Saxophone	French Horn	Trumpet	Trombone	Bass Trombone	Tuba	Baritone	Percussion	Voice	Electronic Tape	Unusual Instruments	Publisher
ANGERER, PAUL *(continued)*																															
Trio 1 (Bruchstücke) (Fragments)						1									1	1															Dobli
ANTHEIL, GEORGE (1900–1959)																															
Bohemian Grove at Night	1952														1	1	1	2	1												Manus
Chamber Concerto	1932														1	1		1	2		1	1	1								Manus
Concertino	1930								1						1				1												Manus
Piano Trio	1950			1		1			1																						Manus
Sonata No. 2	1923			1					1																		1				Manus
String Quartet No. 1	1924			2	1	1																									Manus
String Quartet No. 2	1927			2	1	1																									Manus
String Quartet No. 3	1948			2	1	1																									Manus
Symphony for Five Instruments	1923				1										1				1			1	1								Weint
ANTONIOU, THEODORE (1935–)																															
Chorochronos (Raum-Zeit) III	1975								1																			1	1		Bären
Do-Quintett	1978																				1	2	1		1						Bären
Epilog nach Homer's Odyssee	1963						1		1							1					1						1	3			Bären
Quartetto giocoso, Op 26	1965			1		1			1							1															Bären
Synthesis	1971						1				1					1											1				Bären
APERGHIS, GEORGES (1945–)																															
Ascoltare stanca	1972		10	6	2	2	1		1	1					1	2					2										Salab
La bouteille à la mer (w. actors) *Comment:* Number of actors not specified. *Unus Instr:* Harmonium	1976		60						1												1	1					1			1	Salab
Fragments et essais de reconstitution *Unus Instr:* 2 Bass clarinets	1980		35				2											2			2				2					2	Salab
Il gigante Golia	1975		10	1	1	1	1		1						1	1	1	2	1		1	1	1				2	S			Salab
Histoires de loup *Unus Instr:* Harmonium	1976		120			1	1		1		1				1	2											1			1	Salab
Ilios *Unus Instr:* Bass clarinet, contrabassoon, contrabass tuba	1978		15	1		1	1					1						1	1			2	2		1					3	Salab
Les lauriers sont coupés *Voices:* Soprano and mezzo-soprano	1975		20		1										1		1		1				1					2			Salab
Mouvement pour quintette	1975		8	1	1	1			1									1													Salab
Parenthèses	1977		20	1	1	1	1		1				1		2			2	1		1	1	1				1				Salab
Quatuor				1	1	1															1										Salab
Sports et rebondissements *Voices:* Soprano, 3 mezzos, 2 baritones, and actors	1974		25																				2		1		1	6	1		Salab
Variations	1973		13	2	1	1	1		1			1	1		1	1		1	1		1						1				Salab
APOSTEL, HANS E. (1901–1972)																															
Epigramme (6), Op 33	1962			2	1	1																									Unive
Flischerhaus-Serenade, Op 45	1975			2	1	1	1								1	1		1	1		1	1	1								Dobli
Kleines Kammerkonzert, Op 38 *Comment:* Performance score; 3 copies needed	1964				1							1			1																Dobli
Streichquartett 2, Op 26	1956			2	1	1																									Unive
Studie, Op 29 *Comment:* Performance score; 3 copies needed					1							1			1																Dobli
ARAMBARRI, JESÚS (1902–1960)																															
Intermedio				2	2	2																									UMEsp
ARDEVOL, JOSÉ (1911–1981)																															
String Quartet No. 2	1943		25	2	1	1																									South
ARENSKY, ANTON (1861–1906)																															
Quartett, Op 35	1894			1	1	2																									Kunze
Quintet for Piano and Strings, Op 51	1900	D		2	1	1			1																						Jurge
ARGENTO, DOMINICK (1927–)																															
Elizabethan Songs (6)	1962		19	1		1				1					1	1												H			Boose

	Year Composed or Published	Key	Duration	Violin	Viola	Cello	Double Bass	Gamba	Piano	Harpsicord	Organ	Guitar	Harp	Recorder	Flute/Piccolo	Oboe	English Horn	Clarinet/Bass Clarinet	Bassoon/Contrabassoon	Saxophone	French Horn	Trumpet	Trombone	Bass Trombone	Tuba	Baritone	Percussion	Voice	Electronic Tape	Unusual Instruments	Publisher
ARGENTO, DOMINICK *(continued)*																															
To Be Sung Upon the Water *Unus Instr:* Bass clarinet	1973		25						1									1										H		1	Boose
ARNOLD, MALCOLM (1921–)																															
Oboe Quartet, Op 61	1951			1	1	1										1															Faber
String Quartet No. 2, Op 118	1975			2	1	1																									Faber
Symphony for Brass, Op 123	1979		25																		1	4	3	1	1						Faber
Trevalyan Suite, Op 96	1976		8												3	2		2	2		2										Faber
ARRIAGA, JUAN (1806–1826)																															
Quartets (3)				2	1	1																									VarPb
ARRIEU, CLAUDE (1903–)																															
Dixtuor pour instruments à vent															2	1		2	2		1	1	1								Billa
Quintette		C													1	1		1	1		1										Billa
Suite en quatre															1	1		1	1												Billa
Suite en trio																1		1		1											Billa
ARRIGO, GIROLAMO (1930–)																															
Adiós recuerdos (From "Orden")																							4					6			Ricor
Dalla nébbia verso alla nébbia						6	6																								Ricor
Eclatement/Funérailles (From "Orden")																					6		6								Ricor
ARTEMOV, VYACHESLAV (1940–)																															
Concerto for 13	1967		13						1						2	1		2	1			2	1				3				VAAP
Symphony of Elegies: Elegy III			18	10																							6				VAAP
ARUTYUNIAN, ALEXANDER (1920–)																															
Armenian Sketches *Unus Instr:* Tambourine, tam-tam	1984		12																		1	2	1		1		1			2	VAAP
ASTON, HUGH (1480–1522)																															
Hornpype (arr. Howarth)																					1	2	1		1						Novel
ATTERBERG, KURT (1887–1974)																															
Barocco-Suite 5, Op 23	1922		16		3	1	1								1	1	1														Breit
Barocco-Suite 5 (alt. inst.), Op 23	1922		16	2	1	1	1								1	1		1													Breit
Barocco-Suite 5 (alt. inst. 2), Op 23	1922		16	2	1	1	1								1	1	1														Breit
Suite pastorale in modo antico, Op 34	1931		20	2	1																										Breit
Suite pastorale in modo antico (alt.), Op 34	1931		16	2		1																									Breit
AUBERT, LOUIS F. (1877–1968)																															
L'heure captive				1					1																			1			Duran
AUBIN, TONY (1907–1981)																															
Le calme de la mer									1						1			1													Leduc
Cressida (Fanfare)																			2		4	3	3		1		3				Leduc
Divertissement en 3 mouvements																1		1	1												Leduc
Pièces (2) en sextuor *Comment:* Piano can substitute for harp													1		1	1		1	1		1										Leduc
Prélude, choral et fugue																					1	2	1		1						Leduc
Vitrail (Fanfare)															2						4	3	3		1		4				Leduc
AUSTIN, JOHN (1869–1948)																															
Orpheus and the Maenads	1975		15		1					1					1																AmCom
School Music	1978		15	1	1										1	1		1	1		1		1								AmCom
School Music (alt. inst.)	1978		15												1	1		1	2	1	1		1								AmCom
AUSTIN, LARRY (1930–)																															
Continuum for a Number of Instruments*** *Comment:* For any combination of up to 7 instruments	1964		10																												AmCom

	Year Composed or Published	Key	Duration	Violin	Viola	Cello	Double Bass	Gamba	Piano	Harpsicord	Organ	Guitar	Harp	Recorder	Flute/Piccolo	Oboe	English Horn	Clarinet/Bass Clarinet	Bassoon/Contrabassoon	Saxophone	French Horn	Trumpet	Trombone	Bass Trombone	Tuba	Baritone	Percussion	Voice	Electronic Tape	Unusual Instruments	Publisher
AUSTIN, LARRY *(continued)*																															
Second Fantasy on Ives' Universe Symphony *Unus Instr:* Celesta	1976		16		1				1									1									1		1	1	AmCom
AVNI, TZVI (1927–)																															
Mashav (solo xylophone) *Unus Instr:* Xylophone															2	2		2	2		1	1					2			1	Peter
AVSHALOMOV, JACOB (1919–)																															
Cues from the Little Clay Cart	1953		12		1	1						1			2			1									3				AmCom
AXMAN, EMIL (1887–1949)																															
Streichquartett 1	1936			2	1	1																									Artia
Streichquartett 4	1946			2	1	1																									Artia
Stücke (3)				2					1																						Artia
Variationenfantasie und Scherzo	1944			2	1	1																									Artia
BABBITT, MILTON (1916–)																															
All Set *Unus Instr:* Vibraphone	1957		8				1		1											2		1	1				1			1	AMP
Arie da capo	1974		14	1		1			1						1			1													Peter
Composition for Tenor and 6 Instruments	1960		14	1	1	1				1					1	1												T			AMP
Composition for 4 Instruments	1948			1		1									1			1													Press
Composition for 12 Instruments *Unus Instr:* Celesta	1954		7	1	1	1	1						1		1	1		1	1		1	1					1			1	AMP
The Crowded Air *Unus Instr:* Marimba			10	1	1	1	1		1			1			1	1		1	1								1			1	Peter
Fanfare for Double Brass Sextet			5																		4	4	3		1						Peter
Four Play			13	1		1			1									1													Peter
Groupwise			15	1	1	1			1						1																Peter
Head of the Bed			23	1		1									1			1										S			Peter
Paraphrases *Comment:* Oboe doubles on English horn. *Unus Instr:* Bass clarinet	1979		13						1						1	1	1	2	1		1	1	1		1					1	Peter
A Solo Requiem	1979		25						2																			S			Peter
Sonnets (2)	1955		8		1	1												1										B			Peter
String Quartet No. 1	1954		15	2	1	1																									AMP
String Quartet No. 2	1954		15	2	1	1																									AMP
String Quartet No. 3	1970		19	2	1	1																									Peter
String Quartet No. 4			16	2	1	1																									Peter
String Quartet No. 5			16	2	1	1																									Peter
Woodwind Quartet			12												1	1		1	1												AMP
BACH, FRITZ (1881–1930)																															
Klavierquartett		e		1	1	1			1																						Foeti
BACH, P.D.Q. (1807–1742)																															
Canzon per sonar a sei	1983		3																		2	2	1		1						Press
Capriccio ("La Pucelle de New Orleans")			4												2	2		1	2			1	1					1			Elkan
Diverse Ayres on Sundrie Notions, S.99.44 *Voice:* Bargain-counter tenor. *Unus Instr:* Snake			8	1	1	1				1																		T		1	Elkan
Echo Sonata for 2 Unfriendly Groups, S.99999999			2												1	1			1		1	1	1								Elkan
Fanfare for Fred *Unus Instr:* Timpani	1989		1																		4	4					5			1	Press
Fanfare for the Common Cold																					2	2	1								Press
Fuga Meshuga, S.50% off			3	1											1	1			1												Elkan
The Grossest Fugue, S.50% off			4		1		1								1	1			1				1								Elkan
Iphigenia in Brooklyn, S.52,162 *Voice:* Bargain-counter tenor. *Unus Instr:* Bottle			10	2	1	1				1						3						1						T		1	Elkan

	Year Composed or Published	Key	Duration	Violin	Viola	Cello	Double Bass	Gamba	Piano	Harpsicord	Organ	Guitar	Harp	Recorder	Flute/Piccolo	Oboe	English Horn	Clarinet/Bass Clarinet	Bassoon/Contrabassoon	Saxophone	French Horn	Trumpet	Trombone	Bass Trombone	Tuba	Baritone	Percussion	Voice	Electronic Tape	Unusual Instruments	Publisher
BACH, P.D.Q. *(continued)*																															
The Musical Sacrifice, S.50% off			17	1			1								1	1			1				1								Elkan
No-No Nonette, S.86 *Unus Instr:* Toys																2		2	2		2									3	Press
Octoot for Wind Instruments, S.8			8												2	2		2	2												Press
Safe Sextet *Unus Instr:* Contrabass clarinet, contrabassoon, celesta	1989		6										1		1		1	1	1								1			3	Press
Schleptet, S.0			8	1	1	1									1	1			1		1										Elkan
Sonata for Viola 4-Hands, S.440 *Comment:* For 1 viola, played by two violists					1					1																					Press
Suite from "The Civilian Barber", S.4F			8			1	1												2		2	2	1		1						Elkan
Trio (Sic) Sonata, S.3(4) *Unus Instr:* Tambourine			6												2										1		1			1	Press
"Trite" Quintet, S.6 of 1			19	1	1	1	1		1																						Elkan
BACK, SVEN-ERIK (1919–)																															
Decet	1972		11	1	1	1									1	1		1	1		1										Nordi
Nocturne	1953		15	1	1							1		3													1				Nordi
BACKOFEN, J. G. (1768–1839)																															
Basset Horn Quintet, Op 9 *Unus Instr:* Basset horn		F		2	1	1																								1	Kneus
BADINGS, HENK (1907–1987)																															
Pittsburgh Concerto	1965		18															1			2	2	2				4		1		Peter
Streichquartett 2	1936			2	1	1																									Schot
BADINSKI, NIKOLAI (1937–)																															
Moskauer Bläserquintett	1969														1	1		1	1		1										DeutV
Oktett ("Die Ruinen unter Sofia")	1972			2	1	1	1											1	1		1										DeutV
BAGGIANI, GUIDO (1932–)																															
Memoria for 18 Musicians and Synthesizer *Unus Instr:* Marimbaphone, synthesizer	1983		16	3	1	1	1		1						1	1		2	1		1	1	1	1	1		1			2	Salab
BAHK, JUN SANG (?–)																															
Echo															1	1		1	1		1										Peter
Invocation *Voice:* Soprano (who also dances). *Unus Instr:* Bass clarinet																		1									1	S		1	Peter
BAINES, ANTHONY (1912–)																															
Easy Pieces (9)															2	2		4	1		2										Oxfor
BAIRD, TADEUSZ (1928–1981)																															
Play (String Quartet)	1971		12	2	1	1																									Peter
Variations in Rondo Form			18	2	1	1																									Peter
BAKST, JAMES (?–)																															
String Quartet, Op 2	1938			2	1	1																									Kalmu
BALADA, LEONARDO (1933–)																															
Concerto for Cello and 9 Players	1962		15			1									1	1		1	1		1	2	1				1				GenMu
Cuatris	1969		9						1						1			1	1												GenMu
Cuatris (alt. inst.)	1969		9	1	1	1				1																					GenMu
Geometrías No. 1	1966		9												1	1		1	1			1					1				GenMu
Geometrías No. 2	1967		9	2	1	1																									GenMu
Hangman! Hangman! *Voices:* Narrator, 5 singers, 2 actors	1982		50	1			1		1									1	1			1	1				1	8			Schir
Mosaico, for Brass Quintet	1970		12																		1	2	1	1							GenMu
Sonata for 10 Winds	1980		16												1	1		1	1		2	2	2								Schir
Tresis	1973		7			1						1			1																Schir
Tresis (alt. inst.)	1973		7	1		1						1																			Schir

	Year Composed or Published	Key	Duration	Violin	Viola	Cello	Double Bass	Gamba	Piano	Harpsicord	Organ	Guitar	Harp	Recorder	Flute/Piccolo	Oboe	English Horn	Clarinet/Bass Clarinet	Bassoon/Contrabassoon	Saxophone	French Horn	Trumpet	Trombone	Bass Trombone	Tuba	Baritone	Percussion	Voice	Electronic Tape	Unusual Instruments	Publisher
BALAKIREV, MILY (1837–1910)																															
Octet	1856	c		2	1	1	1								1	1					1										VAAP
BALAY, GUILLAUME (1871–1943)																															
L'Aurore sur la forêt (solo horn)															1	1		1	1		1										Leduc
Petite suite . . . le style du 18e siècle															1	1		1	1		1										Leduc
BAMERT, MATTHIAS (1942–)																															
Introduction and Tarantella	1973								1						1												1				Schir
Woodwind Quintet	1970														1	1		1	1		1										Schir
BARATI, GEORGE (1913–)																															
And the Shadows Were Filled with Light *Unus Instr:* Celesta	1984		14	1					1						1	1		1	1			1					1			1	AmCom
Hawaiian Forest	1971		20	1	1	1									1			1			1						1				AmCom
Indiana Triptych	1983		22		1				1						1	1															AmCom
Quartet *Comment:* Oboe doubles on English horn			18				1			1					1	1	1														Peter
Quartet (alt. vers.)			18			1				1					1	1	1														Peter
Quintet	1961		12	2	1	1										1															AmCom
Spring Serenade	1987		12		1	1									1																AmCom
Trio	1979		20		1							1			1																AmCom
Trio	1988		14	1		1												1													AmCom
The Ugly Duckling *Unus Instr:* Celesta	1983		22	1					1						1			1	1		1	1	1				1			1	AmCom
BARBER, SAMUEL (1910–1981)																															
Dover Beach *Voice:* Medium	1933			2	1	1																						1			Schir
Medea (Cave of the Heart)	1947		25	2	1	1	1		1						1	1		1	1		1										Schir
Serenade, Op 1	1930		10	2	1	1																									Schir
String Quartet, Op 11	1936		17	2	1	1																									Schir
Summer Music	1956		12												1	1		1	1		1										Schir
BARBOTEU, GEORGES Y. (1924–)																															
Esquisse *Comment:* Harp may replace piano									1						1						1										Choud
BARDANASHVILI, IOSEF (?–)																															
Quintet				2	1	1			1																						VAAP
String Quartet				2	1	1																									VAAP
Trio, in Memory of Bizet				1		1			1																						VAAP
BARDIN, MAURICE (?–)																															
Sonatine en trio																					1	1	1								Billa
BARKIN, ELAINE (1932–)																															
Impromptu	1981		8		1	1			1																						AmCom
Inward and Outward Bound	1975		13	1	1	1	1								1	1		1	1		1	1	1		1		2				AmCom
Plus ça change	1972		12	4	2	2	2																				3				AmCom
Refrains *Unus Instr:* Celesta	1967		7	1	1	1									1			1									1			1	AmCom
BARLOW, KLARENZ (1945–)																															
1981 für Klaviertrio	1981			1		1	2		1																						Feedb
BARRAUD, HENRY (1900–)																															
Wind Quintet	1974		16												1	1		1	1		1										Boose
BARRY, GERALD (1952–)																															
"__________" Pianist doubles on harpsichord. *Unus Instr:* Bass clarinet	1979		10		2	2			1	1								3												1	Oxfor
"________" (alt. vers.) *Unus Instr:* Marimba	1979		10		1	1			1									2									1			1	Oxfor
Cork	1985		15	2	1	1																									Oxfor
Handel's Favorite Song	1981		6				1		1			1			1			1				1	1								Oxfor

	Year Composed or Published	Key	Duration	Violin	Viola	Cello	Double Bass	Gamba	Piano	Harpsicord	Organ	Guitar	Harp	Recorder	Flute/Piccolo	Oboe	English Horn	Clarinet/Bass Clarinet	Bassoon/Contrabassoon	Saxophone	French Horn	Trumpet	Trombone	Bass Trombone	Tuba	Baritone	Percussion	Voice	Electronic Tape	Unusual Instruments	Publisher
BARRY, GERALD *(continued)*																															
Oboe Quartet	1988			1	1	1										1															Oxfor
Of Queens' Gardens *Unus Instr:* Glockenspiel, marimba	1986		10	1	1		1		1						1	1		1	1		1	1	1				1			2	Oxfor
Sur les pointes	1985		7						1									2	2	2	2	2	2								Oxfor
Sweet Cork *Voices:* Soprano, bass	1985		7					1		1				1														2			Oxfor
Sweet Punishment	1987		8																		1	2	1		1						Oxfor
Sweet Punishment (version for winds) *Unus Instr:* Contrabassoon	1987		8															3	2											1	Oxfor
Things that Gain by Being Painted *Voices:* Singer, speaker. Props are needed	1977		20			1			1																			2			Oxfor
What the Frog Said *Voices:* Soprano, bass (speaker)	1984		25	1	1	1	1		1						1	1		1	1									2			Oxfor
BARTH, HANS J. (1927–)																															
Bläsermusik 1	1984																					2	2								Merse
Bläsermusik 2	1985																					2	2								Merse
Kirchensonate 1																						2	2								Merse
BARTOK, BÉLA (1881–1945)																															
Contrasts	1938			1					1									1													Boose
Piano Quartet, Op 20	1898	c		1	1	1			1																						Manus
Piano Quintet	1904			2	1	1			1																						EdMus
Pieces (5 from Mikrokosmos, arr. Serly)				2	1	1																									Boose
Quartet No. 1, Op 7	1908	a		2	1	1																									VarPb
Quartet No. 2, Op 17	1917	a	30	2	1	1																									VarPb
Quartet No. 3	1927			2	1	1																									Boose
Quartet No. 4	1928		23	2	1	1																									VarPb
Quartet No. 5	1934			2	1	1																									VarPb
Quartet No. 6	1939			2	1	1																									Boose
Sonata for 2 Pianos and Percussion	1937		25						2																		2				Boose
String Quartet	1898	F		2	1	1																									Manus
Valse (from 14 Bagatelles), Op 6	1908			2	1	1																									Boose
BARTOLOZZI, BRUNO (1911–1980)																															
Concertazioni *** (solo clarinet)	1973				1	1	1					1						1			1	1	1				1				Suvin
BARTOS, FRANTISEK (1905–)																															
Mestak slechticem (Townsman as Nobleman)	1934														1	1		1	1		1										Artia
Streichquartett 2	1935			2	1	1																									Artia
BARTOS, JAN Z. (1908–1981)																															
Klaviertrio 3				1		1			1																						Artia
Streichquartett 2, Op 43	1935			2	1	1																									Artia
Streichquartett 5, Op 66	1952			2	1	1																									Artia
BASNER, VENIAMIN (1925–)																															
Quartet No. 5				2	1	1																									VAAP
BASSETT, LESLIE (1923–)																															
Brass Quintet			14																		1	2	1		1						Peter
Concerto da camera (solo trumpet) *Unus Instr:* Flügelhorn	1981		18	1	1	1			1						1			1				1					1			1	Peter
Nonet	1967		10						1						1	1		1		1	1	1	1		1						Peter
Piano Sextet	1971		19	2	2	1			1																						Peter
Pierrot Songs			12	1		1			1						1			1										S			Peter
Quintet for Piano and Strings	1962		16	2	1	1			1																						AmCom
Sextet *Unus Instr:* Bass clarinet	1979		13			1	1								2			2												1	Peter
String Quartet No. 4	1978			2	1	1																									Press

	Year Composed or Published	Key	Duration	Violin	Viola	Cello	Double Bass	Gamba	Piano	Harpsicord	Organ	Guitar	Harp	Recorder	Flute/Piccolo	Oboe	English Horn	Clarinet/Bass Clarinet	Bassoon/Contrabassoon	Saxophone	French Horn	Trumpet	Trombone	Bass Trombone	Tuba	Baritone	Percussion	Voice	Electronic Tape	Unusual Instruments	Publisher
BASSETT, LESLIE *(continued)*																															
Time and Beyond			9			1			1									1										B			Peter
Trio	1953		15		1				1									1													AmCom
Trio	1980		19	1					1									1													Peter
Wind Music	1975														1	1		1	1	1	1										Press
BAUER, ROSS (1951–)																															
Along the Way			18	1	1	1	1		1						1			1				1					2				Peter
Chimera			12	1	1	1			1				1		1			1			1						1				Peter
Hang Time			14	1					1									1													Peter
BAUERNFEIND, HANS (1908–)																															
Heitere Musik																1		1		1											Dobli
BAUR, JÜRG (1918–)																															
Nonett	1973		21	2	1	1									1	1		1	1		1										Breit
Quintetto sereno	1958		14												1	1		1	1		1										Breit
BAVICCHI, JOHN (1922–)																															
Quartet No. 1 for Brass	1956																					2	2								Oxfor
BAX, ARNOLD (1883–1953)																															
Elegiac Trio	1916				1								1		1																Chest
Piano Quartet (In One Movement)	1922			1	1	1			1																						Murdo
Piano Quintet	1915			2	1	1			1																						Murdo
Piano Trio (In One Movement)	1906			1	1				1																						Chest
Quintet with Harp	1919			2	1	1							1																		Murdo
Quintet with Oboe	1923			2	1	1										1															Murdo
String Quartet No. 1	1918	G		2	1	1																									Murdo
String Quartet No. 2	1926			2	1	1																									Murdo
String Quintet (Lyrical Interlude)	1908			2	1	2																									Murdo
BAZELAIRE, PAUL (1886–1958)																															
Ballade, after Heredia's Anthony	1924			2	1	2			1																						Senar
BAZELON, IRWIN (1922–)																															
Brass Quintet	1963		23																		1	2	2								Boose
Chamber Concerto No. 1	1957		13	1					1						1			1				1			1		1				Manus
Churchill Downs Chamber Concerto Solo sax doubles on clarinet and flute. *Unus Instr:* Fender bass			15				1		1	1	1	1								1	1	3	2				3			1	Boose
Concatenations (solo viola)	1976		15		1																						4				Press
Cross-currents	1978		15																		1	2	1		1		1				Press
Early American Suite	1965		15							1					1	1		1	1		1										Press
Fairy Tale (solo viola)	1989		15		1	1	1		1						1			2			1	1					1				Press
For Tuba with Strings Attached	1982		12	2	1	1																			1						Press
Fusions *Unus Instr:* Bass clarinet	1983		15		1		1		1						1		1	2	1		1	2	1				2			1	Press
Legends and Love Letters	1988		15		1	1			1						1	1											1	S			Press
Phenomena *Comment:* Piano should be "tacky barroom upright"	1972		15	1	1	1	1		1						1	3		1	1		1	1	1				2	S			Press
Quintessentials *Unus Instr:* Marimba	1983		15				1								1			1									2			1	Press
Sound Dreams (In Memory of James Jones)	1977		12		1	1			1						1			1									1				Press
Three Men on a Dis-Course	1979		7			1												1									1				Press
Triple Play	1977		11																				2				1				Press
Woodwind Quintet	1975		19												1	1		1	1		1										Press
BAZZINI, ANTONIO (1818–1897)																															
String Quartet, Op 75		d		2	1	1																									Kunze
BEACH, AMY M. (1867–1944)																															
Pastorale for Woodwind Quintet	1942														1	1		1	1		1										ComPr
Piano Quintet, Op 67	1908	f#		2	1	1			1																						APSch
Piano Trio, Op 150	1939	a		1		1			1																						ComPr

	Year Composed or Published	Key	Duration	Violin	Viola	Cello	Double Bass	Gamba	Piano	Harpsicord	Organ	Guitar	Harp	Recorder	Flute/Piccolo	Oboe	English Horn	Clarinet/Bass Clarinet	Bassoon/Contrabassoon	Saxophone	French Horn	Trumpet	Trombone	Bass Trombone	Tuba	Baritone	Percussion	Voice	Electronic Tape	Unusual Instruments	Publisher
BEACH, AMY M. *(continued)*																															
String Quartet in One Movement, Op 89	1929			2	1	1																									Manus
Theme and Variations, Op 80	1920	a		2	1	1									1																Schir
BEACH, BENNIE (1925–)																															
Music for Brass Quintet																					1	2	1		1						Press
BEALE, JAMES (1924–)																															
Miniatures (3), Op 3	1947		4		1											1		1													AmCom
Piano Trio, Op 5	1948		22		1	1			1																						AmCom
Sextet for Piano and Winds, Op 39	1976		22						1						1	1		1	1		1										AmCom
Still-Lifes (5), Op 32 *Unus Instr:* Vibraphone, celesta													2		2			3	1								1			2	AmCom
BECERRA, GUSTAVO (1925–)																															
String Quartet No. 6				2	1	1																									Oxfor
BECHERT, ERNST (?–)																															
Schattenlinien	1987		11	2	1	1	1											1	1		1										BoteB
BECKER, GÜNTHER (1924–)																															
Ariosi *Unus Instr:* Vibraphone, marimba	1982		13													1	1	2									2			2	Breit
Caprices concertants *Unus Instr:* 5 mandolins, 3 mandolas	1968		10									3															1			8	Breit
Game for Nine *Unus Instr:* Vibraphone	1962		9	1	1	1						1			1			2									2			1	Breit
Un poco giocoso (solo bass tuba) *Unus Instr:* Bass tuba	1983		20	1	1	1	1		1				1		1	1		1	1		1	1	1		1		1			1	Breit
Quasi una fantasmagoria	1981		17															2	2		2										Breit
Serpentinata for Wind Quintet	1967		12												1	1		1	1		1										Breit
Tria Paidia Voliotika	1980		6			1			1									1					1								Breit
BECKER, JOHN J. (1886–1961)																															
Mockery (A Scherzo)	1933		3				1		1						2	1		3		3		2	1				1				AmCom
BEDFORD, DAVID (1937–)																															
The Ones Who Walked Away from Omelas *Unus Instr:* Electric and bass guitars	1976		25	2	1	1						2			1	1		1	1											2	Unive
Symphony for 12 Instruments	1981		23	2	1	1	1								1	2			1		1						2				Unive
When I Heard the Learned Astronomer	1972		15												2	2		2	2		3		1	1	1			T			Unive
BEERMAN, BURTON (1943–)																															
Chamber Music I	1983		9	1		1												1													AmCom
Colors	1968		10	1			1		1				1					1									1				AmCom
Details	1969		10	1	1								1					1													AmCom
Moments 1981	1981		13						1						2			1													AmCom
Points	1969		10	1	1		1								1			1			1						1				AmCom
Secret Gardens	1982		14												1	1		1	1	1	1						1		1		AmCom
Shadows and Figurines	1977		10				1								1			1													AmCom
BEESON, JACK (1921–)																															
Creole Mystery *Voice:* Medium	1974			2	1	1																						1			Boose
The Day's No Rounder than Its Angles Are *Voice:* Medium				2	1	1																						1			Boose
BEETHOVEN, LUDWIG VAN (1770–1827)																															
Bitten (arr. Weingartner), Op 48 *Voice:* Medium		Eb	2	8	3	2	1									1		2	1									1			Unive
Elegischer Gesang, Op 118 *Voices:* Soprano, alto, tenor, bass	1814			2	1	1																						4			VarPb

	Year Composed or Published	Key	Duration	Violin	Viola	Cello	Double Bass	Gamba	Piano	Harpsicord	Organ	Guitar	Harp	Recorder	Flute/Piccolo	Oboe	English Horn	Clarinet/Bass Clarinet	Bassoon/Contrabassoon	Saxophone	French Horn	Trumpet	Trombone	Bass Trombone	Tuba	Baritone	Percussion	Voice	Electronic Tape	Unusual Instruments	Publisher
BEETHOVEN, LUDWIG VAN *(continued)*																															
Folksong Settings *Comment:* English, Irish, Scottish, Welsh, Italian, other.				1		1			1																			1			VarPb
Grosse Fugue, Quartet Movement, Op 133	1825	Bb		2	1	1																									VarPb
Ich liebe dich (arr. Weingartner), WoO 123 *Voice:* Medium	1795	Ab	2	8	3	2	1								1			2	2									1			Unive
Der Küss (arr. Weingartner), Op 128	1822	A	2	8	3	3												2										H			Unive
March	1810	Bb																2	2		2										Breit
Octet for Winds, Op 103	1792															2		2	2		2										VarPb
Piano Quartet (arr. of Quintet, Op. 16), Op 16	1796	Eb		1	1	1			1																						VarPb
Piano Quartet, Op 152 No. 1	1785	Eb		1	1	1			1																						Henle
Piano Quartet, Op 152 No. 2	1785	D		1	1	1			1																						Henle
Piano Quartet, Op 152 No. 3	1785	C		1	1	1			1																						Henle
Piano Trio (arr. from Sextet, Op. 81b)		Eb		1		1			1																						VarPb
Piano Trio, Op 1 No. 1	1795	Eb		1		1			1																						VarPb
Piano Trio, Op 1 No. 2	1795	G		1		1			1																						VarPb
Piano Trio, Op 1 No. 3	1795	c		1		1			1																						VarPb
Piano Trio (arr. of Quintet, Op. 4), Op 63 *Comment:* Probably spurious	1807			1		1			1																						VarPb
Piano Trio, Op 153 *Comment:* Originally attributed to Mozart	1791	Eb		1		1			1																						VarPb
Quintet *Comment:* From Sonata Op. 30 No.3. Probably spurious.	1810			1	2	1									1																VarPb
Quintet, Op 16	1796	Eb							1							1		1	1		1										VarPb
Rondino, Op 146	1792	Eb														2		2	2		2										VarPb
Septet, Op 20	1800	Eb		1	1	1	1											1	1		1										VarPb
Serenade, Op 8	1796	D		1	1	1																									VarPb
Serenade, Op 25	1797	D		1	1										1																VarPb
Sextet, Op 81b	1795	Eb		2	1	1															2										VarPb
String Quartet (arr. from Op. 14 No. 1)	1802	F		2	1	1																									VarPb
String Quartet, Op 18 No. 1	1798	F		2	1	1																									VarPb
String Quartet, Op 18 No. 2	1798	G		2	1	1																									VarPb
String Quartet, Op 18 No. 3	1798	D		2	1	1																									VarPb
String Quartet, Op 18 No. 4	1798	c		2	1	1																									VarPb
String Quartet, Op 18 No. 5	1800	A		2	1	1																									VarPb
String Quartet, Op 18 No. 6	1800	Bb		2	1	1																									VarPb
String Quartet ("Rasumovsky" No. 1), Op 59 No. 1	1806	F		2	1	1																									VarPb
String Quartet ("Rasumovsky" No. 2), Op 59 No. 2	1806	e		2	1	1																									VarPb
String Quartet ("Rasumovsky" No. 3), Op 59 No. 3	1806	C		2	1	1																									VarPb
String Quartet ("The Harp"), Op 74	1809	Eb		2	1	1																									VarPb
String Quartet, Op 95	1810	f		2	1	1																									VarPb
String Quartet, Op 127	1824	Eb		2	1	1																									VarPb
String Quartet, Op 130	1825	Bb		2	1	1																									VarPb
String Quartet, Op 131	1826	c#		2	1	1																									VarPb
String Quartet, Op 132	1825	a		2	1	1																									VarPb
String Quartet, Op 135	1826	F		2	1	1																									VarPb
String Quintet *Comment:* One movement	1817	d		2	2	1																									VarPb

	Year Composed or Published	Key	Duration	Violin	Viola	Cello	Double Bass	Gamba	Piano	Harpsicord	Organ	Guitar	Harp	Recorder	Flute/Piccolo	Oboe	English Horn	Clarinet/Bass Clarinet	Bassoon/Contrabassoon	Saxophone	French Horn	Trumpet	Trombone	Bass Trombone	Tuba	Baritone	Percussion	Voice	Electronic Tape	Unusual Instruments	Publisher
BEETHOVEN, LUDWIG VAN *(continued)*																															
String Quintet *Comment:* Andante Maestoso	1826	C		2	2	1																									VarPb
String Quintet, Op 4	1796	E♭		2	2	1																									VarPb
String Quintet, Op 29	1801	C		2	2	1																									VarPb
String Quintet, Op 104	1817	c		2	2	1																									VarPb
String Quintet, Op 137 *Comment:* Fugue	1817	D		2	2	1																									VarPb
String Trio, Op 3	1792			1	1	1																									VarPb
String Trio, Op 9 No. 1	1798	G		1	1	1																									VarPb
String Trio, Op 9 No. 2	1798	D		1	1	1																									VarPb
String Trio, Op 9 No. 3	1798	c		1	1	1																									VarPb
String Trio, Op 87	1795	C		1	1	1																									VarPb
Trio	1787	G							1						1				1												VarPb
Trio, Op 11	1798	B♭				1			1									1													VarPb
Trio, Op 11, alt. inst.	1798	B♭		1		1			1																						VarPb
Trio, Op 38	1802	E♭				1			1									1													VarPb
Trio, Op 38, alt. inst.	1802	E♭		1		1			1																						VarPb
Trio, Op 70 No. 1	1808	D		1		1			1																						VarPb
Trio, Op 70 No. 2	1808	E♭		1		1			1																						VarPb
Trio, Op 87	1795	C														2	1														VarPb
Trio ("Archduke"), Op 97	1811	B♭		1		1			1																						VarPb
Trio ("Kakadu" variations), Op 121a		G		1		1			1																						VarPb
Trio in One Movement, Op 154	1812	B♭		1		1			1																						VarPb
Variations ("La ci darem")	1797															2	1														VarPb
Variations (14) on an Original Theme, Op 44	1792	E♭		1		1			1																						VarPb
BELL, ELIZABETH (1952–)																															
Perne in a Gyre	1984		14	1		1			1									1													AmCom
BENGUEREL, XAVIER (1931–)																															
Set	1974		14	1	1	1			1						1			1			1										Hanse
BENJAMIN, ARTHUR (1893–1960)																															
String Quartet No. 2	1956		23	2	1	1																									Boose
BENJAMIN, GEORGE (1960–)																															
At First Light *Unus Instr:* Celesta	1982		20	2	1	1	1		1						1	1		1	1		1	1	1				1			1	Faber
Fanfare for Aquarius	1983		1	2	1	1	1		1				1		1	1		1	1		1	1	1				1				Faber
Octet *Unus Instr:* Celesta	1978		10	1	1	1	1								1			1									2			1	Faber
BENNETT, RICHARD R. (1936–)																															
Commedia IV	1973																				1	2	1		1						Novel
Fanfare for the American Wind Symphony *Unus Instr:* Timpani			3																		5	5	5		2		2			1	Peter
Jazz Pastoral *Comment:* Saxophones are alto, tenor, and baritone	1969		25				1		1											3	1	2	1		1		1	1			Unive
Quartett IV	1964			2	1	1																									Unive
BENTZON, NIELS V. (1919–)																															
Chamber Concerto, Op 52	1948		18				1		3									1	1			2					3				Hanse
Climate Changes (solo sax, piano), Op 474	1985		20	2	1	1			1						1	1		1	1	1	1	1	1		1		1				Hanse
Concertino (solo piano), Op 483 *Unus Instr:* Contrabassoon	1986		13												3	2	1	3	3								4			1	Hanse
Sextet, Op 278	1971		20						1						1	1		1	1		1										Hanse
Sinfonia concertante (solo clarinet, violin), Op 100	1956		25	1														1				3	3		1		1				Hanse
Sinfonia da camera, Op 139	1962		20	2	1	1	1		1						1	1		1	1		1		2		1		3				Hanse

	Year Composed or Published	Key	Duration	Violin	Viola	Cello	Double Bass	Gamba	Piano	Harpsicord	Organ	Guitar	Harp	Recorder	Flute/Piccolo	Oboe	English Horn	Clarinet/Bass Clarinet	Bassoon/Contrabassoon	Saxophone	French Horn	Trumpet	Trombone	Bass Trombone	Tuba	Baritone	Percussion	Voice	Electronic Tape	Unusual Instruments	Publisher
BENTZON, NIELS V. *(continued)*																															
Sonata, Op 257	1970		10	1	1	1	1		1						1	1		1	1		1	1	1								Hanse
Sonata diatonica, Op 412			12												1	1		1	1		1				1						Hanse
Watermusic II, Op 528 *Unus Instr:* Bass clarinet	1988		18						1						1	1		2	1		1									1	Hanse
BERENS, HERMANN (1826–1880)																															
String Trio, Op 85 No. 1		D		1	1	1																									Amade
String Trio, Op 85 No. 2		c		1	1	1																									Amade
String Trio, Op 85 No. 3		F		1	1	1																									Amade
BEREZOWSKY, NICOLAY (1900–1953)																															
String Quartet, Op 16	1932			2	1	1																									Boose
Suite, Op 11	1936														1	1		1	1		1										Boose
BERG, ALBAN (1885–1935)																															
Adagio (from Kammerkonzert)	1934		13	1					1									1													Unive
Hier ist Friede, Op 4 No. 5 *Unus Instr:* Harmonium				1		1			1																					1	Unive
Kammerkonzert *Unus Instr:* Piccolo; E♭ and bass clarinets, contrabassoon	1925		32	1					1						2	1	1	3	2		2	1	1							4	Unive
Lyrische Suite (String Quartet)	1926		27	2	1	1																						M			Unive
Streichquartett, Op 3	1910		20	2	1	1																									Unive
Thema und Variationen *Comment:* First movement of Kammerkonzert	1925		9												2	1	1	3	2		2	1	1								Unive
BERG, OLAV (1949–)																															
Concertino (solo guitar)	1979		9	1		1			1			1			1			1													Nordi
Fragments	1977		8		1	1			1						1			1									2				Nordi
Kveita	1987		30	2	1	1			1						1	1		1	1		1										Nordi
BERGER, ARTHUR (1912–)																															
Chamber Music for 13 players *Unus Instr:* Celesta	1960		10	2	1	1	1						1		1	1		1	1		1	1					1			1	Peter
Quartet for Winds	1941	C	10												1	1		1	1												Peter
Septet	1966		12	1	1	1			1						1			1	1												Peter
BERGER, GREGOR (?–)																															
Hommage à Jean Alain											1							1									1				Dobli
Hommage à Maurice Ravel											1							1									1				Dobli
BERGER, JEAN (1909–)																															
The Pied Piper *Unus Instr:* Melodica 26 and 36			35				1		1						1												1	3		2	Schir
BERGER, WILHELM (1861–1911)																															
String Trio, Op 69		g		1	1	1																									Amade
BERGMANN, WALTER (1902–)																															
Music for Wind Quintet															1	1		1	1		1										Dobli
BERGSMA, WILLIAM (1921–)																															
Concerto for Wind Quintet	1958														1	1		1	1		1										Galax
String Quartet No. 3	1953			2	1	1																									CarlF
String Quartet No. 4	1970			2	1	1																									ECSch
Suite for Brass Quartet	1940																					2	1			1					CarlF
Voice of the Coelacanth (Rhapsodic Variations)						1			1												1										ECSch
BERIO, LUCIANO (1925–)																															
Agnus																		3										2			Unive
Air				1	1	1			1																			S			Unive
Autre fois													1		1			1													Unive
Ballade von der Sexuellen Hörigkeit (Weill, arr. Berio) *Unus Instr:* Bass clarinet, vibraphone, accordion	1975		3	1	1	1	1											2									1	M		3	Unive

	Year Composed or Published	Key	Duration	Violin	Viola	Cello	Double Bass	Gamba	Piano	Harpsicord	Organ	Guitar	Harp	Recorder	Flute/Piccolo	Oboe	English Horn	Clarinet/Bass Clarinet	Bassoon/Contrabassoon	Saxophone	French Horn	Trumpet	Trombone	Bass Trombone	Tuba	Baritone	Percussion	Voice	Electronic Tape	Unusual Instruments	Publisher
BERIO, LUCIANO *(continued)*																															
Calmo	1974		3	1	1	1	1								1	1		2	1		1	1	1					S			Unive
Chamber Music ***	1952					1							1					1										S			Suvin
Chemins II Viola Solo. *Unus Instr:* Electric organ	1967		12		2	1					1		1		1			1					1				2			1	Unive
Chemins IV su Sequenza VII	1975		10	3	3	3	2									1															Unive
Circles	1960		20										1														2	F			Unive
Differences	1959		17		1	1							1		1			1											1		Unive
E vó *Unus Instr:* Electric organ	1972		4	1	1	1	1		1		1				1	1		3				1	1				1	S		1	Unive
Folk Songs *Unus Instr:* Piccolo	1964				1	1							1		1			1									2	M		1	Unive
Le grand Lustucru (Weill, arr. Berio)	1972		3	1	1	1	1								1	1		2	1			2					1	M			Unive
Linea *Unus Instr:* Vibraphone and marimba	1974		15						2																		2			2	Unive
El mar la mar *Voices:* Soprano and mezzo. *Unus Instr:* Piccolo, bass clarinet, accordion						1	1						1		1			2										2		3	Unive
Melodrama *Unus Instr:* Electric organ	1970		15	1		1	1		1		1				1			1									1	T		1	Unive
O King				1		1			1						1			1										M			Unive
Opus No. Zoo	1951														1	1		1	1		1										Unive
Quartetto	1955			2	1	1																									Suvin
Recital	1971		35	1	1	1	1		3				1			2		2			2	1	1				1	S			Unive
Sincronie	1964			2	1	1																									Unive
Surabaya Johnny (Weill, arr. Berio)	1972		5	1	1	1	1					1			1			1				1					1	M			Unive
BERKELEY, LENNOX (1903–1989)																															
Diversions, Op 63	1964		18	1	1	1			1							1		1	1		1										Chest
Oboe Quartet				1	1	1										1															Chest
Quartet No. 2				2	1	1																									Chest
Quintet, Op 90	1975								1						1	1		1	1												Chest
Sextet, Op 47	1955			2	1	1												1			1										Chest
String Quartet No. 1	1935		22	2	1	1																									Boose
Trio, Op 44	1954			1					1												1										Chest
BERKELEY, MICHAEL (1948–)																															
Among the Lilies																						4	4								Chest
Chamber Symphony *Unus Instr:* Bass clarinet			20	1	1	1	1		1						3	1		2			1									1	Oxfor
For the Savage Messiah			12	1	1	1	1		1																						Oxfor
The Mayfly (Ballet for Children)				1		1			1						1			1									1				Oxfor
Music from Chaucer			12																		1	2	2								Oxfor
Nocturne			12	1	1	1							1		1																Oxfor
Oboe Quartet				1	1	1										1															Oxfor
Piano Trio			17	1		1			1																						Oxfor
Quintet for Clarinet and Strings			14	2	1	1												1													Oxfor
Rain			8	1		1																						T			Oxfor
String Quartet No. 1			19	2	1	1																									Oxfor
String Quartet No. 2			17	2	1	1																									Oxfor
String Quartet No. 3				2	1	1																									Oxfor
String Trio			15	1	1	1																									Oxfor
BERL, CHRISTINE (1943–)																															
Ab la dolchor	1990			1					1									1										M			Manus
Dark Summer	1989			1	1	1			1																			M			Manus
BERLIOZ, HECTOR (1803–1869)																															
L'ile inconnue (orch. Constant), Op 7 No. 6 *Unus Instr:* Celesta			5	2	1	1	1		1			1			1	1		1	1		1	1	1				3			1	Salab
Sur les lagunes (orch. Koering) *Unus Instr:* Celesta				2	1	1	1		1			1			1	1		1	1		1	1	1				3			1	Salab

	Year Composed or Published	Key	Duration	Violin	Viola	Cello	Double Bass	Gamba	Piano	Harpsicord	Organ	Guitar	Harp	Recorder	Flute/Piccolo	Oboe	English Horn	Clarinet/Bass Clarinet	Bassoon/Contrabassoon	Saxophone	French Horn	Trumpet	Trombone	Bass Trombone	Tuba	Baritone	Percussion	Voice	Electronic Tape	Unusual Instruments	Publisher
BERLIOZ, HECTOR *(continued)*																															
Villanelle (orch. Levinas) *Unus Instr:* Celesta				2	1	1	1		1			1			1	1		1	1		1	1	1				3			1	Salab
BERNARD, EMILE (1843–1902)																															
Quatuor, Op 50		c		1	1	1			1																						Duran
BERNARD, ROBERT (1900–1971)																															
Trio		F♯		1		1			1																						Duran
BERNSTEIN, LEONARD (1918–1991)																															
Fanfare for BIMA	1948																				1	1	1		1						Boose
BERTHELEMY, NORBERT (?–)																															
Rondo pour rire																		2	1												Billa
BERTHOLD, HENRY (1933–)																															
Quintettino															1	1		1	1		1										Peter
BERWALD, FRANZ (1796–1868)																															
Klavierquintett (Larghetto & Scherzo)		A		2	1	1			1																						Bären
Klavierquintett, Op 5		c		2	1	1			1																						Bären
Klavierquintett, Op 6		A		2	1	1			1																						Bären
Klaviertrio	1845	C		1		1			1																						Bären
Klaviertrio	1845	E♭		1		1			1																						Bären
Klaviertrio	1845	d		1		1			1																						Bären
Klaviertrio	1845	f		1		1			1																						Bären
Quartett	1819	E♭							1									1	1		1										Bären
Septett	1817			1	1	1	1											1	1		1										Bären
Streichquartett		E♭		2	1	1																									Bären
Streichquartett		a		2	1	1																									Bären
Streichquartett		g		2	1	1																									Bären
BESSONNET, GEORGES (?–)																															
Quatuors (10)																					1	2	1								Billa
Quatuors (12)																					1	2	1								Billa
Quintettes (10)																					1	2	1		1						Billa
Quintettes (12)																					1	2	1		1						Billa
Trios (10)																					1	1	1								Billa
Trios (12)																					1	1	1								Billa
BEVELANDER, BRIAN E. (1942–)																															
Castle Music *Comment:* Piano 4-hands	1982		8						1																		1		1		AmCom
Fantasy Music	1981		18	1		1			1							1											1				AmCom
BEYDTS, LOUIS (1895–1953)																															
En Arles									1						1													1			Duran
BEYER, FRANK M. (1928–)																															
Bläserquintett	1955														1	1		1	1		1										BoteB
Concertino a tre	1974		14	4	2	2	1									2						1	1								BoteB
Concerto	1968			1		1			1						1			1													BoteB
De lumine	1978		12	1	1	1			1						1			1									1				BoteB
Passacaglia fantastica	1984			1		1			1																						BoteB
Streicherfantasien	1977		14	2	1	1	1																								BoteB
Streichquartett 2	1969			2	1	1																									BoteB
Streichquartett 3 ("Missa")	1985			2	1	1																									BoteB
Trio	1980				1								1			1															BoteB
BEZANSON, PHILIP (1916–1975)																															
Divertimento (Organ, Brass, Percussion)	1964		9								1											2	2				3				AmCom

	Year Composed or Published	Key	Duration	Violin	Viola	Cello	Double Bass	Gamba	Piano	Harpsicord	Organ	Guitar	Harp	Recorder	Flute/Piccolo	Oboe	English Horn	Clarinet/Bass Clarinet	Bassoon/Contrabassoon	Saxophone	French Horn	Trumpet	Trombone	Bass Trombone	Tuba	Baritone	Percussion	Voice	Electronic Tape	Unusual Instruments	Publisher
BEZANSON, PHILIP *(continued)*																															
Divertimento for Brass and Percussion	1964		9																			2	2				1				AmCom
Petite Suite	1973		7												1	1		1	1		1	1	1								AmCom
Piano Trio	1963		14		1	1			1																						AmCom
Sextet for Piano and Winds	1956		15						1						1	1		1	1		1										AmCom
String Quartet No. 1				2	1	1																									Press
Trio for Piano, Clarinet, and Horn	1966		11						1									1			1										AmCom
BHATIA, VANRAJ (1927–)																															
Toy-Seller (Kinguriwali)				1					1																			S			Oxfor
BIALAS, GÜNTER (1907–)																															
Assonanzen (Streichquartett 4)				2	1	1																									Bären
Elegien (3)	1978			1		1									1																Bären
Gesänge (3) nach Lope de Vega	1971											1			1													B			Bären
Pastorale und Rondo (Nonett)	1969			2	1	1	1									1		1	1		1										Bären
Quintett	1984			2	1	1							1																		Bären
Romanza e Danza (Octet after Meyerbeer)	1971															2		2	2		2										Bären
Streichtrio (in Nine Bagatelles)	1984			1	1	1																									Bären
Trio *Comment:* Optional violin	1946				1	1									1																Bären
BINKERD, GORDON (1916–)																															
Portrait intérieur	1972			1		1																						M			Boose
Secret Love						1							1															H			Boose
Songs (3)			18	2	1	1																						M			Boose
String Quartet No. 1	1935		22	2	1	1																									Boose
String Quartet No. 2	1961		14	2	1	1																									Boose
String Trio	1975			1	1	1																									Boose
Trio	1955		23		1	1												1													Boose
BIRTWISTLE, HARRISON (1934–)																															
Secret Theatre *Unus Instr:* Piccolo, contrabassoon, piccolo trumpet	1984		28	2	1	1	1		1						1	1		1	1		1	1	1				1			3	Unive
Songs by Myself *Unus Instr:* Alto flute, vibraphone	1984		10	1	1	1	1		1						1												1	S		2	Unive
Tombeau (In memoriam Igor Stravinsky)	1972		3	2	1	1							1		1			1													Unive
BISCARDI, CHESTER (1948–)																															
Chartres	1973		11	1		1			1							1		1		1							2				AmCom
Di vivere			8	1		1			1						1			1													Peter
Orpha *Unus Instr:* Vibraphone, marimba	1974		7	2	1	1																					2			2	AmCom
Tenzone									1						2																Press
They Had Ceased to Talk			11	1	1				1												1										Peter
BITSCH, MARCEL (1921–)																															
Divertissement															1	1		1	1												Leduc
Sonatine															1	1		1	1		1										Leduc
BLACHER, BORIS (1903–1975)																															
Epitaph (Streichquartett 4), Op 41	1951			2	1	1																									BoteB
Jazz-Coloraturen	1929																		1	1								S			BoteB
Oktett	1965		20	2	1	1	1											1	1		1										BoteB
Pentagramm	1974		22	8	3	3	2																								BoteB
Quintett	1974			1	1	1									1	1															BoteB
Streichquartett 1	1930			2	1	1																									BoteB
Streichquartett 2, Op 16	1940			2	1	1																									BoteB
Streichquartett 3, Op 32	1944			2	1	1																									BoteB
Variationen (Streichquartett 5)	1967			2	1	1																									BoteB

	Year Composed or Published	Key	Duration	Violin	Viola	Cello	Double Bass	Gamba	Piano	Harpsicord	Organ	Guitar	Harp	Recorder	Flute/Piccolo	Oboe	English Horn	Clarinet/Bass Clarinet	Bassoon/Contrabassoon	Saxophone	French Horn	Trumpet	Trombone	Bass Trombone	Tuba	Baritone	Percussion	Voice	Electronic Tape	Unusual Instruments	Publisher
BLACHER, BORIS *(continued)*																															
Virtuose Musik	1966		15										1		2	1		2	1		2	1	1				2				BoteB
BLACKFORD, RICHARD (1954–)																															
Concerto for Seven					1	1			1									1				1	1				1				Oxfor
String Quartet				2	1	1																									Oxfor
BLACKWOOD, EASLEY (1933–)																															
Concertino for 5 instruments	1959			1	1	1									1	1															Schir
Pastoral and Variations	1961		13												1	1		1	1		1										Schir
String Quartet No. 1	1957			2	1	1																									Press
String Quartet No. 2	1959			2	1	1																									AMP
String Quartet No. 4				2	1	1																									Schir
Trio, Op 22	1967			1		1			1																						Schir
Un voyage à Cythere, Op 20	1966		14				1								2	1		2	1		1	1	1					S			Schir
BLAND, ED (1926–)																															
Sketches, Set 1 *Unus Instr:* Timpani	1972		10			2												1				1	1				1			1	AmCom
Sketches, Set 2	1973		6			1												1				1	1								AmCom
BLANK, ALLAN (1925–)																															
13 Ways of Looking at a Blackbird	1965			1		1			1						1			1										S			AMP
Clarinet Quintet	1985		17	2	1	1												1													AmCom
Composition for 11 Players (Section 1)				1		1	1		1				1		1			2			1	1	1								AmCom
Concertino for 5 Players	1986		18	1		1			1						1			1													AmCom
Concertino for 5 Players (alt. inst.) *Unus Instr:* Bass Clarinet	1986		18		1	1			1						1			1												1	AmCom
Paganini Caprice No. 24 (double quintet)															2	2		2	2		2										AMP
Trio	1983		15			1			1						1																AmCom
BLISS, ARTHUR (1891–1975)																															
Clarinet Quintet	1932		26	2	1	1												1													Novel
Conversations	1920		15	1	1	1									1	1															Curwn
Madam Noy	1918		4		1		1						1		1			1	1									S			Chest
Oboe Quintet	1927		20	2	1	1										1															Oxfor
Quartet No. 1	1940			2	1	1																									Novel
Quartet No. 2	1950			2	1	1																									Novel
BLOCH, ERNEST (1880–1959)																															
Concertino *Comment:* Clarinet may replace viola	1948		8		1				1						1																Schir
In the Mountains	1925		5	2	1	1																									CarlF
Night	1925		2	2	1	1																									CarlF
Nocturnes (3)	1924		7	1		1			1																						CarlF
Paysages	1925		6	2	1	1																									CarlF
Piano Quintet No. 1	1923		32	2	1	1			1																						Schir
Piano Quintet No. 2	1956		20	2	1	1			1																						Broud
Pieces (2)	1950		8	2	1	1																									JosWi
Prelude	1925		3	2	1	1																									CarlF
String Quartet No. 1	1916		50	2	1	1																									Schir
String Quartet No. 2, Op 21	1945		33	2	1	1																									Boose
String Quartet No. 3	1951		23	2	1	1																									Schir
String Quartet No. 4	1953		26	2	1	1																									Schir
String Quartet No. 5	1956		30	2	1	1																									Broud
BLOCH, WALDEMAR (1906–)																															
Serenade	1966														1	1		1	1		1										Dobli
BLOCK, STEVEN D. (1952–)																															
Chemical Wedding	1975		20												5						1	1	1	1			3				AmCom
Darkness Songs *Comment:* Narrator optional	1980		15			1	1		1						1	1											1	N			AmCom

	Year Composed or Published	Key	Duration	Violin	Viola	Cello	Double Bass	Gamba	Piano	Harpsicord	Organ	Guitar	Harp	Recorder	Flute/Piccolo	Oboe	English Horn	Clarinet/Bass Clarinet	Bassoon/Contrabassoon	Saxophone	French Horn	Trumpet	Trombone	Bass Trombone	Tuba	Baritone	Percussion	Voice	Electronic Tape	Unusual Instruments	Publisher
BLOCK, STEVEN D. *(continued)*																															
Phantasmagoria	1987		6						1				1		2		1	1	1		1	1					1				AmCom
Players (A Suite for Dancers) *Unus Instr:* Electric piano	1980		22						1						1	1		1	1								1			1	AmCom
Puttin' It Together	1974		10				2													2							1				AmCom
Rockin' Pneumonia	1984		8	1		1			1						1	1		1									1				AmCom
Thelonius Rex	1982		20				1		1									1				1		1			1				AmCom
BOATWRIGHT, HOWARD (1918–)																															
Gypsie Laddie *Voice:* Medium				2																								1			Oxfor
Quartet for Clarinet				1	1	1												1													Oxfor
BOCHMANN, CHRISTOPHER (?–)																															
Chamber Etude No. 1										1						1	1		1												Peter
De Profundis				1		1			1																						Oxfor
BONDON, JACQUES (1927–)																															
Symphonie concertante (Piano and winds)	1978		23						1						2	2		2	2		2										Eschi
BONNARD, ALAIN (?–)																															
Bis															1	1		1		1											Billa
BONNEAU, PAUL (1918–)																															
Fanfare																					3	3	2		1		3				Leduc
Noëls anciens (3) *Comment:* Clarinet can replace English horn																1	1		1												Leduc
BOONE, CHARLES (1939–)																															
Fields/Singing	1976		15	2	1	2	1		1						2	1						1	2				2	S			Salab
Linea meridiana	1975		13			1			1		1		1		1			1									1	1			Salab
Quartet				1	1	1			1																						Salab
San Zeno/Verona *Unus Instr:* Vibraphone, marimba	1976		11	2	1	1	1		1		1				1	1		1	1								2			2	Salab
Second Landscape *Unus Instr:* Xylophone, vibraphone, marimba	1973		14	2	1	1	2		1						1	1		1	1			2					2			3	Salab
Starfish	1966		8	2					1						1			1									2				Salab
String Piece	1978		12	7	2	2	1																								Salab
BORKOVEC, PAVEL (1894–1972)																															
Nonett	1941			1	1	1	1								1	1		1	1		1										Artia
Streichquartett 4	1948			2	1	1																									Artia
BORODIN, ALEXANDER P. (1833–1887)																															
Piano Trio, Op Post.				1		1			1																						Kunze
Quartet on B-la-f (with Liadov, others)	1895			2	1	1																									VarPb
String Quartet (on a theme by Beethoven)	1884	A		2	1	1																									VarPb
String Quartet	1888	D		2	1	1																									VarPb
BORROFF, EDITH (1925–)																															
Piano Trio	1983		16		1	1			1																						AmCom
The Sun and the Wind	1976		43	2	1	1			1	1						2			1		2						2				AmCom
Trio	1982		14						1											1							1				AmCom
BORTOLOTTI, MAURO (1926–)																															
Frammenti 5 (String Quartet)				2	1	1																									Ricor
Studi				1														1			1										Suvin
BOTTESINI, GIOVANNI (1821–1889)																															
Duo concertant (sur themes des "Puritains")						1	1		1																						Billa

	Year Composed or Published	Key	Duration	Violin	Viola	Cello	Double Bass	Gamba	Piano	Harpsicord	Organ	Guitar	Harp	Recorder	Flute/Piccolo	Oboe	English Horn	Clarinet/Bass Clarinet	Bassoon/Contrabassoon	Saxophone	French Horn	Trumpet	Trombone	Bass Trombone	Tuba	Baritone	Percussion	Voice	Electronic Tape	Unusual Instruments	Publisher
BOTTESINI, GIOVANNI *(continued)*																															
Grand duo concertant				1			1		1																						Billa
BOTTJE, WILL G. (1925–)																															
Commentaries (for Solo Guitar)	1983		17	2	1	1	1					1			1	1		2	1		1	1					1				AmCom
Dances, Real and Imagined	1976		20	2	1	1						1																			AmCom
Designs	1974		10			1			1						2																AmCom
Dune Music	1986		14			1			1						1	1															AmCom
Family Music	1989		17			1			1						1							1									AmCom
Fireflies	1981		13	2	1	1				1						1															AmCom
Interplays	1720		20						1	1											1								1		AmCom
Little Sonata III	1979		11	1							1					1															AmCom
Little Sonata III (alt. inst.)	1979		11	1							1					1			1												AmCom
Musica Sonora	1982		20		1					1					1		1														AmCom
Music for a Joyous Occasion III	1975		10			1									2																AmCom
Personalities (Six Portraits)	1979		16			1									1	1															AmCom
Quintet	1954		20	2	1	1									1																AmCom
Quintet (for Winds and Strings)	1983		13	1			1											1	1		1										AmCom
Rooms	1978		15			1			1						1	1					1						1				AmCom
Serenade	1964		17	2	1	1									1	1		1	1		1										AmCom
Sextet	1964		10								1											2	2				1				AmCom
Symbiosis	1974		13			1									2			1											2		AmCom
Trio	1978		16		1	1			1																						AmCom
BOUCARD, MARCEL (?–)																															
Triade															1	1		1													Billa
BOUCOURECHLIEV, ANDRE (1925–)																															
Orion II (with percussion)	1982		20						1													2	2	1			2				Salab
Orion II, for Piano and Brass	1982		20						1													2	2	1			1				Salab
BOUGHTON, RUTLAND (1878–1960)																															
A Cycle of Symbol Songs				2	1	1																						1			Curwn
BOULEZ, PIERRE (1925–)																															
Dérive *Unus Instr:* Vibraphone				1		1			1						1			1									1			1	Unive
explosante-fixe . . . *Unus Instr:* Vibraphone, halaphone	1974		35	1	1	1							1		1			1				1					1			2	Unive
Improvisation sur Mallarmé I *Unus Instr:* Vibraphone, tubular bells									1	1																	4	S		2	Unive
Improvisation sur Mallarmé II *Unus Instr:* Vibraphone, tubular bells, celesta									1	1																	4	S		3	Unive
Le marteau sans maître *Unus Instr:* Vibraphone and xylorimba	1955		34		1							1			1												3	A		2	Unive
Pour le docteur Kalmus	1977		4	1		1			1						1			1													Unive
BOULNOIS, JOSEPH (1884–1918)																															
Piano Trio				1		1			1																						Salab
BOUSCH, FRANÇOIS (1946–)																															
Rêve au soleil des ombres *Unus Instr:* Jazz flute			17	1	1	1									1			1	1								2			1	Ridea
BOUVARD, JEAN (?–)																															
Images (3) *Comment:* Clarinet may replace saxophone				1					1						1					1											Billa
Pièces brèves (3) en trio				1					1						1																Billa
BOWLES, PAUL (1910–)																															
Music for a Farce	1953								1									1				1					1				Weint

	Year Composed or Published	Key	Duration	Violin	Viola	Cello	Double Bass	Gamba	Piano	Harpsicord	Organ	Guitar	Harp	Recorder	Flute/Piccolo	Oboe	English Horn	Clarinet/Bass Clarinet	Bassoon/Contrabassoon	Saxophone	French Horn	Trumpet	Trombone	Bass Trombone	Tuba	Baritone	Percussion	Voice	Electronic Tape	Unusual Instruments	Publisher
BOYD, ANNE (1946–)																															
As All Waters Flow *Unus Instr:* Gong	1976		12						1			2			7												4	F		1	Faber
As It Leaves the Bell	1973		15						1				2														4				Faber
Bencharong	1977		15	7	2	2	1																								Faber
Metamorphoses of Solitary Female Phoenix	1971		14						1						1	1		1	1		1						1				Faber
My Name Is Tian	1979		22		1								1		1												1	S			Faber
BOYKAN, MARTIN (1931–)																															
String Quartet No. 3			15	2	1	1																									Peter
BOZZA, EUGENE (1905–)																															
Aria (solo cello)				2	2	3			1																						Leduc
Bis																					2	2	1		1						Leduc
Fanfare héroïque, Op 46																					4	3	3		1		4				Leduc
Giration																					1	2	1		1						Leduc
Mouvements (3)																					1	2	1		1						Leduc
Octanphonie																2		2	2		2										Leduc
Ouverture pour une cérémonie																					4	3	3	1	1		1				Leduc
Pentaphonie															1	1		1	1		1										Leduc
Pièces (3) pour quatuor de cuivres																					1	2	1								Leduc
Pièces (3) pour septuor																					1	2	3		1						Leduc
Pièces (3) pour une musique de nuit															1	1		1	1												Leduc
Preludé et chaconne																					4	3	3		1		4				Leduc
Quatre mouvements															1	1		1	1		1	1	1								Leduc
Quatuor		a		2	1	1																									Leduc
Scherzo, Op 48															1	1		1	1		1										Leduc
Sérénade															1	1		1	1												Leduc
Sérénade en trio															1			1	1												Leduc
Sonatine															1	1		1	1												Leduc
Sonatine																					1	2	1		1						Leduc
Suite brève en trio																1		1	1												Leduc
Suite française																					1	2	1		1						Leduc
Trilogie																					1	2	1		1						Leduc
Variations sur un thème libre, Op 42															1	1		1	1		1										Leduc
BRACALI, GIANPAOLO (1941–)																															
Sextuor sur un thème de Monteverdi																						3	3				3				Leduc
BRAHMS, JOHANNES (1833–1897)																															
Clarinet Quintet, Op 115	1891	b		2	1	1												1													VarPb
Clarinet Trio, Op 114	1891	a				1			1									1													VarPb
Motet and Fugue—Psalm 51 (arr. Fitzgerald)																					1	2	1		1						Press
Piano Pieces, 4 (arr. Carp)															1	1		1			1										Press
Piano Quartet No. 1, Op 25	1861	g		1	1	1			1																						VarPb
Piano Quartet No. 2, Op 26	1862	A		1	1	1			1																						VarPb
Piano Quartet No. 3, Op 60	1875	c		1	1	1			1																						VarPb
Piano Quintet, Op 34	1864	f		2	1	1			1																						VarPb
Piano Trio No. 1, Op 8	1854	B		1		1			1																						VarPb
Piano Trio No. 2, Op 87	1882	C		1		1			1																						VarPb
Piano Trio No. 3, Op 101	1886	c		1		1			1																						VarPb
Scherzo	1853			1					1									1													Breit
Sextet No. 1, Op 18	1860	B♭		2	2	2																									VarPb
Sextet No. 2, Op 36	1865	G		2	2	2																									VarPb
String Quartet No. 1, Op 51 No. 1	1873	c		2	1	1																									VarPb
String Quartet No. 2, Op 51 No. 2	1873	a		2	1	1																									VarPb
String Quartet No. 3, Op 67	1875	B♭		2	1	1																									VarPb
String Quintet No. 1, Op 88	1882	F		2	2	1																									VarPb

	Year Composed or Published	Key	Duration	Violin	Viola	Cello	Double Bass	Gamba	Piano	Harpsicord	Organ	Guitar	Harp	Recorder	Flute/Piccolo	Oboe	English Horn	Clarinet/Bass Clarinet	Bassoon/Contrabassoon	Saxophone	French Horn	Trumpet	Trombone	Bass Trombone	Tuba	Baritone	Percussion	Voice	Electronic Tape	Unusual Instruments	Publisher
BRAHMS, JOHANNES *(continued)*																															
String Quintet No. 2, Op 111	1890	G		2	2	1																									VarPb
Trio (Horn), Op 40	1865	E♭		1					1												1										VarPb
Trio (alt. inst. 1), Op 40	1865	E♭		1	1				1																						VarPb
Trio (alt. inst. 2), Op 40	1865	E♭		1		1			1																						VarPb
Trio (viola instead of clarinet), Op 114	1891	a			1	1			1																						VarPb
Valse in A (arr. Schwab), Op 39				2	1	1																									CarlF
BRANDMÜLLER, THEO (1948–)																															
Missa Morgenstern *Unus Instr:* Bass clarinet	1978		17	1	1	1			1						1			1									2			1	Breit
Musik der Stille und Obertöne	1978			1		1			1																		1				BoteB
BRAUN, PETER M. (1936–)																															
Chorales (3)	1979					3	1																								BoteB
BREDEMEYER, REINER (1929–)																															
Serenade 3 (für H.E.)					1	1	1		1							1	1						1				1				Peter
Streichquartett				2	1	1																									Peter
Zum 13.7																		1		1							1	S			Peter
BRENET, THÉRÈSE (1935–)																															
Hommage à Signorelli *Unus Instr:* Ondes Martenot			16						1																		1	S		1	Ridea
BRESGEN, CESAR (1913–)																															
Salzburger Divertimento	1965		10												1	1		1	1		1										Dobli
BRETON, TOMÁS (1850–1923)																															
Cuarteto		D		2	1	1																									UMEsp
BRETTINGHAM SMITH, JOLYON (1949–)																															
Dancing Days, Op 13	1975		13	2	1	1			1				1		1	1		1			1	1	1				3	S			BoteB
The Doors of Perception, Op 30	1982		13												1												4				BoteB
O Rise, Op 6	1973		10			1			1	1					1								1				2				BoteB
BRIDGE, FRANK (1879–1941)																															
Divertimenti	1938		7												1	1		1	1												Boose
Phantasie				2	1	1																									Augen
Quartet No. 1		e		2	1	1																									Augen
Quartet No. 2		g		2	1	1																									Augen
Quartet No. 4				2	1	1																									Augen
BRIECE, JACK (1945–1988)																															
Fanfare for Winds	1970		4												1			1		1		1	1		1	1	1				AmCom
Septet *Unus Instr:* Tam-tam, glockenspiel	1985		10						1			1	1								2						2			2	AmCom
BRITTEN, BENJAMIN (1913–1976)																															
Canticle III, Op 55	1954								1												1							T			Boose
Canticle IV, Journey of the Magi	1971								1																			3			Boose
Divertimenti (3)	1936			2	1	1																									Faber
Gemini Variations *Comment:* Piano 4-hands				1					1						1																Faber
Phantasy Quartet, Op 2	1932		15	1	1	1										1															Boose
Quartettino	1930			2	1	1																									Faber
Russian Funeral *Unus Instr:* Contrabass tuba	1936		6																		4	3	2	1	1		1			1	Faber
Scherzo	1955													4																	Boose
Simple Symphony (arr.)				2	1	1																									Oxfor
String Quartet	1931	C		2	1	1																									Boose
String Quartet No. 1, Op 25	1941	D	26	2	1	1																									Boose
String Quartet No. 2, Op 36	1945	C	31	2	1	1																									Boose

	Year Composed or Published	Key	Duration	Violin	Viola	Cello	Double Bass	Gamba	Piano	Harpsicord	Organ	Guitar	Harp	Recorder	Flute/Piccolo	Oboe	English Horn	Clarinet/Bass Clarinet	Bassoon/Contrabassoon	Saxophone	French Horn	Trumpet	Trombone	Bass Trombone	Tuba	Baritone	Percussion	Voice	Electronic Tape	Unusual Instruments	Publisher
BRITTEN, BENJAMIN *(continued)*																															
String Quartet No. 3	1975			2	1	1																									Boose
Sword in the Stone (Concert Suite)	1938		10										1		1			1	1			1	1				1				Faber
BRIZZI, ALDO (1960–)																															
Le erbe nella Thule	1985		30	2	1	1							1		1						1						1	S			Salab
Objet d'art	1980		10	3	2	2	1								1																Salab
BROCKMAN, JANE (1949–)																															
Divergences	1975		7						1						1					1											AmCom
Two-Piano Quartet	1980		11			1			2						1																AmCom
BROOKS, RICHARD (1942–)																															
Serenade	1982		5			1			1						1																AmCom
BROWN, CHARLES (1940–)																															
Trio pour anches																1		1	1												Billa
BROWN, EARLE (1926–)																															
Available Forms I	1961			2	1	1	1		1				1		1	1		2			1	1	1				1				AMP
Centering	1973		20	2	1	1			1						1			1	1		1	1	1								Unive
Hodograph *Unus Instr:* Celesta, vibraphone, marimba, bells	1959								1						1												4			4	AMP
Music	1952			1		1			1																						Unive
Novara				2	1	1			1						1			1				1									Unive
Pentathis	1957			1	1				1				1		1			1				1	1							C	BScho
Sign Sounds *Unus Instr:* Xylophone, vibraphone, marimba, glockenspiel, celesta	1972		18	2	1	1	1		1				1		1			2	1			1	1				5			5	Unive
String Quartet	1965			2	1	1																									Unive
Syntagm III *Comment:* Solo Violin. *Unus Instr:* Celesta, marimba, vibraphone	1970		12	2		1			1				1		1												2			3	Unive
Times 5	1963			1		1							1		1								1						1		Unive
BROWN, J. E. (1937–)																															
1920s	1982		10		1	1			1																						AmCom
Fragments	1966		6	2	1	1			1						1	1		1				1	1				1				AmCom
Quartet for Mixed Instruments *Unus Instr:* Marimba	1967		5						1									1					1				1			1	AmCom
Trio	1966		10						1									1					1								AmCom
BRUCKNER, ANTON (1824–1896)																															
Intermezzo, Op Post				2	2	1																									Inter
Quintet		F		2	2	1																									Inter
BRUGK, HANS M. (1909–)																															
Serenade, Op 22															1	1		1	1		1										VarPb
BRUNIAU, AUGUST (1902–1971)																															
Toi et moi (with clarinet)									1							1		1													Billa
Toi et moi (with clarinet and saxophone)									1									1		1											Billa
Toi et moi (with saxophone)									1							1				1											Billa
BRUNSWICK, MARK (1902–1971)																															
Septet in Seven Movements	1957		12		1	1									1	1		1	1		1										AmCom
BULLER, JOHN (1927–)																															
2 Night Pieces from Finnegans Wake			15			1			1						1			1										S			Oxfor
7 Spazi *Comment:* Clarinet doubles on soprano sax			13	1		1			1									2		1											Oxfor
The Cave			8			1									1			1					1						1		Oxfor
Familiar			13	2	1	1																									Oxfor
The Melian Debate (Thucydides) *Voices:* Tenor and baritone			20			1							1		1		1				1	1						2			Oxfor

	Year Composed or Published	Key	Duration	Violin	Viola	Cello	Double Bass	Gamba	Piano	Harpsicord	Organ	Guitar	Harp	Recorder	Flute/Piccolo	Oboe	English Horn	Clarinet/Bass Clarinet	Bassoon/Contrabassoon	Saxophone	French Horn	Trumpet	Trombone	Bass Trombone	Tuba	Baritone	Percussion	Voice	Electronic Tape	Unusual Instruments	Publisher
BULLER, JOHN *(continued)*																															
Of Three Shakespeare Sonnets			12	2	1	1							1		1			1										M			Oxfor
Le terrazze *Comment:* Oboe doubles on Eng horn; clarinet on sax. *Unus Instr:* Contrabass clarinet, contrabassoon			22	1	1	1	1								1		1	1	1	1	2	1	2				1		1	2	Oxfor
Towards Aquarius			18	2	1	1	1								1	1		1	1		2	1	2				1		1		Oxfor
BUONAVENTURA, CAMARGO (1925–)																															
Il figliol prodigo	1967		35	2	1	1																									Omega
BURGON, GEOFFREY (1941–)																															
Cantata on Medieval Latin Texts *Voice:* Countertenor	1964		7												1	1			1									T			Chest
Gloria	1973		4			1			1						1	1		1			1										Chest
Goldberg's Dream	1975		20						1						1	1		1			1	1	1						1		Chest
Songs of Mary	1970		12		1				1																			S			Chest
Threnody *Comment:* Amplificaton needed	1971		12						1	1																		T			Chest
BURIAN, EMIL F. (1904–1959)																															
Bläserquintett	1933														1	1		1	1		1										Artia
BURKHARD, PAUL (1911–1977)																															
Swiss Nativity																						3	3				3				Schir
BUSBY, GERALD (1935–)																															
Court Dances (Ballet Suite)			23			1				1					1																Peter
BUSCH, ADOLF (1891–1952)																															
Serenade, Op 14	1919	G		2	1	1																									Simro
Streichquartett in einem Satz, Op 29	1925			2	1	1																									Breit
BUSONI, FERRUCIO (1866–1924)																															
Streichquartett 2, Op 26d				2	1	1																									Breit
BUSSER, HENRI P. (1872–1973)																															
Divertissement, Op 119	1951			2	1	1																									Duran
Miseremini mei				1		1	1				1		1															1			Duran
Oraison dominicale											1		1															1			Duran
Le Seigneur vient dans le chemin				1		1					1		1															1			Duran
BUSSOTTI, SYLVANO (1931–)																															
Il Nudo	1964			2	1	1			1																			S			Moeck
Phrase à trois				1	1	1																									Unive
Quartetto Gramsci				2	1	1																									Ricor
Three Lovers' Ballet				1		1			1																						Ricor
Tramonto (Elegiac Dance Scene)															1			1			1										Ricor
BUTTING, MAX (1888–1976)																															
Festschrift für Bach, Op 77	1951			1	1	1									1		1		1												Mitte
Hauskonzert bei Langners, Op 65 *Comment:* Piano 4-hands	1949			1		1			1						1																Mitte
Kleine Kammermusik, Op 70	1950			1		1									1		1														Mitte
Kleine Stücke, Op 26	1924			2	1	1																									Schot
Musik für Feierstunden, Op 85a	1952			2	1	1																									Mitte
La serenata gentile, Op 80	1951			2	1	1									1	1		1	1												Mitte
Streichquartett, Op 18	1919	f		2	1	1																									Wunde
Streichquartett 5, Op 52	1949			2	1	1																									Mitte
Streichquartett 6, Op 90	1955			2	1	1																									Peter
Streichquartett 7, Op 95				2	1	1																									Peter
Streichquartett 8, Op 96				2	1	1																									Peter
Streichquartett 9, Op 97				2	1	1																									Peter
Stücke (3) für Streichtrio, Op 86				1	1	1																									Mitte

	Year Composed or Published	Key	Duration	Violin	Viola	Cello	Double Bass	Gamba	Piano	Harpsicord	Organ	Guitar	Harp	Recorder	Flute/Piccolo	Oboe	English Horn	Clarinet/Bass Clarinet	Bassoon/Contrabassoon	Saxophone	French Horn	Trumpet	Trombone	Bass Trombone	Tuba	Baritone	Percussion	Voice	Electronic Tape	Unusual Instruments	Publisher
CAGE, JOHN (1912–1992)																															
Amores	1960		9						1																		3				Peter
Composition for 3 Voices *** *Comment:* For any 3 (or more) instruments	1934		4																												Peter
Dances (16)	1951		53	1		1			1						1							1					4				Peter
Five *** *Comment:* For any 5 voices or instruments	1988		5																												Peter
Four *** Duration: From 10 to 30 minutes, depending . . .	1989			2	1	1																									Peter
Hymnkus *Unus Instr:* Accordion	1986			1		1			2						1			1	1	2			1				2	1		1	Peter
Music for . . .	1985		30	2	1	1			2						1	1		1			1	1	1				4	1			Peter
Music for Wind Inst. I	1938														1			1	1												Peter
Music for Wind Inst. III	1938														1	1		1	1		1										Peter
Party Pieces	1950								1						1			1	1		1										Peter
Pieces (30) for String Quartet	1984			2	1	1																									Peter
Renga *** *Comment:* For any instruments and/or voices	1976		35																												Peter
Seven			20	1	1	1			1						1			1									1				Peter
Short Inventions (6)	1934		7	1	2	1									1			1				1									Peter
Solo . . . and 6 Short Inventions *** *Comment:* For any 3 instruments, g to g″	1933		15																												Peter
String Quartet in 4 Parts	1950		20	2	1	1																									Peter
Telephones and Birds *** *Comment:* For 3 performers	1977		30																												Peter
Theater Pieces (Parts 1-8) *** *Comment:* For up to 8 musicians, dancers, singers, etc.	1960																														Peter
Variations I and II *** *Comment:* For any number of players, any sound-producing means																															Peter
CALLAWAY, ANN (1949–)																															
Collections-Recollections	1982		18			1			1						1																AmCom
Dramatic Episodes (7)	1976		16			1			1						1																AmCom
CALLERT, G (?–)																															
Micheline gavotte				1	1	1			1																						Kunze
CALTABIANO, RONALD (1959–)																															
Medea	1982		18	1	1	1	1								1	1		2	1		1	1						S			AMP
String Quartet No. 1				2	1	1																									Press
CAMBRELING, SYLVAIN (1948–)																															
Divertissement																					1	2	1		1						Billa
CANNING, THOMAS (1911–)																															
Rondo for Percussion and Brass	1953		8																		2	2	3		1		1				AmCom
CAPLET, ANDRÉ (1878–1925)																															
Conte fantastique *Comment:* Double bass ad lib				2	1	1							1																		Duran
Conte fantastique (alt. inst.) *Comment:* Double bass ad lib				2	1	1			1																						Duran
CARL, ROBERT B. (1954–)																															
Ebb and Flow	1981		18	1		1									1	1		1	1		2	1	1				2				AmCom
Piano Trio ("Always Rising")	1979		15		1	1			1																						AmCom
Time/Memory/Shadow	1988		13	2	1	1			1				1																		AmCom
Time's Filter	1983		5	2	1	1	1								1	1		1	1		1										AmCom
Windriver	1984		9	1		1			1						1			1									1				AmCom

	Year Composed or Published	Key	Duration	Violin	Viola	Cello	Double Bass	Gamba	Piano	Harpsicord	Organ	Guitar	Harp	Recorder	Flute/Piccolo	Oboe	English Horn	Clarinet/Bass Clarinet	Bassoon/Contrabassoon	Saxophone	French Horn	Trumpet	Trombone	Bass Trombone	Tuba	Baritone	Percussion	Voice	Electronic Tape	Unusual Instruments	Publisher
CARL, ROBERT B. *(continued)*																															
Windriver (alt. inst.) *Unus Instr:* Celesta	1984		9	1		1									1			1									1			1	AmCom
CARLSEN, PHILIP (1951–)																															
Penumbra	1987		12	1					1									1													AmCom
CARTER, ELLIOTT (1908–)																															
Brass Quintet	1974		17																		1	2	1	1							AMP
Canon for 3 (In memoriam Igor Stravinsky) *** *Comment:* For 3 equal instruments	1971		2																												AMP
Canon for 4 (Homage to William) *Unus Instr:* Bass clarinet	1984		5	1		1									1			1												1	Hendo
Elegy (orig. for viola and piano)	1943		5	2	1	1																									Peer
Etudes (8) and a Fantasy	1950		23												1	1		1	1												AMP
Fantasy on Purcell's Fantasia	1974		3																		1	2	2								AMP
In Sleep, in Thunder	1981		21	2	1	1	1		1						1		1	1	1		1	1	1				1	T			Hendo
A Mirror on Which to Dwell *Unus Instr:* Bass clarinet	1975		20	1	1	1	1		1						1		1	1									1	S		1	AMP
Poems (3) of Robert Frost (w. harp) *Voice:* Soprano or tenor	1975		6	2	1	1	1						1		1	1		2	1									1			AMP
Poems (3) of Robert Frost *Voice:* Medium	1981		6	2	1	1	1					1			1	1		2	1									1			AMP
Sonata	1952		18			1				1					1	1															AMP
String Quartet No. 1	1951		45	2	1	1																									AMP
String Quartet No. 2	1959		22	2	1	1																									AMP
String Quartet No. 3	1971		22	2	1	1																									AMP
String Quartet No. 4	1986		24	2	1	1																									Hendo
Syringa *Voices:* Mezzo-soprano and narrator	1978		20	1	1	1	1		1			1			1		1	1					1				1	2			AMP
Triple Duo	1983		20	1		1			1						1			1									1				Hendo
Warble for Lilac Time	1946		8	2	1	1							1		1			2	1									S			Peer
Woodwind Quintet	1948		8												1	1		1	1		1										AMP
CASADESUS, FRANCIS (1870–1954)																															
London Sketches	1924		6												2	2		2	2		2										Salab
CASADESUS, ROBERT (1899–1972)																															
Piano Quartet, Op 30				1	1	1			1																						Inter
Sextuor									1						1	1		1	1		1										Duran
CASELLA, ALFREDO (1883–1947)																															
Concerto				2	1	1																									Unive
Serenata				1		1												1	1			1									Unive
Siciliana e burlesca				1		1			1																						Ricor
Sonata a tre, Op 62				1		1			1																						Ricor
CASTELNUOVO-TEDESCO, MARIO (1895–1968)																															
Piano Quintet No. 1				2	1	1			1																						Colom
Piano Quintet No. 2				2	1	1			1																						Colom
Piano Trio No. 1, Op 49	1929	G		1		1			1																						Ricor
Piano Trio No. 2		G		1		1			1																						Colom
Quintet for Guitar and Strings, Op 145				2	1	1						1																			BScho
String Quartet No. 1		G		2	1	1																									Ricor
String Quartet No. 2, Op 139		f		2	1	1																									Affil
CASTERA, RENÉ DE (1873–1955)																															
Piano Trio		d		1		1			1																						Salab
CASTEREDE, JACQUES (1926–)																															
Air Variee *Unus Instr:* Oboe d'amore, heckelphone			8													1	1													2	Peter

	Year Composed or Published	Key	Duration	Violin	Viola	Cello	Double Bass	Gamba	Piano	Harpsicord	Organ	Guitar	Harp	Recorder	Flute/Piccolo	Oboe	English Horn	Clarinet/Bass Clarinet	Bassoon/Contrabassoon	Saxophone	French Horn	Trumpet	Trombone	Bass Trombone	Tuba	Baritone	Percussion	Voice	Electronic Tape	Unusual Instruments	Publisher
CASTEREDE, JACQUES *(continued)*																																
Prelude et danse									1																3		1		1				Leduc
CASTIGLIONI, NICCOLÒ (1932–)																																
Tropi	1960			1		1			1						1			1											1				Suvin
CASTILLON, ALEXIS DE (1838–1873)																																
Quatuor, Op 3				2	1	1																										Duran
Quintette, Op 1				2	1	1			1																							Duran
Trio, Op 4				1		1			1																							Duran
CEELY, ROBERT (1930–)																																
Speculation *Unus Instr:* Bass clarinet	1961		2			1									1	1		2														1	AmCom
CERHA, FRIEDRICH (1926–)																																
Keintate I *Voice:* Medium. *Unus Instr:* Accordion	1982		60	2	1	1	1											2			2						1	1		1	Unive
Keintate II *Voice:* Medium. *Unus Instr:* Accordion	1984		25	2	1	1	1											2			2						1	1		1	Unive
CHABRIER, EMMANUEL (1841–1894)																																
Danse villageoise (arr. Carp)															1	1		1	1		1											Press
Elégie (orch. Français)			4	4	2	2	1								1	1		1	1		1											Eschi
CHAILLEY, JACQUES (1910–)																																
Barcarolle															1	1		1	1		1											Leduc
Pièces contemplatives (3)				2	1	1																										Costa
Suite du 15e siècle *Unus Instr:* Tambourine ad lib				1	1	1																									1	Leduc
Suite du 15e siècle (alt. inst. 1) Oboe may replace English horn. *Unus Instr:* Tambourine ad lib																	1		1		1									1	Leduc
Suite du 15e siècle (alt. inst. 2) Cello may replace viola. *Unus Instr:* Tambourine ad lib					1											1					1									1	Leduc
CHAMINADE, CÉCILE (1857–1944)																																
Trio, Op 11		g		1		1			1																							Duran
CHAPI, RUPERTO (1851–1909)																																
Cuarteto 1				2	1	1																										UMEsp
Cuarteto 2				2	1	1																										UMEsp
Cuarteto 3				2	1	1																										UMEsp
Cuarteto 4				2	1	1																										UMEsp
CHAPPLE, BRIAN (1945–)																																
Venus Fly-Trap	1979		20	2	1	1	1		1						1	1		1	1		1	1	1								Chest
CHAPUIS, AUGUSTE (1858–1933)																																
Trio		g		1		1			1																							Duran
CHAUSHIAN, LEVON (?–)																																
String Quartet No. 3				2	1	1																										VAAP
CHAUSSON, ERNEST (1855–1899)																																
Concerto, Op 21	1891	D		3	1	1			1																							VarPb
Piano Quartet, Op 30		A		1	1	1			1																							VarPb
Piano Trio, Op 3	1882	g		1		1			1																							Salab
Quartet, Op 35	1899	c		2	1	1																										VarPb
CHAVEZ, CARLOS (1899–1978)																																
Cuarteto de arcos	1921			2	1	1																										VarPb
Fuga HAG,C	1964			1	1	1	1																									Boose
Invention No. 2	1965			1	1	1																										Mills

	Year Composed or Published	Key	Duration	Violin	Viola	Cello	Double Bass	Gamba	Piano	Harpsicord	Organ	Guitar	Harp	Recorder	Flute/Piccolo	Oboe	English Horn	Clarinet/Bass Clarinet	Bassoon/Contrabassoon	Saxophone	French Horn	Trumpet	Trombone	Bass Trombone	Tuba	Baritone	Percussion	Voice	Electronic Tape	Unusual Instruments	Publisher
CHAVEZ, CARLOS *(continued)*																															
Melodias indias (4) *Voice:* Soprano or tenor			7	2	1	1	1								1			1										1			CMC
Otros tres exagonos *Voice:* Soprano or tenor	1924				1				1						1	1			1									1			CMC
Soli I	1933		6													1		1	1			1									Boose
Soli II	1961														1	1		1	1		1										Boose
Soli IV	1966		11																		1	1	1								Boose
String Quartet No. 1	1921			2	1	1																									CMC
String Quartet No. 2	1932			2	1	1																									CMC
String Quartet No. 3	1944			2	1	1																									CMC
CHAYNES, CHARLES (1925–)																															
Irradiations	1968			1		1				1																					Leduc
Poèmes (4) de Sappho	1968			1	1	1																						S			Leduc
Séquences pour l'Apocalypse											1										1	2	1		1						Leduc
Sérénade	1954														1	1		1	1		1										Leduc
Tarquinia (3 Frescoes) *Unus Instr:* Ondes Martenot	1973								1																		1			1	Leduc
Visages (11) . . . ou l'antifugue				6	2	2	1																								Leduc
Visions concertantes			20	7	2	2	1																								Ridea
CHEN, QIGANG (?–)																															
Yi				2	1	1												1													Billa
CHENOWETH, GERALD (1943–)																															
Dance Variations	1979		12	1	1	1										1															AmCom
Fantasy Quartet	1973		10	1	1	1									1																AmCom
CHERUBINI, LUIGI (1760–1842)																															
String Quartet, Op 6		a		2	1	1																									Kunze
CHEVILLARD, CAMILLE (1859–1923)																															
Quatuor, Op 16		D♭		2	1	1																									Duran
Quintette, Op 1				2	1	1			1																						Duran
Trio, Op 3		F		1		1			1																						Duran
CHIHARA, PAUL (1938–)																															
The Beauty of the Rose			16										1						1		2						1				Peter
Branches			7																2								1				Peter
Ceremony I			7			2	1									1											1				Peter
Ceremony II (Incantations) *Comment:* Amplification needed			7			2									1												1				Peter
Driftwood			8	1	2	1																									Peter
Driftwood (alt. vers.)			8	2	1	1																									Peter
Piano Trio				1		1			1																						Schir
Primavera			17	2	1	1																									Peter
Sequoia				2	1	1																							1		Peter
String Trio			20	1	1	1																									Peter
Willow, Willow			10												1										1		3				Peter
CHILDS, BARNEY (1926–)																															
Interbalances I *Unus Instr:* Bass clarinet	1962		15				1									1	1	1												1	AmCom
Interbalances I (alt. inst.)	1962		15				1									1	1			1											AmCom
Interbalances III *** (solo cello) *Comment:* For cello and any instruments up to four	1962					1																									AmCom
Music for Winds	1963		12												2	2		2	2	1	1	1	1		1						AmCom
Quartet	1964		17				1								1	1											1				AmCom
Quintet for Strings and Harp	1954		15	2	1	1							1																		AmCom

	Year Composed or Published	Key	Duration	Violin	Viola	Cello	Double Bass	Gamba	Piano	Harpsicord	Organ	Guitar	Harp	Recorder	Flute/Piccolo	Oboe	English Horn	Clarinet/Bass Clarinet	Bassoon/Contrabassoon	Saxophone	French Horn	Trumpet	Trombone	Bass Trombone	Tuba	Baritone	Percussion	Voice	Electronic Tape	Unusual Instruments	Publisher
CHILDS, BARNEY *(continued)*																															
Three Players I	1965		7															1	1		1										AmCom
CHOU, WEN-CHUNG (1923–)																															
Beijing in the Mist *Unus Instr:* Electric bass, electric piano, electric guitar			12				1		2			1								2		1	1				3			3	Peter
Pien (Chamber Concerto) *Comment:* Oboe doubles on English horn	1966		14						1						2	1	1	1	1		1	2	2				4				Peter
Soliloquy of a Bhiksuni			5																		4	1	3		1		3				Peter
Suite for Harp and Wind Quintet			7										1		1	1		1	1		1										Peter
Yu Ko *Unus Instr:* Bass clarinet			5	1					1						1		1	1					2				2			1	Peter
Yun	1969		15						1						1			1	1		1	1	1				2				Peter
CHUDOVA, TATIANA (1944–)																															
Quintet																							4		1						VAAP
CILENSEK, JOHANN (1913–)																															
Mosaic			13	7	3	2	1																								Peter
Woodwind Quintet															1	1		1	1		1										Peter
CLAFLIN, AVERY (1898–1979)																															
Recitativo, aria, e stretta	1958		15	1		1			1												1										AmCom
CLARKE, HENRY L. (1907–)																															
Three from Foster	1980		4		1										1								1								AmCom
Three from Foster (alt. inst.) *Comment:* Other combinations possible	1980		4	1														1	1												AmCom
CLARKE, KEITH R. (?–)																															
Cadences																					1	2	1								Novel
CLARKE, REBECCA (1886–1979)																															
Piano Trio	1921	E♭	25	1		1			1																						Boose
CLAYTON, LAURA (1943–)																															
Cree Songs to the Newborn *Unus Instr:* Xylophone, vibraphone			15			2	1						1		2												2	1		2	Peter
CLEMENTI, ALDO (1925–)																															
Concertino *Unus Instr:* Contrabassoon	1956			1		1	1		1						1	1			2		1									1	Suvin
Piccoli pezzi (3)	1955														1	1		1													Suvin
Sonata									1				1									1									Suvin
Triplum	1960														1	1		1													Suvin
COE, MICHAEL (?–)																															
Miniatures																					1	1	1								Oxfor
COKER, WILSON (1928–)																															
Concertino				1	1	1													1												Press
Woodwind Quintet															1	1		1	1		1										Press
COLE, BRUCE (1947–)																															
Spray of Dead Arrows	1972		20		1				1									1										S			Boose
CONNOLLY, JUSTIN R. (1933–)																															
Cinquepaces																					1	2	1		1						Oxfor
CONSOLI, MARC-ANTON (1941–)																															
Ellipsonics *** *Comment:* Up to 4 players; optional slides, lights, mimes, dancers	1974		10																												AmCom
Interactions	1970		12												1	1		1	1		1	1	1				5				AmCom
Interactions IV (Aftermath)	1975		12				1														1	1	1				1				AmCom
Interactions V (Consequence)	1976		11	2	1	1									1																AmCom

	Year Composed or Published	Key	Duration	Violin	Viola	Cello	Double Bass	Gamba	Piano	Harpsicord	Organ	Guitar	Harp	Recorder	Flute/Piccolo	Oboe	English Horn	Clarinet/Bass Clarinet	Bassoon/Contrabassoon	Saxophone	French Horn	Trumpet	Trombone	Bass Trombone	Tuba	Baritone	Percussion	Voice	Electronic Tape	Unusual Instruments	Publisher
CONSTANT, MARIUS (1925–)																															
L'Eloge de la folie (Ballet) *Unus Instr:* Mandolin, celesta	1966		55				1		2	1	1		1		1	1		1	1		1	2	2				1			2	Salab
Études de concert (4)									1												2	1	1								Leduc
Piano personnage *Unus Instr:* Celesta	1973		20		1	1	1		2		1	1			1	1		3			1	1	1				2			1	Salab
Précis de composition	1982			2	1	1	1											1	1		1								1		Salab
Précis de décomposition	1982			2	1	1													1		1								1		Salab
Psyche									2																		2				Ricor
Stations (14) *Comment:* Percussionist plays 92 instruments. Amplification needed	1970		30	1	1	1				1		1											1				1				Salab
Strings *Unus Instr:* Electric guitar	1972		12	7	2	2	1					1																		1	Salab
Strings (w. harpsichord)			12	7	2	2	1			1																					Salab
Traits *** *Comment:* For up to 20 varied instruments	1969		18																												Salab
Winds	1968		8				1								2	1		2	1		2	2	3								Salab
CONYNGHAM, BARRY (1944–)																															
Basho *Unus Instr:* Piccolo, alto flute, bass clarinet	1981		20	1		1			1						1			1					1							3	Unive
Dwellings *Unus Instr:* Alto flute, bass clarinet	1982		25	1	1	1	1		1			1	1		1	1		1			1	1					1			2	Unive
Sky	1977		12	8	2	2	1																								Unive
String Quartet	1979			2	1	1																									Unive
COOKE, ARNOLD (1906–)																															
Quintet				2	1	1												1													Oxfor
COOPER, PAUL (1926–)																															
Chamber Music I	1982		12	1		1			1						1			2													HanCh
Chamber Music II	1983		15	1		1			1						1			2													HanCh
Concert for Three	1977		16			1			1									1													HanCh
Epitaphs	1969		14				1						1		1																HanCh
Rondels bergamasques *Unus Instr:* Bass clarinet	1988		13		1	1			1						1			1										S		1	HanCh
Silences	1973		12				1								1	1															HanCh
Sonata for Flutes and Piano	1962		12						1						3																HanCh
String Quartet No. 1	1952		14	2	1	1																									HanCh
String Quartet No. 2	1954		15	2	1	1																									HanCh
String Quartet No. 3	1959		13	2	1	1																									HanCh
String Quartet No. 4	1963		11	2	1	1																									HanCh
String Quartet No. 5	1973		18	2	1	1																									HanCh
String Quartet No. 6	1977		21	2	1	1																									HanCh
Voci (3)	1986		13	1		1			1																						HanCh
COPLAND, AARON (1900–1990)																															
As It Fell Upon a Day	1923		6												1			1										S			Boose
The Five Kings (Incidental Music) *Comment:* For 5 instruments	1939																														Manus
Nonet	1960		18	3	3	3																									Boose
Pieces (2) (Rondino; Lento molto)	1928		11	2	1	1																									Boose
Quartet	1950		23	1	1	1			1																						Boose
Quiet City	1939								1									1		1		1									Manus
Quiet City (arr. Kennedy)	1940		10						1								1					1									Boose
Sextet (from Short Symphony)	1937		15	2	1	1			1									1													Boose
Threnody I (Igor Stravinsky, in memoriam)	1971		3	1	1	1									1																Boose
Threnody II (Beatrice Cunningham)	1973		4	1	1	1									1																Boose
Vitebsk	1929		11	1		1			1																						Boose
CORGHI, AZIO (1937–)																															
Stereofonie x 4						1					1				1												1				Ricor

	Year Composed or Published	Key	Duration	Violin	Viola	Cello	Double Bass	Gamba	Piano	Harpsicord	Organ	Guitar	Harp	Recorder	Flute/Piccolo	Oboe	English Horn	Clarinet/Bass Clarinet	Bassoon/Contrabassoon	Saxophone	French Horn	Trumpet	Trombone	Bass Trombone	Tuba	Baritone	Percussion	Voice	Electronic Tape	Unusual Instruments	Publisher
CORIGLIANO, JOHN (1938–)																															
Aria	1985		6	2	1	1										1															Schir
Poem in October	1970		16	2	1	1				1					1	1												T			Schir
Scherzo for oboe and percussion *Unus Instr:* Celesta	1975		6						1				1			1											4			1	Schir
Voyage	1988		8	2	1	1									1																Schir
Wedding Song *** *Voice:* Medium, and any melody instrument	1971		5								1																	1			Schir
CORNILIOS, NICOS (1954–)																															
Peupliers	1983		8	7	2	2	1																								Salab
CORREGIA, ENRICO (1933–)																															
Gial'eolia di notte	1984		9	2	1	1	1		1						1	1		1	1		1	1	1				2				Salab
Interlicht	1983		9	2	2	1									1			1									2				Salab
CORY, ELEANOR (1943–)																															
Concertino II, for Piano and Ensemble *Unus Instr:* Mandolin	1970		16						1				1			1	1	1	1		1		1				4			1	AmCom
Encounters	1986		6	1	1	1									1	1		1													AmCom
Modulations	1972		10	1	1	1	1																				2				AmCom
Septet	1971		12	1	1	1									1	1			1		1										AmCom
Trio	1973		12			1			1									1													AmCom
Trio for Piano and Winds	1977		12						1						1		1														AmCom
COTEK, PAVEL (1922–)																															
Musica a fiato *Unus Instr:* Bass trumpet	1970								1						1							2	1							1	Artia
COUROUPOS, GEORGES (1942–)																															
Abstr'acte, Op 21 *Unus Instr:* Tam-tam	1974		10	1	1	1					1				1	1		1	1		1	1	1		1		1			1	Ridea
COWELL, HENRY D. (1897–1965)																															
Action in Brass	1943																				1	2	2								EdMus
Chrysanthemums	1937			2	1	1														2								S			Manus
A Composition (solo piano)			9	2	1	1			1							1		1	1												Peter
Hymn, Chorale and Fuguing Tune No. 8	1947		8	2	1	1																									AMP
Paragraphs (7)	1925		8	1	1	1																									Peter
Party Pieces	1950								1						1			1	1		1										Peter
Persian Set (Four Movements) *Unus Instr:* Persian drum or tam-tam			15	3		1	1		1			1			1			1									1			1	Peter
Piano Trio	1965		19	1		1			1																						Peter
Polyphonica	1930		4	2	1	1	1								1	1		1	1		1	1	1								AMP
Quartet (w. harp)	1962					1							1		1	1															AMP
Quartet (w. harpsichord)	1954		12			1				1					1	1															AMP
Quartet Romantic	1917			1	1										2																Peter
Rhythm-Harmony Quartet 1					1	1									2																Peter
Rhythm-Harmony Quartet 2	1919		15	2	1	1																									Peter
Rondo			6																		2	3	2								Peter
Sarabande	1937															1		1									1				Manus
Septet *Comment:* For 5 solo wordless voices: 2 Sopranos, alto, tenor, bass	1956								1									1										5			Peter
Set	1953					1				1					1	1															AMP
Set of Five	1951		18	1					1																		1				Peter
Simultaneous Mosaics (26)	1964		9	1		1			1									1									1				Peter
Sinfonietta	1928		14	4	1	1	1								1	1		1	1		1	1	1								AMP
String Quartet No. 1 (Pedantic)	1916		8	2	1	1																									AMP
String Quartet No. 2 (Euphometric)	1919			2	1	1																									Peter
String Quartet No. 3 (Movement)	1928		4	2	1	1																									AMP

	Year Composed or Published	Key	Duration	Violin	Viola	Cello	Double Bass	Gamba	Piano	Harpsicord	Organ	Guitar	Harp	Recorder	Flute/Piccolo	Oboe	English Horn	Clarinet/Bass Clarinet	Bassoon/Contrabassoon	Saxophone	French Horn	Trumpet	Trombone	Bass Trombone	Tuba	Baritone	Percussion	Voice	Electronic Tape	Unusual Instruments	Publisher
COWELL, HENRY D. *(continued)*																															
String Quartet No. 4 (Mosaic)	1935		12	2	1	1																									AMP
String Quartet No. 5 (United)	1936		15	2	1	1																									Peter
String Quartet No. 6	1962		19	2	1	1																									Peter
Suite	1930														1	1		1	1		1										Press
Toccanta	1938					1			1						1													S			Boose
Trio (Four Combinations)			15	1		1			1																						Peter
Trio (Harp)			20	1									1		1																Peter
Vocalise	1928		8						1						1													1			Peter
COYNER, LOU (1931–)																															
A Center Distant *Comment:* Conductor needed	1978		13		1	1	1			1					1			1			1	1	1				1				AmCom
Echoes Upon the Stilled Air *Unus Instr:* Electric piano, bass clarinet	1982		12			1	1		1				1		1	1		1	1		1		1		1		2			2	AmCom
Light that Lingers (Solo Piano)	1983		13			2	1		1				1		2		1										2				AmCom
Occam's Razor (solo harp) *Unus Instr:* Flügelhorn	1989		11		1	1			1				1		1	1		1	1		1		1				1			1	AmCom
Solo Harp with Ensemble *Unus Instr:* Bass clarinet	1985		9	1	1	1	1		1				1				1	1	1	1							1			1	AmCom
Solo Oboe with Ensemble *Unus Instr:* Bass clarinet	1985		9	1	1	1	1		1				1			1		1	1								1			1	AmCom
A Whorl of Time *Comment:* Conductor needed	1982		12			1	1		1						1			1									1				AmCom
Woodenly Booming Along Like a Carved Bee	1972		13						1						1	1		1	1		1										AmCom
CRAS, JEAN E. (1879–1932)																															
Quatuor	1909			2	1	1																									Salab
Quintette	1922	C		2	1	1			1																						Salab
Trio	1907	c		1		1			1																						Duran
CRESTON, PAUL (1906–1985)																															
Concertino for Piano and Wind Quintet, Op 99	1969								1						1	1		1	1		1										Kerby
String Quartet, Op 8	1936			2	1	1																									Shawn
Suite, Op 56	1952				1				1						1																Shawn
Trio, Op 112	1979			1		1			1																						Graph
CREUSOT, JEAN (?–)																															
Pochade																					1	2	1								Billa
CROLEY, RANDELL (1946–)																															
Disquisition (Cyclic Chorale)																					1	2	1		1						Press
CROSSE, GORDON (1937–)																															
Ariadne, Op 31 *Unus Instr:* Celesta, bass clarinet	1972		23	1	1	1	1		1						1			2				1	2				1			2	Oxfor
Canto, Op 4	1963		5												1	1		1	1		1		1								Oxfor
Chime	1983		12																		1	2	1		1						Oxfor
Corpus Christi Carol, Op 5	1964		12	2	1	1												1			1							H			Oxfor
Dreamsongs, Op 35	1973		14						1							1		1	1												Oxfor
Fear No More *Unus Instr:* Oboe d'amore	1981		12													1	1													1	Oxfor
Medieval French Songs, Op 14a			12						1									1									1	1			Oxfor
Oboe Quintet	1988		16	2	1	1										1															Oxfor
Peace for Brass, Op 53	1981		5																		1	4	4		1						Oxfor
String Quartet, Op 47	1980		27	2	1	1																									Oxfor
Studies for String Quartet, Set 1, Op 34a	1973		15	2	1	1																									Oxfor
Studies for String Quartet, Set 2, Op 34b	1977		12	2	1	1																									Oxfor

	Year Composed or Published	Key	Duration	Violin	Viola	Cello	Double Bass	Gamba	Piano	Harpsicord	Organ	Guitar	Harp	Recorder	Flute/Piccolo	Oboe	English Horn	Clarinet/Bass Clarinet	Bassoon/Contrabassoon	Saxophone	French Horn	Trumpet	Trombone	Bass Trombone	Tuba	Baritone	Percussion	Voice	Electronic Tape	Unusual Instruments	Publisher
CROSSE, GORDON *(continued)*																															
Thel (Concertante for solo flute), Op 38	1978		14	4	4	4	2								1						2										Oxfor
Trio	1986		27	1		1			1																						Oxfor
Trio (Rhymes and Reasons), Op 52	1982		35			1			1									1													Oxfor
Verses in memoriam David Munrow *Voice:* Countertenor	1979		9			1				1				1														T			Oxfor
Villanelles, Op 2	1974		12	1		1									1	1		1	1		1										Oxfor
A Wake	1982		10			1			1						1			1													Oxfor
A Wake Again *Voice:* Countertenor						1				1				2														T			Oxfor
Wildboy (Concertante for clarinet), Op 42 *Unus Instr:* Cimbalom	1978		27	1	1	1	1								1			1	1		1						1			1	Oxfor
World Within, Op 40			43	1	1	1			1				1		1			1			1	1					1				Oxfor
CRUMB, GEORGE (1929–)																															
Ancient Voices of Children *Unus Instr:* Electric piano, toy piano, mandolin	1970		25						1				1			1											3	2		3	Peter
Black Angels *Unus Instr:* Electric string quartet	1970		25	2	1	1																								4	Peter
Dream Sequence (Images II) *Unus Instr:* 2 Glass harmonicas, offstage	1976		15	1		1			1																		1			2	Peter
Echoes (11) of Autumn *Unus Instr:* Alto flute	1965		18	1					1						1			1												1	Peter
Federico's Little Songs for Children *Unus Instr:* Piccolo													1		1													S		1	Peter
Idyll for the Misbegotten *Unus Instr:* Amplified flute			15												1												3			1	Peter
Lux Aeterna for 5 Masked Musicians *Unus Instr:* Sitar	1971		15											1	1												2	1		1	Peter
Madrigals, Book I *Unus Instr:* Vibraphone	1965		9				1																				1	S		1	Peter
Madrigals, Book II	1965		7												1												1	S			Peter
Madrigals, Book III	1969		8										1														1	S			Peter
Madrigals, Book IV	1969		9				1						1		1												1	S			Peter
Music for a Summer Evening (Makrokosmos III) *Unus Instr:* Amplified pianos	1974		40						2																		2			2	Peter
Night Music I *Comment:* Celesta may replace piano	1963								1																		1	S			Peter
Night of the Four Moons *Unus Instr:* Alto flute, piccolo, banjo, electric cello	1969		16			1									1												1	A		4	Peter
Songs, Drones, and Refrains of Death *Unus Instr:* Amplified keyboard, electric bass, electric guitar	1968		30				1		1	1		1															2	B		3	Peter
Vox Balaenae for 3 Masked Players *Unus Instr:* Electric flute and cello, amplified piano	1971		18			1			1						1															3	Peter
CRUSELL, BERNHARD H. (1775–1838)																															
Clarinet Quartet, Op 2 No. 1		E♭		1	1	1												1													Kneus
Clarinet Quartet, Op 4		c			1	1	1											1													Kneus
Clarinet Quartet, Op 7				1	1	1												1													Kneus
Flute Quartet, Op 8				1	1		1								1																Kneus
CSEMICZKY, MIKLOS (1954–)																															
String Quartet	1980		20	2	1	1																									Boose
CSERMAK, ANTAL G. (1774–1822)																															
Hungarian Dances (6)				2	1	1																									Dobli

	Year Composed or Published	Key	Duration	Violin	Viola	Cello	Double Bass	Gamba	Piano	Harpsicord	Organ	Guitar	Harp	Recorder	Flute/Piccolo	Oboe	English Horn	Clarinet/Bass Clarinet	Bassoon/Contrabassoon	Saxophone	French Horn	Trumpet	Trombone	Bass Trombone	Tuba	Baritone	Percussion	Voice	Electronic Tape	Unusual Instruments	Publisher
CSERMAK, ANTAL G. *(continued)*																															
String Quartet (Die drohende Gefahr)	1809			2	1	1																									Dobli
CUI, CESAR (1835–1918)																															
Pieces (5), Op 56				1					1						1																Inter
CUSTER, ARTHUR (1923–)																															
Colloquy				2	1	1																									Press
The Ides of March (Incidental Music)	1969		20										1			2					2	3	2		1		1				AmCom
CZERNY, CARL (1791–1857)																															
Grande Serenade Concertante, Op 126						1			1									1			1										MusRa
DAHL, INGOLF (1912–1970)																															
Allegro and arioso															1	1		1	1		1										McGMa
Andante and arioso	1942														1	1		1	1		1										McGMa
Concerto a tre	1946			1		1												1													McGMa
Piano Quartet	1957			1	1	1			1																						McGMa
Piano Trio	1962			1		1			1																						Peer
D'ALESSANDRO, RAFFAELE (1911–1959)																															
String Quartet No. 2, Op 73				2	1	1																									Hug
DALLAPICCOLA, LUIGI (1904–1975)																															
Canti (5) *** *Unus Instr:* Flute in G, clarinet in A, bass clarinet in B♭	1956				1	1			1				1		2			2										B		3	Suvin
Divertimento in quattro esercizi	1934				1	1									1	1		1										S			Caris
Frammenti (5) di Saffo *** *Unus Instr:* Ottavino; piccolo and bass clarinets, celesta	1942			1	1	1	1		1				1		2	1		2	1		1	1					1	S		4	Suvin
Goethe Lieder	1953																	3										S			Suvin
Liriche (2) di Anacreonte *Unus Instr:* Piccolo clarinet in E♭, clarinet in A	1945				1				1									2										S		2	Suvin
Liriche (4) di Antonio Machado *Unus Instr:* Piccolo clarinet, celesta, vibraphone, xylomarimba	1964			2	1	1	1						1		1	1		2	1		1	1					2	S		4	Suvin
Parole di San Paolo *Unus Instr:* Alto flute, bass clarinet, celesta, vibraphone, xylophone	1969				1	1			1				1		1			2									1	M		5	Suvin
Sex Carmina Alcaei	1943			1	1	1			1				1		1	1		1	1		1	1						S			Suvin
DALLINGER, FRIDOLIN (1933–)																															
Bläserquintett															1	1		1	1		1										Dobli
Concertino				1					1									1													Dobli
Fanfare																					2	2	2								Dobli
Suite No. 1 for Wind Quintet															1	1		1	1		1										Dobli
Suite No. 2 for Wind Quintet															1	1		1	1		1										Dobli
DAMAIS, EMILE (1906–)																															
Concert				1	1	1																									Billa
DAMASE, JEAN-MICHEL (1928–)																															
Variations (17)															1	1		1	1		1										Leduc
DANIEL-LESUR, DANIEL (1908–)																															
Lieder (4) *Comment:* A principal violin may replace flute				1	1	1			1				1		1													1			Duran
Suite médiévale				1	1	1							1		1																Duran
Suite pour quatuor à cordes				2	1	1																									Billa

	Year Composed or Published	Key	Duration	Violin	Viola	Cello	Double Bass	Gamba	Piano	Harpsicord	Organ	Guitar	Harp	Recorder	Flute/Piccolo	Oboe	English Horn	Clarinet/Bass Clarinet	Bassoon/Contrabassoon	Saxophone	French Horn	Trumpet	Trombone	Bass Trombone	Tuba	Baritone	Percussion	Voice	Electronic Tape	Unusual Instruments	Publisher
DANIELPOUR, RICHARD (1956–)																															
First Light *Unus Instr:* Timpani	1988		13	2	1	1	1		1				1		1		1	1	1		2	1	1				4			1	AMP
Quintet for Piano and Strings	1988		24	2	1	1			1																						AMP
String Quartet (Requiem)			33	2	1	1																									Peter
Urban Dances	1988		15																		1	2	2								AMP
DANZI, FRANZ (1763–1826)																															
Woodwind Quintet, Op 67 No. 3		E♭													1	1		1	1		1										Kneus
Woodwind Quintet, Op 68 No. 1															1	1		1	1		1										Kneus
Woodwind Quintet, Op 68 No. 2		F													1	1		1	1		1										Kneus
Woodwind Quintet, Op 77 No. 2		e													1	1		1	1		1										Kneus
DAO, NGUYEN T. (1941–)																															
Blessure/Soleil II	1985		17	7	2	2	1								2	2			1		1						1				Salab
Nho *Comment:* Basses play 5 percussion instruments			20			1	5																					S			Salab
Tuyen Lua *Unus Instr:* Timpani			15	2	1	1			1						1												2		1	1	Salab
DARASSE, XAVIER (1934–)																															
Antagonisme II *Unus Instr:* Timpani	1976		15								1										1	1	1		1		2			1	Salab
Antagonisme IV	1976		9																		1	2	1		1						Salab
Étude concertée *Unus Instr:* Vibraphone					2																						1			1	Salab
In memoriam Jean-Pierre Guezec			19								1										1	2	1		1						Salab
DAVID, JOHANN N. (1895–1977)																															
Concerto for Violin and Violoncello, Op 68	1969		19		2		1						1		1			1			1						2				Breit
Concerto No. 1 for Violin, Op 45	1952		32		2	1	1						1		1	1		1	1		1						2				Breit
Introitus, Choral, and Fugue for Organ, Op 25	1939		20								1										4	2	3								Breit
Melancholia for Viola, Op 53	1958		14	4	3	2	1																								Breit
Sinfonia, Op 54	1959		18	4	2	3	1																								Breit
Trio					1							1			1																Dobli
DAVID, THOMAS C. (1925–)																															
Bläserquintett 1															1	1		1	1		1										Dobli
Bläserquintett 2															1	1		1	1		1										Dobli
Concerto for 9 Solo Instruments				1	1	1	1								1	1		1	1		1										Dobli
Quartett				1	1	1										1															Dobli
Quintett				1	1	1	1											1													Dobli
Streichquartett 4				2	1	1																									Dobli
Streichquartett 5	1966			2	1	1																									Dobli
Tricinium *Comment:* Viola may substitute for English horn						1									1		1														Dobli
Trio				1					1									1													Dobli
DAVIDOFF, CARL J. (1838–1889)																															
Streichquartett, Op 38				2	1	1																									Rahte
DAVIDOVSKY, MARIO (1934–)																															
Chacona	1972		10	1		1			1																						EBMar
Noneto	1957		11	2	1	1	1								1	1		1	1												EBMar
Pennplay *Unus Instr:* Bass clarinet			11	1	1	1	1		1						2			2			1	1	1		1		2			1	Peter
Quartetto			11	1	1	1									1																Peter
Romancero			12	1		1									1			1										S			Peter
Salvos *Unus Instr:* Bass clarinet			10	1		1							1		1			1									1			1	Peter
Scenes from Shir Ha-Shirim *Voices:* Soprano, 2 tenors, bass. *Unus Instr:* Oboe d'amore			30	1	1	1	1		1						1	1		1									1	4		1	Peter
String Quartet No. 4			11	2	1	1																									Peter
String Trio			10	1	1	1																									Peter

	Year Composed or Published	Key	Duration	Violin	Viola	Cello	Double Bass	Gamba	Piano	Harpsicord	Organ	Guitar	Harp	Recorder	Flute/Piccolo	Oboe	English Horn	Clarinet/Bass Clarinet	Bassoon/Contrabassoon	Saxophone	French Horn	Trumpet	Trombone	Bass Trombone	Tuba	Baritone	Percussion	Voice	Electronic Tape	Unusual Instruments	Publisher
DAVIDSON, MALCOLM G. (1891–)																															
Beauty Song *Voice:* Medium				2	1	1																						1			Schir
DAVIS, ANTHONY (1951–)																															
Hemispheres *Unus Instr:* Vibraphone, marimba	1983		45	1		1			1						1			1	1			1					1			2	Schir
Lost Moon Sisters	1990		13	1					1																		1	S			Schir
Song Was Sweeter Even So	1987		17	1		1									1			1	1								1		1		Schir
Still Waters III						1			1						1																Schir
Undine	1986		23	1		1			1						1			1	1								1				Schir
Wayang II (Shadow Dance) *Unus Instr:* Vibraphone, marimba	1982		9	1		1			1						1								1				2			2	Schir
Wayang IV *Unus Instr:* Marimba	1981		20	1		1			1						1			1					1				3			1	Schir
DEBUSSY, CLAUDE A. (1862–1918)																															
Chansons de Bilitis *Unus Instr:* Celesta													2		2												1			1	Manus
Golliwog's Cakewalk (arr. Mayer)																					1	2	1		1						Dobli
Le petit negre (trans. Bozza)															1	1		1	1		1										Leduc
Quartet, Op 10	1893	g		2	1	1																									VarPb
Sonata *Comment:* Violin may replace viola	1915				1								1		1																Duran
Trio	1880	G		1		1			1																						Manus
DECOUST, MICHEL (1936–)																															
Aubes incendiées *Unus Instr:* Contrabassoon	1985		20	1	1	1	1		1						1		1	1	1		1		1				1	1		1	Salab
Iambe *Unus Instr:* Contrabassoon, xylophone, glockenspiel, vibraphone, 5-string bass	1976		11				1						1		1		1	2	1					1	1		3			5	Salab
Je, qui d'autre *Voices:* Soprano, tenor, bass. *Unus Instr:* Contrabassoon			45	1	1	2	1						1		1		1	1	1		2			1			2	3		1	Salab
Pour 70 doigts *Comment:* Piano 6-hands	1980		7						1			2						1				1									Salab
Sinfonietta *Unus Instr:* Contrabassoon	1983		19	2	1	1	1								1	1		1	1		1									1	Salab
Sonnet *Unus Instr:* Contrabassoon	1985		17	1	1	1	1		1						1		1	1	1		1		1				1			1	Salab
DeFOTIS, WILLIAM (1953–)																															
Septet (Flute plays offstage)	1974		7		1		1						1		1			1	1		1				1						AmCom
DEGEN, HELMUT (1911–)																															
Klaviertrio				1		1			1																						Bären
DELACHI, PAOLO (?–)																															
Trio		B		1		1			1																						Suvin
DELAGE, MAURICE (1879–1961)																															
Alouette									1						1													1			Duran
Quatuor		d		2	1	1																									Duran
DELANNOY, MARCEL (1898–1962)																															
Ballade concertante for piano, Op 59 *Unus Instr:* Celesta			13	1			1		1						1	1		1	1	1		1	2				2			1	Eschi
Quatuor	1931	E		2	1	1																									Duran
DELAS, JOSÉ L. (1928–)																															
Concetti (Musica para Gesualdo di Venosa) *Unus Instr:* Celesta	1974		15	2	2	1	2		1	1		1	1		2	1		2	1		1	1	1				2			1	Breit
Eilanden *Unus Instr:* Harmonium, celesta	1967		14	2	1					1	1	1	1					1									1		1	2	Breit

	Year Composed or Published	Key	Duration	Violin	Viola	Cello	Double Bass	Gamba	Piano	Harpsicord	Organ	Guitar	Harp	Recorder	Flute/Piccolo	Oboe	English Horn	Clarinet/Bass Clarinet	Bassoon/Contrabassoon	Saxophone	French Horn	Trumpet	Trombone	Bass Trombone	Tuba	Baritone	Percussion	Voice	Electronic Tape	Unusual Instruments	Publisher
DELERUE, GEORGES (1925–)																															
Vitrail																					1	2	2								Billa
DELIUS, FREDERICK (1862–1934)																															
Interludes (2)	1910		4	2	1	1										1															Boose
String Quartet	1916			2	1	1																									ECSch
DELLO JOIO, NORMAN (1913–)																															
Colonial Ballads *Unus Instr:* Timpani	1976		12												1	1		3	1	3	1	1	1		1		2			1	AMP
Satiric Dances for a Comedy *Unus Instr:* Timpani	1975		9												2	2		4	1	3	1	1	1		2		2			1	AMP
DEL TREDICI, DAVID (1937–)																															
Haddocks' Eyes *Voice:* Amplified	1985		20	2	1	1	1		1						1			1			1	1						S			Boose
I Hear an Army	1964		13	2	1	1																						S			Boose
Night Conjure-Verse *Voices:* Soprano and mezzo-soprano or countertenor. *Unus Instr:* Bass clarinet	1965		18	2	1	1									2	1		2	1		1							2		1	Boose
String Trio	1959		8	1	1	1																									Boose
Syzygy, for soprano, horn, and ensemble *Comment:* Soprano voice is amplified. *Unus Instr:* Tubular bells (2 players)	1966		24	2	2	1	1								2	1	1	2	2			2					2	S		2	Boose
DELVINCOURT, CLAUDE (1888–1954)																															
Quatuor				2	1	1																									Duran
DEMBSKI, STEPHEN (1949–)																															
Alba	1980		23	1		1									1			1									1				AmCom
Quartet (with Harpsichord)	1978		8			1				1					1	1															AmCom
Stacked Deck	1979		11	1		1			1						1	1		1	1			1	1				2				AmCom
Trio	1977		15		1	1			1																						AmCom
DEMERSSEMAN, JULES A. (1833–1866)																															
Fantaisie concertante, Op 38									1						1	1															Billa
Guillaume Tell (duo brillant), Op 37									1						1	1															Billa
DENHOFF, MICHAEL (1955–)																															
Chants d'automne	1982		25	2	1	1	1						1		2		1	2	1		2						1	B			Breit
Einsamkeit (In memoriam W. Buchebner) *Unus Instr:* Tam-tam	1982		12	2	1	1							1		1	1		1	1		1	1	1				1			1	Breit
Melancolia (inspired by Dürer) *Unus Instr:* Contrabassoon	1980		21		4	4	2		1				1		1	1	1	2	1								1			1	Breit
Mystiques barcarolles (String Quartet 3)	1982		11	2	1	1																									Breit
O Orpheus singt	1977		16	2	1	1	1											1	1		1										Breit
Quasi una serenata	1978		11												1	1		1	1		1										Breit
Time Proportions	1981		8	1	1	1			1						2												2				Breit
Traumgesicht *Unus Instr:* Tam-tam	1981		12			1			1																		1		1	1	Breit
DENIS, DIDIER (1947–)																															
C'est pas une raison *Voice:* Female. *Unus Instr:* Jazz percussion			17	1		1				1			1		1						1						2	H		1	Ridea
Chants de Tse Yeh *Voice:* Female speaker. *Unus Instr:* Oboe d'amore, celesta, mandolin			10	1		1			1			1	1		1	1					1	1					2	1		3	Ridea
Triangles au soleil à sept branches			20	1											1			1			1	1	1		1		3				Ridea
Trois partout *Unus Instr:* Ondes Martenot			17						1																		1		1	1	Ridea
La vieille danse *Voice:* Deep soprano. *Unus Instr:* Xylophone, timpani			24	1	1	1			1						1			1									1	S		2	Ridea

	Year Composed or Published	Key	Duration	Violin	Viola	Cello	Double Bass	Gamba	Piano	Harpsichord	Organ	Guitar	Harp	Recorder	Flute/Piccolo	Oboe	English Horn	Clarinet/Bass Clarinet	Bassoon/Contrabassoon	Saxophone	French Horn	Trumpet	Trombone	Bass Trombone	Tuba	Baritone	Percussion	Voice	Electronic Tape	Unusual Instruments	Publisher
DENISOV, EDISON (1929–)																															
Concerto piccolo	1977		21																	4							6				VAAP
Crescendo e diminuendo	1965		6	6	3	2	1			1																					VarPb
Diane dans le vent d'automne *Unus Instr:* Vibraphone	1984		9		1		1		1																		1			1	VAAP
Epitaph for 13 Players	1983		6	1	1	1	1		1						1	1		1	1		1	1	1				1				VarPb
Hommage à Pierre *Unus Instr:* Vibraphone	1986			1	1	1			1				1		2			2			1						1			1	Leduc
Music for 11 Wind Instruments & Drums *Unus Instr:* Timpani															1	2		2	2		2	1	1				1			1	Peter
Ode	1968								1									1									1				VAAP
Piano Quintet	1987			2	1	1			1																						VAAP
Piano Trio	1971		20	1		1			1																						VarPb
Pictures (3) of Paul Klee (solo viola) *Unus Instr:* Vibraphone					1		1		1							1					1						1			1	VAAP
Quartet	1989			1	1	1									1																VAAP
Romantic Music	1968		1	1	1	1							1			1															VAAP
Sextet	1984			1	1	1									1	1		1													VAAP
Silhouettes (Cinq portraits des femmes)	1969								2						1												1				VAAP
String Quartet No. 2				2	1	1																									VAAP
Sun of the Incas (Cantata) *Voices:* Soprano, 3 speakers. *Unus Instr:* Marimba, vibraphone, 4 timpani	1964		18	1		1			2						1	1		1			1	1					2	4		6	VarPb
DENNY, WILLIAM (1910–1980)																															
String Quartet No. 2	1952			2	1	1																									Boose
DESENCLOS, ALFRED (1912–1971)																															
Voeux (3) à un nouveau-né	1954			1	1	1																									Leduc
DESORMIERE, ROGER (1898–1963)																															
Danceries (6) du 16e siècle															1		1	1	1		1										Leduc
DESPIC, DEJAN (?–)																															
Vignette, Op 43b	1965		7												1	1		1	1		1										Breit
DESPORTES, YVONNE (1907–)																															
Imageries d'antan																					1	2	1	1							Billa
Images (9) *Comment:* Viola may replace one cello				2		2																									Billa
Images (9) for winds															1	1		1	1												Billa
Sonate pour un baptême *Comment:* English horn may replace alto sax									1						1					1							1	S			Billa
DESSAU, PAUL (1894–1979)																															
Lustige Variationen									1									1	1												Peter
Movements (7) for String Quartet				2	1	1																									Peter
Musik für 15 Streicher	1978		11	9	3	2	1																								BoteB
Partita	1978								1							1		1	1		1										BoteB
Quattrodramma	1965		14			4			2																		2				BoteB
Streichquartett 7	1975			2	1	1																									BoteB
Stücke (3, for brass trio)	1971																					2	1								DeutV
Stücke (3, for wind trio)	1971																	2	1												Bären
Tierverse (after Berthold Brecht) *Unus Instr:* Prepared piano. Guitar may replace piano.	1973					1			1																			1		1	BoteB
DEVILLERS, JEAN-B. (1953–)																															
Clairs obscurs *Unus Instr:* 5-String bass	1983		20	2	1	1	1		1				1		1		1	1	1		1	1	1	1			4			1	Salab

	Year Composed or Published	Key	Duration	Violin	Viola	Cello	Double Bass	Gamba	Piano	Harpsicord	Organ	Guitar	Harp	Recorder	Flute/Piccolo	Oboe	English Horn	Clarinet/Bass Clarinet	Bassoon/Contrabassoon	Saxophone	French Horn	Trumpet	Trombone	Bass Trombone	Tuba	Baritone	Percussion	Voice	Electronic Tape	Unusual Instruments	Publisher
DEWANGER, ANTON (?–)																															
Sextuor				2	2	1			1																						Duran
DIABELLI, ANTON (1781–1858)																															
Pieces (12)																						3					1				Dobli
DIAMOND, DAVID (1915–)																															
Concerto for String Quartet	1936		10	2	1	1																									Peer
Concertpiece for Guitar	1992		15	2	1	1						1																			Peer
Concertpiece for Horn	1978		34	1	1	1			1												1										Peer
Nonet	1962		16	3	3	3																									Peer
Partita	1935		8						1							1			1												Peer
Piano Quartet	1938		34	1	1	1			1																						Manus
Piano Trio	1951		22	1		1			1																						Peer
Quintet	1950		16		2	2												1													Peer
Quintet for Flute, Strings, and Piano	1937		13	1	1	1			1						1																Peer
String Quartet No. 1	1940		18	2	1	1																									Peer
String Quartet No. 2	1943		16	2	1	1																									Peer
String Quartet No. 3	1946		19	2	1	1																									Peer
String Quartet No. 4	1951		30	2	1	1																									Peer
String Quartet No. 5	1960		22	2	1	1																									Peer
String Quartet No. 6	1962		21	2	1	1																									Peer
String Quartet No. 7	1963		23	2	1	1																									Peer
String Quartet No. 8	1964		16	2	1	1																									Peer
String Quartet No. 9	1968		14	2	1	1																									Peer
String Quartet No. 10	1966		16	2	1	1																									Peer
DICHLER, JOSEF (1912–)																															
Music for 2 Violins and Piano				2					1																						Dobli
DICKINSON, PETER (1934–)																															
Fanfares and Elegies											1											3	3								Novel
DIEMER, EMMA L. (1927–)																															
Music for Woodwind Quartet															1	1		1	1												Oxfor
DIERCKS, JOHN (1927–)																															
Brass Quartet																					1	2	1								Press
Figures on China																					1	1	1								Press
Wind Quintet															1	1		1	1		1										Press
DIEREN, BERNARD VAN (1884–1936)																															
Sonetto 7 *Unus Instr:* Cornet				2	2		1								1			2	1		1	1						T		1	Oxfor
DIETHELM, CASPAR (1926–)																															
Clarinet Quartet, Op 167					2	1												1													Amade
Concerto Diletto I, Op 141a				2	2	1																									Amade
Piano Trio, Op 147				1		1			1																						Hug
DILLON, JAMES (1944–)																															
String Quartet			20	2	1	1																									Peter
Überschreiten *Unus Instr:* Contrabassoon				2	1	1	1		1		1				1	1		2	1		1	1	1		1		1			1	Peter
Zone (. . . de Azul)				1	1	1			1									1			1	1	1								Peter
DISTLER, HUGO (1908–1942)																															
Kleine Sommerkantate, post. *Voices:* 2 Sopranos	1942			2	1	1																						2			Bären
Sonata, Op 15a	1935			2					1																						Bären
Streichquartett, Op 20 No. 1	1939	a		2	1	1																									Bären
Streichquartett, Op 20 No. 2		a		2	1	1																									Bären
DITTRICH, PAUL-HEINZ (1930–)																															
Concert avec plusieurs instruments (no.1)	1976		18	1	1	1	1			1					1	1					1										Breit

	Year Composed or Published	Key	Duration	Violin	Viola	Cello	Double Bass	Gamba	Piano	Harpsicord	Organ	Guitar	Harp	Recorder	Flute/Piccolo	Oboe	English Horn	Clarinet/Bass Clarinet	Bassoon/Contrabassoon	Saxophone	French Horn	Trumpet	Trombone	Bass Trombone	Tuba	Baritone	Percussion	Voice	Electronic Tape	Unusual Instruments	Publisher
DITTRICH, PAUL-HEINZ *(continued)*																															
Kammermusik I	1970		15						1						1	1		1	1										1		Unive
Kammermusik II	1973		25			1			1							1													1		Unive
Kammermusik III	1974														1	1		1	1		1							B			Peter
Kammermusik V *Comment:* Live electronics	1977		27												1	1		1	1		1										Peter
Kammermusik VI (Klangtexte für 8)					1	1	1		1							1	1						1				1				Peter
Schlagzeilen	1971		17						2																		2		1		Breit
DJAMBAZIAN, A (?–)																															
Bläserquintett 2, Op 13															1	1		1	1		1										Dobli
DMITRIEV, GEORGY (?–)																															
2 Pieces									1													2									VAAP
String Quartet No. 3				2	1	1																									VAAP
String Quartet No. 4 (in 12 Parables)				2	1	1																									VAAP
DOEHL, FRIEDHELM (1936–)																															
Medea (Monologue for Soprano)	1979		17			1	1		1						1			1				1	1				2	S			Breit
DOHNANYI, ERNST VON (1877–1960)																															
Klavierquintett 1, Op 1	1895	c		2	1	1			1																						VarPb
Klavierquintett 2, Op 26	1914	e♭		2	1	1			1																						Simro
Serenade, Op 10	1902	C		1	1	1																									VarPb
Sextett, Op 37	1933	C		1	1	1			1									1			1										Lengn
Streichquartett 1, Op 7	1899	A		2	1	1																									VarPb
Streichquartett 2, Op 15	1906	D♭		2	1	1																									Simro
Streichquartett 3, Op 33	1926	a		2	1	1																									Rozsa
DOLLARHIDE, THEODORE (1948–)																															
Inner Moons	1974		12		1		1						1		1																AmCom
DOMENICO, OLIVIO DI (?–)																															
Quintetto															1	1		1	1		1										Leduc
DOMHARDT, GERD (1945–)																															
Streichsextett	1980			2	2	2																									DeutV
String Quartet No. 1			9	2	1	1																									Peter
Triosonata	1978														1	1			1												DeutV
DONATO, ANTHONY (1909–)																															
Quartet		e		2	1	1																									Press
DONATONI, FRANCO (1927–)																															
About . . .	1979			1	1							1																			Ricor
For Grilly *Unus Instr:* Bass clarinet	1960			1	1	1									1			2									1			1	Suvin
De Près *Unus Instr:* Ottavinos				3																								F		2	Ricor
Quartetto II	1959			2	1	1																									Suvin
Quartetto IV	1963			2	1	1																									Suvin
DONDEYNE, DÉSIRÉ (1921–)																															
Musique pour cuivres																					1	2	1		1						Billa
Petite musique de cuivres (vol. 1)																					1	2	1		1						Billa
Petite musique de cuivres (vol. 2)																					1	2	1		1						Billa
DONIZETTI, GAETANO (1797–1848)																															
Sinfonia for Winds															1	2		2	2		2										Kunze
String Quartet No. 1		E♭		2	1	1																									Noetz
String Quartet No. 2		A		2	1	1																									Noetz
String Quartet No. 3		c		2	1	1																									Noetz
String Quartet No. 5		e		2	1	1																									Noetz

	Year Composed or Published	Key	Duration	Violin	Viola	Cello	Double Bass	Gamba	Piano	Harpsicord	Organ	Guitar	Harp	Recorder	Flute/Piccolo	Oboe	English Horn	Clarinet/Bass Clarinet	Bassoon/Contrabassoon	Saxophone	French Horn	Trumpet	Trombone	Bass Trombone	Tuba	Baritone	Percussion	Voice	Electronic Tape	Unusual Instruments	Publisher
DONIZETTI, GAETANO *(continued)*																															
String Quartet No. 6		g		2	1	1																									Noetz
String Quartet No. 9		d		2	1	1																									Noetz
DONOVAN, RICHARD F. (1891–1970)																															
Music for Six	1961		10	1		1			1							1		1				1									Peter
Trio	1939			1		1			1																						Arrow
DOPPELBAUER, JOSEF F. (1918–)																															
Bläserquintett															1	1		1	1		1										Dobli
Divertimento (Leobner Trio)				1		1									1																Dobli
Divertimento for Winds (Septet) *Unus Instr:* Bass clarinet															1	1	1	2	1		1									1	Dobli
Miniatures					1	1									1																Dobli
Quartett															1	1		1	1												Dobli
Streichquartett 1	1968		20	2	1	1																									Dobli
Trio															1	1		1													Dobli
Trio																1		1	1												Dobli
Trio					1	1										1															Dobli
Trio																		2	1												Dobli
DOPPLER, FRANZ (1821–1883)																															
Duettino Americain, Op 37				1					1						1																Billa
DORATI, ANTAL (1906–)																															
In the Beginning *Voice:* Bass-baritone	1979		34			1										1											1	B			Boose
String Quartet	1980		30	2	1	1																									Boose
DOWNEY, JOHN (1927–1988)																															
String Quartet No. 2				2	1	1																									Press
DRAKEFORD, RICHARD (?–)																															
Tower Music																					1	2	1		1						Novel
DREW, JAMES (1929–)																															
All Saints' Chorales																					1	2	1								Press
Almost Stationary				1		1			1																						Press
Trio for the Fiery Messengers				1		1			1																						Press
DRIESSLER, JOHANNES (1921–)																															
Aphorismen, Op 7A	1948														1	2		1	1		1										Bären
Serenata a tre, Op 34 No. 2	1955							1		1					1																Bären
Streichquartett, Op 41 No. 1				2	1	1																									Bären
Streichtrio, Op 1 No. 2	1947			1	1	1																									Bären
DRUCKMAN, JACOB (1928–)																															
Animus II	1968		21																								2	1	1		MCA
Animus IV *Unus Instr:* Electric piano	1977		22	1					1		1												1				2	T		1	Boose
Bo *Unus Instr:* Marimba	1979		9															1									1	F		1	Boose
Dark Upon the Harp	1962		22																		1	2	2				1	M			Press
Delizie contente che l'alma beate	1973		11												1	1		1	1		1								1		Boose
Divertimento	1950		20	1	1	1							1					1			1										Boose
Interlude *Unus Instr:* Timpani	1953														1			1									1			1	Manus
Laude *Unus Instr:* Alto flute	1952		12		1	1									1													B		1	Boose
Other Voices	1976		25																		1	2	1	1							Boose
String Quartet No. 1	1948			2	1	1																									Manus
String Quartet No. 2	1966		21	2	1	1																									MCA
String Quartet No. 3	1981		25	2	1	1																									Boose
DUBOIS, PIERRE-MAX (1930–)																															
Le cinéma muet																					1	1	1		1						Leduc

	Year Composed or Published	Key	Duration	Violin	Viola	Cello	Double Bass	Gamba	Piano	Harpsicord	Organ	Guitar	Harp	Recorder	Flute/Piccolo	Oboe	English Horn	Clarinet/Bass Clarinet	Bassoon/Contrabassoon	Saxophone	French Horn	Trumpet	Trombone	Bass Trombone	Tuba	Baritone	Percussion	Voice	Electronic Tape	Unusual Instruments	Publisher
DUBOIS, PIERRE-MAX *(continued)*																															
Fantasia															1	1		1	1		1										Leduc
Huit + un															1	2		2	2		2										Billa
Illustrations (Cinq mouvements)																					1	2	1								Leduc
Lou Cascarelet (Danses provençales) *Comment:* Tambourine ad lib																2	1														Leduc
Mini quatuor *Unus Instr:* 2 Piccolos															2										2					2	Billa
Musique dans l'espace *Unus Instr:* Contrabassoon																			1			4	4				1			1	Billa
Quintette burlesque																					1	2	2								Billa
Septuor																					2	2	2		1						Leduc
Sinfonia da camera *Comment:* A second clarinet can substitute for saxophone															1	1		1	1	1	1										Leduc
Les treteaux									1						1					1											Choud
Trio d'anches																1		1	1												Leduc
Les trois mousquetaires (Divertissement)																1		1	1	1											Leduc
DUBOIS, THÉODORE (1837–1924)																															
Suite															2	1		2	2		1										Leduc
DUBUIS, CLAUDE (?–)																															
Acclamation																						2	2								Billa
DUFAY, GUILLAUME (1400–1474)																															
Pasce tuos (arr. Howarth)																					1	2	1		1						Novel
DUKE, VERNON (1903–1969)																															
Trio (Theme and Variations)	1930								1						1				1												Boose
DUMITRESCU, IANCU (1944–)																															
Cogito trompe-l'oeil *Unus Instr:* Prepared piano, electro-acoustical apparatus, Javanese gong			22						1																					3	Salab
DUPONT, PIERRE (1821–1870)																															
Pièces brèves 3															1	1		1	1		1										Billa
DUREY, LOUIS (1888–1979)																															
Divertissement, Op 107																1		1	1												Billa
Les soirées de Valfere															1	1		1	1		1										Billa
DURIEUX, FREDERIC (1959–)																															
Exil II *Voices:* Coloratura soprano and contralto	1984		21	1	1	1			1				1		1		1	1			1	1					3	2			Salab
DURKO, ZSOLT (1934–)																															
Brass Quartet	1970		8																			2	1		1						Boose
Iconography No. 1	1970		7					2		1																					Boose
Improvvisazioni	1965		7												1	1		1	1		1										Boose
Pieces (11)	1962			2	1	1																									Boose
String Quartet No. 1	1966		10	2	1	1																									Boose
String Quartet No. 2	1969		18	2	1	1																									Boose
DURUFLE, MAURICE (1902–)																															
Prélude, récitatif et variations, Op 3					1				1						1																Duran
DUSAPIN, PASCAL (?–)																															
La conversation	1984		30	1	1	1	1											2	1		1		1								Salab
Fist	1982		13		1	1	1										1	1	1		1	1									Salab
Hop (for 4x3 instruments)	1984		11	1	1	1	1								1	1		2	1		2	1									Salab
Musique captive *Unus Instr:* Contrabass clarinet	1980		3												1	1		2	1	1		2		1						1	Salab
DUSSEK, JAN (1760–1812)																															
Notturno concertante, Op 68 *Comment:* Viola may replace violin		E♭		1					1												1										Bären

	Year Composed or Published	Key	Duration	Violin	Viola	Cello	Double Bass	Gamba	Piano	Harpsicord	Organ	Guitar	Harp	Recorder	Flute/Piccolo	Oboe	English Horn	Clarinet/Bass Clarinet	Bassoon/Contrabassoon	Saxophone	French Horn	Trumpet	Trombone	Bass Trombone	Tuba	Baritone	Percussion	Voice	Electronic Tape	Unusual Instruments	Publisher
DUSSEK, JAN *(continued)*																															
Quintett, Op 41				1	1	1	1		1																						Kunze
DVOŘÁK, ANTONÍN (1841–1904)																															
Bagatelles (with harmonium), Op 47 *Unus Instr:* Harmonium	1878			2	1						1																			1	Inter
Bagatelles (with piano), Op 47	1878			2		1			1																						Inter
Piano Quartet, Op 23	1875	D		1	1	1			1																						VarPb
Piano Quartet, Op 87	1889	E♭		1	1	1			1																						VarPb
Piano Quintet, Op 81	1887	A		2	1	1			1																						VarPb
Piano Trio, Op 21	1875	B♭		1		1			1																						VarPb
Piano Trio, Op 26	1876	g		1		1			1																						VarPb
Piano Trio, Op 65	1883	f		1		1			1																						VarPb
Piano Trio ("Dumky"), Op 90	1891	e		1		1			1																						VarPb
Serenade, Op 44	1878	d				1	1									2		2	2		3										MusRa
Slavonic Dance, Op 46 No. 8									1					3																	Faber
String Quartet, Op 16	1874	a		2	1	1																									VarPb
String Quartet, Op 34	1877	d		2	1	1																									VarPb
String Quartet, Op 51	1879	E♭		2	1	1																									VarPb
String Quartet, Op 61	1881	C		2	1	1																									VarPb
String Quartet, Op 80	1876	E		2	1	1																									VarPb
String Quartet, Op 96	1893	F		2	1	1																									VarPb
String Quartet, Op 105	1895	A♭		2	1	1																									VarPb
String Quartet, Op 106	1895	G		2	1	1																									VarPb
String Quintet, Op 77	1875	G		2	1	1	1																								VarPb
String Quintet, Op 97	1893	E♭		2	2	1																									VarPb
String Sextet, Op 48	1878	A		2	2	2																									VarPb
Terzetto, Op 74	1887			2	1																										VarPb
Waltzes (2, orig. for piano), Op 54	1880			2	1	1																									VarPb
Waltzes (2), Op 54 Nos. 1, 4				2	1	1	1																								Amade
Woodwind Quintet (after Op. 96)															1	1		1	1		1										Billa
EATON, JOHN (1935–)																															
Piano Trio	1971		12	1		1			1																						AMP
Songs for RPB *Unus Instr:* Syn-ket	1964		14						2																			S		1	Shawn
Songs for Ursula *Unus Instr:* Syn-ket	1958		20						1																			S		1	Shawn
Songs of Despair	1986		21	2	1	1	1		1				1		1		1	1	1		1	1	1		1		2	M			AMP
String Quartet	1958		20	2	1	1																									Shawn
Variations für Wind Quintet	1962		18												1	2		2													AMP
EBEN, PETR (1929–)																															
Bläserquintett	1965														1	1		1	1		1										Artia
EBENHÖH, HORST (1930–)																															
Einige Minuten für Klaviertrio, Op 32 No. 1				1		1			1																						Dobli
Festive Pieces (2), Op 48 No. 2																					1	2	1		1						Dobli
Kolloquium, Op 42 No. 2									1														1				1				Dobli
Oktett, Op 43				2	1	1	1											1	1		1										Dobli
Szenen (4) für 6, Op 33				1	1	1									1				1								1				Dobli
Szenen (4) für 10, Op 21 No. 1				2	1	1	1								1	1		1	1								1				Dobli
ECKERT, MICHAEL (1950–)																															
Double Canon	1981		1	1	1										1			1													AmCom
EDEL, YITZHAK (1896–1973)																															
Suite (in memoriam)	1947			1		1			1																						IsrMI
EDER, HELMUT (1916–)																															
Bläserquintett, Op 25	1958														1	1		1	1		1										Dobli
Bläserseptett (Hommage a J. Kepler), Op 55	1970														1	1		1	1		2	1									Dobli
Impressioni, Op 43	1966			2	1	1																									Dobli

	Year Composed or Published	Key	Duration	Violin	Viola	Cello	Double Bass	Gamba	Piano	Harpsicord	Organ	Guitar	Harp	Recorder	Flute/Piccolo	Oboe	English Horn	Clarinet/Bass Clarinet	Bassoon/Contrabassoon	Saxophone	French Horn	Trumpet	Trombone	Bass Trombone	Tuba	Baritone	Percussion	Voice	Electronic Tape	Unusual Instruments	Publisher
EDER, HELMUT *(continued)*																															
Klaviertrio, Op 56	1970			1		1			1																						Dobli
Litzlberg Serenade, Op 67																		2	1		1	1									Dobli
Melismen, Op 58 No. 2 *Comment:* Piano may replace harpsichord										1				3																	Dobli
Notturni, Op 79 No. 1				1	1	1									1	1															Dobli
Otetto Breve, Op 33				2	1	1									1	1		1	1												Dobli
Pastorale, Op 63 No. 1				2	1	1																									Dobli
Piecen, Op 58 No. 1	1972		9							1				1													1				Dobli
Quartett (S.C.H.), Op 80				1	1	1									1																Dobli
Quintett, Op 77				2	1	1												1													Dobli
Septuagesima instrumentalis, Op 51	1969														1	1		1	1		1										Dobli
Streichtrio, Op 28				1	1	1																									Dobli
Suite mit Intermezzi für 11, Op 71 *Unus Instr:* Contrabassoon																2		2	3		4									1	Dobli
EDER DE LASTRA, ERICH (1933–)																															
Bläserquintett															1	1		1	1		1										Dobli
EDLUND, MIKAEL (1950–)																															
Brains and Dancin'	1971		17	2	1	1																									Nordi
Leaves *Unus Instr:* Electric piano	1981		16						2				1														7	F		1	Nordi
Music, for Double Wind Quintet	1984		16												2	2		2	2		2										Nordi
Trio Sun	1980		9						1									1	1												Nordi
EDWARDS, GEORGE (1943–)																															
Bits	1966		9	1	1	1	1		1						1	1		1	1								2				AmCom
Northern Spy	1980		12	1		1	1		1						1	1		1			1	1									AmCom
Trio	1987		10	1					1												1										AmCom
Uroboros *Unus Instr:* Mandolin, celesta	1964		10		2	1				1		1	1		1												1			2	AmCom
Variants *Unus Instr:* Vibraphone, marimba	1964		9	1	1				2				1		1			1				1	1				2			2	AmCom
EINEM, GOTTFRIED VON (1918–)																															
Bläserquintett, Op 46	1975		13												1	1		1	1		1										Boose
Geistliche Sonata, Op 38	1973		15								1											1						S			Boose
Reifliches Divertimento, Op 35a *Unus Instr:* Timpani	1972		5	1	1				1												1						1			1	Boose
Rindlberger March, Op 54 *Unus Instr:* Timpani	1979		4															2	2		2	2	2		1		2			1	BoteB
Streichquartett 1, Op 45	1975		20	2	1	1																									Boose
Streichquartett 2, Op 51	1977			2	1	1																									BoteB
Streichquartett 3	1980		16	2	1	1																									Peter
Streichquartett 4, Op 63				2	1	1																									Unive
EINFELDT, DIETER (1935–)																															
Sizilianische Impressionen									1						1	1		1	1									S			Bosse
Streichquartett 1	1966			2	1	1																									Bosse
EISLER, HANNS (1898–1962)																															
14 Ways of Describing the Rain	1947				1	1			1						1			1													Peter
Divertimento, Op 4	1923														1	1		1	1		1										Unive
Kantate auf den Tod eines Genossen, Op 64					1	1												2										F			Unive
Kantate im Exil, Op 62					1	1												2										F			Unive
Kriegskantate, Op 65					1	1												2										F			Unive
Palmström, Op 5 *Voice:* Reciter. Violin doubles on viola, flute on piccolo				1	1	1									1			1										1			Unive

	Year Composed or Published	Key	Duration	Violin	Viola	Cello	Double Bass	Gamba	Piano	Harpsicord	Organ	Guitar	Harp	Recorder	Flute/Piccolo	Oboe	English Horn	Clarinet/Bass Clarinet	Bassoon/Contrabassoon	Saxophone	French Horn	Trumpet	Trombone	Bass Trombone	Tuba	Baritone	Percussion	Voice	Electronic Tape	Unusual Instruments	Publisher
EISLER, HANNS *(continued)*																															
Präludium und Fuge über B-A-C-H, Op 46	1934			1	1	1																									DeutV
Die römische Kantate, Op 60					1	1												2										F			Unive
Sonatensatz, Op 49	1935												1		1	1															DeutV
Tagebuch (Eine kleine Kantate), Op 9 *Voices:* Soprano, mezzo, alto, tenor				1					1																			4			Unive
EKIMOVSKY, VIKTOR (?–)																															
Chamber Variations *Unus Instr:* Celesta, xylophone, timpani			8	1	1	1	1						1		1	1		1			1	1	1				2			3	VAAP
EL-DABH, HALIM (1921–)																															
A Look at Lightning			14										1		1	1	1														Peter
Mosaic No. 1			6						1																		3				Peter
Mosaic No. 1 (alt. vers.)			6						1																		5				Peter
Tahmeela			9	1											1	1		1	1		1							S			Peter
Thulathiya			8		1				1							1															Peter
Thumaniya (Octet)			8												1	1		1			1	2					2				Peter
ELGAR, EDWARD (1857–1934)																															
Piano Quintet, Op 84	1919	a		2	1	1			1																						Novel
Quintet, Op 6															1	2		1	1												Manus
Serenade				2	1	1			1																						Novel
Speak Music, Op 41	1901			2	1	1																						H			Boose
String Quartet, Op 83	1918	e		2	1	1																									Novel
ELIAS, BRIAN (1948–)																															
Geranos *Comment:* Violin doubles on viola. *Unus Instr:* Bass clarinet	1985		18	1		1			1						1			1									1			1	Chest
ELLINGTON, "DUKE" (1899–1974)																															
Ellington Fantasy (Songs, arr. Chihara)				2	1	1																									Peter
EMMANUEL, MAURICE (1862–1938)																															
Quatuor	1903	B♭		2	1	1																									Duran
ENESCO, GEORGES (1881–1955)																															
Dixtuor, Op 14	1906	D	26												2	1	1	2	2		2										Salab
Octet, Op 7	1900		39	4	2	2																									Enoch
Quatuor, 1er	1920	E♭		2	1	1																									Salab
Quatuor, 2e	1951			2	1	1																									Salab
Rumanian Rhapsody No. 1 (trans. Rudd)	1901			2	2	1			1																						Peer
ENGELMANN, HANS U. (1921–)																															
Les Chansons, Op 47 *Voices:* Unspecified, plus narrator	1982		15		1	1			1						1		1	1										2			Breit
EÖTVÖS, PETER (1944–)																															
Moro lasso *Voices:* 2 Sopranos, alto, tenor, bass	1973										1																	5			Feedb
Pierre-Idyll *Unus Instr:* Oboe d'amore	1984		10	2	1	1	1		1						1	1	1	3	2		2						2			1	Salab
Tartini, Konzert		D		3	1	1	1			1																					Feedb
ERB, DONALD (1927–)																															
Aura				2	1	1																									Press
The Last Quintet	1982														1	1		1	1		1										Press
Saint Valentine's Day Quintet	1981																				1	2	1		1						Press
ERBSE, HEIMO (1924–)																															
Aphorismen (12), Op 13	1956			1					1						1																Litolff

	Year Composed or Published	Key	Duration	Violin	Viola	Cello	Double Bass	Gamba	Piano	Harpsicord	Organ	Guitar	Harp	Recorder	Flute/Piccolo	Oboe	English Horn	Clarinet/Bass Clarinet	Bassoon/Contrabassoon	Saxophone	French Horn	Trumpet	Trombone	Bass Trombone	Tuba	Baritone	Percussion	Voice	Electronic Tape	Unusual Instruments	Publisher
ERBSE, HEIMO *(continued)*																															
Bläserquartett	1961														1	1		1	1												Peter
Das Hohelied Salomo's *Voices:* Soprano, baritone									1																			2			Peter
Klaviertrio, Op 8	1955			1		1			1																						BoteB
Streichquartett 1, Op 5	1954			2	1	1																									BoteB
Trio, Op 37																1		1	1												Dobli
ERDMANN, DIETRICH (1917–)																															
Musica multicolore	1981		15	1	1	1	1									1		1	1		1						1				Breit
Musica per quattro	1979		11													1		1	1								1				Breit
Nuancen	1978		13	1	1	1	1								1			1									1				Breit
ERÖD, IVAN (1936–)																															
Canonic Var. on a Nursery Song				2	1	1																									Dobli
Capriccio for 10 Winds															2	2		2	2		2										Dobli
Divertimento for Brass																					2	6	3		1		1				Dobli
Klaviertrio 1				1		1			1																						Dobli
Klaviertrio 2				1		1			1																						Dobli
Lullaby	1973		2	2	1	1																						1			Boose
Magic Boxes	1973		2	2	1	1																						1			Boose
Milchzahnlieder (Milktooth Songs)	1973		12		1	1			1			1			1													1			Boose
Ricercare ed Aria S.C.H.E.															1	1		1			1										Dobli
Serenade for String Sextet				2	2	2																									Dobli
Streichquartett 1				2	1	1																									Dobli
Streichquartett 2				2	1	1																									Dobli
ESCHER, PETER A. (1915–)																															
Quintet, Op 114																						2	3								Amade
ESTRADA, JULIO (?–)																															
Canto nasciente	1982		16																		2	3	2		1						Salab
ETLER, ALVIN (1913–1973)																															
Concerto for Clarinet	1962		19				2											1				3	3				3				AMP
Concerto for Violin and Wind Quintet	1958		20	1											1	1		1	1		1										AMP
Quintet for Brass	1963		15																		1	2	1		1						AMP
Quintet No. 2 (for Woodwinds)	1957		16												1	1		1	1		1										AMP
Sextet			16	1	1	1										1		1	1												AMP
ETTI, KARL (1912–)																															
Variations and Fugue															1	1		1	1		1										Dobli
EVANGELISTA, JOSÉ (1943–)																															
Clos de vie *Unus Instr:* Clavichord, banjo, vibraphone	1983		15	2		1	1		1			1	1														1			3	Salab
Immobilis in mobili	1978		10	1	1	1			2						1	1		1									1				Salab
Motionless Move for 14 *Unus Instr:* 3 Synthesizers, electric piano, electric guitar	1980		13	1	1	1			2			1			1	1		1									2			5	Salab
EVETT, ROBERT (1922–1975)																															
Concerto for Harpsichord *Unus Instr:* Celesta			20	3	3	3				1												1					2			1	Peter
Fantasia on a Theme by Handel	1967		13		1	1			1																						AmCom
The Little Ones *Unus Instr:* 5 Timpani	1970		7	1		1																					1			5	AmCom
Mary Dyer	1968		8		1	1			1																						AmCom
Piano Quartet	1961		25	1	1	1			1																						AmCom
Piano Quintet	1954		20	2	1	1			1																						AmCom
EYBLER, JOSEPH (1765–1846)																															
Quintett, Op 61				1	2	1	1																								Kunze
Trio, Op 2				1	1	1																									Kunze

	Year Composed or Published	Key	Duration	Violin	Viola	Cello	Double Bass	Gamba	Piano	Harpsicord	Organ	Guitar	Harp	Recorder	Flute/Piccolo	Oboe	English Horn	Clarinet/Bass Clarinet	Bassoon/Contrabassoon	Saxophone	French Horn	Trumpet	Trombone	Bass Trombone	Tuba	Baritone	Percussion	Voice	Electronic Tape	Unusual Instruments	Publisher
EYCHENNE, MARC (1933–)																															
Cantilène et danse				1					1											1											Billa
FAILLENOT, MAURICE (?–)																															
Divertissement dans le style ancien																					1	1	1								Billa
FALIK, YURI (1936–)																															
An English Diversion	1978		5												1			1	1												Boose
FALLA, MANUEL DE (1876–1946)																															
Concerto for Harpsichord	1926	D	12	1		1				1					1	1		1													Eschi
Concerto (alt. inst.)	1926	D	12	1		1			1						1	1		1													Eschi
Pantomime and Ritual Fire Dance			11	2	1	1	1		1																						Chest
Psyche	1924		8	1	1	1							1		1													M			Chest
FARIÑAS, CARLOS (1934–)																															
Capriccio stravagante a 4 (quodlibet)				2	1	1	1																								Kunze
FAURÉ, GABRIEL U. (1845–1925)																															
Piano Quartet No. 1, Op 15	1879	c		1	1	1			1																						VarPb
Piano Quartet No. 2, Op 45	1886	g		1	1	1			1																						VarPb
Piano Quintet No. 1, Op 89	1895	d		2	1	1			1																						Schir
Piano Quintet No. 2, Op 115	1921	c		2	1	1			1																						Duran
Piano Trio, Op 120	1923	d		1		1			1																						Duran
Songs (3, arr. Carp)															1	1		1	1		1										Press
String Quartet, Op 121	1924	e		2	1	1																									Duran
FAVRE, GEORGES (1905–)																															
Gouaches (Watercolors)																1		1	1												Duran
Métope															1	1		1	1		1										Duran
FELD, JINDRICH (1925–)																															
Miniatursuite *Comment:* Cello ad lib	1964			3					1																						Artia
Nonetto (Suite de chambre)	1956			1	1	1	1								1	1		1	1		1										Leduc
Quintette	1970																				1	2	1		1						Leduc
FELDMAN, HERBERT B. (1931–)																															
String Quartet No. 1, Op 39				2	1	1																									McGin
FELDMAN, MORTON (1926–)																															
Atlantis *Unus Instr:* Bass clarinet, contrabassoon, xylophone, vibraphone	1959					1	1		1				1		3			2	2		1	1	1		1		2			4	Peter
Between Categories *Unus Instr:* Chimes	1969			2		2			2																		2			1	Peter
Clarinets (3), Cello and Piano	1971					1			1									3													Unive
Durations I	1960			1		1			1						1																Peter
Durations III	1961			1					1																1						Peter
Durations IV *Unus Instr:* Vibraphone	1961			1		1																					1			1	Peter
Durations V *Unus Instr:* Vibraphone, celesta	1961			1		1			1				1								1						1			2	Peter
False Relationships & Extended Ending *Unus Instr:* Chimes	1968		16	1		1			3														1							1	Peter
First Principles	1967		16	2		3	2		4				1		1						1		1		2		2				Peter
For Frank O'Hara *Unus Instr:* Glockenspiel, xylophone, vibraphone	1973		15	1		1			1						1			1									2			3	Unive
For Franz Kline *Unus Instr:* Chimes	1962			1		1			1												1							S		1	Peter
I Met Heine on the Rue Fürstenberg				1		1									1			1									1	1			Unive
Instruments (4) *Unus Instr:* Chimes	1965			1		1			1																		1			1	Peter
Instruments (11) *Unus Instr:* Vibraphone	1953			1		1			1						2						1	2	1		1		1			1	Peter
Instruments I *Unus Instr:* Piccolo and alto flute; glockenspiel, marimbaphone, xylophone, vibraphone	1974		17												1	1	1						1				2			6	Unive

	Year Composed or Published	Key	Duration	Violin	Viola	Cello	Double Bass	Gamba	Piano	Harpsicord	Organ	Guitar	Harp	Recorder	Flute/Piccolo	Oboe	English Horn	Clarinet/Bass Clarinet	Bassoon/Contrabassoon	Saxophone	French Horn	Trumpet	Trombone	Bass Trombone	Tuba	Baritone	Percussion	Voice	Electronic Tape	Unusual Instruments	Publisher
FELDMAN, MORTON *(continued)*																															
Intervals *Voice:* Bass-baritone. *Unus Instr:* Vibraphone	1961					1																	1				1	B		1	Peter
Ixion (Summerspace, a Ballet)	1958		11			1	1		1						3			1			1	1	1								Peter
Journey to the End of Night	1949														1			2	1									S			Peter
De Kooning	1963			1		1			1												1						1				Peter
Madame Press Died Last Week at Ninety *Unus Instr:* Bells, celesta. Bass clarinet may replace tuba	1970		4			2	2								2						1	1	1		1		1			2	Unive
Numbers *Unus Instr:* Celesta	1964			1		1	1		1						1						1		1		1		1			1	Peter
O'Hara Songs *Voice:* Bass-baritone. *Unus Instr:* Chimes	1962			1	1	1			1																		1	B		1	Peter
Pieces (2)	1961			2	1	1												1													Peter
Pieces (2, for 6 inst.)	1956			1		1									2						1	1									Peter
Pieces (3)	1956			2	1	1																									Peter
Projection II	1951			1		1			1						1							1									Peter
Projection V	1951					3			2						3							1									Peter
Rabbi Akiba *Unus Instr:* Celesta	1963					1	1		1						1		1				1	1	1		1		1	S		1	Peter
Routine Investigations	1976		16		1	1	1		1							1						1									Unive
Songs (4) to e.e. cummings	1951					1			1																			S			Peter
Straits of Magellan	1961		5				1		1			1	1		1						1	1									Peter
Structures	1951		6	2	1	1																									Peter
Vertical Thoughts III *Unus Instr:* Celesta	1963			1		1	1		1						1						1	1	1		1		2	S		1	Peter
Vertical Thoughts V *Unus Instr:* Celesta	1963			1																					1		1	S		1	Peter
Voices and Instruments II *Voices:* High	1972		12			2	1								1													3			Unive
FELLEGARA, VITTORIO (1927–)																															
Ottetto	1953														1	1		1	1		1	2	1								Suvin
Serenata *Unus Instr:* Bass clarinet	1960			2	1	1			1						1			2									1			1	Suvin
Serenata (alt. inst.)	1960			2	1	1			1						1			1	1								1				Suvin
FENNELLY, BRIAN (1937–)																															
Canzona and Dance	1982		9	1	1	1			1									1													AmCom
Empirical Rag	1980		5			1			1									1					1								AmCom
Empirical Rag (alt. vers.)	1980		5		1	1			1																						AmCom
Evanescences	1969		23	1		1									1			1											1		AmCom
Trio No. 2 *Comment:* Piano may replace harpsichord	1987		17	1		1				1																					AmCom
Triple Play	1984		11		1	1			1																						AmCom
Tropes and Echoes (solo clarinet)	1986		15	1	1	1			1						1	1	1	1	1		1						1				AmCom
Two Movements for Wind Quartet	1963		7													1		1				1	1								AmCom
FERNEYHOUGH, BRIAN (1943–)																															
Adagíssimo	1982		2	2	1	1																									Peter
Carceri d'invenzione I *Comment:* Oboe doubles on English horn. *Unus Instr:* Bass clarinet, contrabassoon, euphonium	1982		13	2	1	1	1		1						1	1	1	2	1		1	1	1		1		1			3	Peter
La chute d'Icare (solo clarinet) *Unus Instr:* Vibraphone, marimba			11	1		1			1						1	1		1									1			2	Peter
Etudes transcendantales			27			1				1					1	1												S			Peter
Funérailles, I and II	1980		20	2	2	2	1						1																		Peter
Prometheus	1967		20												1	1	1	1	1		1										Peter
Sonatas for String Quartet	1967		40	2	1	1																									Peter
Sonatina			7															3	1												Peter
String Quartet No. 2	1980		11	2	1	1																									Peter
String Quartet No. 3				2	1	1																									Peter

	Year Composed or Published	Key	Duration	Violin	Viola	Cello	Double Bass	Gamba	Piano	Harpsicord	Organ	Guitar	Harp	Recorder	Flute/Piccolo	Oboe	English Horn	Clarinet/Bass Clarinet	Bassoon/Contrabassoon	Saxophone	French Horn	Trumpet	Trombone	Bass Trombone	Tuba	Baritone	Percussion	Voice	Electronic Tape	Unusual Instruments	Publisher
FERRITTO, JOHN (1937–)																															
Concertino, Op 15	1976		11				1									1				1							2				AmCom
Diversioni, 4	1966		9	1					1									1													AmCom
Frammento, Op 10 *Unus Instr:* Vibraphone	1970		11				1															1					1			1	AmCom
Quartetto, Op 13	1974		10	1					1						1						1										AmCom
Sextet, for Piano and Winds	1980		16						1						1	1		1	1		1										AmCom
FERROUD, PIERRE O. (1900–1936)																															
Quatuor	1936	C		2	1	1																									Duran
Trio	1934															1		1	1												Duran
FIALA, JOSEPH (1748–1816)																															
Divertimento III		E♭															2		2		3										Kunze
FIBICH, ZDENEK (1850–1900)																															
Klavierquintett, Op 42 *Comment:* Also written for violin, clarinet, French horn, cello, piano	1894	D		2	1	1			1																						Artia
FINE, IRVING (1914–1962)																															
Notturno for Strings and Harp	1951		15	10	3	3	1						1																		Schir
Partita for Wind Quintet	1948														1	1		1	1		1										Schir
String Quartet	1955			2	1	1																									SPAM
FINE, VIVIAN (1913–)																															
Quintet (after paintings by E. Munch)			12	1		1			1							1		1													Peter
FINKE, FIDELIO F. (1891–1968)																															
Acht Musiken	1923			2	1																										NeueM
Streichquartett 1	1914			2	1	1																									Breit
Streichquartett 2 (Der zerstörte Tasso)				2	1	1																						H			Bären
FINNEY, ROSS L. (1906–)																															
Concerto for Strings	1977		18	6	2	5	2																								Peter
Divertimento									1							1											1				Peter
Narrative (cello plus 14)	1976		14	2	1	1	1								1	1		3			2	2	1								Peter
Piano Quartet	1948	a	20	1	1	1			1																						Peter
Piano Quintet			20	2	1	1			1																						Peter
Piano Quintet No. 2	1961			2	1	1			1																						ECSch
Piano Trio No. 2	1954		19	1		1			1																						CarlF
Quartet	1979		15			1			1							1											1				Peter
String Quartet No. 4	1950			2	1	1																									SPAM
String Quartet No. 6		E	25	2	1	1																									Peter
String Quintet	1958		20	2	1	2																									Peter
Two Acts for Three Players	1970		16						1									1									1				Peter
Variations on a Memory	1975		7						1						2			2		1	2	1	1				1				Peter
FINNISSY, MICHAEL (1946–)																															
Alongside	1979		15		1	1			1						1	1		1	1		1	1	1				1				Unive
A Beuk o' Newcassel Sangs	1989								1									1										S			Oxfor
Le Lay de la Fonteinne *Unus Instr:* Vibraphone	1990														1	1											1	M		1	Oxfor
Nowhere Else to Go *Unus Instr:* Synthesizer	1989					1												1				1					1		1	1	Oxfor
Obrecht Motetten I	1989			1	1	1									1			1	1			1	1				1				Oxfor
Obrecht Motetten II *Unus Instr:* Mandolin	1989											1	1																	1	Oxfor
Obrecht Motetten III (solo viola)				2	1	1	1								1	1		1	1		1	1	1				1				Oxfor
Obrecht Motetten IV																					1	2	2								Oxfor
Piano Concerto No. 3 *Unus Instr:* Bass clarinet, tenor trombones. Oboe doubles on English horn	1978					1	1		1							1	1	1					2							2	Unive

	Year Composed or Published	Key	Duration	Violin	Viola	Cello	Double Bass	Gamba	Piano	Harpsicord	Organ	Guitar	Harp	Recorder	Flute/Piccolo	Oboe	English Horn	Clarinet/Bass Clarinet	Bassoon/Contrabassoon	Saxophone	French Horn	Trumpet	Trombone	Bass Trombone	Tuba	Baritone	Percussion	Voice	Electronic Tape	Unusual Instruments	Publisher
FINNISSY, MICHAEL *(continued)*																															
Piano Concerto No. 5 *Unus Instr:* Alto flute, oboe d'amore, vibraphone	1980		22						1						1	1											1			3	Unive
Unknown Ground	1990			1		1			1																			B			Oxfor
FINZI, GERALD (1901–1956)																															
By Footpath and Stile, Op 2	1922		25	2	1	1																						B			Boose
Interlude, Op 21	1936		8	2	1	1										1															Boose
Prelude and Fugue, Op 24	1936		8	1	1	1																									Boose
FIRSOVA, ELENA (1950–)																															
Amoroso (String Quartet No. 4), Op 40	1989			2	1	1																									VAAP
Earthly Life (Cantata)			20	3	1	1	1						1		1												1	S			VAAP
Misterioso (String Quartet No. 3), Op 24	1980		10	2	1	1																									VAAP
Petrarca's Sonnets, Op 17 *Unus Instr:* Celesta	1976		16	1	1	1							1		1	1					1						1			1	VAAP
FISCHER, IRWIN (1903–1977)																															
Divertimento	1963	D	24	1		1	1								1			1	1		1										AmCom
Trio	1928	d	22		1	1			1																						AmCom
FISHER, STEPHEN (1940–)																															
String Quartet No. 1			20	2	1	1																									Peter
FITELBERG, JERZY (1903–1951)																															
Capriccio *Comment:* Bassoon may replace trombone	1929														1	1		2					1								Omega
String Quartet No. 2	1931			2	1	1																									Unive
FOERSTER, JOSEF B. (1859–1951)																															
Nonett, Op 147	1931			1	1	1	1								1	1		1	1		1										Artia
Streichquartett 4, Op 182	1949	F		2	1	1																									Artia
FOLPRECHT, ZDENEK (1900–1961)																															
Concertino, Op 21	1940			1	1	1	1								1	1		1	1		1										Artia
FONTYN, JACQUELINE (1930–)																															
Halo (for Harp and 16 Instruments)	1978		16	2	1	1	1		1				1		1	1		2			2	1	1				2				BoteB
Pour onze archets	1971		13	6	2	2	1																								Schir
FORET, FÉLICIEN (?–)																															
Suite en trio																1		1	1												Billa
FORTIN, V. (?–)																															
Steirische Tänze (12)												1		4																	Dobli
FORTNER, WOLFGANG (1907–1987)																															
Streichquartett 3	1950			2	1	1																									BScho
FOSS, LUKAS (1922–)																															
Cave of the Winds	1972		15												1	1		1	1		1										Salab
Divertissement pour Mica (2e Quatuor)	1972			2	1	1																									Salab
Echoi	1963					1			1									1									1				CarlF
MAP (Men at Play) *** *Comment:* For 5 instruments	1970																														Pembr
Paradigm *** *Comment:* Harp and 3 unspecified instruments. Percussionist conducts ensemble	1969											1															1		1		CarlF
Phorion *Comment:* All 3, electric instruments	1967								1		1	1																			CarlF
Round a Common Center (quartet) *Comment:* Narrator is optional	1980			1	1	1			1																			N			CarlF

	Year Composed or Published	Key	Duration	Violin	Viola	Cello	Double Bass	Gamba	Piano	Harpsicord	Organ	Guitar	Harp	Recorder	Flute/Piccolo	Oboe	English Horn	Clarinet/Bass Clarinet	Bassoon/Contrabassoon	Saxophone	French Horn	Trumpet	Trombone	Bass Trombone	Tuba	Baritone	Percussion	Voice	Electronic Tape	Unusual Instruments	Publisher
FOSS, LUKAS *(continued)*																															
Round a Common Center (quintet) *Comment:* Narrator is optional	1980			2	1	1			1																			N			CarlF
String Quartet No. 3	1947			2	1	1																									Salab
FOSSA, FRANÇOIS DE (1775–1849)																															
Quatuors (3), Op 19				1	1	1						1																			Chant
Trios concertans (3), Op 18				1	1							1																			Chant
FOSTER, STEPHEN (1826–1864)																															
Best-Loved Songs (12, arr. Carp)				2	1	1																									Press
FOULDS, JOHN (1880–1939)																															
Music Pictures (Group IV), Op 55 *Comment:* Also available as Piano Trio or Piano Quintet	1917		10	1	1	1			1																						Boose
FOURESTIER, LOUIS (1892–1976)																															
Quatuor "de Venise"				2	1	1																									Duran
FOWLER, JENNIFER (1939–)																															
Arrows of St. Sebastian	1982		20	2	1	1			1						1	1		1	1		1	1	1		1						Unive
Chimes, Fractured *Unus Instr:* Dudelsack	1971		9								1				2	2		2	2								6			1	Unive
FRACKENPOHL, ARTHUR R. (1924–)																															
Chorale and Canon																				4											Press
Short Pieces (3)				2	1	1																									Schir
FRANÇAIX, JEAN (1912–)																															
Divertissement	1954															1		1	1												BScho
Quatuor	1938			2	1	1																									BScho
Quatuor	1955														1	1		1	1												BScho
Quintette	1951														1	1		1	1		1										BScho
Tema con variazioni	1976		7	6	2	2	1											1													Eschi
Trio	1935			1	1	1																									BScho
FRANCK, CESAR (1822–1890)																															
Piano Quintet	1879	f		2	1	1			1																						VarPb
Piano Trio No. 1, Op 1 No. 1	1840	f♯		1		1			1																						VarPb
Piano Trio No. 2, Op 1 No. 2	1840	B♭		1		1			1																						VarPb
Piano Trio No. 3, Op 1 No. 3	1840	b		1		1			1																						VarPb
Piano Trio No. 4	1842			1		1			1																						VarPb
Prelude, Aria, Final (arr. Woollett)	1900			1		1			1																						Hamel
String Quartet	1889	D		2	1	1																									VarPb
FRANCO, JOHAN (1908–)																															
The Bells of Zion *Unus Instr:* Bells	1969		5																			3					1			1	AmCom
Divertimento	1946		6	2	1	1									1																AmCom
Pilgrim's Progress	1969		60						1						1		1	1	1			3	1				1				AmCom
Pilgrim's Progress (alt. vers.)	1969		60				1						1		1		1	1	1			3	1				1				AmCom
Psalm for Brasses	1965		5										1								1	3	1								AmCom
FRANK, ANDREW (1946–)																															
Sonate da camera	1978		12	1					1						1																AmCom
FRANKE, BERND (1959–)																															
Quartett	1979				1		1											1									1				DeutV
FREED, ISADORE (1900–1960)																															
Triptych	1943			1	1	1			1																						Press
FRITSCH, JOHANNES (1941–)																															
Bestandteile des Vorüber *Unus Instr:* Bass clarinet	1963						3											1	1		1		2		1			H		1	Feedb

	Year Composed or Published	Key	Duration	Violin	Viola	Cello	Double Bass	Gamba	Piano	Harpsicord	Organ	Guitar	Harp	Recorder	Flute/Piccolo	Oboe	English Horn	Clarinet/Bass Clarinet	Bassoon/Contrabassoon	Saxophone	French Horn	Trumpet	Trombone	Bass Trombone	Tuba	Baritone	Percussion	Voice	Electronic Tape	Unusual Instruments	Publisher
FRITSCH, JOHANNES *(continued)*																															
Filigranfalter *Comment:* For high voice and 12 strings	1963																											H			Feedb
Fragmente über den Tod *Voices:* Soprano and speaker					1	1			1																			2			Feedb
Hochtöner *Unus Instr:* Synthesizer	1974				1										1												1			1	Feedb
Klaviertrio 1	1964			1		1			1																						Feedb
Klaviertrio 2	1985			1		1			1																						Feedb
Laudate Dominum *Voices:* Soprano, mezzo-suprano, alto, tenor, bass				2	1	1	1																					5			Feedb
Modulation 1	1965			1	1	1	1		1																						Feedb
Modulation 2 *Comment:* 13 Instruments	1966																														Feedb
Musik für Sankt Georg	1985						1				1																2				Feedb
Nachtmusik	1963			1	1	1	1																								Feedb
September 70	1970								1						4																Feedb
Streichquintett	1984			2	1	1	1																								Feedb
Testament vivier *Unus Instr:* Bass clarinet									1						1		1	1	1		1								1	1	Feedb
Trio *Unus Instr:* Synthesizer	1977				1				1														1							1	Feedb
FROHLOFF, ERICH-KARL (1921–)																															
Kleine Serenade, Op 6 No. 3				4		2	1																								Krono
FROHNE, VINCENT S. (1936–)																															
Streichquartett 1			28	2	1	1																									BoteB
FROMM, HERBERT (1905–)																															
String Quartet				2	1	1																									Boose
FROMM-MICHAELS, ILSE (1888–)																															
Musica Larga	1958			2	1	1												1													Sikor
FROSCHAUER, HELMUTH (1933–)																															
Sextett	1962														1	1		2	1		1										Dobli
FROUNBERG, IVAR (1950–)																															
. . . en vue de Roesnaes *Unus Instr:* Celesta	1981		7		1				1							1		2					1				1			1	Hanse
FUCHS, ROBERT (1847–1927)																															
Clarinet Quintet, Op 102				2	1	1												1													Kunze
Streichtrio, Op 94		A		1	1	1																									Kunze
Terzett, Op 107				2	1																										Kunze
FUGA, SANDRO (1906–)																															
Quartetto I	1943			2	1	1																									Suvin
Quartetto II	1945			2	1	1																									Suvin
Quartetto III	1948			2	1	1																									Suvin
Quartetto IV	1965			2	1	1																									Suvin
Trio	1943			1		1			1																						Suvin
FULEIHAN, ANIS (1900–1970)																															
Piano Quintet	1964			2	1	1			1																						Boose
FÜRST, PAUL W. (1926–)																															
Apropos Wind Quintet, Op 49															1	1		1	1		1										Dobli
Bläserquartett, Op 40															1	1		1	1												Dobli
Bläserquintett 3, Op 29															1	1		1	1		1										Dobli
Konzertante Musik, Op 25															1	1		1	1		1										Dobli
Petitionen, Op 51					1				1									1													Dobli
Streichquartett, Op 34	1964			2	1	1																									Dobli

	Year Composed or Published	Key	Duration	Violin	Viola	Cello	Double Bass	Gamba	Piano	Harpsicord	Organ	Guitar	Harp	Recorder	Flute/Piccolo	Oboe	English Horn	Clarinet/Bass Clarinet	Bassoon/Contrabassoon	Saxophone	French Horn	Trumpet	Trombone	Bass Trombone	Tuba	Baritone	Percussion	Voice	Electronic Tape	Unusual Instruments	Publisher
FUSS, JOHANN E. (1777–1819)																															
Notturno en quatuor, Op 3					3	1																									Kunze
Notturno en quatuor (alt. inst.)					2	1												1													Kunze
FUSSELL, CHARLES (1938–)																															
Eurydice for Soprano and 9 Players	1984		29	1		1			1						1			1			1	1	1				1	S			Schir
Processionals (3) *Unus Instr:* Contrabassoon	1973		9										1		2	1	1	3	2		2	2	2				4			1	Schir
FUTTERER, CARL (1873–1927)																															
Octet	1921			2	1	1	1										1	1	1												Amade
Woodwind Quartet	1921	F														1		1	1		1										Kneus
Woodwind Quintet															1	1		1	1		1										Kneus
GABAYE, PIERRE (1903–)																															
Quintette															1	1		1	1		1										Leduc
Recreation									1												1	1	1								Leduc
GAL, HANS (1890–1987)																															
Divertimento												1		2																	Dobli
Streichquartett 3, Op 95	1970			2	1	1																									Simro
GALLOIS-MONTBRUN, RAYMOND (1918–)																															
Tableaux indochinois	1951			2	1	1																									Leduc
GANGE, KENNETH (?–)																															
Rag Burlesque																					1	2	1		1						Novel
GARANT, SERGE (1929–)																															
Offrande III	1971		14			3			1				2														2				Salab
GARCIN, GERARD (1947–)																															
Encore plus tard *Unus Instr:* Contrabassoon	1985		20	1	1	1	1								1			1	1								1			1	Salab
Nacimento for 11 Instruments *Unus Instr:* Vibraphone	1985		25	2	1	1	1								1	1		1	1		1						1			1	Salab
GARDNER, JOHN L. (1917–)																															
Theme and Variations																					1	2	1								Oxfor
GATTERMANN, P. (?–)																															
Fantaisie concertante *Comment:* Also available for 9 other sets of instruments				1					1						1																Billa
GATTERMEYER, HEINRICH (1923–)																															
Divertimento, Op 114					1				1									1													Dobli
Divertimento, Op 116 No. 1																					2	2	2				1				Dobli
Kammermusik I für Blechbläser *Comment:* For feast or festival; tuba, alternative instrument																					1	2	2								Dobli
Kammermusik II für Blechbläser *Comment:* Dances from Near and Far; tuba, alternative instrument																					1	2	2								Dobli
Kammermusik III für Blechbläser																					1	2	2								Dobli
Quartett, Op 81 No. 2																1		1	1		1										Dobli
Trio, Op 62 No. 2																1		1	1												Dobli
GAUDIBERT, ERIC (1936–)																															
Astrance	1980														1	1		1	1		1										Foeti
GAUL, HARVEY B. (1881–1945)																															
Tennessee Devil Tunes	1936			2	1	1																									JFisc
GEBAUER, ETIENNE (1777–1823)																															
Trio, Op 33 No. 3				1		1													1												MusRa

	Year Composed or Published	Key	Duration	Violin	Viola	Cello	Double Bass	Gamba	Piano	Harpsicord	Organ	Guitar	Harp	Recorder	Flute/Piccolo	Oboe	English Horn	Clarinet/Bass Clarinet	Bassoon/Contrabassoon	Saxophone	French Horn	Trumpet	Trombone	Bass Trombone	Tuba	Baritone	Percussion	Voice	Electronic Tape	Unusual Instruments	Publisher
GEBAUER, FRANÇOIS R. (1773–1845)																															
3 Wind Trios, Op 42															1			1	1												Kunze
Wind Quartet, Op 41															1			1	1		1										Kunze
GEHLHAAR, ROLF (1943–)																															
Camera Oscura	1978																				1	2	1		1						Feedb
Fluid				1		1			1									1													Feedb
Helix	1967						1		1											1			1				1				Feedb
Das Mädchen aus der Ferne									1						1													S			Feedb
Musi-Ken	1971			2	1	1																									Feedb
Pixels	1981					2									2			2			2										Feedb
Spektra	1974																						4	4							Feedb
Strangeness, Charm, and Colour	1978								1													2	1								Feedb
GEISSLER, FRITZ (1921–1984)																															
Bläserquintet	1957														1	1		1	1		1										Peter
Impromptus	1979			1		1			1																						DeutV
Klaviertrio	1970			1		1			1																						DeutV
Ode an eine Nachtigall	1968			2	1	1									1	1		1	1		1										DeutV
Quintett (Frühlingsquintett)	1976			2	1	1												1													DeutV
Streichquartett 2	1972			2	1	1																									DeutV
GENG, CHARLES (?–)																															
Mélodie duettino (vers. 1) *Comment:* Also available in 6 other versions				1					1									1													Billa
GENIN, PAUL A. (1829–1904)																															
Grand duo concertant (with clarinet)									1						1			1													Billa
Grand duo concertant (with oboe)									1						1	1															Billa
GENTILUCCI, ARMANDO (1939–)																															
Cantata: Siamo prossimi al risveglio	1968						1		1																		1	B			Ricor
Cile	1973														1	1		1	1		1										Ricor
Crescendo	1971			1		1			1																						Ricor
Diario II	1971														1	1		1	1		1										Ricor
E ho alzato gli occhi				2	1																										Ricor
Momenti (string quartet)				2	1	1																									Ricor
GENZMER, HARALD (1909–)																															
Capriccio for Chamber Orchestra			12	2	2	1										1		1	1		1										Peter
Cello Concerto	1950		21			1	1									2		3	2		4										Peter
Music for Four Wind Instruments			7																			2	2								Peter
Nonet			12	2	1	1	1									1		1	1		1										Peter
Notturno (solo French horn) *Comment:* Viola may substitute for French horn			5	3																	1										Peter
Piano Trio	1964		20	1		1			1																						Peter
Quintet for Brass			8																		1	2	1		1						Peter
Quintet for Winds	1959		15												1	1		1	1		1										Peter
Sextet			10															2	2		2										Peter
Trio			15							1					1				1												Peter
Trio (with Harp)			21		1								1		1																Peter
GERBER, RENÉ (1908–)																															
Suite	1948								1						1	1															Amade
GERBER, STEVEN R. (1948–)																															
Concertino in 2 Movements	1984		12	2	1	1			1																						AmCom
GERHARD, ROBERTO (1896–1970)																															
The Akond of Swat (words by Lear)	1956		5																								2	S			Oxfor
Concert for Eight *Unus Instr:* Mandolin, accordion	1962		11				1		1			1			1			1									1			2	Oxfor

	Year Composed or Published	Key	Duration	Violin	Viola	Cello	Double Bass	Gamba	Piano	Harpsicord	Organ	Guitar	Harp	Recorder	Flute/Piccolo	Oboe	English Horn	Clarinet/Bass Clarinet	Bassoon/Contrabassoon	Saxophone	French Horn	Trumpet	Trombone	Bass Trombone	Tuba	Baritone	Percussion	Voice	Electronic Tape	Unusual Instruments	Publisher
GERHARD, ROBERTO *(continued)*																															
Hymnody	1963		17						2						1	1		1			1	1	1		1		2				Oxfor
Leo *Unus Instr:* Celesta	1969		20	1					1						1			1			1	1	1				2			C	Oxfor
Libra	1968		15	1					1			1			1			1									1				Oxfor
String Quartet No. 1	1955		19	2	1	1																									Boose
String Quartet No. 2	1962		13	2	1	1																									Oxfor
GERSCHEFSKI, EDWIN (1909–)																															
"America" Variations (Piano and Winds)	1963		2						1						1			1	1	1		1									AmCom
"America" Variations, Op 44 No. 1	1963		2						1						1			1	1												AmCom
"America" Variations (for Winds), Op 44 No. 10	1963		2												1			1	1			1									AmCom
"America" Variations (for Wind Sextet), Op 45 No. 2	1963		2												1	1		1	1			1			1						AmCom
"America" Variations (Trio with Piano), Op 45 No. 4	1963		2						1						1			1													AmCom
"America" Variations (Quartet with Piano), Op 45 No. 8 *Unus Instr:* Contrabassoon	1963		2						1							1			2											1	AmCom
"America" Variations (Winds and Perc.), Op 45 No. 10	1963		2												1	1		1	1			1			1		1				AmCom
Music for Strings, Op 69, Nos.1-6	1972		9	2	1	1																					1				AmCom
Piano Quintet in 4 Movements, Op 16	1935		22	2	1	1			1																						AmCom
Piano Trio, Op 43	1960		13		1	1			1																						AmCom
Prelude, Op 6 No. 5	1957		4										1		2	2		2	1								3				AmCom
Rhapsody, Op 46	1963		12		1	1			1																						AmCom
Song Without Words	1939		4	2	1				1				1		1																AmCom
GERSHWIN, GEORGE (1898–1937)																															
5 Songs (arr. Silverman)				2	1	1																									Schir
GEWICKSMANN, VITALI A. (1924–)																															
Japanese Elegies *Unus Instr:* Bass clarinet							1		1	1					1			2			1						5	S		1	Peter
String Quartet No. 2				2	1	1																									Peter
GHEDINI, GIORGIO F. (1892–1965)																															
Concerto à cinque									1						1	1		1	1												Ricor
Musica per tre stromenti	1963					1			1						1																Ricor
Quartetto I	1927			2	1	1																									Suvin
Ricercari, 7	1946			1		1			1																						Suvin
GHENT, EMMANUEL (1925–)																															
Dithyrambos	1965																				1	2	2								Oxfor
Dithyrambos (alt. vers.)	1965																				2	4	3		1						Oxfor
Quartet	1960														1	1		1	1												Oxfor
Triality I	1964			1															1			1									Oxfor
Triality II	1964			1															1			1									Oxfor
GIBBS, CECIL A. (1889–1960)																															
Henry Brocken	1937			2	1	1			1																						Boose
Miniature Quartet, Op 74	1934			2	1	1																									Boose
Peacock Pie *Comment:* Also for 3 violins and cello; double bass ad lib	1933		9	2	1	1																									Boose
Piano Trio, Op 97	1940	D	19	1		1			1																						Boose
String Quartet, Op 73	1933	A		2	1	1																									Boose
The Three Graces (Light Suite), Op 92	1941		11	1		1			1																						Boose
GIDEON, MIRIAM (1906–)																															
Fantasy on Irish Folk Tunes	1975		13		1											1			1								1				AmCom

	Year Composed or Published	Key	Duration	Violin	Viola	Cello	Double Bass	Gamba	Piano	Harpsicord	Organ	Guitar	Harp	Recorder	Flute/Piccolo	Oboe	English Horn	Clarinet/Bass Clarinet	Bassoon/Contrabassoon	Saxophone	French Horn	Trumpet	Trombone	Bass Trombone	Tuba	Baritone	Percussion	Voice	Electronic Tape	Unusual Instruments	Publisher
GIDEON, MIRIAM *(continued)*																															
Fantasy on Irish Folk Tunes (alt. inst.)	1975		13		1	1										1											1				AmCom
The Shooting Starres Attend Thee				1		1									1													H			Peter
Spirit Above the Dust (Song Cycle)			15	2	1	1									1	1			1		1							1			Peter
Trio	1978		6			1			1									1													AmCom
Wing'd Hour (Song Cycle) *Unus Instr:* Vibraphone			10	1		1									1	1											1	H		1	Peter
GIELEN, MICHAEL (1927–)																															
String Quartet ("Un vieux souvenir")			37	2	1	1																									Peter
GIESEKING, WALTER (1895–1956)																															
Quintet	1920	B♭							1							1		1	1		1										Boose
GILBERT, PIA (1921–)																															
Food *Voices:* Soprano and baritone			7						1													1					1	2			Peter
Interrupted Suite			10						3									1													Peter
Spirals and Interpolations			12						1							1				1							1				Peter
GINASTERA, ALBERTO (1916–1983)																															
Cantos del Tucuman *Unus Instr:* 2 Indian drums	1938			1									1		1												1	1		2	Boose
Impresiones de la Puna	1942			2	1	1									1																Barry
Piano Quintet, Op 29	1963		20	2	1	1			1																						Boose
Serenata, Op 42 *Unus Instr:* Xylophone, vibraphone	1972					1							1		1	1		1	1		1						2	B		2	Boose
String Quartet No. 1	1948			2	1	1																									Boose
String Quartet No. 2, Op 26	1958		27	2	1	1																									Boose
String Quartet No. 3 (with voice), Op 40	1973		25	2	1	1																						S			Boose
GIRAUD, SUZANNE (1958–)																															
La dernière lumière	1958		11	1		1			1						1			1			1						2	S			Salab
L'Offrand à Venus	1985		7	2	1	1							1		1			1									1				Salab
GIULIANI, MAURO (1781–1829)																															
Grand Concerto, Op 36		A		2	1	1						1																			Schro
Introduction, Variation, und Polonaise, Op 65				2	1	1						1																			Schro
Serenade, Op 19				1		1						1																			Schro
GLANERT, DETLEV (1960–)																															
Norden (Five Pictures) *Unus Instr:* Bass clarinet	1986		12		1	1	1		1						1			1									1			1	BoteB
GLASS, PHILIP (1937–)																															
Brass Sextet																					2	2	1		1						Novel
Company	1983		8	2	1	1																									Ms/Dn
Façades	1982		7	2	1	1														2											Ms/Dn
Floe	1983		7						1						1					2	2										Ms/Dn
Glassworks	1981		40		1	1			1						2					2	2										MS/Dn
Habeve Song	1983		8															1	1									S			Ms/Dn
Modern Love Waltz *Unus Instr:* Vibraphone	1979		12						2				1		1			1									1			1	Ms/Dn
String Quartet No. 1	1966		16	2	1	1																									Ms/Dn
String Quartet No. 2 (from "Company")	1983		8	2	1	1																									Ms/Dn
String Quartet No. 3 (from "Mishima"), Op 18	1985		18	2	1	1																									Ms/Dn
String Quartet No. 4 (from "Boczak")	1989		20	2	1	1																									Ms/Dn

	Year Composed or Published	Key	Duration	Violin	Viola	Cello	Double Bass	Gamba	Piano	Harpsicord	Organ	Guitar	Harp	Recorder	Flute/Piccolo	Oboe	English Horn	Clarinet/Bass Clarinet	Bassoon/Contrabassoon	Saxophone	French Horn	Trumpet	Trombone	Bass Trombone	Tuba	Baritone	Percussion	Voice	Electronic Tape	Unusual Instruments	Publisher
GLASSER, S (?–)																															
Trio																						2	1								MusRa
GLAZUNOFF, ALEXANDER K. (1865–1936)																															
Novelettes (5), Op 15	1894			2	1	1																									VarPb
String Quartet No. 1, Op 1	1882	D		2	1	1																									Belai
String Quartet No. 2, Op 10	1884	F		2	1	1																									Belai
String Quartet No. 4, Op 64	1899	a		2	1	1																									Belai
String Quartet No. 5, Op 70	1900	d		2	1	1																									Belai
String Quartet No. 6, Op 106	1937	B♭		2	1	1																									Belai
String Quartet No. 7, Op 107	1931	C		2	1	1																									Belai
String Quintet, Op 39	1895	A		2		2	1																								Belai
GLIÈRE, REINHOLD (1875–1956)																															
String Quartet, Op 2		A		2	1	1																									Inter
GLINKA, MICHAIL I. (1804–1857)																															
String Quartet No. 1	1824	D		2	1	1																									Kunze
String Quartet No. 2	1830	F		2	1	1																									Kunze
Trio pathétique *Comment:* Cello may replace bassoon	1827								1									1	1												VarPb
GLINSKY, ALBERT V. (1952–)																															
Masquerade	1982		25	1		1	1						1		1	1		1	1		1						1				AmCom
GLOBOKAR, VINKO (1934–)																															
Accord			15			1					1				1								1				1	S			Peter
Airs de voyages vers l'interieur *Voices:* 2 each sopranos, altos, tenors, basses. Amplification	1972		23															1					1					8			Peter
Discours VI				2	1	1																									Peter
Fluide *Unus Instr:* Flügelhorn	1967		15																		3	2	2		1		3			1	Peter
Un jour comme un autre			60			1	1					1						1									1	S			Peter
La ronde *** *Comment:* For any number of melody instruments			20																												Peter
Vendre le vent			35						1						1	1		1	1	1	1	1	1		1		1				Peter
GODARD, BENJAMIN (1849–1895)																															
2e Trio, Op 72		F		1		1			1																						Duran
GODFREY, DANIEL (1949–)																															
Aubade	1978		8										1		1				1												AmCom
Impromptu	1970		7			1			1									1													AmCom
Septet	1973		5	2	1	1											1				1	1									AmCom
GOEB, ROGER (1914–)																															
Black on White (Clarinet Quintet)	1985		15	2	1	1												1													AmCom
Concertant Ib	1948		14						1						1	1		1													AmCom
Concertant IIb	1951		12	2	1	1													1												AmCom
Concertant IIIb	1951		15		1										1	1		1	1		2	2	1		1						AmCom
Concertant IVb	1951		16	2	1	1			1									1													AmCom
Declarations	1961		12			1									1	1			1		1										AmCom
Flute Quintet	1983		16	2	1	1									1																AmCom
Hurry *Unus Instr:* Vibraphone	1985		8		1	1	1								1	1		1			1	1					1			1	AmCom
Kinematic Trio	1985		15		1	1			1																						AmCom
Oboe Quartet	1964		15	1	1	1										1															AmCom
Octet	1980		18	2	1	1	1											1	1		1										AmCom
Piano Quintet	1955		21	2	1	1			1																						AmCom
Processionals (3)	1951		11								1											2	3								AmCom
Trombone Quintet (Concertino)	1949		13	2	1	1																	1								AmCom
Winds Playing	1988		16												1	1		1	1		2	2	1		1						AmCom
GOETZ, HERMANN (1840–1876)																															
Klavierquartett, Op 6	1867	E		1	1	1			1																						Kunze

	Year Composed or Published	Key	Duration	Violin	Viola	Cello	Double Bass	Gamba	Piano	Harpsicord	Organ	Guitar	Harp	Recorder	Flute/Piccolo	Oboe	English Horn	Clarinet/Bass Clarinet	Bassoon/Contrabassoon	Saxophone	French Horn	Trumpet	Trombone	Bass Trombone	Tuba	Baritone	Percussion	Voice	Electronic Tape	Unusual Instruments	Publisher
GOETZ, HERMANN *(continued)*																															
Klavierquintett, Op 16	1874	c		1	1	1	1		1																						Kunze
Klaviertrio 1, Op 1	1863	g		1		1			1																						Kunze
GOLD, ERNEST (1921–)																															
String Quartet No. 1				2	1	1																									Press
GOLDMAN, RICHARD F. (1910–1980)																															
Chamber Music Suite				2		1			1						1																Press
Chamber Music Suite (alt. vers.)				2					1							1			1												Press
GOLDMANN, FRIEDRICH (1941–)																															
Sonata for Wind Quintet and Piano	1970								1						1	1		1	1		1										Peter
So und so	1972						1										1						1								DeutV
String Quartet	1975			2	1	1																									Peter
Trio	1967								1						1												1				DeutV
Zusammenstellung *Unus Instr:* Bass clarinet, contrabassoon	1976		28												1		1	1	1		1									2	Peter
GOLDSCHMIDT, BERTHOLD (1903–)																															
Clarinet Quartet	1983		20	1	1	1												1													Boose
Piano Trio	1985		16	1		1			1																						Boose
String Quartet No. 2	1936		28	2	1	1																									Boose
GOLESTAN, STAN (1875–1956)																															
Petite suite bucolique																1		1	1												Duran
Quatuor	1932			2	1	1																									Duran
GOLUB, PETER (1952–)																															
Flying Colors	1978		9			3	1								5												3				AmCom
The Gemini Sonata	1984		13						1						1			1													AmCom
Jupiter Transit	1982		8			1			1																		1				AmCom
Shadows	1979		12	2	1	1	1		1												1	1	1				1				AmCom
Song	1976		12	1		1			1									1													AmCom
GOOSSEN, FREDERIC (1927–)																															
Concertato (for Solo Organ)	1975		5								1				1			1	2			1	2								AmCom
GOOSSENS, EUGENE (1893–1962)																															
Fantasy	1924														1	1		2	2		2	1									Leduc
Pastorale et arlequinade	1924								1						1	1															Leduc
String Quartet No. 2, Op 59	1940		34	2	1	1																									Boose
GORECKI, HENRYK M. (1933–)																															
Concerto (for 9 instruments), Op 11 *Unus Instr:* Xylophone, mandolin	1957		10	2	1	1									1			1				1					1			2	Boose
Genesis I (Elementi), Op 19 No. 1	1962		13	1	1	1																									Boose
Genesis II (Canti strumentali), Op 19 No. 2 *Unus Instr:* Mandolin	1962		8	3	3				1			1			2							1					2			1	Boose
Monologhi, Op 16 *Unus Instr:* Glockenspiel, vibraphone	1960		17										2														3	S		2	Boose
La musiquette 2me (Muzycka II), Op 23	1967		7						2													4	4				5				Boose
La musiquette 4me (Trombone Concerto), Op 28	1970					1			1									1					1								Schot
Quartettino, Op 5	1956		8	1											2	1															Boose
Recitatives and Ariosos (Lerchenmusik), Op 53	1986		35			1			1									1													Boose
GOULD, MORTON (1913–)																															
Bird Movements (from Audubon) *Unus Instr:* Contrabassoon			12				1								3	1	1	3	3						1		1			1	Schir
Concerto concertante (for violin)	1982		22	1					1						1	1		1	1		1										Schir

	Year Composed or Published	Key	Duration	Violin	Viola	Cello	Double Bass	Gamba	Piano	Harpsicord	Organ	Guitar	Harp	Recorder	Flute/Piccolo	Oboe	English Horn	Clarinet/Bass Clarinet	Bassoon/Contrabassoon	Saxophone	French Horn	Trumpet	Trombone	Bass Trombone	Tuba	Baritone	Percussion	Voice	Electronic Tape	Unusual Instruments	Publisher
GOULD, MORTON *(continued)*																															
Elegy (from TV series, "Holocaust")	1978		4	10	3	3	3																								Schir
Swanee River (in style of Ellington)			4				1		1			1						1	1	3	2	2	1				1				Schir
GOUNOD, CHARLES (1818–1893)																															
Petite symphonie	1888														1	2		2	2		2										Billa
GRAAP, LOTHAR (1933–)																															
Divertimento	1964														1	1			1												DeutV
GRABNER, HERMANN (1866–1969)																															
Der Herr ist mein Hirte (Psalm 23) *Voices:* Soprano and alto				2							1																	2			Merse
GRAINGER, PERCY (1882–1961)																															
I'm Seventeen Come Sunday *Unus Instr:* Euphonium	1912		3																		4	3	3		1		2			1	Schir
GRANADOS, ENRIQUE (1867–1916)																															
Pequeña romanza, Op Post.				2	1	1																									UMEsp
Trio				1		1			1																						UMEsp
GRANT, WILLIAM P. (1910–)																															
The Ballet Master's Dream, Op 5	1973		21	2	1	1			1																						AmCom
GREENBAUM, MATTHEW (1950–)																															
Commedia	1986			1	1	1	1		1				1									1	1		1						AmCom
GREENBURG, LAURA (1942–)																															
Piano Trio	1984		11		1	1			1																						AmCom
GREGSON, EDWARD (1945–)																															
Quintet for Brass																					1	2	1		1						Novel
GRIEG, EDVARD (1843–1907)																															
Danses norvegiennes (4), Op 35	1881														1	1		1	1		1										Billa
String Quartet, Op 27	1879	g		2	1	1																									Peter
Unfinished Quartet, Op Posthumous	1908	F		2	1	1																									Peter
GROOT, H. DE (?–)																															
Variations on a French folksong																1		1	1												Harmo
GROSS, ROBERT (1914–)																															
Octet *Unus Instr:* Bass clarinet	1970		8	1		1	1		1						1	1		2												1	AmCom
Trivarow	1976		9	1					1									1													AmCom
GROSSKOPF, ERHARD (1934–)																															
Concerto (Flecktreue Raritatenkunst) *Unus Instr:* Electrical apparatus	1969		21	1	1		1		1						1	1					1						2			1	BoteB
Divertimento	1974		15																		1	2	2								AMP
Quartet No. 3	1968		19	2	1	1																									AMP
Recollections	1982		21						1						1	1		1	1		1										AMP
Variations	1984		21	1	1	1			1																						AMP
GROSSMANN, FERDINAND (1887–1970)																															
Streichtrio				1	1	1																									Dobli
GRUBER, HEINZ K. (1943–)																															
Bossa Nova quintet (from MOB-Stücken), Op 21e															1	1		1	1		1										Dobli
Bossa Nova trio (from MOB-Stücken), Op 21e	1968								1						1				1												Dobli
Cello Concerto	1989		21	2	1	2	1		1						1	1		1	1		1	1	1				1				Boose
The Expulsion from Paradise *Voices:* 1 male, 1 female; or 3 male and 1 female	1979		20				1		1						1					1	1						1	2			Boose

	Year Composed or Published	Key	Duration	Violin	Viola	Cello	Double Bass	Gamba	Piano	Harpsicord	Organ	Guitar	Harp	Recorder	Flute/Piccolo	Oboe	English Horn	Clarinet/Bass Clarinet	Bassoon/Contrabassoon	Saxophone	French Horn	Trumpet	Trombone	Bass Trombone	Tuba	Baritone	Percussion	Voice	Electronic Tape	Unusual Instruments	Publisher
GRUBER, HEINZ K. *(continued)*																															
Frankenstein!!	1979		28	2	2	1			1						1			1	1		1	1					1				Boose
MOB Pieces (3) *** *Comment:* For 7 interchangeable instruments and percussion	1977																														Boose
Nebelsteinmusik (Violinkonzert 2)	1988		16	5	2	2	1																								Boose
Phantom-Bilder	1977		13	2	1	1	1		1			1			1	1		1				1	1				1				Boose
GRUENBERG, LOUIS (1884–1964)																															
Daniel Jazz, Op 21	1924		18	2	1	1			1									1				1					1	T			Unive
Diversions (4), Op 32	1930		8	2	1	1																									CosCb
Indiscretions (4), Op 20	1922		6	2	1	1																									Unive
Quintet for Piano and Strings	1929		20	2	1	1			1																						Manus
GRÜNAUER, INGOMAR (1938–)																															
Bläserquartett															1	1		1	1												Dobli
GUBAIDULINA, SOFIA (1931–)																															
Concerto for Bassoon and Low Strings	1975		30			8	6												1												VAAP
Etudes (5)	1965						1						1														1				VAAP
Garden of Joy and Sadness (Trio)	1980				1								1		1													N			VarPb
Perception *Voices:* Soprano and baritone; ensemble of 7 strings																												2	1		VarPb
Piano Quintet				2	1	1			1																						VAAP
String Quartet No. 1	1971		21	2	1	1																									VAAP
String Quartet No. 2	1987		10	2	1	1																									VarPb
String Quartet No. 3	1987		15	2	1	1																									VarPb
GUDMUNDSEN-HOLMG'N, PELLE (1932–)																															
reTurning	1987		18						1				1		1			1									1				Hanse
GUEZEC, JEAN-PIERRE (1934–1971)																															
Architectures colorées	1964		8	2	1	1	1								1	1		2			1	1	1				3				Salab
Forme-Couleurs for 2 Harps	1969		9										2		2	1		2			1	1					2				Salab
Successif-Simultane for 12 Solo Strings	1968		13	7	2	2	1																								Salab
Textures enchainées	1967		9										1		2	1		2			2	2	2	1			3				Salab
GUILLOU, JEAN (1930–)																															
Cantilia	1961					4			1				1														1				Leduc
Colloques no. 1	1954			1					1						1	1															Leduc
Colloques no. 4	1965								1		1																1				Leduc
GURIDI, JESÚS (1886–1961)																															
Cuarteto 2	1957	A		2	1	1																									UMEsp
GURSCHING, ALBRECHT (1934–)																															
Streichquartett 3	1966			2	1	1																									Bosse
GUYARD, CHRISTOPHE (?–)																															
Voyager III				1					1									1													Billa
GYROWETZ, ADALBERT (1763–1850)																															
Quartet				1	1	1												1													Kunze
HABA, ALOIS (1893–1973)																															
Nonett 3, Op 82	1953			1	1	1	1								1	1		1	1		1										Artia
Streichquartett 7, Op 73	1951			2	1	1																									Artia
Streichquartett 12, Op 90	1960			2	1	1																									Artia
Streichquartett 14, Op 94	1963			2	1	1																									Artia
HABA, KAREL (1898–1972)																															
Klaviertrio, Op 24	1940			1		1			1																						Artia

	Year Composed or Published	Key	Duration	Violin	Viola	Cello	Double Bass	Gamba	Piano	Harpsicord	Organ	Guitar	Harp	Recorder	Flute/Piccolo	Oboe	English Horn	Clarinet/Bass Clarinet	Bassoon/Contrabassoon	Saxophone	French Horn	Trumpet	Trombone	Bass Trombone	Tuba	Baritone	Percussion	Voice	Electronic Tape	Unusual Instruments	Publisher
HABA, KAREL *(continued)*																															
Streichquartett 2, Op 5	1924			2	1	1																									Artia
HADAMOWSKY, HANS (1906–)																															
Variations on a Folk Song																2	1														Dobli
HADER, WILDMAR (1941–)																															
Hör meinen Protest *Voice:* Bass	1970										1											1						1			Bosse
HAGERUP BULL, EDVARD (1922–)																															
Ad usum amicorum	1957			1		1			1						1																Billa
HALFFTER, CRISTOBAL (1930–)																															
Antiphonismoi *Comment:* Flute doubles on alto flute, oboe on English horn	1967		17	1	1	1			1						1	1	1	1													Unive
Brecht-Lieder (4)	1967								2																			1			Unive
Concierto para flauta y sexteto de cuerda	1982		26	2	2	2									1																Unive
Noche pasiva del sentido	1971																										2	S	1		Unive
Oda para felicitar a un amigo *Unus Instr:* Alto flute, bass clarinet, celesta	1969		5		1	1									1			2									1			3	Unive
Planto por las victimas de la violencia	1971		25	2	1	1			1						3	3		3									4				Unive
Pourquoi	1975		24	6	3	2	1																								Unive
Le retour de l'enfant prodigue									2																			1			Unive
Streichquartett 2 (Mémoires 1870)				2	1	1																									Unive
Streichquartett 3				2	1	1																									Unive
Tiempo para espacios	1974		18	6	3	2	1			1																					Unive
Variaciones sobre la resonancia de un grito *Comment:* Piano and harpsichord have "ring modulator"	1977		26			3			1	1	1							3					3								Unive
HALLER, HERMANN (1914–)																															
Pieces (5) in the Form of Variations	1980														1	1		1	1		1										Hug
HAMANN, ERICH (1898–)																															
Piano Quartet, Op 35				1	1	1			1																						Dobli
Piano Trio, Op 27				1		1			1																						Dobli
Sicilian Suite, Op 36				2		1																									Dobli
String Quartet, Op 14				2	1	1																									Dobli
String Quartet, Op 25 No. 1				2	1	1																									Dobli
String Quartet, Op 25 No. 2				2	1	1																									Dobli
String Quartet, Op 39				2	1	1																									Dobli
String Quintet, Op 34				2	1	2																									Dobli
String Trio, Op 28				1	1	1																									Dobli
String Trio, Op 30				1	1	1																									Dobli
String Trio, Op 37				2	1																										Dobli
Trio, Op 38				1	1				1																						Dobli
HAMBRAEUS, BENGT (1928–)																															
Gioco del cambio, Op 33 *Unus Instr:* Bass clarinet	1954		18						1	1					1		1	1									1			1	Nordi
Introduzione, sequenze, coda	1959		20												3												6				Nordi
HAMEL, PETER M. (1947–)																															
Adagio und Finale	1985			2	1	1							1		1			1													Bären
Fragment von Jean Gebser *Unus Instr:* Vibraphone	1979					1			1						1												1	F		1	Bären
Klaviertrio in 3 Sätzen	1985			1		1			1																						Bären
So fern (Drei Gedichte von W. Bachler) *Unus Instr:* Celesta	1985					1			1						1												1	S		1	Bären

	Year Composed or Published	Key	Duration	Violin	Viola	Cello	Double Bass	Gamba	Piano	Harpsicord	Organ	Guitar	Harp	Recorder	Flute/Piccolo	Oboe	English Horn	Clarinet/Bass Clarinet	Bassoon/Contrabassoon	Saxophone	French Horn	Trumpet	Trombone	Bass Trombone	Tuba	Baritone	Percussion	Voice	Electronic Tape	Unusual Instruments	Publisher
HAMEL, PETER M. *(continued)*																															
Streichquartett 1	1989			2	1	1																									Bären
Streichquartett 2	1986			2	1	1																									Bären
HAMPTON, CALVIN (1938–)																															
Triple Play *Unus Instr:* Ondes Martenot			8						2																					1	Peter
HANNAY, ROGER (1930–)																															
Fantôme	1967		12		1				1									1													Peter
HANUS, JAN (1915–)																															
Fantasie, Op 6	1939			2	1	1																									Artia
Suita domestica, Op 57	1964														1	1		1	1		1										Artia
HARBISON, JOHN (1938–)																															
Bermuda Triangle *Unus Instr:* Amplified cello	1970		9			1					1									1										1	AMP
Book of the Hours and Seasons *Voice:* Mezzo-soprano or tenor	1975		15			1			1						1													1			AMP
Chorale Preludes, 2	1987		8																		1	2	2								AMP
Christmas Vespers (Movement II)	1988		27																		1	2	2								AMP
Concerto	1985		13	2	1	1										1		1													AMP
Confinement	1965		15	1	1	1	1		1						1	1	1	1		1		1	1				1				AMP
Dumbshows (from The Winter's Tale)	1974		12	1	1				1						1			1													AMP
Exequien for Calvin Simmons *Unus Instr:* Vibraphone	1982		5		2	1			1						1			1									1			1	AMP
Fanfare for Foley's	1986		2																		4	4	3		1		2				AMP
Die Kurze	1970		11	1		1			1						1			1													AMP
Little Fantasy (12 Days of Christmas)	1988		4																		1	2	2								AMP
Magnum misterium, Op 16	1987		16																		1	2	2								AMP
Merchant of Venice (Incidental Music)	1971		12	2	2	1																									AMP
Mirabai Songs for Soprano *Unus Instr:* Marimba	1982		15	1	1	1	1						1		1			1									1	S		1	AMP
Moments of Vision *Voices:* Soprano and tenor. Renaissance-style ensemble. *Unus Instr:* Crumhorn	1975		15					1				1		1														2		1	AMP
Music for 18 Winds	1986		10												2	2		2	2	1	4	2	1	1	1						AMP
The Natural World	1987		12	1		1			1						1			1										S			AMP
Nocturne, 1989	1989		6																		1	2	2								AMP
November 19, 1828	1988		16	1	1	1			1																						AMP
Organum for Paul Fromm *Unus Instr:* Vibraphone, marimba	1981		4			1			1				1														2			2	AMP
Piano Quintet	1981		22	2	1	1			1																						AMP
Piano Trio	1969		9	1		1			1																						AMP
Preludes, 4 (from "December Music")	1967			1											1	1		1													McGin
Samuel Chapter (for high voice) *Voice:* Soprano or tenor. *Unus Instr:* Vibraphone	1978		12		1	1			1						1			1									1	1		1	AMP
Serenade for Six Players *Unus Instr:* Bass clarinet	1968		11	1	1	1									1			2												1	AMP
String Quartet No. 1	1985		11	2	1	1																									AMP
String Quartet No. 2	1987		26	2	1	1																									AMP
The Three Wise Men (Christmas Concerto) *Voice:* Reader	1988		16																		1	2	2					1			AMP
Twilight Music	1985		17	1					1												1										AMP

	Year Composed or Published	Key	Duration	Violin	Viola	Cello	Double Bass	Gamba	Piano	Harpsicord	Organ	Guitar	Harp	Recorder	Flute/Piccolo	Oboe	English Horn	Clarinet/Bass Clarinet	Bassoon/Contrabassoon	Saxophone	French Horn	Trumpet	Trombone	Bass Trombone	Tuba	Baritone	Percussion	Voice	Electronic Tape	Unusual Instruments	Publisher
HARBISON, JOHN *(continued)*																															
Variations	1982			1					1									1													AMP
HARPER, EDWARD (1941–)																															
Fantasia II (for 11 solo strings)			16	6	2	2	1																								Oxfor
Fantasia III			10																		1	2	1	1							Oxfor
Intrada after Monteverdi			5	1	1	1	1		1				1		1			2			1	1					1				Oxfor
Quintet			10	1		1			1						1			1													Oxfor
Ricercari in memoriam Luigi Dallapiccola			16	1		1	1		1				1		1			2			1	1					1				Oxfor
String Quartet No. 2			22	2	1	1																									Oxfor
HARRIS, MATTHEW (1956–)																															
Ancient Greek Melodies *Unus Instr:* Bass clarinet	1985		17	1		1									1			1									2			1	AmCom
Music After Rimbaud			8	1		1									1			1													Peter
Starry Night (7 Paintings)			21	1		1			1																						Peter
HARRIS, ROY (1898–1979)																															
4 Minutes, 20 seconds	1942			2	1	1									1																Manus
Abraham Lincoln Walks at Midnight	1953			1		1			1																			M			AMP
Canticle of the Sun (Cantata)	1961		37	3	2	1			1						1		1	2										H			AMP
Childhood Memories of Ocean Moods	1966			2	1	1	1		1																						Manus
Concerto for piano, Op 2	1927		20	2	1	1			1									1													CosCb
Fantasy	1932								1						1	1		1	1		1										CosCb
Piano Quintet	1936			2	1	1			1																						Schir
Piano Trio	1933			1		1			1																						Press
Sextet	1932		10						1						1	1		1	1		1										CosCb
String Quartet	1929		24	2	1	1																									CosCb
String Quartet No. 2	1933			2	1	1																									CosCb
String Quartet No. 3	1937			2	1	1																									Mills
String Quintet	1935			2	2	1																									Schir
String Sextet	1932			2	2	2																									CosCb
Variations (3) on a Theme				2	1	1																									Schir
HARRIS, RUSSELL (1914–)																															
Dance Group, Op 13	1941		12	1					2									1	1												AmCom
HARRISON, JULIUS (1885–1963)																															
Widdicombe Faire (Humoresque), Op 22				2	1	1																									Boose
HARRISON, LOU (1917–)																															
Alma Redemptoris Mater *Unus Instr:* Tack piano			2	1					1														1					B		1	Peer
Avalokiteshvara *Unus Instr:* Jalataranga (2 players)			3										1																	2	Manus
Beverly's Troubadour Piece			2										1														2				Manus
Concerto for Violin	1959		15	1																							5				Peter
Concerto in slendro *Unus Instr:* 2 Tackpianos, celesta, washtubs, garbage pails	1961		11	1					2																		2			5	Peter
Concerto No. 1 for Flute			10												1												2				Peter
Double Concerto (solo violin, cello) *Unus Instr:* Gamelan			23	1		1																								1	Peter
Haiku *Voices:* Unison chorus. *Unus Instr:* Shiao			2										1														1	6		1	Manus
A Joyous Procession, a Solemn Procession *Comment:* Employs chorus of high and low voices																							1				1	8			Peter

	Year Composed or Published	Key	Duration	Violin	Viola	Cello	Double Bass	Gamba	Piano	Harpsicord	Organ	Guitar	Harp	Recorder	Flute/Piccolo	Oboe	English Horn	Clarinet/Bass Clarinet	Bassoon/Contrabassoon	Saxophone	French Horn	Trumpet	Trombone	Bass Trombone	Tuba	Baritone	Percussion	Voice	Electronic Tape	Unusual Instruments	Publisher
HARRISON, LOU *(continued)*																															
Party Pieces	1950								1						1			1	1		1										Peter
Peace Piece Two			7	2	2	1							2														3	T			Manus
Pied Beauty *Comment:* Cello may substitute for trombone															1								1				1	1			Manus
Siciliana			3												1	1		1	1		1										Manus
Solstice *Unus Instr:* Tack piano, celesta			30			2	1		1						1	1						1								2	Peer
String Trio			3	1	1	1																									Peter
Suite for Violin *Unus Instr:* Tack piano, celesta			10	1		2	1		1				1		2	1											1			2	AMP
Suite No. 2			12	2	1	1																									Merry
HARSANYI, TIBOR (1898–1954)																															
Concertino for Piano	1931		21	2	1	1			1																						Salab
Divertimento No. 1 (Concertino)	1941			2					1																						Salab
L'Histoire du petit tailleur *Unus Instr:* Timpani	1939		25	1		1									1			1	1			1					2	N		1	Eschi
Nonette	1927		24	2	1	1									1	1		1	1		1										Eschi
HARTIG, HEINZ F. (1907–1969)																															
Composizione per cinque, Op 50				1	1	1									1	1															BoteB
HARTLEY, WALTER S. (1927–)																															
Brass Quintet																					1	2	1		1						Press
Quartet for Brass *Unus Instr:* Euphonium																					1	1	1		1					1	Press
Solemn Music																					1	2	1								Press
Suite for Diverse Trumpets *Unus Instr:* Flügelhorn																						5								1	Press
HARTWELL, HUGH (1945–)																															
Matinée d'ivresse				1		1			1									1									1				Oxfor
Septet *Unus Instr:* Bass clarinet				1	1	1												3			1									1	Oxfor
HARTZELL, EUGENE (1932–)																															
Companion Pieces to a Wind Quintet															1	1		1	1		1										Dobli
Projections for Wind Quintet															1	1		1	1		1										Dobli
Trio				1					1									1													Dobli
Trio for Piano and Winds *Comment:* Bassoon may replace bass clarinet									1						1			1													Dobli
HARVEY, JONATHAN (1939–)																															
Album (7 Miniatures for Wind Quintet) *Comment:* Oboist doubles on oboe d'amore, English horn	1979		18												1	1	1	1	1		1									1	Faber
Bhakti *Unus Instr:* Piccolo trumpet	1982		50	3	1	1			1				1		1		1	2			1	1	1				1			1	Faber
Concelebration	1980		16			1			1						1			1									1				Faber
Smiling Immortal *Comment:* Amplification needed	1977		17	2	1	1			1						1	1		1			1	1					1		1		Faber
Song Offerings	1985		17	2	1	1	1								1			1										S			Faber
String Quartet	1977			2	1	1																									Faber
HASELBACH, JOSEF (1936–)																															
Fragen an die Nacht				2	2	1																									Hug
HASHAGEN, KLAUS (1924–)																															
Septalie Studie für 7 Spieler *Comment:* Violin, viola, cello are alternative instruments	1966								1						1	1		1	1			1	1								Bosse
HASLAM, HERBERT (1928–)																															
Antimasque																					1	2	1								Press
HASQUENOPH, PIERRE (1922–1982)																															
Concerto de Nuremberg (comp. Werner), Op 43a	1982		14	7	2	2	1													1											Eschi

	Year Composed or Published	Key	Duration	Violin	Viola	Cello	Double Bass	Gamba	Piano	Harpsicord	Organ	Guitar	Harp	Recorder	Flute/Piccolo	Oboe	English Horn	Clarinet/Bass Clarinet	Bassoon/Contrabassoon	Saxophone	French Horn	Trumpet	Trombone	Bass Trombone	Tuba	Baritone	Percussion	Voice	Electronic Tape	Unusual Instruments	Publisher
HASQUENOPH, PIERRE *(continued)*																															
Divertissement																					3	3	3		1		1				Dobli
Divertissement pour dixtuor					2	1	1	1							1	1		1	1		1										Dobli
HAUBENSTOCK-RAMATI, ROMAN (1919–)																															
Blessings *Unus Instr:* Celesta	1952			4					1				1		1												1	S		1	Unive
Cantando *Unus Instr:* Celesta. Score calls for celesta or harpsichord	1984		20			1			1	1			1		1												1			1	Unive
La comedie *Comment:* Sprechgesang. *Voices:* 2 Female, 1 male	1969																										3	3			Unive
Credentials (Think, Think Lucky) *Comment:* Sprechgesang. *Unus Instr:* Celesta, vibraphone, glockenspiel	1960			1					1									1									2	1		3	Unive
Mobile for Shakespeare *Voice:* Soprano or mezzo. *Unus Instr:* Celesta, vibraphone									1																		3	1		2	Unive
Rounds *Unus Instr:* Vibraphone	1969		2		1	1			1						1			1									1			1	Unive
Streichquartett 2	1978			2	1	1																									Unive
Trio (Ricercari)	1950			1	1	1																									Unive
HAUER, JOSEF M. (1883–1959)																															
Kammermusik (January 24, 1957) *Unus Instr:* Bass clarinet	1957			2	1	1			1						1	1		1	1											1	Dobli
Zwölftonspiel (April 27, 1951) *Unus Instr:* Bass clarinet	1951			2	1	1			1						1			2	1											1	Dobli
Zwölftonspiel (June 15, 1957) Piano 4 hands. *Unus Instr:* Bass clarinet	1957			2	1	1			1						1	1		1	1											1	Dobli
Zwölftonspiel (July 26, 1957) *Unus Instr:* Bass clarinet	1957			2	1	1									1	1		1	1											1	Dobli
Zwölftonspiel (Aug. 17, 1957)	1957			2					1																						Dobli
Zwölftonspiel (Sept. 1957)	1957			1	1				1																						Dobli
Zwölftonspiel mit Zwölftonreihe *Comment:* Zwölftonreihe von W. Kammerländer	1948			2	1	1			1																						Dobli
HAUFRECHT, HERBERT (1909–)																															
Divertimento	1975		11	1		1			1			1																			AmCom
Fantasy for 4 on Haitian Themes	1973		13		1				1									1									1				AmCom
Piano Trio	1989		15		1	1			1																						AmCom
Trio	1985		17			1			1									1													AmCom
Whoa, Little Horses, and Other Pieces *Unus Instr:* Celesta	1947		6	2	1	1	1		1						1			1									1			1	AmCom
HAXTON, KENNETH (1919–)																															
Eclogue	1975		8	2	1	1										1															AmCom
HECHTEL, HERBERT (1937–)																															
Streichquartett 3 "retrouvent une scene lyrique"	1963			2	1	1																									Bosse
HEIDEN, BERNHARD (1910–)																															
Quintet	1952		16	2	1	1															1										AMP
Serenade	1910		24	1	1	1													1												AMP
Trio	1956			1		1			1																						AMP
HEIDER, WERNER (1930–)																															
Commission			10	1		1	1		1		1				1								1				2	B			Peter
Passatempo per 7 solisti	1967		13	1			1											1	1			1	1				1				Peter
Picasso-Musik	1966		10	1					1									1										M			Peter
Plan			6	6	3	2	1																								Peter

	Year Composed or Published	Key	Duration	Violin	Viola	Cello	Double Bass	Gamba	Piano	Harpsicord	Organ	Guitar	Harp	Recorder	Flute/Piccolo	Oboe	English Horn	Clarinet/Bass Clarinet	Bassoon/Contrabassoon	Saxophone	French Horn	Trumpet	Trombone	Bass Trombone	Tuba	Baritone	Percussion	Voice	Electronic Tape	Unusual Instruments	Publisher
HEIDER, WERNER *(continued)*																															
Pyramide for Igor Stravinsky			2	2	1	1	1		1				1		1	1		1	1		1	1	1				1				Peter
Pyramide for Igor Stravinsky (with harpsichord)			2	2	1	1	1			1			1		1	1		1	1		1	1	1				1				Peter
Strophen			9	2	1	1	1		1				1		1		1	2	1		1	1			1		2				Peter
HEILMAN, WILLIAM C. (1877–1946)																															
Trio, Op 7				1	1	1																									Press
HEILNER, IRWIN (1908–1991)																															
Badinerie *Unus Instr:* Cornetto, lute	1980		4					1				1																		2	AmCom
Capriccio *Unus Instr:* Cornetto, lute	1980		4					1				1																		2	AmCom
HEISS, JOHN (1938–)																															
Songs of Nature	1975		14	1	1	1									1			1										M			Boose
HELLER, DUANE L. (1951–)																															
Variations on a Theme of Paganini	1978		22	1	1	1				1					1			1													AmCom
HELLERMANN, WILLIAM (1939–)																															
Columbus Circle *** *Comment:* For piano, and any 3 woodwinds	1971		25						1																						AmCom
HELLMESBERGER, JOSEPH (1855–1907)																															
Romanze, Op 43 No. 2				4					1																						Dobli
HELM, EVERETT (1913–)																															
String Quartet No. 2				2	1	1																									BoteB
HELPS, ROBERT (1928–)																															
Postlude (No. 3 of Serenade)	1948		8	1					1												1										AmCom
Quintet	1975		13	1		1			1						1			1													AmCom
Serenade in 3 Movements	1964		23	2	1	1			1												1										AmCom
Trio	1957		12		1	1			1																						AmCom
HEMPEL, ROLF (1932–)																															
Movimento	1966														1	1		1	1		1										Bosse
HENGARTNER, MAX (?–)																															
Little Suite for String Quartet				2	1	1																									Kunze
HENNING, ERVIN A. (1910–)																															
Badinage															1	1		1	1												Press
HENRIQUES, FINI V. (1867–1940)																															
Quartet	1936	a		2	1	1																									Hanse
HENZE, HANS W.. (1926–)																															
Kammermusik 1958	1958			2	1	1			1									1	1		1							T			BScho
Kammer-Sonate 1948	1948			1		1			1																						BScho
Quattro fantasie (Octet)	1958			2	1	1	1											1	1		1										BScho
Quintett	1952														1	1		1	1		1										BScho
Streichquartett 1	1947			2	1	1																									BScho
Streichquartett 2	1952			2	1	1																									BScho
HERCHET, JÖRG (1943–)																															
Komposition	1978								1						1	1		1	1		1										DeutV
HERRMANN, HUGO (1896–1967)																															
Streichquartett 3 (Der Frühling), Op 101	1956		20	2	1	1																									Sikor
HERRMANN, PETER (1941–)																															
Klavierquintett				2	1	1			1																						DeutV
Streichquartett	1964			2	1	1																									DeutV
Trio No. 2	1972			1		1			1																						DeutV

	Year Composed or Published	Key	Duration	Violin	Viola	Cello	Double Bass	Gamba	Piano	Harpsicord	Organ	Guitar	Harp	Recorder	Flute/Piccolo	Oboe	English Horn	Clarinet/Bass Clarinet	Bassoon/Contrabassoon	Saxophone	French Horn	Trumpet	Trombone	Bass Trombone	Tuba	Baritone	Percussion	Voice	Electronic Tape	Unusual Instruments	Publisher
HERSCHMANN, HEINZ (1924–)																															
Meditations																						4	2	1							Kunze
HERTEL, THOMAS (?–)																															
Imitations for String Quartet				2	1	1																									Peter
HERVIG, RICHARD (1917–)																															
Chamber Music for 6 Players *Unus Instr:* Bass clarinet	1976		11	1			1		1						1			1									1			1	AMP
HERZOGENBERG, HEINRICH (1834–1900)																															
Klavierquartett, Op Post.				1	1	1			1																						Kunze
HESPOS, HANS-JOACHIM (1938–)																															
einander-bedingendes *Unus Instr:* Tenor saxophone	1966				1							1			1			1		1										1	Bosse
HESS, ERNST (1912–1968)																															
Bassethorn Quartet *Unus Instr:* Basset horn				1	1	1																								1	Amade
HESS, WILLY (1859–1939)																															
Divertimento, Op 82				1	1										1																Amade
Quintet, Op 63 *Unus Instr:* Contrabassoon				2	1	1													1											1	Amade
Quintet, Op 95 *Unus Instr:* Basset horn. May be replaced by clarinet				1	1	1	1																							1	Amade
Serenade for 11 Instruments, Op 19				2	1	1									1	1		1	2		2										Amade
Trio, Op 75																		2	1												Amade
Trio, Op 76				1	1	1																									Amade
HESSENBERG, KURT (1908–)																															
Sieben Leben möcht ich haben, Op 64 *Comment:* Flute may replace violin	1955			1	1	1								1														A			Bären
Variationen-Suite, Op 86			15	2	1	1	1									1		1	1		1										Breit
HEUGTEN, H. VAN (?–)																															
Music for Brass																						2	1		1						Harmo
Music for Brass (alt. vers.)																					1	1			1						Harmo
Quartet																		1		3											Harmo
HEYN, VOLKER (1938–)																															
Nachtschicht	1982		17			1	1																				3				Breit
Phryh			11	3	2	2	1		1																						Breit
Rozs	1983		7	1	1	1														1		1	1								Breit
HIBBARD, WILLIAM (1939–)																															
Gestures *Unus Instr:* Marimba	1963		7				1								1												1			1	AmCom
Pieces (4) *Unus Instr:* Vibraphone	1962		7	1			1		1						1			1			1		1				1			1	AmCom
Stabiles for 13 Instruments *Unus Instr:* Vibraphone	1969		8	1	1	1	1		1				1		2			2				1	1				1			1	AMP
HIDALGO, MANUEL (1956–)																															
Hacia *Unus Instr:* Timpani	1980			2	1	1																					1			1	Breit
La inercia y la mierda *Unus Instr:* Timpani	1981		16	2	2	2												3									3			1	Breit
L'Obvio	1983		12	1	1	1	1								1			2									2				Breit
Seguirizas d'Estutgar					1	1	1																								Breit
HILLER, Jr., LEJAREN (1924–)																															
String Quartet No. 7			25	2	1	1																									Peter
HILLIARD, JOHN S. (1947–)																															
Menhir	1982		15						1													1					1				AmCom
Samadhi *Unus Instr:* Bass clarinet	1979		9	2	1	1									1		1	2									4			1	AmCom

	Year Composed or Published	Key	Duration	Violin	Viola	Cello	Double Bass	Gamba	Piano	Harpsicord	Organ	Guitar	Harp	Recorder	Flute/Piccolo	Oboe	English Horn	Clarinet/Bass Clarinet	Bassoon/Contrabassoon	Saxophone	French Horn	Trumpet	Trombone	Bass Trombone	Tuba	Baritone	Percussion	Voice	Electronic Tape	Unusual Instruments	Publisher
HINDEMITH, PAUL (1895–1963)																															
Die junge Magd (Six Poems), Op 23 No. 2	1922			2	1	1									1			1										A			BScho
Kammermusik 2 ***, Op 36 No. 1 *Comment:* And 12 instruments	1924								1																						BScho
Kammermusik 3 ***, Op 36 No. 2 *Comment:* And 10 instruments	1925					1																									BScho
Klavierquintett, Op 7	1917			2	1	1			1																						BScho
Kleine Kammermusik, Op 24 No. 2	1922														1	1		1	1		1										BScho
Melancholie, Op 13	1918			2	1	1																						A			BScho
Minimax (Parody)	1923			2	1	1																									BScho
Oktett	1958			1	2	1	1											1	1		1										BScho
Quartet	1938			1		1			1									1													BScho
Quintett, Op 30	1923			2	1	1												1													BScho
Die Serenaden (A Cantata), Op 35	1925				1	1										1												S			BScho
Streichquartett, Op 2	1915	C		2	1	1																									BScho
Streichquartett 1, Op 10	1919	f		2	1	1																									BScho
Streichquartett 2, Op 16	1921	C		2	1	1																									BScho
Streichquartett 3, Op 22	1922			2	1	1																									BScho
Streichquartett 4, Op 32	1923			2	1	1																									BScho
Streichtrio 1, Op 34	1924			1	1	1																									BScho
Streichtrio 2	1933			1	1	1																									BScho
String Quartet No. 5	1943	E♭		2	1	1																									AMP
String Quartet No. 6	1946			2	1	1																									BScho
Stücke (3) für 5 *** *Comment:* 5 instruments	1925																														BScho
Des Todes Tod, Op 23 No. 1	1922				2	2																						F			BScho
Trio, Op 47 *Unus Instr:* Heckelphone	1928				1				1																					1	BScho
HIRSCH, HANS L. (1937–)																															
Aubade, Gigue, and Nocturne			10	2	1	1	1						1		1	1															Peter
HLOBIL, EMIL (1901–)																															
Quartetto, Op 23 *Comment:* Piano may replace harpsichord	1943			1	1	1				1																					Hudeb
HODDINOTT, ALUN (1929–)																															
Divertimento	1963															1		1	1		1										Oxfor
Divertimento for 8 Instruments	1968			1	1	1	1								1			1	1		1										Oxfor
Nocturnes and Cadenzas				1		1												1													Oxfor
Quintet	1972			2	1	1			1																						Oxfor
Ritornelli (solo trombone)	1974														1	1		2	1		1	1	1								Oxfor
Ritornelli II	1974																				1	2	1								Oxfor
Roman Dream									1				1														3	S			Oxfor
Scena				2	1	1																									Oxfor
Septet	1956			1	1	1			1									1	1		1										Oxfor
Sextet	1960			1	1	1									1			1	1												Oxfor
String Quartet No. 1	1966			2	1	1																									Oxfor
Variations	1962			2	1	1							1		1			1													Oxfor
HODKINSON, SYDNEY (1934–)																															
Echo Preludes *Unus Instr:* 2 Euphoniums, 2 flügelhorns			18			1															4	4	3		1					4	AMP
Elegia in tempore belli *Unus Instr:* Timpani	1984		15				1														1	2	1		1		1			1	AmCom
Hidden Cave (Nuevas Canciones, Bk I)	1982		18	2	1	1															1						1	L			AMP
Papillons	1984		20		1								1		1																AmCom
Poems (2, for solo cello)	1989		22			1			1																		1				AmCom

	Year Composed or Published	Key	Duration	Violin	Viola	Cello	Double Bass	Gamba	Piano	Harpsicord	Organ	Guitar	Harp	Recorder	Flute/Piccolo	Oboe	English Horn	Clarinet/Bass Clarinet	Bassoon/Contrabassoon	Saxophone	French Horn	Trumpet	Trombone	Bass Trombone	Tuba	Baritone	Percussion	Voice	Electronic Tape	Unusual Instruments	Publisher
HODKINSON, SYDNEY *(continued)*																															
Sea Hours (Nuevas Canciones, Bk II)	1982		20			8							1															H			AMP
Sonata, Das Lebewohl	1984		25		1	1			1																						AmCom
Stanzas (Nine Miniatures)	1959		12		1	1			1																						AmCom
The Steps of Time (solo cello)	1984		15	2	1	1																					1				AmCom
The Steps of Time (with solo trombone)	1984		15	2	1																		1				1				AmCom
String Trio (alla marcia)	1983		20	1	1	1																									AMP
Trinity *** *Comment:* For any 3 treble instruments	1972		7																												AmCom
HOERE, ARTHUR (1897–1979)																															
Septet			10	2	1	1			1						1													F			Eschi
HOFFER, BERNARD (?–)																															
The River			30																	4							1				Schir
HOFFMANN, ERNST (1776–1822)																															
Trio	1809	E		1		1			1																						DeutV
HOIBY, LEE (1926–)																															
Overture: To a Song, Op 48	1988		6	1	1	1			1							1															Schir
Sextet	1974		20						1						1	1		1	1		1										Schir
HOLLANDER, BENNOIT (1853–1942)																															
Quatuor, 2e, Op 30				2	1	1																									Duran
HÖLLER, KARL (1907–1987)																															
Chamber Concerto for Harpsichord, Op 19	1958		17	1	1	1	1			1					1	1															Leuck
Concerto for Organ, Op 15 *Unus Instr:* Timpani	1966		28			1	1				1										2	2	2		1		1			1	Leuck
Piano Quartet				1	1	1			1																						Peter
Piano Trio			32	1		1			1																						Peter
Streichquartett 6, Op 51	1957	e	30	2	1	1																									Sikor
HÖLLER, YORK (1944–)																															
Antiphon	1976		13	2	1	1																							1		Breit
Arcus	1978		20	2	1	1	1		1		1				1		1	2	2		1	1	1				2		1		Breit
HOLLOWAY, ROBIN (1934–)																															
Aria, Op 44 *Comment:* Oboe doubles on English horn	1980		17	2	1	1	1		1						1	1	1	1	1		1	1	1				1				Boose
Brass Quintet (Divertimento No. 5), Op 67	1987																				1	2	1		1						Boose
Concertino No. 3, Op 29	1975		9	2											1			1	1	1	1	1	1				2				Boose
Conundrums (Divertimento No. 4), Op 33b	1979		17												1	1		1	1		1							S			Boose
Divertimento No. 2 (Wind Nonet), Op 18	1972		15												1	1	1	2	2		2										Boose
Evening with Angels, Op 17 *Unus Instr:* Celesta	1983		25	2	1	1	1								2	1	1	2	1		1	1	1	1			1			1	Boose
Fantasy-Pieces, Op 16	1971		28	2	1	1	1		1						2	1		1	1		1	1									Boose
Garden Music, Op 1	1982		18	1		1			1						1	1		1	1		1						1				Boose
Music for "Sweeney Agonistes", Op 4 *Voices:* Speakers in the play. Clarinet doubles on sax	1965		8												1			1		1		1	1				2	4			Boose
Nursery Rhymes (Divertimento No. 3), Op 33a	1977		25												1	1		1	1		1							S			Boose
Poems (3) of William Epson, Op 3 *Comment:* Clarinet doubles on sax	1965		20				1			1					1			1		1							7				Boose

	Year Composed or Published	Key	Duration	Violin	Viola	Cello	Double Bass	Gamba	Piano	Harpsicord	Organ	Guitar	Harp	Recorder	Flute/Piccolo	Oboe	English Horn	Clarinet/Bass Clarinet	Bassoon/Contrabassoon	Saxophone	French Horn	Trumpet	Trombone	Bass Trombone	Tuba	Baritone	Percussion	Voice	Electronic Tape	Unusual Instruments	Publisher
HOLLOWAY, ROBIN *(continued)*																															
Rivers of Hell, Op 34 Oboe doubles on English horn. *Unus Instr:* Xylophone, vibraphone	1977		31		1	1			1						1	1	1	1									1			2	Boose
Serenade, Op 41	1979	C	24	2	1	1	1											1	1		1										Boose
Serenade, Op 57	1983	E♭	20	2	1	1	1								1	1		1	1		1										Boose
Serenade, Op 64	1986	G	12	2	2	2	1																								Boose
Showpiece (Concertino No. 4), Op 53	1983		8	2	1	1	1		1						1	1		1	1		1	1	1				1				Boose
HOLST, GUSTAV (1874–1934)																															
Wind Quintet, Op 14	1903	A♭													1	1		1	1		1										Faber
HOLST, IMOGEN (1907–1984)																															
String Quintet	1982			2	2	1																									Faber
HOLSTEIN, JEAN-PAUL (1939–)																															
Peut être . . . le jour (Hommage à Ravel)				2	1	1																									Leduc
HOLTEN, BO (1948–)																															
Venetian Rhapsody	1974		10	2	1	1									1	1			1		1	3	2								Hanse
HONEGGER, ARTHUR (1892–1955)																															
Chansons (3) (La petite sirene)	1924		3	2	1	1																						1			Salab
Concerto da camera									1						1		1														Salab
Contrepoints (3)	1923			1		1									1		1														Hanse
Quatuor à cordes	1917			2	1	1																									Eschi
Quatuor à cordes	1936			2	1	1																									Salab
Quatuor à cordes	1937			2	1	1																									Salab
Rhapsodie	1917			2	1				1																						Salab
HOPKINS, JOHN (1949–)																															
13 Ways of Looking at a Blackbird *Unus Instr:* Celesta	1978		21	1	1	1				1			1				1										1			1	Schir
Allelujah	1980		4	1		1			1									1									1				Schir
Angelus *Unus Instr:* 2 Euphoniums	1980		20																		2	4	4		2		1			2	Schir
Cantilever *Unus Instr:* Bass clarinet			20	1	1	1			1						1		1	1			1									1	Schir
Cloud of Unknowing *Unus Instr:* Celesta	1978		23	1		1			1						1			1									1			1	Schir
For the Far Journey	1981			1		1				1					1			1										S			Schir
Fuga canonica *Unus Instr:* Bass clarinet	1981		5	1		1				1					1			1												1	Schir
Noche oscura *Unus Instr:* Bass clarinet	1976		15		1	1						1			1			1										S		1	Schir
Ra *** *Comment:* Flexible instrumentation	1979		5																												Schir
Round	1974		8		1	1			1						1			1													Schir
Se la face ay pale *Unus Instr:* Bass clarinet	1977		9	1		1									1			1									1			1	Schir
Stone Circle	1981		25	1		1									1			1									1				Schir
HORNE, DAVID (1970–)																															
Splintered Unisons	1988		11	1		1			1									1													Boose
String Quartet	1988		10	2	1	1																									Boose
towards dharma . . .	1989		17		1	1			1						1	1											1				Boose
HOROVITZ, JOSEPH (1926–)																															
Music Hall Suite																					1	2	1		1						Novel
HORVATH, JOSEF M. (1931–)																															
4 Songs *Voice:* Soprano or tenor			9		1	1									1			1										1			Peter
Redundanz 1 (for Wind Octet)																2		2	2		2										Dobli

	Year Composed or Published	Key	Duration	Violin	Viola	Cello	Double Bass	Gamba	Piano	Harpsicord	Organ	Guitar	Harp	Recorder	Flute/Piccolo	Oboe	English Horn	Clarinet/Bass Clarinet	Bassoon/Contrabassoon	Saxophone	French Horn	Trumpet	Trombone	Bass Trombone	Tuba	Baritone	Percussion	Voice	Electronic Tape	Unusual Instruments	Publisher
HORVATH, JOSEF M. *(continued)*																															
Redundanz 2 (for String Quartet)				2	1	1																									Dobli
Redundanz 3 (Wind Octet and String Quartet) *Comment:* Players double on English horn, bass clarinet, contrabassoon				2	1	1										2	1	2	2		2									2	Dobli
HOUDY, PIERICK (?–)																															
Divertissement									1												1	1									Leduc
HOVHANESS, ALAN (1911–)																															
Bacchanale, Op 203A *Unus Instr:* 2 Vibraphones, glockenspiel, chimes, giant tamtam			4																								5			5	Peter
Bagatelles (4) for String Quartet, Op 30			6	2	1	1																									Peter
The Burning House Overture, Op 185A			5												1												4				Peter
Canzona and Fugue, Op 72			5																		1	2	1								Peter
Canzona and Fugue (alt. inst.), Op 72			5																		1	2			1						Peter
Consolations (2), Op 232				2	1	1																									Peter
Dance of Black-Haired Mountain Storm, Op 183A *Unus Instr:* Xylophone			5												1												3			1	Peter
Dances (6), Op 79	1967		7																		1	2	1		1						Peter
Divertimento, Op 61 No. 5			12													1		1	1		1										Peter
Fantasies (5) for Brass Choir, Op 70			15																		1	2	1		1						Peter
The Flowering Peach, Op 125 *Unus Instr:* Celesta, timpani, tam-tam, vibraphone, glockenspiel			19										1					1		1							4			5	AMP
Hanna, Op 101 *Comment:* Piano 4-hands			10						2									2													Peter
Khaldis. Concerto for Piano, Op 91 *Comment:* With 4 trumpets, or any multiples of 4			18						1													4					1				RKing
Koke No Niwa (Moss Garden), Op 181	1954		7										1				1										2				Peter
Koke No Niwa (Moss Garden, alt. inst.), Op 181	1954		7										1					1									2				Peter
Mountains and Rivers Without End, Op 225 *Unus Instr:* Timpani			25										1		1	1		1				1	1				4				Peter
Mysterious Horse Before the Gate, Op 205			3																				1				5				Peter
October Mountain, Op 135 *Unus Instr:* Glockenspiel, 2 marimbas, timpani, tam-tam			11																								6			5	Peter
Orbit No. 1, Op 92 No. 1 *Unus Instr:* Celesta	1952		4										1		1												2			1	Peter
Piano Quintet, Op 9	1962		10	2	1	1			1																						Peter
Piano Quintet No. 2, Op 109	1964		15	2	1	1			1																						Peter
Piano Trio, Op 3	1935	e	9	1		1			1																						Peter
Quartet No. 1, Op 97			8			1				1					1	1															Peter
Quartet No. 2, Op 112			14			1			1						1	1															Peter
Requiem and Resurrection, Op 224			15																		4	2	3		1		4				Peter
Saturn, Op 243			25						1									1										S			Peter
Sextet, Op 108	1966		15	1																							5				Peter
Sextet, Op 164			10	2	1	1				1				1																	Peter
Sharagan and Fugue, Op 58																					1	2	1			1					RKing

	Year Composed or Published	Key	Duration	Violin	Viola	Cello	Double Bass	Gamba	Piano	Harpsicord	Organ	Guitar	Harp	Recorder	Flute/Piccolo	Oboe	English Horn	Clarinet/Bass Clarinet	Bassoon/Contrabassoon	Saxophone	French Horn	Trumpet	Trombone	Bass Trombone	Tuba	Baritone	Percussion	Voice	Electronic Tape	Unusual Instruments	Publisher
HOVHANESS, ALAN *(continued)*																															
Sonata, Op 130			10								1					2															Peter
String Quartet No. 1, Op 8	1936		13	2	1	1																									Peter
String Quartet No. 2, Op 147	1950		12	2	1	1																									Peter
String Quartet No. 3, Op 208 No. 1	1968		10	2	1	1																									Peter
String Quartet No. 4, Op 208 No. 2	1970			2	1	1																									Peter
String Trio, Op 201	1962		6	1	1	1																									Peter
Suite, Op 99 *Unus Instr:* Celesta, tam-tam, xylophone			15	1					1																		1			3	Peter
Symphony for Metal Orchestra			23												6								3				5				Peter
Tower Music (Suite), Op 129			10												1	1		1	1		2	1	1		1						Rongw
Upon Enchanted Ground, Op 90 No. 1 *Unus Instr:* Tam-tam			4			1							1		1												1			1	Peter
Vibration Painting, Op 226	1969		12	7	3	2	1																								Peter
Wind Quintet, Op 159	1960		17												1	1		1	1		1										Peter
The World Beneath the Sea (I), Op 133 No. 1 *Unus Instr:* Vibraphone			10										1							1							3			1	Peter
The World Beneath the Sea (II), Op 133 No. 2 *Unus Instr:* Timpani; bells, chimes, or glockenspiel			15				1						1					1									2			2	Peter
HOWARTH, ELGAR (1935–)																															
English Dances of the 16th Century																					1	2	1		1						Novel
Variations for Brass Quintet																					1	2	1		1						Novel
HOWE, MARY (1882–1964)																															
Elegiaca	1941			1		1			1																						IIMus
HRABOVSKY, LEONID (1935–)																															
Concerto misterioso *Unus Instr:* Crotales	1977		17	1	1	1				1			1		1			1	1								1			1	VAAP
Constanti			14	1					4																		6				VAAP
Kogda (When)			18	5		4	4		1									1									1	M			VAAP
HUBEAU, JEAN (1917–)																															
Sonatine									1						1			1			1										Billa
HUBER, HANS (1852–1921)																															
Senfkom	1975			1	1	1				1						1												S			Sikor
HUBER, KLAUS (1924–)																															
Auf die ruhige Nachtzeit	1958				1	1									1													S			Bären
Kleine Meditationen, 3 *Comment:* From "Kleine deutsche Messe"	1969			1	1	1							1																		Bären
Moteti-Cantiones	1963			2	1	1																									BScho
Sätze (3) in zwei Teilen	1959														1	1		1	1		1										Bären
HUBER, NICOLAUS A. (1939–)																															
Chronogramm	1966			1		1			1									1													Bosse
Demi jour	1985		16			1			1							1															Breit
La force du vertige	1985		16	1		1			1						1			1									1				Breit
Mimus	1965								1												2	2	2		1		2				Bosse
Streichquartett (Informationen über e-f)	1966			2	1	1																									Bären
von . . . bis . . . *Unus Instr:* Harmonium	1966				1				1		1																1			1	Bären
HUEBLER, KLAUS K. (1956–)																															
Feuerzauber	1981		6			1							1		3																Breit
Streichquartett 3	1982		13	2	1	1																									Breit
HUFSCHMIDT, WOLFGANG (1934–)																															
Alt-testamentliche Spruche (3)	1965				1										1													S			Bären
Exercitien III (Das Prinzip Hoffnung) *Comment:* Alternate insts: Harpsichord or organ; tuba	1976			1					1						1						1						1	M			Bären

	Year Composed or Published	Key	Duration	Violin	Viola	Cello	Double Bass	Gamba	Piano	Harpsicord	Organ	Guitar	Harp	Recorder	Flute/Piccolo	Oboe	English Horn	Clarinet/Bass Clarinet	Bassoon/Contrabassoon	Saxophone	French Horn	Trumpet	Trombone	Bass Trombone	Tuba	Baritone	Percussion	Voice	Electronic Tape	Unusual Instruments	Publisher
HUFSCHMIDT, WOLFGANG *(continued)*																															
Ich stehe an deiner Krippen hier *Voices:* Soprano and tenor	1960			2		1																						2			Bären
Trio 3 *Voice:* Speaker	1977											3				3												1			Bären
Verwandlungen	1969			2	1	1																									Bären
HUGGLER, JOHN (1928–)																															
Bittere Nüsse			9	1	1	1									1			1										S			Peter
Capriccio sregolato *Unus Instr:* Bass clarinet			10	1	1	1			1						1			1												1	Peter
Music for 13 Instruments, Op 75			6			1									2	1		3	2		2	1	1								Peter
Music in Two Parts, Op 63			6	1			1		1						1			2				2					2				Peter
HUGHES, MARK (1934–)																															
Divertimento																					1	1	1								Press
HUGON, GEORGES (1904–1980)																															
Quatuor à cordes				2	1	1																									Duran
HUMEL, GERALD (1931–)																															
Flashes *Unus Instr:* Celesta	1968		9	1	1	1	1		1				1		3	1		2			1	1	1				1			1	BoteB
Temno for Violoncello and Ensemble	1969		16	1	1	1	1		1				1		1	1		1	1		1	1	1								BoteB
HUMMEL, JOHANN N. (1778–1837)																															
Quintett, Op 87				1	1	1	1		1																						Kunze
String Trio *Comment:* Violin may replace 1 viola		E♭			2	1																									Peter
String Trio *Comment:* Violin may replace 1 viola		G			2	1																									Peter
Trio, Op 78						1			1						1																Kunze
HUPFER, KONRAD (1935–)																															
Streichquartett	1972			2	1	1																									Bosse
HURD, MICHAEL (1928–)																															
Harlequin Suite																					1	2	1		1						Novel
HUSA, KAREL (1921–)																															
Concerto	1965		25						1												1	2	1		1						AMP
Divertimento for Brass and Percussion	1958		15																		4	3	3		1		2				AMP
Divertimento for Brass Quintet	1968		16																		2	1	2								AMP
Evocations of Slovakia	1952		15		1	1												1													BScho
Fanfare for Brass and Percussion *Unus Instr:* Timpani	1980		6																		4	3	2	1	1		1			1	AMP
Intradas and Interlude	1980		18																			7					1				AMP
Landscapes for Brass Quintet	1977		22																		1	2	1		1						AMP
Preludes (2)	1966		12												1			1	1												Leduc
Recollections	1981		21						1						1	1		1	1		1										AMP
Serenade	1963		15						1						1	1		1	1		1										Leduc
Sonata a tre	1981		20	1					1									1													AMP
String Quartet	1943			2	1	1																									BScho
String Quartet No. 1	1948		18	2	1	1																									BScho
String Quartet No. 2	1954		20	2	1	1																									BScho
String Quartet No. 3	1968		19	2	1	1																									AMP
Variations	1984		21	1	1	1			1																						AMP
HUTCHESON, JERE (1938–)																															
Designs for Fourteen			10																		2	4	3		2		3				Peter
Nocturnes of the Inferno	1976		22	1					1									1													AmCom
IANNACCONE, ANTHONY (1943–)																															
Mythical Sketches (3)																					1				2	1					Press

	Year Composed or Published	Key	Duration	Violin	Viola	Cello	Double Bass	Gamba	Piano	Harpsicord	Organ	Guitar	Harp	Recorder	Flute/Piccolo	Oboe	English Horn	Clarinet/Bass Clarinet	Bassoon/Contrabassoon	Saxophone	French Horn	Trumpet	Trombone	Bass Trombone	Tuba	Baritone	Percussion	Voice	Electronic Tape	Unusual Instruments	Publisher
IBERT, JACQUES (1890–1962)																															
Aria				1					1						1																Leduc
Aria (arr. Hoeree) *Comment:* Oboe may replace flute									1						1			1													Leduc
Interludes (2) *Comment:* Harp may replace harpsichord				1						1					1																Leduc
Mouvements (2)	1923														2			1	1												Leduc
Mouvements (2, for alt. inst.)	1923														1	1		1	1												Leduc
Pièces brèves (3)	1930														1	1		1	1		1										Leduc
Quatuor à cordes	1944			2	1	1																									Leduc
Trio	1944			1		1							1																		Leduc
ICHIYANAGI, TOSHI (1933–)																															
Distance *Comment:* Score calls for Noh actor						1			1						1			1									1		1		Peter
Sapporo *** *Comment:* For up to 15 players, and any number of instruments																															Peter
Stanzas *** *Comment:* For any number of string instruments																															Peter
IMBRIE, ANDREW (1921–)																															
Dandelion Wine	1967		7	2	1	1			1							1		1													Shawn
Dream Sequence *Comment:* Oboe doubles on English horn. *Unus Instr:* Bass clarinet			17	1	1	1			1						1	1	1	1									1			1	Peter
Pilgrimage				1		1			1						1			1									1				Peter
Serenade	1952				1				1						1																Shawn
String Quartet No. 1	1942			2	1	1																									Shawn
String Quartet No. 2	1953			2	1	1																									Shawn
String Quartet No. 3	1957			2	1	1																									Shawn
String Quartet No. 4	1969			2	1	1																									Shawn
String Quartet No. 5	1987			2	1	1																									Shawn
To a Traveller	1971			1					1									1													Shawn
INDY, VINCENT D' (1851–1931)																															
Chansons et danses (Divertissement), Op 50	1899														1	1		2	2		1										Duran
Quatuor, Op 7	1878	a		1	1	1			1																						Duran
Quatuor à cordes, Op 35	1891			2	1	1																									Hamel
Quatuor à cordes, Op 45	1898			2	1	1																									Duran
Quatuor à cordes, Op 96	1929			2	1	1																									Heuge
Quintette, Op 81	1925	g		2	1	1			1																						Senar
Sextuor à cordes, Op 92	1928			2	2	2																									Heuge
Suite dans le style ancien, Op 24		D		2	1	1									2							1									Leduc
Suite en parties (obbligato flute), Op 61				1	1	1							1		1																Heuge
Trio, Op 29	1888					1			1									1													VarPb
Trio, Op 98	1929	G		1		1			1																						Salab
INGHELBRECHT, DÉSIRÉ E. (1880–1965)																															
Fanfares (4) *Unus Instr:* Timpani	1932																				4	3	3		1		2			1	Salab
Quatuor à cordes				2	1	1																									Duran
Quintette		c		2	1	1							1																		Leduc
IOACHIMESCU, CALIN (1949–)																															
Oratio II *Comment:* Each performer must have a wooden flute	1984		14												1	1		1			1	1	1				1				Salab
IOANNIDIS, YANNIS (1930–)																															
Actina	1969		10																		1	2	2								Breit

	Year Composed or Published	Key	Duration	Violin	Viola	Cello	Double Bass	Gamba	Piano	Harpsicord	Organ	Guitar	Harp	Recorder	Flute/Piccolo	Oboe	English Horn	Clarinet/Bass Clarinet	Bassoon/Contrabassoon	Saxophone	French Horn	Trumpet	Trombone	Bass Trombone	Tuba	Baritone	Percussion	Voice	Electronic Tape	Unusual Instruments	Publisher
IOANNIDIS, YANNIS *(continued)*																															
Actina (for Wind Quintet)	1969		10												1	1		1	1		1										Breit
IRELAND, JOHN (1879–1962)																															
Phantasie (Piano Trio No. 1)	1906	a		1		1			1																						ECSch
Piano Trio No. 2	1917			1		1			1																						ECSch
Piano Trio No. 3	1938	E	26	1		1			1																						Boose
String Quartet No. 1, Op Post.	1895	d	26	2	1	1																									Boose
String Quartet No. 2, Op Post.	1897	c	36	2	1	1																									Boose
ISRAEL, BRIAN M. (1951–)																															
Tower Music																					1	1	1								Press
ISTVAN, MILOSLAV (1928–)																															
Ritmi ed antiritmi	1966								2																		1				Artia
IVES, CHARLES (1874–1954)																															
Adagio cantabile (The Innate)	1908		3	2	1	1			1																						Peer
Adagio sostenuto (At Sea)			3	2	2	1			1																						Peer
Aeschylus and Sophocles			4	2	1	1			1																			1			Mercu
Allegretto sombroso (Incantation)			1	2	2	1			1																						Peer
From the Steeples and the Mountains *Unus Instr:* Chimes	1902		4						1													1	1				1			1	Peer
Hallowe'en				2	1	1			1																						Bomar
In re con moto et al			4	2	1	1			1																						Peer
Largo	1902			1					1									1													Peer
Largo risoluto No. 1			3	2	1	1			1																						Peer
Largo risoluto No. 2			2	2	1	1			1																						Peer
Let There Be Light			3								1												4								Peer
Let There Be Light (alt. vers.)			3	4							1																				Peer
Remembrance				2	2	1			1																						Peer
Scherzo				2	1	1																									Peer
Scherzo (All the Way Around and Back)	1907		2	2	2	1			1																						Peer
Scherzo (All the Way Around . . .) *Unus Instr:* Bugle, bells	1907			1					1						1												1			2	Peer
Scherzo (Over the Pavements) *Unus Instr:* Cymbal			5												1			1	1			1	3				2			1	Peer
The See'r (from Set No. 2) *Unus Instr:* Cornet	1908		3						1									1				1				1	1			1	AMP
Set	1914		26	2	1	1			1																						Peer
Song for the Harvest Season *Unus Instr:* Cornet			3				1				1											1						1		1	Mercu
String Quartet No. 1	1896		21	2	1	1																									Peer
String Quartet No. 2	1913		28	2	1	1																									Peer
Sunrise			6	1					1																			1			Peter
Trio	1911		13	1		1			1																						Peer
JACKSON, AMBROSE (?–)																															
Quatuor pour cuivres, No. 1																						2	2								Billa
JACOB, GORDON (1895–1984)																															
3 Songs of Innocence				1	1	1																						S			Oxfor
Divertimento		E♭														2		2	2		2										MusRa
Quintet No. 2															1	1		1	1		1										MusRa
Sextet									1						1	1		1	1		1										MusRa
Trio																1		1	1												MusRa
Trio					1				1									1													MusRa
JACOB, WERNER (1938–)																															
. . . sine nomine super nomina . . . *Unus Instr:* Timpani	1985		20								1																3			1	Breit
Telos Nomou (Das Ende des Gesetzes)	1970		11						1	1	1				1		1				1		1				3	N			Breit

	Year Composed or Published	Key	Duration	Violin	Viola	Cello	Double Bass	Gamba	Piano	Harpsicord	Organ	Guitar	Harp	Recorder	Flute/Piccolo	Oboe	English Horn	Clarinet/Bass Clarinet	Bassoon/Contrabassoon	Saxophone	French Horn	Trumpet	Trombone	Bass Trombone	Tuba	Baritone	Percussion	Voice	Electronic Tape	Unusual Instruments	Publisher
JACOBI, FREDERICK (1891–1952)																															
Quartet on Indian Themes				2	1	1																									Press
String Quartet No. 2				2	1	1																									Press
JADIN, LOUIS (1768–1853)																															
Nocturne No. 3		G													1			1	1		1										Kneus
JAHN, THOMAS (1940–)																															
Tango habañera (Violin Concerto) *Unus Instr:* Vibraphone	1977		16				1		1			1	1		1		1	1	1	1		1					2			1	Schir
JANÁČEK, LEOS (1854–1928)																															
Ave Maria *Voice:* Soprano or tenor			3	1					1																			1			Unive
Capriccio	1926								1						1							2	3		1						Artia
Concertino	1925			2	1				1									1	1		1										VarPb
Kinderreime (Rikadla) *Voice:* Just 1, or 6-9 soloists	1927		15		1				1																			1			Unive
Mladi (Youth) *Unus Instr:* Bass clarinet	1924														1	1		2	1		1									1	Artia
Rikadla (Kinderreime) *Unus Instr:* Ocarina, child's drum, piccolo, E♭ clarinet, contrabassoon	1925		15				1		1						2			2	2									9		5	Unive
Streichquartett 1	1923			2	1	1																									Artia
Streichquartett 2 ("Intimate Letters")	1928			2	1	1																									Artia
JAROCH, JIRI (1920–)																															
Nonett (Detska suita [Children's Suite])	1952			1	1	1	1								1	1		1	1		1										Artia
JARZEBSKI, ADAM (?–1649)																															
4 Canzoni																						2	2								Billa
JEKIMOWSKI, VIKTOR (1947–)																															
Komposition 7 (1970)	1970			2	1	1																									DeutV
JENEY, ZOLTAN (1943–)																															
Round	1972		11						1	1			1																		Boose
Twelve Songs			27	1					1																			F			Boose
JEREMIAS, OTAKAR (1892–1962)																															
Klavierquartett, Op 5	1911	e		1	1	1			1																						Artia
JETTEL, RUDOLF (1905–)																															
Bläserquintett															1	1		1	1		1										Dobli
Bläserquintett 3															1	1		1	1		1										Kunze
Streichquartett		C		2	1	1																									Dobli
Trio		c		1	1													1													Dobli
JIRAK, KAREL B. (1891–)																															
Klaviertrio, Op 89	1966			1		1			1																						Artia
Streichquartett 1, Op 9		c		2	1	1																									Artia
Streichquartett 3, Op 41				2	1	1																									Artia
JIRASEK, IVO (1920–)																															
Musik für Sopran, Flöte und Harfe													1		1													S			Artia
JOHNSON, A. P. (1955–)																															
Autumn Trio	1980		15			1			1						1																AmCom
Cento No. 2 *Unus Instr:* Marimba	1985		12						1						1	1		1	1		1	1	1				1			1	AmCom
Magic Mirage	1973		12	1			1		1						1			1	1	1		1	1		1		1				AmCom
Summer Trio	1985		12			1			1						1																AmCom
JOHNSON, DAVID N. (1922–)																															
Stücke (3)	1966			2	1	1																									Feedb
Triangles (3 Ringmodulationen)	1975					1									1			1													Feedb
JOHNSON, JAMES J. (1924–)																															
Diversions *Unus Instr:* Celesta, rhythm section			9										1										6				1			2	Peter

	Year Composed or Published	Key	Duration	Violin	Viola	Cello	Double Bass	Gamba	Piano	Harpsicord	Organ	Guitar	Harp	Recorder	Flute/Piccolo	Oboe	English Horn	Clarinet/Bass Clarinet	Bassoon/Contrabassoon	Saxophone	French Horn	Trumpet	Trombone	Bass Trombone	Tuba	Baritone	Percussion	Voice	Electronic Tape	Unusual Instruments	Publisher
JOHNSON, SHERLAW (1932–)																															
Quintet				1	1	1			1									1													Oxfor
String Quartet No. 2				2	1	1																									Oxfor
Triptych				1		1			1						1			1									2				Oxfor
JOLAS, BETSY (1926–)																															
D'un opéra de poupée *Unus Instr:* 2 Ondes Martenot, 4 electric keyboards, synthesizer	1982		19	1		1			1			1			1			1			1						1			7	Salab
O Wall (d'un opéra de poupée)	1989														1	1		1	1		1										Leduc
Plupart du temps II	1990					1														1								T			Leduc
Quatuor IV ("Menus propos")	1990			2	1	1																									Leduc
JOLIVET, ANDRÉ (1905–1974)																															
Alla rustica	1963		4										1		2																Boose
Chant de Linos (solo flute) *Comment:* Piano can substitute for harp				1	1	1							1		1																Leduc
Madrigal *Voices:* Soprano, alto, tenor, bass	1963				1										1		1		1									4			Boose
Messe pour le jour de la paix *Unus Instr:* Tambourine.	1940										1																1	1		1	Heuge
Pastorale de Noël	1949												1		1				1												Heuge
Pastorale de Noël (alt. vers.) *Comment:* Cello can substitute for viola	1949			1	1								1																		Heuge
Quatuor à cordes, Op 52	1934			2	1	1																									Heuge
Sérénade	1945														1	1		1	1		1										Billa
Suite liturgique	1942						1						1			1	1											1			Duran
Suite pour trio à cordes	1930			1	1	1																									Billa
Yin-Yang *** *Comment:* For 11 solo strings	1974																														EMTra
JONES, CHARLES (1910–)																															
Lyric Waltz Suite	1948		11												1	1		1	1												Peter
String Quartet No. 6	1970		15	2	1	1																									Peter
JONES, KELSEY (1922–)																															
Quintet for Winds	1968		14												1	1		1	1		1										Peter
Sonata da camera	1957		10							1					1	1															Peter
JONGEN, JOSEPH (1873–1953)																															
Quatuor, Op 23	1901	E♭		1	1	1			1																						Duran
Trio (Prélude, variations, et final), Op 30	1907			1	1				1																						Duran
JOPLIN, SCOTT (1868–1917)																															
7 Rags (arr. Zinn)				2	1	1	1																								Press
The Entertainer (arr. Beyer) Alt. Inst.: 3 Flutes for recorders; guitar for piano. Bass ad libitum.	1902								1					3																	Amade
The Strenuous Life Alt. inst.: 3 Flutes for recorders; guitar for piano. Bass ad libitum.									1					3																	Amade
JOSEPHS, WILFRED (1927–)																															
String Trio	1966			1	1	1																									Oxfor
Trio of Trios, Op 87	1974		24	1		1			1																						Boose
JOUBERT, CLAUDE H. (?–)																															
Partita				1	1	1									1	1															Billa
JULLIEN, RENÉ (?–)																															
Novelettes (4), Op 17	1914			2	1	1																									Simro
JUNG, HELGE (1943–)																															
Suite für Blechbläser, Op 5	1967																				1	2	1								DeutV

	Year Composed or Published	Key	Duration	Violin	Viola	Cello	Double Bass	Gamba	Piano	Harpsicord	Organ	Guitar	Harp	Recorder	Flute/Piccolo	Oboe	English Horn	Clarinet/Bass Clarinet	Bassoon/Contrabassoon	Saxophone	French Horn	Trumpet	Trombone	Bass Trombone	Tuba	Baritone	Percussion	Voice	Electronic Tape	Unusual Instruments	Publisher
JUNGK, KLAUS (1916–)																															
Alterationen				1		1			1																						Peter
KAGEL, MAURICIO (1931–)																															
Acustica (II)*** *Comment:* For 2-5 musicians and electronic tape	1970		75																										2		Unive
Acustica (III)*** *Comment:* For 2-5 instrumentalists	1970		25																												Unive
Aus dem Nachlass					1	1	1																								Peter
Exotica*** *Comment:* For 6 players and at least 60 non-European instruments, plus stereo tapes and loudspeakers	1972		50																												Unive
Kontra—Danse*** *Comment:* For 7 instrumentalists or singers	1970																														Unive
Marches (10) in Order to Miss Victory			10												1			1	1	1		1			1		1				Peter
Mare Nostrum *Voices:* Countertenor, baritone. Flute doubles on piccolo, oboe on English horn, guitar on mandolin and lute. Singers also play accordions.	1975		60			1						1	1		1	1	1										1	2		4	Unive
Musik aus Diaphonie*** *Comment:* For 6-10 singers and/or instrumentalists. Electronic tape ad libitum	1964		15																										1		Unive
Musik aus Tremens*** *Comment:* For 5 performers	1965		20																												Unive
Piano Trio				1		1			1																						Peter
Prince Igor, Stravinsky *Voice:* Bass			18		1												1				1				1		2	1			Peter
Der Schall*** *Comment:* For 5 players, and innumerable instruments	1968		40																												Unive
Sextett				2	2	2																									Unive
Sonant *Unus Instr:* 2 Membranophones			16				1					1	1														2			2	Peter
Streichquartett 1	1967			2	1	1																									Unive
Streichquartett 2				2	1	1																									Unive
Tango alemán *Unus Instr:* Bandoneon				1					1																			1		1	Peter
Unter Strom*** *Comment:* For 3 performers			30																												Unive
Variété *Unus Instr:* Accordion			60			1			1		1							1		1		1					1			1	Peter
KAHN, ERICH I. (1905–1956)																															
Actus tragicus	1946		13	2	1	1	1								1	1		1	1		1										AmCom
Divertimento	1927		5	1						1					1																AmCom
Triple Concerto	1955		7		1	1			1																						AmCom
KAHOWEZ, GÜNTER (1940–)																															
Bläserquintett 2, Op 52															1	1		1	1		1										Dobli
Streichquartett 1	1960			2	1	1																									Dobli
Structures pour 6 instruments									1						1	1		1	1		1										Dobli
KALMAR, LASZLO (1931–)																															
Morfeo	1977		5	2	1	1																									EMBud
KALOMIRIS, MANOLIS (1883–1962)																															
Piano Trio, Op 22				1		1			1																						Salab
KANITZ, ERNST (1894–1978)																															
Notturno	1950			1	1										1																Valle

	Year Composed or Published	Key	Duration	Violin	Viola	Cello	Double Bass	Gamba	Piano	Harpsicord	Organ	Guitar	Harp	Recorder	Flute/Piccolo	Oboe	English Horn	Clarinet/Bass Clarinet	Bassoon/Contrabassoon	Saxophone	French Horn	Trumpet	Trombone	Bass Trombone	Tuba	Baritone	Percussion	Voice	Electronic Tape	Unusual Instruments	Publisher
KAPLAN, ELLIOTT (?–)																															
Suite for Woodwind Trio															1			1	1												Press
KAPR, JAN (1914–)																															
Barvy tichka (Farben der Stille)	1973			1	1	1	1			1					1	1			1												Bären
Rotazione 9	1967			1	1	1			1																						Artia
KARCHIN, LOUIS S. (1951–)																															
Capriccio (solo violin) *Unus Instr:* Bass clarinet	1977		11	1	1	1			1						1	1		1												1	AmCom
Trio	1972		10			1			1						1																AmCom
KARKOSCHKA, ERHARD (1923–)																															
Psylex	1968														1													M	1		Bosse
KARLINS, M. W. (1932–)																															
Catena II *Unus Instr:* Flügelhorn	1981		14																	1	1	1	1		1					1	AmCom
Celebration	1970		8							1					1	1															AmCom
Fanfare with Fugato (solo amplified cello) *Unus Instr:* Amplified cello	1981		4			1																2	2							1	AmCom
Fantasy and Passacaglia	1961		10		1		1								1						1										AmCom
Music *Unus Instr:* Bass clarinet	1966		7						1							1		1												1	AmCom
Saxtuper	1989		9																	1					1		1				AmCom
Trio	1960		12	1		1									1																AmCom
Variations	1963		9	1	1	1												1													AmCom
Variations on obiter dictum	1965		11			1			1																		1				AmCom
KATZER, GEORG (1935–)																															
Divertissement à trois *** *Comment:* For strings or winds, and keyboard	1969																														DeutV
Kommen und Gehen	1981								1						1	1		1	1		1										DeutV
Lieder nach Leising *Voice:* Male	1983					1			1						1			1									1	1			DeutV
Streichmusik I	1971			7	3	2	2																								Peter
Streichmusik II	1972		14	11	3	3	1																								Peter
Streichquartett 1	1966			2	1	1																									DeutV
KAUER, FERDINAND (1751–1831)																															
New Hungarian Dances (12)				2			1																								Dobli
KAUFFMANN, JEAN (?–)																															
Quintettino															1	1		1	1		1										Billa
KAUFMAN, FREDRICK (1936–)																															
A Bud for Bloom	1988		10						1						1	1															AmCom
Concerto for Clarinet	1987		15	2	2	1												1													AmCom
Seascape *Unus Instr:* Celesta	1985		10	8		3	2						1														4			1	AmCom
KAUFMANN, ARMIN (1902–1980)																															
Drosser Trio, Op 101				1					1						1																Dobli
Klaviertrio, Op 57 No. 2				1		1			1																						Dobli
Streichquartett 4, Op 17				2	1	1																									Dobli
Streichquartett 4 (trans.), Op 17				1	1	1									1																Dobli
Streichquartett 6, Op 81				2	1	1																									Dobli
Suite, Op 93				3					1																						Dobli
Trio, Op 60				1	1	1																									Dobli
KAUFMANN, SERGE (?–)																															
Triade															1	1		1													Billa
KAUN, HUGO (1863–1932)																															
Quintet for Piano and Strings, Op 39	1902	f		2	1	1			1																						Rahte
KEATS, DONALD (1929–)																															
String Quartet No. 1	1951			2	1	1																									Boose
String Quartet No. 2	1965			2	1	1																									Boose

	Year Composed or Published	Key	Duration	Violin	Viola	Cello	Double Bass	Gamba	Piano	Harpsicord	Organ	Guitar	Harp	Recorder	Flute/Piccolo	Oboe	English Horn	Clarinet/Bass Clarinet	Bassoon/Contrabassoon	Saxophone	French Horn	Trumpet	Trombone	Bass Trombone	Tuba	Baritone	Percussion	Voice	Electronic Tape	Unusual Instruments	Publisher
KELDORFER, ROBERT (1901–1980)																															
Musik für 5 Bläser															1	1		1	1		1										Dobli
Ricordo di Faedis *Unus Instr:* Bass clarinet, basset horn																		3												2	Dobli
Trio															1			1	1												Dobli
KELEMEN, MILKO (1924–)																															
Entrances	1966		10																		2	2	1								Peter
Entrances (Woodwind Quintet)	1966		12												1	1		1	1		1										Peter
Epitaph *Unus Instr:* Vibraphone			6		1																						3	M		1	Peter
Motion	1968		12	2	1	1																									Peter
Musik für Heissenbüttel			5	1		1			1									1										M			Peter
Radiant *Unus Instr:* Celesta	1961		12		1				1				1		1												1			1	Peter
Splintery				2	1	1																									Peter
Surprise			6	7	3	3	1																								Peter
Varia Melodia	1972		14	2	1	1																									Peter
KELLER, HOMER (1915–)																															
Declaration	1966		9		1	1			1																						AmCom
Interplay	1970		11												1						1						1				AmCom
Reduktion	1974					1				1					1																Hug
KELLY, BRYAN G. (1934–)																															
Fanfares and Sonatina																					2	2	2								Novel
Suite Parisienne																					1	2	1		1						Novel
KELLY, ROBERT (1917–)																															
Concerto	1960		24		1	1			1																						AmCom
Concerto (solo viola), Op 53	1976		22		1				1																		1				AmCom
Fantasia (solo harp), Op 62	1984		16	2	1	1							1		1	1															AmCom
Fluctuations *Unus Instr:* Timpani	1973		21								1										4	4	3		1		3			1	AmCom
Introduction and Dialogue	1951		8			1			1												1										AmCom
Quintet for Clarinet and Strings	1956		13	2	1	1												1													AmCom
Theme and Variations (Nobody Knows de Trouble)	1947		14	1	1				1																						AmCom
Variant, Op 45	1967		8		1	1			1																						AmCom
KELTERBORN, RUDOLF (1931–)																															
5 Fantasien	1958					1				1					1																Bären
6 Short Pieces	1984				1							1			1																BoteB
Consort Music	1975		9	1	1	1	1								1			1									1	S			BoteB
Fantasie a tre	1967			1		1			1																						Bären
Kammermusik für fünf Bläser *Comment:* Flute doubles on piccolo	1974														1	1		1	1		1										Bären
Kana/Auferstehung *Subtitle:* Zwei Gesänge nach Herbert Meier	1964			2							1																	B			Bären
Lyrische Kammermusik	1959			1	1													1													Bären
Oktett	1969			2	1	1	1											1	1		1										BoteB
Sonata sacra	1966																				3	3	3		1						Bären
Streichquartett 2	1952			2	1	1																									Bären
Streichquartett 3	1962			2	1	1																									Bären
Streichquartett 4	1970			2	1	1																									Bären
Tableaux encadres	1974			7	3	2	1																								Bären
KENNAN, KENT W. (1913–)																															
Quintet for Piano and Strings	1940			2	1	1			1																						Schir
KERNIS, AARON J. (1960–)																															
Brilliant Sky, Infinite Sky	1990			1					1																		1	B			AMP
Death Fugue *Voice:* Bass-baritone	1981		11				1																				1	1			AMP
Delicate Songs	1988		18	1		1									1																AMP
Invisible Mosaics I	1987		30	1		1			1									1													AMP

	Year Composed or Published	Key	Duration	Violin	Viola	Cello	Double Bass	Gamba	Piano	Harpsicord	Organ	Guitar	Harp	Recorder	Flute/Piccolo	Oboe	English Horn	Clarinet/Bass Clarinet	Bassoon/Contrabassoon	Saxophone	French Horn	Trumpet	Trombone	Bass Trombone	Tuba	Baritone	Percussion	Voice	Electronic Tape	Unusual Instruments	Publisher
KERNIS, AARON J. *(continued)*																															
Music for Trio (Cycle IV)	1982		22			1			1						1																AMP
Nocturne *Unus Instr:* 2 Glockenspiels	1982		5						2													1					2	S		2	AMP
String Quartet (Musica celestis)	1990		35	2	1	1																									AMP
KESNAR, MAURITS (1900–1957)																															
Intermezzo																					1	2	1								Press
KESSLER, THOMAS (1937–)																															
Stücke, 4				2	1	1																									Bosse
Trio	1968			1	1	1																									BoteB
KHACHATURIAN, ARAM (1903–1978)																															
Piano Trio (with viola)	1932			1	1				1																						Inter
Trio (with clarinet)	1932			1					1									1													Peter
KHACHATURIAN, KARAN (1920–)																															
String Quartet	1969			2	1	1																									VAAP
KIEL, FRIEDRICH (1821–1885)																															
Klaviertrio, Op 3				1		1			1																						Kunze
String Quartet, Op 53 No. 1		a		2	1	1																									Simro
String Quartet, Op 53 No. 2		E♭		2	1	1																									Simro
KIESEWETTER, TOMASZ (1911–)																															
Szenen									1						1	1															Bosse
KIEVMAN, CARSON (1949–)																															
California Mystery Park (Overture)				3	1	2	2		1			1			1	2		1	1								4				AMP
The Earth Only Endures	1975		13												2			1									2	5			AMP
J.P. (Confessions of a Saxophone) *Unus Instr:* Toy piano	1976		15				1		1							1	1	2	1	3							2			1	AMP
Multinationals and the Heavens	1976		25	2	1	1																					4				AMP
Piano Concert *Unus Instr:* Bass tuba, choir bells. Amplification needed									1						2	2		3	1		2	2	1		1		1			2	AMP
Sirocco, Op 4	1975														1	1		1	1		1										AMP
KING, JOHN L. (1953–)																															
Piano Trio No. 1	1978		14		1	1			1																						AmCom
Quartet	1979		24	1		1			1									1													AmCom
KINGMA, P (?–)																															
Serenata Gemini				1		1									1	1															Harmo
KIRCHNER, LEON (1919–)																															
Concerto for Violin, Violoncello *Unus Instr:* Celesta	1960		19												1	1		1	2		1	2	2				4			1	AMP
Lily (for Soprano and Ensemble) *Unus Instr:* Celesta	1973		22	1	1	1			1						1	1		1	1		1						1	S	1	1	AMP
Music for Twelve	1985		10	1	1	1	1		1						1	1		1	1		1	1	1								AMP
Piano Trio	1954		15	1		1			1																						AMP
String Quartet No. 1	1949		20	2	1	1																									AMP
String Quartet No. 2	1958		19	2	1	1																									AMP
String Quartet No. 3	1966		16	2	1	1																									AMP
KIRCHNER, THEODOR (1823–1903)																															
"Nur Tropfen" (Little Pieces)				2	1	1																									Amade
KITZKE, JEROME P. (1955–)																															
The Big Gesture *Unus Instr:* Bass clarinet	1987		13													1		1									1			1	AmCom
A Day of Dappled Seaborne Clouds *Voices:* Soprano and narrator	1978		50			1													1								1	2			AmCom

	Year Composed or Published	Key	Duration	Violin	Viola	Cello	Double Bass	Gamba	Piano	Harpsicord	Organ	Guitar	Harp	Recorder	Flute/Piccolo	Oboe	English Horn	Clarinet/Bass Clarinet	Bassoon/Contrabassoon	Saxophone	French Horn	Trumpet	Trombone	Bass Trombone	Tuba	Baritone	Percussion	Voice	Electronic Tape	Unusual Instruments	Publisher
KITZKE, JEROME P. *(continued)*																															
A Keening Wish *Unus Instr:* Bass clarinet, bass drum	1988		10				1											2									1	N		2	AmCom
Mad Coyote Madly Sings *Voices:* 4 Speakers. *Unus Instr:* Tenor sax, drum set	1991		9				1													1							1	4		2	Manus
Present Music *Unus Instr:* Vibraphone, xylophone	1982		14	1		1			1						1			1									1			2	AmCom
KIVA, OLEH (1947–)																															
Chamber Cantata No. 1			15	3	2	1	1		1	1			1		2						2						2	S			VAAP
Chamber Cantata No. 3 *Unus Instr:* Celesta			18	4	2	1	1		1				1		1	1		1									1	S		1	VAAP
Chamber Cantata No. 4 *Voices:* Soprano and baritone			16	8	2	2	1								1													2			VAAP
Poems (3) for Baritone Voice *Unus Instr:* Celesta			12	4	2	1	1		1				1		1	1		1									1	B		1	VAAP
KLEBE, GISELHER (1925–)																															
Al rovescio, Op 67 *Unus Instr:* Metallidiophone	1972								1				1		1												1			1	Bären
Bagatelles (7), Op 35 *Unus Instr:* Basset horn													1										1				1			1	BoteB
Concerto a cinque, Op 50	1965						1		1	1			1														1				Bären
Divertissement joyeux, Op 5	1949		11	4	3	2	2											1	1		1	1	1				1				BoteB
Elegia appassionata, Op 22	1955			1		1			1																						BoteB
Gratulations-Tango, Op 40a *Unus Instr:* Harmonium										1	1									1		1								1	BoteB
Klavierquintett ("quasi una fantasia"), Op 53	1966			2	1	1			1																						Bären
Missa "Miserere Nobis", Op 45	1964		20												2	2		3	2		3	2	3		1						BoteB
Quattrofonia, Op 89	1982								2																		2				Bären
Scene und Arie, Op 54	1968					8			2													3	3								Bären
Streichquartett 1, Op 9	1949			2	1	1																									BoteB
Streichquartett 2, Op 42	1963			2	1	1																									BoteB
Streichquartett 3, Op 87	1981			2	1	1																									Bären
Tennen No Bi (Die Schönheit der Natur), Op 62						1	1		1				1		1	1		1													Bären
KLOSE, HYACINTHE (1808–1880)																															
La somnambule (clarinet and bassoon) *Comment:* Also available for various pairs of wind instruments and piano									1										1												Billa
KLUSSMANN, ERNST G. (1901–)																															
Spielmusik 1 (Variations)				3		1																									Sikor
KNAB, ARMIN (1881–1951)																															
Sonate *Comment:* Piano may replace harpsichord										1				2																	Bären
Wo du hingehst, da will ich auch	1947			1							1																	S			Merse
KNAIFEL, ALEXANDER (1943–)																															
The Canterville Ghost *Unus Instr:* Flexaton, celesta, xylophone, timpani, bells			45	2	2	1			1		1				1	1		2	1		1	1	1		1		5			5	VAAP
Da! *Unus Instr:* Celesta, flexaton, cymbals	1980		15	1	1	1	1			1				1	1	1		1		1		1					1		1	3	VAAP
KNIGHT, MORRIS (1933–)																															
Cassation																					1	1	1								Press
Selfish Giant Suite															1			1	1												Press

	Year Composed or Published	Key	Duration	Violin	Viola	Cello	Double Bass	Gamba	Piano	Harpsicord	Organ	Guitar	Harp	Recorder	Flute/Piccolo	Oboe	English Horn	Clarinet/Bass Clarinet	Bassoon/Contrabassoon	Saxophone	French Horn	Trumpet	Trombone	Bass Trombone	Tuba	Baritone	Percussion	Voice	Electronic Tape	Unusual Instruments	Publisher
KNIGHT, MORRIS *(continued)*																															
Selfish Giant Suite (alt. vers.)															1			1					1								Press
KNUSSEN, OLIVER (1952–)																															
Cantata, Op 15	1977			1	1	1										1															Faber
Coursing, Op 17	1979		6	1	1	1	1		1						1	1		1	1		1	1	1				1				Faber
Hums and Songs of Winnie-the-Pooh, Op 6 *Unus Instr:* Bass clarinet	1983		12			1									1		1	1									1			1	Faber
Little Fantasies (3), Op 6a	1976		7												1	1		1	1		1										Faber
Océan de terre *Unus Instr:* Celesta	1976		12	1		1	1		1						1			1									2			1	Faber
Ophelia Dances, Op 13	1975			1	1	1			1						1		1	1			1						1				Faber
Pantomime			12	2	1	1									1	1		1	1		1										Faber
Processionals, Op 2	1968		10	2	1	1									1	1		1	1		1										Faber
Puzzle Music, Op 11	1973		9									1	1		1			1									2				Schir
Puzzle Music (alt. inst.), Op 11 *Unus Instr:* Mandolin	1973		9										1		1			1									2			1	Schir
Rosary Songs, Op 9	1972				1				1									1										S			Faber
Trumpets, Op 12	1975																	3										S			Faber
KOCH, JOHANNES H. (1918–)																															
Nach dem Winter da kommt der Sommer																						3	2								Bären
Sinfonietta																						3	3				1				Bären
KOCHAN, GUNTER (1930–)																															
String Quartet	1974			2	1	1																									Peter
KODALY, ZOLTAN (1882–1967)																															
Intermezzo	1905		5	1	1	1																									EMBud
Serenade, Op 12	1920	F		2	1																										Unive
String Quartet No. 1, Op 2	1909	c	38	2	1	1																									EMBud
String Quartet No. 2, Op 10	1918	D		2	1	1																									Unive
Trio	1899			2	1																										Many
KOECHLIN, CHARLES (1867–1950)																															
Epitaph de Jean Harlow, Op 164	1937								1						1					1											Eschi
Le jeu de la Nativité, Op 177	1941		13		1	1					1				1	2			1			1	1								Eschi
Le jeu de la Nativité (alt. vers.), Op 177	1941		13		1	1			1		1				1	2			1			1	1								Eschi
Primavera Quintet, Op 156	1936		15	1	1	1							1		1																Eschi
Quatuor à cordes, Op 51	1921	D		2	1	1																									Senar
Quintet, Op 80	1921		40	2	1	1			1																						Eschi
Sonate à sept, Op 221	1949		15	2	1	1				1					1	1															Eschi
Sonate à sept (alt. inst.), Op 221	1949		15	2	1	1							1		1	1															Eschi
Sonatine No. 1, Op 194 No.1 *Unus Instr:* Oboe d'amore	1942		10	2	2	2				1					2	1		1												1	Eschi
Sonatine No. 1 (alt. inst.), Op 194 No. 1	1942		10	2	2	2				1					2			1		1											Eschi
Sonatine No. 2, Op 194 No. 2 *Unus Instr:* Oboe d'amore	1942			2	2	2				1					2	1		1												1	Eschi
Sonatine No. 2 (alt. inst.), Op 194 No. 2	1942			2	2	2				1					2			1		1											Eschi
Trio, Op 92	1924														1			1	1												Senar
Victoire de la vie, Op 167	1938			2	1	1			1						1	1		1	1		1	1					2				Eschi
KOERING, RENÉ (1940–)																															
Le bouleversement du Prince Henri *Unus Instr:* Timpani	1982		15						1						1	1		1	1		2	2	2				2			1	Salab
Quatuor à cordes, 2e				2	1	1																									Salab
KÖHLER, SIEGFRIED (1927–1984)																															
Streichquartett 1 ("Synthesen"), Op 65				2	1	1																									DeutV

	Year Composed or Published	Key	Duration	Violin	Viola	Cello	Double Bass	Gamba	Piano	Harpsichord	Organ	Guitar	Harp	Recorder	Flute/Piccolo	Oboe	English Horn	Clarinet/Bass Clarinet	Bassoon/Contrabassoon	Saxophone	French Horn	Trumpet	Trombone	Bass Trombone	Tuba	Baritone	Percussion	Voice	Electronic Tape	Unusual Instruments	Publisher
KOHOUTEK, CTIRAD (1929–)																															
Suite für Bläserquintett	1959														1	1		1	1		1										Artia
KOHS, ELLIS B. (1916–)																															
Burlesca I *Unus Instr:* Timpani	1945		3												1			1	1				1				2			1	AmCom
Burlesca II	1945		3		1													1			1										AmCom
Burlesca III	1945		3	1			1																		1		1				AmCom
Night Watch *Unus Instr:* Kettledrum	1943		5												1						1						1			1	AmCom
Quartet (Studies in Variation, Part 3)	1962		20	1	1	1			1																						AmCom
KOKKONEN, JOONAS (1921–)																															
Durch einen Spiegel . . . Metamorphosis	1977			7	2	2	1			1																					Schir
String Quartet No. 3	1976			2	1	1																									Schir
KOLB, BARBARA (1939–)																															
Chansons bas	1966												1														2	S			CarlF
Chromatic Fantasy *Unus Instr:* Amplified instruments; vibraphone	1979		13									1			1	1				1		1					1	N		1	Boose
Chromatic Fantasy (alt. inst.) *Unus Instr:* Amplified instruments; vibraphone, electric harpsichord	1979		13							1					1	1				1		1					1	N		2	Boose
Millefoglie *Unus Instr:* Vibraphone, marimba	1987		20			1							1		1	1		2					1				2		1	2	Boose
The Point that Divides the Wind *Voices:* Male. *Unus Instr:* Bells, gongs, xylophone	1982		13								1																4	3		3	Boose
Songs Before an Adieu	1979		18									1			1													S			Boose
Soundings	1978		16	2	1	1							1		1	1		1	1		1						1		1		Boose
Three Place Settings	1968			1			1											1									1	N			CarlF
Time . . . and Again	1985		16	2	1	1										1													1		Boose
Trobar Clus *Unus Instr:* Amplified harpsichord; vibraphone, marimba	1970		12	1	2	1				1		1			1							1	2				2			3	Boose
KONDO, JO (1947–)																															
An Elder's Hocket *Comment:* Piano doubles on marimba			4						1						1			1									1			1	Peter
Sight Rhythmics *Unus Instr:* Banjo, steel drum				1					1																1		1			2	Peter
KONINK, SERVAAS VAN (?–1718)																															
Suite (arr. Koch)		B♭		2		1																									Harmo
KONT, PAUL (1920–)																															
Blechmusik I (1. Trio)																					1	1	1								Dobli
Blechmusik I (2. Quartett)																					1	1	1	1							Dobli
Blechmusik I (3. Quartettino)																					2	1	1								Dobli
Concerto lirico in maniera pura, Op 61 No. 2				1	1	1									1			1													Dobli
Quintett in memoriam Franz Danzi															1	1		1	1		1										Dobli
Septett in gemischten Manier, Op 61 No. 3	1964			1	1	1	1								1			1	1												Dobli
Serenata a tre in maniera materiale, Op 61 No. 1				1	1										1																Dobli
Trio (with guitar)					1							1			1																Dobli
Trio (with piano)				1		1			1																						Dobli
KOPELENT, MAREK (1932–)																															
Agnus Dei	1982		20	1	1	1			1		1				1			1					1				2	S			Breit
Musica oder eine uralte Geschichte *Voices:* Soprano and 2 speakers	1979									1					1	1												3			Bären

	Year Composed or Published	Key	Duration	Violin	Viola	Cello	Double Bass	Gamba	Piano	Harpsicord	Organ	Guitar	Harp	Recorder	Flute/Piccolo	Oboe	English Horn	Clarinet/Bass Clarinet	Bassoon/Contrabassoon	Saxophone	French Horn	Trumpet	Trombone	Bass Trombone	Tuba	Baritone	Percussion	Voice	Electronic Tape	Unusual Instruments	Publisher
KOPELENT, MAREK *(continued)*																															
Musik für 5	1966		7		1				1							1		1	1												Breit
Quintett	1972		15																		1	2	2								Breit
Streichquartett 4	1967		8	2	1	1																									Breit
Streichquartett 5	1979		16	2	1	1																									Breit
KOPPRASCH, C. (?–)																															
Kornukopia (10 Romantic Etudes) *Comment:* For brass quintet																					1	2	2								Faber
KORDA, VIKTOR (1900–)																															
Capriccio												1		3																	Dobli
Divertimento															1	1		1	1		1										Dobli
Quartettino															1			1			1	1									Dobli
Snapshots (10)																		1	1		1		1								Dobli
Trio-Suite																			1			1					1				Dobli
KORF, ANTHONY (1951–)																															
Oriole	1983		20	1	1	1			1							1															AmCom
KORN, PETER J. (1922–)																															
Prelude and Scherzo, Op 22	1953																				1	2	2								Boose
Quintet for Winds, Op 40			14												1	1		1	1		1										Peter
KORNAUTH, EGON (1891–1959)																															
Kammermusik, Op 31	1925			2	1	1	1								1	1		1			1										Dobli
Klavierquartett, Op 18	1921	c		1	1	1			1																						Dobli
Klavierquintett, Op 35a				2	1	1			1																						Dobli
Kleine Abendmusik, Op 14	1926			2	1	1																									Dobli
Quintett, Op 33	1943	f♯		2	1	1												1													Dobli
Streichquartett, Op 26	1924	g		2	1	1																									Dobli
Suite, Op 45 Alternative instrument: Viola				1		1			1																						Dobli
KORNDORF, NIKOLAI (1947–)																															
Confessions (Chamber Symphony)	1979		21	1	1	1	1								1	1		1	1		1	1	1				1		1		VAAP
KORNGOLD, ERICH W. (1897–1957)																															
Sextett, Op 10	1917	D		2	2	2																									BScho
Streichquartett, Op 16	1922	A		2	1	1																									BScho
Suite, Op 23 *Comment:* Piano part for left hand only	1930			2		1			1																						BScho
Trio, Op 1	1910			1		1			1																						Unive
KOTONSKI, WLODZIMIERZ (1925–)																															
Trio	1960											1			1												1				PWP
KOUBA, JOSEF (1880–)																															
Streichquartett		c		2	1	1																									Artia
KOVACH, F. (?–)																															
Trio No. 1 (Musique d'automne)												1			1			1													Kunze
KRAFT, LEO (1922–)																															
Concerto No. 2	1972														1	1		1	1		1	1	1				1				AMP
KRAFT, WALTER (1905–1977)																															
Heinzelmännchen-Ballade				1	1	1									1													S			Bären
O lux beata Trinitas *Voices:* 4 Sopranos				4		1	1				1																	4			Bären
KRATOCHWIL, HEINZ (1933–)																															
Klaviertrio, Op 29				1		1			1																						Dobli
Partita ritmica (with flute), Op 92															1	1		1													Dobli
Partita ritmica (with saxophone), Op 92																		2		1											Dobli

	Year Composed or Published	Key	Duration	Violin	Viola	Cello	Double Bass	Gamba	Piano	Harpsicord	Organ	Guitar	Harp	Recorder	Flute/Piccolo	Oboe	English Horn	Clarinet/Bass Clarinet	Bassoon/Contrabassoon	Saxophone	French Horn	Trumpet	Trombone	Bass Trombone	Tuba	Baritone	Percussion	Voice	Electronic Tape	Unusual Instruments	Publisher
KRATOCHWIL, HEINZ *(continued)*																															
Vergnügliche Kurzgeschichten, Op 133																					1	2	1		1						Dobli
Vergnügliche Kurzgeschichten (alt. inst.), Op 133																						3	1		1						Dobli
KRATZSCHMAR, WILFRIED (1944–)																															
Anakreontische Phantasie	1976														1	1		1	1		1										DeutV
KRAUZE, ZYGMUNT (1938–)																															
Arabesque *Unus Instr:* 2 Soprano and 2 alto melodicas	1983		13	4	4	2	1		1						1	1		1	1		1	1	1							4	Unive
Quatuor pour la naissance	1984		20	1		1			1									1													Unive
Tableau vivant	1982		15	2	2	1	1		1						1	1		2	1		1	1	1								Unive
KREIGER, ARTHUR V. (1945–)																															
Chamber Concerto for Piano and 12 Instruments	1986		157	1	1	1	1		1						1	1		2			1	1					2				AmCom
Composition	1973		8				1		1						1												2				AmCom
Nocturne *Comment:* Conductor needed	1976		12		1	1												2			1				1		2		1		AmCom
KREISLER, FRITZ (1875–1962)																															
String Quartet	1921	a		2	1	1																									CarlF
KREJCI, ISA (1904–1968)																															
Streichquartett 2	1953	d		2	1	1																									Artia
Streichquartett 3	1960			2	1	1																									Artia
Streichquartett 4	1962			2	1	1																									Artia
KREJCI, MIROSLAV (1891–1964)																															
Streichquintett, Op 15	1926	B♭		2	2	1																									Artia
KREK, UROS (1922–)																															
La journée d'un bouffon	1973		15																		1	2	1		1						Breit
KREMEN, ISRAEL (?–1949)																															
Forms (4) for Four *Unus Instr:* Bass clarinet	1984		15						1						1			1		1										1	AmCom
Trio	1981		7		1	1			1																						AmCom
KREMER, CLEMENS (1930–)																															
Aphorismen (3)	1967																					2	2								Bosse
ŘRENEK, ERNST (1900–)																															
Alpbach Quintett, Op 180	1962														1	1		1	1		1						1				Unive
Aulokithara, Op 213a *Comment:* English horn may replace oboe	1972												1			1													1		Bären
La corona (Cantate), Op 91 *Voices:* Mezzo-soprano and baritone											1																1	2			Bären
Fibonacci mobile, Op 187 *Comment:* Piano 4-hands, plus coordinator				1	1	1			1																						Bären
Lustige Märsche (3), Op 44	1926		10												1	1		4			2	2	1		1		2				Unive
Pentagramm, Op 163	1957														1	1		1	1		1										Bären
Quintina über die fünf Vokale, Op 191 *Unus Instr:* Vibraphone, xylophone	1965				1							1		1													2	1		2	Bären
Serenade, Op 4	1919			1	1	1												1													Assma
Sestina, Op 161	1957			1					1			1			1			1				1						S			Bären
Streichquartett 1, Op 6	1921			2	1	1																									Unive
Streichquartett 2, Op 8	1921			2	1	1																									Assma
Streichquartett 3, Op 20	1923			2	1	1																									Unive
Streichquartett 4, Op 24	1924			2	1	1																									Unive
Streichquartett 5, Op 65	1930			2	1	1																									Unive

	Year Composed or Published	Key	Duration	Violin	Viola	Cello	Double Bass	Gamba	Piano	Harpsicord	Organ	Guitar	Harp	Recorder	Flute/Piccolo	Oboe	English Horn	Clarinet/Bass Clarinet	Bassoon/Contrabassoon	Saxophone	French Horn	Trumpet	Trombone	Bass Trombone	Tuba	Baritone	Percussion	Voice	Electronic Tape	Unusual Instruments	Publisher
KŘENEK, ERNST *(continued)*																															
Streichquartett 6, Op 78	1936			2	1	1																									Unive
Streichquartett 7, Op 96	1943			2	1	1																									Unive
Streichquartett 8, Op 233	1981			2	1	1																									Bären
Streichtrio, Op 65	1948			1	1	1																									Hanse
Trio, Op 108	1946		8	1					1									1													BoteB
KREUTZER, JOSEPH (1778–1832)																															
Trio, Op 9 No. 3		D		1								1			1																Dobli
KREUTZER, KONRADIN (1780–1849)																															
Clarinet Quartet		E♭		1	1	1												1													VarPb
Septet, Op 62		E♭		1	1	1	1											1	1		1										Dobli
Trio					1													2													Kunze
Waltzes (6) for Wind Sextet (Biba)																		2	2		2										Amade
KREUTZER, RODOLPHE (1766–1831)																															
Trio *Comment:* Can use clarinet for oboe, cello for bassoon					1											1			1												Kunze
KRICKA, JAROSLAV (1882–1969)																															
Streichquartett 3, Op 97	1949			2	1	1																									Artia
KRIST, JOACHIM (1948–)																															
Kreuzwege	1976			1	1	1			1																						Feedb
KROEGER, KARL (1932–)																															
Sonata Breve																			1		1	1									Press
KROL, BERNHARD (1920–)																															
Auferstehungskonzert, Op 89											1										4	2	3								BoteB
Divertissement classique, Op 58 *Unus Instr:* Contrabass tuba	1975		17																		4	4	4		1					1	BoteB
Elegia passionata, Op 69 *Comment:* Piano may replace harpsichord							1			1							1														BoteB
Konsonanzen-Quintett, Op 71									1							1		1	1		1										BoteB
Kronungs-Fantasie, Op 76											1											1	1								BoteB
Linzer Harmoniemusik, Op 67	1978		17													2		2	2		2										BoteB
Promenade parisienne, Op 78																					1	2	2								BoteB
KROLL, WILLIAM (1901–)																															
Cantio *Voice:* Baritone						2	1				1																	B			Bosse
Magnificat *Unus Instr:* Bass clarinet	1958					1	1									1		2		1								S		1	Bosse
KROMMER, FRANTISEK V. (1759–1831)																															
Pieces (13), Op 47					1													2													Kneus
Quartet		C		1	1	1										1															MABoh
Quartet		F		1	1	1										1															MABoh
Quartet, Op 75		D		1	1	1									1																Kunze
String Quartet, Op 5 No. 1		E♭		2	1	1																									MABoh
Variations on a Theme of Pleyel		F														2	1														Kneus
KROPFREITER, AUGUSTINUS F. (1936–)																															
Bläserquintett															1	1		1	1		1										Dobli
Divertimento II																1		1	1		1										Dobli
Divertimento III															1	1		1	1		1										Dobli
Konzertante Musik											1										4	3	3								Dobli
KRUL, ELI (1926–1970)																															
String Quartet			14	2	1	1																									Peter
KUBELIK, RAFAEL (1914–)																															
String Quartet No. 2			12	2	1	1																									Peter

	Year Composed or Published	Key	Duration	Violin	Viola	Cello	Double Bass	Gamba	Piano	Harpsicord	Organ	Guitar	Harp	Recorder	Flute/Piccolo	Oboe	English Horn	Clarinet/Bass Clarinet	Bassoon/Contrabassoon	Saxophone	French Horn	Trumpet	Trombone	Bass Trombone	Tuba	Baritone	Percussion	Voice	Electronic Tape	Unusual Instruments	Publisher
KUBELIK, RAFAEL *(continued)*																															
String Quartet No. 5			20	2	1	1																									Peter
KUBIK, GAIL (1914–)																															
Divertimento	1985				1				1						1	1		1				1									Leduc
KUBIZEK, AUGUSTIN (1918–)																															
Kammerquintett, Op 15	1962														1	1		1	1		1										Dobli
Quartetto da camera, Op 24a												1				1		1	1												Dobli
Sinfonia da camera (Nonet), Op 26b				1	1	1	1								1	1		1	1		1										Dobli
Trio, Op 26a						1			1									1													Dobli
Vergnügliche Miniaturen (12-Ton Reihe), Op 28a				1														1	1				1								Dobli
KUBO, MAYAKO (1947–)																															
Miniatur I	1981		16	1			1		1									1	1								2				Breit
KUHLAU, FRIEDRICH (1786–1832)																															
Quintet, Op 51 No. 3		A		1	2	1									1																Kunze
Trio, Op 119						1			1						1																Billa
Trio, Op 119				1					1						1																Billa
KUHN, MAX (1896–)																															
Serenata notturna															1	1		1	1		1										Kunze
KUNAD, RAINERN (1936–)																															
Commedia "Die Ehe" (Conatum 46)	1969								1							1			1												DeutV
Melodie, die ich verloren hatte	1968				2	2									1													S			DeutV
Musik für Bläser in 3 Sätzen	1965														1	1		1	1		1										DeutV
Streichquartett 2 (Conatum 39)	1916			2	1	1																									DeutV
KUPFERMAN, MEYER (1926–)																															
Little Symphony	1952		19	2	1	1	1								1	2			2		2										Weint
KURI-ALDANA, MARIO (1931–)																															
Candelaria (Suite)	1965														1	1		1	1		1										MusRa
Cantares	1961								1						1			1													MusRa
KURKA, ROBERT (1921–1957)																															
The Good Soldier Schweik Suite, Op 22 *Unus Instr:* Contrabassoon			20												2	1	1	2	2		3	2	1				2			1	Weint
Music for Five, Op 14				1			1											1			1	1									Weint
Polka and Waltz (from "Schweik") *Unus Instr:* Contrabassoon			20												2	1	1	2	2		3	2	1				1			1	Weint
KURTAG, GYORGY (1926–)																															
Bagatelles, Op 14b	1981		15				1		1						1																Boose
Hommage à Mihaly Andras, Op 13	1978		9	2	1	1																									Boose
The Little Fix, Op 15b *Unus Instr:* Piccolo	1978		6									1			1								1							1	Boose
Quartetto per archi	1964			2	1	1																									Zenem
Scenes from a Novel, Op 19 *Unus Instr:* Cimbalom	1982		20	1			1																				1	S		1	Boose
Wind Quintet, Op 2	1959		7												1	1		1	1		1										Boose
KVANDAL, JOHAN (1919–)																															
Night Music, Op 57	1981		20				1									2		2	2		2										Nordi
Octet, Op 54 *Comment:* Optional double bass	1980		15													2		2	2		2										Nordi
LABEY, MARCEL (1875–1968)																															
Quatuor	1911	g		1	1	1			1																						Duran
Quatuor à cordes, Op 17	1919	a		2	1	1																									Duran
LABROCA, MARIO (1896–1973)																															
Quartetto II	1934			2	1	1																									Suvin
Quartetto III				2	1	1																									Suvin

	Year Composed or Published	Key	Duration	Violin	Viola	Cello	Double Bass	Gamba	Piano	Harpsicord	Organ	Guitar	Harp	Recorder	Flute/Piccolo	Oboe	English Horn	Clarinet/Bass Clarinet	Bassoon/Contrabassoon	Saxophone	French Horn	Trumpet	Trombone	Bass Trombone	Tuba	Baritone	Percussion	Voice	Electronic Tape	Unusual Instruments	Publisher
LABURDA, JIRI (1931–)																															
6 Inventions																						2	1								Press
LACHENMANN, HELMUT (1935–)																															
Gran torso	1972		20	2	1	1																									Breit
temA	1968		14			1									1													M			Breit
Trio fluido	1966		16		1													1									1				Breit
LACHNER, FRANZ (1803–1890)																															
Frauenliebe und Leben									1												1							1			MusRa
Frauenliebe und Leben (Intermezzo), Op 82									1									1										1			MusRa
'Nachts in der Kajute,' 'Waldvoglein' *Comment:* Clarinet may replace French horn									1												1							1			MusRa
Notte soave delizia									1												1							1			MusRa
Quintet No. 2		E♭													1	1		1	1		1										MusRa
Die Seejungfern									1												1							1			MusRa
LACHNER, IGNAZ (1807–1895)																															
Piano Trio, Op 89		d		1	1				1																						Amade
Quartett, Op 106		C		3	1																										Kunze
Quintett, Op 121		c		2	1	2																									Kunze
Trio, Op 45				1	1				1																						Kunze
Trio, Op 102		E♭		1	1				1																						Amade
LACOUR, GUY (?–)																															
Divertissement																				1							6				Billa
LADERMAN, EZRA (1924–)																															
Cadence	1978		9	2	1	1									2																Schir
Cadence	1978		10	4	1	2	1								2																Schir
Celestial Bodies				2	1	1									1																Oxfor
Clarinet Quintet	1988		27	2	1	1												1													Schir
Double Helix				2	1	1									1	1															Oxfor
MBL Suite	1988		20	2	1	1									2																Schir
Nonette				1		1			1						1			1	1		1	1	1								Oxfor
Octet (double string quartet)	1986		28	4	2	2																									Schir
Octet (for winds)																2		2	2		2										Oxfor
Piano Quintet	1990		30	2	1	1			1																						Schir
Single Voice				2	1	1										1															Oxfor
Song of Songs	1977		30		1	1									1													S			Schir
String Quartet No. 1				2	1	1																									Oxfor
String Quartet No. 2				2	1	1																									Oxfor
String Quartet No. 3				2	1	1																									Oxfor
String Quartet No. 4	1974		22	2	1	1																									Schir
String Quartet No. 5	1976		43	2	1	1																									Schir
String Quartet No. 6	1980		19	2	1	1																									Schir
String Quartet No. 7	1984		21	2	1	1																									Schir
String Quartet No. 8	1988		23	2	1	1																									Schir
Talkin'-Lovin'-Leavin'	1990		10	2	1	1								1																	Schir
Theme, Variations, and Finale				1	1	1	1								1			1	1		1										Oxfor
Trio				1	1				1																						Oxfor
LAJTHA, LASZLO (1892–1963)																															
Études (5) pour quatuor à cordes, Op 20	1934			2	1	1																									Leduc
Hommages (4)															1	1		1	1												Leduc
Marionettes, Op 26	1937			1	1	1							1		1																EMBud
Quatuor à cordes, Op 49	1950			2	1	1																									Leduc
Quatuor à cordes, Op 53	1951			2	1	1																									Leduc

	Year Composed or Published	Key	Duration	Violin	Viola	Cello	Double Bass	Gamba	Piano	Harpsicord	Organ	Guitar	Harp	Recorder	Flute/Piccolo	Oboe	English Horn	Clarinet/Bass Clarinet	Bassoon/Contrabassoon	Saxophone	French Horn	Trumpet	Trombone	Bass Trombone	Tuba	Baritone	Percussion	Voice	Electronic Tape	Unusual Instruments	Publisher
LAJTHA, LASZLO *(continued)*																															
Quatuor à cordes, Op 57	1953			2	1	1																									Leduc
Quintette, Op 46				1	1	1							1		1																Leduc
Trio, Op 22	1935					1							1		1																Leduc
Trio, Op 47	1949					1							1		1																Leduc
Trio à cordes, Op 18	1927			1	1	1																									Leduc
LALO, EDOUARD (1823–1892)																															
Quatuor à cordes, Op 45	1880	e		2	1	1																									Hamel
Trio, 1er, Op 7		c		1		1			1																						Billa
Trio, 2e		b		1		1			1																						Hamel
Trio, 3e, Op 26	1880	a		1		1			1																						Duran
LAMPE, GÜNTER (1925–)																															
Permutazioni															1	1		1	1		1										DeutV
LANCHBERY, JOHN (1923–)																															
Three Girls for Five Brass																					1	2	1		1						Novel
LANG, ISTVAN (1933–)																															
Acufenos I (solo trombone) *Unus Instr:* Vibraphone	1966		11						1						1			1					1				1			1	EMBud
Constellations	1975		15	1	1	1										1															EMBud
Prelude, 3 Mobiles, and a Postlude	1980		7																		1	2	1		1						EMBud
Quartetto d'archi No. 2	1978		8	2	1	1																									EMBud
Woodwind Quintet No. 1	1964		10												1	1		1	1		1										EMBud
Woodwind Quintet No. 2 (Trasfigurazioni)	1965		10												1	1		1	1		1										EMBud
Woodwind Quintet No. 3	1975		10												1	1		1	1		1										EMBud
LANGE, SAMUEL DE (1840–1911)																															
Streichquartett 3, Op 67	1895	g		2	1	1																									Rahte
LANNOY, EDUARD VON (1787–1853)																															
Quintet No. 2		E♭							1							1		1	1		1										Kunze
LANTIER, PIERRE L. (1910–)																															
Quatuor				2	1	1																									Billa
Quatuor				2	1	1																									Duran
LAUERMANN, HERBERT (1955–)																															
String Quartet				2	1	1																									Dobli
LAWSON, PETER (?–)																															
Valentia extramaterial			8						1						1												2				Peter
LAYTON, BILLY J. (1924–)																															
Divertimento, Op 6	1960		11	1		1				1								1	1				1				1				Schir
LAZAROF, HENRI (1932–)																															
Bläseroktett *Unus Instr:* Bass clarinet	1969		10												1	1		2	1		1	1	1							1	BoteB
Cadence III	1970			1																							2				BoteB
Concertazione *Unus Instr:* Flügelhorn	1973					1							1		1			1			1						1		1	1	Press
Espaces *Unus Instr:* Bass clarinet	1966		17		2	2			2						2			2												1	AMP
Partita for Brass Quintet and Tape	1971		12																		1	2	1		1				1		AMP
Serenade				2	2	2																									Press
String Quartet				2	1	1																									Press
Tempi concertati (Double concerto) *Unus Instr:* Xylophone, vibraphone, celesta	1964		27	1	1				1	1			1		1												2			3	AMP
Trio for Winds															1	1		1													Press
LeBARON, ANNE (1953–)																															
Fertility Dance	1971		6				1								1												2				AmCom

	Year Composed or Published	Key	Duration	Violin	Viola	Cello	Double Bass	Gamba	Piano	Harpsicord	Organ	Guitar	Harp	Recorder	Flute/Piccolo	Oboe	English Horn	Clarinet/Bass Clarinet	Bassoon/Contrabassoon	Saxophone	French Horn	Trumpet	Trombone	Bass Trombone	Tuba	Baritone	Percussion	Voice	Electronic Tape	Unusual Instruments	Publisher
LeBARON, ANNE *(continued)*																															
Giuoco piano	1971		9				1								2							2	2								AmCom
Music for peyote cactus	1973		10	1												1				1							1				AmCom
Passacaglia	1971		3	1		1									1	1		1	1												Amcom
Resonances *Unus Instr:* Timpani	1971		4						1				1														1			1	AmCom
LECHNER, KONRAD (1911–)																															
Cantica II	1971		9			1									1												1	M	1		Breit
Cantica II (alt. inst.)			9			1				1					1													S			Breit
LECHTHALER, JOSEF (1891–1948)																															
Trio, Op 57 *Comment:* A cello may replace the gamba, and a piano the harpsichord				1				1		1																					Dobli
LEES, BENJAMIN (1924–)																															
Miniatures, 2	1974														1	1		1	1		1										Boose
Piano Trio	1983			1		1			1																						Boose
String Quartet No. 1	1952		16	2	1	1																									Boose
String Quartet No. 2	1955		20	2	1	1																									Boose
Variables, 3	1955		9						1							1		1			1										Boose
LEFEBVRE, CLAUDE (1931–)																															
Cheminements	1982		16	8	3	3	2																								Salab
Ivresse-absence for 19 Brass	1977		17																		8	5	5		1						Salab
Suite for Baritone	1961		20	2	1	1	1		1						1			1	1									B			Salab
LEFEVRE, JEAN X. (1763–1829)																															
Trio		B♭																2	1												Kunze
LEGE, GÜNTER (1935–)																															
Ubi caritas (Concertino) *Voices:* Tenor, baritone, and bass	1967				4										1													3			Bosse
LEHMANN, HANS U. (1937–)																															
". . . zu streichen"				2	2	2																									Hug
LEITERMEYER, FRITZ (1925–)																															
Capriccio strumentale, Op 19				1	1	1																									Dobli
Divertimento for Wind Quintet, Op 38															1	1		1	1		1										Dobli
Divertimento for 12 Winds, Op 53 *Unus Instr:* Piccolo, bass clarinet, and contrabassoon															2	1	1	2	2		2	1	1							3	Dobli
Pezzo per ottoni (Piece for Brass)																						4	4		1						Dobli
Streichquartett 2, Op 27			20	2	1	1																									Dobli
Tiento (Fantasie), Op 62					1				1									1													Dobli
LEITNER, E. L. (?–)																															
Intrada for Organ											1										2	2	2		1						Dobli
LEKEU, GUILLAUME (1870–1894)																															
Piano Trio				1		1			1																						Salab
LEMAIRE, FELIX (?–)																															
Mini-trio																1		1	1												Billa
LEMELAND, AUBERT (1932–)																															
Divertissement															1			1		1											Billa
Mouvement concertant				1	1	1									1	1															Billa
Musique nocturne															1	1		1	1		1										Billa
Pastorale																1		1	1												Billa
Quintette à vent, Op 101															1	1		1	1		1										Billa
Symphonie pour cuivres																					1	2	2		1						Billa
Terzetto																1		1		1											Billa
Trio à cordes, Op 75				1	1	1																									Billa
LENNON, JOHN A. (1950–)																															
Voices			20	2	1	1																									Peter

	Year Composed or Published	Key	Duration	Violin	Viola	Cello	Double Bass	Gamba	Piano	Harpsicord	Organ	Guitar	Harp	Recorder	Flute/Piccolo	Oboe	English Horn	Clarinet/Bass Clarinet	Bassoon/Contrabassoon	Saxophone	French Horn	Trumpet	Trombone	Bass Trombone	Tuba	Baritone	Percussion	Voice	Electronic Tape	Unusual Instruments	Publisher
LENOT, JACQUES (1945–)																															
À l'aube, le rivage															1		1	1	1		2		1								Salab
Bientôt le soleil (for harp)			5	2	1	1	1						1		2		1	2	1		2	1	1				1				Salab
La bourrasque (for cello) *Unus Instr:* Celesta			3	2	1	2	1								1	1		1	1		1	1	1				1			1	Salab
Espace de conflict	1978		20	1		1			1						1			1										M			Salab
Espace latent	1978		11						1						2	1		1	1		1	1	1								Salab
Exergue (for cello)	1977		12	3	1	1	1		1				1		1	1		2	1		1	1	1				1				Salab
Un grand principe de violence *Unus Instr:* Piccolo clarinet, bass clarinet, celesta	1980		20	1	1	1			1				1		2	1	1	2	2		2						4			3	Salab
The Julian Trio				1					1						1																Salab
Lied 5 *Unus Instr:* Oboe d'amore	1985		21	2	2	2			1							1	1				1									1	Salab
La mer (for clarinet) *Unus Instr:* Celesta			3	2	1	1	1								1		1	4	1		2						1			1	Salab
Nuit d'été II (alt. inst.)	1984		45	2	1	1	1		2						1	1	1	1	1		1	1	1		1		1				Salab
Nuit d'été II (for cello)	1984		45	2	1	1	1		1		1				1	1	1	1	1		1	1	1				1				Salab
Ou la brume *Unus Instr:* Celesta			7	1	1	1			1				1		2			3	1								1			1	Salab
Stabat Mater *Voices:* 2 High tenors, 2 baritones, bass. *Unus Instr:* Sackbut	1983		45					3			1																	5		1	Salab
Utopia glossa quinta						1			1						1			1													Salab
Utopia parafrasi *Comment:* Woodwinds play diverse instruments	1983		25	2	1	1	1		1						1	1	1	1	1		2	1	1				1				Salab
Le vent du soir *Unus Instr:* Celesta			6	2	1	1	1		1				1		2	1		3	1		2	1	1				1			1	Salab
LEROUX, PHILIPPE (?–)																															
Le jardin ouvert																1			1		1				1						Billa
LESSARD, JOHN (1920–)																															
Movements V	1978		8	1		1																1									AmCom
Movements VI	1978		15		1	1																1					1				AmCom
Movements VIII *Unus Instr:* Marimba, vibraphone	1984		9																			1					2			2	AmCom
LEUKAUF, ROBERT (1902–)																															
Bläserquintett, Op 25															1	1		1	1		1										Dobli
Quintett, Op 32a				1	1	1									1	1															Dobli
LEVI, PAUL A. (1941–)																															
Progressions (5) for 3 Instruments	1971		15		1										1			1													AmCom
LEVINAS, MICHAEL (1949–)																															
Appels *Comment:* Microphone is needed for every instrument but percussion	1974		9				1		1						1	1		1	1		1		1				2				Salab
Le choeur des arches (3e Arcade)	1984		10		4	5	2		1																		1		1		Salab
Concerto pour piano (Espace)	1976		12			1			1						2							2	3						1		Salab
Concerto pour un piano (Espace 2)	1980		13			1			1						1						1	1					1		1		Salab
Strettes tournantes-migrations	1978		10		1	1	1								1			1	1		2	1									Salab
La voix des voix *Unus Instr:* Bass clarinet, synthesizer	1984		20				1								1			1	1		1	1	1				2			2	Salab
LEWIN, FRANK (1925–)																															
Dunlap's Creek	1953		4	2	1	1										1						1									AmCom
Dunlap's Creek (for winds)	1953		4												1	1	1	1	1			1									AmCom
LEWIS, PETER T. (1932–)																															
Alcazar III *** *Comment:* For 4 or more instruments	1972		5																												AmCom
Epigrams (3) *Unus Instr:* Contrabassoon	1961		4	2	1	1									2	1	1	2	2		2									1	AmCom

	Year Composed or Published	Key	Duration	Violin	Viola	Cello	Double Bass	Gamba	Piano	Harpsicord	Organ	Guitar	Harp	Recorder	Flute/Piccolo	Oboe	English Horn	Clarinet/Bass Clarinet	Bassoon/Contrabassoon	Saxophone	French Horn	Trumpet	Trombone	Bass Trombone	Tuba	Baritone	Percussion	Voice	Electronic Tape	Unusual Instruments	Publisher
LEWIS, PETER T. *(continued)*																															
Lament for Mrs. Bridge *Unus Instr:* Mandolin, piccolo, contrabassoon, cymbals, celesta	1963		1				3						1		2	1			1		2	1	1				1			5	AmCom
Lament for Mrs. Bridge (alt. inst.) *Unus Instr:* Piccolo, contrabassoon, mandolin, vibraphone, celesta, cymbals	1963		1				3								2	1			1		2	1	1				2			6	AmCom
Manestar	1970		23	1	1	1			1						1								1				1		1		AmCom
Piano Trio (with viola)	1960		9		1	1			1																						AmCom
Terribilitá *** *Comment:* For diverse instruments	1977		10																										1		AmCom
LEWIS, ROBERT H. (1926–)																															
Tangent for Double Brass Quartet																					2	4	2								Press
Trio				1					1									1													Dobli
LEWKOVITCH, BERNHARD (1927–)																															
Cantata sacra	1959		8			1									1			1	1				1					1			Hanse
Songs of Solomon	1959		8															1			1			1				T			Hanse
Tres orationes	1957		7													1			1									T			Hanse
LEYENDECKER, ULRICH (1946–)																															
Cancion ultima, for Alto *Unus Instr:* Vibraphone	1984		11		1	1			1				1		1		1	1			1	1					1	A		1	Sikor
Streichquartett (exempla nova 71)				2	1	1																									Sikor
LIADOFF, ANATOLE (1855–1914)																															
Mazurka (String Quartet)				2	1	1																									Belai
LICKL, JOHANN G. (1769–1843)																															
Quintetto concertante		F													1	1		1	1		1										Kneus
Trio																		1	1		1										Kunze
LIDHOLM, INGVAR (1921–)																															
Music for Strings				2	1	1																									Nordi
LIEBERMAN, GLENN (1947–)																															
Alii termini	1982		7			1			1														1								AmCom
Concertino *Unus Instr:* Synthesizer	1987		19		1		1		1						3			1												1	AmCom
Dialectic	1978		11			1										1		1									1				AmCom
Fanfare *Unus Instr:* Military drum	1981		4												6							4					4			1	AmCom
Generation of Leaves	1981		13									1			1			1													AmCom
Immaculate Obsession	1985		10	1			1					1																			AmCom
Passacaglia *Unus Instr:* Bass clarinet	1979		13	1	1	1	1		1						1	1		2									1			1	AmCom
Sextet	1976		7	1	1	1			1						1	1															AmCom
Termini *Unus Instr:* Bass clarinet	1975		8			1							1					1												1	AmCom
Trio	1973		12			1									1			1													AmCom
Trio Sonata *Unus Instr:* Vibraphone	1980		11	1																					1		1			1	AmCom
LIEBERSON, GODDARD (1911–1977)																															
String Quartet				2	1	1																									Oxfor
LIEBERSON, PETER (1946–)																															
Accordance *Unus Instr:* Vibraphone or celesta	1977		12		1		1		1				1		1			1									1			1	AMP
Concerto for Violoncello *Unus Instr:* Mandolin	1977		13	2	1		1		1				1		1	1		1				1					1			1	AMP
Concerto for 4 Groups	1973		9	2	1	1	1		1						1	1		1	1		1										AMP
Feast Day	1985		20			1			1						1	1															AMP
Lalita (Chamber Variations) *Unus Instr:* Bass clarinet	1984		18	1	1	1	1		1						1	1		1			1						1			1	AMP

	Year Composed or Published	Key	Duration	Violin	Viola	Cello	Double Bass	Gamba	Piano	Harpsicord	Organ	Guitar	Harp	Recorder	Flute/Piccolo	Oboe	English Horn	Clarinet/Bass Clarinet	Bassoon/Contrabassoon	Saxophone	French Horn	Trumpet	Trombone	Bass Trombone	Tuba	Baritone	Percussion	Voice	Electronic Tape	Unusual Instruments	Publisher
LIEBERSON, PETER *(continued)*																															
Motetti di Eugenio Montale *Voices:* Soprano, alto. *Unus Instr:* Bass clarinet									1				1					2										2		1	AMP
Raising the Gaze	1988		9	1	1				1						1			1									2				AMP
Songs (3) for Soprano	1982		10	2	1	1			1				1		1	1		1	1		1	1	1					S			AMP
Tashi Quartet	1979		30	1		1			1									1													AMP
Wind Messengers *Unus Instr:* 2 Bass clarinets	1990		8												3	2		4	2		2									2	AMP
Ziji	1987		10	1	1	1			1									1			1										AMP
LIGETI, GYORGY (1923–)																															
Aventures *Voices:* Coloratura soprano, alto, and baritone			11			1	1		1	1					1						1						1	3			Peter
Cello Concerto			16	2	1	2	1						1		1	1		2	1		1	1	1								Peter
LINDBERG, MAGNUS (1958–)																															
UR *Unus Instr:* Bass clarinet, Yamaha keyboards, live electronics	1986		15	1		1			1									1												3	Hanse
LINDBERG, NILS (1933–)																															
Blues for Bill			5																	4							1				Nordi
Brand New			3																	4							1				Nordi
Curbits			5																	4							1				Nordi
Zodiac			4																	4							1				Nordi
LINDBLAD, FREDRIK (1801–1878)																															
Streichquintett		F		2	2	1																									Kunze
Trio, Op 10				1	1				1																						Kunze
LINDENFELD, HARRIS (1945–)																															
Combinations (Last Gold of Perished Star)	1974		10																			1					2				AmCom
Combinations II (Leones somnians)	1975		12																				1				2				AmCom
From "Le grotte des combarelles"	1978		10		1	1			1																						AmCom
Réflexion sur la paysage	1978		11						1									1									1				AmCom
Die Totenglocken	1979		12	1		1			1									1	1								1				AmCom
LINKE, NORBERT (1933–)																															
Profit tout clair	1967		13	1	1	1	1									1		1	1		1										Breit
LIPP, CHARLES (?–1945)																															
Amorous Perspective	1974		4		1										1			1							1						AmCom
LIPTAK, DAVID (1949–)																															
Chamber Concerto (solo clarinet)	1978		13															1									4				AmCom
Giovine vagha i non senti	1986		11	1		1			1													1	1								AmCom
Mixed Doubles	1985		14	1			1															1			1						AmCom
LISCHKA, RAINER (1942–)																															
Kontakte *Unus Instr:* Flute in A, vibraphone	1973						1								1												1			2	DeutV
LISZT, FRANZ (1811–1886)																															
Movements, 2 *Comment:* Double bass ad libitum				2	1	1																									Amade
LIVIABELLA, LINO (1902–1964)																															
Quartetto		f		2	1	1																									Suvin
LLOYD, JONATHAN (1948–)																															
Ben's Boogie (from 3 Dances)			5												1	1		1	1		1										Boose
Brass Quintet	1982		5																			2	2		1						Boose
Don't Mention the War *Unus Instr:* Glockenspiel, xylophone	1982		15		1	1	1		1							1	1						1				1			2	Boose
Fancy Free (from 3 Dances)	1982		3	1	1	1	1								1		1	1	1		1										Boose

	Year Composed or Published	Key	Duration	Violin	Viola	Cello	Double Bass	Gamba	Piano	Harpsicord	Organ	Guitar	Harp	Recorder	Flute/Piccolo	Oboe	English Horn	Clarinet/Bass Clarinet	Bassoon/Contrabassoon	Saxophone	French Horn	Trumpet	Trombone	Bass Trombone	Tuba	Baritone	Percussion	Voice	Electronic Tape	Unusual Instruments	Publisher
LLOYD, JONATHAN *(continued)*																															
Keir's Kick (from 3 Dances)	1982		5	2	1	1																									Boose
One Step More *Unus Instr:* Oboe d'amore	1986		11			1				1					1	1														1	Boose
Songs (3)	1980		12		1				1																			H			Boose
String Quintet No. 1	1982		8	2	2	1																									Boose
String Quintet No. 2 *Unus Instr:* Mandolin	1982		7				1					2	1																	1	Boose
Waiting for Gozo *Comment:* Oboe doubles on English horn. *Unus Instr:* Contrabassoon	1981		12	2	1	1	1								1	1	1	1	1		1	1	1							1	Boose
Wind Quintet	1982		4												1	1		1	1		1										Boose
Won't It Ever Be Morning *Comment:* Oboe doubles on English horn. *Unus Instr:* Bass clarinet	1980		12	2	1	1			1			1			1	1	1	1	1	1	2	1	1				1			1	Boose
LOCKWOOD, NORMAND (1906–)																															
Clarinet Quintet	1959		25	2	1	1												1													AmCom
String Quartet No. 3				2	1	1																									Press
Trio	1978		30		1								1		1																AmCom
LOEFFLER, CHARLES M. (1861–1935)																															
Music for Four Stringed Instruments				2	1	1																									Press
Psalm 137 (By the Waters of Babylon)	1907					1					1		1		2													1			Schir
LOGOTHETIS, ANESTIS (1921–)																															
Styx *** *Comment:* Variable instrumentation, graphically notated			10																												Breit
LOHSE, FRED (?–)																															
Piano Trio			22	1		1			1																						Peter
Woodwind Quintet															1	1		1	1		1										Peter
LOLINI, RUGGIERO (?–)																															
Forme e silenzi				2	1																										Ricor
LOMBARDO, ROBERT (1932–)																															
Yes!	1971		9			1												1				1					1				AmCom
LONDON, EDWIN (1929–)																															
Bebop Dreams (solo horn)			5	2	1	1	1		1				1								1						1				Peter
Brass Quintet			14																		1	2	1		1						Peter
Portrait of Three Ladies *Comment:* Clarinet doubles on sax. *Voices:* Narrator and mezzo-soprano. *Unus Instr:* Bass clarinet			21	1		1	1								1	1		2		1	1	2	1		1		2	2		1	Peter
Psalm of These Days III *Voices:* 2 Tenors, baritone, bass			16		1		1		1						1			1				1	1		1		1	4			Peter
LORA, ANTONIO (1899–1965)																															
Trio			25		1	1			1																						AmCom
LORENTZEN, BENT (1935–)																															
Contorni	1978		13	1		1			1																						Hanse
Mambo	1982		10			1			1									1													Hanse
Paesaggio	1983		12	1	1										1	1		1	1		1										Hanse
Paradiesvogel (Bird of Paradise)	1983		12	1		1			1			1			1			1									1				Hanse
Quadrata	1963		8	2	1	1																									Hanse
Quartetto Rustico	1972		10	2	1	1																									Hanse
Samba	1980		7			1			1									1					1								Hanse
Studies for Three *Comment:* Guitar may replace percussion	1968		20			1																					1	S			Hanse

	Year Composed or Published	Key	Duration	Violin	Viola	Cello	Double Bass	Gamba	Piano	Harpsicord	Organ	Guitar	Harp	Recorder	Flute/Piccolo	Oboe	English Horn	Clarinet/Bass Clarinet	Bassoon/Contrabassoon	Saxophone	French Horn	Trumpet	Trombone	Bass Trombone	Tuba	Baritone	Percussion	Voice	Electronic Tape	Unusual Instruments	Publisher
LORENTZEN, BENT *(continued)*																															
Syncretism	1970		6			1			1									1					1								Hanse
Wunderblümen	1982		14	2	1	1	1		1						1	1		1	1												Hanse
LORENZO, LEONARDO DE (1875–1962)																															
I quattro virtuosi, Op 8			12												1	1		1	1												Peter
Trio eccentrico, Op 76			7												1			1	1												Peter
Trio romantico, Op 78			12												1	1		1													Peter
LOTHAR, FRIEDRICH W. (1885–)																															
Streichtrio, Op 65				1	1	1																									Bären
LOTHAR, MARK (1902–)																															
Haiku (8)					1				1						1												1	S			Amade
LOUCHEUR, RAYMOND (1899–1979)																															
Portraits																1		1	1												Billa
LOUVIER, ALAIN (1945–)																															
Pièces, 5																					1	2	1		1						Leduc
Portraits, 5 et une image (solo sax)																1		1	1	1											Leduc
LOVENDUSKY, JAMES (1957–)																															
Danse macabre	1984		5	1		1			1						1			1									1				AmCom
Implosion *Unus Instr:* Bass clarinet. Electronic tape available from publisher.	1983		15												1		1	1	1								1		1	1	AmCom
Rhapsody on a Windy Night	1979		8		1	1			1																						AmCom
Sextet *Unus Instr:* Electric keyboard	1983		10	1		1			1																		2			1	AmCom
LUDEWIG, WOLFGANG (1926–)																															
Apokaliptische Vision	1972			1		1			1									1													BoteB
Concertino	1979									1					1				1												BoteB
Mosaik	1974														1	1		1	1		1										BoteB
Movimento variatio	1981				1							1			1																BoteB
Reflexionen	1975					1			1						1																BoteB
LUEDEKE, RAYMOND (1944–)																															
Acrostic	1979		7						1											4											AmCom
Macchu Picchu	1978		24	1	1				1						1																AmCom
The Moon in the Labyrinth	1984		25	2	1	1							1																		AmCom
Serenade	1982		12			1			1							1															AmCom
Variations	1971		7	1	1	1										1															AmCom
LUENING, OTTO (1900–)																															
Bass with the Delicate Air	1940		6												1	1		1	1												Highg
Brass Trio	1969		6																		1	1	1								Peter
Cartoons (4; "Short Suite")	1974		4												1			1	1												Highg
Dealer's Choice	1990		10	1	1	1																									Phant
Dealer's Choice (Divertimento) *Comment:* Flute may replace oboe	1990		10													1		1	1												Phant
Divertimento	1988		10	1	1	1										1															AmCom
Divertimento for Brass Quintet	1988		15																		1	2	1		1						AmCom
Easy March	1950		2						1					1	1	1															Juill
Elegy for the Lonesome Ones *Comment:* Can also be played with 2 clarinets	1974		6	2	1	1	1											1									1				AmCom
Elegy for the Lonesome Ones (alt. inst.) *Comment:* Trumpets are muted	1974		6	2	1	1	1											2				2									AmCom
Entrance and Exit Music *Unus Instr:* Cymbals	1964		5																			3	3				1			1	Peter

	Year Composed or Published	Key	Duration	Violin	Viola	Cello	Double Bass	Gamba	Piano	Harpsicord	Organ	Guitar	Harp	Recorder	Flute/Piccolo	Oboe	English Horn	Clarinet/Bass Clarinet	Bassoon/Contrabassoon	Saxophone	French Horn	Trumpet	Trombone	Bass Trombone	Tuba	Baritone	Percussion	Voice	Electronic Tape	Unusual Instruments	Publisher
LUENING, OTTO *(continued)*																															
Erster Verlust	1928		5						1						1													S			AmCom
Fanfare for a Festive Occasion *Unus Instr:* Bells, timpani, cymbals	1965		4																		3	3	3				3			3	Peter
Fantasia brevis	1936		5	1	1	1																									Scree
Fantasia for Piano Trio	1981		10		1	1			1																						AmCom
Fuguing Tune	1939		4												1	1		1	1		1										AMP
Green Mountain Evening, July 25, 1988	1988		6			2			1						1	1		1													AmCom
Mexican Serenades *Unus Instr:* Piccolo, bass clarinet	1974		10				1								2	1	1	2	1		1						2			2	Highg
Piano Trio	1921		13	1		1			1																						Highg
Potowatomi Legends	1980		18	1		1	1		2						1	1		1	1		1	1	1				3				AmCom
Prelude and Fugue	1974		4												1			1	1												Highg
Serenade	1983		17		1	1			1																						AmCom
Sextet	1918		17	1	1	1									1			1			1										Bardi
Song, Poem, and Dance	1958		10	2	1	1									1																Highg
The Soundless Song *Comment:* With optional movement and light	1924		17	2	1	1			1						1			1										1			Highg
String Quartet No. 1 *Comment:* Optional clarinet obbligato in last movement	1920		40	2	1	1																									Highg
String Quartet No. 2	1924		9	2	1	1																									Peter
String Quartet No. 3	1928		16	2	1	1																									Peter
Suite (4 Cartoons)	1966		4	1	1	1																									Highg
Suite	1976		11						1						2																Scree
Theatre Piece No. 2 *Voices:* Narrator and recorded soprano	1956		35												2			2	1		2	2	2		1		1	2	1		Manus
Triadic Canon with Variations	1976		6	2											1																AmCom
Trio (for Brass)	1969		6																		1	1	1								Peter
Trio (with Flute and Cello)	1962		10			1			1						1																Peter
Trio (with Flute and Violin)	1952		14	1					1						1																Highg
Trio (with Flute and Voice)	1924		6	1											1													S			Highg
LUMSDAINE, DAVID (1931–)																															
Annotations of Auschwitz *Unus Instr:* Bass flute	1964			1		1			1						1						1	1						S		1	Unive
LUNDBORG, ERIK (1948–)																															
Butte Chord for 8 Players	1975		12	1		1			1			1			1			1	1								1				AmCom
Ghost Sonatine *Unus Instr:* Bass clarinet	1983		14	1		1			1						1			1												1	AmCom
Soundsoup *Unus Instr:* Contrabass clarinet	1976		12						1						1			2	1			1			1		1			1	AmCom
LUPPI, GIAN P. (?–)																															
Specchi				2	1	1												1													Peter
LUSTIG, MOSHE (1922–1958)																															
Introduction, Interlude, and Conclusion	1954			2	1	1							1																		IsrMI
LUTOSLAWSKI, WITOLD (1913–)																															
Chain 1 *Comment:* Oboe doubles on English horn	1983		11	2	1	1	1		1						1	1	1	1	1		1	1	1				1				Chest
Dance Preludes (3rd version)	1959		7	2	1	1									1	1		1	1		1										Chest
Mini Overture	1982		3																		1	2	2								Chest
Prelude and Fugue *Comment:* For 13 Solo Strings	1971																														Chest
Slides *Comment:* Piano doubles on celesta	1988		4	1	1	1	1		1						1	1		1	1		1						1			1	Chest

	Year Composed or Published	Key	Duration	Violin	Viola	Cello	Double Bass	Gamba	Piano	Harpsicord	Organ	Guitar	Harp	Recorder	Flute/Piccolo	Oboe	English Horn	Clarinet/Bass Clarinet	Bassoon/Contrabassoon	Saxophone	French Horn	Trumpet	Trombone	Bass Trombone	Tuba	Baritone	Percussion	Voice	Electronic Tape	Unusual Instruments	Publisher
LUTOSLAWSKI, WITOLD *(continued)*																															
String Quartet	1964		25	2	1	1																									Chest
LYBBERT, DONALD (1923–1981)																															
Fanfare			1																			4	4								Peter
Lines for the Fallen			8						2																			S			Peter
Praeludium			6																			3	3				2				Peter
Trio for Winds			15															1	1		1										Peter
MAASZ, GERHARD (1906–)																															
Concertino *Comment:* Piano may replace harpsichord	1954			1		1				1					1																Bären
Divertimento *Comment:* Oboe may replace flute	1955			2	1	1									1																Sikor
Serenades (2)				1	1										1																Amade
MacBRIDE, DAVID H. (1951–)																															
It Figures *Unus Instr:* Xylophone	1976		12		1				1									1									1			1	AmCom
Litany for Gabrielle	1983		5						1						1												1				AmCom
Melody Wave (to Obata) *Unus Instr:* Bass clarinet	1977		10				1								2			2		1						1	1			1	AmCom
Quadrumane	1984		13				4																				4				AmCom
Twin (for 2 identical ensembles)	1983		2																			2					2				AmCom
Wintersong *** *Comment:* For solo melody instrument, and up to 20 others	1986		7																												AmCom
MACCOMBIE, BRUCE (1943–)																															
Canto marmerim	1972		12	1	1	1	1		1																		2	S		C	AMP
Parkside Music *Unus Instr:* Prepared piano	1978		14	1					2									1									1			1	AMP
MACDOWELL, EDWARD (1860–1908)																															
2 Woodland Sketches (trans.)																				4											Press
MACERO, TEO (1925–)																															
One-Three Quarters			8	1		1			2						2								1		1						Peter
MACHE, FRANÇOIS B. (1935–)																															
Rituel d'oublie for Tape and Ensemble *Unus Instr:* Contrabass clarinet	1969		33												2	2		5	2			3	3	1			3		1	1	Salab
Safous mele *Unus Instr:* Suspended and Chinese cymbals, snare drum, tam-tam	1959		15										1		2	2											1	9		4	Salab
MACHOVER, TOD (1953–)																															
Soft Morning, City!							1																					S	1		Ricor
String Quartet No. 1				2	1	1																									Ricor
MacKEY, STEVEN (1956–)																															
Piano Quartet	1982		16	1	1	1			1																						AmCom
MacMILLAN, ERNEST (1893–1973)																															
Sketches (2) on French Canadian Airs				2	1	1																									Oxfor
MACONCHY, ELIZABETH (1907–)																															
Quintet				2	1	1												1													Oxfor
Reflections					1								1			1		1													Oxfor
String Quartet No. 8	1967			2	1	1																									Faber
String Quartet No. 9	1969		14	2	1	1																									Chest
String Quartet No. 10	1972		15	2	1	1																									Chest
String Quartet No. 11	1976		16	2	1	1																									Chest

	Year Composed or Published	Key	Duration	Violin	Viola	Cello	Double Bass	Gamba	Piano	Harpsicord	Organ	Guitar	Harp	Recorder	Flute/Piccolo	Oboe	English Horn	Clarinet/Bass Clarinet	Bassoon/Contrabassoon	Saxophone	French Horn	Trumpet	Trombone	Bass Trombone	Tuba	Baritone	Percussion	Voice	Electronic Tape	Unusual Instruments	Publisher
MACONCHY, ELIZABETH *(continued)*																															
String Quartet No. 12	1979		13	2	1	1																									Chest
String Quartet No. 13 (Quartetto Corto)	1984		8	2	1	1																									Chest
Wind Quintet	1980		19												1	1		1	1		1										Chest
MADERNA, BRUNO (1920–1973)																															
Quartetto				2	1	1																									Suvin
MADJERA, GOTTFRIED (1905–)																															
String Quartet				2	1	1																									Peter
MAHLER, GUSTAVE (1860–1911)																															
Ich atmet'einen Linden Duft *Unus Instr:* Celesta	1901	F	2	1	1								1		1	1		1	1		3						1			1	Unive
Klavierquartett	1876			1	1	1			1																						Sikor
Lieder eines fahrenden Gesellen *Unus Instr:* Glockenspiel, harmonium	1884		25	2	2	1			1						1			1									1	L		2	Unive
Der Tambours'gsell	1901	e	5			1	1									2		3	3		4				1		4				Unive
MAIGUASHCA, MESIAS (1938–)																															
Oeldorf 8 *Unus Instr:* Synthesizer	1974			1		1					1							1											1	1	Feedb
Quarteto de Cuerdas	1964			2	1	1																									Feedb
MAINARDI, ENRICO (1897–1976)																															
Notturno				1		1			1																						Suvin
Quartetto				2	1	1																									Suvin
Trio				1		1			1																						Suvin
MALEC, IVO (1925–)																															
Arco 11 (for 11 String Soloists)	1975		19	6	2	2	1																								Salab
Lumina	1968		15	7	2	2	1																						1		Salab
Miniatures pour Lewis Carroll	1964		11	1									1		1												2				Breit
Vox, vocis *Voices:* 2 Sopranos and mezzo-soprano	1978		26	2	1	1	1						1									1					2	3			Salab
MALIPIERO, GIAN F. (1882–1973)																															
Dialogo no. 4 *Comment:* For 5 "strumenti a perdifiato"																															Ricor
Endecatode *Unus Instr:* Xylophone, celesta	1966		15	2	2	1			1						1	1		1	1		1	1	1				3			2	Unive
Quartetto No. 2 (Stornelli e ballate)	1923			2	1	1																									Ricor
Quartetto No. 5 (Dei Capricci)				2	1	1																									Suvin
Quartetto No. 6 (L'Arca di Noe)	1947			2	1	1																									Ricor
Quartetto No. 7	1950			2	1	1																									Ricor
Quartetto No. 8 (Per Elisabetta)	1964			2	1	1																									Ricor
Serenata mattutina *Unus Instr:* Celesta	1959		13		2										1	1		1	2		2						1			1	Unive
Sonata a cinque				1	1	1			1						1																Ricor
Sonata a cinque	1934			1	1	1							1		1																Ricor
MALIPIERO, RICCARDO (1914–)																															
Musica da camera	1959														1	1		1	1		1										Suvin
Quartetto I	1941			2	1	1																									Suvin
Quartetto II	1954			2	1	1																									Suvin
Quartetto III	1960			2	1	1																									Suvin
Quintetto	1957			2	1	1			1																						Suvin
MAMANGAKIS, NIKOS (1929–)																															
Tetraktys	1966		10	2	1	1																									Breit
MAMLOK, URSULA (1928–)																															
5 Bagatelles			7	1		1												1													Peter
5 Songs from Stray Birds						1									1													S			Peter

	Year Composed or Published	Key	Duration	Violin	Viola	Cello	Double Bass	Gamba	Piano	Harpsicord	Organ	Guitar	Harp	Recorder	Flute/Piccolo	Oboe	English Horn	Clarinet/Bass Clarinet	Bassoon/Contrabassoon	Saxophone	French Horn	Trumpet	Trombone	Bass Trombone	Tuba	Baritone	Percussion	Voice	Electronic Tape	Unusual Instruments	Publisher
MAMLOK, URSULA *(continued)*																															
Der Andreas Garten													1		1													M			Peter
Composition for 7 Players *Unus Instr:* Bass clarinet	1963		4	1	1	1												2				1					1			1	AmCom
Concertino			11	2	1	1	1								1	1		1	1		1						1				Peter
Concert Piece for Four	1964		8		1										1	1											1				AmCom
Divertimento	1975		9			1									1												2				AmCom
Festive Sounds			8												1	1		1	1		1										Peter
From My Garden II	1983		7						1							1					1										AmCom
Die Laterne			5	1		1			1						1			1										S			Peter
Movements	1966		9				1								1												1				AmCom
Panta Rhei			8	1		1			1																						Peter
Sextet			12	1			1		1						1			2													Peter
When Summer Sang			9	1		1			1						1			1													Peter
MANNINO, FRANCO (1924–)																															
Ballata drammatica, Op 67				1	1	1			1																						Ricor
Enigma				2	1	1																									Ricor
Improvisazione, Op 57				1					1												1										Ricor
MANOURY, PHILIPPE (1952–)																															
Numero cinq (for Piano)			25	2	1	1			1						1	1	1		1		1	2	1								Ridea
MANSURIAN, TIGRAN (1939–)																															
2 Girls	1984					1			1						1													1			VAAP
Concerto for Violin			18	11	4	3	1																								VAAP
Concerto No. 2 for Cello			25	10	4	4	1																								VAAP
Tovem *Unus Instr:* Bass drum			10	2	2	1			1						1	1		1	1		1	1	1				2			1	VAAP
MANZIARLY, MARCELLE DE (1899–)																															
Trio						1			1						1																Duran
MANZONI, GIACOMO (1932–)																															
Epodo															1	1		1	1		1										Ricor
Percorso a otto															2	2		2	2												Ricor
Quartetto				2	1	1																									Ricor
MARCKHL, ERICH (1902–)																															
8 Tänze				2	1	1																									Dobli
Sonata for Wind Quintet															1	1		1	1		1										Dobli
Streichquartett		c#		2	1	1																									Dobli
MARCO, TOMÁS (1942–)																															
Aura				2	1	1																									Salab
MARCOS, MIKLOS (1943–)																															
Descort	1971		7				1								1													S			Nordi
Pantomim	1970		12			1			1	1	1																		1		Nordi
Spel	1969		15			1												1					1				1				Nordi
MARKEVITCH, IGOR (1912–1983)																															
L'Envol d'Icare	1933		24						2																		3				Boose
Serenade	1931		18	1														1	1												Boose
MARTEAU, HENRI (1874–1934)																															
String Quartet No. 2, Op 9	1905			2	1	1																									Simro
MARTELLI, HENRI (1895–1980)																															
Trio																1		1	1												Billa
MARTI, HEINZ (1934–)																															
Response				1	1	1																									Hug
MARTIN, FRANK (1890–1974)																															
Ballade *Unus Instr:* Piccolo, bass clarinet, contrabassoon	1972		13		1					1			1		2	1	1	2	2		2	2	1				3			3	Unive

	Year Composed or Published	Key	Duration	Violin	Viola	Cello	Double Bass	Gamba	Piano	Harpsicord	Organ	Guitar	Harp	Recorder	Flute/Piccolo	Oboe	English Horn	Clarinet/Bass Clarinet	Bassoon/Contrabassoon	Saxophone	French Horn	Trumpet	Trombone	Bass Trombone	Tuba	Baritone	Percussion	Voice	Electronic Tape	Unusual Instruments	Publisher
MARTIN, FRANK *(continued)*																															
Klaviertrio über irländische Volkslieder				1		1			1																						Hug
Minnelieder (3)	1960		9		1	1									1													S			Unive
Pièce brève *Comment:* Harpsichord may replace harp	1957												1		1	1															Hug
Poemes de la mort *Voices:* Tenor, baritone. Electric guitars	1971		17									3																2			Unive
Quartett				2	1	1																									Unive
Rhapsodie	1935		14	2	2		1																								Unive
Sonnets, 4	1921				1	1									1													M			Hug
Streichtrio	1936			1	1	1																									Unive
Le vin herbé (Der Zaubertrank)	1941		105	2	2	2	1		1																			12			Unive
Weihnachtslieder (3)									1						1													H			Unive
MARTINO, DONALD (1931–)																															
Canoni (7) Enigmatici *Comment:* May also be played by 2 violas and 2 cellos or bassoons	1955			2	1	1																									ECSch
Concerto for Wind Quintet	1964		16												1	1		1	1		1										IoneP
Notturno	1973		16	1		1			1						1			1									1				IoneP
Quartet	1957		23	1	1	1												1													IoneP
Trio	1959			1		1			1																						ECSch
MARTINON, JEAN (1910–1976)																															
Domenon 4															1	1		1	1		1										Billa
Sonatine, 4e																1		1	1												Billa
String Quartet No. 2				2	1	1																									Press
Trio, Op 32 No. 2				1	1	1																									Billa
MARTINS, MARIA (1926–)																															
Trio	1961			1		1			1																						Gulben
MARTINŮ, BOHUSLAV (1890–1959)																															
Bergerettes				1		1			1																						Peer
Concerto da camera (String Quartet)				2	1	1																									Peer
Concerto pour clavecin	1935		17	3	1	1	1		1	1					1				1												Unive
Fantasy for Ondes Martenot *Unus Instr:* Ondes Martenot	1944		15	2	1	1			1							1														1	Eschi
Madrigal Sonata	1942			1					1						1																AMP
Mazurka-Nocturne	1949			2		1										1															Eschi
Musique de chambre No. 1	1959		18	1	1	1			1				1					1													Eschi
Pastorals	1951			2		1								5				1													Bären
Piano Quartet No. 1	1942			1	1	1			1																						AMP
Piano Quintet No. 1	1933		19	2	1	1			1																						Eschi
Piano Quintet No. 2	1944			2	1	1			1																						AMP
Piano Trio		d		1		1			1																						Eschi
Piano Trio No. 3				1		1			1																						Eschi
Promenades	1940			1						1					1																Bären
Quartett II				2	1	1																									Unive
Quatuor à cordes, 3e				2	1	1																									Leduc
La revue de cuisine, ballet fantaisie				1		1			1									1	1			1									Leduc
Sérénade *Unus Instr:* Clarinet in C	1951		21	1	1	1												2												1	Eschi
Sonate	1936			1					1						1																Bären
Sonatine				2					1																						Leduc
String Quintet	1927		18	2	2	1																									Eschi
Trio	1944		20			1			1						1																AMP
MARTIRANO, SALVATORE (1927–)																															
Octet	1963		15	2	1	1									1	1		1	1												Schir

	Year Composed or Published	Key	Duration	Violin	Viola	Cello	Double Bass	Gamba	Piano	Harpsicord	Organ	Guitar	Harp	Recorder	Flute/Piccolo	Oboe	English Horn	Clarinet/Bass Clarinet	Bassoon/Contrabassoon	Saxophone	French Horn	Trumpet	Trombone	Bass Trombone	Tuba	Baritone	Percussion	Voice	Electronic Tape	Unusual Instruments	Publisher
MARTIRANO, SALVATORE *(continued)*																															
Octet *Unus Instr:* Marimba, celesta	1984		15	1		1	1								1			2									2			2	Schir
MARX, JOSEPH (1882–1964)																															
Quartetto chromatico (2nd version)	1937	A		2	1	1																									Dobli
Streichquartett (in modo antico)	1938			2	1	1																									Dobli
Streichquartett (in modo classico)	1941			2	1	1																									Dobli
MARX, KARL (1897–1985)																															
Botschaft, Op 41 *Comment:* Violin, flute, may replace recorders									1					2														S			Bären
Divertimento, Op 21a		F		1	1	1			1						1																Bären
Frühlingstau in deinen Augen, Op 38 *Comment:* Violin or flute may replace recorder									1					1														A			Bären
Kammermusik, Op 56	1955			1	1	1		1		1					1	1															Bären
Liebeslieder, 3, Op 42a				2	1	1																						S			Bären
Reifende Frucht, Op 23									1																			2			Bären
Turmmusik, Op 37 No. 1 *Comment:* Percussion ad libitum	1938																					3	2								Bären
Variationen, 18, Op 30				1	1	1								2		1															Bären
MASEK, VACLAV V. (1755–1831)																															
Serenada		D♭														2		2	2		2										MABoh
MASELLI, GIANFRANCO (1929–)																															
4 Movimenti				2	1	1																									Suvin
Divertimento				1			1			1					1	1						1	1								Suvin
MASON, BENEDICT (1954–)																															
Adagio con molto sentimento d'affetto	1988		11			2			1																						Chest
Brass Quintet	1989		15																		1	2	1		1						Chest
Double Concerto for Horn, Trombone	1988		19	2	1	1	1		1				1		1	1		1	1		1	1	1		1		1				Chest
The Hinterstoisser Traverse	1986		13	1	1	1			1						1	1		1	1		1	1	1				1				Chest
Horn Trio	1987		25	1					1												1										Chest
Imposing a . . . Pattern in Chaos . . .	1990		15	2	1	1	1		1						1	1		1				1					1				Chest
Nodding Trillums and Curve Lined Angles *Unus Instr:* DX7 (doubled on piano)	1990		20	2	1	1	1		1						1	1		1	1		2	1	1				4			1	Chest
String Quartet	1987		35	2	1	1																									Chest
MASON, DANIEL G. (1873–1953)																															
Divertimento, Op 26	1927		14												1	1		1	1		1										CarlF
Fanny Blair (folksong fantasy)	1929			2	1	1																									Oxfor
Pastorale, Op 8	1913		9	1					1									1													Matho
Pieces (3), Op 13	1922		10	2	1	1							1		1																SPAM
Quartet, Op 7	1912		30	1	1	1			1																						Schir
Serenade	1929			2	1	1																									CarlF
String Quartet on Negro Themes, Op 19	1919		27	2	1	1																									SPAM
Variations on a John Powell Theme, Op 24	1926		13	2	1	1																									CarlF
MASON, JOHN (?–)																															
Canonic Device	1960																	2	1												ComPr
MASSEUS, JAN (1913–)																															
Tango						1			1						3																Harmo
MASSIAS, GÉRARD (1933–)																															
Variations							1									1		1		1											Billa

	Year Composed or Published	Key	Duration	Violin	Viola	Cello	Double Bass	Gamba	Piano	Harpsicord	Organ	Guitar	Harp	Recorder	Flute/Piccolo	Oboe	English Horn	Clarinet/Bass Clarinet	Bassoon/Contrabassoon	Saxophone	French Horn	Trumpet	Trombone	Bass Trombone	Tuba	Baritone	Percussion	Voice	Electronic Tape	Unusual Instruments	Publisher
MASSIS, AMABLE (1893–)																															
Theme et variations															1	1		1	1		1										Billa
MASSON, GÉRARD (1936–)																															
Alto tambour (for 2 Violas) *Unus Instr:* 5-String bass	1985		23	7	4	2	1																							1	Salab
Gymnastique de l'éponge	1985		28	2	1	1	1		1							1	1	2	1												Salab
Ouest 1	1967		15	1		1			1				1		1			2	1			1	1								Salab
Quatuor a cordes				2	1	1																									Salab
MASSONEAU, LOUIS (?–)																															
Quartets, 3				1	1		1									1															Amade
MATHIAS, WILLIAM (1934–)																															
Ceremony after Fire Raid (Dylan Thomas) *Voices:* Soprano, alto, tenor, baritone, bass									1																		1	5			Oxfor
Concertino, Op 65 *Comment:* Recorder may replace flute; piano, harpsichord	1964		12							1					1	1			1												Oxfor
Divertimento, Op 24	1963		10						1						1	1															Oxfor
Investiture Anniversary Fanfare *Unus Instr:* 2 Bass trumpets. Bass trumpets may be replaced by trombones			4																			6		1			4			2	Oxfor
Piano Trio, Op 30			15	1		1			1																						Oxfor
Quintet, Op 22	1963		17												1	1		1	1		1										Oxfor
Soundings	1988																				1	2	2								Oxfor
String Quartet, Op 38	1967		18	2	1	1																									Oxfor
String Quartet No. 2, Op 84			19	2	1	1																									Oxfor
String Quartet No. 3	1987		29	2	1	1																									Oxfor
Zodiac Trio, Op 70			16		1								1		1																Oxfor
MATSUDAIRA, YORI-AKI (1931–)																															
Variazioni				1		1			1																						Suvin
MATTHEWS, COLIN (1946–)																															
Ceres, Op 4 *Unus Instr:* Indian bells, vibraphone	1972		15			2	1					1			3												2			2	Faber
Divertimento, Op 21a	1982		21	4	2	2																									Faber
The Great Journey, Parts 1 and 2, Op 22	1983		22		1	1	1		1						1			1			1						1	B			Faber
Little Suite No. 1, Op 18a	1979		6	4	2	2	1								1	1		2	1		1	1									Faber
Little Suite No. 2, Op 18b *Unus Instr:* Vibraphone, glockenspiel	1979		6	4	2	2	1								1	1	1	3	1		1	1					1			2	Faber
Night's Mask (for Soprano), Op 26	1984				1	1			1				1		1			1			1							S			Faber
Oboe Quartet	1981			1	1	1										1															Faber
Rainbow Studies, Op 12 *Unus Instr:* Bass clarinet	1978		17						1						1		1	1	1											1	Faber
String Quartet No. 1	1979			2	1	1																									Faber
Sun's Dance *Unus Instr:* Contrabassoon	1985		17	2	2	1									1		1	1	1		1									1	Faber
Triptych, Op 25a	1984		6	2	1	1			1																						Faber
MATTHEWS, WILLIAM (1950–)																															
Ferns (B)	1976		10	1		1			1						1																AmCom
Letters from Home (Antiphonal Music) *Comment:* Conductor needed	1976		12		1		1		1	1					1			1	1								1				AmCom
MATTHUS, SIEGFRIED (1934–)																															
Streichquartett	1971			2	1	1																									DeutV

	Year Composed or Published	Key	Duration	Violin	Viola	Cello	Double Bass	Gamba	Piano	Harpsicord	Organ	Guitar	Harp	Recorder	Flute/Piccolo	Oboe	English Horn	Clarinet/Bass Clarinet	Bassoon/Contrabassoon	Saxophone	French Horn	Trumpet	Trombone	Bass Trombone	Tuba	Baritone	Percussion	Voice	Electronic Tape	Unusual Instruments	Publisher
MATTHUS, SIEGFRIED *(continued)*																															
Trio	1972				1								1		1																DeutV
MAURER, LUDWIG W. (1789–1878)																															
12 Little Pieces (Book I)																					1	2	2								Novel
12 Little Pieces (Book II)																					1	2	2								Novel
MAVES, DAVID (1937–)																															
A Bestiary *Voices:* 2 Sopranos, 2 altos			9																								2	4			Peter
Oktoechos			8															1			1						1				Peter
MAW, NICHOLAS (1935–)																															
Double Canon for Stravinsky (alt. vers.)	1967		1	2	1	1																									Boose
Double Canon for Stravinsky (for winds) *Unus Instr:* Bass clarinet	1967		1												2			2												1	Boose
Double Canon for Stravinsky's Birthday	1967		1		1								1		1																Boose
Flute Quartet	1981			1	1	1									1																Faber
String Quartet No. 1	1965		35	2	1	1																									Boose
MAXWELL DAVIES, PETER (1934–)																															
Agnus Dei *Voices:* 2 Sopranos	1984		5		1	1																						2			Chest
All Sons of Adam (realization) *Unus Instr:* Celesta, marimba	1974		7		1	1						1			1			1									2			2	Boose
Antechrist	1967		6	1		1									1			1									2			B	Boose
Ave Maris Stella *Unus Instr:* Marimba	1975		32		1	1			1						1			1									1			1	Boose
The Bairns of Brugh *Unus Instr:* Marimba	1981		5		1	1			1						1			1									1			1	Boose
Birthday Music for John	1983		9		1	1									1																Chest
The Blind Fiddler *Comment:* Array of percussion instruments	1975		43	1		1				1		1			1			1									1	M			Boose
Brass Quintet	1981		25																		1	2	1		1						Chest
Brass Quintet	1981		33																		1	2	2								Chest
Canon in memoriam Igor Stravinsky *Comment:* Puzzle canon, lasts till puzzle is solved	1972			2	1	1							1		1			1													Boose
Dances from "Two Fiddlers" (solo vln)	1978			1		1			1						1			1									1				Boose
Fantasia on a Ground and Two Pavans *Comment:* Based on works by Purcell	1968		12	1		1				1					1			1									1				Boose
Fiddlers at the Wedding *Unus Instr:* Mandolin	1974		19									1			1												1	M		1	Boose
From Stone to Thorn	1971		13							1		1						1									1	M			Boose
Gesualdo Motets (2)	1982		3																		1	2	2								Chest
Hymn to St. Magnus	1972		37		1	1			1						1			1									1	M			Boose
Image, Reflection, Shadow *Unus Instr:* Cimbalom	1982		30	1		1			1						1			1									1			1	Chest
In Nomine (7)	1965		21	2	1	1							1		1	1		1	1		1										Boose
Jimmack the Postie *Unus Instr:* Timpani	1986		11	1	1	1	1								1	1			1		1	1					1			1	Chest
Kinloche his Fantassie (realization) *Unus Instr:* Glockenspiel	1975		5	1		1				1					1			1									1			1	Boose
Little Quartet No. 1 *Comment:* In memoriam Oriel Glock	1980		8	2	1	1																									Boose

	Year Composed or Published	Key	Duration	Violin	Viola	Cello	Double Bass	Gamba	Piano	Harpsicord	Organ	Guitar	Harp	Recorder	Flute/Piccolo	Oboe	English Horn	Clarinet/Bass Clarinet	Bassoon/Contrabassoon	Saxophone	French Horn	Trumpet	Trombone	Bass Trombone	Tuba	Baritone	Percussion	Voice	Electronic Tape	Unusual Instruments	Publisher
MAXWELL DAVIES, PETER *(continued)*																															
Little Quartet No. 2	1981			2	1	1																									Boose
March: The Pole Star	1982		3																		1	2	2								Chest
A Mirror of Whitening Light *Unus Instr:* Crotales, glockenspiel, marimbaphone, celesta	1977		22	2	1	1	1								1		1	1	1		1	1	1				1			4	Boose
Missa super l'Homme armè *Unus Instr:* Harmonium or harpsichord, celesta, or out-of-tune piano	1971		20	1		1					1				1		1										1	1		1	Boose
My Lady Lothian's List *Unus Instr:* Glockenspiel, marimba	1975		7	1		1									1			1									2	M		2	Boose
Our Father Whiche in Heaven Art *Comment:* Realization after John Angus. *Unus Instr:* Celesta, marimba	1977		5	1		1									1			1									2			2	Boose
Points and Dances from "Taverner" (Act I)	1970		9		1	1				1		1			1			1													Boose
Points and Dances from "Taverner" (Act II) *Unus Instr:* Positive organ, regal; contrabassoon	1970		10								1				1			1	1			1	1				1			3	Boose
Prelude and Fugue in c# (J.S. Bach) *Comment:* From Bach's Well-Tempered Clavier, BWV 849, Book I. *Unus Instr:* Marimba	1972		5		1	1				1					1			1									1			1	Boose
Prelude and Fugue in C# (J.S. Bach) *Comment:* From The Well-tempered Clavier, Book I. *Unus Instr:* Marimba	1974		5		1	1				1					1			1									1			1	Boose
Psalm 124 (realization) *Comment:* Realization after Peebles, Fethy, and Anon. *Unus Instr:* Glockenspiel, marimba	1974		10	1		1						1			1			1									2			2	Boose
Quartet Movement	1952		5	2	1	1																									Chest
Renaissance Scottish Dances *Comment:* Arranged after anonymous originals. *Unus Instr:* Glockenspiel, marimba	1973		10	1		1						1			1			1									1			2	Boose
Revelation and Fall *Comment:* Array of percussion instruments. *Unus Instr:* Contrabassoon	1980		25	2	1	1	1						1		1	1		1	1		1	1	1				3	S		1	Boose
Runes from a Holy Island *Unus Instr:* Celesta	1977		10		1	1									1			1									1			1	Chest
Shakespeare Music *Unus Instr:* Contrabassoon	1964		12		1		1					1			1	1		1	1		1		1				1			1	Boose
Si Quis Diligit Me (realization) *Comment:* Arranged after Peebles and Heagy. *Unus Instr:* Celesta	1973		4		1	1									1			1									2			1	Boose
Stedman Caters	1968		15		1	1				1					1			1									1				Boose
Tallis Voluntaries (4)	1982		4																		1	2	2								Chest
Unbroken Circle *Unus Instr:* Bass clarinet	1984		6		1	1			1						1			1												1	Chest
Veni sancte—Veni Creator spiritus *Comment:* Transcription of an original by Dunstable, and a free fantasia. *Unus Instr:* Glockenspiel	1972		9		1	1				1					1			1									1			1	Boose
A Welcome to Orkney	1980		3	4	2	2									1	1		1	1		1										Boose

	Year Composed or Published	Key	Duration	Violin	Viola	Cello	Double Bass	Gamba	Piano	Harpsicord	Organ	Guitar	Harp	Recorder	Flute/Piccolo	Oboe	English Horn	Clarinet/Bass Clarinet	Bassoon/Contrabassoon	Saxophone	French Horn	Trumpet	Trombone	Bass Trombone	Tuba	Baritone	Percussion	Voice	Electronic Tape	Unusual Instruments	Publisher
MAYER, B (?–)																															
3 Light Movements on a Folksong *Comment:* "Fein Sein, beinander bleiben"																					1	2	1		1						Dobli
Blues for Five																					1	2	1		1						Dobli
Christmas Songs for Brass Quintet																					1	2	1		1						Dobli
Kein schöner Land																					1	2	2								Dobli
Little Fantasy on a Folksong																					1	2	1		1						Dobli
Turmbläsen fur Weihnachtszeit																						2	2								Dobli
MAYER, WILLIAM (1925–)																															
Country Fair																						2	1								Press
MAYR, GIOVANNI (1763–1845)																															
12 Bagatelles *Unus Instr:* Basset horn (may be replaced by clarinet)															1				1											1	Kneus
MAYUZUMI, TOSHIRO (1929–)																															
Metamusic *Comment:* Conductor needed				1					1											1											Peter
Microcosmos *Unus Instr:* Claveoline, musical saw, vibraphone, xylophone			13						1			1															1			4	Peter
Olympics (Ballet in One Act)			20				1		1												2	2	2				2				Peter
Pieces for Prepared Piano and Strings *Unus Instr:* Prepared piano			13	2	1	1			1																					1	Peter
Prelude			12	2	1	1																									Peter
Sphenogrammes *Unus Instr:* Marimba			20	1		1			1						1					1							1	A		1	Peter
McBRIDE, ROBERT (1911–)																															
Chipanecas	1973		2	1		1							1																		AmCom
Cielito lindo	1968		3	1		1							1																		AmCom
Comfortable Flight	1958		5	2	1	1											1														AmCom
Home on the Range	1961		3	1		1							1																		AmCom
Quintet	1958		5	2	1	1										1															AmCom
I Ride an Old Paint *Unus Instr:* Garden hose in F#	1973		2																			1	1							1	AmCom
Rudiments of Rugcutting (Quartet)	1950		3	2		1			1																						AmCom
Rudiments of Rugcutting (Trio)	1950		3						1							1		1													AmCom
Wise-Apple Five	1944		5	2	1	1												1													AmCom
McCABE, JOHN (1939–)																															
Rounds for Brass Quintet																					1	2	1		1						Novel
McEWEN, JOHN (1868–1948)																															
Nugae (Seven Bagatelles)	1912		16	2	1	1																									Boose
String Quartet	1921	e	23	2	1	1																									Boose
McGUIRE, JOHN (1942–)																															
Cadenza	1967			2	1	1																									Feedb
McKAY, GEORGE F. (1899–1970)																															
Joyful Dance															1	1		1	1		1										Press
McLEAN, EDWIN (1906–1951)																															
Big Variations *Unus Instr:* Xylophone	1977		8	2	1	1									2			2			1	1	1				1			1	AmCom
Box Car Bertha													1		1													S			AMP
Trio *Unus Instr:* Electric bass	1981		1				1		1																		1			1	AmCom
McPHEE, COLIN (1901–1964)																															
Concerto for Piano and Wind Octet	1928		18						1						2	1		1	1		1	1	1								AMP
MEALE, RICHARD (1932–)																															
Las alboradas	1963		13	1					1						1						1										Boose
Incredible Floridas *Unus Instr:* Bass clarinet. Violin doubles on viola	1971		33	1		1			1						1			1									1			1	Unive

	Year Composed or Published	Key	Duration	Violin	Viola	Cello	Double Bass	Gamba	Piano	Harpsicord	Organ	Guitar	Harp	Recorder	Flute/Piccolo	Oboe	English Horn	Clarinet/Bass Clarinet	Bassoon/Contrabassoon	Saxophone	French Horn	Trumpet	Trombone	Bass Trombone	Tuba	Baritone	Percussion	Voice	Electronic Tape	Unusual Instruments	Publisher
MEFANO, PAUL (1937–)																															
Estampes japonaises *Voice:* Light soprano or coloratura. *Unus Instr:* Celesta or glockenspiel			10	2	1	1			1				1		2			2									1	S		1	Salab
Et l'unique cordeau des trompettes marin	1962						1		1									1					1				1	S			Salab
L'Infirmité du feu *Unus Instr:* Hyoshi				1	1	1			1							1		1					1					S		1	Salab
Mouvement calme				2	1	1																									Salab
Ondes, espaces mouvants *Unus Instr:* Heckelphone	1976			2											1		1	1	1		1	1	1				1			1	Salab
La Scene 1 (for Four Voices) *Voices:* Soprano, mezzo-soprano, tenor, bass. *Unus Instr:* Celesta	1986			1	1	1	1		1						2	1			1	2	1	2					3	4		1	Salab
La Scene 3 (for Voice) *Unus Instr:* Celesta	1984		20	1	1	1	1		1						2	1			1	2	1	2					3	1		1	Salab
Signes-Oubli, I *Unus Instr:* Piccolo trumpet	1972		4	1	1	1	1				2				1			2				1		1			1			1	Salab
Signes-Oubli, II *Unus Instr:* Contrabass tuba	1972		4	1	1	1	1					1				1	1		1		1				1		1			1	Salab
MEIER, JOST (1939–)																															
2 Canzonen																						2	2								Billa
MELBY, JOHN (1941–)																															
And I Remembered the Cry of the Peacocks	1988		14	1	1	1											1												1		AmCom
MELLNÄS, ARNE (1933–)																															
Cabrillo	1970					1												1					1				1				Peter
Capricorn Flakes *Unus Instr:* Vibraphone, glockenspiel	1970								1	1																	1			2	Peter
Ceremus	1973						1								1			1				1	1				1				Peter
Gardens	1986			1		1			1						1			1									1				Nordi
Per Caso	1962			1			1													1			1				2				Tonos
Quasi niente *Comment:* Can be played 2, 3, or 4 to a part	1968		10	1	1	1																									Peter
Siamfoni	1964																				1	1	1								Peter
MENDELSSOHN, FELIX (1809–1847)																															
Concerted Pieces (2) *Unus Instr:* Basset horn									1									1												1	VarPb
Octet for Strings, Op 20	1825	E♭		4	2	2																									VarPb
Piano Quartet, Op 1	1822	c		1	1	1			1																						VarPb
Piano Quartet No. 2, Op 2	1823	f		1	1	1			1																						VarPb
Piano Quartet No. 3, Op 3	1825	b		1	1	1			1																						VarPb
Piano Trio No. 1, Op 49	1839	d		1		1			1																						VarPb
Piano Trio No. 2, Op 66	1845	c		1		1			1																						VarPb
Pieces (4)	1847			2	1	1																									Breit
Pieces, 3 (arr. Naumann)						1			1									1													Amade
Scherzo, from "Midsummer Night's Dream" (arr. Gabler), Op 61 No. 1															1	1		1	1		1										Dobli
Sextet, Op 110	1824	D		1	2	1	1		1																						VarPb
String Quartet, Op 12	1829	E♭		2	1	1																									VarPb
String Quartet, Op 13	1827	a		2	1	1																									VarPb
String Quartet, Op 44 No. 1	1838	D		2	1	1																									VarPb
String Quartet, Op 44 No. 2	1837	e		2	1	1																									VarPb
String Quartet, Op 44 No. 3	1838	E♭		2	1	1																									VarPb
String Quartet, Op 80	1847	f		2	1	1																									VarPb

	Year Composed or Published	Key	Duration	Violin	Viola	Cello	Double Bass	Gamba	Piano	Harpsicord	Organ	Guitar	Harp	Recorder	Flute/Piccolo	Oboe	English Horn	Clarinet/Bass Clarinet	Bassoon/Contrabassoon	Saxophone	French Horn	Trumpet	Trombone	Bass Trombone	Tuba	Baritone	Percussion	Voice	Electronic Tape	Unusual Instruments	Publisher
MENDELSSOHN, FELIX *(continued)*																															
String Quintet, Op 18	1832	A		2	2	1																									VarPb
String Quintet, Op 87	1845	B♭		2	2	1																									VarPb
MENEELY-KYDER, SARAH (1945–)																															
Rob Peter to Pay Paul	1983		20						1						1	1		1	1		1										AmCom
MENNIN, PETER (1923–1983)																															
Voices *Unus Instr:* Timpani	1975		25						1	1			1														6	S		1	Schir
MENOTTI, GIAN C. (1911–)																															
Cantilena and Scherzo	1977		12	2	1	1							1																		Schir
Nocturne (for High Voice)	1982		6	2	1	1							1															H			Schir
MENU, PIERRE (?–)																															
Sonatine				2	1	1																									Duran
MERILAEINEN, USKO (1930–)																															
Impressions	1965		6		1	1	1		1						1	1		1	1		1						1				BoteB
MERSSON, BORIS (1921–)																															
Odyssée à quatre																1		1	1	1											Kunze
MESSIAEN, OLIVIER (1908–1992)																															
Mass for 8 Sopranos and 4 Violins	1933			4																								8			Unive
La mort du nombre *Voices:* Soprano and tenor	1930			1					1																			2			Duran
Oiseaux exotiques *Unus Instr:* Glockenspiel, xylophone, temple blocks	1956		14						1						2	1		4	1		2	1					7			3	
Quatuor pour la fin du temps	1941			1		1			1									1													Duran
METSK, JURO (1954–)																															
Sestetto	1982			1	1										1				1		1						1				DeutV
METZLER, FRIEDRICH (1910–)																															
3 Hymnen *Unus Instr:* Glockenspiel											1																5			1	Merse
MEYER, ERNST H. (1905–)																															
Clarinet Quintet				2	1	1												1													Peter
String Quartet No. 4				2	1	1																									Peter
Trio 1948				1		1			1																						Peter
MEYER, JEAN (?–)																															
3 Interludes en sextuor *Comment:* Percussion ad lib																					2	2	2				1				Leduc
Choral et fuga cantabile																					1	3	1		1						Leduc
Hymne à l'Aurore *Comment:* Percussion ad lib																					2	2	2		1		1				Leduc
Negro Spiritual																					2	2	2		1						Billa
Variations sur un thème classique *Comment:* Oboe may replace flute															1			2													Leduc
MICHAEL, FRANK (1943–)																															
Trio, Op 58	1985		19	1					1						1																BoteB
Yantra, Op 41				1		1			1																						BoteB
MICHEELSEN, HANS F. (1902–1973)																															
Ei, du feiner Reiter (5 Variations)																						2	3								Bären
Singet dem Herrn *Comment:* Harpsichord may replace organ											1				1													S			Bären
Was betrübst du dich				1							1																	A			Bären
Wenn ich mit Menschen und mit Engels zun *Voice:* Alto or bass				1							1																	1			Bären
MIEG, PETER (1906–)																															
Quintet	1969			2		1				1					1																Amade

	Year Composed or Published	Key	Duration	Violin	Viola	Cello	Double Bass	Gamba	Piano	Harpsicord	Organ	Guitar	Harp	Recorder	Flute/Piccolo	Oboe	English Horn	Clarinet/Bass Clarinet	Bassoon/Contrabassoon	Saxophone	French Horn	Trumpet	Trombone	Bass Trombone	Tuba	Baritone	Percussion	Voice	Electronic Tape	Unusual Instruments	Publisher
MIEREANU, COSTIN (1943–)																															
Couleurs du temps				2	1	1																									Salab
Enlacements infinis *Unus Instr:* Celesta	1985		15	1		1			1						1			2			1	1	1				2	S		1	Salab
Kammerkonzert I *Unus Instr:* Mandolin	1985		16	1			1					1	1		1			1		1							2			1	Salab
Labyrinthes d'Adrien *Unus Instr:* Ondes Martenot, synthesizer, electric keyboards	1981		18			1			2		3	2			1			1			1							S		3	Salab
MIGOT, GEORGES (1891–1976)																															
1er Livre de divertissement (Conclusion)													1		1			1													Leduc
Concert *Comment:* Violin, piano can substitute for flute and harp						1							1		1																Leduc
Mouvements d'eau, 5				2	1	1																									Leduc
Quintette, Op 350															1	1		1	1		1										Leduc
Threne																1		1	1												Leduc
Trio																1		1	1												Leduc
Trio (ou suite à trois)				1		1			1																						Leduc
MIHALOVICI, MARCEL (1898–1985)																															
Concerto quasi una fantasia (for violin), Op 33	1930			1		1	1		1						2	2		2	2			2	1		1						Eschi
MILHAUD, DARIUS (1892–1974)																															
Der 129 Psalm, Op 53	1919		8	4	2	2	2						1		2	1		2	1			1					1	B			Unive
Actualités, Op 104	1928		7	2	2	2	1											2				2	1				1				Unive
Cantate de l'enfant et de la mère, Op 185 *Voice:* Reciter	1938			2	1	1			1																			1			Heugel
Cantate del'homme *Voices:* Soprano, alto, tenor, bass	1937		20						1						1	1			1	1							2	4		T	Salab
Cantate de Psaumes, Op 425 *Unus Instr:* Piccolo, bass clarinet	1967		18	4	2	2	1						1		1			1	1			1					3	B		2	Unive
Caramel Mou ("Shimmy" for Jazz band), Op 68 *Voice:* Optional	1920								1									1				1	1				1	1			Eschi
Chamber Concerto, Op 389	1961		15	2	1	1	1		1						1	1		1	1		1										Eschi
Concerto for Percussion, Op 109	1930		7	6	2	2	1								2			2			1		1				1				Unive
Concerto for Viola			15	2	2	1									2	1		2	1		1	1	1				1				Unive
La creation du monde (Ballet), Op 81a *Unus Instr:* Timpani	1923		15	2		1	1		1						2	1		2	1	1	1	2	1				2			1	Eschi
La creation du monde (Suite de concert), Op 81b	1926		15	2	1	1			1																						Eschi
Études sur des thèmes liturgiques			11	2	1	1																									Eschi
L'Homme et son désir, Op 48	1918		20	2	1	1	1						1		2	2		2	1		1	2					2				Unive
Machines agricoles, Op 56	1919		12	1	1	1	1								1			1	1									M			Unive
Mesures (150, for Heugel's 150th anniv.)																						2	1								Heuge
Music for the Ars Nova, Op 432 *Unus Instr:* Bass clarinet	1969		12	1		1			1				1		1			2	1		1	1	1				2			1	Eschi
Musique pour Graz, Op 429	1969		15	1	1	1	1								1	1		1	1			1									Unive
Octuor (Quartets 14 and 15)	1949			4	2	2																									Heuge
Pan et Syrinx *Voices:* Soprano, baritone, and vocal quartet	1934		20						1						1	1			1	1								2			Salab
Pan et Syrinx (alt. inst.) *Voices:* Soprano, baritone, and vocal quartet	1934		20						1						1		1		1	1								6			Salab
Pastorale, Op 147	1935															1		1	1												Monde
Quartett VI	1922	G		2	1	1																									Unive

	Year Composed or Published	Key	Duration	Violin	Viola	Cello	Double Bass	Gamba	Piano	Harpsichord	Organ	Guitar	Harp	Recorder	Flute/Piccolo	Oboe	English Horn	Clarinet/Bass Clarinet	Bassoon/Contrabassoon	Saxophone	French Horn	Trumpet	Trombone	Bass Trombone	Tuba	Baritone	Percussion	Voice	Electronic Tape	Unusual Instruments	Publisher
MILHAUD, DARIUS *(continued)*																															
Quartett VII	1925	B♭		2	1	1																									Unive
Quatuor				1	1	1			1																						Duran
Quatuor à cordes, 1er, Op 5	1912			2	1	1																									Duran
Quatuor à cordes, 2e, Op 16	1915			2	1	1																									Duran
Quatuor à cordes, 3e, Op 32	1916			2	1	1																							1			Duran
Quatuor à cordes, 4e, Op 46	1918			2	1	1																									Salab
Quatuor à cordes, 5e, Op 64	1920			2	1	1																									Salab
Quatuor à cordes, 10e, Op 218	1940			2	1	1																									Salab
Quatuor à cordes, 11e, Op 232	1942			2	1	1																									Salab
Quatuor à cordes, 12e, Op 252	1945			2	1	1																									Salab
Quatuor à cordes, 13e, Op 268	1946			2	1	1																									Salab
Quatuor à cordes, 14e, Op 291	1948			2	1	1																									Heuge
Quatuor à cordes, 15e, Op 291	1949			2	1	1																									Heuge
Quatuor à cordes, 16e	1949			2	1	1																									Heuge
Quatuor à cordes, 17e, Op 307	1951			2	1	1																									Heuge
Quatuor à cordes, 18e, Op 308	1952			2	1	1																									Heuge
Quintette, Op 443	1973		17												1	1		1	1		1										Eschi
Quintette à cordes, 1er				2	1	1			1																						Heuge
Quintette à cordes, 2e, Op 316	1953			2	2	1																									Heuge
Quintette à cordes, 3e				2	2	1																									Heuge
Quintette à cordes, 4e, Op 350	1956			2	1	2																									Heuge
Les rêves de Jacob, Op 294	1954			1	1	1	1									1															Heuge
Scaramouche (solo saxophone)	1937		10												1	1		1	1	1	1										Salab
Septuor à cordes	1964			2	2	2	1																								Heuge
Sextuor à cordes, Op 368	1959			2	2	2																									Heuge
Sketches (2)															1	1		1	1		1										Press
Sonate, Op 15	1914			2					1																						Duran
Sonate, Op 47	1918								1						1	1		1													Duran
Sonatine à trois				1	1	1																									Press
Stanford Serenade (for Oboe), Op 430	1969		12	2	1	1	1						1		1			1	1			1					1				Eschi
Suite, Op 157b	1937			1					1									1													Salab
Suite des quatrains	1962		12	1		1	1						1		1			1		1								N			Salab
Suite des sonnets, Op 401 *Voices:* Soprano, countertenor, tenor, bass	1963		17		1					1					1	1			1				1					4			Eschi
Symphonie 1: Le Printemps, Op 43 *Unus Instr:* Piccolo	1917		4	2	1	1							1		2	1		1												1	Unive
Symphonie 2: Pastorale, Op 49	1918		4	1	1	1	1								1		1		1												Unive
Symphonie 3: Serenade, Op 71	1921		3	1	1	1	1								1			1	1												Unive
Symphonie 4: Dixtuor à cordes, Op 74	1921		6	4	2	2	2																								Unive
Symphonie 5: Dixtuor d'instruments à vent, Op 75 *Unus Instr:* Piccolo, bass clarinet	1922		5												2	1	1	2	2		2									2	Unive
Symphonie 6, Op 79 *Voices:* Soprano, alto, tenor, bass	1923		6			1										1												4			Unive
Trio à cordes, Op 274	1947			1	1	1																									Heuge
MILLER, EDWARD (1930–)																															
Around *** *Comment:* For any odd number of players above 5	1973																														AmCom
Fantasy-Concerto for Alto Sax	1971		10												2	2		2	2		2	2	2		1	1					AmCom
Going Home *Unus Instr:* Electric bass and electric piano, vibraphone	1985		5				1		1									1									1			3	AmCom
Piano Trio	1984		13		1	1			1																						AmCom
Quartet-Variations *** *Comment:* For any four musicians, and 35 mm slides	1972		20																												AmCom

	Year Composed or Published	Key	Duration	Violin	Viola	Cello	Double Bass	Gamba	Piano	Harpsicord	Organ	Guitar	Harp	Recorder	Flute/Piccolo	Oboe	English Horn	Clarinet/Bass Clarinet	Bassoon/Contrabassoon	Saxophone	French Horn	Trumpet	Trombone	Bass Trombone	Tuba	Baritone	Percussion	Voice	Electronic Tape	Unusual Instruments	Publisher
MILLER, EDWARD *(continued)*																															
Serenade (All Ill-Lit Night)	1982		8												2	2		2	2		1	1	1								AmCom
MILLS, CHARLES (1914–)																															
The Brass Piano	1964		4																			3	3				1				AmCom
Chamber Concerto	1942		15	2	1	1									1	1		1	1		2										AmCom
The Fourth Joyful Mystery	1945		3	2		1			1																						AmCom
Music (Minor Bird Blues)	1963	a	3				1							1						1											AmCom
Paul Bunyan Jump	1964		5				1		1											1		1					1				AmCom
Piece	1963		5	1	1	1								1	1																AmCom
Serenade, Op 68	1946		5						1						1						1										AmCom
MIROGLIO, FRANCIS (1924–)																															
Chicanes	1984		20	1		1							1		1		1	1			1	1	1				1				Salab
Espaces				2	1	1	1								1	1		1	1												Suvin
Fluctuances													1		1												2				Suvin
Horizons courbés ***	1977		18	1		1	1								1	1		1			1		1								Salab
Horizons courbés *** (w. ad lib inst.) *Unus Instr:* Sitar, marimba	1977		18	2		1	1		1	1		1	1		1	1		1			1		1				2			2	Salab
MITCHELL, DARLEEN C. (1942–)																															
Translucent Unreality No. 1 *Unus Instr:* Wind chimes	1978		8						1						1												1			1	AmCom
Translucent Unreality No. 3 *Comment:* Amplification	1974		8						1									1			1										AmCom
Translucent Unreality No. 4	1978		8			1			1												1										AmCom
Translucent Unreality No. 6 *Unus Instr:* Wind chimes, glockenspiel	1976		8						1												1						2			2	AmCom
Translucent Unreality No. 7 *Unus Instr:* Glockenspiel	1978		6			1			1						1			1			1						1			1	AmCom
MITREA-CELARIAN, MIHAIL (1935–)																															
A-OU-S (for 5 Voices) *Unus Instr:* Synthesizer and mandolin or other plucked instrument	1985		21	2	1	1	1		1						1	1		1		1			1				1	5		2	Salab
Em (Cantata) *Voices:* Soprano and tenor. *Unus Instr:* Basset horn, a mouth organ, and claviette	1983		22		1		1									1					1						1	2		3	Salab
Et la lune *Unus Instr:* Synthesizer	1984		7				1																				7			1	Salab
Et la lune (alt. inst.) *Unus Instr:* Electric clavichord, 5-string bass. Percussionists play 12 rattles	1984		7				1																				7			2	Salab
Janvier *Unus Instr:* Vibraphone	1985		14				2								1			1	2	2			1							1	Salab
Milchstrassenmusik *Unus Instr:* Celesta, marimba, vibraphone. Tuba ad lib.	1984		21	2	1	1	1				1				1	1		1	2		2	1	1		1		2			3	Salab
Seth	1969		9				1		1		1				1			1				1	1				1				Salab
Seth (alt. inst.) *Unus Instr:* Ocarina	1969		9				1		1		1							1				1	1				1			1	Salab
MITTERGRADNEGGER, G (?–)																															
Canciones for Recorder Quintet														5																	Dobli
MOENE, ALAIN (1942–)																															
Babylone (Recitations for Five) *Voices:* Soprano, alto, tenor, baritone, and bass	1984		55	1	1	1									1	1		1					4					5			Salab
MOESCHINGER, ALBERT (1897–)																															
Capricci e danze	1945															1		1	1												Hug
Divertimento, Op 10				1	1	1																									Hug

	Year Composed or Published	Key	Duration	Violin	Viola	Cello	Double Bass	Gamba	Piano	Harpsicord	Organ	Guitar	Harp	Recorder	Flute/Piccolo	Oboe	English Horn	Clarinet/Bass Clarinet	Bassoon/Contrabassoon	Saxophone	French Horn	Trumpet	Trombone	Bass Trombone	Tuba	Baritone	Percussion	Voice	Electronic Tape	Unusual Instruments	Publisher
MOESCHINGER, ALBERT *(continued)*																															
Images				1		1									1					1											Billa
MOLIQUE, BERNHARD (1802–1869)																															
Quintett, Op 35				1	2	1									1																Kunze
MOLLICONE, HENRY (1946–)																															
Run, Jimmy, Run *Unus Instr:* Flügelhorn, synthesizer	1978		19						1			1										1					1			2	AmCom
Strobe *** *Comment:* For any instruments, and lights	1971		20																												AmCom
Tender Granite *Unus Instr:* Bass clarinet	1976		15	1		1			1			1			1			1												1	AmCom
MOMIGNY, JEROME DE J. (1762–1838)																															
Streichquartett		D		2	1	1																									Bären
MONTSALVATGE, XAVIER (1912–)																															
Invocaciones (5) al crucificado *Unus Instr:* Celesta	1969		23				1		1				1		1	2		2	1		2	1					1			1	UMEsp
MOORE, DOROTHY R. (1940–)																															
Trio No. 1	1970		15		1	1			1																						AmCom
MOORE, DOUGLAS S. (1893–1969)																															
Trio	1953			1		1			1																						ECSch
MORERA, ENRIQUE (1865–1942)																															
4 Sardanas (Catalan Dances)																					1	2	2								Faber
MORITZ, EDVARD (1891–)																															
Divertimento																		1		2											Press
Divertimento (alt. vers.)																		2		1											Press
String Quartet, Op 27	1926			2	1	1																									Benja
MORRICONE, ENNIO (1928–)																															
Immobile																		4			1										Salab
MORRIS, HAROLD (1890–1964)																															
Piano Quintet	1929			2	1	1			1																						Manus
Piano Trio	1917		15	1		1			1																						Manus
Piano Trio No. 2	1952			1		1			1																						SPAM
String Quartet	1928			2	1	1																									Manus
MORTARI, VIRGILIO (1902–)																															
Quintet				2	1	1			1																						Caris
Serenata ("La Diavolessa")				1	1	1																									Leduc
MORYL, RICHARD (1929–)																															
Summer's Music	1977		8									1			1	1															AmCom
MOSSOLOV, ALEXANDER (1900–1973)																															
Advertisements (for Voice) *Unus Instr:* Marimba and vibraphone			4	1	1	1	1		1				1		1	1		1	1		1	1	1				2	1		2	VAAP
MOTTE, DIETHER LA (1928–)																															
Charaktere, 1-5	1977			1					1												1										Bären
Gesammelte Werke *Voices:* 2 Sopranos	1973								1						1													2			Bären
Konzert für 7 Instrumente *Unus Instr:* Bass clarinet	1973					1			1						3			2												1	Bären
Die Niemandsrose	1966			1	1	1							1		1			1	1									B			Bären
Septett	1965			1			1											1	1			1	1				1				Bären

	Year Composed or Published	Key	Duration	Violin	Viola	Cello	Double Bass	Gamba	Piano	Harpsicord	Organ	Guitar	Harp	Recorder	Flute/Piccolo	Oboe	English Horn	Clarinet/Bass Clarinet	Bassoon/Contrabassoon	Saxophone	French Horn	Trumpet	Trombone	Bass Trombone	Tuba	Baritone	Percussion	Voice	Electronic Tape	Unusual Instruments	Publisher
MOURANT, WALTER (1910–)																															
Burletta	1964		4	1	1	1												1													AmCom
MOURAVIEFF, LEON (1905–)																															
Dance-Metamorphoses			12		2	2																									Peter
MOYSE, LOUIS (1912–)																															
Quintet															1	1		1	1		1										McGMa
MOZART, WOLFGANG A. (1756–1791)																															
Pieces from "Don Giovanni" (arr. Wendt)																2	2		2		2										Bären
MOZART, Jr., WOLFGANG A. (1791–1844)																															
Piano Quartet		g		1	1	1			1																						Dobli
MUCZYNSKI, ROBERT (1929–)																															
Second Piano Trio				1		1			1																						Press
String Trio				1	1	1																									Press
MÜLLER, IWAN (1786–1854)																															
Concertante									1									1		1											Billa
Concertante									1						1	1															Billa
Concertante									1						1	1															Billa
Concertante									1							1		1													Billa
MULLER, PETER (1791–1877)																															
Quintet No. 1		E♭													1	1		1	1		1										MusRa
Quintet No. 2		E♭													1	1		1	1		1										MusRa
Quintet No. 3		A													1	1		1	1		1										MusRa
MÜLLER-HERMANN, JOHANNE (1878–1941)																															
Streichquartett, Op 6	1912	E♭		2	1	1																									Unive
MÜLLER-HORNBACH, GERHARD (1951–)																															
Bewegte Stille *Unus Instr:* Bass clarinet	1979		40	1	1	1									1	1														1	Breit
Klaviertrio	1978		15	1		1			1																						Breit
Passacaglia II *Unus Instr:* Bass clarinet	1981		15	2	1	1	1								1	1		1	1		1	1	2							1	Breit
Streichquartett	1984		20	2	1	1																									Breit
MÜLLER-WEINBERG, ACHIM (1933–)																															
Streichquartett 2	1978			2	1	1																									DeutV
Szenen	1980			1												1			1												DeutV
MÜLLER-ZÜRICH, PAUL (1898–)																															
Serenata turicensis *Unus Instr:* Basset horn					1	1																								1	Amade
String Quartet No. 2, Op 64				2	1	1																									Hug
String Trio, Op 46				1	1	1																									Amade
MUÑOZ MOLLEDA, JOSÉ (1905–)																															
Cuarteto 1		f		2	1	1																									UMEsp
MUNTZING, A (?–)																															
Serenade for Two Young String Players (A)				1		1			1																						Dobli
Serenade for Two Young String Players (B)					1	1			1																						Dobli
Serenade for Two Young String Players (C)						2			1																						Dobli

	Year Composed or Published	Key	Duration	Violin	Viola	Cello	Double Bass	Gamba	Piano	Harpsicord	Organ	Guitar	Harp	Recorder	Flute/Piccolo	Oboe	English Horn	Clarinet/Bass Clarinet	Bassoon/Contrabassoon	Saxophone	French Horn	Trumpet	Trombone	Bass Trombone	Tuba	Baritone	Percussion	Voice	Electronic Tape	Unusual Instruments	Publisher
MURAIL, TRISTAN (1947–)																															
Desintegrations	1984		22	2	1	1	1		1						2	1		2	1		1	1	1				2				Salab
MUSGRAVE, THEA (1928–)																															
Chamber Concerto No. 1	1962		11	1	1	1										1		1	1		1	1	1								Chest
Chamber Concerto No. 2 (Homage to Ives) *Comment:* Flute doubles on piccolo and alto flute; clarinet on bass clarinet; violin on viola	1966		14	1		1			1						1			1												3	Chest
Chamber Concerto No. 3	1966		24	2	1	1	1											1	1		1										Chest
Serenade	1961		13		1	1							1		1			1													Chest
String Quartet	1958		16	2	1	1																									Chest
Trio	1978		10						1						1	1															Chest
NARITA-YOSHIDA, KAZUKO (1957–)																															
Arbre mécanique *Unus Instr:* Vibraphone, marimba	1984		12						1						1	1		1	1								2			2	Salab
NAULAIS, JEROME (?–)																															
Esquisses																					1	2	1		1						Billa
NAUMANN, ERNST (1910–)																															
Duo-Suite							2		1																						McGMa
Serenade (Nonet), Op 10				2	1	1	1								1	1			1		1										Amade
String Quartet No. 2	1955			2	1	1																									UnWas
NAWRATIL, KAREL (1867–1936)																															
String Quartet No. 2, Op 21		d		2	1	1																									Rahte
NEDBAL, MANFRED J. (1902–)																															
Kleines Streichtrio				1	1	1																									Dobli
Kleines Trio						1												1	1												Dobli
Quartettino (Sonatine)				2	1	1																									Dobli
Streichquartett				2	1	1																									Dobli
NEIKRUG, MARC (1946–)																															
Concertino	1977		17	1	1	1			1						1	1		1													Chest
Mobile	1982		15	2	2	1			1						2	1		3									2				Chest
Stars the Mirror	1989			2	1	1																									CheHa
Streichquartett	1966			2	1	1																									Bären
String Quartet No. 2	1972		16	2	1	1																									Chest
Voci	1988			1		1			1									1													Chest
NEJEDLY, VIT (1912–1945)																															
Streichquartett, Op 12	1937			2	1	1																									Artia
NEMIROFF, ISAAC (1912–1977)																															
4 Treble Suite *Comment:* Oboe may replace one flute															2			2													McGMa
Perspectives															1	1			1												McGMa
Variations to a Theme *Comment:* Bassoon may replace cello						1									1	1															McGMa
NEUBERT, GOTTFRIED (1926–)																															
Nun singet und seid froh											1											2	2								Merse
NEUBERT, GÜNTER (1936–)																															
Musikalische Essays *Voice:* Speaker	1982						1										1						1					1			DeutV
Musik für Bläserquintett	1968														1	1		1	1		1										DeutV
Triptychon in Erinnerung an Max Beckmann	1984				1		1					1					1														DeutV
NEWELL, ROBERT M. (1940–)																															
Panharmonium *Comment:* Piano 4-hands	1978		7						1												2		2				2				AmCom
Panharmonium (alt. vers.) *Comment:* Flutes, oboe, mandolin are optional, off-stage	1978		7						1						4	1					2		2				2			1	AmCom

	Year Composed or Published	Key	Duration	Violin	Viola	Cello	Double Bass	Gamba	Piano	Harpsicord	Organ	Guitar	Harp	Recorder	Flute/Piccolo	Oboe	English Horn	Clarinet/Bass Clarinet	Bassoon/Contrabassoon	Saxophone	French Horn	Trumpet	Trombone	Bass Trombone	Tuba	Baritone	Percussion	Voice	Electronic Tape	Unusual Instruments	Publisher
NEWLIN, DIKA (1923–)																															
Piano Quintet	1941		30	2	1	1			1																						AmCom
Piano Trio No. 2	1948		15		1	1			1																						AmCom
NICULESCU, STEFAN (1927–)																															
Formants (Music in a Mobile Form)	1968		12	9	4	3	1																								Salab
Ison I *Unus Instr:* 5-string bass, contrabassoon	1973			2	1	1	1								1	1		3	1		1	1	1							2	Salab
Octuplum *Unus Instr:* Mandolin	1985		13		1	1						1			1			1		1							1			1	Salab
Scenes *Unus Instr:* Celesta, xylophone, vibraphone	1965						2		1						2		1	2	1			1	1				2			3	Salab
Sinchronie I, for 6-12 Inst. *Unus Instr:* Celesta, bells, vibraphone, marimba	1983		10	1	1	1			1						1	1		1	1								3			4	Salab
NIELSEN, CARL (1865–1931)																															
Bläserquintett, Op 43	1923		25												1	1		1	1		1										Hanse
Quintett	1888	G		2	1	1			1																						Samfu
Serenata in vano	1914		11			1	1											1	1		1										Hanse
Streichquartett 1, Op 13	1888		25	2	1	1																									Hanse
Streichquartett 2, Op 5	1890		30	2	1	1																									Hanse
Streichquartett 3, Op 14	1898		35	2	1	1																									Hanse
Streichquartett 4, Op 44	1906			2	1	1																									Hanse
Streichquintett	1888			2	2	1																									Samfu
Ved en ung Kunstners Baare	1942			2	1	1	1																								SKABO
NIELSON, LEWIS J. (1950–)																															
Between	1982		15												1												2				AmCom
Sole Survivor	1976		9				1													1		1					2				AmCom
Suspension and Silence *Unus Instr:* Vibraphone	1980		12			1			1						1												1			1	AmCom
White Rose *Unus Instr:* Vibraphone	1983		15							1					1												1			1	AmCom
NIHASHI, (1ST NAME UNK.) (?–)																															
Banka. Chant funebres	1987															1		1	1	1											Leduc
NILSSON, BO (1937–)																															
Déjà connu	1973		10												1	1		1	1		1										Nordi
For Strings Only	1954		12	1	1	1	1																								Nordi
Stunde eines Blocks	1958		15	1	1																						1	S			Nordi
Zeitpunkte *Unus Instr:* Alto flute, bass clarinet, alto and tenor saxophones, contrabassoon	1956		5												2	1	1	2	2	2										5	Unive
NONO, LUIGI (1924–)																															
Fragmente-Stille, an Diotima	1980			2	1	1																									Ricor
Quando stanno morendo . . . Live electronics. *Voices:* Female	1982					1									1													4			Ricor
NORDEN, HUGO (1909–)																															
Impromptu	1961			1		1			1																						Humph
NORDENSTROM, GLADYS (1924–)																															
Bläserquintett *Unus Instr:* Piccolo	1977														1	1		1	1		1									1	Bären
NORDHEIM, ARNE (1931–)																															
Epigram	1955		9	2	1	1																									Hanse
Partita I	1963		9		1					1																	1				Hanse
String Quartet	1956		18	2	1	1																									Hanse
Tractatus (solo flute) *Unus Instr:* Bass clarinet, contrabassoon, celesta	1986		13	2	1	1	1		1				1		1		1	1	1								2			3	Hanse
NORGARD, PER (1932–)																															
Prelude and Ant Fugue with Crab Canon *Unus Instr:* Mandolin	1982		7	1			1					1			1			1									1			1	Hanse

	Year Composed or Published	Key	Duration	Violin	Viola	Cello	Double Bass	Gamba	Piano	Harpsicord	Organ	Guitar	Harp	Recorder	Flute/Piccolo	Oboe	English Horn	Clarinet/Bass Clarinet	Bassoon/Contrabassoon	Saxophone	French Horn	Trumpet	Trombone	Bass Trombone	Tuba	Baritone	Percussion	Voice	Electronic Tape	Unusual Instruments	Publisher
NORGARD, PER *(continued)*																															
Prelude to Breaking (Wave Music) *Unus Instr:* Bass clarinet	1986			2	1	1			1						1			1									1	M		1	Hanse
Quartet No. 1 (Quartetto brioso)	1958		20	2	1	1																									Hanse
Quartet No. 2 (In 3 Spheres)	1965		10	2	1	1																									Hanse
Quartet No. 3: Inscape	1969		17	2	1	1																									Hanse
Quintet	1951		25	1	1	1			1						1																Hanse
Sanger fran Aftonland	1956		30	1	1	1							1		1													A			Hanse
Spell						1			1									1													Hanse
Tintinnabulary (String Quartet No. 4)				2	1	1																									Hanse
Trio	1955		25			1			1									1													Hanse
Trio No. 2	1974					1			1									1													Hanse
Whirls World	1970		12												1	1		1	1		1										Hanse
NOSTRAND, BURR VAN (?–1945)																															
Emergency Plumber's Manual	1976		18						1												1	2	1		1						AmCom
Factory Manual for Urban Survival *Unus Instr:* Prepared baby grand piano	1972		40			1			1						1															1	AmCom
NOVAK, JIRI F. (1913–)																															
11 Miniaturen, Op 109	1970				1																2										Artia
NOVAK, VITESLAV (1870–1949)																															
Klavierquintett, Op 12				2	1	1			1																						Artia
Streichquartett 3, Op 66				2	1	1																									Artia
NOWAK, ALISON (1948–)																															
Canzonet	1984		3		1	1			1																						AmCom
Equinox	1977		10	1	1		1											1	1		1										AmCom
Home Fire	1985		6	4					1																						AmCom
Musica composita I	1974		8	1		1			1						1			1	1			1									AmCom
Quartet	1974		7	1		1									1			1													AmCom
Quintet	1973		6	1					1			1			1				1												AmCom
Setting Out	1985		5	2					1																						AmCom
NOWAK, LIONEL (1911–)																															
Concertpiece *Unus Instr:* Kettledrum	1961		12	2	1	1	1																				6			1	AmCom
Festival (A Processional) *Unus Instr:* Timpani	1963		7																			4	4				5			1	AmCom
Piano Trio	1954		17		1	1			1																						AmCom
Quartet	1952		17	1	1	1										1															AmCom
Soundscape	1970		9	1					1																		1				AmCom
Suite	1954		17			1			1									1													AmCom
Trio	1951		14	1		1												1													AmCom
NYSTEDT, KNUT (1915–)																															
The Moment *Unus Instr:* Celesta	1962		8																								1	S		1	Nordi
Rhapsody in Green	1978		13																		1	2	2								Nordi
String Quartet No. 2	1948		25	2	1	1																									Nordi
String Quartet No. 3	1956		23	2	1	1																									Nordi
String Quartet No. 4	1966		14	2	1	1																									Hanse
OEHRING, WOLFGANG (1941–)																															
Ich wollt, dass ich daheime wär				2	1	1																						S			Bären
OKUMURA, HAJIME (1925–)																															
Jahresanfang in Japan. Trio	1969					1			1						1																Bosse
OLAH, TIBERIU (1928–)																															
Perspective *Unus Instr:* Bass clarinet	1970			1	1	1	1								1		1	1			1	1	1				3			1	Salab
Translations	1969		13	7	4	3	2																								Salab
OLAN, DAVID (1948–)																															
4 Studies	1973		8	1					1									1									1				AmCom

	Year Composed or Published	Key	Duration	Violin	Viola	Cello	Double Bass	Gamba	Piano	Harpsicord	Organ	Guitar	Harp	Recorder	Flute/Piccolo	Oboe	English Horn	Clarinet/Bass Clarinet	Bassoon/Contrabassoon	Saxophone	French Horn	Trumpet	Trombone	Bass Trombone	Tuba	Baritone	Percussion	Voice	Electronic Tape	Unusual Instruments	Publisher
OLAN, DAVID *(continued)*																															
Fantasy	1983		9			1				1					1		1														AmCom
Gathering	1972		12	1		1			1						1							1	1				2				AmCom
Music	1966		8	1	1	1									1			1	1		1	1	1				4				AmCom
Octet	1979		11	1	1		1		1						2			1							1						AmCom
Satz	1977		9	1	1	1			1						1			1											1		AmCom
Septet	1975		7				1		1						1	1					1	1					1				AmCom
Starting Winter	1974		8	1											1			1													AmCom
OLIVER, STEPHEN (1950–)																															
Suite from Nicholas Nickleby																					1	2	1		1						Novel
OLLONE, MAX D' (1875–1959)																															
Trio		a		1		1			1																						Duran
OLSEN, POUL R. (1922–1982)																															
Patet (per nove musici), Op 55 *Unus Instr:* Xylophone, marimbaphone	1968		8	1	1	1						1			1			1									3			2	BoteB
OREFICE, GIACOMO (1865–1922)																															
Trio		c		1		1			1																						Ricor
ORR, BUXTON D. (1924–)																															
Divertimento																						2	2	1							Novel
ORTIZ, WILLIAM (1947–)																															
Amor, cristal y piedra	1960		16							1		1	1																		AmCom
Composición	1982		8		1	1			1																						AmCom
Un jardin chino de serenidad	1973		10	1	1	1							1		1												1				AmCom
Suite, Tercer mundo (Third World) *Unus Instr:* Xylophone	1977		15									2		1	1												3			1	AmCom
OSTENDORF, JENS-PETER (1944–)																															
String Quartet (Exempla nova 13)				2	1	1																									Sikor
OTANO, NEMESIO (1880–1956)																															
Zortzico				1		1			1																						UMEsp
Zortzico (alt. vers.)				2	2	2																									UMEsp
OTTERLOO, WILLEM VAN (1907–)																															
String Trio	1949			1	1	1																									Donem
OVERTON, HALL (1920–1972)																															
Fantasy	1961		10						1												1	2	1		1		1				AmCom
Nonage	1951		15	2	1	1	1		1						1	1		1	1		1	1									AmCom
Pulsations	1971		17	1		1	1		1				1		1			1	1		1	1	1				1				AmCom
String Quartet No. 2				2	1	1																									ECSch
PABLO, LUIS DE (1930–)																															
Drunken Elephants (II)	1973		12	2	1	1	1						1		1	1		1	1	1	2	1	1				1				Salab
Imaginario I	1967									1																	3				Salab
Masque	1973								1						1			1									1				Salab
Modulus III *Unus Instr:* Celesta, glockenspiel, mandolin, vibraphone, 2 xylophones, timpani	1967		18						2		1	1	2									4					5			7	Salab
Modulus IV (Version I)	1965			2	1	1																									Salab
Polar *Unus Instr:* Bass clarinet	1961																	1		1							1	1		1	Salab
Symphonies for 17 Brass *Unus Instr:* 2 Bugles	1966		14																		4	5	3	1	2					2	Salab
PACCIONE, PAUL (1952–)																															
Grid-work *Unus Instr:* Bass clarinet	1980		10	1		1			1									2												1	AmCom
Radical Ears	1989		5						1												1	2	1		1						AmCom
Stabile *Unus Instr:* Vibraphone	1976		8									1						1									1			1	AmCom

	Year Composed or Published	Key	Duration	Violin	Viola	Cello	Double Bass	Gamba	Piano	Harpsicord	Organ	Guitar	Harp	Recorder	Flute/Piccolo	Oboe	English Horn	Clarinet/Bass Clarinet	Bassoon/Contrabassoon	Saxophone	French Horn	Trumpet	Trombone	Bass Trombone	Tuba	Baritone	Percussion	Voice	Electronic Tape	Unusual Instruments	Publisher
PACCIONE, PAUL *(continued)*																															
Radical Ears	1989		5						1												1	2	1		1						AmCom
Stabile *Unus Instr:* Vibraphone	1976		8									1						1									1			1	AmCom
PACKER, RANDALL (1933–)																															
Phosphores chanteurs	1978		6	1		1							1		1	1											1				AmCom
PAGANINI, NICCOLÒ (1782–1840)																															
Caprice No. 9 (arr. Zinn)				2	1	1																									Press
Caprice No. 24 (arr. Zinn)				2	1	1																									Press
PALESTER, ROMAN (1907–)																															
Secondo trio				1	1	1																									Suvin
PALMER, ROBERT (1915–)																															
Piano Quintet				2	1	1			1																						Peter
PANIZZA, ETTORE (1875–1967)																															
Quartetto		c		2	1	1																									Suvin
PANUFNIK, ANDRZEJ (1914–1991)																															
Arbor Cosmica (Evocations for 12 Strings)	1983		40	6	3	2	1																								Boose
Paean *Comment:* Organ ad lib. Optional fanfare trumpets	1980		3								1										6	6	6								Boose
Piano Trio	1934		20	1		1			1																						Boose
Piano Trio	1977		20	1		1			1																						Boose
String Quartet No. 1	1976		20	2	1	1																									Boose
String Quartet No. 2 ("Messages")	1980		20	2	1	1																									Boose
Triangles	1972		16			3									3																Boose
PARK, JAMES (1942–)																															
Narratio melica (in memoriam familiae)	1986		7			1						1			1																AmCom
Old Ethan's Dreams	1983		20		1	1			1																						AmCom
PARRIS, ROBERT (1924–)																															
3 Chorale Preludes (Bach) *Comment:* Other keyboard instruments may replace piano	1983		9						1													1	1								AmCom
Book of Imaginary Beings (Part I)	1972		25	1		1			1						1												2				AmCom
Book of Imaginary Beings (Part II)	1983		22	1	1	1												1									2				AmCom
Concerto	1977		18	1		1			1																		1				AmCom
Dirge for the New Sunrise *Unus Instr:* Timpani	1970		9	1		1									1												4			1	AmCom
Four Pieces	1965		10															1	1		1										AmCom
The Golden Net *Unus Instr:* Timpani	1968		14	1	1	1									1	1		1	1		1	1					1			1	AmCom
Lamentations and Praises			10																		2	3	3		1						Peter
Lamentations and Praises (alt. vers.)																					2	3	3		1		3				Peter
Quintet	1957		15	1		1									1	1			1												AmCom
Rite of Passage (solo clarinet) *Unus Instr:* Celesta	1978		20			1	1		1			1	1					1									7			1	AmCom
St. Winifred's Well *Unus Instr:* 4 Timpani	1967		8			2			1						1												1			4	AmCom
Trio	1959		23			1			1									1													AmCom
PÄRT, ARVO (1935–)																															
An den Wassern zu Babel (Psalm 137) *Voices:* Soprano, alto, tenor, bass	1984		9	1	1	1	1								1	1		1	1		1							4			Unive
Quintettino (Woodwind Quintet)	1964														1	1		1	1		1										Peter
Ein Wallfahrtslied (Psalm 121) *Voice:* Lyric tenor or baritone	1984		8	2	1	1																						1			Unive

	Year Composed or Published	Key	Duration	Violin	Viola	Cello	Double Bass	Gamba	Piano	Harpsicord	Organ	Guitar	Harp	Recorder	Flute/Piccolo	Oboe	English Horn	Clarinet/Bass Clarinet	Bassoon/Contrabassoon	Saxophone	French Horn	Trumpet	Trombone	Bass Trombone	Tuba	Baritone	Percussion	Voice	Electronic Tape	Unusual Instruments	Publisher
PASCAL, ANDRÉ (1894–)																															
Quatuor				2	1	1																									Duran
Sonatine				2					1																						Duran
PASCAL, CLAUDE (1921–)																															
Octuor															2	1		1	2		1	1									Duran
Quatuor				2	1	1																									Duran
PAUBON, PIERRE (1910–)																															
Colloque à trois															1	1		1													Billa
PAUER, JIRI (1919–)																															
Bläserquintett	1960														1	1		1	1		1										Artia
PAVLYENKO, SERGEI (1952–)																															
Symphony No. 3 *Unus Instr:* Celesta	1982		15	2	2	1			1				1		1	1		1	1		1	1	1				3			1	VAAP
PAYNE, ANTHONY (1936–)																															
Consort Music	1987		16	2	1	1																									Chest
A Day in the Life of a Mayfly	1983		13	1		1			1						1			1									1				Chest
Echoes of Courtly Love (Homage to Dufay)	1987																				1	2	2								Chest
Paraphrases and Cadenzas	1969		15		1				1									1													Chest
A Sea-change	1988		12	2	1	1							1		1			1													Chest
Sonatas and Ricercars	1970		14																		1	2	2								Chest
The Stones and Lonely Places Sing	1979			1	1	1			1						1			1			1										Chest
String Quartet	1978		20	2	1	1																									Chest
PEETERS, FLOR (1903–1986)																															
Trio, Op 80			10												1			1	1												Peter
PEIXINHO, JORGE R. (1940–)																															
Episodios	1961			2	1	1																									Gulbe
Memoires-miroirs, for Harpsichord	1983		23	6	2	2	2			1																					Salab
PENDERECKI, KRZYSTOF (1933–)																															
Quartetto	1960			2	1	1																									PWP
String Quartet No. 2	1968			2	1	1																									PWP
PENNISI, FRANCESCO (1934–)																															
Corteggio						1				1					1																Ricor
Nuit sans étoiles	1977			2	1					1																					Ricor
PERAGALLO, MARIO (1910–)																															
Musica per doppio quartetto	1949			3	2	2	1																								Unive
PERLE, GEORGE (1915–)																															
String Quartet No. 7	1973			2	1	1																									Boelk
Wind Quintet No. 1	1959														1	1		1	1		1										Press
Wind Quintet No. 2	1960														1	1		1	1		1										Press
Wind Quintet No. 3	1967														1	1		1	1		1										Press
PERLEA, JONEL (1900–1970)																															
Streichquartett, Op 10	1924			2	1	1																									Rahte
PERLONGO, DANIEL (1942–)																															
3 Tempi	1971		11	1		1									1			1			1										AmCom
A Day at Xochimilco	1987		17						1						1	1		1	1		1										AmCom
Improvisation for Four *Unus Instr:* Accordion	1965		7															1				1			1					1	AmCom
Movement for 8 Players *Unus Instr:* Vibraphone	1967		5	1		1						1			1			1				1	1							1	AmCom
Process 7, 5, 3 for 6 in 12	1969		12												1	1		1									3				AmCom
PERRIN, JEAN-CHARLES (1920–)																															
Quatuor																						2	2								Billa

	Year Composed or Published	Key	Duration	Violin	Viola	Cello	Double Bass	Gamba	Piano	Harpsicord	Organ	Guitar	Harp	Recorder	Flute/Piccolo	Oboe	English Horn	Clarinet/Bass Clarinet	Bassoon/Contrabassoon	Saxophone	French Horn	Trumpet	Trombone	Bass Trombone	Tuba	Baritone	Percussion	Voice	Electronic Tape	Unusual Instruments	Publisher
PERSICHETTI, VINCENT (1915–1987)																															
King Lear (Septet), Op 35	1948								1						1	1		1	1		1						1				Elkan
Parable II	1968																				1	2	1		1						Elkan
Parable X (String Quartet No. 4)	1972			2	1	1																									Elkan
Parable XXIII	1981			1		1			1																						Elkan
Pastoral (for Wind Quintet)	1943														1	1		1	1		1										Schir
Serenade No. 1 (10 Winds)	1929														1	1		1	1		2	2	1		1						Elkan
Serenade No. 3	1941			1		1			1																						Peer
Serenade No. 6	1950				1	1																	1								Elkan
String Quartet No. 1	1939			2	1	1																									Elkan
String Quartet No. 2	1944			2	1	1																									Elkan
String Quartet No. 3	1959			2	1	1																									Elkan
String Quartet No. 4 (Parable X)	1972			2	1	1																									Elkan
PETERKA, RUDOLF (?–)																															
Streichquartett	1924			2	1	1																									Simro
PETERS, RUDOLF (1902–1962)																															
Streichquartett, Op 8	1923			2	1	1																									Simro
PETIT, JEAN-LOUIS (1937–)																															
Octuor pour Guernesey															1	1		1	1		1	2	1								Billa
PETIT, PIERRE Y. (1922–)																															
Les quatre vents																					2	1			1						Leduc
PETRASSI, GOFFREDO (1904–)																															
Quartetto	1958			2	1	1																									Suvin
Serenata	1958				1		1			1					1												1				Suvin
Trio	1960			1	1	1																									Suvin
PETROVICS, EMIL (1930–)																															
Cassazione	1953		7																			3	1		1						EMBud
String Quartet	1958		25	2	1	1																									EMBud
Wind Quintet	1964		15												1	1		1	1		1										EMBud
PETTERSSON, ALLAN (1911–)																															
Concerto (solo violin)	1949		32	3	1	1																									Nordi
PETYREK, FELIX (1892–1951)																															
Ave Maria zart (Variations)				1	1	1																									Dobli
Gute Nacht, o Welt																1		1	1		1										Dobli
PFAUTSCH, LLOYD (1921–)																															
Festival Prelude	1985																				1	2	2								RKing
PFISTER, HEIDI (1927–1978)																															
"Mobili a tre" (Trio)									1						1			1													Kunze
Ottobeuren Quintett															1	1		1	1		1										Kunze
PFITZNER, HANS (1869–1949)																															
Streichquartett	1886	d		2	1	1																									Bären
String Quartet No. 4, Op 36	1925	c#	27	2	1	1																									Boose
PFUNDT, REINHARD (1951–)																															
Serenade *Comment:* Violin may replace one flute	1979					1									2																DeutV
Streichquartett	1974			2	1	1																									DeutV
PHILIPPOT, MICHEL (1925–)																															
Commentarioulus Copernicae	1972		17	1		1			1						1			1	1		1	1					1				Salab
Octet	1974		12	2	2	1												1	1		1										Salab
PHILLIPS, IVAN (?–)																															
Short Arrangements (6)																1		1	1												Oxfor
PHILLIPS, PETER (1930–)																															
Music for a Ballet *Comment:* This work takes up an entire evening. *Unus Instr:* Timpani				7	3	2	1			1																	2			1	AMP

	Year Composed or Published	Key	Duration	Violin	Viola	Cello	Double Bass	Gamba	Piano	Harpsicord	Organ	Guitar	Harp	Recorder	Flute/Piccolo	Oboe	English Horn	Clarinet/Bass Clarinet	Bassoon/Contrabassoon	Saxophone	French Horn	Trumpet	Trombone	Bass Trombone	Tuba	Baritone	Percussion	Voice	Electronic Tape	Unusual Instruments	Publisher
PICHA, FRANTISEK (1893–1964)																															
Streichquartett 2, Op 30	1943	G		2	1	1																									Artia
Trio quasi una fantasia, Op 21	1934			1		1			1																						Artia
PICHAUREAU, CLAUDE (1940–)																															
Marine			8	1					1														1								Ridea
PICHLER, ERNST (1908–)																															
Music for Brass																					2	2	2								Dobli
PICK, CARL-HEINZ (1929–)																															
Auf den Spuren des Roten Oktober				2	1	1																									DeutV
PICKER, TOBIAS (1954–)																															
Septet *Unus Instr:* Contrabassoon, vibraphone, glockenspiel	1975		10	1					1						1				1			1	1				1			3	AmCom
Sextet No. 2 (Halles Ravine) *Unus Instr:* Vibraphone, glockenspiel	1976		10	1		1			1							1		1									1			2	AmCom
PICK-MANGIAGALLI, RICCARDO (1882–1949)																															
3 Fughe				2	1	1																									Suvin
PIER, GEORG (?–)																															
Etüden									1									1				1					1				Dobli
Etüden (3)	1955								1									1									1				Dobli
PIERNÉ, GABRIEL (1863–1937)																															
3 Pièces en trio				1	1	1																									Leduc
Giration (Choreographic Divertissement)	1929		9	3	1	1	1		1						1			1	1			1	1								Salab
Marche des petits soldats de plomb, Op 14 No. 6															1	1		1	1		1										Leduc
Pastorale, Op 14															1	1		1	1		1										Leduc
Pastorale variée, Op 30															1	1		1	2		1	1									Duran
Preludio et fughetta, Op 40 No. 1															2	1		1	2		1										Hamel
Sonata da camera, Op 48						1			1						1																Duran
Trio, Op 45				1		1			1																						Duran
Voyage au pays du tendre				1	1	1							1		1																Leduc
PIERNÉ, PAUL (1874–1952)																															
Bucolique variée																1		1	1												Billa
Suite pittoresque															1	1		1	1		1										Leduc
PIETRI, GIUSEPPE (1886–1946)																															
Serenata elbana				1		1			1																						Suvin
PIJPER, WILLEM (1894–1947)																															
Pezzi antichi (4)	1947			3		1																									Donem
Quintet	1949														1	1		1	1		1										Donem
PILATI, MARIO (1903–1938)																															
Quintetto		D		2	1	1			1																						Ricor
PILLNEY, KARL H. (1896–1980)																															
Divertimento, Op 2♭ *Unus Instr:* Tenor banjo			13	1		1	1		1						1	1		1	1	1	1	1	1				1			1	Tisch
PILLOIS, JACQUES (1877–1935)																															
5 Hai-kai				1	1	1							1		1																Duran
PILSS, KARL (1902–)																															
Octet		c		2	1	1	1											1	1		1										Dobli
Serenade for Wind Quintet		G													1	1		1	1		1										Dobli
PINKHAM, DANIEL (1923–)																															
Brass Trio			5																		1	1	1								Peter
Concertante			12								1	1		1													1				Peter

	Year Composed or Published	Key	Duration	Violin	Viola	Cello	Double Bass	Gamba	Piano	Harpsicord	Organ	Guitar	Harp	Recorder	Flute/Piccolo	Oboe	English Horn	Clarinet/Bass Clarinet	Bassoon/Contrabassoon	Saxophone	French Horn	Trumpet	Trombone	Bass Trombone	Tuba	Baritone	Percussion	Voice	Electronic Tape	Unusual Instruments	Publisher
PINKHAM, DANIEL *(continued)*																															
Concertante for Organ and Brass			12								1											2	2				2				Peter
Concertante with Celesta *Unus Instr:* Celesta			12								1																2			1	Peter
Fanfare, Aria, and Echo *Unus Instr:* Timpani			6																		2						1			1	Peter
Merry Christmas (Adeste Fideles) *Unus Instr:* Timpani			3								1											2	2				2			1	Peter
Merry Christmas (Coventry Carol) *Comment:* Flute, oboe, violin, and cello may replace recorders			3							1				3																	Peter
Merry Christmas (God Rest You) *Unus Instr:* Timpani			2								1											2	2				1			1	Peter
Merry Christmas (In dulce jubilo) *Comment:* Other melody instruments may replace violins			5	2	1	1	1				1												1								Peter
Prelude	1944		5	1	1	1									1																AmCom
Prelude, Adagio, and Chorale			7																		1	2	1		1						Peter
Sonata *Unus Instr:* Cornetto	1947		14								1											2	1			1				1	AmCom
PIRCKMAYER, GEORG (1918–1977)																															
Transition 56/71				1		1			1																						Dobli
PISK, PAUL A. (1893–1990)																															
Envoy, Op 104	1964		8	1	1	1										1		1	1												AmCom
Moresca Figures	1934		16	1					1									1													AmCom
Perpetuum mobile	1968		8								1											2	2								AmCom
Suite, Op 85	1955		12												1	1		1													AmCom
PISTON, WALTER (1894–1976)																															
Ceremonial Fanfare	1969		2																		6	4	3		1		2				AMP
Counterpoints (3)	1973		10	1	1	1																									AMP
Divertimento	1946		11	2	1	1	1								1	1		1	1												AMP
Fanfare for the Fighting French	1943																				4	3	3		1		2				Boose
Partita	1944		16	1	1						1																				AMP
Piano Quartet	1964		16	1	1	1			1																						AMP
Piano Quintet	1949		20	2	1	1			1																						AMP
Piano Trio No. 1	1935		17	1		1			1																						AMP
Piano Trio No. 2	1966		17	1		1			1																						AMP
Pieces (3)	1926		9												1			1	1												AMP
Quintet	1942		17	2	1	1									1																AMP
Quintet for Winds	1956		18												1	1		1	1		1										AMP
Souvenir	1967		4	1									1		1																AMP
String Quartet No. 1	1933		20	2	1	1																									Schir
String Quartet No. 2	1935		22	2	1	1																									AMP
String Quartet No. 3	1947			2	1	1																									Boose
String Quartet No. 4	1951		20	2	1	1																									AMP
String Quartet No. 5	1962		16	2	1	1																									AMP
String Sextet	1944		18	2	2	2																									AMP
PIZZETTI, ILDEBRANDO (1889–1968)																															
Canzoni (3)	1926			2	1	1																						1			Ricor
Quartetto	1933	D		2	1	1																									Ricor
Trio	1925	A		1		1			1																						Ricor
PLACHETA, HUGO (1892–)																															
Divertimento for Wind Quintet, Op 8															1	1		1	1		1										Dobli
Quartett, Op 10	1963															1		1	1		1										Dobli

	Year Composed or Published	Key	Duration	Violin	Viola	Cello	Double Bass	Gamba	Piano	Harpsicord	Organ	Guitar	Harp	Recorder	Flute/Piccolo	Oboe	English Horn	Clarinet/Bass Clarinet	Bassoon/Contrabassoon	Saxophone	French Horn	Trumpet	Trombone	Bass Trombone	Tuba	Baritone	Percussion	Voice	Electronic Tape	Unusual Instruments	Publisher
PLANEL, ROBERT (1908–)																															
Quatuor				2	1	1																									Duran
PLATZ, ROBERT (1951–)																															
Flötenstücke	1983		10		1	1							1		2			1			1	1									Breit
PLESKOW, RAOUL (1931–)																															
4 Pieces	1980		9			1			1						1																AmCom
4 Short Pieces	1981		5	2	1	2									1			1													AmCom
Bagatelles *Unus Instr:* Bass clarinet	1981		10	1		1	1		1						1			2												1	AmCom
Bagatelles (alt. inst.)	1981		10	1		1	1		1						1			1	1												AmCom
Bagatelles No. 2	1966		5		1				1						1																AmCom
Crossplay *Unus Instr:* Vibraphone	1963		10	1		1			1						1			1									1			1	AmCom
Divertimento	1983		9	1		1			1						1			1													AmCom
Fantasia (sopra Ave Regina Coelorum)	1975		10	1	1	1	1		1						1	1		1	1						1		1				AmCom
For Flute, Violin, and Guitar	1984		8	1								1			1																AmCom
For 4 Instruments	1986		13	1		1									1			1													AmCom
Intrada	1984		6	1		1									1			1													AmCom
Movement	1966		8	1					1							1															AmCom
Movement for 9 Players *Unus Instr:* Celesta	1967		10	1		1	1		1						1			1				1					2			1	AmCom
Music	1964		7				1		1						1												1				AmCom
Music for 7 Players	1965		12	1		1			1				1		1			1									1				AmCom
Quatrain on a Choral Tune *** *Comment:* For 2 treble and 1 tenor instrument, and keyboard	1985		4						1																						AmCom
Sextet	1963		9	1		1			1						1	1		1													AmCom
Trio	1977		8			1			1						1																AmCom
PLEYEL, IGNAZ J. (1757–1831)																															
Grand Trio						1			1						1																MusRa
Quartet		E♭		1	2	1																									MusRa
String Sextet				2	2	1	1																								Kunze
String Trios (Vol. 1, Nos. 1-3)				2		1																									VarPb
Trio for flute, clarinet, and bassoon		C													1			1	1												Bären
Trio for flute, clarinet, and bassoon (No. 2)		C													1			1	1												MusRa
Trio for flute, violin, and cello, Op 73 No. 1				1		1									1																Amade
Trio for flute, violin, and cello, Op 73 No. 2 *Comment:* Bassoon may replace cello		C		1		1									1																VarPb
Trio for 2 clarinets and bassoon, Op 20 No. 2		E♭																2	1												MusRa
Trios Concertant (3), Op 10				1	1	1																									VarPb
PODESVA, JAROMIR (1927–)																															
Z Moravy (Streichquartett)	1952			2	1	1																									Artia
POLIN, CLAIRE (1926–)																															
Cader Idris	1971																				1	2	2								Schir
POLZELLI, A (?–)																															
Trio, Op 4					1	1												1													Kunze
PONCE, MANUEL (1886–1948)																															
String Quartet				2	1	1																									Peer
POOT, MARCEL (1901–)																															
Concertino	1958														1	1		1	1		1										Leduc
Quatuor	1952			2	1	1																									Eschi
PORENA, BORIS (1927–)																															
Neumi *Unus Instr:* Vibraphone, marimba															1												2			2	Suvin

	Year Composed or Published	Key	Duration	Violin	Viola	Cello	Double Bass	Gamba	Piano	Harpsicord	Organ	Guitar	Harp	Recorder	Flute/Piccolo	Oboe	English Horn	Clarinet/Bass Clarinet	Bassoon/Contrabassoon	Saxophone	French Horn	Trumpet	Trombone	Bass Trombone	Tuba	Baritone	Percussion	Voice	Electronic Tape	Unusual Instruments	Publisher
PORTER, QUINCY (1897–1966)																															
Divertimento			18												1	1		1	1		1										Peter
Quintet	1961		24	2	1	1				1																					AmCom
Quintet on a Childhood Theme	1940		6	2	1	1									1																AmCom
String Quartet No. 3			18	2	1	1																									Peter
String Quartet No. 6			16	2	1	1																									Peter
POSER, HANS (1917–1970)																															
Streichquartett No. 1, Op 20				2	1	1																									Sikor
Streichquartett 2, Op 38	1956			2	1	1																									Sikor
POSSINGER, ALEXANDER (?–)																															
Trio		D			1										1						1										Amade
Trio, Op 16		F			1	1										1															Amade
POSSINGER, F A. (1767–1827)																															
Trio		F														2	1														Kneus
POULENC, FRANCIS (1899–1963)																															
Aubade (Choreographic Concerto for Piano) *Unus Instr:* 3 Timpani	1929		21		2	2	2		1						2	2		2	2		2	1					1			3	Salab
Le bal masqué (Profane Cantata)	1932		17	1	1				1							1		1	1		1						1	B			Salab
Le bestiaire (Cortège d'Orphée—6 Songs)	1920		6	2	1	1									1			1	1									F			Salab
Eiffel Tower Polka									1													2									Salab
L'Invitation au château	1947		14	1					1									1													Eschi
Leocadia Tableau I (Overture)	1940			1			1		1									1	1												Eschi
Leocadia Tableau II (Valse)				1			1		1									1	1									1			Eschi
Musique pour faire plaisir (arr. Francaix) *Unus Instr:* Contrabassoon	1981		10												2	1	1	2	2		2									1	Eschi
Sextuor	1945								1						1	1		1	1		1										Hanse
Sonata	1925																				1	1	1								Chest
Trio									1							1			1												Hanse
POUSSEUR, HENRI (1929–)																															
Chants sacré (3) ***	1951			1	1	1																						1			Suvin
Echos II de Votre Faust	1969					1			1						1													M			Unive
Quintetto	1955			1		1			1									2												B	Suvin
Symphonies à 15 solistes	1955		13	2	1	1			1				2		1	1		1	1		2	1	1								Unive
POWELL, MEL (1923–)																															
Filigree Setting	1959		6	2	1	1																									Schir
Immobile 5 (tape and diverse inst.) *** *Comment:* For any number and combination of listed instruments. *Unus Instr:* Vibraphone, marimba	1967		5	1	1	1			1				1		1	1		1				1					2		1	2	Schir
Improvisation	1962		5		1				1									1													Schir
Little Companion Pieces	1979		12	2	1	1																						S			Schir
Miniatures for Baroque Ensemble, Op 8	1957		12	1	1	1				1					1	1															Schir
Piano Quintet	1958			2	1	1			1																						Schir
Piano Trio	1954			1		1			1																						Schir
Prayer Settings (2)	1963			1	1	1										1												T			Schir
Settings (for Soprano)	1979		14			1			1				1		1			1				1					1	S			Schir
String Quartet	1982		12	2	1	1																									Schir
Die Violine	1989		3	1					1																			S			Schir
Woodwind Quintet	1985		8												1	1		1	1		1										Schir
POWERS, ANTHONY (1953–)																															
Another Part of the Island *Unus Instr:* Basset clarinet, marimba, glockenspiel, crotales	1980		28	1		1			1						1			1									1			4	Oxfor

	Year Composed or Published	Key	Duration	Violin	Viola	Cello	Double Bass	Gamba	Piano	Harpsicord	Organ	Guitar	Harp	Recorder	Flute/Piccolo	Oboe	English Horn	Clarinet/Bass Clarinet	Bassoon/Contrabassoon	Saxophone	French Horn	Trumpet	Trombone	Bass Trombone	Tuba	Baritone	Percussion	Voice	Electronic Tape	Unusual Instruments	Publisher
POWERS, ANTHONY *(continued)*																															
Chamber Concerto *Comment:* Oboe doubles on English horn. *Unus Instr:* Bass clarinet, vibraphone, marimba	1984		23	2	1	1	1		1						1	1	1	1	1		1	1	1				1			3	Oxfor
Etudes-Tableaux (Book 1)	1986		17	1		1			1																						Oxfor
Etudes-Tableaux (Book 2)	1986			1	1	1	1		1																						Oxfor
Music for Strings (2 solo violins) *Comment:* Violins: 12. Ensemble includes string quartet	1984		23	12	3	3	1																								Oxfor
Nocturnes Book 1	1981		14	1			1															1									Oxfor
Nympheas *Unus Instr:* Glockenspiel, vibraphone	1983			2	1	1	1		1			1	1		2			1									1			2	Oxfor
Quintet *Unus Instr:* Bass clarinet	1983		15	1	1	1									1			1												1	Oxfor
Sonata	1981		13			1				1					1	1															Oxfor
String Quartet	1987			2	1	1																									Oxfor
Venexiana I	1983		18	2		1				1																		T			Oxfor
Winter Festivals *Unus Instr:* Contrabassoon. Winds double on other instruments	1985		32		1	1	1						1		1	1	1	1	1		1							M		1	Oxfor
POWNING, GRAHAM (?–)																															
Trio No. 1	1972															2	1														McGMa
Trio No. 2	1974															2	1														McGMa
PRAETORIUS, MICHAEL (1571–1621)																															
Suite from Terpsichore (arr. Dean)															1	1		1	1		1										Press
PREMRU, RAYMOND (1934–)																															
Concertino															1	1		1	1				1								MusRa
PRESSER, WILLIAM (1916–)																															
Minuet, Sarabande, and Gavotte															1	1		1	1		1										Press
Second Suite																					1	2	1								Press
Trio																2	1														Press
Trio for Winds																1		1	1												Press
Wind Quintet															1	1		1	1		1										Press
PREVIN, ANDRÉ (1929–)																															
A Different Kind of Blues				1			1		1			1															1				Hanse
It's a Breeze				1			1		1			1															1				Hanse
Outings (4) for Brass Quintet			12																		1	2	2								Hanse
PRIN, YVES (1933–)																															
Actions simultanées (Version I) *Unus Instr:* Bass clarinet, contrabassoon, contrabass tuba			14						1									1	1		1				1		3			3	Ridea
Concerto for Percussion and Brass *Unus Instr:* Contrabass tuba																					4	4		3	2		6			1	Ridea
Mobile I *Unus Instr:* Musette			13													1	1										1		1	1	Ridea
PRINZ, ALFRED (1930–)																															
Danzas (for Wind Octet)																2		2	2		2										Dobli
Moments Musicaux (Reminiscences)															1	1		1	1		1										Dobli
Moment Musicaux II									1						1				1												Dobli
Quintet				2	1	1									1																Dobli
PRIULI, GIOVANNI (1575–1629)																															
Canzone a 7 *Comment:* Alt. version: 2 Fr. horns, 3 trumpets, 2 trombones																						4	3								Amade
PROBST, DOMINIQUE (?–)																															
Les plaisirs de l'ile enchantée				1								1		1													1				Billa

	Year Composed or Published	Key	Duration	Violin	Viola	Cello	Double Bass	Gamba	Piano	Harpsicord	Organ	Guitar	Harp	Recorder	Flute/Piccolo	Oboe	English Horn	Clarinet/Bass Clarinet	Bassoon/Contrabassoon	Saxophone	French Horn	Trumpet	Trombone	Bass Trombone	Tuba	Baritone	Percussion	Voice	Electronic Tape	Unusual Instruments	Publisher
PROCTER, LELAND H. (1914–)																															
Quintet	1949		20	2	1	1			1																						AmCom
PROKOFIEV, SERGE (1891–1953)																															
Overture on Hebrew Themes, Op 34	1919			2	1	1			1									1													VarPb
Quintet, Op 39	1924	g	22	1	1		1									1		1													Boose
String Quartet No. 1, Op 50	1930	b	25	2	1	1																									VarPb
String Quartet No. 2, Op 92	1941	F		2	1	1																									VarPb
PROSPERI, CARLO (1921–)																															
4 Invenzioni				1	1								1					1													Suvin
In nocte secunda *Unus Instr:* Clavichord				6								1																		1	Ricor
PUCCINI, GIACOMO (1858–1924)																															
Minuetto No. 2				2	1	1																									Bocca
Quartetto		D		2	1	1																									Bocca
Scherzo		a		2	1	1																									Bocca
PURCELL, HENRY (1659–1695)																															
Chacony in g (arr. Britten)			7	2	1	1																									Boose
Restoration Suite (arr. Lewis)			12	2	1	1																									Boose
QUARANTA, FELICE (1910–)																															
Strofe X 5/3				1		1			1			1															1				Ricor
QUERAT, MARCEL (?–)																															
Magie															1			1		1											Billa
Magie (alt.)															1			1	1												Billa
RABEY, R (?–)																															
Tes yeux				1					1																			1			Duran
RACHMANINOFF, SERGEI (1873–1943)																															
Songs (6, arr. Leonardi)				1		1			1																						Boose
String Quartets (2)	1947			2	1	1																									Russi
Trio		g		1		1			1																						Kunze
Trio élégiaque, Op 9	1893		46	1		1			1																						VarPb
Vocalise (arr. Conus), Op 34	1915		4	1		1			1																						Boose
RADAUER, IRMFRIED (1928–)																															
Siau-Tschu *Voices:* Soprano and narrator. *Unus Instr:* Celesta	1962			1			1					1	1		2		1			1							3	2		1	Peter
RADULESCU, MICHAEL (1934–)																															
Bläserquintett															1	1		1	1		1										Dobli
Streichtrio				1	1	1																									Dobli
RAFF, JOACHIM (1822–1882)																															
Sinfonietta for 10 Winds, Op 188															2	2		2	2		2										VarPb
RAGWITZ, ERHARD (1933–)																															
3 Sätze, Op 22	1969			2	1	1																									Breit
Klaviertrio 1, Op 10	1965			1		1			1																						DeutV
Klaviertrio 2, Op 30	1975			1		1			1																						DeutV
RAKOWSKI, DAVID (?–)																															
Slange			16	1	1	1	1		1									2			1										Peter
RAMEAU, JEAN P. (1683–1764)																															
Suite (arr. Nakagawa)		G													1	1		1	1		1										Press
RAMOUS, GIANNI (1930–)																															
Quartetto	1963			2	1	1																									Suvin
RAMOVS, PRIMOZ (1921–)																															
Antworten	1974		9												1	1		1	1		1										Breit
Con sordino	1974		8						1													1	1								Breit

	Year Composed or Published	Key	Duration	Violin	Viola	Cello	Double Bass	Gamba	Piano	Harpsicord	Organ	Guitar	Harp	Recorder	Flute/Piccolo	Oboe	English Horn	Clarinet/Bass Clarinet	Bassoon/Contrabassoon	Saxophone	French Horn	Trumpet	Trombone	Bass Trombone	Tuba	Baritone	Percussion	Voice	Electronic Tape	Unusual Instruments	Publisher
RAMOVS, PRIMOZ *(continued)*																															
Triptychon				2	1	1																									Breit
RANDS, BERNARD (1935–)																															
Canti del sole	1983		25	2	1	1			1						1			1				1	1				2	1			Unive
Canti lunatici *Unus Instr:* Piccolo and alto flutes	1980		28	1	1	1			1						1			1				1					2	S		2	Unive
Serenata 75 *Unus Instr:* Celesta, electric piano, electric organ	1976		15	1		1			2		1				1			1									1			3	Unive
RAPF, KURT (1922–)																															
6 Pieces for Wind Quintet															1	1		1	1		1										Dobli
Requiem for Organ and Brass											1										4	4	3		1		2				Dobli
RAPHAEL, GÜNTHER (1903–1960)																															
My Dark Hands (Five Songs)							1		1																		1	B			Breit
Palmström Sonata *Comment:* Percussion ad libitum				1			1		1									1										T			Breit
Sonatina, Op 65 No. 1					1								1		1																Breit
Trio, Op 70						1			1									1													Breit
RASMUSSEN, KARL A. (1947–)																															
A Ballad of Game and Dreams	1974		19			1			1			1																			Hanse
Ballo in Maschera	1981		8												1	1		1	1		1										Hanse
Berio Mask	1977		13	1		1						1																			Hanse
Encore VIII *Unus Instr:* Vibraphone	1983		14						1									1									1			1	Hanse
Fugue Fuga *Unus Instr:* Vibraphone	1984		14						1									1									1			1	Hanse
Italiensk Koncert	1981		14	1		1			1			1																			Hanse
Love Is in the World	1974		18									1															1	1			Hanse
Parts Apart	1978		16	2	1	1									1	1															Hanse
Pianissimo furioso	1982		7	1		1			1			1																			Hanse
Protocol and Myth *Unus Instr:* Accordion	1971		42									1															1			1	Hanse
Solos and Shadows	1983		19	2	1	1																									Hanse
Surrounded by Scales	1985		18	2	1	1																									Hanse
This Moment *Voices:* 3 Sopranos	1966														1												1	3			Hanse
Le tombeau de Père Igor	1977		11			1			1									1													Hanse
RATHAUS, KYRIL (1895–1954)																															
Gallant Serenade	1947		5												1	1		1	1		1										Boose
Streichquartett 5	1954			2	1	1																									Unive
String Quartet No. 3				2	1	1																									Oxfor
String Quartet No. 4, Op 59	1956			2	1	1																									SPAM
Tower Music for Brass																					1	2	2								AMP
RATIU, HORIA (?–)																															
Altitudes (for 15 Players)	1982		15	2	1	1	1								2	1		1	1		1	1		1			2				Salab
RAUTAVAARA, EINOJUHANI (1928–)																															
String Quartet No. 2, Op 12			22	2	1	1																									Breit
RAVEL, MAURICE (1875–1937)																															
Chansons madécasses	1926					1			1						1													1			Duran
Introduction et Allegro	1906	G♭		2	1	1							1		1			1													Duran
Pièce en forme de habanera (arr. Kessler)	1907														1	1		1	1		1										Leduc
Poèmes (3) de Mallarmé *Unus Instr:* Bass clarinet	1913			2	1	1			1						2			2										F		1	Duran
Quatuor	1903	F		2	1	1																									VarPb
Le tombeau de Couperin (trans. Jones)	1917														1	1		1	1												Duran
Trio	1914	a		1		1			1																						Duran

	Year Composed or Published	Key	Duration	Violin	Viola	Cello	Double Bass	Gamba	Piano	Harpsicord	Organ	Guitar	Harp	Recorder	Flute/Piccolo	Oboe	English Horn	Clarinet/Bass Clarinet	Bassoon/Contrabassoon	Saxophone	French Horn	Trumpet	Trombone	Bass Trombone	Tuba	Baritone	Percussion	Voice	Electronic Tape	Unusual Instruments	Publisher
RAVENOR, TERENCE (?–)																															
Renaissance Quartets (3)																						2	2								Oxfor
Renaissance Quartets, 3 (alt. vers.)																					1	2				1					Oxfor
RAWSTHORNE, ALAN (1905–1971)																															
Clarinet Quartet	1948			1	1	1												1													Oxfor
Oboe Quartet	1970			1	1	1										1															Oxfor
Piano Quintet	1968			2	1	1			1																						Oxfor
Quintet	1971			1		1			1									1			1										Oxfor
String Quartet No. 1 (Theme and Vars.)	1939			2	1	1																									Oxfor
String Quartet No. 3	1965			2	1	1																									Oxfor
Suite	1970				1								1		1																Oxfor
Tankas of the Four Seasons	1965			1		1										1		1	1									T			Oxfor
Trio	1962			1		1			1																						Oxfor
RAXACH, ENRIQUE (1932–)																															
Paraphrase for Alto Voice			15	1	1	1							1		1			1	1		1	1					2	A			Peter
RAYKI, GYÖRGY (1921–)																															
Burleske für 11 Bläser *Unus Instr:* Piccolo	1958		9												1	1		2	2		3	1	1							1	Unive
RAZZI, FAUSTO (1932–)																															
Invenzione a tre *Unus Instr:* Piccolo clarinet																1		2												1	Suvin
READ, GARDNER (1913–)																															
Nine by Six	1951		16												1		1	1	1		1	1									Peter
Sinfonia da chiesa			11								1										1	2	2								Peter
READ, THOMAS L. (1938–)																															
5 Sketches	1961		4		1										1			1													AmCom
Corrente			11													1		1	1												Peter
Corridors (Overture)	1977		7	1		1										1					1	1	1								AmCom
Fanfare for the Marble Court	1978		7																		2	2	2				6				AmCom
Isochronisms No. 3 *Unus Instr:* Vibraphone, timpani	1972		8																		4	6	4	2			2			2	AmCom
Naming the Changes			26			1			1						1	1											2	S			Peter
RECK, DAVID (1935–)																															
Number, Op 2 *Voice:* Actress			18	1			1					1			1			1									1	1			Peter
REDEL, MARTIN C. (1947–)																															
Dispersion *Unus Instr:* Typewriter	1972		11	1	1	1			1						1	1		1									1			1	BoteB
Epilogue, Op 15 *Voice:* Bass-baritone	1971											1			1													1			BoteB
Espressioni, Op 29									1							1		1	1		1										BoteB
Interplay, Op 23 *Unus Instr:* Vibraphone, xylophone	1975		10	1	1	1			1						1			1									2			2	BoteB
Piano Trio, Op 19	1972			1		1			1																						BoteB
Reliefs, Op 14	1970					1							1			1	1				1						1				BoteB
String Quartet No. 1, Op 7	1967			2	1	1																									BoteB
String Quartet No. 2, Op 25	1977			2	1	1																									BoteB
REGER, MAX (1873–1916)																															
Klavierquartett, Op 113		d		1	1	1			1																						BoteB
Klavierquartett, Op 133	1916	a		1	1	1			1																						VarPb
Klavierquintett, Op 64	1902	c		2	1	1			1																						Peter
Maria Wiegenlied, Op 76 No. 52 *Voice:* Medium. Cello may replace violin	1912			1							1																	1			BoteB
Quintett, Op 146	1916	A		2	1	1												1													VarPb
Serenade, Op 77a	1904	D		1	1										1																BoteB

	Year Composed or Published	Key	Duration	Violin	Viola	Cello	Double Bass	Gamba	Piano	Harpsicord	Organ	Guitar	Harp	Recorder	Flute/Piccolo	Oboe	English Horn	Clarinet/Bass Clarinet	Bassoon/Contrabassoon	Saxophone	French Horn	Trumpet	Trombone	Bass Trombone	Tuba	Baritone	Percussion	Voice	Electronic Tape	Unusual Instruments	Publisher
REGER, MAX *(continued)*																															
Serenade, Op 141a	1915	G		1	1										1																Peter
Sextett, Op 118	1911	F		2	2	2																									BoteB
Streichquartett, Op 54 No. 1	1902	g		2	1	1																									AiblV
Streichquartett, Op 54 No. 2	1902	A		2	1	1																									AiblV
Streichquartett, Op 74	1904	d		2	1	1																									BoteB
Streichquartett, Op 109	1909	E♭		2	1	1																									BoteB
Streichquartett, Op 121	1911	f♯		2	1	1																									Peter
Streichquartett, Op Post. S365	1889	d		2	1	1																									BoteB
Streichtrio, Op 77b	1904	a		1	1	1																									BoteB
Trio, Op 2	1911	b		1	1				1																						BScho
Trio, Op 102	1908	e		1		1			1																						LautK
Trio No. 2, Op 141b	1915	d		1	1	1																									Peter
Wind Serenade, First Movement		B♭	5												2	2		2	2		4										Breit
REICH, STEVE (1936–)																															
Different Trains	1988		25	2	1	1																							1		Boose
Drumming (Part 2) *Unus Instr:* 3 Marimbas (9 players)	1971		22																								3	F		3	Boose
Drumming (Part 3) *Unus Instr:* 3 Glockenspiel (4 players) and whistling	1971		14												1												3			3	Boose
Eight Lines *Comment:* Revised version of Octet. *Unus Instr:* Bass clarinet	1983		17	4	2	2	1		2						2			2												1	Boose
Music for Mallet Inst., Voices, Organ *Unus Instr:* 4 Marimbas, 2 glockenspiels, vibraphone	1973		18								1																4	F		7	Boose
Music for 18 Musicians *Voice:* wordless. *Unus Instr:* 3 Marimbas, 2 xylophones, vibraphone	1976		55	1		1			4																		6	4		4	Boose
Octet	1979		17	2	1	1			2						2			2													Boose
Sextet *Unus Instr:* 3 Marimbas, 2 vibraphones, tam-tam, 2 bass drums	1985		28						2																		4			8	Boose
REICHA, ANTONIN J. (1770–1836)																															
Clarinet Quintet		B♭		2	1	1												1													MusRa
Fantasy, Op 51		G		1		1									1																Amade
Flute Quartet, Op 98 No. 1		g		1	1	1									1																MABoh
Flute Quartet, Op 98 No. 2		C		1	1	1									1																MABoh
Flute Quartet, Op 98 No. 3		G		1	1	1									1																MABoh
Flute Quintet, Op 105		A		2	1	1									1																Amade
Flute Trio		G		1		1									1																Amade
Horn Quintet, Op 106		E		2	1	1															1										MusRa
Oboe Quintet, Op 107		F		2	1	1										1															MusRa
Octet, Op 96 *Comment:* Flute may replace oboe		E♭		2	1	1	1									1		1			1										MusRa
String Trio		F		1	1	1																									Kunze
Variations (arr. Foerster)				1		1									1																Amade
Woodwind Quintet, Op 88 No. 1		e													1	1		1	1		1										Kneus
Woodwind Quintet, Op 88 No. 3															1	1		1	1		1										MABoh
Woodwind Quintet, Op 88 No. 4		d													1	1		1	1		1										Kneus
Woodwind Quintet, Op 88 No. 6		F													1	1		1	1		1										Kneus
Woodwind Quintet, Op 91 No. 1		C													1	1		1	1		1										Kneus
Woodwind Quintet, Op 91 No. 2		a													1	1		1	1		1										Kneus
Woodwind Quintet, Op 91 No. 3		D													1	1		1	1		1										Kneus
Woodwind Quintet, Op 91 No. 4															1	1		1	1		1										Billa
Woodwind Quintet, Op 91 No. 5		A													1	1		1	1		1										Kneus

	Year Composed or Published	Key	Duration	Violin	Viola	Cello	Double Bass	Gamba	Piano	Harpsicord	Organ	Guitar	Harp	Recorder	Flute/Piccolo	Oboe	English Horn	Clarinet/Bass Clarinet	Bassoon/Contrabassoon	Saxophone	French Horn	Trumpet	Trombone	Bass Trombone	Tuba	Baritone	Percussion	Voice	Electronic Tape	Unusual Instruments	Publisher
REICHA, ANTONIN J. *(continued)*																															
Woodwind Quintet, Op 91 No. 6		c													1	1		1	1		1										Kneus
Woodwind Quintet, Op 91 No. 9															1	1		1	1		1										MABoh
Woodwind Quintet, Op 91 No. 11															1	1		1	1		1										MABoh
Woodwind Quintet, Op 99 No. 2		E♭													1	1		1	1		1										MusRa
Woodwind Quintet, Op 99 No. 6		G													1	1		1	1		1										Kneus
Woodwind Quintet, Op 100 No. 4		e													1	1		1	1		1										Kneus
REIMANN, ARIBERT (1936–)																															
Monumenta for Winds and Timpani *Unus Instr:* Timpani	1960		8												2	1	1	2	2		3	2	2				1			1	BoteB
REINECKE, CARL (1824–1910)																															
Clarinet Trio, Op 264					1				1									1													Amade
Horn Trio, Op 274 *Comment:* Viola may replace French horn									1									1			1										MusRa
REINER, HERBERT A. (?–)																															
Eichendorff Octet *Comment:* Soprano or tenor voice ad libitum	1955			1	1	1	1								1	1		1	1									1			Amade
String Quartet No. 2	1958			2	1	1																									Amade
REINER, KAREL (1910–1979)																															
Trio *Unus Instr:* Bass clarinet	1964														1			1									1			1	Artia
REINHOLD, OTTO (1899–)																															
Klaviertrio				1		1			1																						Bären
REISER, ALOIS (1887–1977)																															
Piano Quintet				2	1	1			1																						Press
String Quartet, Op 16	1920			2	1	1																									VarPb
REITER, ALBERT (1905–)																															
Music for Brass *Unus Instr:* Tenor horn																					2	3	2		1					1	Dobli
Music for Solo Trombone and 5 Horns																					5		1								Dobli
Music for Trumpet, Tenor Horns, and Tuba *Unus Instr:* 2 Tenor horns																					3	1			1					2	Dobli
Music for Winds															1	1		1	1		1										Dobli
Piano Trio				1		1			1																						Dobli
REIZENSTEIN, FRANZ (1911–1968)																															
Wind Quintet, Op 5	1934		15												1	1		1	1		1										Boose
REMACHA, FERNANDO (1898–)																															
Cuarteto				2	1	1																									UMEsp
RENIE, HENRIETTE (1875–1956)																															
Trio *Comment:* Piano can substitute for harp				1		1							1																		Leduc
RENOSTO, PAOLO (1935–)																															
Al(do)us Quartet				2	1	1																									Ricor
Fast				2	1																										Ricor
Gesta				6	2	2	1																								Ricor
RESPIGHI, OTTORINO (1879–1936)																															
Quartetto dorico	1925			2	1	1																									Unive
Suite della tabacchiera									1						2	2			2												Ricor
Il tramonto				2	1	1																						M			Ricor
REVERDY, MICHELE (1943–)																															
El corro infrangible	1984		15	1	1	1	1								1	1		2	1		1	1	1								Salab
Scenic Railway *Unus Instr:* Contrabass clarinet	1983		17				1								2		1	3	2		2	1	1		1		3			1	Salab

	Year Composed or Published	Key	Duration	Violin	Viola	Cello	Double Bass	Gamba	Piano	Harpsicord	Organ	Guitar	Harp	Recorder	Flute/Piccolo	Oboe	English Horn	Clarinet/Bass Clarinet	Bassoon/Contrabassoon	Saxophone	French Horn	Trumpet	Trombone	Bass Trombone	Tuba	Baritone	Percussion	Voice	Electronic Tape	Unusual Instruments	Publisher
REVUELTAS, SILVESTRE (1899–1940)																															
Little Serious Piece No. 1															1	1		1		1		1									Peer
Little Serious Piece No. 2															1	1		1		1		1									Peer
Música de feria (Festival Music)				2	1	1																									Peer
Ocho por radio				1	1	1	1											1	1			1					1				Peer
Sensemaya *Unus Instr:* Bass clarinet			7	2			1		1						1			2	1			2	1				5			1	Schir
String Quartet No. 1				2	1	1																									Peer
String Quartet No. 2				2	1	1																									Peer
Toccata Without a Fugue *Unus Instr:* Bass clarinet				1											1			3			1	1					1			1	Peer
REYNOLDS, ROGER (1934–)																															
Again *Voices:* 2 Sopranos (wordless). Needed: amplification system, lighting	1974		27				2								2								2				2	2	1		Peter
Coconino — a Shattered Landscape	1985			2	1	1																									Peter
Compass *Voices:* Tenor and bass. Needed: amplification	1974		30			1	1																					2	1	1	Peter
Emperor of Ice Cream	1974		14				1		1																		1	8			Peter
Gathering	1965		10												1	1		1	1		1										Peter
Less Than Two	1979		22						2																		2		1		Peter
Mistral *Comment:* Amplification needed	1985		19	2		2	2			1											2	2	2								Peter
Not Only Night	1988			1		1			1						1			1										S	1		Peter
Personae (violin solo) *Unus Instr:* Piccolo, bass clarinet. Two- or 4-channel tape	1990		25	1	1	1	1		1						1			1			1			1			1		1	2	Peter
Ping *Comment:* Performance includes projections and film	1968		24						1						1												1		1		Peter
Promises of Darkness	1976		22	1		1	1		1						1			1	1		1	1	1				1				Peter
Quick Are the Mouths of Earth	1965		18			3			1						3	1						1	1	1			2				Peter
The Serpent-Snapping Eye	1979		19						1													1					1		1		Peter
Shadowed Narrative	1982		23	1		1			1									1													Peter
String Quartet No. 2	1961		14	2	1	1																									Peter
Traces	1968		25			1			1						1														3		Peter
Transfigured Wind III			35	1	1	1	1		1						1	1		2	1		1	1	1				2		1		Peter
Wedge *Unus Instr:* Piccolo	1961		9				1		1						2							2	2				1			1	Peter
REZNICEK, EMIL (1860–1945)																															
Streichquartett	1923	d		2	1	1																									Birnb
Streichquartett	1932	B♭		2	1	1																									Birnb
RHEINBERGER, JOSEF G. (1839–1901)																															
Concerto (Suite), Op 149				1		1					1																				Amade
Nonet, Op 139		E♭		1	1	1	1								1	1		1	1		1										MusRa
RHENE-BATON, RENÉ (1879–1940)																															
Aubade															1	1		2	2		1										Duran
Trio	1923	c		1		1			1																						Duran
RHODES, PHILLIP (1940–)																															
Autumn Setting			11	2	1	1																						S			Peter
Ensemble Etudes	1967		9	2	1	1									1	1		1	1		1										AmCom
Museum Pieces			18	2	1	1												1													Peter
Quartet (with flute and harp)			14	1		1							1		1																Peter
String Trio			9	1	1	1																									Peter
Trio				1	1	1																									Peter
Visions of Remembrance *Voices:* Soprano, mezzo-soprano			22	1	1	1			1						1		1	1			1	1	1					2			Peter

	Year Composed or Published	Key	Duration	Violin	Viola	Cello	Double Bass	Gamba	Piano	Harpsicord	Organ	Guitar	Harp	Recorder	Flute/Piccolo	Oboe	English Horn	Clarinet/Bass Clarinet	Bassoon/Contrabassoon	Saxophone	French Horn	Trumpet	Trombone	Bass Trombone	Tuba	Baritone	Percussion	Voice	Electronic Tape	Unusual Instruments	Publisher
RICHTER, MARGA (1926–)																															
Dusseldorf Concerto	1982		20	2	3	1							1		1												1				Schir
RIDIL, CHRISTIAN (?–)																															
Mobile musicale																2			1												Breit
RIDKY, JAROSLAV (1897–1956)																															
Klaviertrio, Op 44	1951			1		1			1																						Artia
Streichquartett 5, Op 34	1937			2	1	1																									Artia
RIEGGER, WALLINGFORD (1885–1961)																															
Canons (3) for Woodwinds, Op 9 *Unus Instr:* Piccolo	1931		10												1	1		1	1											1	Merio
Concerto for Piano, Op 53	1952		15						1						1	1		1	1		1										AMP
Divertissement, Op 15	1933		14			1							1		1																Peter
Duos for 3 Woodwinds, Op 35	1943		20												1	1		1													NewMu
Movement, Op 66	1957		5						1													2	1								Peer
Nonet, Op 49	1951		9																		2	3	3		1						AMP
Piano Quintet, Op 47	1951		25	2	1	1			1																						AMP
Piano Trio, Op 1	1933		20	1		1			1																						Schir
Prelude and Fugue, Op 52 *Unus Instr:* Euphonium	1953														1	1		3	1	3	1	5	1		2		2			1	AMP
Romanza, Op 56a			5	2	1	1																									AMP
String Quartet No. 1, Op 30	1939		16	2	1	1																									AMP
String Quartet No. 2, Op 43	1948		18	2	1	1																									AMP
Woodwind Quintet, Op 51	1952		8												1	1		1	1		1										BScho
RIES, FERDINAND (1784–1838)																															
Clarinet Trio, Op 28						1			1									1													Kunze
Flute Trio, Op 63		E♭				1			1						1																VarPb
Octet, Op 128				1	1	1	1		1									1	1		1										MusRa
Piano Quintet, Op 74				1	1	1	1		1																						Kunze
RIESMAN, MICHAEL (1943–)																															
Chamber Concerto			30	2	1	1	1		1						1	1		1	1		1						1				Schir
RIETI, VITTORIO (1898–)																															
Madrigal en quatre parties	1927		15	2	1	1	1		1						1	1		1	1		1	1									Salab
Quatuor à cordes	1926	F		2	1	1																									Salab
Woodwind Quintet	1957														1	1		1	1		1										AMP
RIHM, WOLFGANG (1952–)																															
Bild	1984		9		1	1	1		1												1	1	1				2				Unive
Chiffre I *Unus Instr:* Bass clarinet	1982		8			2	1		1									1	1			1	1							1	Unive
Chiffre III *Unus Instr:* Bass clarinet, contrabassoon, bass trumpet	1983		6			2	1		1								1	1	1		1	1	1				2			3	Unive
Chiffre IV *Unus Instr:* Bass clarinet	1984		9			1			1									1												1	Unive
Chiffre VI *Unus Instr:* E♭ and bass clarinets, contrabassoon	1985		6	2	1	1	1											1	1		1									3	Unive
Erscheinung *Comment:* Piano ad libitum	1978		14	3	3	3																									Unive
Klaviertrio	1972		9	1		1			1																						Breit
Segmente, Op 12			10																												Breit
Streichquartett 2, Op 10	1970		13	2	1	1																									Breit
Streichtrio, Op 9				1	1	1																									Breit
RIHOVSKY, VOJTECH (1870–1950)																															
Pohadka, Op 51				1		1			1																						Artia
RIISAGER, KNUDAGE (1897–1974)																															
Conversatione																1		1	1												Engst
Divertimento															1	1			1		1										Engst

	Year Composed or Published	Key	Duration	Violin	Viola	Cello	Double Bass	Gamba	Piano	Harpsicord	Organ	Guitar	Harp	Recorder	Flute/Piccolo	Oboe	English Horn	Clarinet/Bass Clarinet	Bassoon/Contrabassoon	Saxophone	French Horn	Trumpet	Trombone	Bass Trombone	Tuba	Baritone	Percussion	Voice	Electronic Tape	Unusual Instruments	Publisher
RIISAGER, KNUDAGE *(continued)*																															
Sonatina, Op 55a				1		1			1																						Engst
RILEY, DENNIS (1943–)																															
Apparitions	1984				1								1		1																Peter
Cantata I *Unus Instr:* Vibraphone	1966		7			1			1											1								M		1	Peter
Concertante Music I	1970		9	3		1	1		1				1		2			2				1	1				1				Peter
Concertante Music II	1972		18	1	1	1									1			1					1				2				Peter
Concertante Music IV	1978		13	1		1	1		1						1			2	1		1						1				Peter
Concertino	1976		13			1			1				1									1					2				Peter
Dances and Interludes			13	1	1	1												1													Peter
Fantasia after Gibbons	1983					1										1		1													Peter
Fantasia after Gibbons (alt. inst.)	1983					1									1			1													Peter
Masques	1982														1	1		1	1		1										Peter
Poems (5) of Marilyn Hacker	1986		24	1	1	1				1					1	1			1								1	S			Peter
Songs (5) on Japanese Haiku	1963			1		1												1										S			Peter
Summer Music	1979		8									1			1													M			Peter
Variations II (Trio)	1968		8	1	1	1																									Peter
RIMSKY-KORSAKOV, NIKOLAI (1844–1908)																															
Flight of the Bumble Bee (arr. Walter)															1	1		1	1		1										Billa
Quintet, Op Post.									1						1			1	1		1										VarPb
String Quartet, Op 12		F		2	1	1																									RusMV
String Sextet, Op Post.		A		2	2	2																									RusMV
Theme and Variations on a Chorale				2	1	1																									Kunze
RINEHART, JOHN M. (1937–)																															
Capriccio	1966		7		1	1			1																						AmCom
RINGGER, ROLF U. (1935–)																															
Souvenirs de Capri				2	2	2															1							S			Hug
RIVIER, JEAN (1896–1987)																															
Capriccio															1	1		1	1		1										Billa
ROCCA, LODOVICO (1895–)																															
Storiella									1				1						1				2								Ricor
ROCHBERG, GEORGE (1918–)																															
Contra mortem et tempus				1					1						1			1													Press
Piano Quartet				1	1	1			1																						Press
Piano Trio				1		1			1																						Press
Quintet				2	1	2																									Press
String Quartet No. 1				2	1	1																									Press
To the Dark Wood															1	1		1	1		1										Press
Trio for Piano and Winds									1									1			1										Press
RODGERS, LOU (?–)																															
Quintet	1959		9	2	1	1																1									AmCom
RODRIGUEZ, ALBERT (?–)																															
Cuarteto				1	1	1						1																			UMEsp
ROGER-DUCASSE, JEAN J. (1873–1954)																															
Quatuor	1909	d		2	1	1																									Duran
Quatuor	1910	g		1	1	1			1																						Duran
Quatuor à cordes, 2e		D		2	1	1																									Duran
ROLAND-MANUEL, ALEXIS (1891–1966)																															
Suite dans le goût espagnol										1						1			1			1									Duran
Suite dans le goût espagnol (alt. inst.)									1							1			1			1									Duran

	Year Composed or Published	Key	Duration	Violin	Viola	Cello	Double Bass	Gamba	Piano	Harpsicord	Organ	Guitar	Harp	Recorder	Flute/Piccolo	Oboe	English Horn	Clarinet/Bass Clarinet	Bassoon/Contrabassoon	Saxophone	French Horn	Trumpet	Trombone	Bass Trombone	Tuba	Baritone	Percussion	Voice	Electronic Tape	Unusual Instruments	Publisher
ROLLA, ALESSANDRO (1757–1841)																															
Serenata				2	2																										Amade
String Trio		C		2	1																										Kunze
String Trio		F		2	1																										Kunze
String Trio		d		2	1																										Kunze
ROMANOVSKY, ERICH M. (1929–)																															
Trio															1			1	1												Dobli
ROMBERG, ANDREAS (1767–1821)																															
Quintett, Op 41 No. 1				1	2	1									1																Kunze
ROMBERG, BERNHARD (1767–1841)																															
String Trio, Op 38 No. 1				1	1	1																									Kunze
ROOSEVELT, JOSEPH W. (1918–)																															
Flute and Fiddle (4 Duos)	1975		12	1	1										5																AmCom
Serenade	1955		12		1	1										1															AmCom
Song and Dance Suite	1975		13		1											1		1													AmCom
ROPARTZ, GUY (1864–1955)																															
Lamento for Oboe and Wind Ensemble			5												2	1		2	2		1										Salab
Pièces (2)															1	1		1	1		1										Duran
Prélude, marine, et chansons				1	1	1							1		1																Duran
Quatuor à cordes, 1er	1893	g		2	1	1																									Rouar
Quatuor à cordes, 2e	1912	d		2	1	1																									Duran
Quatuor à cordes, 3e	1925	G		2	1	1																									Duran
Quatuor à cordes, 4e	1934	E		2	1	1																									Duran
Quatuor à cordes, 5e	1940	D		2	1	1																									Duran
Quatuor à cordes, 6e	1951	F		2	1	1																									Duran
Sérénade				2	1	1																									Rouar
Trio	1918	a		1		1			1																						Duran
Trio	1935	a		1	1	1																									Duran
ROREM, NED (1923–)																															
Ariel	1971		17						1									1										S			Boose
Bright Music	1988			2		1			1						1																Boose
End of Summer	1985		18	1					1									1													Boose
Last Poems of Wallace Stevens	1972					1			1																			1			Boose
Lovers	1964		17			1				1							1										5				Boose
Mourning Scene from Samuel			6	2	1	1																						1			Peter
Santa Fe Songs *Voice:* Medium	1980		25	2	1	1			1																			1			Boose
Serenade on 5 English Poems	1975		16	1	1				1																			1			Boose
Sinfonia for Wind Symphony Orchestra			9												3	2	1	4	3		2										Peter
Sinfonia for Wind Symphony Orchestra (alt. inst.) *Unus Instr:* Celesta			9						1						3	2	1	4	3		2						2			1	Peter
String Quartet No. 2				2	1	1																									Peer
Trio	1960		18			1			1						1																Peter
Winter Pages	1981		36	1		1			1									1	1												Boose
ROSEMAN, RONALD A. (1933–)																															
Concertino	1982		15	1		1				1					1	1			1												AmCom
Sonata	1980		17							1						2															AmCom
Trio	1985		15						1							1							1								AmCom
ROSEN, JEROME (1921–)																															
Clarinet Quintet	1960		18	2	1	1												1													AmCom

	Year Composed or Published	Key	Duration	Violin	Viola	Cello	Double Bass	Gamba	Piano	Harpsicord	Organ	Guitar	Harp	Recorder	Flute/Piccolo	Oboe	English Horn	Clarinet/Bass Clarinet	Bassoon/Contrabassoon	Saxophone	French Horn	Trumpet	Trombone	Bass Trombone	Tuba	Baritone	Percussion	Voice	Electronic Tape	Unusual Instruments	Publisher
ROSEN, JEROME *(continued)*																															
Quintet (with Saxophone)	1974		15	2	1	1														1											AmCom
ROSENFELD, GERHARD (1931–)																															
Quartettino				2	1	1																									Peter
ROSENMAN, LEONARD (1924–)																															
Chamber Music IV (w. Solo Contrabass) *Unus Instr:* Contrabass	1976		15	8	4	4	1																							1	Schir
Chamber Music V	1979		22	1		1			1						1			1									2				Schir
ROSSE, FRANÇOIS (?–)																															
Mad'son 5 (Trio)													1		1													1			Billa
ROSSINI, GIOACCHINO A. (1792–1868)																															
Barber of Seville Overture and 3 Arias (arr. Sedlak) *Unus Instr:* Contrabassoon	1816															2		2	3		2	2								1	MusRa
Flute Quartet No. 1		G		1	1	1									1																VarPb
Flute Quartet No. 2		A		1	1	1									1																VarPb
Flute Quartet No. 3				1	1	1									1																VarPb
Flute Quartet No. 4		D		1	1	1									1																VarPb
Sonata No. 1 for Strings *Comment:* Viola may replace a violin	1804	G		2		1	1																								Dobli
Sonata No. 2 for Strings *Comment:* Viola ad libitum	1804	A		2		1	1																								Dobli
Sonata No. 3 for Strings *Comment:* Viola may replace a violin	1804	C		2		1	1																								Dobli
Sonata No. 4 for Strings *Comment:* Viola ad libitum	1804	B♭		2		1	1																								Dobli
Sonata No. 5 for Strings *Comment:* Viola ad libitum	1805	E♭		2		1	1																								Dobli
Sonata No. 6 for Strings *Comment:* Viola ad libitum	1806	D		2		1	1																								Dobli
ROSZAVOLGYI, MARK R. (1790–1848)																															
Drei Csardas				2	1	1																									Dobli
ROT, M (?–)																															
Die Legende vom lieben Augustin, Op 8																					1	2	1		1						Dobli
ROTA, NINO (1911–1979)																															
Petite offrande musicale															1	1		1	1		1										Leduc
Trio	1958			1					1						1																Ricor
RÖTSCHER, KONRAD (1910–)																															
Divertimento, Op 22	1952			1		1									1			1													BoteB
Quintett, Op 41															1	1		1	1		1										BoteB
RÖTTGER, HEINZ (1909–1977)																															
Chamber Music									1									1									1				Peter
Constellationen	1958			2	1	1																									DeutV
ROUSE, CHRISTOPHER (1949–)																															
Subjectives VIII *Comment:* Conductor needed	1972		6																			5					3				AmCom
ROUSSAKIS, NICOLAS (1934–)																															
Concertino	1973		11												1	1		1	1								2				AmCom
Sextet	1964		12	1	1	1			1						1			1													AmCom
Trigono *Unus Instr:* Vibraphone	1986		15																				1				6			1	AmCom
ROUSSEL, ALBERT (1869–1937)																															
Divertissement, Op 6	1905								1						1	1		1	1		1										Rouar

	Year Composed or Published	Key	Duration	Violin	Viola	Cello	Double Bass	Gamba	Piano	Harpsicord	Organ	Guitar	Harp	Recorder	Flute/Piccolo	Oboe	English Horn	Clarinet/Bass Clarinet	Bassoon/Contrabassoon	Saxophone	French Horn	Trumpet	Trombone	Bass Trombone	Tuba	Baritone	Percussion	Voice	Electronic Tape	Unusual Instruments	Publisher
ROUSSEL, ALBERT *(continued)*																															
Flute Trio, Op 40	1929				1	1									1																Duran
Piano Trio, Op 2	1902			1		1			1																						Salab
Quatuor, Op 45	1932	D		2	1	1																									Duran
Sérénade, Op 30	1925			1	1	1							1		1																Duran
String Trio, Op 58	1937			1	1	1																									Duran
ROVICS, HOWARD (1936–)																															
Cybernetic Study No. 2	1968		4						1									1	1												AmCom
Events II *Unus Instr:* Bass clarinet	1972		7	1		1	1		1							1		2				1					1			1	AmCom
Quartet	1966		7							1					1	1			1												AmCom
Transactions	1973		17	1		1	1		1						1			1									1				AmCom
Trio	1983		7		1	1			1																						AmCom
ROWLEY, ALEC (1892–1958)																															
Short Trio on French Tunes				1		1			1																						Peter
ROY, KLAUS G. (1924–)																															
Sterlingman Suite															1	1		1	1												Press
ROZKOSNY, JOSEF (1833–1913)																															
Reverie (solo cello)				3	2	3	1																								Urban
ROZSA, MIKLOS (1907–)																															
Piano Quintet, Op 2	1928	f		2	1	1			1																						Breit
Sinfonia concertante, Op 29				1		1			1																						Breit
String Quartet No. 1, Op 22				2	1	1																									Breit
String Trio No. 1, Op 1				1	1	1																									Breit
Tema con variazione (from Sinfonia concertante)				1		1			1																						Breit
RUBIN, MARCEL (1905–)																															
Divertimento				1		1			1																						Dobli
Serenade															1	1		1	1		1										Dobli
Streichquartett 1				2	1	1																									Dobli
Streichquartett 2				2	1	1																									Dobli
Streichtrio				1	1	1																									Dobli
Variations on a French Revolutionary Air				2	1	1	1											1	1		1	1	1				1				Dobli
RUBINSTEIN, ANTON (1829–1894)																															
Quartet, Op 17 No. 2		c		2	1	1																									Breit
Quartet, Op 17 No. 3		F		2	1	1																									Breit
Quintetto, Op 59				2	2	1																									Senff
RUDERS, POUL (1949–)																															
4 Compositions *Unus Instr:* Bass clarinet	1980		25	2	1	1	1		1						1			1			1									1	Hanse
Break-Dance	1984		7						1													2	3								Hanse
Dance (4) in One Movement *Comment:* Oboe doubles on English horn	1983		18	2	1	1	1		1						1	1	1	1	1		1	1	1				1				Hanse
Diferencias *Unus Instr:* Vibraphone	1980		8	1		1			1			1			1			1									1			1	Hanse
Dramaphonia (solo piano) *Unus Instr:* Piccolo; E♭ and bass clarinets, contrabassoon, piccolo trumpet	1987			1		1	1		1						1	1		1	1		1	1	1				1			5	Hanse
Greeting Concertino *Unus Instr:* Cornet	1982		10	1		1	1		1												1	1	1				1			1	Hanse
Medieval Variations *Unus Instr:* Cornet	1974		35		1	1			1	1					1					1			1							1	Hanse
Nightshade *Unus Instr:* Banjo	1987		10	1			1		1						1			1			1		1				1			1	Hanse
Pestilence Songs *Unus Instr:* Saloon piano	1975		15						1			1																S		1	Hanse

	Year Composed or Published	Key	Duration	Violin	Viola	Cello	Double Bass	Gamba	Piano	Harpsicord	Organ	Guitar	Harp	Recorder	Flute/Piccolo	Oboe	English Horn	Clarinet/Bass Clarinet	Bassoon/Contrabassoon	Saxophone	French Horn	Trumpet	Trombone	Bass Trombone	Tuba	Baritone	Percussion	Voice	Electronic Tape	Unusual Instruments	Publisher
RUDERS, POUL *(continued)*																															
Rondeau	1976		8	1		1			1			1			1			1									1				Hanse
Stabat Mater *Unus Instr:* Bells	1974		20						1		1																1	S		1	Hanse
String Quartet No. 1 (Rastlose Mensch)	1971		25	2	1	1																									Hanse
String Quartet No. 2	1979		12	2	1	1																									Hanse
String Quartet No. 3	1979		7	2	1	1																									Hanse
Tattoo for Three	1984		7			1			1									1													Hanse
Vox in Rama *Unus Instr:* Electric violin	1983		10	1					1									1												1	Hanse
Wind Drumming	1979		12												1	1		1	1		1						4				Hanse
RUDHYAR, DANE (1895–1985)																															
Nostalgia (Nonet)	1983		19	3	1	1	1		1						1												1				AmCom
RUDOLPH, JOHANN J. (1788–1831)																															
Trio *Comment:* Archduke Rudolph, Beethoven's patron, friend, and pupil						1			1									1													MusRa
RUEFF, JEANINE (1922–)																															
3 Pièces																1		1	1												Leduc
Quatuor, Op 2				2	1	1																									Duran
RULON, C. B. (1954–)																															
Dances for Oboe Quartet	1984		12	1	1	1										1															AmCom
Oh, Rampant Punk *Unus Instr:* Synthesizer	1988		16	1		1			1						1			1									2			1	AmCom
RUTTER, JOHN (1943–)																															
Ding! Dong! Merrily on High																					1	2	1		1		1				Oxfor
We Wish You a Merry Christmas																					1	2	1		1		1				Oxfor
RUZICKA, PETER (1948–)																															
. . . fragment . . .				2	1	1																									Sikor
Introspezione (exempla nova 23)				2	1	1																									Sikor
SAARIAHO, KAIJA (1952–)																															
Io *Unus Instr:* Celesta (doubled on piano) and bass flute	1987		18	2	1	1	1		1				1		3						2		1		1		2			2	Hanse
SABON, E. (?–)																															
Charité *Comment:* Violin may replace clarinet									1						1			1													Billa
Les cloches bleues									1							1			1												Billa
Helvétie									1							1	1														Billa
SADLER, HELMUT (1921–)																															
Quartettino															1	1		1	1												SudDM
Sinfonia concertante (for 15 Winds) *Unus Instr:* Contrabassoon	1980		20												2	2		2	2		2	2	2		1		2			1	Breit
SAINT-MARTIN, LEONCE DE (1886–1954)																															
In memoriam. Paraphrase of National Hymn											1											3	3								Duran
SAINT-SAENS, CAMILLE (1835–1921)																															
Caprice sur des airs danois et russes, Op 79									1						1	1		1													VarPb
Feuillet d'album															1	1		2	2		2										Duran
La muse et le poète, Op 132				1		1			1																						Duran
Quatuor, Op 41	1875	B♭		1	1	1			1																						Duran
Quatuor, 1er, Op 112	1900	e		2	1	1																									Duran

	Year Composed or Published	Key	Duration	Violin	Viola	Cello	Double Bass	Gamba	Piano	Harpsicord	Organ	Guitar	Harp	Recorder	Flute/Piccolo	Oboe	English Horn	Clarinet/Bass Clarinet	Bassoon/Contrabassoon	Saxophone	French Horn	Trumpet	Trombone	Bass Trombone	Tuba	Baritone	Percussion	Voice	Electronic Tape	Unusual Instruments	Publisher
SAINT-SAENS, CAMILLE *(continued)*																															
Quatuor, 2e, Op 153	1919	G		2	1	1																									Duran
Quintette, Op 14 *Comment:* Double-bass ad lib	1855	A		2	1	1			1																						VarPb
Septet, Op 65	1881	E♭		2	1	1	1		1													1									VarPb
Sérénade, Op 15				1	1				1		1																				Duran
Sérénade (alt. inst.)				1		1			1		1																				Duran
Tarentelle, Op 6									1						1			1													VarPb
Trio, Op 65		E♭		1		1			1																						Duran
Trio, 1er, Op 18	1863	F		1		1			1																						VarPb
Trio, 2e, Op 92	1892	e		1		1			1																						Duran
SAMAZEUILH, GUSTAVE (1877–1967)																															
Cantabile et capriccio	1948			2	1	1																									Duran
Divertissement et musette	1912			2	1	1									1	1		1	1		1										Duran
Quatuor	1911	D		2	1	1																									Duran
Suite en trio	1938			1	1	1																									Duran
SAMMONS, ALBERT E. (1886–1957)																															
Phantasy Quartet	1915	B		2	1	1																									Boose
SAMUEL-ROUSSEAU, MARCEL (1882–1955)																															
Pièces, 2				2	1	1																									Duran
SAMYN, NOEL (?–)																															
Trio, 1er																		2		1											Billa
Trio, 2e																		2		1											Billa
Trio, 3e																		2		1											Billa
Trio, 4e																		2		1											Billa
Trio, 5e																		2		1											Billa
SANDER, PETER (1933–)																															
Brass Quintet No. 1																					1	2	1		1						Kunze
String Quartet No. 1				2	1	1																									Kunze
Wind Quintet															1	1		1	1		1										Kunze
SAPIEYEVSKI, JERZY (1945–)																															
Concerto for Trumpet															2	1		1	2		1	1					1				Peter
Games for Percussion and Brass			7																		4	3	4		1		1				Peter
Mazurka (Quartet)				2	1	1																									Press
SAPP, ALLEN D. (1922–)																															
Trio No. 1	1949		14		1	1			1																						AmCom
SARY, LASZLO (1940–)																															
Quartetto *Unus Instr:* Cimbalon	1968			1											1												1	S		1	Boose
SATIE, ERIC (1866–1925)																															
La messe des pauvres			8	1		1			1				1		1			2	1		1	1	1				2				Salab
Musique d'ameublement	1920		3	2	2	1									1			1	1			1					1				Salab
Parade: Ragtime *Unus Instr:* Cornet	1917			3	1	1	1								1	1		1	1		1	1	1				1			1	Salab
Les patins dansent	1913		3	2	1	1	1								1	1		1	1		1	1									Salab
Le piège de Méduse *Unus Instr:* Tambourine	1913			1		1	1											1				1	1				1			1	Salab
Quatuor intime et secret (arr. Caby)				2	1	1																									Salab
Sarabande, 1er																					1	2	2								Salab
SAUGUET, HENRI (1901–)																															
Chants (3) de contemplation sur . . . Lao Tseu *Voices:* Contralto and bass																					1	2	1					2			Leduc

	Year Composed or Published	Key	Duration	Violin	Viola	Cello	Double Bass	Gamba	Piano	Harpsicord	Organ	Guitar	Harp	Recorder	Flute/Piccolo	Oboe	English Horn	Clarinet/Bass Clarinet	Bassoon/Contrabassoon	Saxophone	French Horn	Trumpet	Trombone	Bass Trombone	Tuba	Baritone	Percussion	Voice	Electronic Tape	Unusual Instruments	Publisher
SAUGUET, HENRI *(continued)*																															
Chants (3) de contemplation sur . . . Lao Tseu *Voices:* Contralto and bass														4														2			Leduc
Quatuor à cordes, 2e	1950	A		2	1	1																									Heuge
SAUTEREAU, C. (?–)																															
Quatuor				2	1	1																									Duran
SAXTON, ROBERT (1953–)																															
Cantata No. 2	1980		8						1							1												T			Chest
Canzona in memoriam Igor Stravinsky	1978		13	1	1	1							1		1	1		1			1										Chest
Choruses to Apollo *Unus Instr:* Celesta	1980		15						1				1														1			1	Chest
Circles of Light	1985		19	2	1	1	1		1						1	1		1	1		1	1	1				1				Chest
Echoes of the Glass Bead Game	1975		12												1	1		1	1		1										Chest
Eloge	1980		14	2	1	1		1							1	1		1			1										Chest
Piccola musica per Luigi Dallapiccola	1981		5		1	1			1						1	1															Chest
Processions and Dances	1981		12	1	1	1			1				1		1	1		1													Chest
The Sentinel of the Rainbow *Comment:* Piano doubles on celesta, oboe on English horn, clarinet on bass clarinet	1984			1		1			1						1	1	1	1									1			2	Chest
String Quartet	1979		13	2	1	1																									Chest
Traumstadt	1980		11	1	1	1	1		1																						Chest
What Does the Song Hope For?	1974		13	1	1	1			1						1	1		1											1		Chest
SAYGUN, AHMED A. (1907–)																															
String Quartet No. 1, Op 27	1947			2	1	1																									South
SCELSI, GIACINTO (1905–)																															
1er Quatuor	1944		28	2	1	1																									Salab
Anagamin, for 12 Strings	1965		6	7	7																										Salab
Anahit (for Violin)	1965		11	1	2	2	2								3		1	2		1	2	1	2								Salab
Khoom (for Soprano)	1962		20	2	1	1																					2	S			Salab
Kya (for Solo Clarinet)	1959		11		1	1											1	2			1	1	1								Salab
Pranam I (for Voice)	1972		8	2	1	1									1		1	1	1	1	1	1	1					1	1		Salab
Pranam II	1976		6	1	1	1	1				1				2			1			1										Salab
I presagi	1958		10																	1	2	2	2		2		1				Salab
Yamaon, for Bass Voice *Voice:* Bass. *Unus Instr:* Contrabassoon	1958		10				1												1	2							1	1		1	Salab
SCHACHT, THEODOR (1748–1823)																															
Fuga sopra'l do-re-mi-fa-sol-la				2	1	1																									Bosse
SCHAFER, R M. (1933–)																															
Arcana *Comment:* Flute doubles on piccolo, piano on electric organ	1972			1		1			1		1		1		1			1				1	1				1	1		2	Unive
Streichquartett	1970			2	1	1																									Unive
SCHEDL, GERHARD (?–)																															
Nachtstück															1	1		1	1		1										Dobli
Schall und Rauch (Drei Parodien), Op 13				1			1		1									1	1			1	1								Dobli
Songs over "Deh veni alla finestra", Op 4				1		1			1																						Dobli
Der Totentanz für Anno Neun, Op 14 *Unus Instr:* Bass clarinet				1		1	1								1	1		2												1	Dobli
SCHELB, JOSEF (1894–1977)																															
Musik zu "Der gestutzte Eros"									1			1						1									1				Bären
SCHELLE, MICHAEL (1950–)																															
Cry Wolf *Comment:* Conductor needed	1981		10			1			1																		5				AmCom

	Year Composed or Published	Key	Duration	Violin	Viola	Cello	Double Bass	Gamba	Piano	Harpsicord	Organ	Guitar	Harp	Recorder	Flute/Piccolo	Oboe	English Horn	Clarinet/Bass Clarinet	Bassoon/Contrabassoon	Saxophone	French Horn	Trumpet	Trombone	Bass Trombone	Tuba	Baritone	Percussion	Voice	Electronic Tape	Unusual Instruments	Publisher
SCHELLE, MICHAEL *(continued)*																															
Double Quartet *Unus Instr:* Bass clarinet	1980		16												1	1		3	1		2									1	AmCom
Music for the Kid from Alabama	1984		13	1	1	1			1						1	1		1	1								1				AmCom
Music for the Last Days of Strindberg	1979		17	1	1	1			1						1	1		1	1								1				AmCom
Songs Without Words	1977		9		1	1			1																						AmCom
SCHENKER, FRIEDRICH (1942–)																															
Epitaph für Neruda				10	4	3	1																								Peter
Frammenti di "Orfeo—dramma per musica" *Comment:* English horn may replace oboe	1978														1	1			1												DeutV
Solo-Duo-Trio *Comment:* Oboe may replace violin				1		1			1																						Bären
String Quartet				2	1	1																									Peter
Trioballade *Comment:* Cello may replace bassoon	1968								1							1			1												DeutV
SCHERCHEN, HERMANN (1891–1966)																															
Streichquartett 1, Op 1	1920			2	1	1																									Stein
SCHERCHEN-HSIAO, TONA (1938–)																															
Ziguidor *Unus Instr:* Tape recorder	1977		20												1	1		1	1		1									1	Boose
SCHIBLER, ARMIN (1920–)																															
Epitaph, Furioso, and Epilog				1	1	1									1																Kunze
Pieces (5) for Wind Quintet															1	1		1	1		1										Kunze
Quintet: Recitativi e danze				2	1	2																									Kunze
SCHICKELE, PETER (1935–)																															
7 Bagatelles	1959		6												1	1		1	1												Elkan
Aspendicitis *Unus Instr:* Drums	1961		3				2								3								2				1			1	AmCom
Commedia	1977		7													2			1												Elkan
Dances for Three	1980		14															2	1												Elkan
Diversions	1963		9													1		1	1												AmCom
Dream Dances	1988		12			1									1	1															Elkan
Fanfare for a Lost Cause	1960		2	1	1	1									1	1		1					1								AmCom
Little London Trio	1985		8	2	1																										Elkan
A Little Mosey Music (Brass Sextet)	1983		3																		2	2	1		1						Elkan
Mozart on Parade (Brass Quintet)	1983		4																		1	2	1		1						Elkan
Music for an Evening *Comment:* Piano 4 hands			15	2	1	1			1																						Elkan
Nellermojo	1984		5						1											3		1	1				1				Elkan
Part-Time Invention *Unus Instr:* Drums	1964		4				1			1					1												1			1	AmCom
Piano Concerto No. 2 (Ole!)	1978		8						1												1	2	1		1						Elkan
Polka from "Hornsmoke"	1976		2																		1	2	1		1						Elkan
Quartet	1982		20	1		1			1									1													Elkan
Scenes (3) for 5 Instruments	1965		15	1						1					1	1			1												AmCom
Serenade for 11 Instruments	1981		21	2	1	1	1		1						1	1		1	1		1										Elkan
String Quartet No. 1 ("American Dreams")	1983		28	2	1	1																									Elkan
String Quartet No. 2 ("In Memoriam")	1987		24	2	1	1																									Elkan
String Quartet No. 3 ("The Four Seasons")			16	2	1	1																									Elkan
String Sextet	1990		27	2	2	2																									Elkan
String Trio	1960		12	1	1	1																									AmCom

	Year Composed or Published	Key	Duration	Violin	Viola	Cello	Double Bass	Gamba	Piano	Harpsicord	Organ	Guitar	Harp	Recorder	Flute/Piccolo	Oboe	English Horn	Clarinet/Bass Clarinet	Bassoon/Contrabassoon	Saxophone	French Horn	Trumpet	Trombone	Bass Trombone	Tuba	Baritone	Percussion	Voice	Electronic Tape	Unusual Instruments	Publisher
SCHICKELE, PETER *(continued)*																															
Summer Trio	1966		16			1			1						1																Elkan
Trio Serenade	1979		13						1						2																Elkan
Variations on a Joke	1984		5																		1	2	1		1						Elkan
SCHIDLOWSKY, LEON (1931–)																															
11 Grabsteine (Eleven Tombstones)	1972																				1	2	1		1		1	1	1		IsrMI
SCHIEDERMAYER, JOHANN B. (1779–1840)																															
6 Intradas																						4					1				Harmo
SCHIFF, HELMUT (1893–)																															
Divertimento	1966															1		1	1												Dobli
SCHIFRIN, LALO (1932–)																															
Variants on a Madrigal by Gesualdo *Unus Instr:* Celesta	1969		18	2	1	1				1					1	1		1	1		1	1	1		1		1			1	AMP
SCHILLINGS, MAX (1868–1933)																															
Streichquartett, Op 1b	1906	e		2	1	1																									Simro
Streichquintett, Op 32	1917	E♭		2	2	1																									Unive
SCHISKE, KARL (1916–1969)																															
Bläserquintett, Op 24	1959														1	1		1	1		1										Dobli
Divertimento (Transformationen), Op 49	1963		15	2	1	1	1											1	1		1	1	1								Dobli
Sonatine (Piano Trio), Op 34				1		1			1																						Dobli
Streichquartett 1, Op 4	1937		16	2	1	1																									Dobli
Triosonata, Op 41				1	1	1																									Dobli
SCHLUMPF, MARTIN (1947–)																															
String Quartet	1975			2	1	1																									Hug
SCHMIDEK, KURT (1919–)																															
Sonatina für 5 Bläser, Op 31															1	1		1	1		1										Dobli
Streichtrio, Op 39				1	1	1																									Dobli
SCHMIDT, CHRISTFRIED (1932–)																															
Kammermusik 7 (Epitaph auf einen Bohemie)	1974								1						1	1		1	1		1										DeutV
Streichquartett 2	1970			2	1	1																									DeutV
SCHMIDT, FRANZ (1874–1939)																															
Klavierquintett	1954	G		2	1	1			1																						Weinb
Streichquartett 2	1927	G		2	1	1																									Dobli
Tullnerbacher Blasmusik *Voice:* Bass																2					3	2					1	1			Dobli
SCHMITT, FLORENT (1870–1958)																															
Andante et Scherzo, Op 35	1906			2	1	1							1																		Salab
Andante religioso, Op 109				2	1	1																									Duran
A tour d'anches, Op 97	1939								1							1		1	1												Duran
Chants alizés, Op 125	1939														1	1		1	1		1										Duran
Hasards, Op 96				1	1	1			1																						Duran
Lied et Scherzo (solo horn), Op 54	1910														2	2		2	2		2										Duran
Pour presque tous les temps, Op 134				1		1			1						1																Duran
Quatuor (brass)																							3	1							Billa
Quatuor (strings), Op 112	1948	g#		2	1	1																									Duran
Quintette, Op 51	1908		50	2	1	1			1																						Salab
Sonatine (piano trio), Op 85b				1		1			1																						Duran
Sonatine en trio, Op 85										1					1			1													Duran
Suite en rocaille, Op 84	1934			1	1	1							1		1																Duran
Trio, Op 105	1944			1	1	1																									Duran
SCHMITT, MEINRAD (1935–)																															
Fantasia piccola	1971			2	1	1																									Bosse

	Year Composed or Published	Key	Duration	Violin	Viola	Cello	Double Bass	Gamba	Piano	Harpsicord	Organ	Guitar	Harp	Recorder	Flute/Piccolo	Oboe	English Horn	Clarinet/Bass Clarinet	Bassoon/Contrabassoon	Saxophone	French Horn	Trumpet	Trombone	Bass Trombone	Tuba	Baritone	Percussion	Voice	Electronic Tape	Unusual Instruments	Publisher
SCHNABEL, ARTHUR (1882–1951)																															
Streichquartett 1	1927			2	1	1																									Unive
String Quartet No. 3	1924		40	2	1	1																									Boose
String Trio, Op 30	1925		18	1	1	1																									Boose
SCHNEIDER, GARU M. (1957–)																															
Timeless Footsteps *Unus Instr:* Windchimes	1980		9						1									1									1			1	AmCom
SCHNITTKE, ALFRED (1934–)																															
Concerto Grosso No. 3 *Unus Instr:* Celesta			17	10	3	2	1			1																	1			1	VarPb
Dialogue (for Violoncello and 7 Inst.) *Unus Instr:* Vibraphone, xylophone, marimba	1965		10			1			1						1	1		1			1	1					1			3	VarPb
Hymnus I *Unus Instr:* Timpani	1974		10			1							1														1			1	VAAP
Hymnus III *Unus Instr:* Timpani or bells	1975		4			1				1									1								1			1	VAAP
Konzert No. 3 für Violine *Unus Instr:* Piccolo. Harp ad libitum	1964		28	2	1	1	1						1		2	1	1	3	3		2	1	1							1	Unive
Labyrinth *Unus Instr:* Celesta, bells, 2 tom-toms, marimba, xylophone			35	6	3	3	1			1																	3			6	VAAP
Madrigals (3) *Unus Instr:* Vibraphone	1980		8	1	1		1			1																	1	S		1	VAAP
Piano Quartet (after Mahler)	1988		8	1	1	1			1																						VarPb
Piano Quintet	1976		29	2	1	1			1																						VarPb
Septet	1981			1	1	1				1					1			2													VarPb
Serenade	1968			1			1		1									1									1				Unive
Streichquartett 1	1966			2	1	1																									VarPb
Streichquartett 2	1981		22	2	1	1																									VarPb
Streichquartett 3	1983			2	1	1																									VarPb
Streichquartett 4				2	1	1																									VAAP
Streichtrio				1	1	1																									Unive
SCHOBER, BRIAN (1951–)																															
Antiphonal	1978		10						1						1	1		1	1		1	2	1				1				AmCom
Mosaic (solo cello) *Unus Instr:* Bells, crotales, celesta, vibraphone, marimba	1974		25			1			1							1											5			5	AmCom
SCHOECK, OTHMAR (1886–1957)																															
Gaseln (for Baritone Voice), Op 38	1923		16						1						1	1		1				1					1	B			Breit
Notturno (5 Sätze), Op 47	1933		45	2	1	1																						B			Unive
Serenade, Op 1	1907			2	1	1									1	1		1	1		1										Hug
Streichquartett, Op 23	1913	D		2	1	1																									Hug
Streichquartett Satz		B		2	1	1																									Amade
SCHOENBERG, ARNOLD (1874–1951)																															
Alle, welche Dich suchen *Unus Instr:* Contrabassoon			2			3	1						1		4		1	5	1											1	Unive
Die eiserne Brigade				2	1	1			1																						Unive
Funiculi, Funicula (Denza, arr. Schoenberg) *Unus Instr:* Mandolin				1	1	1						1						1												1	Unive
Herzgewächse, Op 20 *Unus Instr:* Celesta	1911										1		1															S		1	Unive
Kammersymphonie (arr. Webern), Op 9 *Comment:* Violin, viola, may replace flute, clarinet in A			22	1		1			1						1			1													Unive
Kammersymphonie, Op 9 *Unus Instr:* Clarinets in D, Eb; bass clarinet; contrabassoon	1906		22	2	1	1	1								1	1	1	3	2		2									4	Unive

	Year Composed or Published	Key	Duration	Violin	Viola	Cello	Double Bass	Gamba	Piano	Harpsicord	Organ	Guitar	Harp	Recorder	Flute/Piccolo	Oboe	English Horn	Clarinet/Bass Clarinet	Bassoon/Contrabassoon	Saxophone	French Horn	Trumpet	Trombone	Bass Trombone	Tuba	Baritone	Percussion	Voice	Electronic Tape	Unusual Instruments	Publisher
SCHOENBERG, ARNOLD *(continued)*																															
Lied der Waldtaube (from Gurre-Lieder) *Voice:* Medium. *Unus Instr:* Harmonium	1911		13	2	1	1	1		1						1	2		3	2		2							1		1	Unive
Nachtwandler *Unus Instr:* Piccolo, snare drum									1						1							1					1	1		2	Unive
Ode to Napoleon Buonaparte *Voice:* Reciter	1942		16	2	1	1			1																			1			Schir
Pieces for Orchestra (arr. Greissler)			20	1	1	1	1		1		1				1	1		1	1		1										Peter
Pierrot Lunaire, Op 21 *Unus Instr:* Bass clarinet	1912		40	1	1	1									1			2										1		1	Unive
Quintett, Op 26	1924														1	1		1	1		1										Unive
Scherzo für Streichquartett	1897	F		2	1	1																									Unive
Serenade, Op 24 *Unus Instr:* Mandolin	1924			1	1	1						1						2										1		1	Unive
Ständchen (Schubert, arr. Schoenberg) *Unus Instr:* Mandolin				1	1	1						1						1												1	Unive
Ein Stelldichein				1		1			1							1		1													Unive
Streichquartett	1897	D		2	1	1																									Faber
Streichquartett 1, Op 7	1905	d		2	1	1																									Unive
Streichquartett 2 (with voice), Op 10	1908	F♯		2	1	1																						1			Unive
Streichquartett 3, Op 30	1927			2	1	1																									Unive
String Quartet No. 4, Op 37	1936		33	2	1	1																									Schir
String Trio, Op 45	1946			1	1	1																									Bomar
Suite, Op 29 *Unus Instr:* Piccolo clarinet, bass clarinet	1926			1	1	1			1									3												2	Unive
Verklärte Nacht, Op 4	1899			2	2	2																									Unive
Weihnachtsmusik für Kammerensemble *Unus Instr:* Harmonium				2		1			1																					1	Unive
Weil i a alter Draher bin (Sioly, arr. Schoenberg) *Unus Instr:* Mandolin				1	1	1						1						1												1	Unive
SCHOLLUM, ROBERT (1913–)																															
Halbturner Abendmusik, Op 95				1		1			1																						Dobli
Mosaic, Op 75	1967								1							1											1				Dobli
Oktett in 8 Skizzen, Op 63	1960			1	1	1	1								1	1		1	1												Dobli
Streichquartett 1, Op 40	1949		17	2	1	1																									Dobli
Streichquartett 2, Op 72	1966		13	2	1	1																									Dobli
Stücke (5) für Bläserquintett															1	1		1	1		1										Dobli
Trio for Flute, Bassoon, and Piano, Op 45 *Comment:* Cello may replace bassoon									1						1				1												Dobli
Trio for Harp and Strings, Op 85				1	1								1																		Dobli
Trio for Oboe, Clarinet, and Piano, Op 71									1							1		1													Dobli
SCHÖNBACH, DIETER (1931–)																															
Lyric Songs No. 2									2																			1			Peter
SCHROEDER, HERMANN (1904–)																															
Chamber Music				2	1																										Peter
SCHRÖTER, HEINZ (1907–)																															
Klaviertrio, Op 2				1		1			1																						BoteB
SCHUBERT, FRANZ (1797–1828)																															
Adagio and Rondo Concertante, Op D487	1816	F		1	1	1			1																						VarPb

	Year Composed or Published	Key	Duration	Violin	Viola	Cello	Double Bass	Gamba	Piano	Harpsicord	Organ	Guitar	Harp	Recorder	Flute/Piccolo	Oboe	English Horn	Clarinet/Bass Clarinet	Bassoon/Contrabassoon	Saxophone	French Horn	Trumpet	Trombone	Bass Trombone	Tuba	Baritone	Percussion	Voice	Electronic Tape	Unusual Instruments	Publisher
SCHUBERT, FRANZ *(continued)*																															
Deutsche (5) mit Coda und 7 Trios, Op D90	1813			2	1	1																									VarPb
German Dances (4-part)				2	1	1																									VarPb
German Dances (5-part)				2	1	1	1																								Dobli
Menuette (6), Nos. 1-3 (arr. Weinmann), Op D2D	1811															2		2	2		2	1									Bären
Menuette (6), Nos. 4-6, Op D2D	1811														1	1		2	2		2										Bären
Menuette (5) und 6 Trios, Op D89	1813			2	1	1																									VarPb
Nocturne, Op D897	1828	E♭		1		1			1																						VarPb
Octet, Op D803	1824	F		2	1	1	1											1	1		1										VarPb
Quintet (Trout), Op 114	1819	A		1	1	1	1		1																						VarPb
Quintet, Op D956	1828	C		2	1	2																									VarPb
Shepherd Music (arr. Schoenbach)															1	1		1	1		1										Press
Sonata Movement, Op D28	1812	B♭		1		1			1																						VarPb
String Quartet No. 1, Op D18	1811			2	1	1																									Dobli
String Quartet No. 2, Op D32	1812	C		2	1	1																									VarPb
String Quartet No. 3, Op D36	1812	B♭		2	1	1																									VarPb
String Quartet No. 4, Op D46	1813	C		2	1	1																									VarPb
String Quartet No. 5, Op D68	1814	B♭		2	1	1																									VarPb
String Quartet No. 6	1813	D		2	1	1																									VarPb
String Quartet No. 7, Op D87 *Comment:* Opus 125 No. 1	1817	E♭		2	1	1																									VarPb
String Quartet No. 8, Op D94	1814	D		2	1	1																									VarPb
String Quartet No. 9, Op D112 *Comment:* Opus 168	1814	B♭		2	1	1																									VarPb
String Quartet No. 10, Op D173	1815	g		2	1	1																									VarPb
String Quartet No. 11, Op D353 *Comment:* Opus 125 No. 2	1817	E		2	1	1																									VarPb
String Quartet No. 12 (Quartettsatz), Op D703	1820	c		2	1	1																									VarPb
String Quartet No. 13, Op D804	1824	a		2	1	1																									VarPb
String Quartet No. 14, w. Variations, Op D810 *Comment:* "Death and the Maiden"	1826	d		2	1	1																									VarPb
String Quartet No. 15, Op D887 *Comment:* Opus 161	1826	G		2	1	1																									VarPb
Trio	1816	B♭		2	1																										Cefes
Trio, Op D898	1828	B♭		1		1			1																						VarPb
Trio, Op D929	1827	E♭		1		1			1																						VarPb
Trio No. 1	1817	B♭		1	1	1																									VarPb
Trio No. 2, Op D581	1817	B♭		1	1	1																									VarPb
Wind Octet, Op D72	1813	F														2		2	2		2										McGMa
SCHUBERT, MANFRED (1937–)																															
Capricciettì (3 Stücke)	1969			2	1	1																									DeutV
Moments musicaux	1967														1	1		1	1		1										DeutV
Musik für 7 Instrumente				1	1	1			1						1			1	1												IMBib
Streichquartett 1	1963			2	1	1																									NeueM
Streichquartett 2 (Laager Quartett)	1970			2	1	1																									DeutV
SCHUBROW, MANUEL (1954–)																															
Streichquartett 1	1975			2	1	1																									DeutV
SCHULLER, GUNTHER (1925–)																															
12 by 11 *Unus Instr:* Vibraphone and drums	1955		8				1						1		1			1	1	1	1		1				2			2	ModJQ
Abstraction	1959		5	2	1	1	2					1								1							1				ModJQ
Adagio for Flute and String Trio			5	1	1	1									1																AMP

	Year Composed or Published	Key	Duration	Violin	Viola	Cello	Double Bass	Gamba	Piano	Harpsicord	Organ	Guitar	Harp	Recorder	Flute/Piccolo	Oboe	English Horn	Clarinet/Bass Clarinet	Bassoon/Contrabassoon	Saxophone	French Horn	Trumpet	Trombone	Bass Trombone	Tuba	Baritone	Percussion	Voice	Electronic Tape	Unusual Instruments	Publisher
SCHULLER, GUNTHER *(continued)*																															
Aphorisms	1967		14	1	1	1									1																AMP
Atonal Jazz Study for Jazz Ensemble	1948						1		1						1			1		3	2	1	1		1		1				Manus
Automation, for a Real or Imaginary Film *Unus Instr:* Bass clarinet	1963		7	1			1		1				1		1			1	1		1						2			1	Margu
Blues	1945		4				1														2	1	2				1				Margu
Bouquet for Collage	1988		16	1		1			1						1			1									1				Margu
Chimeric Images *Unus Instr:* Celesta, doubled on piano	1988		15	1	1	1	1		1				1		1			1	1											1	Margu
Composition for Carillon *Unus Instr:* Glockenspiel, vibraphone, chimes	1962										1																3			3	Margu
Conversations *Unus Instr:* Vibraphone and drums	1959		12	2	1	1	1		1																		2			2	MJQ
Curtain Raiser	1960		2						1						1			1			1										Margu
Densities No. 1 *Unus Instr:* Vibraphone	1963		4				1					1						1									1			1	MJQ
Double Quintet	1961		12												1	1		1	1		2	2	1		1						AMP
Fanfare	1962		1																			4	4								Margu
Fanfare pour Wolf Trap *Unus Instr:* 2 Flügelhorns	1989		3																		4	4	4		2		3			2	Margu
Fantasia concertante No. 2	1947		15						1														3								Margu
Fantasia concertante No. 4	1946		11						1							3															Margu
Impromptus (5)	1989		12	2	1	1											1														AMP
Impromptus and Cadenzas *Comment:* Oboe doubles on English horn	1990		20	1		1										1	1	1	1		1										AMP
Jumpin' in the Future. Saxophones: Soprano, alto, tenor	1948		5				1		1						1	1				3	2	1	1		1						Margu
Eine kleine Posaunenmusik *Unus Instr:* Contrabass clarinet	1980		17				1						1		2	1	1	3	1		2	2	3		1		1			1	AMP
Eine kleine Posaunenmusik (alt. inst.) *Unus Instr:* Celesta	1980		17				1						1		2	1	1	3	1		2	2	3		1		1			1	AMP
Lifelines	1960		7									1			1												1				AMP
Little Music for 4 Brasses	1962		5																		1	1	1		1						Mento
Movements (2)	1952			1	1	1									1																Margu
Music for Brass Quintet	1961		12																		1	2	1		1						AMP
Music for Young People	1991		9	1		1			1						1																AMP
Music from "Yesterday in Fact" *Unus Instr:* Bass clarinet, drums	1963			1		1	1		1						1			1		1	1	1					1			2	Margu
Music-Symbiosis *Comment:* Dancer needed	1957		18	1					1																		1				AMP
Night Music	1962		4	1			1					1						1											1		ModJQ
Octet for Winds and Strings	1979		36	2	1	1	1											1	1		1										AMP
On Light Wings (for Piano Quartet)	1984		20	1	1	1			1																						AMP
Paradigm Exchanges	1991		20	1		1			1						1			1													AMP
Perpetuum mobile *Comment:* Tuba may replace bassoon. Horns are muted.	1948		4																1		4										Margu
Piano Trio	1984		20	1		1			1																						AMP
Renaissance Lyrics (6) *Voice:* Lyric tenor	1962		15	1	1	1	1		1						1	1												T			AMP
Romantic Sonata	1941		13						1									1			1										Margu
Sandpoint Rag	1986		4	2	1	1	1		1						1	1		1	1		1	1	1		1		1				Margu
Sandpoint Rag (Sextet)	1986		4																		2	2	1		1						Margu

	Year Composed or Published	Key	Duration	Violin	Viola	Cello	Double Bass	Gamba	Piano	Harpsicord	Organ	Guitar	Harp	Recorder	Flute/Piccolo	Oboe	English Horn	Clarinet/Bass Clarinet	Bassoon/Contrabassoon	Saxophone	French Horn	Trumpet	Trombone	Bass Trombone	Tuba	Baritone	Percussion	Voice	Electronic Tape	Unusual Instruments	Publisher
SCHULLER, GUNTHER *(continued)*																															
Sextet	1988		16	2	1	1			1										1												Margu
Sonata serenata	1978		16	1		1			1									1													AMP
String Quartet No. 1	1957		18	2	1	1																									Unive
String Quartet No. 2	1965		14	2	1	1																									AMP
String Quartet No. 3	1986		22	2	1	1																									Margu
Suite (Quintet)	1958														1	1		1	1		1										AMP
Symphonie für Blechbläser	1950		19																		4	6	3		1	2	3				Unive
Tear Drop *Comment:* Clarinet doubles on baritone sax	1967		12				1					1			1			3		1	1	1	1		1		1			1	Margu
Transformation *Unus Instr:* Tenor sax, vibraphone and drums	1956		61				1		1				1		1			1	1	1	1		1				2			3	Margu
The Trial *Comment:* Oboe doubles on English horn	1989		25	2	1	1	1		1				1		1	1	1	1				1	1				1				Margu
Trio	1948		11		1											1					1										AMP
Trio Setting	1990		16	1					1									1													AMP
Variants on a Theme of John Lewis *Unus Instr:* Vibraphone, timpani	1960			2	1	1	2					2			1					1							2			2	Malco
Variants on a Theme of Thelonius Monk *Unus Instr:* Vibraphone, drums	1960		15	2	1	1	2		1			1			1					2							2			2	Margu
SCHUMAN, WILLIAM (1910–1992)																															
Amaryllis Variations	1964			1	1	1																									Press
American Hymn	1980		9																		1	2	1	1							Merio
Cooperstown Fanfare	1987		1																			2	2								Merio
Dances (Divertimento)	1985		10												1	1		1	1		1										Merio
In Sweet Music *Unus Instr:* Piccolo and alto flute	1978		23		1								1		1													1		2	Merio
String Quartet No. 1	1936			2	1	1																									Withd
String Quartet No. 2	1937		16	2	1	1																									Hendo
String Quartet No. 3	1939			2	1	1																									Press
String Quartet No. 4	1950		28	2	1	1																									Schir
String Quartet No. 5	1937		30	2	1	1																									Merio
The Young Dead Soldiers *Unus Instr:* Bass clarinet	1976		15		4	4	1									2	1	3	2											1	Merio
SCHUMANN, CLARA (1819–1896)																															
Klaviertrio, Op 17				1		1			1																						Kunze
SCHUMANN, ROBERT (1810–1856)																															
Andante and Variations, Op 46		B♭				2			2												1										VarPb
Fantasiestücke, 3, Op 73	1849			1					1									1													VarPb
Fantasiestücke, 3, Op 73	1849					1			1									1													VarPb
Für die Jugend (arr. Henning), Op 68				2		1																									Bären
Märchenerzählungen (Fairy Tales), Op 132 *Comment:* Violin may replace clarinet	1854				1				1									1													VarPb
Phantasiestücke, 4, Op 88	1850			1		1			1																						VarPb
Piano Quartet, Op 47	1845	E♭		1	1	1			1																						VarPb
Piano Quintet, Op 44	1843	E♭		2	1	1			1																						VarPb
Piano Trio No. 1, Op 63	1848	d		1		1			1																						VarPb
Piano Trio No. 2, Op 80	1850	F		1		1			1																						VarPb
Piano Trio No. 3, Op 110	1852	g		1		1			1																						VarPb
String Quartet, Op 41 No. 1	1849	a		2	1	1																									VarPb
String Quartet, Op 41 No. 2	1849	F		2	1	1																									VarPb
String Quartet, Op 41 No. 3	1849	A		2	1	1																									Bären

	Year Composed or Published	Key	Duration	Violin	Viola	Cello	Double Bass	Gamba	Piano	Harpsicord	Organ	Guitar	Harp	Recorder	Flute/Piccolo	Oboe	English Horn	Clarinet/Bass Clarinet	Bassoon/Contrabassoon	Saxophone	French Horn	Trumpet	Trombone	Bass Trombone	Tuba	Baritone	Percussion	Voice	Electronic Tape	Unusual Instruments	Publisher
SCHWAEN, KURT (1909–)																															
Concertino Apollineo *Unus Instr:* Bass clarinet									1						1	1	1	1	1		1	1								1	Peter
Octet				2	1	1	1											1	1		1										Peter
SCHWANTNER, JOSEPH (1943–)																															
Canticle of the Evening Bells			20	1	1	1	1		1						1		1	1	1		1	1	1				1				Peter
Consortium I			9	1	1	1									1			1													Peter
Diaphonia intervallum			12	2	1	2	1		1						1					1											Peter
Elixir (Consortium VIII)			15	1	1	1			1						1			1													Peter
Wild Angels of the Open Hills *Comment:* Soprano, doubling on chimes, tambourine, etc.			28										1		1												1	S		5	Peter
SCHWARTZ, ELLIOTT S. (1936–)																															
Eclipse I (Enigma Variations)	1971		13	1		1			1									2	2			1	1				1				AmCom
Jet Piece *** *Comment:* For piano and any 3 melody instruments	1980		12						1																						AmCom
Octet	1971		13	1		1			2						1	1		1									1				AmCom
Spirals *Unus Instr:* Electric piano	1985		15	2	1	1	1		1						1			1												1	AmCom
SCHWARZ-SCHILLING, REINHARD (1904–1985)																															
Streichquartett	1932	f		2	1	1																									Bären
SCHWEINITZ, WOLFGANG VON (1953–)																															
Adagio, Op 22 *Unus Instr:* Basset horn	1983																1		1		1									1	Boose
Englische Serenade, Op 24	1984																	2	2		2										Boose
SCHWEIZER, KLAUS (1939–)																															
Kammermusik	1971			1		1				1					1		1														Bären
SCHWEIZER, ROLF (1936–)																															
Bläsermusik *Comment:* For 4 to 6 trumpets and trombones		d																													Bären
SCHWERTBERGER, G. (?–)																															
Mississippi Suite														3																	Dobli
SCHWERTSIK, KURT (1935–)																															
Austrian Quodlibet, Op 14	1967		15	1			1				1	1	1		1				1			1			1		1				Boose
Bagatellen für Klaviertrio, Op 36	1979		11	1		1			1																						Boose
Blechpartie im neuesten Geschmack, Op 43	1986		11																		1	2	1		1						Boose
Iba di gaunz oaman Fraun (8 Songs), Op 49	1983		16				1		1																		1	S			Boose
Ich sein Blumenbein (11 Songs), Op 38 *Comment:* Composer specifies "keyboards"	1980		16						1			1																1			Boose
Kleine Blasmusik, Op 32	1977		6																			2	2								Boose
Macbeth (Dance-Theatre)	1988		90						2																		1				Boose
Musik vom Mutterland MU	1974			1	1	1	1								1	1		2	1		1										Dobli
Neues von Eu-Sirius, Op 55	1988		15	2	1																										Boose
Proviant for Wind Sextet	1965														1	1		1	1		1	1									Dobli
Querschnitt durch eine Operette	1969		10												1	1		1	1		1										Dobli
Skizzen und Entwürfe, Op 25	1974		18	2	1	1																									Boose
Sotto voce (Gedämpfte Unterhaltung), Op 39	1980		12	1		1						1			1																Boose
Streichquartett, Op 4	1961			2	1	1																									EdMod
Stückwerk, Op 12 *Unus Instr:* Contrabassoon	1966		12				1		1								1	1	1				1					S		1	Boose
Twilight Music (A Celtic Serenade), Op 30	1976		14	2	1	1	1											1	1		1										Boose

	Year Composed or Published	Key	Duration	Violin	Viola	Cello	Double Bass	Gamba	Piano	Harpsicord	Organ	Guitar	Harp	Recorder	Flute/Piccolo	Oboe	English Horn	Clarinet/Bass Clarinet	Bassoon/Contrabassoon	Saxophone	French Horn	Trumpet	Trombone	Bass Trombone	Tuba	Baritone	Percussion	Voice	Electronic Tape	Unusual Instruments	Publisher
SCIARRINO, SALVATORE (1947–)																															
Quintettino No. 1				2	1	1												1													Ricor
Quintettino No. 2															1	1		1	1		1										Ricor
Trio				1		1			1																						Ricor
SCIORTINO, PATRICE (1922–)																															
Toca Senh																					1	2	2		1						Billa
SCOTT, CYRIL (1879–1970)																															
Piano Quartet, Op 16	1900	e		1	1	1			1																						Boose
SCRIABIN, ALEXANDER (1872–1915) and others																															
Variations on a Russian Folk Song				2	1	1																									Inter
SCULTHORPE, PETER (1929–)																															
Chorales (from Rites of Passage)	1973		43			3	2																		2		3				Faber
Music for String Quartet				2	1	1																									Faber
Song of Tailitnama	1974		10			6																					2	H			Faber
String Quartet No. 6				2	1	1																									Faber
String Quartet No. 8	1969			2	1	1																									Faber
String Quartet No. 9	1975			2	1	1																									Faber
Tabuh Tabuhan	1968		24												1	1		1	1		1						2				Faber
SEARCH, FREDERICK P. (1899–)																															
Sextet	1934	f		2	2	2																									SPAM
SEARLE, HUMPHREY (1915–1982)																															
The Owl and the Pussy Cat *Voice:* Speaker						1						1			1													1			Oxfor
Sinfonietta, Op 49	1969		18	1		1	1								1	1		1	1		1										Faber
Songs (3) of Jocelyn Brooke, Op 25b	1954		18	2	1	1	1		1				1		2	1		2	1		1	1						H			Faber
SECHTER, SIMON (1788–1867)																															
Streichquartett		G		2	1	1																									Dobli
SEGERSTAM, LEIF (1944–)																															
Another of Many Nnnnooooowwwws	1973														1	1		1	1		1										Schir
SEIBER, MATYAS (1905–1960)																															
4 Medieval French Songs *** *Comment:* For 3 instruments																												1			Suvin
Fantasia				2	1	1									1						1										Suvin
Quartetto I				2	1	1																									Suvin
Quartetto II				2	1	1																									Suvin
SEMEGEN, DARIA (1946–)																															
Jeux des quatres	1970		12			1			1									1					1								AmCom
SEMMLER-COLLERY, ARMAND (?–)																															
Offrande (quartet)																						2	2								Billa
Offrande (quintet)																					1	2	1		1						Billa
SEREBRIER, JOSÉ (1938–)																															
Fantasia (String Quartet No. 4)				2	1	1																									Peer
SESSIONS, ROGER (1896–1985)																															
String Quartet No. 1	1936			2	1	1																									EBMar
String Quartet No. 2	1954			2	1	1																									EBMar
String Quintet	1958			2	2	1																									Boose
SETER, MORDECAI (1916–)																															
Elegy	1954			2	1	1												1													IsrMI
SEYFRIT, MICHAEL E. (1947–)																															
Continuum, Vacuum, Residuum *Unus Instr:* Prepared piano, 6-hands	1971		15						1								1	1					1							1	AmCom

	Year Composed or Published	Key	Duration	Violin	Viola	Cello	Double Bass	Gamba	Piano	Harpsicord	Organ	Guitar	Harp	Recorder	Flute/Piccolo	Oboe	English Horn	Clarinet/Bass Clarinet	Bassoon/Contrabassoon	Saxophone	French Horn	Trumpet	Trombone	Bass Trombone	Tuba	Baritone	Percussion	Voice	Electronic Tape	Unusual Instruments	Publisher
SEYFRIT, MICHAEL E. *(continued)*																															
Dusk to Dusk *Comment:* Percussion: 12	1976		17			1											1	1			1										AmCom
In Search of . . . *Unus Instr:* Marimba	1975		19				1											1									1			1	AmCom
Latent Images *Unus Instr:* Marimba	1973		20	1		1			1									1	1								1			1	AmCom
Refuge *** *Comment:* Ensemble includes 3 additional unspecified instruments	1974					1	1		1								1	1		1			1								AmCom
SHATIN, JUDITH (1949–)																															
Legends	1972		18			1									1	1											1				AmCom
Soundspecs *** *Comment:* For any group of strings	1981																														AmCom
Werther	1983		9	1		1			1						1			1													AmCom
SHCHEDRIN, RODION (1922–)																															
The Frescoes of Dionysius *Unus Instr:* Celesta	1981		13		1	1									1		1	1	1		1						1			1	VarPb
A Musical Offering for Organ, 9 Winds			120								1				3				3		3										VarPb
SHEINKMAN, MORDECHAI (1926–)																															
Divertimento	1957												1					1				1	1								Peter
SHEPHERD, ARTHUR (1880–1958)																															
Quartet		e		2	1	1																									Press
Quartet for Strings	1935	e		2	1	1																									SPAM
Triptych	1926			2	1	1																						H			Press
SHERIFF, NOAM (1935–)																															
Musik für Holzbläser	1961						1		1														1								IsrMI
SHIFRIN, SEYMOUR (1926–1979)																															
In Eius memoriam	1968		6	1		1			1						1			1													Peter
Satires of Circumstance	1964		17	1		1	1		1						1			1										S			Peter
Serenade	1954		20		1				1							1		1			1										Peter
String Quartet No. 1	1949			2	1	1																									BoteB
String Quartet No. 2	1962		18	2	1	1																									Peter
String Quartet No. 3	1966		13	2	1	1																									Peter
String Quartet No. 4	1967		18	2	1	1																									Peter
String Quartet No. 5	1972		17	2	1	1																									Peter
SHIMAZU, TAKEHITO (1949–)																															
Chromosom	1978			2	1	1																									DeutV
Moire	1980								1						2																DeutV
Neoplasma	1979														1	1		1	1		2										DeutV
SHIPLEY, EDWARD (?–)																															
Rite of Lucifrage																					1	2	1		1						Oxfor
SHORT, DAVID (?–)																															
Brass Quintet																					1	2	1		1						Billa
SHOSTAKOVICH, DMITRI (1906–1975)																															
Adagio and Allegretto				2	1	1																									VAAP
Piano Quintet, Op 57	1940	g		2	1	1			1																						VarPb
Pieces (2) for String Octet, Op 11	1925		11	4	2	2																									VarPb
Songs (7)	1967			1		1			1																			S			VAAP
String Quartet No. 1, Op 49	1938	C	15	2	1	1																									VarPb
String Quartet No. 2, Op 68	1944	A	32	2	1	1																									VarPb
String Quartet No. 3, Op 73	1946			2	1	1																									VarPb
String Quartet No. 4, Op 83	1949	D	22	2	1	1																									VarPb

	Year Composed or Published	Key	Duration	Violin	Viola	Cello	Double Bass	Gamba	Piano	Harpsicord	Organ	Guitar	Harp	Recorder	Flute/Piccolo	Oboe	English Horn	Clarinet/Bass Clarinet	Bassoon/Contrabassoon	Saxophone	French Horn	Trumpet	Trombone	Bass Trombone	Tuba	Baritone	Percussion	Voice	Electronic Tape	Unusual Instruments	Publisher
SHOSTAKOVICH, DMITRI *(continued)*																															
String Quartet No. 5, Op 92	1952	B♭	30	2	1	1																									VarPb
String Quartet No. 6, Op 101	1956	G	25	2	1	1																									VarPb
String Quartet No. 7, Op 108	1960	f♯	12	2	1	1																									VarPb
String Quartet No. 8, Op 110	1960			2	1	1																									VarPb
String Quartet No. 9, Op 117	1964			2	1	1																									Sikor
String Quartet No. 10, Op 118	1964	A♭	22	2	1	1																									VarPb
String Quartet No. 11, Op 122	1966			2	1	1																									VarPb
String Quartet No. 12, Op 133	1968			2	1	1																									VarPb
String Quartet No. 13, Op 138	1970			2	1	1																									VAAP
String Quartet No. 14, Op 142	1973			2	1	1																									VarPb
String Quartet No. 15, Op 144	1974			2	1	1																									VarPb
Trio No. 1, Op 8	1923			1		1			1																						VarPb
Trio No. 2, Op 67	1944	e	24	1		1			1																						VarPb
Violin Duets with Piano Accompaniment				2					1																						Peter
SHUT, VLADISLAV (1941–)																															
Romantic Messages			15	8	2	2	1		1						1				1												VAAP
Sinfonia da camera No. 3 *Unus* *Instr:* Vibraphone, marimba			18	6	2	2	2								1	1											3			2	VAAP
SIBELIUS, JEAN (1865–1957)																															
Suite mignonne, Op 98A	1921	g		2	1	1	1								2																Chapp
Voces Intimae (String Quartet), Op 56	1909	d		2	1	1																									VarPb
SIEGL, OTTO (1896–1978)																															
Bläserquintett	1972														1	1		1	1		1										Dobli
Burlesque (Streichquartett 1 movement), Op 29	1924			2	1	1																									Dobli
Divertimento, Op 44	1926			1	1	1																									Dobli
Klaviertrio, Op 37				1	1				1																						Dobli
Klaviertrio, Op 94				1	1				1																						Dobli
Kleine Kammersuite				2		1																									Dobli
Quintett Serenade	1961			1	1	1												1	1												Dobli
Streichquartett, Op 77				2	1	1																									Dobli
Streichquintett	1958	G		2	2	1																									Dobli
Streichsextett (1 movement), Op 28				2	2	2																									Dobli
Streichtrio, Op 130	1944	B♭		1	1	1																									Dobli
Streichtrio 1, Op 134a	1944	a		2	1																										Dobli
SIERRA, ROBERTO (1953–)																															
Concierto nocturnal	1985		14	1		1				1					1	1		1													Salab
SIGURBJORNSSON, THORKELL (1938–)																															
For Renée	1973		11	1					1						1												1				Boose
SILSBEE, ANN L. (1930–)																															
And Who So Witnessed	1984		14	1	1	1			1						1			1									1				AmCom
Pharos II	1979		10			1			1																		1				AmCom
Quartet	1980		115	1		1			1									1													AmCom
Trialogue	1976		9	1					1									1													AmCom
SILVESTROV, VALENTIN (1937–)																															
Drama	1971		40	1		1			1																						VAAP
Ode to the Nightingale (Cantata)				2	1	1	1						1		1	1		1			1	1	1		1		1	S			VAAP
Piano Quintet	1961		20	2	1	1			1																						VAAP
Postludium D-S-C-H	1981			1		1			1																			S			VAAP
Serenade for 2 Solo Violins and Strings			15	10	4	3	2																								VAAP

	Year Composed or Published	Key	Duration	Violin	Viola	Cello	Double Bass	Gamba	Piano	Harpsicord	Organ	Guitar	Harp	Recorder	Flute/Piccolo	Oboe	English Horn	Clarinet/Bass Clarinet	Bassoon/Contrabassoon	Saxophone	French Horn	Trumpet	Trombone	Bass Trombone	Tuba	Baritone	Percussion	Voice	Electronic Tape	Unusual Instruments	Publisher
SILVESTROV, VALENTIN *(continued)*																															
String Quartet	1974		18	2	1	1																									VAAP
Symphony No. 2	1965		24	8	3	2	1		1						1												2				VAAP
SIMONS, NETTY (1913–)																															
Facets 4				2	1	1																									Press
SIMPSON, ROBERT (1921–)																															
String Quartet No. 8	1979			2	1	1																									Faber
SIMS, EZRA (1928–)																															
II (Variations)	1973		5	1	1	1										1															AmCom
Flourish	1975		2	1	1	1										1															AmCom
From an Oboe Quartet	1971		7	1	1	1										1															AmCom
Longfellow Sparrow	1976		30												5			5				3	5								AmCom
Night Piece (In girum imus nocte . . .) *Comment:* Needed: Computer-generated sound	1989		116		1	1									1			1												1	AmCom
Phenomena	1981		18	1	1	1									1			1													AmCom
Quartet	1982		13	1	1	1									1																AmCom
Sextet (for Clarinets and String Trio)	1983		20	1	1	1												3													AmCom
Sextet (for Winds and String Trio)	1981		20	1	1	1												1		1	1										AmCom
String Quartet (sic) No. 2	1974		30	1	1	1									1			1													AmCom
Yr Obdt Servt II *Unus Instr:* 2 Marimbas	1977		10	2	1	1	1					1						4			1		1				2			2	AmCom
SINDING, CHRISTIAN (1856–1941)																															
Quintett, Op 5	1884	e		2	1	1			1																						Hanse
Streichquartett, Op 70	1904	a		2	1	1																									Peter
Trio, Op 64	1902	a		1		1			1																						Peter
SITSKY, LARRY (1934–)																															
Woodwind Quartet	1963														1	1		1	1												Boose
SKOLNIK, WALTER (1934–)																															
Pastorale															1	1		1	1		1										Press
SKORZENY, FRITZ (1900–1965)																															
Klaviertrio		A		1		1			1																						Dobli
Eine Nachtmusik für 5 Bläser	1963														1	1		1	1		1										Dobli
Pro Juventute	1969			2	1																										Dobli
Streichtrio	1963			1	1	1																									Dobli
Suite 1	1957			1	1		1																								Dobli
Suite 2	1958			1	1		1																								Dobli
Trio					1							1			1																Dobli
SLAVENSKI, JOSIP S. (1896–1955)																															
Quartett, Op 3	1923			2	1	1																									BScho
SLAVICKY, KLEMENT (1910–)																															
Trialog	1966			1					1									1													Artia
SLONIMSKY, SERGEI (1932–)																															
Antiphons (String Quartet No. 1)			12	2	1	1																									VAAP
Dialogues (Inventions)	1964		20												1	1		1	1		1										VAAP
Exotic Suite *Unus Instr:* Electric guitar	1976		33	2								2								1							1			1	VAAP
SMALLEY, ROGER (1943–)																															
Melody Study I *** *Comment:* For 4 melody instruments	1970		12																												Faber
Melody Study II *** *Comment:* For 4-12 melody instruments	1970		15																												Faber
Missa parodia II	1967		16	1	1				1						1	1		1			1	1	1								Faber

	Year Composed or Published	Key	Duration	Violin	Viola	Cello	Double Bass	Gamba	Piano	Harpsicord	Organ	Guitar	Harp	Recorder	Flute/Piccolo	Oboe	English Horn	Clarinet/Bass Clarinet	Bassoon/Contrabassoon	Saxophone	French Horn	Trumpet	Trombone	Bass Trombone	Tuba	Baritone	Percussion	Voice	Electronic Tape	Unusual Instruments	Publisher
SMALLEY, ROGER *(continued)*																															
Strata	1971		30	10	2	2	1																								Faber
String Sextet	1965		11	2	2	2																									Faber
SMETANA, BEDRICH (1824–1884)																															
Piano Trio, Op 15	1880	g		1		1			1																						VarPb
Quartet No. 1 (Aus meinem Leben), Op 116	1881	e	26	2	1	1																									VarPb
Quartet No. 2	1889	d		2	1	1																									VarPb
SMIRNOV, DMITRI (1948–)																															
The Moonlight Story *Unus Instr:* Bass clarinet					1	1	1								1			1												1	VarPb
Piano Trio, Op 23	1977			1		1			1																						VAAP
The Seasons, Op 28	1979		22		1								1		1													1			Schir
The Sorrow of Past Days (Vocal Cycle)	1975			1		1									1												1	1			VAAP
String Quartet No. 1, Op 11	1973			2	1	1																									VAAP
String Quartet No. 2	1985			2	1	1																									VAAP
SMITH, DAVID S. (1877–1949)																															
Quartet No. 6				2	1	1																									Press
Quintet				2	1	1			1																						Oxfor
SMITH, HALE (1925–)																															
2 Love Songs of John Donne	1958		8	2	1	1									1	1		1	1		1							S			HalsC
Dialogues and Commentaries *Unus Instr:* Bass clarinet	1991		18	1	1	1			1						1			1									1			1	Manus
Introductions, Cadenzas, Interludes	1974		13	1	1	1			1				1		1	1		1													Press
Solemn Music	1979		9								1										4	4	3								Peter
Variations for Six Players	1975		10						1						1	1		1	1		1										Press
SMITH, JOHN S. (1750–1836)																															
The Star Spangled Banner				2	1	1																									Press
SMITH, JULIA (1911–)																															
Quartet for Strings	1964			2	1	1																									Press
Trio (Cornwall)	1955			1		1			1																						Press
SMITH, LELAND (1925–)																															
Arabesque (solo tenor sax and bassoon) *Unus Instr:* Vibraphone	1969		9	2	1	1									2			1	1	1	1	1	1				1			1	AmCom
Introduction and Divertimento	1949		8	1	1	1												1				1									AmCom
Quartet	1961		20	1		1			1												1										AmCom
Suite for Trio	1947		10	1														1				1									AmCom
Trio	1947		13			1			1						1																AmCom
Trio (alt. inst.)	1947		13	1		1			1																						AmCom
SMITH, LEO (1941–)																															
The Burning of Stones	1978		10										3									1									AmCom
Mutumishi *** *Comment:* For any instruments, at the performers' discretion	1970		12																												AmCom
Peldimxy No. 1	1972		12				1		1											2		1					1				AmCom
Song of the Universe is the Signature . . . *Unus Instr:* Vibraphone	1980		24				1								1							1					1			1	AmCom
We Are for Freedom—Now	1980		20	1		1	1		1						1			2				1	1		1						AmCom
SMITH BRINDLE, REGINALD (1917–)																															
Death of Antigone *Voices:* Mezzo-soprano, bass, 1 or 2 speakers			27	1					1						1												1	3			Peter
Genesis Dream			14						1						1			2				1					3	F			Peter
SMYTH, ETHEL (1858–1944)																															
String Quartet	1914	e		2	1	1																									Unive

	Year Composed or Published	Key	Duration	Violin	Viola	Cello	Double Bass	Gamba	Piano	Harpsicord	Organ	Guitar	Harp	Recorder	Flute/Piccolo	Oboe	English Horn	Clarinet/Bass Clarinet	Bassoon/Contrabassoon	Saxophone	French Horn	Trumpet	Trombone	Bass Trombone	Tuba	Baritone	Percussion	Voice	Electronic Tape	Unusual Instruments	Publisher
SOLLBERGER, HARVEY (1938–)																															
Chamber Variations *Comment:* Conductor needed	1964		17	1	1	1	1		1						2	1		1	1								2				AmCom
Divertimento	1970		13			1			1						1																AmCom
Original Substance/Manifests/Traces	1987		15						1			1	1		1												1				AmCom
Riding the Wind (solo flute, clarinet) *Comment:* Amplification needed	1974		17	1		1			1						1			1													AmCom
The Two and the One	1972		12			1																					2				AmCom
SOMMER, VLADIMIR (1921–)																															
Streichquartett		d		2	1	1																									Artia
SONZOGNO, GIULIO C. (1906–1976)																															
Pastorale, Allegro e Aria				2	1	1			1																						Suvin
SOPRONI, JOSZEF (1930–)																															
Musica da camera no. 2	1976		11	1		1			1									1													EMBud
String Quartet No. 4	1971		17	2	1	1																									EMBud
SORENSEN, BENT (1958–)																															
Adieu (String Quartet No. 2)	1986		9	2	1	1																									Hanse
Alman (String Quartet No. 1)	1984		14	2	1	1																									Hanse
Angel's Music (String Quartet No. 3)	1988		16	2	1	1																									Hanse
Clairobscur	1987		10	2	1	1	1								1	1	1	1	1		1										Hanse
Cyprianius	1982		15															2									2	F			Hanse
Donne	1983		9	1								1																1			Hanse
Garnet to Garnet	1985		9									1															1	1			Hanse
Madelein	1985		11												1	1		1	1		1										Hanse
Trotto	1983		9	1		1										1			1		1										Hanse
Les tuchins *Unus Instr:* 2 Electric guitars	1986		9			2						2											1							2	Hanse
SORESINA, ALBERTO (1911–)																															
Ciaccona e variazione	1947			1	1	1			1																						Ricor
SOURIS, ANDRÉ (1899–1970)																															
Choral, marche et galop	1956																					2	2								Maure
Comptines pour enfants sinistres *** *Voices:* Soprano, mezzo-soprano	1948			1					1									1										2			Suvin
Rengaine	1937														1	1		1	1		1										Leduc
SOUSA, JOHN P. (1854–1932)																															
Stars and Stripes Forever (arr. Zinn)				2	1	1																									Press
The Thunderer March (arr. Zinn)				2	1	1																									Press
Washington Post March (arr. Zinn)				2	1	1																									Press
SOWERBY, LEO (1895–1968)																															
Serenade	1916	G	8	2	1	1																									SPAM
SPELMAN, TIMOTHY M. (1891–1970)																															
Quartet		d		2	1	1																									Suvin
SPEZZAFERRI, GIOVANNI (1888–1963)																															
Preludio e fuga																						2	1								Suvin
SPIES, CLAUDIO (1925–)																															
Sonata No. 2	1963														1	1		1	1		1										IMBib
SPINNER, LEOPOLD (1906–1980)																															
Quintet	1963		8				1					1						1	1		1										Boose
Sonatina, Op 23	1971		11													1		1	1		1										Boose
String Quartet No. 1	1930			2	1	1																									Boose
String Quartet No. 2, Op 2	1941			2	1	1																									Boose

	Year Composed or Published	Key	Duration	Violin	Viola	Cello	Double Bass	Gamba	Piano	Harpsicord	Organ	Guitar	Harp	Recorder	Flute/Piccolo	Oboe	English Horn	Clarinet/Bass Clarinet	Bassoon/Contrabassoon	Saxophone	French Horn	Trumpet	Trombone	Bass Trombone	Tuba	Baritone	Percussion	Voice	Electronic Tape	Unusual Instruments	Publisher
SPINNER, LEOPOLD *(continued)*																															
String Quartet No. 3, Op 7	1952		12	2	1	1																									Boose
Trio				1		1			1																						Press
Trio	1935					1			1									1													Boose
Trio	1940				1	1												1													Boose
SPOHR, LOUIS (1784–1859)																															
Deutsche Lieder, 6, Op 103									1									1										H			Bären
Doppel-Quartett 1, Op 65	1890	d		4	2	2																									VarPb
Fantasie and Var. on a Theme by Danzi, Op 81				2	1	1												1													MusRa
Grand Nonetto, Op 31	1876			1	1	1	1								1	1		1	1		1										Litol
Klaviertrio, Op 133	1848	B♭		1		1			1																						Bären
Oktett, Op 32	1890	E		1	2	1	1											1			2										VarPb
Quartett (solo violin & trio), Op 61	1890	b		2	1	1																									Kunze
Quintet, Op 52		c							1						1			1	1		1										VarPb
Septet, Op 147	1855	A		1		1			1						1			1	1		1										VarPb
Streichquartett, Op 15 No. 1		E♭		2	1	1																									VarPb
Streichquartett, Op 15 No. 2		D		2	1	1																									VarPb
Streichquartett, Op 29 No. 1		E♭		2	1	1																									Bären
Trio, WoO28		f		1		1							1																		Merse
SPRONGL, NORBERT (1892–)																															
Bläserquintett, Op 90	1965														1	1		1	1		1										Dobli
SROM, KAREL (1904–)																															
Streichquartett 3	1966			2	1	1																									Artia
STADLMAIR, HANS (1929–)																															
Octet																2		2	2		2										Peter
STAEPS, HANS U. (1909–)																															
Arcadian Scenes														5																	Dobli
Ariettas, 4									1					5																	Dobli
Aubade und Tanz									1			1		6																	Dobli
Auf unserm Hof daheim														3																	Dobli
Des Einhorns Anmut (Unicornis gratia)														4																	Dobli
Frau Nachtigall, mach dich bereit														4																	Dobli
Lieder der Liebenden									1					1														1			Dobli
Das Lied tont fort														3														1			Dobli
Das Lied tont fort (strings)				2	1																							1			Dobli
Partita (Dort nied'n in jenem Holze)														4																	Dobli
Tänze, 7														4																	Dobli
Triludi														3																	Dobli
Trio														3																	Dobli
STALLAERT, ALPHONSE (1920–)																															
Quintet for saxophone and strings				2	1	1														1											Billa
STALLCOP, GLENN (1950–)																															
Calypso Round *Unus Instr:* Marimba	1981		12				1						1		1						1						1			1	AmCom
Fanfare	1981		7				1														1						1				AmCom
Lullaby	1980		12										1		1						1										AmCom
Midsummer Night *Unus Instr:* Marimba	1982		23	1					1																					1	AmCom
Trio	1983		26		1				1						1																AmCom
STALVEY, DORRANCE (1930–)																															
Points, Lines, Circles							1					1	1					1									3				Salab
STANKOVICH, YEVHEN (1942–)																															
Chamber Symphony No. 1 *Unus Instr:* Timpani				1					1				1		1			1					1				3			1	VAAP

	Year Composed or Published	Key	Duration	Violin	Viola	Cello	Double Bass	Gamba	Piano	Harpsicord	Organ	Guitar	Harp	Recorder	Flute/Piccolo	Oboe	English Horn	Clarinet/Bass Clarinet	Bassoon/Contrabassoon	Saxophone	French Horn	Trumpet	Trombone	Bass Trombone	Tuba	Baritone	Percussion	Voice	Electronic Tape	Unusual Instruments	Publisher
STANKOVICH, YEVHEN *(continued)*																															
Chamber Symphony No. 3				7	2	2	1								1																VAAP
STARER, ROBERT (1924–)																															
Annapolis Suite	1985												1								1	2	2								RKing
Concertino *Voices:* Soprano, baritone	1953			1					1																			2			IsrMP
Dirge																					1	2	1								Press
Fanfare in Five	1985																					3	3								RKing
String Quartet	1947			2	1	1																									Press
STAUB, VOLKER (?–)																															
Number 8	1986																						2				1				Feedb
STEARNS, PETER P. (1931–)																															
Chamber Set II	1959		9	1			1													1		1									AmCom
Concertino da camera (solo guitar)	1983		18			1	1					1						1			1										AmCom
Quartet for the Annunciation	1982		18	1		1			1									1													AmCom
Septet	1959		10	1	1	1	1											1		1	1										AmCom
Serenade for 15 Winds	1956		15												3	3		3	2		3				1						AmCom
Sextet	1962		20	1	1	1									1			1			1										AmCom
Sounding Solitude (A Tone Poem) *Unus Instr:* Bells	1984		9									1						1									1			1	AmCom
There Is a River Whose Streams	1982		10		1							1			1																AmCom
Trio *Unus Instr:* Bass clarinet	1964		10				1								1			1												1	AmCom
Trio Variations *Unus Instr:* Bass clarinet	1965		6	1														1				1								1	AmCom
STEFFEN, WOLFGANG (1923–)																															
Gertrud-Kolmar Trilogy, Op 35									1						1			1									1	S			BoteB
Music for Piano, Op 44	1975		11	1	1	1	1		1						1			1									1				BoteB
Polychromie (for Piano), Op 38	1970		11	2	1	1			1						1	1		1	1		1						1				BoteB
Trio, Op 37						1			1						1																BoteB
Triplum 72, Op 39									1						1												1				BoteB
STEIN, LEON (1910–)																															
Song and Dance	1981		14		1	1			1																						AmCom
Three for Nine	1982		16	1	1	1	1								1	1		1	1		1										AmCom
STETKA, FRANZ (?–)																															
Kleine Suite		a										1		2																	Dobli
Suite				1										3																	Dobli
Thema mit Variationen *Comment:* Piano may replace guitar		C										1		2																	Dobli
STEVENS, HALSEY (1908–1989)																															
Septet	1957		19		2	2												1	1		1										AmCom
STEWART, ROBERT (1918–)																															
Heart Attack	1973		9																						1		2				AmCom
Hydra	1963		10	1		1			1						1	1			1												AmCom
Movements (5) for Bassoon & 5 Inst. *Unus Instr:* Flügelhorn	1963		10				1		1						1				1											1	AmCom
Nonet	1964		12	1	1	1			1						1			1	1		1	1									AmCom
Trio No. 4	1962		9	1		1									1																AmCom
Trio No. 5	1963		10		1													1					1								AmCom
STIBILJ, MILAN (1929–)																															
Condensation	1967								2														1				1				Bären
STILL, WILLIAM G. (1895–1978)																															
Danzas de Panama				2	1	1																									Peer
STOCK, DAVID (1939–)																															
Flashback *Unus Instr:* Gong	1968		12	1	1	1	1			1					1	1			1		1	1	1				1			1	AmCom
Keep the Change *** *Comment:* For any 5 treble-clef instruments	1981		6																												AmCom

	Year Composed or Published	Key	Duration	Violin	Viola	Cello	Double Bass	Gamba	Piano	Harpsicord	Organ	Guitar	Harp	Recorder	Flute/Piccolo	Oboe	English Horn	Clarinet/Bass Clarinet	Bassoon/Contrabassoon	Saxophone	French Horn	Trumpet	Trombone	Bass Trombone	Tuba	Baritone	Percussion	Voice	Electronic Tape	Unusual Instruments	Publisher
STOCK, DAVID *(continued)*																															
Kennedy Center Tonight Theme	1981		2												1	1		1			3	3	3				3				AmCom
Night *Comment:* Optional dancer	1980		4	1		1												1													AmCom
Noro *** *Comment:* A game piece for up to any 4 instruments	1966		5																												AmCom
Parallel Worlds *Unus Instr:* Marimba	1984		16			1	1						1		1	1		1	1		1	1					1			1	AmCom
Persona *Comment:* Two optional dancers	1980		6	1		1			1									1									1				AmCom
The Philosopher's Stone (solo violin)	1980		15	1		1	1		1						1	1		1	1								2				AmCom
Quick Opener *Unus Instr:* Marimba	1987		7	1	1	1	1		1				1		1	1		1	1		1	1	1							1	AmCom
Quintet	1966		14	2	1	1												1									1				AmCom
Serenade for 5 Instruments	1964		7		1	1									1			1			1										AmCom
Sliberty Stomp	1985		4												1	1		3		2	1	3	1								AmCom
Sulla spiaggia *Unus Instr:* Electric piano, bass clarinet, vibraphone	1985		10						1						1		1	1									1			3	AmCom
Yerusha (solo clarinet) *Unus Instr:* Bass clarinet	1986		7	1			1											2	1			1	1							1	AmCom
STOCKHAUSEN, KARLHEINZ (1928–)																															
Adieu															1	1		1	1		1										Unive
Aus den Sieben Tagen***, Op 26	1968																														Unive
Dr. K Sextett, Op 29 *Unus Instr:* Bass clarinet	1969		4		1	1			1						1			1									1			1	Unive
Kontra-Punkte, Op 1 *Unus Instr:* Bass clarinet	1953		14	1		1			1				1		1			2	1			1	1							1	Unive
Kreuzspiel, Op 1/7 *Unus Instr:* Bass clarinet, woodblock	1951		12						1							1		1									3			2	Unive
Plus-Minus, Op 14	1968					1			3									1					1								Unive
Refrain, Op 11 *Unus Instr:* Celesta, vibraphone, antique cymbals	1959		12						1																		2			3	Unive
Stop (Paris version: 18 instruments in 6 groups), Op 18 1/2 *Unus Instr:* Electric cello, alto flute, clarinet in E♭, bass clarinet, basset horn, vibraphone, elektronium	1969		21	1	2	2			1						1	1		2	1		1	1	1		1		1			7	Unive
Zeitmasse, Op 5 *Unus Instr:* Bass clarinet	1957														1	1	1	1	1											1	Unive
STOCKMEIER, WOLFGANG (1931–)																															
Variationen											1											2	3								Bären
STOJANTSCHEW, STOJAN (1931–)																															
Trio	1977											1			1												1				DeutV
STOUT, ALAN (1932–)																															
Canticum canticorum	1962		9		1								1		1	1		1	1		1						1	S		C	Peter
Fanfare for the Peninsula Music Festival	1972		3																		3	2	2				2				AmCom
Movements	1960		11	2	1	1												1													AmCom
Suite for Flute and Percussion	1962		15												1												4				Peter
Velut umbra, Op 35a	1960		11	1	1	1	1		1						1							4	2		1		1				AmCom
STRANG, GERALD (1908–1983)																															
Concerto for Cello	1951		14			1			1						1	1		1	1												AmCom
Concerto Grosso	1950		20	1	1	1									1			1	1		1										AmCom
Divertimento for 4 Instruments *** *Comment:* Group must include cello, or clarinet, or bassoon	1948		6																												AmCom

	Year Composed or Published	Key	Duration	Violin	Viola	Cello	Double Bass	Gamba	Piano	Harpsicord	Organ	Guitar	Harp	Recorder	Flute/Piccolo	Oboe	English Horn	Clarinet/Bass Clarinet	Bassoon/Contrabassoon	Saxophone	French Horn	Trumpet	Trombone	Bass Trombone	Tuba	Baritone	Percussion	Voice	Electronic Tape	Unusual Instruments	Publisher
STRANG, GERALD *(continued)*																															
Variations for 4 Instruments *** *Comment:* For any combination of woodwinds and strings	1956		6																												AmCom
STRANZ, ULRICH (1946–)																															
Streichquartett 1	1976			2	1	1																									Bären
Trio d'anches	1980															1		1	1												Bären
STRAUSS, RICHARD (1864–1949)																															
Klavierquartett, Op 13	1886	c		1	1	1			1																						VarPb
Meinem Kinde, Op 37 No. 3	1897		2	2	2	1	1						1		2				2									1			Unive
Serenade, Op 7	1881	E♭	10												2	2		2	3		4										Unive
Streichquartett, Op 2	1880	A		2	1	1																									Unive
Suite, Op 4 *Unus Instr:* Contrabassoon	1884	B♭	25												2	2		2	3		4									1	Leuck
Suite (alt. inst.), Op 4	1884	B♭	25												2	2		2	2		4				1						Leuck
Till Eulenspiegel (arr. Carp)	1895								1						1	1		1	1		1										Press
Till Eulenspiegel einmal anders (arr. Hasenoehrl)				1			1											1	1		1										Peter
STRAUSS, WOLFGANG (1927–)																															
Trio, Op 58	1971			1		1			1																						DeutV
STRAUSS, Jr., JOHANN (1825–1899)																															
Annen-Polka (arr. Halffter), Op 117	1852			2	1	1									1	1		1	1												Unive
Roses from the South (arr. Schoenberg), Op 388 *Unus Instr:* Harmonium	1880			2	1	1			1																					1	Unive
Schatzwalzer (arr. Webern), Op 418 *Unus Instr:* Harmonium	1886			2	1	1			1																					1	Unive
Wine, Women, and Song (arr. Berg), Op 333 *Unus Instr:* Harmonium	1869			2	1	1			1																					1	Unive
STRAVINSKY, IGOR (1882–1971)																															
Berceuses du chat	1914		5															3										1			Chest
Concertino for String Quartet	1920		7	2	1	1																									Chest
Concertino for 12 Instruments	1952		10	1		1									1	1	1	1	2			2	2								Hanse
Double Canon (Raoul Dufy in memoriam)	1959		2	2	1	1																									Boose
Elegy for J.F.K.	1964		2															3										B			Boose
Epitaphium	1959		2										1		1			1													Boose
In memoriam Dylan Thomas	1954			2	1	1																	4					T			Boose
Instrumental Miniatures, 8	1962		6	2	2	2									2	2		2	2		1										Chest
Introitus (T.S. Eliot in memoriam) *Voices:* 6 male voices. *Unus Instr:* Tam-tam	1965				1		1		1				1														2	6		1	Boose
Octet for Winds	1923														1			1	2			2	1		1						Boose
Pastorale	1933			1												1	1	1	1												BScho
Pastorale (for Soprano)	1923															1	1	1	1									S			BScho
Pieces, 3	1918		8	2	1	1																									Boose
Poems from the Japanese, 3	1913			2	1	1									2			2										S			Boose
Pribaoutki (Peasant Songs) *Comment:* Oboe doubles on English horn	1919			1	1	1	1								1	1	1	1	1									1			Chest
Ragtime *Unus Instr:* Cimbalom	1918		6	2	1		1								1			1			1	1	1				1			1	Chest
Septet	1952			1	1	1			1									1	1		1										Boose
The Soldier's Tale *Voices:* 3 Readers	1918		60	1			1											1	1			1	1				1	3			Chest
The Soldier's Tale (Suite)	1918		25	1			1											1	1			1	1				1				Chest
The Soldier's Tale (for trio)	1919		15	1					1									1													VarPb

	Year Composed or Published	Key	Duration	Violin	Viola	Cello	Double Bass	Gamba	Piano	Harpsicord	Organ	Guitar	Harp	Recorder	Flute/Piccolo	Oboe	English Horn	Clarinet/Bass Clarinet	Bassoon/Contrabassoon	Saxophone	French Horn	Trumpet	Trombone	Bass Trombone	Tuba	Baritone	Percussion	Voice	Electronic Tape	Unusual Instruments	Publisher
STRAVINSKY, IGOR *(continued)*																															
Songs from William Shakespeare, 3	1953		7		1										1			1										M			Boose
Songs, 4	1954		6									1	1		1													1			Chest
STRAVINSKY, SOULIMA (1910–)																															
String Quartet			13	2	1	1																									Peter
Trio			25	1		1			1																						Peter
STREET, TISON (1943–)																															
Odds and Ends, from "So Much Depends" *Voices:* Soprano and tenor	1973		20	2	1	1			1																			2			AMP
String Quartet	1972		12	2	1	1																									AMP
Variations	1964		7			1						1			1																AMP
STREIFF, PETER (1944–)																															
Partikel 1-7 *** *Comment:* For ensemble of 2 to 12 players																															Hug
STRNISTE, JIRI (1914–)																															
Octet	1975															2		2	2		2										Artia
Suite per quartetto di ottoni	1973																					2	2								Artia
STROBL, L (?–)																															
Musik für Blechbläser																					2	3	2		1		1				Dobli
Suite 1 für Bläserquintett															1	1		1	1		1										Dobli
STROE, AUREL (1932–)																															
Musique de concert	1964		13						1												4	4	4				4				Salab
STROMHOLM, FOLKE (1941–)																															
In memoriam Alban Berg	1965		6	2	1	1																									Nordi
Karakeino, Farewell	1978		8	1		1			1									1													Nordi
Music	1970		10															1									2				Nordi
Noai'di	1973		8												1	1	1	1	1												Nordi
Wind Quintet	1968		8												1	1	1	1	1												Nordi
STUCKY, STEVEN E. (1949–)																															
Divertimento	1971		11						1									8									2				AmCom
Quartet	1973		17		1	1			1									1													AmCom
SUBEN, JOEL E. (1946–)																															
2 Reveries from Under Milkwood *Unus Instr:* Glockenspiel	1968		5	1	1	1			1				1		1	1		1	1		1	1			1		2			1	AmCom
2 Reveries (alt. inst.) *Unus Instr:* Bass clarinet, celesta, glockenspiel	1968		5	1	1	1				1			1		1	1		1	1		1	1			1		1			3	AmCom
SUBOTNICK, MORTON (1933–)																															
A Fluttering of Wings				2	1	1																									Press
A Fluttering of Wings (alt. vers.)				2	1	1																							1		Press
SUCHON, EUGEN (1908–)																															
Stücke (6) für Streichquartett	1965			2	1	1																									Artia
SUDER, JOSEPH (1892–1980)																															
String Quartet No. 2	1939	e		2	1	1																									Amade
Wind Quintet															1	1		1	1		1										Amade
SUGAR, MIKLOS (1952–)																															
Parcornussion																					2						1				EMBud
SUGAR, REZSO (1919–)																															
Frammenti musicali	1963								1						1	1		1	1		1										EMBud
SURINACH, CARLOS (1915–)																															
Apasionada (Ballet)	1961		35				1		1							1		1	1		1	1					2				AMP
Cantos berberes (3)	1952		10		1	1							1		1	1		1													Peer
David and Bathsheba (Ballet) *Unus Instr:* Piccolo			23				2		1				1		2	2	1				2	2					2			1	AMP

	Year Composed or Published	Key	Duration	Violin	Viola	Cello	Double Bass	Gamba	Piano	Harpsicord	Organ	Guitar	Harp	Recorder	Flute/Piccolo	Oboe	English Horn	Clarinet/Bass Clarinet	Bassoon/Contrabassoon	Saxophone	French Horn	Trumpet	Trombone	Bass Trombone	Tuba	Baritone	Percussion	Voice	Electronic Tape	Unusual Instruments	Publisher
SURINACH, CARLOS *(continued)*																															
Doppio concertino *Unus Instr:* Piccolo, English horn			16	1			1		1						1	1		1	1		1	1					2			2	Rongw
Hieroglyphics *Unus Instr:* 2 Piccolos, bass clarinet			10			4	2								4		1	3			1									3	AMP
Hollywood Carnival *Unus Instr:* Piccolo, timpani			8				1								1			1				1					3			2	Rongw
Ritmo Jondo *Unus Instr:* Xylophone and 3 hand clappers	1952		6															1				1					3			4	AMP
String Quartet	1974		25	2	1	1																									AMP
Tientos	1953		9							1							1										1				AMP
SUTER, HERMANN (1870–1926)																															
String Quartet, Op 1		D		2	1	1																									VarPb
SUTER, ROBERT (1919–)																															
Sonata	1975			1		1			1																						Hug
Sonatina	1966									1						1			1												Hug
SWAN, ALFRED J. (1890–1970)																															
Trio	1936	a							1						1			1													Belai
SWANSON, HOWARD (1907–1978)																															
Soundpiece for Brass Quintet	1952																				1	2	2								Weint
Vista No. 2 (String Octet)	1969			4	2	2																									Weint
SYDEMAN, WILLIAM (1928–)																															
Concerto da camera III	1965		14	1			1											1				2					2				Schir
Concerto da camera III (alt. inst.) *Unus Instr:* Contrabassoon	1965		14	1			1												1			2					2			1	AMP
Music			13		1							1			1												1				Peter
Quintet No. 2	1959														1	1		1	1		1										McGMa
Trio				1			1								1																McGMa
SYVERUD, STEPHEN L. (1938–)																															
Five Pieces	1964		8			1									1			1													AmCom
SZABO, XAVER F. (1902–1969)																															
Sestetto per archi, Op 98	1965			2	2	2																									Zenem
SZELL, GEORGE (1897–1970)																															
Klavierquintett, Op 2	1912	E		2	1	1			1																						Unive
SZOKOLAY, SANDOR (1931–)																															
Alliterations	1977		4																			3	1		1						EMBud
String Quartet No. 1	1973			2	1	1																									Peter
SZYMANOWSKI, KAROL (1882–1937)																															
Streichquartett 1, Op 37	1917	C		2	1	1																									Unive
Streichquartett 2, Op 56	1927			2	1	1																									Unive
SZYMANSKI, PAWEL (1954–)																															
2 Illusory Constructions	1984		13			1			1									1													Chest
2 Pieces	1982		13	2	1	1																									Chest
Appendix (solo piccolo)	1983		12		2	2									1						1		1				2				Chest
Quasi una sinfonietta	1990			2	1	1	1		1						1	1		1	1		1	1	1				1				Chest
String Quartet	1975		11	2	1	1																									Chest
Villanelle *Voices:* Alto and tenor	1981		10		2					1																		2			Chest
TAFFANEL, PAUL (1844–1908)																															
Quintette															1	1		1	1		1										Leduc
TAILLEFERRE, GERMAINE (1892–1983)																															
Quatuor	1918			2	1	1																									Duran
TAIRA, YOSHIHISA (1938–)																															
Clea			14	7	2	2	1																								Ridea

	Year Composed or Published	Key	Duration	Violin	Viola	Cello	Double Bass	Gamba	Piano	Harpsicord	Organ	Guitar	Harp	Recorder	Flute/Piccolo	Oboe	English Horn	Clarinet/Bass Clarinet	Bassoon/Contrabassoon	Saxophone	French Horn	Trumpet	Trombone	Bass Trombone	Tuba	Baritone	Percussion	Voice	Electronic Tape	Unusual Instruments	Publisher
TAIRA, YOSHIHISA *(continued)*																															
Fusion			13												2												3				Ridea
Hiérophone II			16		4		2		1				1		3												4				Ridea
Ignescence			18						2																		2				Ridea
Luisances *Unus Instr:* 2 Ondes Martenot			11									1															1			2	Ridea
Pentalpha for 5 Soloists *Unus Instr:* Marimba			11												1			1	1								1			1	Ridea
Radiance, for Piano			11	1	1	1			1				1		4	1		1			1	1					1				Ridea
Sonomorphie II			13			1							1			1											1	S			Ridea
TAKACS, JENO (1902–)																															
Divertimento (Eine kleine Tafelmusik), Op 74															1	1		1	1		1										Dobli
Oktett, Op 96				1		1	1								1	1		1	1		1										Dobli
Serenade after old Graz contradances, Op 83a															1	1		1	1		1										Dobli
Trio Rhapsodie, Op 11				1		1			1																						Dobli
TAKAHASHI, YUJI (1938–)																															
Bridges I *Unus Instr:* Electric harpsichord	1967		7			1				1																	2			1	Peter
Bridges II	1968		4		3											2		2				2									Peter
Chromamorphe I *Unus Instr:* Vibraphone	1963		4	1			1								1						1	1	1				1			1	Peter
Nikité	1971		8			1	1									1		1				1	1								Peter
TAKEMITSU, TŌRU (1930–)																															
Bryce *Unus Instr:* Marimba	1976		10										2		1												1			1	Salab
Eucalyptus II	1970												1		1	1															Salab
Garden Rain (for Brass Ensemble)	1974		8																		1	2	2	1	1						Salab
Landscape 1	1960			2	1	1																									Salab
Quatrain II	1976			1		1			1									1													Salab
Ring *Unus Instr:* Lute	1962											2			1															1	Ongak
Waves	1976		10															1			1		2				1				Salab
TALMA, LOUISE (1906–)																															
All the Days of My Life	1965					1			1									1									1	T			Manus
Ambient Air	1983			1		1			1						1																CarlF
Diadem (Song Cycle)	1979			1		1			1						1			1										T			CarlF
Episodes, 7					1				1						1																Peter
Full Circle *Unus Instr:* Timpani	1985			8	3	2	1		1						2			2									2			1	CarlF
Have You Heard, Do You Know? *Voices:* Soprano, mezzo-soprano, and tenor	1980			1	1	1	1		1						1			1	1			1					1	3			CarlF
String Quartet	1954			2	1	1																									Manus
Summer Sounds	1973			2	1	1												1													CarlF
Variations on "13 Ways of Looking at a Blackbird" *Voice:* Soprano or tenor. Flute or violin may replace oboe	1979								1							1												1			CarlF
TAMBA, AKIRA (1932–)																															
Complex simple (for 2 Ondes Martenot) *Unus Instr:* 2 Ondes Martenot. Violin must be amplified			11	1	1	1	1								1			1			1	1	1				4			3	Ridea
Concerto da camera (for flute)			14	6	2	2	1								1																Ridea
Ennea			19	2	1	1	1		1						1			1										1			Ridea
Resurgence (for Harpsichord)			20	7	2	2	1			1																					Ridea
TANENBAUM, ELIAS (1924–)																															
Blurred Visions	1985		14		1								1		1												1				AmCom

	Year Composed or Published	Key	Duration	Violin	Viola	Cello	Double Bass	Gamba	Piano	Harpsicord	Organ	Guitar	Harp	Recorder	Flute/Piccolo	Oboe	English Horn	Clarinet/Bass Clarinet	Bassoon/Contrabassoon	Saxophone	French Horn	Trumpet	Trombone	Bass Trombone	Tuba	Baritone	Percussion	Voice	Electronic Tape	Unusual Instruments	Publisher
TANENBAUM, ELIAS *(continued)*																															
A Bubble in My Eye	1985		14						1														1				1				AmCom
Chamber Piece No. 1	1956		16			1			1						1			1									1				AmCom
Clarinet Trio with Tape	1980		10	1		1												1											1		AmCom
Consort	1970					1	1					1			1		1			1							1				AmCom
Further Reflections	1978		11	1		1			1																				1		AmCom
Jazz Set	1969		8				1		1											1		1					1		1		AmCom
Music for 3 Chamber Groups	1961		15	2	1	1							1		1	1		1	2		2	1	1		1		3				AmCom
Nove	1963		16	1			1		1						1			1	1	1		1	1				1				AmCom
Remembrance	1975		16	1		1	1								1					1							2		1		AmCom
Side-by-Side	1980		13	1	1	1									1	1		1		1							1		1		AmCom
The Three of Us	1983		12						1						1												1				AmCom
Trio	1958		15			1									1									1							AmCom
Trio (alt. inst.)	1964		13			1			1									1													AmCom
Trio for Flute, Tenor and Bass Violins *Comment:* Strings are tenor violin, and bass violin	1958		15	1			1								1																AmCom
Trio I, II, III	1967		14	1	1	1	1								1	1		1		1							1				AmCom
Twelve with Tape *Unus Instr:* Bass clarinet	1978		15	2	1	1	1											2		1		1	1				2		1	1	AmCom
Words or Blues for Us *Unus Instr:* Vibraphone	1977		10				1													1							1			1	AmCom
TANSMAN, ALEXANDRE (1897–1986)																															
Le bateau (Nous jouons pour Maman)				1		1			1																						Eschi
Music for Clarinet and String Quartet	1982		10	2	1	1												1													Eschi
Music for Six	1977		20	2	1	1			1									1													Eschi
Music for Strings (Quartet No. 7)	1948		22	2	1	1																									Eschi
Serenade	1930			1		1			1																						Leduc
String Quartet No. 2				2	1	1																									Salab
Triptych	1930		16	2	1	1																									Eschi
TARANU, CORNEL (1934–)																															
Guirlandes *Unus Instr:* Celesta	1979								1				1		1	1		1	1		1	1	1				4			1	Salab
Offrandes I	1978														1												3				Salab
Offrandes II	1979			1	1	1	1		1						1												3				Salab
Rime de Michelangelo *Voice:* Bass-baritone	1977			1	1	1	1		1						1			1			1	1	1					1			Salab
TATE, PHYLLIS (1911–1987)																															
Air and Variations	1958			1					1									1													Oxfor
Apparitions *Unus Instr:* Harmonica	1968			2	1	1			1																			T		1	Oxfor
The Ballad of Reading Gaol	1980					1					1																	B			Oxfor
Creatures Great and Small	1973						1					1															1	M			Oxfor
The Lady of Shalott *Unus Instr:* Celesta	1956			1					2																		3	T		1	Oxfor
Movements for String Quartet *Comment:* Revised version of String Quartet (1952)	1982			2	1	1																									Oxfor
The Rainbow and the Cuckoo	1974			1	1	1										1															Oxfor
Scenes from Tyneside	1978								1									1										M			Oxfor
TAUB, BRUCE J. (1948–)																															
California Music (Concertino)	1976		12			1			1			1			1			1	1												AmCom
Chamber Variations IV *Comment:* Conductor needed	1973		24	1	1	1	1		1						1	1		1	1				1				1				AmCom
Extremities (Quintet III)			12	1		1			1						1			1													Peter

	Year Composed or Published	Key	Duration	Violin	Viola	Cello	Double Bass	Gamba	Piano	Harpsicord	Organ	Guitar	Harp	Recorder	Flute/Piccolo	Oboe	English Horn	Clarinet/Bass Clarinet	Bassoon/Contrabassoon	Saxophone	French Horn	Trumpet	Trombone	Bass Trombone	Tuba	Baritone	Percussion	Voice	Electronic Tape	Unusual Instruments	Publisher
TAUB, BRUCE J. *(continued)*																															
Extremities II (Quintet V)				1		1			1						1			1													Peter
Fragile Lady (Improvisation)			9				1		1																		1	S			Peter
Nocturnal Voices (Quintet IV)	1981		15		1	1	1		1						1																AmCom
Of the Wings of Madness	1985		10	1	1	1	1		1						1	1		1	1		1	1	1				2				AmCom
Passion, Poison, and Petrification *Voices:* Soprano, tenor, bass, and four actors			35	1		1			1			1			1			1	1								1	7			Peter
Quartet	1970		12	1		1									1				1												AmCom
Quintet (I)	1972		15	1		1			1						1			1													AmCom
Quintet (II)	1972		8	1					1			1			1				1												AmCom
Variations Four String Quartet			10	2	1	1																									Peter
Variations 11.7.3.3.4	1970		15	1	1	1			1				1		2																AmCom
TAUBERT, ERNST E. (1838–1934)																															
Quartet, Op 32 No. 1		D		2	1	1																									Raabe
Quartet, Op 32 No. 2		E♭		2	1	1																									Raabe
Quartet, Op 63		d		2	1	1																									Simro
TAUSINGER, JAN (1921–)																															
Canto di speranza	1965			1	1	1			1																						Artia
Hochwalder Nonett	1974			1	1	1	1								1	1		1	1		1										Artia
TAVENER, JOHN (1944–)																															
Abbasid Songs, 6	1979		20												3												1	T			Chest
Canciones españolas *Voices:* 2 Countertenors or 2 sopranos	1972		15							1	1				2												1	2			Chest
Trisagion	1981		12																		1	2	2								Chest
TAYLOR, CLIFFORD (1923–)																															
Islands (A Chamber Concerto)	1985		17	1		1							1					1			1						2				AmCom
Movement for 3	1968		9		1	1			1																						AmCom
Quintet No. 3	1981		15		1											1		1	1		1										AmCom
Trio	1960		15			1			1									1													AmCom
TCHAIKOVSKY, BORIS (1925–)																															
Partita for Violoncello *Unus Instr:* Glockenspiel, xylophone, vibraphone, timpani						1			1	1		1															5			4	VAAP
TCHAIKOWSKY, PETER I. (1840–1893)																															
Andante cantabile (solo cello)				2	2	2																									Kunze
Elégie																					1	2	1		1						Billa
Humoresque (arr. Aaron)															1	1		1	1												Schir
Humoresque, Op 10 No. 2																					1	2	1								Press
Piano Pieces, 3 (arr. Carp)															1	1		1	1		1										Press
Piano Trio, Op 50	1882	a		1		1			1																						VarPb
Souvenir de Florence, Op 70	1887	d		2	2	2																									Inter
String Quartet No. 1, Op 11	1871	D		2	1	1																									VarPb
String Quartet No. 2, Op 22	1874	F		2	1	1																									VarPb
String Quartet No. 3, Op 30	1876	e♭		2	1	1																									VarPb
String Quartet, Op Post.		B♭		2	1	1																									Kunze
Tchaikovsky Variations (arr. Hoiby) *Comment:* Includes original variations by Hoiby for oboe			18						1						1	1		1	1		1										Aguar
TCHEREPNIN, ALEXANDER (1899–1977)																															
Brass Quintet, Op 105			12																		1	2	1		1						Peter
Children's Trio	1960			1		1									1																Amade
Mystère, Op 37 No. 2 *Unus Instr:* 2 Cornets	1923		10	4	2	3	2								1				1		2	2					1			2	Unive

	Year Composed or Published	Key	Duration	Violin	Viola	Cello	Double Bass	Gamba	Piano	Harpsicord	Organ	Guitar	Harp	Recorder	Flute/Piccolo	Oboe	English Horn	Clarinet/Bass Clarinet	Bassoon/Contrabassoon	Saxophone	French Horn	Trumpet	Trombone	Bass Trombone	Tuba	Baritone	Percussion	Voice	Electronic Tape	Unusual Instruments	Publisher
TCHEREPNIN, ALEXANDER *(continued)*																															
Quatuor, 2e, Op 40	1926			2	1	1																									Duran
Stücke (3) für Kammerorchester, Op 37 *Unus Instr:* 2 Cornets	1923		32	4	2	3	2								1				1		2	2					1			2	Unive
Trio	1925			1		1			1																						Duran
Woodwind Quintet			14												1	1		1	1		1										Peter
TEMPLETON, ALEC (1909–1963)																															
Passepied															1	1	1	2	1												Press
TERTERIAN, AVET (1929–)																															
String Quartet	1964	C		2	1	1																									VAAP
TERZAKIS, DIMITRI (1938–)																															
Erotikon	1979		10	1		1												1										S			Breit
Hommage à Morse	1970		6	2	1	1									1	1		1					1								Breit
Notturni *Voices:* 2 Sopranos, alto, 2 tenors, bass	1976			1														1									1	6			Bären
Nuances	1970				1				1																		1	A	1		Bären
Numoi *Voice:* Male. *Unus Instr:* Santouri	1975					1												1									2	1		1	Bären
Der Raub der Europa *Unus Instr:* Vibraphone	1985		15	2	1	1									1	1		1	1		1							S		1	Breit
Streichquartett 2	1976			2	1	1																									Bären
TESSIER, ROBERT (1939–)																															
Isomerie			17	9	3	2	1																								Salab
Mobile-immobile *Unus Instr:* Ondes Martenot, vibraphone, xylophone, glockenspiel, celesta	1982			1	1	1	1		1				1		1		1	1	1		1	1	1				2			5	Salab
Motition, for Soprano	1984		12	1	1	1									1			1			1							S			Salab
TESTI, FLAVIO (1923–)																															
Cantata 4. Viens, mon beau chat, Op 31																		2										B			Ricor
THÄRICHEN, WERNER (1921–)																															
Concerto for Oboe, Op 46 *Unus Instr:* Timpani	1967		24			4	2						1			1											5			1	BoteB
Oktett, Op 40				2	2	1												1	1		1										BoteB
Streichquartett 1, Op 31				2	1	1																									BoteB
THIELE, SIEGFRIED (1934–)																															
Praeludia et cantus	1978			1	1	1									1																DeutV
Proportionen	1971					1			1							1															DeutV
Serenade	1969			1		1									1																DeutV
Streichquartett	1983			2	1	1																									DeutV
THILMAN, JOHANNES P. (1906–1973)																															
Aspekte					1								1		1																Peter
Clarinet Quintet, Op 731	1956			2	1	1												1													Peter
Dramatic Scenes for String Quartet				2	1	1																									Peter
Kammerspiel for String Quartet				2	1	1																									Peter
Ostinati					1	1							1		1												1				Peter
Streichquartett, Op 81		D		2	1	1																									Hofme
String Quartet No. 2, Op 62	1955			2	1	1																									Peter
Trio piccolo *Unus Instr:* Bass clarinet					1										1			1												1	Peter
THOMAS, ANDREW (1929–)																															
Alexander's Dark Band	1978		10	1					1						1			2			1	1			1		3				AmCom
Black Mamba	1979		12			1			1									1									1				AmCom
Elegy (in Memory of Max Pollikoff)	1985		5			1											1	1													AmCom

	Year Composed or Published	Key	Duration	Violin	Viola	Cello	Double Bass	Gamba	Piano	Harpsicord	Organ	Guitar	Harp	Recorder	Flute/Piccolo	Oboe	English Horn	Clarinet/Bass Clarinet	Bassoon/Contrabassoon	Saxophone	French Horn	Trumpet	Trombone	Bass Trombone	Tuba	Baritone	Percussion	Voice	Electronic Tape	Unusual Instruments	Publisher
THOMAS, ANDREW *(continued)*																															
Night Prelude	1980		5			1			1									1									1				AmCom
St. Teresa in the Eye of the Storm	1986		4															1	1		1										AmCom
THOMAS-MIFUNE, WERNER (1941–)																															
Big Train				4		2																									Kunze
Big Train (alt.)				4	2																										Kunze
Kleine Eisenbahn				1	1	1									1																Kunze
THOMPSON, RANDALL (1899–1984)																															
Quintet	1920				1	1			1						1			1													Schir
Scherzino *Unus Instr:* Flageolet	1920			1	1										1															1	ECSch
Septette	1927			2	1	1			1						1			1													ECSch
String Quartet No. 1	1941	d		2	1	1																									ECSch
String Quartet No. 2	1967			2	1	1																									ECSch
Suite	1940				1											1		1													ECSch
The Wind in the Willows	1924			2	1	1																									Manus
THOMSON, VIRGIL (1896–)																															
Barcarolle (Portrait of George Hugnet)															1	1	1	1	1												Schir
Family Portrait	1975		10																		1	2	2								AMP
Four Saints: An Olio *Unus Instr:* Glockenspiel, accordion	1982		20	2	1	1	1								2	2	1	2	2		2	1	1				2			2	Schir
Parson Weems and the Cherry Tree *Unus Instr:* Flügelhorn, xylophone, glockenspiel; optional timpani	1975		25	1			1								1			1				1		1			3			3	Schir
Party Pieces	1950								1						1			1	1		1										Peter
Sonata da chiesa	1926		15		1													1			1	1	1								Boose
Stabat Mater	1931		6	2	1	1																						S			Boose
String Quartet No. 1	1931		22	2	1	1																									Boose
String Quartet No. 2	1932		28	2	1	1																									Boose
THORNE, FRANCIS (1922–)																															
Chamber Concerto (solo cello)	1975		19	1	1	1	1								1			1	1			1	1				2				AmCom
Divertimento No. 3 for Wind Quintet	1983														1	1		1	1		1										AMP
Evensong *Unus Instr:* Celesta	1975		16									1	1		1												1			1	AmCom
Head Music	1975		16			1			1									1													AmCom
Lyric Variations No. 7	1982		17	1		1			1									1	1		1	1									AmCom
Prufrock Ballet Music *Unus Instr:* Banjo	1974		30			1						1			1			1	1			1					1			1	AmCom
Rhapsodic Variations No. 2	1985		14	1		1												1													AmCom
Set Pieces, 7	1967		20		2		1		1									2	2			2	1				2				AmCom
THORNE, NICHOLAS (1953–)																															
Night Elegy	1979		12						1							1		1													Hanse
Quartet	1986		16	1		1			1									1													Hanse
Songs from the Mountains	1985		18	1		1			1						1			1									1				Hanse
TILLIS, FREDERICK C. (1930–)																															
Music	1972		11		1	1			1																						AmCom
Music for an Experimental Lab Ensemble	1967		2	1					1											2	1				1						AmCom
Three Plus One	1969		8	1								1						1											1		AmCom
TIPEI, SEVER (1943–)																															
Never Mind *** *Comment:* For any instruments up to 6	1977		20																												AmCom
Single Tone *** *Comment:* For any 5 instruments	1971		5																												AmCom

	Year Composed or Published	Key	Duration	Violin	Viola	Cello	Double Bass	Gamba	Piano	Harpsicord	Organ	Guitar	Harp	Recorder	Flute/Piccolo	Oboe	English Horn	Clarinet/Bass Clarinet	Bassoon/Contrabassoon	Saxophone	French Horn	Trumpet	Trombone	Bass Trombone	Tuba	Baritone	Percussion	Voice	Electronic Tape	Unusual Instruments	Publisher
TIPPETT, MICHAEL (1905–)																															
Crown of the Year *Comment:* Flutes or recorders may replace violins	1958			2	1	1			1									1													BScho
String Quartet No. 1	1944			2	1	1																									BScho
String Quartet No. 2	1943			2	1	1																									BScho
String Quartet No. 3	1946			2	1	1																									BScho
String Quartet No. 4	1979			2	1	1																									BScho
TIRCUIT, HEUWELL (1931–)																															
Cantata No. 3 (on Poems of Stephen Crane)			23			1			1						1													S			AMP
Concerto for Violin *Unus Instr:* Bass clarinet			22	1											2	2		2	2		2									1	AMP
Halcyon for Flute			5	8	2	2	2				1				1				1			1					1				AMP
Halcyon for Flute (alt. vers.)			5	8	2	2	2								1												1				AMP
String Quartet No. 3			20	2	1	1																									AMP
TISCHHAUSER, FRANZ (1921–)																															
Octet				2	1	1	1											1	1		1										Amade
Omaggi a Mälzel	1963		12	7	2	2	1																								Peter
TISHCHENKO, BORIS (1939–)																															
Concerto No. 1 for Violoncello *Unus Instr:* Timpani	1963		25			1					1					3		3	3		2	3	2		1		2			1	VAAP
String Quartet No. 2				2	1	1																									VAAP
String Quartet No. 4, Op 77	1980		42	2	1	1																									VAAP
String Quartet No. 5, Op 90	1984		32	2	1	1																									VAAP
Symphony No. 3 *Voices:* Soprano, baritone. *Unus Instr:* Timpani			31	1	1	1	1		1						2	2		2	1		1	1	1				2	2		1	VAAP
TISNE, ANTOINE (1932–)																															
Caractères	1965			2	2	1									1	1		1	1		1						1				Billa
Disparates	1968														1	1		1	1		1										Billa
Episodes New-Yorkais				1		1			1						1			1													Billa
Musique en trio				1		1			1																						Billa
Quatuor à cordes	1963			2	1	1																									Billa
Stances minoennes																					1	2	1		1						Leduc
Tosatti				1	1	1												1	1												Ricor
TITTEL, ERNST (1910–)																															
Intrada für Orgel und Blechbläser											1											3	3								Dobli
Sonata for Like/Unlike Instruments, Op 30 *Comment:* Cello may substitute for viola				2	1																										Dobli
TOCH, ERNEST (1887–1964)																															
Piano Quintet	1938			2	1	1			1																						VarPb
"Spitzweg" Serenade	1917			2	1																										Tisch
Tanz Suite	1923			1	1		1								1			1									1				Tisch
TOGNI, CAMILLO (1922–)																															
Aubade *Unus Instr:* Vibraphone	1965					1				1			1		1			1									1			1	Suvin
TOLDRA, EDUARDO (1895–1962)																															
Vistas al mar				2	1	1																									UMEsp
TOMASI, HENRI (1901–1971)																															
Danses profanes et sacrées (5)															1	1		1	1		1										Leduc
Etre ou ne pas être (Hamlet's soliloquy)																							3		1						Leduc
Fanfares liturgiques																					4	3	4				4				Leduc
Pastorale inca				2											1																Leduc
Pastorales provençales												2			1																Leduc
Printemps															1	1		1	1	1			4		1						Leduc

	Year Composed or Published	Key	Duration	Violin	Viola	Cello	Double Bass	Gamba	Piano	Harpsicord	Organ	Guitar	Harp	Recorder	Flute/Piccolo	Oboe	English Horn	Clarinet/Bass Clarinet	Bassoon/Contrabassoon	Saxophone	French Horn	Trumpet	Trombone	Bass Trombone	Tuba	Baritone	Percussion	Voice	Electronic Tape	Unusual Instruments	Publisher
TOMASI, HENRI *(continued)*																															
Recuerdos de las Baleares												3				1											1				Leduc
Variations sur un thème corse															1	1		1	1		1										Leduc
TOOVEY, ANDREW (1962–)																															
Ate	1986		12	2	1	1	1		1				1		1		1	1	1		1	1	1				2				Boose
Black Light *Comment:* Oboe doubles on English horn. *Unus Instr:* Bass clarinet, contrabassoon	1989		10	2	1	1	1		1				1		1	1	1	1	1		1	1	1				2			2	Boose
Shining Bright	1988		14	1	1	1																									Boose
Shining Forth	1987		16	1		1			1																						Boose
Snow Flowers *Unus Instr:* Piccolo	1988		10		1								1		1															1	Boose
Untitled String Quartet	1985		15	2	1	1																									Boose
White Fire *Unus Instr:* Contrabassoon (optional)	1988		10	1		1			1									1	1											1	Boose
Winter Solstice *Comment:* Oboe doubles on English horn	1988		16	1	1	1									1	1	1	1									1	M			Boose
TOPLIFF, ROGER (?–)																															
Reflections																		2	1												Press
TORKE, MICHAEL (1961–)																															
Ceremony of Innocence	1983		7	1		1			1						1			1													Boose
The Harlequins Are Looking at You			12	1		1			1																						Boose
Patterns in Sand (from "Ceremony")	1983		9	1		1			1						1			1													Boose
The Yellow Pages	1984		7	1		1			1						1			1													Boose
TOSI, DANIEL (1953–)																															
Scordatura *** *Comment:* For 9 to 14 strings, optional tape	1984		16																										1		Salab
Verstimmung (reorch. of Scordatura) *Unus Instr:* Marimba	1985		15	1		1									1			1	1		1	1	1			1				1	Salab
TOUCHE, J. C. (?–)																															
Quintette				2	1	1			1																						Duran
TOURNIER, MARCEL L. (1879–1951)																															
Nocturne *Comment:* Piano may replace harp						1					1		1																		Leduc
TOVEY, DONALD F. (1875–1940)																															
Trio, Op 8	1906								1									1			1										MusRa
TOWER, JOAN (1938–)																															
Amazon I	1977		13	1		1			1						1			1													AMP
Black Topaz (solo piano) *Unus Instr:* Bass clarinet	1976		12						1						1			1				1	1				2			1	AMP
Breakfast Rhythms 1 and 2 (for Clarinet)	1975		15	1		1			1						1												1				AMP
Brimset	1965		6												2												2				AmCom
Fanfare for the Uncommon Woman *Unus Instr:* Timpani	1986		3																		4	3	2	1	1		3			1	Schir
Island Prelude (solo oboe)	1989		10												1	1		1	1		1										AMP
Island Prelude (solo oboe and strings)	1989		10	2	1	1	1									1															AMP
Noon Dance	1982		17	1		1			1						1			1									1				AMP
Petroushskates	1980		5	1		1			1						1			1													AMP
Prelude for 5 Players	1970		5						1						1	1		1	1												AmCom
Prelude for 5 Players (alt. inst.)	1971		6	1		1			1						1			1													AmCom
TOWNSEND, DOUGLAS (1921–)																															
8x8 (Vars. on a Theme by Milhaud), Op 3 No. 1			4			1			1					1								1									Peter
8x8 (alt. inst.), Op 3 No. 1			4						1						1	1			1												Peter

	Year Composed or Published	Key	Duration	Violin	Viola	Cello	Double Bass	Gamba	Piano	Harpsicord	Organ	Guitar	Harp	Recorder	Flute/Piccolo	Oboe	English Horn	Clarinet/Bass Clarinet	Bassoon/Contrabassoon	Saxophone	French Horn	Trumpet	Trombone	Bass Trombone	Tuba	Baritone	Percussion	Voice	Electronic Tape	Unusual Instruments	Publisher
TOWNSEND, DOUGLAS *(continued)*																															
Chamber Symphony			15												1	1		1	1		2	1	1		1						Peter
TREMBLAY, GILLES (1932–)																															
Champs II "Souffles"	1968		16				1		1						2	1		1			1	2	2				2				Salab
Compostelle I	1978		18	3			3						2		2			1			1		2				4				Salab
Envoi (Concerto for Piano)			30	2			1		1						2			2			1	2	2				3				Salab
Oralleluiants *Unus Instr:* Microphone	1975		23				3								1			1			1						2	S		1	Salab
Vers (Champs III)	1969		24	3			1								2			1			1	1					3				Salab
Vers le soleil	1977		16	7	2	2	1		1						2	1		1	1		2	1	2				3				Salab
TRIEBENSEE, J. (1772–1846)																															
Trio		B♭														2	1														Kneus
Trio		F														2	1														Kneus
Variations on a Theme of Haydn																2	1														Kneus
TRIEBMANN, KARL O. (1936–)																															
String Quartet				2	1	1																									Peter
Symphonic Essay No. 2 (for 10 Inst.)				2	1	1	1								1	1		1	1		1										Peter
Symphonic Essay No. 3 (for 8 Inst.)					1	1	1		1							1	1						1				1				Peter
TRIEDER, JAN (1957–)																															
Ricercare (Doch meine Stimme)	1977			2	1	1																									DeutV
TRIMBLE, LESTER (1923–)																															
Fragments from Canterbury Tales			16							1					1			1										S			Peter
Fragments (alt. inst.)			16						1						1			1										S			Peter
Nonet for Winds and Strings			18	2	1	1	1								1	1		1	1												Peter
Notturno			7	2	1	1																									Peter
Panels I *Unus Instr:* Electric harpsichord and electric guitar	1973			1	1	1	1			1	1	1			1					1							2			2	Peter
Petit Concert *Voice:* Medium			10	1						1						1												1			Peter
Petit Concert (alt. inst.) *Voice:* Medium			10	1					1							1												1			Peter
String Quartet No. 1	1950			2	1	1																									Press
TROJAHN, MANFRED (1949–)																															
Déplorations (Sept scènes de ballet, I) *Comment:* English horn may replace oboe. *Unus Instr:* Bass clarinet	1982														1	1		1									2			1	Bären
Die Nachtigall	1984																	3										3			Bären
Pièces brèves (2)	1973			2	1	1																									Bären
. . . stiller Gefährt der Nacht *Comment:* Piano may replace celesta	1978					1									1												1	S		1	Bären
Streichquartett 2 (mit Klarinett und Mezzo)	1980			2	1	1												1										M			Bären
Streichquartett 3	1983			2	1	1																									Bären
TROMBLY, PRESTON A. (1945–)																															
Aperçu	1978		10						1									1	1												AmCom
Chamber Concerto (solo piano)	1975		12	1	1		1						1		1	1		1			1	1	1				1				AmCom
In memoriam: Igor Stravinsky	1972		15		1		1								1	1		1	1												AmCom
Trio (in 3 Movements)	1973		10				1								1												1				AmCom
Trio da camera	1975		7			1			1						1																AmCom
TSONTAKIS, GEORGE (1951–)																															
3 Mood Sketches	1989		14												1	1		1	1		1										Press
Birdwind Quintet	1983		20												1	1		1	1		1										Press
Brass Quintet	1991		25																		1	2	2								Press

	Year Composed or Published	Key	Duration	Violin	Viola	Cello	Double Bass	Gamba	Piano	Harpsicord	Organ	Guitar	Harp	Recorder	Flute/Piccolo	Oboe	English Horn	Clarinet/Bass Clarinet	Bassoon/Contrabassoon	Saxophone	French Horn	Trumpet	Trombone	Bass Trombone	Tuba	Baritone	Percussion	Voice	Electronic Tape	Unusual Instruments	Publisher
TSONTAKIS, GEORGE *(continued)*																															
Galway Kinnell Songs	1987		12	2	1	1			1																			M			Press
Heartsounds	1990		27	1	1	1	1		1																						Press
The Past, the Passion *Comment:* Oboe doubles on English horn, flute on piccolo	1987		15	1	1	1	1		1				1		1		1	1			2	1	1				1				AmCom
Preludio et fantasia (solo cello)			12			1			1												1	2	2								Press
String Quartet No. 1 ("Mother's Hymn")	1980		11	2	1	1																									Press
String Quartet No. 2 ("Emerson")	1984		25	2	1	1																									Press
String Quartet No. 3 ("Coraggio")	1986		24	2	1	1																									Press
String Quartet No. 4, ("Thy Tenderness")	1988		28	2	1	1																									Press
TULL, FISHER (1934–)																															
Coup de Brass Encore																					2	1	1		1						Boose
Fusion	1982		9						1						1								1								Boose
TURCHI, GUIDO (1916–)																															
Concerto breve	1955			2	1	1																									Suvin
Trio	1946				1										1			1													Suvin
TURINA, JOAQUIN (1882–1949)																															
La Anunciacion				2	2	2																									UMEsp
Calliope (Himno)				2	1	1			1																						UMEsp
Circulo, Op 91	1936			1		1			1																						UMEsp
Erato (Trovas y saetas)				2	1	1																									UMEsp
La oración del torero, Op 34	1925		8	2	1	1																									UMEsp
Piano Quartet, Op 67	1931	a		1	1	1			1																						Salab
Piano Trio No. 1, Op 35	1926			1		1			1																						Salab
Piano Trio No. 2, Op 76	1933			1		1			1																						Salab
Scène andalouse (solo viola)	1912			2	2	1			1																						Salab
Serenata	1935			2	1	1																									UMEsp
Talia (Naranjos y olivos)				2	1	1																									UMEsp
TURNER, CHARLES (1921–)																															
Ballad of Barnaby			45	1		1									1			1									1				Schir
TUROK, PAUL (1929–)																															
Elegy in Memory of Karel Rathaus																					2	3	3		1			1			MusRa
UHL, ALFRED (1909–)																															
Jubiläums Quartett	1961			2	1	1																									Dobli
Kleines Konzert	1936				1				1									1													Dobli
Kleines Konzert	1972			1		1			1																						Dobli
Streichquartett 1	1946			2	1	1																									Dobli
Trio				1	1							1																			Dobli
ULLRICH, HERMANN (1888–)																															
Trio-Fantasie, Op 20				1					1												1										Dobli
ULTAN, LLOYD (1929–)																															
Quintet	1967		18	2	1	1						1																			AmCom
Suite	1987																				1	2	2								RKing
UNG, CHINARY (1942–)																															
Mohori			14			1			1				1		1	1											2	M			Peter
Spiral			14			1			1																		1				Peter
Tall Wind			6			1						1			1	1												S			Peter
URAY, ERNST L. (1906–)																															
Alpenländische Spielmusik I																					1	2	1								Dobli
Alpenländische Spielmusik II																		2			1		1								Dobli
Duo for two violins and piano				2					1																						Dobli
Fanfare for Feast and Festival																						2	2								Dobli

	Year Composed or Published	Key	Duration	Violin	Viola	Cello	Double Bass	Gamba	Piano	Harpsicord	Organ	Guitar	Harp	Recorder	Flute/Piccolo	Oboe	English Horn	Clarinet/Bass Clarinet	Bassoon/Contrabassoon	Saxophone	French Horn	Trumpet	Trombone	Bass Trombone	Tuba	Baritone	Percussion	Voice	Electronic Tape	Unusual Instruments	Publisher
URAY, ERNST L. *(continued)*																															
Hommage à Johann Strauss															1	1		1	1		1										Dobli
Musik für Bläserquintett															1	1		1	1		1										Dobli
Schladminger Dances															1			1	1		1	1									Dobli
URBANNER, ERICH (1936–)																															
Aphorismen (8)	1966														1			1	1												Dobli
Etüde für Bläserquintett															1	1		1	1		1										Dobli
Improvisation III	1969			2	1	1	1								1	1		1	1								1				Dobli
Improvisation IV	1969														1	1		1	1		1										Dobli
"Lyrica" für Kammerensemble *Unus Instr:* Celesta	1971			1			1		1				1		1			1			1		1				1			1	Dobli
Nocturne														6																	Dobli
Sextett	1973			1		1				1					1	1			1												Dobli
Streichquartett 2	1957			2	1	1																									Dobli
Streichquartett 3	1972			2	1	1																									Dobli
"Takes" für Klaviertrio				1		1			1																						Dobli
USMANBAS, ILHAN (1921–)																															
String Quartet	1947			2	1	1																									Boose
USTVOLSKAYA, GALINA (1919–)																															
Octet *Unus Instr:* Timpani	1949			4					1							2											1			1	VAAP
Trio	1949			1					1									1													VAAP
VALEN, FARTEIN (1887–1952)																															
Quartet No. 1, Op 10	1936			2	1	1																									Hanse
Quartet No. 2, Op 13	1931			2	1	1																									Hanse
VALERA, ROBERTO (?–)																															
Movimiento concertante (solo guitar) *Unus Instr:* Bass and contrabass clarinets, 2 contrabassoons, vibraphone			9												3	1		3	4		1						2			5	Peter
VAN DE VATE, NANCY H. (1930–)																															
Sound Pieces, 3	1973		10																		2	2	2		1		6				AmCom
Trio	1980		14						1										1								1				AmCom
VANDOR, IVAN (1932–)																															
Quartetto				2	1	1																									Suvin
Serenata *Unus Instr:* Bass clarinet					1	1							1		1			1			1									1	Suvin
VARÈSE, EDGAR (1883–1965)																															
Ecuatorial *Voice:* Bass. *Unus Instr:* Thereminovox	1934								1		1											4	4				1	1		1	Colom
Octandre							1								1	1		1	1		1	1	1								Colom
VASKS, PETERIS (1946–)																															
Episodi e canto perpetuo	1985			1		1			1																						VarPb
Music for a Deceased Friend	1977		10												1	1		1	1		1										VarPb
String Quartet No. 2 (Summer Singing)	1984			2	1	1																									VAAP
VAUGHAN WILLIAMS, RALPH (1872–1958)																															
Christmas Tunes, 3																						2	2								Oxfor
Double Trio for String Sextet	1939			2	2	2																									Withd
Household Music—3 Preludes on Welsh Hymn Tunes *** *Comment:* For string quartet or any combination of instruments. French horn ad libitum	1943			2	1	1																									Oxfor
Hymns, 4	1914		11		1				1																			T			Boose

	Year Composed or Published	Key	Duration	Violin	Viola	Cello	Double Bass	Gamba	Piano	Harpsicord	Organ	Guitar	Harp	Recorder	Flute/Piccolo	Oboe	English Horn	Clarinet/Bass Clarinet	Bassoon/Contrabassoon	Saxophone	French Horn	Trumpet	Trombone	Bass Trombone	Tuba	Baritone	Percussion	Voice	Electronic Tape	Unusual Instruments	Publisher
VAUGHAN WILLIAMS, RALPH *(continued)*																															
Merciless Beauty (Three Rondels)	1921		8	1	1	1																						H			Curwn
On Wenlock Edge	1909			2	1	1			1																			T			Boose
Phantasy Quintet	1912			2	2	1																									VarPb
Piano Quintet	1905	c		1	1	1	1		1																						BrLib
Quintet	1900	D		1		1			1									1			1										BrLib
String Quartet	1898	c		2	1	1																									BrLib
String Quartet No. 1	1921	g	28	2	1	1																									Curwn
String Quartet No. 2	1944	a		2	1	1																									Oxfor
VEIGL, W (?–)																															
5 Aphorismen *Unus Instr:* Xylophone, glockenspiel, vibraphone, marimba																											4			4	Dobli
VELLONES, PIERRE (1889–1939)																															
Trio					1								1		1																Duran
Trio (alt. inst.)													1		1	1															Duran
VELTEN, KLAUS (1937–)																															
4 Sudamerikanische Tänze															1	1		1	1												Bosse
Variationen über ein altes Volkslied															1	1		1	1												Bosse
VERDI, GIUSEPPE (1813–1901)																															
Quartetto	1873	e		2	1	1																									VarPb
VERESS, SANDOR (1907–)																															
Quartetto I	1931			2	1	1																									Suvin
Quartetto II	1937			2	1	1																									Suvin
Sonatina	1931															1		1	1												Suvin
Trio	1954			1	1	1																									Suvin
Trio (Tre quadri)	1962			1		1			1																						Suvin
VERETTI, ANTONIO (1900–1978)																															
Divertimento for Piano and Winds									1						1	1		1	1												Ricor
Elegie in friulano	1963			1								1						1										1			Ricor
VERRALL, JOHN (1908–)																															
3 Nocturnes	1987		15		1	1			1																						AmCom
Divertimento	1971		12												1			1	1												AmCom
Introduction, Variations, and Adagio	1974		14	1		1			1						1	1															AmCom
Nonette	1970		10	2	1	1									1	1		1	1		1										AmCom
Pastoral Elegy (solo oboe)	1970		7												1	1		3	1		1	1	3		1						AmCom
Quintet	1953		17	2	1	1			1																						AmCom
Serenade															1	1		1	1		1										Press
Serenade No. 2															1	1		1	1		1										Press
String Quartet No. 4	1949			2	1	1																									Press
VERRALL, PAMELA M. (1915–)																															
Old English Music *Comment:* A second clarinet may replace oboe																1		1	1												Oxfor
VIERNE, LOUIS (1870–1937)																															
Marche triomphale for Napoleon *Unus Instr:* 3 Timpani	1921		9								1											3	3				1			3	Salab
VIERU, ANATOLE (1926–)																															
Iossef et ses frères *Unus Instr:* Contrabassoon	1979		17										1		1	1		1	2		1	1	1				2			1	Salab
Museum Music for Harpsichord *Unus Instr:* Japanese bells and maracas	1968		12	7	2	2	1			1																	1			2	Salab
Steps of Silence	1966		16	2	1	1																					1				Salab
VIEUXTEMPS, HENRI (1820–1881)																															
Duo brillant *Comment:* Viola can replace violin				1		1			1																						BScho

	Year Composed or Published	Key	Duration	Violin	Viola	Cello	Double Bass	Gamba	Piano	Harpsicord	Organ	Guitar	Harp	Recorder	Flute/Piccolo	Oboe	English Horn	Clarinet/Bass Clarinet	Bassoon/Contrabassoon	Saxophone	French Horn	Trumpet	Trombone	Bass Trombone	Tuba	Baritone	Percussion	Voice	Electronic Tape	Unusual Instruments	Publisher
VILLA-LOBOS, HEITOR (1887–1959)																															
Bachianas Brasileiras No. 5	1945		11			8																						S			AMP
Cançoes tipicas: Mokoce ce maka	1935				1	1									1	1	1	1	1									1			Eschi
Choros No. 3 ("Pica-Pao") *Comment:* May be performed with men's chorus	1925		6															1	1	1	3		1								Eschi
Choros No. 4 for 3 Horns and Trombone	1926		4																		3	1									Eschi
Choros No. 7 (Setemino) *Unus Instr:* Tam-tam	1927		10	1		1									1	1		1	1	1										1	Eschi
Divagação *Unus Instr:* Tambourine			2			1			1																		1			1	Eschi
Fantasie concertante *Unus Instr:* Clarinet in C			15						1									1	1											1	Eschi
Piano Trio No. 1	1911		20	1		1			1																						Eschi
Piano Trio No. 2	1916		20	1		1			1																						Eschi
Piano Trio No. 3	1929		25	1		1			1																						Eschi
Poema da criança e su mama	1923		6			1									1			1										1			Eschi
Quatuor	1928		20												1	1		1	1												Eschi
Quatuor (with women's chorus) *Unus Instr:* Celesta	1921		22										1		1					1							1	Ch		1	Eschi
Quintette en forme de choros	1928		12												1	1	1	1	1												Eschi
Quintette en forme de choros (alt. inst.)	1928		12												1	1		1	1		1										Eschi
Quintette instrumental	1957		20	1	1	1							1		1																Eschi
Sextuor mystique *Unus Instr:* Celesta	1917		15									1	1		1			1		1							1			1	Eschi
String Quartet No. 1	1915			2	1	1																									Peer
String Quartet No. 2	1915		23	2	1	1																									Eschi
String Quartet No. 3	1916		20	2	1	1																									Eschi
String Quartet No. 4	1917		20	2	1	1																									AMP
String Quartet No. 5	1931		22	2	1	1																									AMP
String Quartet No. 6	1938		24	2	1	1																									AMP
String Quartet No. 7	1942			2	1	1																									AMP
String Quartet No. 8	1944			2	1	1																									Ricor
String Quartet No. 9	1945			2	1	1																									Peer
String Quartet No. 10	1946			2	1	1																									Peer
String Quartet No. 11	1948			2	1	1																									Peer
String Quartet No. 12			25	2	1	1																									AMP
String Quartet No. 13	1952			2	1	1																									Eschi
String Quartet No. 14	1953			2	1	1																									Eschi
String Quartet No. 15	1954			2	1	1																									Eschi
String Quartet No. 16	1955			2	1	1																									Eschi
String Quartet No. 17	1958			2	1	1																									Eschi
String Trio	1940		20	1	1	1																									Eschi
Trio			10													1		1	1												Eschi
VINE, CARL (1954–)																															
Aria *Unus Instr:* Celesta	1984		9			1			1						1												1	1		1	Chest
Cafe concertino	1984		11	1	1	1			1						1			1													Chest
Elegy	1985		8			1			1						1								1				1				Chest
Miniature III	1983		12						1						1										1		1				Chest
Miniature IV	1988		15	1	1	1			1						1			1													Chest
String Quartet No. 2	1984		15	2	1	1																									Chest
VINTER, GILBERT (1909–1969)																															
2 Miniatures	1950		7												1	1		1	1		1										Boose
VIOLETTE, ANDREW (1953–)																															
Chaconne *Unus Instr:* Marimba	1984		17	1																							2			1	AmCom

	Year Composed or Published	Key	Duration	Violin	Viola	Cello	Double Bass	Gamba	Piano	Harpsicord	Organ	Guitar	Harp	Recorder	Flute/Piccolo	Oboe	English Horn	Clarinet/Bass Clarinet	Bassoon/Contrabassoon	Saxophone	French Horn	Trumpet	Trombone	Bass Trombone	Tuba	Baritone	Percussion	Voice	Electronic Tape	Unusual Instruments	Publisher
VIOLETTE, ANDREW *(continued)*																															
Quintet	1983		25	1		1			1						1			1													AmCom
Worldes Blis *Unus Instr:* 4 Timpani	1982		25																		1	3	2				4			4	AmCom
VIVIER, CLAUDE (1948–1983)																															
3 Airs pour un opera imaginaire	1982		15	2	1	1	1								2	2		1			1						1	S			Salab
Wo bist du, Licht?	1981		23	11	4	3	2																				1				Salab
VOGEL, ERNST (1926–)																															
Klaviertrio				1		1			1																						Dobli
Musik für Blechbläser und Schlagzeug																					4	2	3		1		1				Dobli
Oktett				2	1	1	1											1	1		1										Dobli
Sonate									1							1		1													Dobli
Spiel und Zwischenspiel											1										1	2	1	1							Dobli
Spiel und Zwischenspiel (with tuba)											1										1	2	1		1						Dobli
Streichquartett 2				2	1	1																									Dobli
VOGEL, ROGER C. (1947–)																															
Trio	1985		14		1	1			1																						AmCom
VOGEL, WLADIMIR (1896–1984)																															
Concertino				2	1	1									1																Kunze
Dal quaderno di Francine	1957								1						1													S			Suvin
Ticinella	1941														1	1		1	1	1											Suvin
Trio (1975)	1975														1			1	1												Kunze
Varietudes (12)	1942			1		1									1			1													Suvin
VOGT, GUSTAV (1781–1870)																															
Adagio religioso																2	1														Billa
Adagio religioso (version 2)																		2		1											Billa
VOGT, HANS (1911–)																															
Dialogue	1960			1		1			1																						BoteB
Streichquartett 1	1960			2	1	1																									BoteB
Streichquartett 2	1975			2	1	1																									BoteB
Streichquartett 3 (alla fantasia)	1977			2	1	1																									BoteB
Streichquartett 4	1982			2	1	1																									BoteB
VOLANS, KEVIN (1949–)																															
Chevron	1989			2	1	1			1						2	1		2	1		1	1		1							Chest
Hunting: Gathering (String Quartet 2)	1987		20	2	1	1																									Chest
Into Darkness	1986		13	1		1			1									2									2				Chest
Notes d'un peintre	1987		5	2	1	1																									Chest
The Songlines (String Quartet No. 3)	1988			2	1	1																									Chest
Walking Song *Comment:* Needed: 2 Hand clappers	1984		8							1					1																Chest
White Man Sleeps	1982		22					1		2																	1				Chest
White Man Sleeps	1986		24	2	1	1																									Chest
VOSS, FRIEDRICH (1930–)																															
Capriccioso (solo flute)	1965		7												2	1		1	1												Breit
Klaviertrio	1957		10	1		1			1																						Breit
Serenade	1959		10	1									1		1																Breit
Streichquartett 1	1906		10	2	1	1																									Breit
VRANICKY, ANTONIN (1761–1820)																															
Lovecke pochody (Hunter's March) *Unus Instr:* Contrabassoon																2		2	3		2	2								1	Artia
VRANICKY, PAVEL (1756–1808)																															
Klaviertrio		G		1		1			1																						Artia
VUSTIN, ALEXANDER (1943–)																															
Nocturnes *Unus Instr:* Vibraphone, xylophone			12	1			1		1		1		2			1		1				1					3	1	1	2	VAAP

	Year Composed or Published	Key	Duration	Violin	Viola	Cello	Double Bass	Gamba	Piano	Harpsicord	Organ	Guitar	Harp	Recorder	Flute/Piccolo	Oboe	English Horn	Clarinet/Bass Clarinet	Bassoon/Contrabassoon	Saxophone	French Horn	Trumpet	Trombone	Bass Trombone	Tuba	Baritone	Percussion	Voice	Electronic Tape	Unusual Instruments	Publisher
WAGGONER, ANDREW (1960–)																															
Going . . . *Unus Instr:* Contrabassoon	1987		10	1			1								1				1											1	AmCom
WAGHALTER, IGNATZ (1882–1949)																															
Quartet, Op 3	1913	D		2	1	1																									Simro
WAGNER, RICHARD (1813–1883)																															
Adagio for clarinet				2	2	1												1													Breit
Quartet Movement (reconstructed by Gerald Abraham)				2	1	1																									Oxfor
Siegfried Idyll	1870			2	1	1	1								1	1		2			2	1									Breit
WAHREN, KARL H. (1933–)																															
Increase *Unus Instr:* Marimba	1971										1				1												1			1	BoteB
L'art pour l'art	1968					1			1						1																BoteB
Messing-Klange	1978										1												4								BoteB
Soundscreen (Klangraster)	1975														1												2				BoteB
Tango noir	1978		12	1	1	1	1								1			1									1				BoteB
WALKER, JAMES (1929–)																															
Woodwind Quintet			19												1	1		1	1		1										Schir
WALLACH, JOELLE (1929–)																															
Quartet Movement	1967		7	1		1									1			1													AmCom
WALTER, JOHANNES (1964–)																															
Musik für Cello						1																					2				Feedb
WALTON, WILLIAM (1902–1983)																															
Anniversary Fanfare *Unus Instr:* Timpani	1973		1																			9	4	3			2			1	Oxfor
Façade Entertainment *Voice:* Reciter. Second cello is optional	1922		45			2									1			1		1		1					1	1			Oxfor
Façade Suite (arr. Palmer)						2									1			1		1		1					1				Oxfor
Façade 2 (8 new sections) *Voice:* Reciter. Second cello is optional			12			2									1			1		1		1					1	1			Oxfor
Fanfare for a Great Occasion (adapted Sargent)			1																		4	3	3		1		3				Oxfor
Introduction to the British National Anthem *Comment:* As many snare drums as possible																						3	3								Oxfor
Pieces, 6 (arr. de Jongh), Set 1																						2	2								Oxfor
Pieces, 6 (arr. de Jongh), Set 2 *Comment:* Horn is optional																					1	3	3								Oxfor
Quartet for Piano and Strings	1918		27	1	1	1			1																						Oxfor
A Queen's Fanfare	1959		1																			8	2	2							Oxfor
String Quartet	1922			2	1	1																									Oxfor
String Quartet	1947	a	29	2	1	1																									Oxfor
WALZEL, LEOPOLD M. (1902–1970)																															
Parallelen-Quintet, Op 27				1	1	1	1		1																						Dobli
Quintetto impetuoso, Op 42															1	1		1	1		1										Dobli
Trio passionato, Op 32				1	1	1																									Dobli
WANGENHEIM, VOLKER (1928–)																															
Klangspiel II *Comment:* E♭ and bass clarinets and sax ad lib. Celesta may replace piano	1972		15			1			1						1			1									1				Peter
WARD, ROBERT (1917–)																															
String Quartet No. 1	1965			2	1	1																									ECSch

	Year Composed or Published	Key	Duration	Violin	Viola	Cello	Double Bass	Gamba	Piano	Harpsicord	Organ	Guitar	Harp	Recorder	Flute/Piccolo	Oboe	English Horn	Clarinet/Bass Clarinet	Bassoon/Contrabassoon	Saxophone	French Horn	Trumpet	Trombone	Bass Trombone	Tuba	Baritone	Percussion	Voice	Electronic Tape	Unusual Instruments	Publisher
WARFIELD, GERALD A. (1940–)																															
Fantasy Quintet	1978		10	1		1			1						1			1													AmCom
Fantasy Quintet (alt. inst.)	1978		10	1		1			1							1		1													AmCom
Romances and Metamorphoses	1978		12	1		1			1						1			1													AmCom
Romances and Metamorphoses (alt. inst.)	1978		10	1		1			1							1		1													AmCom
WARLOCK, PETER (1894–1930)																															
As Ever I Saw	1918			2	1	1																						1			Boose
Balulalow	1919			2	1	1																						S			Oxfor
The First Mercy	1927			2	1	1																						1			Boose
Mourn No Moe	1919			2	1	1																						1			Boose
My Gostly Fader	1918			2	1	1																						1			Boose
Sleep	1922			2	1	1																						B			Oxfor
Take, O Take Those Lips Away	1917			2	1	1																						1			Boose
WASHBURN, ROBERT (1928–)																															
3 Pieces for 3 Woodwinds *Comment:* A bass clarinet may replace bassoon															1			1	1												Oxfor
5 Miniatures for 5 Brasses	1980		12																		1	2	2								Boose
Concertino for Brass and Wind Quintets															1	1		1	1		2	2	1		1						Oxfor
Quintet for Brass																					1	2	1		1						Oxfor
Serenade for Strings	1966			2	1	1																									Oxfor
String Quartet				2	1	1																									Oxfor
Suite for Strings				2	1	1																									Oxfor
Woodwind Quintet															1	1		1	1		1										Oxfor
WEAIT, CHRISTOPHER (1939–)																															
Marches (4) from the American Revolution *Comment:* Alternative instruments: Piccolo, English horn, clarinet																2			2												McGMa
WEBER, ALAIN (1930–)																															
Liminaire																					1	2	1		1						Billa
Quintette	1954														1	1		1	1		1										Leduc
Variantes	1964								1																		2				Leduc
WEBER, BEN (1916–1979)																															
Aubade	1949		4			1							1		1																AmCom
Ballet (Pool of Darkness), Op 26	1950		15	1		1			1						1				1			1									AmCom
Chamber Fantasie (solo violin), Op 51 *Unus Instr:* Bass clarinet	1959		18			2	1						1					3												1	AmCom
Concertino, Op 11b	1941		7	1		1												1													AmCom
Concerto (solo piano), Op 32	1950		18			1			1						1	1		1	1		1										AmCom
Image in the Snow (film score) *Unus Instr:* Celesta	1952		20			1																	1							1	AmCom
Serenade, Op 39	1953		9			1				1					1	1															AmCom
Serenade (alt. inst.), Op 39	1953			1	1	1			1																						AmCom
Variations, Op 11a	1941		6	1		1			1									1													AmCom
WEBER, CARL MARIA VON (1786–1826)																															
Adagio and Rondo																		2	2		2										MusRa
Clarinet Quintet, Op 34	1815	B♭		2	1	1												1													VarPb
Concertino (10 Winds)		C														1		4	2		2	1									MusRa
Concertino (12 winds)															1	1		4	2		2	1	1								Kunze
Introduction, Theme, and Variations				2	1	1												1													Liena
March	1826														1	2		2	2		2	2	1								VarPb
Natur und Liebe (Cantata), Op 61 *Voices:* 2 Sopranos, 2 tenors, 2 basses	1818								1																			6			VarPb

	Year Composed or Published	Key	Duration	Violin	Viola	Cello	Double Bass	Gamba	Piano	Harpsicord	Organ	Guitar	Harp	Recorder	Flute/Piccolo	Oboe	English Horn	Clarinet/Bass Clarinet	Bassoon/Contrabassoon	Saxophone	French Horn	Trumpet	Trombone	Bass Trombone	Tuba	Baritone	Percussion	Voice	Electronic Tape	Unusual Instruments	Publisher
WEBER, CARL MARIA VON *(continued)*																															
Piano Quartet, Op 8	1809	B♭		1	1	1			1																						VarPb
Piano Trio, Op 63	1819	g		1		1			1																						VarPb
Quintet, Op 34		B♭		2	1	1												1													VarPb
Scottish Folk Songs (10)	1825			1		1			1						1													1			Manus
Tema con variazioni							1								1			4	2		2	1	1								MusRa
Waltz with Trio		E♭													1			2	2		2	1									Kunze
Waltzes, 6															1			4	2		2		1								MusRa
Wo nehm' ich Blumen her?	1823								1																			3			VarPb
WEBERN, ANTON VON (1883–1945)																															
Bagatelles (6), Op 9	1913			2	1	1																									Univе
Canons (5, on Latin texts), Op 16 *Unus Instr:* Bass clarinet	1924																	2										S		1	Unive
Concerto for 9 Instruments, Op 24	1934			1	1				1						1	1		1			1	1	1								Unive
Geistliche Lieder (5), Op 15 *Voice:* High soprano. *Unus Instr:* Bass clarinet. Violin doubles on viola	1922		5	1	1								1		1			1				1						1		1	Unive
Konzert, Op 24	1934		12	1	1				1						1	1		1			1	1	1								Unive
Lieder (2, poems by Rilke), Op 8 *Voice:* Medium. *Unus Instr:* Bass clarinet, celesta	1910			1	1	1							1					1			1	1						1		2	Unive
Lieder (3), Op 18 *Unus Instr:* Eb clarinet	1925											1						1										1		1	Unive
Lieder (6, poems by Trakl), Op 14 *Unus Instr:* Bass clarinet	1921			1		1												2										H		1	Unive
Piano Quintet (one movement)	1907			2	1	1			1																						Boelk
Pieces (5) for String Quartet, Op 5	1909			2	1	1																									Unive
Quartett, Op 22	1930			1					1									1		1											Unive
Streichquartett (one movement), Op 28	1905			2	1	1																									Unive
Streichquartett, Op 28	1938			2	1	1																									Unive
Streichtrio, Op 20	1927			1	1	1																									Unive
Traditional Rhymes (3), Op 17 *Unus Instr:* Bass clarinet	1925			1														2										1		1	Unive
WEHRLI, WERNER (1892–1944)																															
Trio, Op 11				1					1												1										Amade
WEIGL, KARL (1881–1949)																															
Capriccio (Intermezzo No. 2)	1947			2	1	1																									Blake
Interrupted Serenading (Intermezzo No. 3)	1947			2	1	1																									Blake
Short Pieces, 4	1941		8						1									4													AmCom
Short Pieces, 4 (alt. inst.)	1941		8	4					1																						AmCom
Trio	1939		26		1	1			1																						AmCom
WEIGL, VALLY (1894–1982)																															
Brief Encounters (Wind Quartet)	1979		21													1		1	1		1										AmCom
Brief Encounters (Wind Quartet alt. inst.)	1979		21														1		1		1	1									AmCom
Brief Encounters (wind trio)	1979		21													1		1			1										AmCom
Cherry Tree (Version II, with flute)	1968		3						1						1						1										AmCom
Cherry Tree (Version II, with oboe)	1968		3						1							1					1										AmCom
Contemplation, from Trialogue	1978		4		1				1						1																AmCom
Dance Fragments, from Trialogue	1978		4		1				1						1																AmCom
Dear Earth	1956		14	1		1			1												1										AmCom
Echoes from Poems by Patricia Benton *Comment:* Version exists for French horn instead of clarinet	1956		14	1					1									1													AmCom

	Year Composed or Published	Key	Duration	Violin	Viola	Cello	Double Bass	Gamba	Piano	Harpsicord	Organ	Guitar	Harp	Recorder	Flute/Piccolo	Oboe	English Horn	Clarinet/Bass Clarinet	Bassoon/Contrabassoon	Saxophone	French Horn	Trumpet	Trombone	Bass Trombone	Tuba	Baritone	Percussion	Voice	Electronic Tape	Unusual Instruments	Publisher
WEIGL, VALLY *(continued)*																															
Enigma	1979		5		1				1						1																AmCom
Enigma (alt. inst.)	1978		5		1								1		1																AmCom
Escapade, from Trialogue	1978		4		1				1						1																AmCom
Lyrical Suite *Voice:* Medium			14			1			1						1													1			Peter
Lyrical Suite (alt. inst.) *Voice:* Medium			14			1			1									1										1			Peter
New England Suite	1953		18			1			1									1													AmCom
Old Time Divertimento	1977		4																1		1	1									AmCom
Old Time Divertimento (alt. inst.)	1977		4															1	1		1										AmCom
Petite Suite	1981		11												1	1			1		1										AmCom
Prelude for Three, from Trialogue	1978		4		1				1						1																AmCom
Trialogue (with harp)	1978		16		1								1		1																AmCom
Trialogue (with piano)	1978		16		1				1						1																AmCom
WEILL, KURT (1900–1950)																															
Ballade von Der Sexuellen Hörigkeit *Unus Instr:* Bass clarinet, vibraphone, accordion	1928		3	1	1	1	1											2									1			3	Unive
Berlin im Licht-Song *Unus Instr:* Banjo	1928		5	1																3		2	2					H		1	Unive
Frauentanz, Op 10	1924				1										1			1	1		1							S			Unive
Le Grand Lustucru (arr. Berio) *Unus Instr:* Piccolo	1934		3	1	1	1	1								1	1		2	1			2					1	M		1	Unive
Konzert für Violine, Op 12	1924		33	1			1								2	1		2	2		2	1					1				Unive
Der neue Orpheus, Op 15	1925		18	1	1	1	1						1		2	2		2	2			2	2				1	S			Unive
Öl-Musik (arr. Drew)	1928		4	1					1						1					1		1	1				5	1			Unive
Pantomime aus "Der Protagonist"	1925														2			2	2			2									Unive
Streichquartett, Op 8	1923			2	1	1																									Unive
Surabaya Johnny (arr. Berio)	1929		5	1	1	1	1					1			1			1				1					1	M			Unive
Vom Tod im Wald, Op 23 *Voice:* Bass. *Unus Instr:* Contrabassoon	1927		8															2	2		2	2	1	1				1		1	Unive
WEINER, STANLEY (1925–)																															
Suite for Brass Quintet																					1	2	1		1						Billa
Trio No. 2																					1	1	1								Billa
WEINGARDEN, LOUIS (1943–)																															
Fantasy and Funeral Music						1			2																		1				Oxfor
Things Heard and Seen in Summer				1		1			1																						Oxfor
WEINGARTNER, FELIX VON (1863–1942)																															
Klaviersextett, Op 33		e		2	1	1	1		1																						Breit
Octett		G		2	1	1			1									1	1		1										Unive
Quintett, Op 40		C		2		1										2															Breit
Quintett, Op 50		g		1	1	1			1									1													Breit
Serenata				2	1	1	1																								Ricor
Streichquartett, Op 24		d		2	1	1																									Breit
Streichquartett, Op 26		f		2	1	1																									Breit
Streichquartett, Op 34		F		2	1	1																									Breit
Streichquartett, Op 62	1918	D		2	1	1																									Unive
WEINSTEIN, MICHAEL H. (1960–)																															
"As You Like It" *Voices:* 2 Tenors and 2 baritones	1982		4						1												1							4			Micha
Brass Quintet	1986		12																		2	2	1								Micha
Elegy	1983		6						1												1							T			Micha
Piano Quintet	1985		18	1		1			1									1			1										Micha
Piano Trio	1987		15	1		1			1																						Micha

	Year Composed or Published	Key	Duration	Violin	Viola	Cello	Double Bass	Gamba	Piano	Harpsicord	Organ	Guitar	Harp	Recorder	Flute/Piccolo	Oboe	English Horn	Clarinet/Bass Clarinet	Bassoon/Contrabassoon	Saxophone	French Horn	Trumpet	Trombone	Bass Trombone	Tuba	Baritone	Percussion	Voice	Electronic Tape	Unusual Instruments	Publisher
WEINSTEIN, MICHAEL H. *(continued)*																															
Quartet for Trombone and String Trio	1987		10	1	1	1																	1								Micha
Waldeck Quartet	1983								1						1						1							1			Micha
"Wedding Bells"	1983		5																		1		1					T			Micha
Woodwind Quintet	1987		13												1	1		1	1		1										Micha
WEIR, JUDITH (1954–)																															
Distance and Enchantment	1989		12	1		1			1																						Chest
Lovers, Learners, and Libations *Voices:* Mezzo-soprano, tenor. *Unus Instr:* Vielle, rebec	1987		16										1	1														2		2	Chest
The Romance of Count Arnaldos	1989		5		1	1	1											2										S			Chest
Sederunt principes *Unus Instr:* Xylophone	1987		10	3	2	1	1		1				1		1	1		2	1		1		1				1			1	Chest
String Quartet	1990		13	2	1	1																									Chest
WEISBERG, ARTHUR (1931–)																															
Clarinet Quintet	1986		17	2	1	1												1													AmCom
Horn Quintet	1976		14	2	1	1															1										AmCom
Piano Quintet	1988		17	2	1	1			1																						AmCom
Trio	1985		13		1	1			1																						AmCom
WEISGALL, HUGO (1912–)																															
Holiday Dance No. 1 (Hanukkah)															1	1		1	1		1										Press
Lines															1	1		1	1												Press
Pastorale															1	1		1	1								1				Press
WEISMANN, JULIUS (1879–1950)																															
Streichquartett, Op 14	1906	F		2	1	1																									Rahte
WEISS, MANFRED (1935–)																															
Erfüllund der Zeiten	1982					1			1																			B			DeutV
Klaviertrio 2	1973			1		1			1																						DeutV
Streichquartett	1965			2	1	1																									DeutV
Stücke, 4	1972			2	1	1																									DeutV
WELLESZ, EGON (1885–1974)																															
Oktett, Op 67	1949			2	1	1	1											1	1		1										Dobli
Pastorale *Unus Instr:* Triangle			5	2		1	1								1	1				1							1			1	Unive
Sonette der Elisabeth Barrett-Browning, Op 52	1934		24	2	1	1																						S			Unive
Streichquartett 6, Op 64	1947			2	1	1																									Dobli
Streichquartett 7, Op 66	1948			2	1	1																									Dobli
Streichquartett 9, Op 97	1966			2	1	1																									Dobli
Stücke (4) für Streichquartett, Op 103				2	1	1																									Dobli
Stücke (4) für Streichquintett, Op 109				2	2	1																									Dobli
Stücke (4) für Streichtrio, Op 105				1	1	1																									Dobli
WELLMAN, SAMUEL (1951–)																															
Suite	1984		18	1									1					1					1								AmCom
WENZEL, EBERHARD (1896–1982)																															
Nun freut euch, lieben Christen gmein	1978										1											2	2								Bären
Sollt ich meinem Gott nicht singen	1974										1											2	2								Bären
Sonatine für Bläser und Orgel	1977										1											2	2								Merse
Weihnachtskonzert	1976										1											2	3								Bären
WENZEL, HANS J. (1939–)																															
Streichquartett 2	1969			2	1	1																									DeutV
Streichquartett 3	1970			2	1	1																									DeutV

	Year Composed or Published	Key	Duration	Violin	Viola	Cello	Double Bass	Gamba	Piano	Harpsicord	Organ	Guitar	Harp	Recorder	Flute/Piccolo	Oboe	English Horn	Clarinet/Bass Clarinet	Bassoon/Contrabassoon	Saxophone	French Horn	Trumpet	Trombone	Bass Trombone	Tuba	Baritone	Percussion	Voice	Electronic Tape	Unusual Instruments	Publisher
WERNER, FRITZ (1898–)																															
Concertino						1			1						1																Duran
WERNER, JEAN-JACQUES (1935–)																															
Trio d'anches																1		1	1												Billa
WERNER, JOSEF (1837–1922)																															
Elégie, Op 21					1	3																									Amade
Quartet, Op 6					1	3																									Amade
WERNERT, WOLFGANG (1936–)																															
Psalm 116 *Unus Instr:* Vibraphone															1												1	S		1	Bosse
WESTERGAARD, SVEND (1922–)																															
Quartetto per archi, Op 28	1966		17	2	1	1																									Hanse
WETZ, RICHARD (1875–1935)																															
Quartet No. 2, Op 49	1924			2	1	1																									Simro
WETZLAR, HORST (1936–)																															
Volkslieder (8) im einfachen Bläsersatz	1973																					2	2								Merse
WHITNEY, JOHN C. (1942–)																															
Junk Food Blues				2	1	1																									Press
WHITTENBERG, CHARLES (1927–)																															
Variations for Nine			14	1			1								1	1		1	1		1	1	1								Peter
WIDOR, CHARLES M. (1844–1937)																															
Quatuor, Op 66		a		1	1	1			1																						Duran
WIENHORST, RICHARD W. (1920–)																															
Divertimento	1958		10												2												1				AmCom
Intradas (6) for Chamber Instruments	1984		6												3	1		2	1			3	1		2						AmCom
WIGGLESWORTH, FRANK (1918–)																															
After Summer Music	1983		15		1							1			1																AmCom
Earth Smoke and Blazing Stars	1985		6												1	1		1			1										AmCom
Serenade	1952		10		1							1			1																AmCom
WILBY, PHILIP (1949–)																															
"and I move around the Cross . . . "	1985		8												2	2		2	2		2										Chest
Classic Images	1988		12																		1	2	2								Chest
Easter Wings	1988		4		1	1	1											2										S			Chest
Et surrexit Christus	1979		65	1	1	1			1		1				1			2										S			Chest
Green Man Dancing	1988		10												1	1		1	1		1										Chest
WILDBERGER, JACQUES (1922–)																															
Double Refrain *Unus Instr:* Bass flute	1972		15									1			1		1												2	1	Breit
In My End Is My Beginning *Voices:* Soprano and tenor. *Unus Instr:* Celesta	1964		14		1	1	1		1	1			1		1	1		1	1		1	1					2	2		1	Breit
Quartett	1967		13						1				1		1	1															Breit
WILDGANS, FRIEDRICH (1913–1965)																															
Festive Music for 12 Brass Instruments																						4	6		2						Dobli
Kleine Stücke (3)				1	1	1																									Dobli
Kleines Kammertrio																1	1		1												Dobli
Kleines Trio	1961														1			1	1												Dobli

	Year Composed or Published	Key	Duration	Violin	Viola	Cello	Double Bass	Gamba	Piano	Harpsicord	Organ	Guitar	Harp	Recorder	Flute/Piccolo	Oboe	English Horn	Clarinet/Bass Clarinet	Bassoon/Contrabassoon	Saxophone	French Horn	Trumpet	Trombone	Bass Trombone	Tuba	Baritone	Percussion	Voice	Electronic Tape	Unusual Instruments	Publisher
WILLIAMS, JOHN (1932–)																															
The Cantina Band *Unus Instr:* Vibraphone, xylophone							1		1									1		3		1					5			2	WrnBr
WILLIS, RICHARD (1819–1900)																															
String Quartet No. 2				2	1	1																									Press
WILSON, DONALD (1937–)																															
Doubles			7		1		1											1	1												Peter
Figuration	1981					1			1									1													Peter
Sett *** *Comment:* For 3 low instruments, 1-3 low voices	1963		10																									B			AmCom
Stabile II *** *Comment:* For 2 or more high and 1 or more low instruments	1965		19																												AmCom
WIMBERGER, GERHARD (1923–)																															
Phantasie für 8 Spieler	1982			2	1	1	1											1	1		1										Bären
Songs, 4 *Voice:* Medium	1970						1		1																		1	1			Bären
Streichquartett	1978			2	1	1																									Bären
WINBECK, HEINZ (1946–)																															
Blick in den Strom	1981			2	1	2																									Bären
Poco a poco . . .	1974			1	1	1			1																						Bären
Streichquartett 2 (Tempi notturni)	1979			2	1	1																									Bären
Streichquartett 3	1984			2	1	1																									Bären
WINSLOW, WALTER K. (1947–)																															
The Bells of Eola	1977		17		1		1																				3				AmCom
Divertimento *Unus Instr:* Celesta	1975		25	1		1									1				1								1			1	AmCom
Nachtwanderlied *Unus Instr:* Celesta	1970		18	1		1	1						1		1			1			1						2			1	AmCom
Sinfonia for Eleven *Unus Instr:* Vibraphone, timpani	1968		22						1						2				1		1	1					5			2	AmCom
Sylvan Dances	1987		14	1		1	1						1					1			1						1				AmCom
Unified Field	1979		15	1		1			1									1													AmCom
WINTER, PETER (1754–1825)																															
10 Divertimenti				2	1	1																									Hug
Festfanfare *Unus Instr:* Timpani																						3	3		1		1			1	Peter
WIREN, DAG (1905–)																															
String Quartet, Op 9	1939			2	1	1																									Nordi
WITKOWSKI, GEORGES M. (1867–1943)																															
Quatuor	1902			2	1	1																									Duran
WITTINGER, ROBERT (1945–)																															
Compensazioni, Op 9	1967		11	1	1										1	1		1			1	1	1								Breit
Concerto for Oboe and Harp, Op 24	1972			8	3	3	1						1			1															Breit
Costruzioni, Op 8	1966		11	2	1	1																									Breit
Streichquartett 3, Op 20	1970		11	2	1	1																									Breit
Tendenze, Op 14 *Unus Instr:* Celesta. Piano doubles on celesta and harpsichord	1969		11		1				1	1																	1			1	Breit
Tensioni, Op 15	1970		9												1	1		1	1		1										Breit
Tolleranza, Op 16 *Unus Instr:* Celesta	1969		7													1											1			1	Breit
WOHLGEMUTH, GERARD (1920–)																															
String Quartet No. 1				2	1	1																									Peter
String Quartet No. 2 (Doelauer Quartet)				2	1	1																									Peter
WOLF, HUGO (1860–1903)																															
Italian Serenade	1892			2	1	1																									VarPb

	Year Composed or Published	Key	Duration	Violin	Viola	Cello	Double Bass	Gamba	Piano	Harpsicord	Organ	Guitar	Harp	Recorder	Flute/Piccolo	Oboe	English Horn	Clarinet/Bass Clarinet	Bassoon/Contrabassoon	Saxophone	French Horn	Trumpet	Trombone	Bass Trombone	Tuba	Baritone	Percussion	Voice	Electronic Tape	Unusual Instruments	Publisher
WOLF, HUGO *(continued)*																															
Serenade	1887	G		1	1	1	1																								Stein
WOLFF, CHRISTIAN (1934–)																															
Bowery Preludes									1						1								1				1				Peter
Braverman Music *** *Comment:* For 4 or more players, and 1 or 2 pianos			25						1																						Peter
Changing the System *** *Comment:* For 8 or more players, some melody and some low instruments																															Peter
Digger Song (for J.C.'s 76th)				1	1	1																					1				Peter
Edges *** *Comment:* For any number of players and instruments																															Peter
Eisler Ensemble Pieces *Unus Instr:* Bass clarinet			11	1		1			1									1												1	Peter
Electric Spring I *Unus Instr:* Electric bass							1					1									1									1	Peter
Electric Spring II												2		1									1								Peter
Electric Spring II (alt. vers.)												2		1									1	1							Peter
Electric Spring III *Unus Instr:* Electric bass				1								1									1									E	Peter
Emma					1	1			1																						Peter
Exercises 15-18 *Comment:* For any number of instruments, including solos																															Peter
For 1, 2, or 3 People *** *Comment:* For any instruments	1964																														Peter
For 5 or 10 Players *** *Comment:* For any group of 5 or 10 players	1962																														Peter
For Morty *** *Unus Instr:* Glockenspiel, vibraphone									1																		2			2	Peter
I Like to Think of Harriet Tubman *** *Voice:* Female, with alto and low bass instruments			7																									1			Peter
In Between Pieces *** *Comment:* For any 3 players	1963																														Peter
Leaning Forward *Voices:* Soprano, baritone. *Unus Instr:* Bass clarinet						1												1										2		1	Peter
Lines *Comment:* Also for quartet of any stringed instruments				2	1	1																									Peter
Long Peace March *Unus Instr:* Contrabassoon					1	1	1								1	1		1		1	1		1				1			1	Peter
Nine *Unus Instr:* Celesta	1951					2			1						1			1			1	1	1							1	Peter
Pairs *** *Comment:* For 2, 4, 6, or 8 players, on any instruments																															Peter
Peace March 2			9			1			1						1			1									1				Peter
Peace March 3 (The Sun Is Burning)			8			1									1												1				Peter
Piano Trio			9	1		1			1																						Peter
Septet *** *Comment:* For 7 players (of any instruments)	1964																														Peter
String Quartet Exercises	1975			2	1	1																									Peter
Summer	1961			2	1	1																									Peter
Trio I	1951		5			1									1							1									Peter
Trio II *Comment:* Piano 4-hands									1																		1			1	Peter
WOLF-FERRARI, ERMANNO (1876–1948)																															
Kammersymphonie, Op 8	1903	B♭		2	1	1	1		1						1	1		1	1		1										Rahte

	Year Composed or Published	Key	Duration	Violin	Viola	Cello	Double Bass	Gamba	Piano	Harpsicord	Organ	Guitar	Harp	Recorder	Flute/Piccolo	Oboe	English Horn	Clarinet/Bass Clarinet	Bassoon/Contrabassoon	Saxophone	French Horn	Trumpet	Trombone	Bass Trombone	Tuba	Baritone	Percussion	Voice	Electronic Tape	Unusual Instruments	Publisher
WOLF-FERRARI, ERMANNO *(continued)*																															
Klaviertrio 1, Op 5	1930	D		1		1			1																						Leuck
Klaviertrio 2, Op 7	1901	F♯		1		1			1																						Rahte
Streichquartett, Op 23	1940	e		2	1	1																									Leuck
WÖLFL, JOSEPH (1773–1812)																															
Trio		B♭																2	1												Kunze
Trio		E♭																2	1												Kunze
WOLPE, STEFAN (1902–1972)																															
Piece for Trumpet and Seven Instruments	1971		14	1	1	1	1									1			1		1	1									Peter
WOLPERT, FRANZ A. (1917–1978)																															
Andante (Trauermusik), Op 8 No. 3	1948			2	1	1																									Breit
WOLSCHINA, REINHARD (1952–)																															
5 Caprichios	1973														1	1		1	1		1										DeutV
Pezzo capriccioso per trio	1974			1		1			1																						DeutV
WOOD, CHARLES (1866–1926)																															
Wind Quintet		F	20												1	1		1	1		1										Boose
WOOD, HUGH (1932–)																															
Horn Trio	1989		15	1					1												1										Chest
Piano Trio	1884		18	1		1			1																						Chest
String Quartet No. 1, Op 4	1962			2	1	1																									Chest
String Quartet No. 2, Op 13	1970			2	1	1																									Chest
String Quartet No. 3, Op 20	1978			2	1	1																									Chest
WOOD, JOSEPH (1915–)																															
Quintet	1954		16	2	1	1			1																						AmCom
WOOLLEN, RUSSELL (1923–)																															
Piano Quartet	1952	A	23	1	1	1			1																						AmCom
Quartet	1953		23	1	1	1									1																AmCom
Suite	1979		18	1	1	1									1																AmCom
Trio	1967		15		1	1			1																						AmCom
Triptych for Brass Choir			8																		2	4	3		1						Peter
WOYRSCH, FELIX VON (1860–1944)																															
String Quartet, Op 64	1929	E♭		2	1	1																									Simro
WRANITZKY, ANTON (1761–1820)																															
Trio		C														2	1														Kneus
WRIGHT, MAURICE (1949–)																															
Aulos	1972		12	4	2	2	1									1															AmCom
Music for 10 Players and Electronic Sounds *Unus Instr:* Tam-tam	1981		25	1	1	1	1		1						1	1		1	1								1		1	1	AmCom
Riverside *Unus Instr:* Bass clarinet	1981		12	1		1			1						1			1											1	1	AmCom
WUORINEN, CHARLES (1938–)																															
Ancestors	1978		9	2	2	2	1		1							1			1		1						1				Peter
Arabia Felix *Unus Instr:* Vibraphone	1973		11	1					1			1			1				1								1			1	Peter
Archaeopteryx *Unus Instr:* Marimba	1978		15						1						3			2			2			1	1					1	Peter
Archangel	1977		12	2	1	1																		1			1				Peter
Bassoon Variations *Unus Instr:* Timpani	1972		11										1						1								1			1	Peter
Bearbeitungen (Das Glogauer Liederbuch)	1962		7	1			1								1			1													Peter
Beast 708 *Unus Instr:* Vibraphone	1980			1			1		1						1			1			2		2				1			1	Peter
Canzona to the Memory of Igor Stravinsky *Unus Instr:* Vibraphone	1971		14	1	1	1	1		1				1		1		1	1	1			1					1			1	Peter

	Year Composed or Published	Key	Duration	Violin	Viola	Cello	Double Bass	Gamba	Piano	Harpsicord	Organ	Guitar	Harp	Recorder	Flute/Piccolo	Oboe	English Horn	Clarinet/Bass Clarinet	Bassoon/Contrabassoon	Saxophone	French Horn	Trumpet	Trombone	Bass Trombone	Tuba	Baritone	Percussion	Voice	Electronic Tape	Unusual Instruments	Publisher
WUORINEN, CHARLES *(continued)*																															
Chamber Concerto (solo cello)	1963		17	1	1	1	1		1						1		1	1	1								2				Peter
Chamber Concerto (solo flute) *Unus Instr:* Celesta	1964		14				1		1	1		1	1		1												4			1	Peter
Chamber Concerto (solo oboe) *Unus Instr:* Timpani	1965		17				1		1				1			1									1		5			1	Peter
Chamber Concerto (solo tuba) *Comment:* Percussionist plays 12 drums. *Unus Instr:* Contrabassoon	1970		17												4	1	1		2		4				1		1			1	Peter
Composition for Violin and 10 Inst. *Unus Instr:* Bass clarinet	1964		11	1			1		1							2		1			2		2				1			1	Peter
Concertino, for 15 Solo Instruments	1984		16				1								2	2		4	2		4										Peter
Divertimento	1982			2	1	1																									Peter
Doleful Dompe on Deborah's Departure	1986		4	1		1											1														Peter
Double Solo for Horn Trio	1985		14	1					1												1										Peter
Evolutio Transcripta	1961		9	4	2	2	1		1						1	1		1	1		1	1	1								Peter
Fanfare for Rutgers University	1986		2																		2	2	2								Peter
Fortune	1979		17	1		1			1									1													Peter
Harp Variations	1972		12	1	1	1							1																		Peter
Horn Trio	1981		11	1					1												1										Peter
Horn Trio Continued	1985		10	1					1												1										Peter
Hyperion	1975		16	1	1	1	1		1						1	1		1	1		1	1	1								Peter
Joan's	1979		6	1		1			1						1			1													Peter
Madrigali spirituale sopra salmo secundo *Voices:* Tenor and baritone	1960		5	2		1	1			1						2												2			Peter
Message to Denmark Hill	1970		26				1		1						1													B			Peter
Movement for Wind Quintet			4												1	1		1	1		1										Press
New York Notes *Comment:* Optional computer-generated track	1982		20	1		1			1						1			1									1			1	Peter
Octet	1962		14	1		1	1		1							1		1			1	1									McGMa
On Alligators	1972		17	2	1	1									1	1		1	1												Peter
Piano Trio	1983		11	1		1			1																						Peter
Politics of Harmony (A Masque) *Voices:* Alto, tenor, and bass	1967		35	2			2		1				2		2										2		1	3			Peter
Salve Regina (two settings by John Bull) *Unus Instr:* Timpani	1966		8	1	1	1			1						2	1	1	1			1	1	2				1			1	Peter
Songs (6) for 2 Voices *Voices:* Countertenor and tenor	1977		16	1		1										1			1		2							2			Peter
Speculum Speculi	1972		15				1		1						1	1		1									1				Peter
Spinoff *Unus Instr:* Congas	1983		7	1			1																				1			1	Peter
String Quartet No. 1	1971		21	2	1	1																									Peter
String Quartet No. 2	1979		19	2	1	1																									Peter
String Quartet No. 3	1987		26	2	1	1																									Peter
String Sextet	1989		20	2	2	2																									Peter
String Trio	1968		15	1	1	1																									Peter
Tashi (chamber version)	1975		31	1		1			1									1													Peter
Tiento sobre Cabezon	1961		4	1	1	1			1	1					1	1															Peter
Trio for Bass Instruments	1981		9				1																	1	1						Peter
Trio No. 1	1961		5			1			1						1																AmCom
Trio No. 2 (Piece for Stefan Wolpe)	1962		9			1			1						1																Peter
Trio No. 3	1973		17			1			1						1																Peter
Trombone Trio *Unus Instr:* Vibraphone, marimba	1985		8						1														1				1			2	Peter
Turetzky Pieces	1960		13				1								1			1													Peter
Wind Quintet	1977		15												1	1		1	1		1										Peter

	Year Composed or Published	Key	Duration	Violin	Viola	Cello	Double Bass	Gamba	Piano	Harpsicord	Organ	Guitar	Harp	Recorder	Flute/Piccolo	Oboe	English Horn	Clarinet/Bass Clarinet	Bassoon/Contrabassoon	Saxophone	French Horn	Trumpet	Trombone	Bass Trombone	Tuba	Baritone	Percussion	Voice	Electronic Tape	Unusual Instruments	Publisher
WUORINEN, CHARLES *(continued)*																															
The Winds	1977		15						1						1	1		2	1			1	1		1						Peter
Winter's Tale	1991		25	1	1	1			1									1			1							S			Peter
WÜRDINGER, E (?–)																															
Bläserquintett, Op 8															1	1		1	1		1										Dobli
WYNER, YEHUDI (1929–)																															
Passage	1983		11	1	1	1			1						1			1				1									AmCom
Romances, 2	1980		15	2	1	1			1																						AmCom
Serenade	1958		15		1	1			1						1						1	1	1								AmCom
Tanz and Maissele	1981		14	1		1			1									1													AmCom
XENAKIS, IANNIS (1922–)																															
Akanthos (for Soprano)	1977		11	2	1	1	1		1						1			1										S			Salab
Akea *Unus Instr:* Contrabasoon	1986		12	2	1	1			1																					1	Salab
À l'île de Gorée	1986		14	2	1	1	1								1	1		1	1		1	1	1								Salab
Anaktoria	1969		11	2	1	1	1											1	1		1										Salab
Analogues A and B	1959		7	6		2	1																						1		Salab
Aroura	1971		12	7	2	2	1																								Salab
Atrees *Unus Instr:* Bass clarinet	1960		15	2		1									1			2			1	1	1				1			1	Salab
Epei	1976		13				1										1	1				1	2								Salab
Jalons *Unus Instr:* Contrabassoon	1986		15	2	1	1	1						1		1	1		2	1		1	1	1		1					1	Salab
Khal Perr (Brass Quintet, Percussion) *Unus Instr:* Piccolo trumpet	1983		11																		1	2	1		1		1			1	Salab
Morsima-Amorsima	1962		11	1		1			1																						Boose
N'shima			17			1															2		2					M			Salab
Palimpsest	1979		11	2	2	1			1								1	1	1		1						1				Salab
Phlegra	1975		14	1	1	1	1								1	1		1	1		1	1	1								Salab
ST/4-1 080262	1962		12	2	1	1																									Boose
Syrmos	1959		14	12		4	2																								Salab
Thallein	1984		17	2	1	1	1		1						1	1		1	1		1	1	1				1				Salab
YANNATOS, JAMES (1929–)																															
5 Epigrams	1966		5	2	1	1																									AMP
YAVELOW, CHRISTOPHER J. (1950–)																															
Dimension-L	1973		9				1		1										1				1								AmCom
Fanfare	1973		2																			2					3				AmCom
Intercosmos *Comment:* A film is part of the performance	1972		6	1		1									1				1			1		1			5				AmCom
Introspections	1971		17	1	1	1												2	1			2	1								AmCom
Monday Morning Fantasy	1979		12												2	1	1	2			1		1								AmCom
Monday Morning Fantasy (alt. inst.)	1979		12												2	1		2	1	1	1										AmCom
Phi-lings	1976		14	1		1			1									1													AmCom
Quintet *Comment:* Quintet includes a reed instrument	1971		15	2	1	1																									AmCom
Ritual and Sabotage of the 20th Century	1982		19		1	1			1																						AmCom
Sermon *Comment:* Needed: slides, costumes	1973		10	3	3													1			1	3	1								AmCom
YSAŸE, THÉOPHILE (1865–1918)																															
Piano Quintet, Op 5	1913			2	1	1			1																						Salab
YTTREHUS, ROLV (1926–)																															
Music for Winds, Percussion, and Viola *Unus Instr:* Xylophone	1961		10		1				1						1			1			1	1	1				1			1	AmCom
Sextet	1974		14	1			1		1												1	1					1				Peter
YUN, ISANG (1917–)																															
Clarinet Quintet	1984			2	1	1												1													BoteB

	Year Composed or Published	Key	Duration	Violin	Viola	Cello	Double Bass	Gamba	Piano	Harpsicord	Organ	Guitar	Harp	Recorder	Flute/Piccolo	Oboe	English Horn	Clarinet/Bass Clarinet	Bassoon/Contrabassoon	Saxophone	French Horn	Trumpet	Trombone	Bass Trombone	Tuba	Baritone	Percussion	Voice	Electronic Tape	Unusual Instruments	Publisher
YUN, ISANG *(continued)*																															
Concertino *Unus Instr:* Accordion	1983			2	1	1																								1	BoteB
Harmonia for 16 Winds, Harp, Percussion *Comment:* English horn, 3rd clarinet ad lib. Piano may replace harp	1974		12										1		2	2	1	2	3		4		1				1				BoteB
Images	1968			1		1									1	1															BoteB
Klaviertrio	1975			1		1			1																						BoteB
Konzertante Figuren	1972		22	4	2	2	1								2	2		1	1		2	1	1								BoteB
Loyang *Comment:* Strings may be doubled	1962		14	1		1							1		1	1		1	1								2				BoteB
Memory	1974																										1	3			BoteB
Music for Seven Instruments	1959		12	1		1									1	1		1	1		1										BoteB
Novelette *Comment:* Cello can replace viola	1980			1	1								1		1																BoteB
Oktett *Unus Instr:* Bass clarinet	1978			2	2	1												1	1		1									1	BoteB
Piece concertante	1976		15	1	1	1	1		1						1			1									1				BoteB
Quintet No. 1	1986		24	2	1	1									1																BoteB
Rencontre	1986		13			1							1					1													BoteB
Sonata *Comment:* Cello can replace viola. *Unus Instr:* Oboe d'amore	1979				1								1			1														1	BoteB
Streichquartett 3	1960			2	1	1																									BoteB
ZADOR, EUGEN (1894–1977)																															
Suite for Winds																					4	4	3		1						Kunze
ZAFRED, MARIO (1922–)																															
III Trio	1955			1		1			1																						Ricor
Quintet	1952														1	1		1	1		1										Ricor
Sestetto	1967			2	2	2																									Ricor
ZAGORTSEV, VASILY (?–)																															
Dimensions				1					1									1		1		1									VAAP
ZAHLER, NOEL B. (1951–)																															
Trio	1984		9		1	1			1																						AmCom
ZBAR, MICHEL (1942–)																															
Apex II			8	7	2	2	1																								Ridea
La miniature de sable *Unus Instr:* Jazz bass			11				1																				1	1	1	1	Ridea
ZECHLIN, RUTH (1926–)																															
Aktionen für vier Solostreicher	1978			2	1	1																									DeutV
Hommages à PHL	1973			2	2	1																					2				DeutV
Katharsis	1981					1										1											1				DeutV
Trio	1957				1	1										1															Peter
ZELENKA, ISTVAN (1936–)																															
Chronologie *Unus Instr:* Bass clarinet															1	1		1	1		1									1	Dobli
ZELJENKA, ILJA (1932–)																															
Streichquartett	1963			2	1	1																									Artia
ZEMLINSKY, ALEXANDER VON (1871–1942)																															
Klarinetten Trio, Op 3 *Comment:* Violin may replace clarinet	1897	d				1			1									1													Simro
Quartett, Op 4	1898	A		2										1	1																Simro
Streichquartett 2, Op 15	1916	D		2	1	1																									Unive
Streichquartett 3, Op 19	1924			2	1	1																									Unive
ZENDER, HANS (1936–)																															
3 Rondels (after Mallarmé)	1961				1										1													A			BoteB

	Year Composed or Published	Key	Duration	Violin	Viola	Cello	Double Bass	Gamba	Piano	Harpsicord	Organ	Guitar	Harp	Recorder	Flute/Piccolo	Oboe	English Horn	Clarinet/Bass Clarinet	Bassoon/Contrabassoon	Saxophone	French Horn	Trumpet	Trombone	Bass Trombone	Tuba	Baritone	Percussion	Voice	Electronic Tape	Unusual Instruments	Publisher
ZENDER, HANS *(continued)*																															
Hölderin lesen *Comment:* Speaking voice ad lib	1979			2	1	1																						1			BoteB
Kantate *Unus Instr:* Alto flute	1980					1				1					1													A		1	BoteB
Lo-Shu I	1977					1									1												1				BoteB
Modelle *** *Comment:* Variable instrumentation	1973																														BoteB
Muji no kyo *Comment:* Voice and cello ad lib	1975		17	1		1			1						1													1			BoteB
Muji no kyo (alt. inst.) *Comment:* Voice and each instrument ad lib	1975		17			1			1						1													1			BoteB
Quartett	1965					1			1						1												1				BoteB
Quintett	1950														1	1		1	1		1										BoteB
Trifolium	1966					1			1						1																BoteB
ZIKA, RICHARD (1897–1947)																															
Streichquartett	1949			2	1	1																									Artia
ZILLIG, WINFRIED (1905–1963)																															
Lustspielsuite	1934														1	1		1	1		1										Bären
Streichquartett 1	1927			2	1	1																									Bären
Streichquartett 2	1944			2	1	1																									Bären
Tema con var. zu Goethes "Clavigo"				2	1	1																									Bären
Theater Music: Anni Nabels Boxschau *Unus Instr:* Harmonium											1							1				1					1			1	Bären
Theater Music: As You Like It				1	1										1	1															Bären
Theater Music: Camino Real *Unus Instr:* Mandolin							1		1			1										1	1				1			1	Bären
Theater Music: Comedy of Errors															1	1		1	1		1										Bären
Theater Music: Hamlet														1	1		1				1	1	1				1				Bären
Theater Music: Leonce und Lena				1	1	1									1																Bären
Theater Music: Life of Edward II *Unus Instr:* Harmonium											1					1	1				1	1	1							1	Bären
Theater Music: Penthesilea																					1	1	1		1		1				Bären
ZIMMERMANN, BERND-ALOIS (1918–1970)																															
Capricci (5) di Frescobaldi *Unus Instr:* Lute, oboe d'amore	1962							3				1		3		1						3	3							2	Bären
ZIMMERMANN, UDO (1943–)																															
Hymne an die Sonne	1977									1					1													S			DeutV
ZINN, WILLIAM (?–)																															
Kol Nidrei Memorial				2	1	1																									Press
ZINZADSE, SULCHAN F. (1925–)																															
String Quartet No. 7				2	1	1																									VAAP
ZIPP, FRIEDRICH (1914–)																															
Choralevorspiele																						2	2								Merse
Jauchzet Gott, alle Lände, Op 38 No. 2 *Comment:* Flute may replace violin				1							1																	H			Merse
O du lieber Augustin *Comment:* Double bass ad libitum	1980			2	1	1	1																								Merse
Sonata *Comment:* Percussion ad libitum	1977																					3	3		1						Bären
Wie schön blüht uns der Maien				2											1													2			Merse
Das Wort ward Fleisch, Op 38 No. 1 *Comment:* Flute may replace violin				1							1																	H			Merse
ZOEPHEL, KLAUS (1929–)																															
Woodwind Quintet															1	1		1	1		1										Peter

	Year Composed or Published	Key	Duration	Violin	Viola	Cello	Double Bass	Gamba	Piano	Harpsicord	Organ	Guitar	Harp	Recorder	Flute/Piccolo	Oboe	English Horn	Clarinet/Bass Clarinet	Bassoon/Contrabassoon	Saxophone	French Horn	Trumpet	Trombone	Bass Trombone	Tuba	Baritone	Percussion	Voice	Electronic Tape	Unusual Instruments	Publisher
ZONN, PAUL (1938–)																															
Canzoni, overo sonate (solo oboe) *Unus Instr:* Flügelhorn, vibraphone	1974		14				1		1				1		1	1						1	1				1			2	AmCom
Concerto (alt. inst.)	1970		17		1	1			1						1	1	1		1		2	1	1				3				AmCom
Concerto (solo viola)	1970		17		1	1			1						1	2			1		2	1	1				3				AmCom
Divertimento	1964		11				1																		1		2				AmCom
Divertimento No. 2	1965		12				1											1									3		1		AmCom
Liberata I *Unus Instr:* Bass clarinet	1968		10						1						1		1	1												1	AmCom
Liberata II	1968		18	1	1	1			1																						AmCom
Melos	1969		14		1	1			1																						AmCom
Microditties	1967		4	1	1	1										1															AmCom
One Slow Turn of the World *Unus Instr:* Bass clarinet	1971		11				1								1	1		1									1			1	AmCom
Periphrasis	1966		10			1										1		1													AmCom
Sonorum I *Unus Instr:* Vibraphone, marimba	1967		10	1	1		1								1	1		1			1	1	1				3			2	AmCom
The Voyage of Columbus (solo trumpet) *Unus Instr:* Flügelhorn	1975		14	1			1		1						1	1				1			1				2			1	AmCom
ZUPKO, RAMON (1932–)																															
Fantasies for Woodwind Quintet			20												1	1		1	1		1										Peter
Fixations *Comment:* Conductor needed	1974		15	1		1			1																				1		Peter
Pro and Contra Dances			20																		1	2	1		1						Peter
ZWILICH, ELLEN T. (1939–)																															
Double Quartet				4	2	2																									Press
String Trio				1	1	1																									Press

PART III

Master Quick-Reference Index

	3 Strings	4 Strings	5 Strings	3 Winds	4 Winds	5 Winds	3 Brass	4 Brass	5 Brass	2 Strings & Keyboard	3 Strings & Keyboard	4 Strings & Keyboard	2 Winds & Keyboard	3 Winds & Keyboard	4 Winds & Keyboard	Brass & Keyboard	Misc. Ensembles (3 to 5)	Strings, Wind Keyboard Trio	Strings, Wind Keyboard Quartets	Strings, Wind Keyboard Quintets	Sextets & Larger Ensembles	Ensemble with Guitar/Harp	Ensembles with Keyboard	Ensembles with Percussion	Ensembles with Unusual Instruments	Ensemble with Voice
ABBADO, MARCELLO (1926–)														✓												
ABEL, KARL F. (1723–1787)																	✓									
ABENDROTH, WALTER (1896–1973)	✓	✓																								
ABRAHAMSEN, HANS (1952–)		✓							✓								✓				✓	✓	✓	✓	✓	✓
ACKER, DIETER (1940–)		✓							✓	✓								✓			✓		✓	✓		
ADAM, ADOLPHE (1803–1856)																							✓			✓
ADAMS, JOHN (1947–)																					✓					
ADDISON, JOHN (1920–)																	✓									
ADLER, SAMUEL (1928–)		✓								✓						✓	✓		✓			✓		✓		
ADOLPHE, BRUCE (1955–)										✓							✓		✓	✓						
ADOLPHUS, MILTON (1913–)													✓				✓				✓					
ADOMIAN, LAN (1905–1979)																	✓						✓	✓	✓	✓
ADSON, JOHN (?–1640)																					✓					
AESCHBACHER, WALTHER (1901–1969)	✓																✓							✓		
AICHINGER, GREGOR (1564–1628)		✓						✓								✓										
AITKEN, HUGH (1924–)		✓																								✓
AITKEN, ROBERT (1939–)																						✓		✓	✓	
ALAIN, JEHAN (1911–1940)				✓													✓									
ALBERT, STEPHEN (1941–1992)																						✓	✓	✓	✓	✓
ALBICASTRO, HENRICUS (1661–1738)										✓													✓			✓
ALBIN, ROGER (1920–)																							✓			
ALBINONI, TOMASO (1671–1750)									✓	✓	✓												✓			
ALBRECHTSBERGER, ANTON (?–)	✓																									
ALBRECHTSBERGER, JOHANN G. (1736–1809)	✓	✓	✓														✓				✓				✓	
ALBRIGHT, WILLIAM (1944–)																	✓						✓	✓		✓
ALFANO, FRANCO (1875–1954)		✓								✓		✓														
ALKAN, CHARLES V. (1813–1888)										✓																
ALLANBROOK, DOUGLAS (1921–)																	✓									
ALTMANN, EDO (?–)																					✓					
ALWYN, WILLIAM (1905–)																								✓		
AMBROSIUS, HERMANN (1897–)																					✓					
AMELLER, ANDRE (1912–)								✓	✓												✓					
AMES, WILLIAM (1901–1987)										✓	✓	✓	✓				✓	✓			✓	✓	✓	✓		
AMFITEATROV, DANIELE (1901–1983)										✓																
AMON, JOHANN A. (1763–1825)		✓															✓									
AMRAM, DAVID (1930–)		✓							✓	✓	✓						✓			✓		✓	✓	✓		✓
AMY, GILBERT (1936–)																						✓	✓	✓	✓	✓
ANCELIN, PIERRE (1934–)									✓																	
ANDERSON, BETH (1950–)										✓						✓		✓				✓	✓	✓		
ANDERSON, THOMAS J. (1928–)																		✓				✓	✓	✓	✓	
ANDREAE, VOLKMAR (1879–1962)																	✓									
ANDRES, DANIEL (?–)								✓																		
ANDRIESSEN, HENDRICK (1892–1981)	✓																									
ANDRIEU, MIHAIL G. (?–)																					✓					
ANGERER, PAUL (1927–)		✓		✓						✓			✓				✓	✓			✓	✓	✓	✓		
ANTES, JOHN (1740–1811)	✓																									
ANTHEIL, GEORGE (1900–1959)		✓								✓			✓				✓				✓		✓	✓		
ANTONIOU, THEODORE (1935–)									✓										✓				✓	✓		✓
APERGHIS, GEORGES (1945–)																	✓			✓		✓	✓	✓	✓	✓
APOSTEL, HANS E. (1901–1972)		✓																			✓	✓				
ARAMBARRI, JESÚS (1902–1960)																					✓					

	3 Strings	4 Strings	5 Strings	3 Winds	4 Winds	5 Winds	3 Brass	4 Brass	5 Brass	2 Strings & Keyboard	3 Strings & Keyboard	4 Strings & Keyboard	2 Winds & Keyboard	3 Winds & Keyboard	4 Winds & Keyboard	Brass & Keyboard	Misc. Ensembles (3 to 5)	Strings, Wind Keyboard Trio	Strings, Wind Keyboard Quartets	Strings, Wind Keyboard Quintets	Sextets & Larger Ensembles	Ensemble with Guitar/Harp	Ensembles with Keyboard	Ensembles with Percussion	Ensembles with Unusual Instruments	Ensemble with Voice
ARDEVOL, JOSÉ (1911–1981)		✓																								
ARENSKY, ANTON (1861–1906)		✓										✓														
ARGENTO, DOMINICK (1927–)																							✓		✓	✓
ARIOSTI, ATTILIO (1666–1729)																							✓			✓
ARNOLD, MALCOLM (1921–)		✓															✓				✓					
ARRIAGA, JUAN (1806–1826)		✓																								
ARRIEU, CLAUDE (1903–)					✓												✓				✓					
ARRIGO, GIROLAMO (1930–)																					✓					✓
ARTEMOV, VYACHESLAV (1940–)																							✓	✓		
ARUTYUNIAN, ALEXANDER (1920–)																								✓	✓	
ASTON, HUGH (1480–1522)									✓																	
ATTERBERG, KURT (1887–1974)	✓																				✓					
AUBERT, LOUIS F. (1877–1968)																							✓			✓
AUBIN, TONY (1907–1981)				✓					✓				✓									✓		✓		
AUSTIN, JOHN (1869–1948)																		✓			✓					
AUSTIN, LARRY (1930–)																							✓	✓	✓	
AVNI, TZVI (1927–)																								✓	✓	
AVSHALOMOV, JACOB (1919–)																						✓		✓		
AXMAN, EMIL (1887–1949)		✓								✓																
BABBITT, MILTON (1916–)		✓			✓												✓		✓	✓	✓	✓	✓	✓	✓	✓
BACH, C. P. E. (1714–1788)										✓	✓							✓	✓		✓		✓			
BACH, FRITZ (1881–1930)											✓															
BACH, J. C. (1732–1795)																			✓							
BACH, JOHANN C. (1735–1782)	✓	✓								✓	✓		✓				✓	✓		✓	✓		✓			
BACH, JOHANN S. (1685–1750)	✓	✓								✓			✓					✓	✓			✓	✓		✓	✓
BACH, P.D.Q. (1807–1742)									✓			✓					✓				✓	✓	✓	✓	✓	✓
BACH, WILHELM F. (1710–1784)													✓					✓								
BACK, SVEN-ERIK (1919–)																					✓	✓		✓		
BACKOFEN, J. G. (1768–1839)																									✓	
BADINGS, HENK (1907–1987)		✓																						✓		
BADINSKI, NIKOLAI (1937–)																	✓				✓					
BAGGIANI, GUIDO (1932–)																							✓	✓	✓	
BAHK, JUN SANG (?–)																	✓							✓	✓	✓
BAINES, ANTHONY (1912–)																					✓					
BAIRD, TADEUSZ (1928–1981)		✓																								
BAKST, JAMES (?–)		✓																								
BALADA, LEONARDO (1933–)		✓							✓		✓			✓							✓	✓	✓	✓		✓
BALAKIREV, MILY (1837–1910)																					✓					
BALAY, GUILLAUME (1871–1943)																	✓									
BAMERT, MATTHIAS (1942–)																	✓						✓	✓		
BARATI, GEORGE (1913–)																	✓		✓	✓		✓	✓	✓	✓	
BARBER, SAMUEL (1910–1981)		✓															✓						✓			✓
BARBOTEU, GEORGES Y. (1924–)																							✓			
BARDANASHVILI, IOSEF (?–)		✓								✓		✓														
BARDIN, MAURICE (?–)							✓																			
BARGAGNI, O (?–?)								✓																		
BARKIN, ELAINE (1932–)										✓														✓	✓	
BARLOW, KLARENZ (1945–)												✓														
BÄRMANN, HEINRICH (1784–1847)																	✓									
BARRAUD, HENRY (1900–)																	✓									
BARRY, GERALD (1952–)		✓							✓								✓					✓	✓	✓	✓	✓
BARTH, HANS J. (1927–)								✓																		
BARTOK, BÉLA (1881–1945)		✓									✓	✓						✓					✓	✓		
BARTOLINI, ORINDIO (1580–1640)																					✓					
BARTOLOZZI, BRUNO (1911–1980)																						✓		✓		

	3 Strings	4 Strings	5 Strings	3 Winds	4 Winds	5 Winds	3 Brass	4 Brass	5 Brass	2 Strings & Keyboard	3 Strings & Keyboard	4 Strings & Keyboard	2 Winds & Keyboard	3 Winds & Keyboard	4 Winds & Keyboard	Brass & Keyboard	Misc. Ensembles (3 to 5)	Strings, Wind Keyboard Trio	Strings, Wind Keyboard Quartets	Strings, Wind Keyboard Quintets	Sextets & Larger Ensembles	Ensemble with Guitar/Harp	Ensembles with Keyboard	Ensembles with Percussion	Ensembles with Unusual Instruments	Ensemble with Voice
BARTOS, FRANTISEK (1905–)		✓															✓									
BARTOS, JAN Z. (1908–1981)		✓								✓																
BASNER, VENIAMIN (1925–)		✓																								
BASSANI, GIOVANNI B. (1647–1716)											✓															
BASSETT, LESLIE (1923–)		✓							✓			✓						✓			✓		✓	✓	✓	✓
BAUER, ROSS (1951–)																		✓				✓	✓	✓		
BAUERNFEIND, HANS (1908–)																	✓									
BAUR, JÜRG (1918–)																	✓				✓					
BAVICCHI, JOHN (1922–)								✓																		
BAX, ARNOLD (1883–1953)		✓	✓							✓	✓	✓					✓					✓				
BAZELAIRE, PAUL (1886–1958)																							✓			
BAZELON, IRWIN (1922–)									✓								✓					✓	✓	✓	✓	✓
BAZZINI, ANTONIO (1818–1897)		✓																								
BEACH, AMY M. (1867–1944)		✓								✓		✓					✓									
BEACH, BENNIE (1925–)									✓																	
BEALE, JAMES (1924–)										✓							✓					✓	✓	✓	✓	
BECERRA, GUSTAVO (1925–)		✓																								
BECHERT, ERNST (?–)																					✓					
BECKER, GÜNTHER (1924–)																	✓				✓	✓	✓	✓	✓	
BECKER, JOHN J. (1886–1961)																							✓	✓		
BEDFORD, DAVID (1937–)																						✓		✓	✓	✓
BEECKE, IGNAZ VON (1733–1803)		✓															✓									
BEER, JOHANN (1655–1700)																							✓			
BEERMAN, BURTON (1943–)														✓			✓					✓	✓	✓		
BEESON, JACK (1921–)																										✓
BEETHOVEN, LUDWIG VAN (1770–1827)	✓	✓	✓	✓						✓	✓		✓				✓	✓			✓		✓			✓
BELL, ELIZABETH (1952–)																			✓							
BENDA, JIRI A. (1722–1795)										✓																
BENGUEREL, XAVIER (1931–)																							✓			
BENJAMIN, ARTHUR (1893–1960)		✓																								
BENJAMIN, GEORGE (1960–)																						✓	✓	✓	✓	
BENNETT, RICHARD R. (1936–)		✓							✓														✓	✓	✓	✓
BENTZON, NIELS V. (1919–)																					✓		✓	✓	✓	
BERENS, HERMANN (1826–1880)	✓																									
BEREZOWSKY, NICOLAY (1900–1953)		✓															✓									
BERG, ALBAN (1885–1935)		✓																✓			✓		✓		✓	✓
BERG, OLAV (1949–)																						✓	✓	✓		
BERGER, ARTHUR (1912–)					✓																	✓	✓	✓	✓	
BERGER, GREGOR (?–)																							✓	✓		
BERGER, JEAN (1909–)																							✓	✓	✓	✓
BERGER, WILHELM (1861–1911)	✓																									
BERGMANN, WALTER (1902–)																	✓									
BERGSMA, WILLIAM (1921–)		✓						✓									✓						✓			
BERIO, LUCIANO (1925–)		✓															✓				✓	✓	✓	✓	✓	✓
BERKELEY, LENNOX (1903–1989)		✓													✓		✓				✓		✓			
BERKELEY, MICHAEL (1948–)	✓	✓							✓	✓		✓					✓				✓	✓	✓	✓	✓	✓
BERL, CHRISTINE (1943–)																							✓			✓
BERLIOZ, HECTOR (1803–1869)																						✓	✓	✓	✓	
BERNARD, EMILE (1843–1902)											✓															
BERNARD, ROBERT (1900–1971)										✓																
BERNHARD, CHRISTOPH (1627–1692)																							✓			✓
BERNIER, NICOLAS (1664–1734)																							✓			✓
BERNSTEIN, LEONARD (1918–1991)								✓																		

	3 Strings	4 Strings	5 Strings	3 Winds	4 Winds	5 Winds	3 Brass	4 Brass	5 Brass	2 Strings & Keyboard	3 Strings & Keyboard	4 Strings & Keyboard	2 Winds & Keyboard	3 Winds & Keyboard	4 Winds & Keyboard	Brass & Keyboard	Misc. Ensembles (3 to 5)	Strings, Wind Keyboard Trio	Strings, Wind Keyboard Quartets	Strings, Wind Keyboard Quintets	Sextets & Larger Ensembles	Ensemble with Guitar/Harp	Ensembles with Keyboard	Ensembles with Percussion	Ensembles with Unusual Instruments	Ensemble with Voice
BERTALI, ANTONIO (1605–1669)																			✓				✓			
BERTHELEMY, NORBERT (?–)				✓																						
BERTHOLD, HENRY (1933–)																	✓									
BERWALD, FRANZ (1796–1868)		✓								✓		✓									✓		✓			
BESOZZI, ALESSANDRO (1702–1793)				✓													✓									
BESSONNET, GEORGES (?–)							✓	✓	✓																	
BEVELANDER, BRIAN E. (1942–)																							✓	✓		
BEYDTS, LOUIS (1895–1953)																							✓			✓
BEYER, FRANK M. (1928–)		✓	✓							✓							✓			✓	✓	✓	✓	✓		
BEZANSON, PHILIP (1916–1975)		✓								✓											✓		✓	✓		
BHATIA, VANRAJ (1927–)																							✓			✓
BIALAS, GÜNTER (1907–)	✓	✓															✓				✓	✓				✓
BIBER, HEINRICH (1644–1704)																							✓	✓		✓
BIECHTELER, MATTHIAS S. (1668–1743)										✓																
BINKERD, GORDON (1916–)	✓	✓															✓					✓				✓
BIRTWISTLE, HARRISON (1934–)																						✓	✓	✓	✓	✓
BISCARDI, CHESTER (1948–)													✓							✓			✓	✓	✓	
BITSCH, MARCEL (1921–)					✓												✓									
BLACHER, BORIS (1903–1975)		✓															✓				✓	✓		✓		✓
BLACKFORD, RICHARD (1954–)		✓																					✓	✓		
BLACKWOOD, EASLEY (1933–)		✓								✓							✓									✓
BLAND, ED (1926–)																	✓							✓	✓	
BLANK, ALLAN (1925–)																	✓	✓		✓	✓	✓	✓		✓	✓
BLISS, ARTHUR (1891–1975)		✓															✓					✓				✓
BLOCH, ERNEST (1880–1959)		✓								✓		✓						✓								
BLOCH, WALDEMAR (1906–)																	✓									
BLOCK, STEVEN D. (1952–)																						✓	✓	✓	✓	✓
BOATWRIGHT, HOWARD (1918–)																	✓									✓
BOCCHERINI, LUIGI (1743–1805)	✓	✓	✓														✓									
BOCHMANN, CHRISTOPHER (?–)										✓				✓												
BODINUS, SEBASTIAN (1700–1753)																							✓			
BOISMORTIER, JOSEPH B. (1689–1755)													✓	✓				✓								
BONDON, JACQUES (1927–)																							✓			
BONNARD, ALAIN (?–)																	✓									
BONNEAU, PAUL (1918–)				✓																				✓		
BONPORTI, FRANCESCO A. (1672–1749)										✓																
BOONE, CHARLES (1939–)											✓										✓	✓	✓	✓	✓	✓
BORKOVEC, PAVEL (1894–1972)		✓																			✓					
BORODIN, ALEXANDER P. (1833–1887)		✓								✓																
BORROFF, EDITH (1925–)										✓													✓	✓		
BORTOLOTTI, MAURO (1926–)		✓															✓									
BOTTESINI, GIOVANNI (1821–1889)										✓																
BOTTJE, WILL G. (1925–)										✓						✓	✓	✓	✓		✓	✓	✓	✓		
BOUCARD, MARCEL (?–)				✓																						
BOUCOURECHLIEV, ANDRE (1925–)																							✓	✓		
BOUGHTON, RUTLAND (1878–1960)																										✓
BOULEZ, PIERRE (1925–)																				✓		✓	✓	✓	✓	✓
BOULNOIS, JOSEPH (1884–1918)										✓																
BOUSCH, FRANÇOIS (1946–)																								✓	✓	
BOUVARD, JEAN (?–)																		✓					✓			
BOWLES, PAUL (1910–)																							✓	✓		

	3 Strings	4 Strings	5 Strings	3 Winds	4 Winds	5 Winds	3 Brass	4 Brass	5 Brass	2 Strings & Keyboard	3 Strings & Keyboard	4 Strings & Keyboard	2 Winds & Keyboard	3 Winds & Keyboard	4 Winds & Keyboard	Brass & Keyboard	Misc. Ensembles (3 to 5)	Strings, Wind Keyboard Trio	Strings, Wind Keyboard Quartets	Strings, Wind Keyboard Quintets	Sextets & Larger Ensembles	Ensemble with Guitar/Harp	Ensembles with Keyboard	Ensembles with Percussion	Ensembles with Unusual Instruments	Ensemble with Voice
BOYD, ANNE (1946–)																					✓	✓	✓	✓	✓	✓
BOYKAN, MARTIN (1931–)		✓																								
BOZZA, EUGENE (1905–)		✓		✓	✓			✓	✓								✓				✓		✓	✓		
BRACALI, GIANPAOLO (1941–)																								✓		
BRADE, WILLIAM (1560–1630)			✓																		✓				✓	
BRAHMS, JOHANNES (1833–1897)		✓	✓						✓	✓	✓	✓					✓	✓			✓		✓			
BRANDMÜLLER, THEO (1948–)																							✓	✓	✓	
BRAUN, PETER M. (1936–)		✓																								
BREDEMEYER, REINER (1929–)		✓																					✓	✓		✓
BRENET, THÉRÈSE (1935–)																							✓	✓	✓	✓
BRESCIANELLO, GIOVANNI A. (1690–1757)	✓																									
BRESGEN, CESAR (1913–)																	✓									
BRETON, TOMÁS (1850–1923)		✓																								
BRETTINGHAM SMITH, JOLYON (1949–)																						✓	✓	✓		✓
BRIDGE, FRANK (1879–1941)		✓			✓																					
BRIECE, JACK (1945–1988)																						✓	✓	✓	✓	
BRITTEN, BENJAMIN (1913–1976)		✓			✓												✓	✓				✓	✓	✓	✓	✓
BRIZZI, ALDO (1960–)																					✓	✓		✓		✓
BROCKMAN, JANE (1949–)																			✓				✓			
BROOKS, RICHARD (1942–)																		✓								
BROWN, CHARLES (1940–)				✓																						
BROWN, EARLE (1926–)		✓								✓												✓	✓	✓	✓	
BROWN, J. E. (1937–)										✓													✓	✓	✓	
BRUCKNER, ANTON (1824–1896)			✓																							
BRUGK, HANS M. (1909–)																	✓									
BRUNETTI, GAETANO (1744–1798)																	✓									
BRUNIAU, AUGUST (1902–1971)													✓										✓			
BRUNSWICK, MARK (1902–1971)																					✓					
BULLER, JOHN (1927–)		✓															✓					✓	✓	✓	✓	✓
BUNS, BENEDICTUS (1642–1716)										✓																
BUONAMENTE, GIOVANNI B. (1600–1642)																									✓	
BUONAVENTURA, CAMARGO (1925–)		✓																								
BURGON, GEOFFREY (1941–)																							✓			✓
BURIAN, EMIL F. (1904–1959)																	✓									
BURKHARD, PAUL (1911–1977)																								✓		
BUSBY, GERALD (1935–)																		✓								
BUSCH, ADOLF (1891–1952)		✓																								
BUSONI, FERRUCIO (1866–1924)		✓																								
BUSSER, HENRI P. (1872–1973)		✓																				✓	✓			✓
BUSSOTTI, SYLVANO (1931–)	✓	✓								✓							✓						✓			✓
BUTTING, MAX (1888–1976)	✓	✓															✓		✓		✓					
BUXTEHUDE, DIETRICH (1637–1707)										✓													✓			✓
CAGE, JOHN (1912–1992)		✓		✓													✓				✓		✓	✓	✓	✓
CALDARA, ANTONIO (1670–1736)										✓	✓												✓			
CALLAWAY, ANN (1949–)																		✓								
CALLERT, G (?–)											✓															
CALTABIANO, RONALD (1959–)		✓																								✓
CAMBINI, GIUSEPPE M. (1746–1825)				✓																						
CAMBRELING, SYLVAIN (1948–)									✓																	
CANNABICH, CHRISTIAN (1731–1798)											✓						✓									
CANNING, THOMAS (1911–)																								✓		

	3 Strings	4 Strings	5 Strings	3 Winds	4 Winds	5 Winds	3 Brass	4 Brass	5 Brass	2 Strings & Keyboard	3 Strings & Keyboard	4 Strings & Keyboard	2 Winds & Keyboard	3 Winds & Keyboard	4 Winds & Keyboard	Brass & Keyboard	Misc. Ensembles (3 to 5)	Strings, Wind Keyboard Trio	Strings, Wind Keyboard Quartets	Strings, Wind Keyboard Quintets	Sextets & Larger Ensembles	Ensemble with Guitar/Harp	Ensembles with Keyboard	Ensembles with Percussion	Ensembles with Unusual Instruments	Ensemble with Voice
CAPLET, ANDRÉ (1878–1925)												✓										✓				
CAPRICORNUS, SAMUEL (1628–1665)																							✓			✓
CARL, ROBERT B. (1954–)										✓											✓	✓	✓	✓	✓	
CARLSEN, PHILIP (1951–)																		✓								
CARTER, ELLIOTT (1908–)		✓			✓				✓								✓		✓			✓	✓	✓	✓	✓
CASADESUS, FRANCIS (1870–1954)																					✓					
CASADESUS, ROBERT (1899–1972)											✓												✓			
CASELLA, ALFREDO (1883–1947)		✓								✓							✓									
CASTELNUOVO-TEDESCO, MARIO (1895–1968)		✓								✓		✓										✓				
CASTERA, RENÉ DE (1873–1955)										✓																
CASTEREDE, JACQUES (1926–)																							✓	✓	✓	
CASTIGLIONI, NICCOLÒ (1932–)																							✓	✓		
CASTILLON, ALEXIS DE (1838–1873)		✓								✓		✓														
CAVACCIO, GIOVANNI (1556–1626)								✓																		
CAZZATI, MAURIZIO (1620–1677)											✓															
CEELY, ROBERT (1930–)																									✓	
CERHA, FRIEDRICH (1926–)																								✓	✓	✓
CESARE, GIOVANNI M. (1590–1667)																✓										
CHABRIER, EMMANUEL (1841–1894)																	✓				✓					
CHAILLEY, JACQUES (1910–)		✓															✓								✓	
CHAMINADE, CÉCILE (1857–1944)										✓																
CHAPI, RUPERTO (1851–1909)		✓																								
CHAPPLE, BRIAN (1945–)																							✓			
CHAPUIS, AUGUSTE (1858–1933)										✓																
CHARPENTIER, MARC-ANTOINE (1645–1704)										✓											✓					
CHAUSHIAN, LEVON (?–)		✓																								
CHAUSSON, ERNEST (1855–1899)		✓								✓	✓												✓			
CHAVEZ, CARLOS (1899–1978)	✓	✓					✓										✓						✓			✓
CHAYNES, CHARLES (1925–)										✓							✓				✓		✓	✓	✓	✓
CHEN, QIGANG (?–)																	✓									
CHENOWETH, GERALD (1943–)																	✓									
CHERUBINI, LUIGI (1760–1842)		✓																								
CHEVILLARD, CAMILLE (1859–1923)		✓								✓		✓														
CHIHARA, PAUL (1938–)	✓	✓								✓												✓		✓		
CHILDS, BARNEY (1926–)																	✓				✓	✓		✓	✓	
CHILESE, BASTIAN (?–?)																					✓					
CHOU, WEN-CHUNG (1923–)																						✓	✓	✓	✓	
CHUDOVA, TATIANA (1944–)									✓																	
CILENSEK, JOHANN (1913–)																	✓				✓					
CIMA, GIOVANNI P. (1570–?)																							✓		✓	
CLAFLIN, AVERY (1898–1979)																							✓			
CLARKE, HENRY L. (1907–)																	✓									
CLARKE, KEITH R. (?–)								✓																		
CLARKE, REBECCA (1886–1979)										✓																
CLAYTON, LAURA (1943–)																						✓		✓	✓	✓
CLEMENTI, ALDO (1925–)				✓																		✓	✓		✓	
CLERAMBOULT, LOUIS N. (1676–1749)										✓																
COE, MICHAEL (?–)							✓																			
COKER, WILSON (1928–)																	✓									
COLE, BRUCE (1947–)																							✓			✓
COLISTA, LELIO (1629–1680)											✓															
CONNOLLY, JUSTIN R. (1933–)									✓																	

	3 Strings	4 Strings	5 Strings	3 Winds	4 Winds	5 Winds	3 Brass	4 Brass	5 Brass	2 Strings & Keyboard	3 Strings & Keyboard	4 Strings & Keyboard	2 Winds & Keyboard	3 Winds & Keyboard	4 Winds & Keyboard	Brass & Keyboard	Misc. Ensembles (3 to 5)	Strings, Wind Keyboard Trio	Strings, Wind Keyboard Quartets	Strings, Wind Keyboard Quintets	Sextets & Larger Ensembles	Ensemble with Guitar/Harp	Ensembles with Keyboard	Ensembles with Percussion	Ensembles with Unusual Instruments	Ensemble with Voice
CONSOLI, MARC-ANTON (1941–)																	✓							✓		
CONSTANT, MARIUS (1925–)																✓					✓	✓	✓	✓	✓	
CONYNGHAM, BARRY (1944–)		✓																			✓	✓	✓	✓	✓	
COOKE, ARNOLD (1906–)																	✓									
COOPER, PAUL (1926–)		✓								✓				✓			✓	✓				✓	✓		✓	✓
COPERARIO, GIOVANNI (1575–1626)	✓																									
COPLAND, AARON (1900–1990)		✓								✓	✓						✓				✓		✓			✓
CORBETT, W (?–?)													✓										✓			
CORELLI, ARCANGELO (1653–1713)		✓								✓												✓	✓			
CORGHI, AZIO (1937–)																							✓	✓		
CORIGLIANO, JOHN (1938–)																	✓					✓	✓	✓	✓	✓
CORNILIOS, NICOS (1954–)																					✓					
CORREGIA, ENRICO (1933–)																							✓	✓		
CORRETTE, MICHEL (1709–1795)											✓			✓					✓							
CORY, ELEANOR (1943–)													✓					✓			✓	✓	✓	✓	✓	
COTEK, PAVEL (1922–)																							✓		✓	
COUPERIN, FRANÇOIS (1668–1733)		✓	✓							✓	✓								✓		✓		✓			
COUROUPOS, GEORGES (1942–)																							✓	✓	✓	
COWELL, HENRY D. (1897–1965)	✓	✓							✓	✓							✓		✓		✓	✓	✓	✓	✓	✓
COYNER, LOU (1931–)																						✓	✓	✓	✓	
CRAS, JEAN E. (1879–1932)		✓								✓		✓														
CRESTON, PAUL (1906–1985)		✓								✓								✓					✓			
CREUSOT, JEAN (?–)								✓																		
CROLEY, RANDELL (1946–)									✓																	
CROSSE, GORDON (1937–)		✓							✓	✓				✓			✓	✓	✓		✓	✓	✓	✓	✓	✓
CRUMB, GEORGE (1929–)																						✓	✓	✓	✓	✓
CRUSELL, BERNHARD H. (1775–1838)																	✓									
CSEMICZKY, MIKLOS (1954–)		✓																								
CSERMAK, ANTAL G. (1774–1822)		✓																								
CUI, CESAR (1835–1918)																		✓								
CUSTER, ARTHUR (1923–)		✓																				✓		✓		
CZERNY, CARL (1791–1857)																							✓			
DAHL, INGOLF (1912–1970)										✓	✓						✓									
D'ALESSANDRO, RAFFAELE (1911–1959)		✓																								
DALL'ABACO, EVARISTO F. (1675–1742)										✓																
DALLAPICCOLA, LUIGI (1904–1975)																						✓	✓	✓	✓	✓
DALLINGER, FRIDOLIN (1933–)																	✓	✓			✓					
DAMAIS, EMILE (1906–)	✓																									
DAMASE, JEAN-MICHEL (1928–)																	✓									
D'ANDRIEU, JEAN F. (1684–1740)											✓															
DANIEL-LESUR, DANIEL (1908–)		✓																				✓	✓			✓
DANIELPOUR, RICHARD (1956–)		✓							✓			✓										✓	✓	✓	✓	
DANZI, FRANZ (1763–1826)																	✓									
DAO, NGUYEN T. (1941–)																							✓	✓	✓	✓
DARASSE, XAVIER (1934–)									✓														✓	✓	✓	
DAVID, JOHANN N. (1895–1977)																					✓	✓	✓	✓		
DAVID, THOMAS C. (1925–)		✓															✓	✓			✓					
DAVIDOFF, CARL J. (1838–1889)		✓																								
DAVIDOVSKY, MARIO (1934–)	✓	✓								✓							✓				✓	✓	✓	✓	✓	✓
DAVIDSON, MALCOLM G. (1891–)																										✓
DAVIS, ANTHONY (1951–)																		✓					✓	✓	✓	✓
DEBUSSY, CLAUDE A. (1862–1918)		✓							✓	✓							✓					✓		✓	✓	✓
DECOUST, MICHEL (1936–)																						✓	✓	✓	✓	✓

	3 Strings	4 Strings	5 Strings	3 Winds	4 Winds	5 Winds	3 Brass	4 Brass	5 Brass	2 Strings & Keyboard	3 Strings & Keyboard	4 Strings & Keyboard	2 Winds & Keyboard	3 Winds & Keyboard	4 Winds & Keyboard	Brass & Keyboard	Misc. Ensembles (3 to 5)	Strings, Wind Keyboard Trio	Strings, Wind Keyboard Quartets	Strings, Wind Keyboard Quintets	Sextets & Larger Ensembles	Ensemble with Guitar/Harp	Ensembles with Keyboard	Ensembles with Percussion	Ensembles with Unusual Instruments	Ensemble with Voice
DE FESCH, WILLEM (1687–1757)													✓													
DEFOTIS, WILLIAM (1953–)																						✓				
DEGEN, HELMUT (1911–)										✓																
DELACHI, PAOLO (?–)										✓																
DELAGE, MAURICE (1879–1961)		✓																					✓			✓
DELALANDE, MICHEL (1657–1726)								✓															✓	✓		
DELANNOY, MARCEL (1898–1962)		✓																					✓	✓	✓	
DELAS, JOSÉ L. (1928–)																						✓	✓	✓	✓	
DELERUE, GEORGES (1925–)									✓																	
DELIUS, FREDERICK (1862–1934)		✓															✓									
DELLO JOIO, NORMAN (1913–)																								✓	✓	
DEL TREDICI, DAVID (1937–)	✓																						✓	✓	✓	✓
DELVINCOURT, CLAUDE (1888–1954)		✓																								
DEMBSKI, STEPHEN (1949–)										✓									✓				✓	✓		
DEMERSSEMAN, JULES A. (1833–1866)													✓													
DENHOFF, MICHAEL (1955–)		✓															✓				✓	✓	✓	✓	✓	✓
DENIS, DIDIER (1947–)																						✓	✓	✓	✓	✓
DENISOV, EDISON (1929–)		✓								✓		✓					✓				✓	✓	✓	✓	✓	✓
DENNY, WILLIAM (1910–1980)		✓																								
DESENCLOS, ALFRED (1912–1971)	✓																									
DESORMIERE, ROGER (1898–1963)																	✓									
DESPIC, DEJAN (?–)																	✓									
DESPORTES, YVONNE (1907–)		✓			✓				✓														✓	✓		✓
DESSAU, PAUL (1894–1979)		✓		✓			✓						✓								✓		✓	✓	✓	✓
DEVIENNE, FRANÇOIS (1759–1803)	✓			✓													✓	✓					✓			
DEVILLERS, JEAN-B. (1953–)																						✓	✓	✓	✓	
DEWANGER, ANTON (?–)																							✓			
DIABELLI, ANTON (1781–1858)																								✓		
DIAMOND, DAVID (1915–)	✓	✓								✓	✓		✓				✓			✓	✓					
DICHLER, JOSEF (1912–)										✓																
DICKINSON, PETER (1934–)																							✓			
DIEMER, EMMA L. (1927–)					✓																					
DIERCKS, JOHN (1927–)							✓	✓									✓									
DIEREN, BERNARD VAN (1884–1936)																									✓	✓
DIETHELM, CASPAR (1926–)			✓							✓							✓									
DILLON, JAMES (1944–)		✓																					✓	✓	✓	
DISTLER, HUGO (1908–1942)		✓								✓																✓
DITTERSDORF, KARL D. VON (1739–1799)	✓							✓																		
DITTRICH, PAUL-HEINZ (1930–)															✓		✓	✓					✓	✓		✓
DJAMBAZIAN, A (?–)																	✓									
DMITRIEV, GEORGY (?–)		✓														✓										
DOEHL, FRIEDHELM (1936–)																							✓	✓		✓
DOHNANYI, ERNST VON (1877–1960)	✓	✓										✓											✓			
DOLLARHIDE, THEODORE (1948–)																						✓				
DOMENICO, OLIVIO DI (?–)																	✓									
DOMHARDT, GERD (1945–)		✓		✓																	✓					
DONATO, ANTHONY (1909–)		✓																								
DONATONI, FRANCO (1927–)		✓																				✓		✓	✓	✓
DONDEYNE, DÉSIRÉ (1921–)									✓																	
DONIZETTI, GAETANO (1797–1848)		✓																			✓					
DONOVAN, RICHARD F. (1891–1970)										✓													✓			

	3 Strings	4 Strings	5 Strings	3 Winds	4 Winds	5 Winds	3 Brass	4 Brass	5 Brass	2 Strings & Keyboard	3 Strings & Keyboard	4 Strings & Keyboard	2 Winds & Keyboard	3 Winds & Keyboard	4 Winds & Keyboard	Brass & Keyboard	Misc. Ensembles (3 to 5)	Strings, Wind Keyboard Trio	Strings, Wind Keyboard Quartets	Strings, Wind Keyboard Quintets	Sextets & Larger Ensembles	Ensemble with Guitar/Harp	Ensembles with Keyboard	Ensembles with Percussion	Ensembles with Unusual Instruments	Ensemble with Voice
DOPPELBAUER, JOSEF F. (1918–)		✓		✓	✓												✓								✓	
DOPPLER, FRANZ (1821–1883)																		✓								
DORATI, ANTAL (1906–)		✓																						✓		✓
DOWNEY, JOHN (1927–1988)		✓																								
DRAKEFORD, RICHARD (?–)									✓																	
DREW, JAMES (1929–)								✓		✓																
DRIESSLER, JOHANNES (1921–)	✓	✓																✓			✓					
DRUCKMAN, JACOB (1928–)		✓							✓								✓					✓	✓	✓	✓	✓
DRUSCHETZKY, GEORG (1745–1819)								✓													✓					
DUBOIS, PIERRE-MAX (1930–)				✓				✓	✓								✓				✓		✓	✓	✓	
DUBOIS, THÉODORE (1837–1924)																					✓					
DUBUIS, CLAUDE (?–)								✓																		
DUFAY, GUILLAUME (1400–1474)									✓																	
DUKE, VERNON (1903–1969)													✓													
DUMITRESCU, IANCU (1944–)																							✓		✓	
DUPONT, PIERRE (1821–1870)																	✓									
DUREY, LOUIS (1888–1979)				✓													✓									
DURIEUX, FREDERIC (1959–)																						✓	✓	✓		✓
DURKO, ZSOLT (1934–)		✓						✓		✓							✓									
DURUFLE, MAURICE (1902–)																		✓								
DUSAPIN, PASCAL (?–)																					✓				✓	
DUSSEK, JAN (1760–1812)												✓											✓			
DVOŘÁK, ANTONÍN (1841–1904)	✓	✓	✓							✓	✓	✓		✓			✓				✓		✓		✓	
EATON, JOHN (1935–)		✓				✓				✓												✓	✓	✓	✓	✓
EBEN, PETR (1929–)																	✓									
EBENHÖH, HORST (1930–)									✓	✓											✓		✓	✓		
ECKERT, MICHAEL (1950–)																	✓									
EDEL, YITZHAK (1896–1973)										✓																
EDER, HELMUT (1916–)	✓	✓								✓				✓			✓				✓		✓	✓	✓	
EDER DE LASTRA, ERICH (1933–)																	✓									
EDLUND, MIKAEL (1950–)		✓											✓								✓	✓	✓	✓	✓	✓
EDWARDS, GEORGE (1943–)																						✓	✓	✓	✓	
EGENOLF, CHRISTIAN (1502–1555)		✓																								
EINEM, GOTTFRIED VON (1918–)		✓															✓						✓	✓	✓	✓
EINFELDT, DIETER (1935–)		✓																					✓			✓
EISLER, HANNS (1898–1962)	✓																✓			✓		✓	✓			✓
EKIMOVSKY, VIKTOR (?–)																						✓		✓	✓	
EL-DABH, HALIM (1921–)																		✓				✓	✓	✓		✓
ELER, J (?–?)				✓																						
ELGAR, EDWARD (1857–1934)		✓				✓						✓														✓
ELIAS, BRIAN (1948–)																							✓	✓	✓	
ELLINGTON, "DUKE" (1899–1974)		✓																								
EMMANUEL, MAURICE (1862–1938)		✓																								
ENESCO, GEORGES (1881–1955)		✓																			✓		✓			
ENGELMANN, HANS U. (1921–)																							✓			✓
EÖTVÖS, PETER (1944–)																							✓	✓	✓	✓
ERB, DONALD (1927–)		✓							✓								✓									
ERBSE, HEIMO (1924–)		✓		✓	✓					✓								✓					✓			✓
ERDMANN, DIETRICH (1917–)																								✓		
ERLEBACH, PHILIPP H. (1657–1714)										✓																
ERÖD, IVAN (1936–)		✓								✓							✓				✓	✓	✓	✓		✓
ESCHER, PETER A. (1915–)									✓																	
ESTRADA, JULIO (?–)																					✓					
ETLER, ALVIN (1913–1973)									✓								✓				✓			✓		
ETTI, KARL (1912–)																	✓									
EVANGELISTA, JOSÉ (1943–)																						✓	✓	✓	✓	

	3 Strings	4 Strings	5 Strings	3 Winds	4 Winds	5 Winds	3 Brass	4 Brass	5 Brass	2 Strings & Keyboard	3 Strings & Keyboard	4 Strings & Keyboard	2 Winds & Keyboard	3 Winds & Keyboard	4 Winds & Keyboard	Brass & Keyboard	Misc. Ensembles (3 to 5)	Strings, Wind Keyboard Trio	Strings, Wind Keyboard Quartets	Strings, Wind Keyboard Quintets	Sextets & Larger Ensembles	Ensemble with Guitar/Harp	Ensembles with Keyboard	Ensembles with Percussion	Ensembles with Unusual Instruments	Ensemble with Voice
EVETT, ROBERT (1922–1975)										✓	✓	✓											✓	✓	✓	
EYBLER, JOSEPH (1765–1846)	✓		✓																							
EYCHENNE, MARC (1933–)																							✓			
FAILLENOT, MAURICE (?–)							✓																			
FALIK, YURI (1936–)				✓																						
FALLA, MANUEL DE (1876–1946)																						✓	✓			✓
FARINA, CARLO (1600–1640)																							✓			
FARIÑAS, CARLOS (1934–)			✓																							
FASCH, JOHANN F. (1688–1758)					✓													✓	✓							
FAURÉ, GABRIEL U. (1845–1925)		✓								✓	✓	✓					✓									
FAVRE, GEORGES (1905–)				✓													✓									
FELD, JINDRICH (1925–)									✓		✓										✓					
FELDMAN, HERBERT B. (1931–)		✓																								
FELDMAN, MORTON (1926–)		✓															✓		✓	✓	✓	✓	✓	✓	✓	✓
FELLEGARA, VITTORIO (1927–)																					✓		✓	✓	✓	
FENNELLY, BRIAN (1937–)										✓							✓			✓			✓	✓		
FERNEYHOUGH, BRIAN (1943–)		✓			✓																✓	✓	✓	✓	✓	✓
FERRABOSCO, ALFONSO (1575–1628)		✓	✓																							
FERRITTO, JOHN (1937–)																		✓					✓	✓	✓	
FERROUD, PIERRE O. (1900–1936)		✓		✓																						
FIALA, JOSEPH (1748–1816)																					✓					
FIBICH, ZDENEK (1850–1900)												✓														
FINE, IRVING (1914–1962)		✓															✓					✓				
FINE, VIVIAN (1913–)																				✓						
FINGER, GOTTFRIED (1660–?)																							✓			
FINKE, FIDELIO F. (1891–1968)	✓	✓																								✓
FINNEY, ROSS L. (1906–)		✓	✓							✓	✓	✓									✓		✓	✓		
FINNISSY, MICHAEL (1946–)									✓													✓	✓	✓	✓	✓
FINZI, GERALD (1901–1956)	✓																✓									✓
FIRSOVA, ELENA (1950–)		✓																				✓		✓	✓	✓
FISCHER, IRWIN (1903–1977)										✓											✓					
FISCHER, JOHANN K. (1670–1746)		✓		✓						✓		✓														
FISHER, STEPHEN (1940–)		✓																								
FITELBERG, JERZY (1903–1951)		✓															✓									
FOERSTER, JOSEF B. (1859–1951)		✓																			✓					
FOLPRECHT, ZDENEK (1900–1961)																					✓					
FONTANA, GIOVANNI B. (?–1630)										✓								✓								
FONTYN, JACQUELINE (1930–)																					✓	✓	✓	✓		
FORET, FÉLICIEN (?–)				✓																						
FÖRSTER, EMANUEL A. (1748–1823)		✓																								
FÖRSTER, KASPAR (1617–1673)														✓												
FORTIN, V. (?–)																						✓				
FORTNER, WOLFGANG (1907–1987)		✓																								
FOSS, LUKAS (1922–)		✓															✓					✓	✓	✓		✓
FOSSA, FRANÇOIS DE (1775–1849)																						✓				
FOSTER, STEPHEN (1826–1864)		✓																								
FOULDS, JOHN (1880–1939)											✓															
FOURESTIER, LOUIS (1892–1976)		✓																								
FOWLER, JENNIFER (1939–)																							✓	✓	✓	
FRACKENPOHL, ARTHUR R. (1924–)		✓						✓																		
FRANÇAIX, JEAN (1912–)	✓	✓		✓	✓												✓				✓					
FRANCK, CESAR (1822–1890)		✓								✓		✓														
FRANCK, JOHANN W. (1644–1710)																							✓			✓
FRANCK, MELCHIOR (1579–1639)								✓																		
FRANCO, JOHAN (1908–)																	✓					✓	✓	✓	✓	

	3 Strings	4 Strings	5 Strings	3 Winds	4 Winds	5 Winds	3 Brass	4 Brass	5 Brass	2 Strings & Keyboard	3 Strings & Keyboard	4 Strings & Keyboard	2 Winds & Keyboard	3 Winds & Keyboard	4 Winds & Keyboard	Brass & Keyboard	Misc. Ensembles (3 to 5)	Strings, Wind Keyboard Trio	Strings, Wind Keyboard Quartets	Strings, Wind Keyboard Quintets	Sextets & Larger Ensembles	Ensemble with Guitar/Harp	Ensembles with Keyboard	Ensembles with Percussion	Ensembles with Unusual Instruments	Ensemble with Voice
FRANK, ANDREW (1946–)																		✓								
FRANKE, BERND (1959–)																								✓		
FREED, ISADORE (1900–1960)											✓															
FRESCOBALDI, GIROLAMO (1583–1643)								✓	✓												✓					
FRITSCH, JOHANNES (1941–)		✓	✓							✓		✓			✓								✓	✓	✓	✓
FROHLOFF, ERICH-KARL (1921–)																					✓					
FROHNE, VINCENT S. (1936–)		✓																								
FROMM, HERBERT (1905–)		✓																								
FROMM-MICHAELS, ILSE (1888–)																	✓									
FROSCHAUER, HELMUTH (1933–)																					✓					
FROUNBERG, IVAR (1950–)																							✓	✓	✓	
FUCHS, ROBERT (1847–1927)	✓																✓									
FUGA, SANDRO (1906–)		✓								✓																
FULEIHAN, ANIS (1900–1970)												✓														
FÜRST, PAUL W. (1926–)		✓			✓												✓	✓								
FUSS, JOHANN E. (1777–1819)		✓															✓									
FUSSELL, CHARLES (1938–)																						✓	✓	✓	✓	✓
FUTTERER, CARL (1873–1927)																	✓				✓					
FUX, JOHANN J. (1660–1741)										✓			✓													
GABAYE, PIERRE (1903–)																✓	✓									
GABRIELI, ANDREA (1510–1586)					✓			✓																		
GABRIELI, DOMENICO (1659–1690)										✓																
GABRIELI, GIOVANNI (1557–1612)								✓	✓												✓		✓			
GAL, HANS (1890–1987)		✓																				✓				
GALLOIS-MONTBRUN, RAYMOND (1918–)		✓																								
GANGE, KENNETH (?–)									✓																	
GARANT, SERGE (1929–)																						✓	✓	✓		
GARCIN, GERARD (1947–)																								✓	✓	
GARDNER, JOHN L. (1917–)								✓																		
GASSMANN, FLORIAN L. (1729–1774)	✓									✓							✓									
GATTERMANN, P. (?–)																		✓								
GATTERMEYER, HEINRICH (1923–)				✓					✓								✓	✓						✓		
GAUDIBERT, ERIC (1936–)																	✓									
GAUL, HARVEY B. (1881–1945)		✓																								
GEBAUER, ETIENNE (1777–1823)																	✓									
GEBAUER, FRANÇOIS R. (1773–1845)				✓													✓									
GEHLHAAR, ROLF (1943–)		✓							✓							✓			✓		✓		✓	✓		✓
GEISSLER, FRITZ (1921–1984)		✓								✓							✓				✓					
GEMINIANI, FRANCESCO (1687–1762)										✓																
GENG, CHARLES (?–)																		✓								
GENIN, PAUL A. (1829–1904)													✓													
GENTILUCCI, ARMANDO (1939–)	✓	✓								✓							✓						✓	✓		✓
GENZMER, HARALD (1909–)								✓	✓	✓			✓				✓				✓	✓				
GERBER, RENÉ (1908–)													✓													
GERBER, STEVEN R. (1948–)												✓														
GERHARD, ROBERTO (1896–1970)		✓																				✓	✓	✓	✓	✓
GERSCHEFSKI, EDWIN (1909–)										✓		✓	✓	✓			✓				✓	✓	✓	✓	✓	
GERSHWIN, GEORGE (1898–1937)		✓																								
GERVAISE, CLAUDE (1540–1560)								✓																		
GEWICKSMANN, VITALI A. (1924–)		✓																					✓	✓	✓	✓
GHEDINI, GIORGIO F. (1892–1965)		✓								✓					✓			✓								

	3 Strings	4 Strings	5 Strings	3 Winds	4 Winds	5 Winds	3 Brass	4 Brass	5 Brass	2 Strings & Keyboard	3 Strings & Keyboard	4 Strings & Keyboard	2 Winds & Keyboard	3 Winds & Keyboard	4 Winds & Keyboard	Brass & Keyboard	Misc. Ensembles (3 to 5)	Strings, Wind Keyboard Trio	Strings, Wind Keyboard Quartets	Strings, Wind Keyboard Quintets	Sextets & Larger Ensembles	Ensemble with Guitar/Harp	Ensembles with Keyboard	Ensembles with Percussion	Ensembles with Unusual Instruments	Ensemble with Voice
GHENT, EMMANUEL (1925–)					✓				✓								✓				✓					
GIBBONS, ORLANDO (1583–1625)	✓																				✓					
GIBBS, CECIL A. (1889–1960)		✓								✓		✓														
GIDEON, MIRIAM (1906–)																		✓						✓	✓	✓
GIELEN, MICHAEL (1927–)		✓																								
GIESEKING, WALTER (1895–1956)																							✓			
GILBERT, PIA (1921–)																							✓	✓		✓
GINASTERA, ALBERTO (1916–1983)		✓										✓					✓					✓		✓	✓	✓
GIORDANI, TOMMASO (1730–1806)										✓																
GIRAUD, SUZANNE (1958–)																						✓	✓	✓		✓
GIULIANI, MAURO (1781–1829)																						✓				
GLANERT, DETLEV (1960–)																							✓	✓	✓	
GLASS, PHILIP (1937–)		✓																			✓	✓	✓	✓	✓	✓
GLASSER, S (?–)							✓																			
GLAZUNOFF, ALEXANDER K. (1865–1936)		✓	✓																							
GLETLE, JOHANN M. (1626–1683)																							✓			✓
GLIÈRE, REINHOLD (1875–1956)		✓																								
GLINKA, MICHAIL I. (1804–1857)		✓											✓													
GLINSKY, ALBERT V. (1952–)																						✓		✓		
GLOBOKAR, VINKO (1934–)		✓																				✓	✓	✓	✓	✓
GLUCK, CHRISTOPH W. (1714–1787)								✓		✓																
GODARD, BENJAMIN (1849–1895)										✓																
GODFREY, DANIEL (1949–)																		✓			✓	✓				
GOEB, ROGER (1914–)										✓		✓		✓			✓				✓		✓	✓	✓	
GOETZ, HERMANN (1840–1876)										✓	✓	✓														
GOLD, ERNEST (1921–)		✓																								
GOLDMAN, RICHARD F. (1910–1980)																				✓						
GOLDMANN, FRIEDRICH (1941–)		✓															✓						✓	✓	✓	
GOLDSCHMIDT, BERTHOLD (1903–)		✓								✓							✓									
GOLESTAN, STAN (1875–1956)		✓		✓																						
GOLUB, PETER (1952–)													✓						✓				✓	✓		
GOOSSEN, FREDERIC (1927–)																							✓			
GOOSSENS, EUGENE (1893–1962)		✓											✓								✓					
GORECKI, HENRYK M. (1933–)	✓																✓	✓				✓	✓	✓	✓	✓
GOULD, MORTON (1913–)																					✓	✓	✓	✓	✓	
GOUNOD, CHARLES (1818–1893)																					✓					
GRAAP, LOTHAR (1933–)				✓																						
GRABNER, HERMANN (1866–1969)																							✓			✓
GRAINGER, PERCY (1882–1961)																								✓	✓	
GRANADOS, ENRIQUE (1867–1916)		✓								✓																
GRANT, WILLIAM P. (1910–)												✓														
GRAUN, CARL H. (1704–1759)																									✓	
GRAUN, JOHANN G. (1703–1771)										✓			✓					✓								
GRAUPNER, CHRISTOPH (1683–1760)		✓											✓										✓		✓	✓
GREENBAUM, MATTHEW (1950–)																						✓	✓			
GREENBURG, LAURA (1942–)										✓																
GREGSON, EDWARD (1945–)									✓																	
GRIEG, EDVARD (1843–1907)		✓															✓									
GRILLO, GIOVANNI B. (?–1622)																					✓					
GROOT, H. DE (?–)				✓																						
GROSS, ROBERT (1914–)																		✓					✓		✓	
GROSSKOPF, ERHARD (1934–)		✓							✓		✓												✓	✓	✓	
GROSSMANN, FERDINAND (1887–1970)	✓																									

	3 Strings	4 Strings	5 Strings	3 Winds	4 Winds	5 Winds	3 Brass	4 Brass	5 Brass	2 Strings & Keyboard	3 Strings & Keyboard	4 Strings & Keyboard	2 Winds & Keyboard	3 Winds & Keyboard	4 Winds & Keyboard	Brass & Keyboard	Misc. Ensembles (3 to 5)	Strings, Wind Keyboard Trio	Strings, Wind Keyboard Quartets	Strings, Wind Keyboard Quintets	Sextets & Larger Ensembles	Ensemble with Guitar/Harp	Ensembles with Keyboard	Ensembles with Percussion	Ensembles with Unusual Instruments	Ensemble with Voice
GRUBER, HEINZ K. (1943–)													✓				✓				✓	✓	✓	✓		✓
GRUENBERG, LOUIS (1884–1964)		✓										✓											✓	✓		✓
GRÜNAUER, INGOMAR (1938–)					✓																					
GUAMI, GIOSEFFO (1540–1612)								✓													✓					
GUBAIDULINA, SOFIA (1931–)		✓										✓									✓	✓		✓		✓
GUDMUNDSEN-HOLMG'N, PELLE (1932–)																						✓	✓	✓		
GUEZEC, JEAN-PIERRE (1934–1971)																					✓	✓		✓		
GUILLOU, JEAN (1930–)																			✓			✓	✓	✓		
GURIDI, JESÚS (1886–1961)		✓																								
GURSCHING, ALBRECHT (1934–)		✓																								
GUSSAGO, CESARIO (?–?)																					✓					
GUYARD, CHRISTOPHE (?–)																		✓								
GYROWETZ, ADALBERT (1763–1850)																	✓									
HABA, ALOIS (1893–1973)		✓																			✓					
HABA, KAREL (1898–1972)		✓								✓																
HADAMOWSKY, HANS (1906–)				✓																						
HADER, WILDMAR (1941–)																							✓			✓
HAFFNER, WALTHER (?–?)																✓										
HAGERUP BULL, EDVARD (1922–)																			✓							
HALFFTER, CRISTOBAL (1930–)		✓																			✓		✓	✓	✓	✓
HALLER, HERMANN (1914–)																	✓									
HALTENBERGER, BERNHARD (1748–1780)																	✓									
HAMANN, ERICH (1898–)	✓	✓	✓							✓	✓															
HAMBRAEUS, BENGT (1928–)																							✓	✓	✓	
HAMEL, PETER M. (1947–)		✓								✓												✓	✓	✓	✓	✓
HAMMERSCHMIDT, ANDREAS (1611–1675)																							✓			✓
HAMPTON, CALVIN (1938–)																							✓		✓	
HÄNDEL, GEORG F. (1685–1759)										✓			✓		✓		✓	✓				✓	✓	✓		✓
HANFF, JOHANN N. (1665–1711)																							✓			✓
HANNAY, ROGER (1930–)																		✓								
HANUS, JAN (1915–)		✓															✓									
HARBISON, JOHN (1938–)		✓	✓						✓	✓	✓	✓					✓	✓		✓	✓	✓	✓	✓	✓	✓
HARPER, EDWARD (1941–)		✓							✓											✓	✓	✓	✓	✓		
HARRIS, MATTHEW (1956–)										✓							✓							✓	✓	
HARRIS, ROY (1898–1979)		✓	✓							✓		✓					✓				✓		✓			✓
HARRIS, RUSSELL (1914–)																				✓						
HARRISON, JULIUS (1885–1963)		✓																								
HARRISON, LOU (1917–)	✓	✓															✓					✓	✓	✓	✓	✓
HARSANYI, TIBOR (1898–1954)										✓		✓									✓			✓	✓	✓
HARTIG, HEINZ F. (1907–1969)																	✓									
HARTLEY, WALTER S. (1927–)								✓	✓																✓	
HARTWELL, HUGH (1945–)																							✓	✓	✓	
HARTZELL, EUGENE (1932–)													✓				✓	✓								
HARVEY, JONATHAN (1939–)		✓																				✓	✓	✓	✓	✓
HASELBACH, JOSEF (1936–)			✓																							
HASHAGEN, KLAUS (1924–)																							✓			
HASLAM, HERBERT (1928–)								✓																		
HASQUENOPH, PIERRE (1922–1982)																					✓			✓		
HASSE, JOHANN A. (1699–1783)										✓												✓				
HASSLER, HANS L. (1564–1612)																					✓					
HAUBENSTOCK-RAMATI, ROMAN (1919–)	✓	✓																				✓	✓	✓	✓	✓
HAUER, JOSEF M. (1883–1959)										✓		✓											✓		✓	

	3 Strings	4 Strings	5 Strings	3 Winds	4 Winds	5 Winds	3 Brass	4 Brass	5 Brass	2 Strings & Keyboard	3 Strings & Keyboard	4 Strings & Keyboard	2 Winds & Keyboard	3 Winds & Keyboard	4 Winds & Keyboard	Brass & Keyboard	Misc. Ensembles (3 to 5)	Strings, Wind Keyboard Trio	Strings, Wind Keyboard Quartets	Strings, Wind Keyboard Quintets	Sextets & Larger Ensembles	Ensemble with Guitar/Harp	Ensembles with Keyboard	Ensembles with Percussion	Ensembles with Unusual Instruments	Ensemble with Voice
HAUFRECHT, HERBERT (1909–)										✓								✓				✓	✓	✓	✓	
HAXTON, KENNETH (1919–)																	✓									
HAYDN, JOSEF (1732–1809)	✓	✓		✓						✓			✓				✓	✓			✓	✓	✓	✓	✓	
HAYDN, MICHAEL (1737–1806)		✓															✓				✓					
HECHTEL, HERBERT (1937–)		✓																								
HEIDEN, BERNHARD (1910–)										✓							✓									
HEIDER, WERNER (1930–)																					✓	✓	✓	✓		✓
HEILMAN, WILLIAM C. (1877–1946)	✓																									
HEILNER, IRWIN (1908–1991)																						✓			✓	
HEINICHEN, JOHANN D. (1683–1729)																		✓					✓			✓
HEISS, JOHN (1938–)																										✓
HELLER, DUANE L. (1951–)																							✓			
HELLERMANN, WILLIAM (1939–)																							✓			
HELLMESBERGER, JOSEPH (1855–1907)												✓														
HELM, EVERETT (1913–)		✓																								
HELPS, ROBERT (1928–)										✓										✓			✓			
HEMPEL, ROLF (1932–)																	✓									
HENGARTNER, MAX (?–)		✓																								
HENNING, ERVIN A. (1910–)					✓																					
HENRIQUES, FINI V. (1867–1940)		✓																								
HENZE, HANS W.. (1926–)		✓								✓							✓				✓		✓			✓
HERCHET, JÖRG (1943–)																							✓			
HERRMANN, HUGO (1896–1967)		✓																								
HERRMANN, PETER (1941–)		✓								✓		✓														
HERSCHMANN, HEINZ (1924–)																					✓					
HERTEL, THOMAS (?–)		✓																								
HERVIG, RICHARD (1917–)																							✓	✓	✓	
HERZOGENBERG, HEINRICH (1834–1900)											✓															
HESPOS, HANS-JOACHIM (1938–)																						✓			✓	
HESS, ERNST (1912–1968)																									✓	
HESS, WILLY (1859–1939)	✓			✓													✓				✓				✓	
HESSENBERG, KURT (1908–)																					✓					✓
HEUGTEN, H. VAN (?–)							✓	✓									✓									
HEYN, VOLKER (1938–)																					✓		✓	✓		
HIBBARD, WILLIAM (1939–)																						✓	✓	✓	✓	
HIDALGO, MANUEL (1956–)	✓																							✓	✓	
HILLER, JR., LEJAREN (1924–)		✓																								
HILLIARD, JOHN S. (1947–)																							✓	✓	✓	
HILTON, JOHN (1599–1657)	✓																									
HINDEMITH, PAUL (1895–1963)	✓	✓										✓					✓		✓		✓		✓		✓	✓
HINGESTON, JOHN (?–1688)																✓										
HIRSCH, HANS L. (1937–)																						✓				
HLOBIL, EMIL (1901–)											✓															
HÖCKH, C (?–?)											✓															
HODDINOTT, ALUN (1929–)		✓						✓				✓					✓				✓	✓	✓	✓		✓
HODKINSON, SYDNEY (1934–)	✓									✓												✓	✓	✓	✓	✓
HOERE, ARTHUR (1897–1979)																							✓			✓
HOFFER, BERNARD (?–)																								✓		
HOFFMANN, ERNST (1776–1822)										✓																
HOFFMANN, LEOPOLD (1738–1793)										✓																
HOIBY, LEE (1926–)																				✓			✓			
HOLLANDER, BENNOIT (1853–1942)		✓																								
HÖLLER, KARL (1907–1987)		✓								✓	✓												✓	✓	✓	
HÖLLER, YORK (1944–)		✓																					✓	✓		

	3 Strings	4 Strings	5 Strings	3 Winds	4 Winds	5 Winds	3 Brass	4 Brass	5 Brass	2 Strings & Keyboard	3 Strings & Keyboard	4 Strings & Keyboard	2 Winds & Keyboard	3 Winds & Keyboard	4 Winds & Keyboard	Brass & Keyboard	Misc. Ensembles (3 to 5)	Strings, Wind Keyboard Trio	Strings, Wind Keyboard Quartets	Strings, Wind Keyboard Quintets	Sextets & Larger Ensembles	Ensemble with Guitar/Harp	Ensembles with Keyboard	Ensembles with Percussion	Ensembles with Unusual Instruments	Ensemble with Voice
HOLLOWAY, ROBIN (1934–)									✓												✓		✓	✓	✓	✓
HOLST, GUSTAV (1874–1934)																	✓									
HOLST, IMOGEN (1907–1984)			✓																							
HOLSTEIN, JEAN-PAUL (1939–)		✓																								
HOLTEN, BO (1948–)																					✓					
HONEGGER, ARTHUR (1892–1955)		✓									✓		✓				✓									✓
HOPKINS, JOHN (1949–)																				✓		✓	✓	✓	✓	✓
HORNE, DAVID (1970–)		✓																	✓				✓	✓		
HOROVITZ, JOSEPH (1926–)									✓																	
HORVATH, JOSEF M. (1931–)		✓																			✓				✓	✓
HOTTETERRE, JACQUES (1674–1762)													✓									✓				
HOUDY, PIERICK (?–)																✓										
HOVHANESS, ALAN (1911–)	✓	✓						✓	✓	✓		✓	✓				✓		✓		✓	✓	✓	✓	✓	✓
HOWARTH, ELGAR (1935–)									✓																	
HOWE, MARY (1882–1964)										✓																
HRABOVSKY, LEONID (1935–)																						✓	✓	✓	✓	✓
HUBEAU, JEAN (1917–)																							✓			
HUBER, HANS (1852–1921)																							✓			✓
HUBER, KLAUS (1924–)		✓															✓					✓				✓
HUBER, NICOLAUS A. (1939–)		✓																✓	✓				✓	✓	✓	
HUEBLER, KLAUS K. (1956–)		✓																				✓				
HUFSCHMIDT, WOLFGANG (1934–)		✓																				✓	✓	✓		✓
HUGGLER, JOHN (1928–)																					✓		✓	✓	✓	✓
HUGHES, MARK (1934–)							✓																			
HUGON, GEORGES (1904–1980)		✓																								
HUMEL, GERALD (1931–)																						✓	✓	✓	✓	
HUMMEL, JOHANN N. (1778–1837)	✓											✓						✓								
HUPFER, KONRAD (1935–)		✓																								
HURD, MICHAEL (1928–)									✓																	
HUSA, KAREL (1921–)		✓		✓					✓		✓						✓	✓					✓	✓	✓	
HUTCHESON, JERE (1938–)																		✓						✓		
IANNACCONE, ANTHONY (1943–)								✓																		
IBERT, JACQUES (1890–1962)		✓			✓								✓				✓	✓				✓				
ICHIYANAGI, TOSHI (1933–)																							✓	✓		
IMBRIE, ANDREW (1921–)		✓																✓					✓	✓	✓	
INDY, VINCENT D' (1851–1931)		✓								✓	✓	✓						✓			✓	✓				
INGHELBRECHT, DÉSIRÉ E. (1880–1965)		✓																				✓		✓	✓	
IOACHIMESCU, CALIN (1949–)																								✓		
IOANNIDIS, YANNIS (1930–)									✓								✓									
IRELAND, JOHN (1879–1962)		✓								✓																
ISRAEL, BRIAN M. (1951–)							✓																			
ISTVAN, MILOSLAV (1928–)																							✓	✓		
IVES, CHARLES (1874–1954)		✓								✓		✓				✓		✓					✓	✓	✓	✓
JACCHINI, GIUSEPPE (1670–1727)																✓										
JACKSON, AMBROSE (?–)								✓																		
JACOB, GORDON (1895–1984)				✓													✓	✓			✓		✓			✓
JACOB, WERNER (1938–)																							✓	✓	✓	✓
JACOBI, FREDERICK (1891–1952)		✓																								
JADIN, LOUIS (1768–1853)																	✓									
JAHN, THOMAS (1940–)																						✓	✓	✓	✓	
JANÁČEK, LEOS (1854–1928)		✓																					✓		✓	✓
JAROCH, JIRI (1920–)																					✓					
JARZEBSKI, ADAM (?–1649)								✓																		
JEKIMOWSKI, VIKTOR (1947–)		✓																								
JENEY, ZOLTAN (1943–)																						✓	✓			✓

	3 Strings	4 Strings	5 Strings	3 Winds	4 Winds	5 Winds	3 Brass	4 Brass	5 Brass	2 Strings & Keyboard	3 Strings & Keyboard	4 Strings & Keyboard	2 Winds & Keyboard	3 Winds & Keyboard	4 Winds & Keyboard	Brass & Keyboard	Misc. Ensembles (3 to 5)	Strings, Wind Keyboard Trio	Strings, Wind Keyboard Quartets	Strings, Wind Keyboard Quintets	Sextets & Larger Ensembles	Ensemble with Guitar/Harp	Ensembles with Keyboard	Ensembles with Percussion	Ensembles with Unusual Instruments	Ensemble with Voice
JENKINS, JOHN (1592–1678)		✓																			✓					
JEREMIAS, OTAKAR (1892–1962)											✓															
JETTEL, RUDOLF (1905–)		✓															✓									
JIRAK, KAREL B. (1891–)		✓								✓																
JIRASEK, IVO (1920–)																						✓				✓
JOHNSON, A. P. (1955–)																		✓					✓	✓	✓	
JOHNSON, DAVID N. (1922–)		✓															✓									
JOHNSON, JAMES J. (1924–)																						✓		✓	✓	
JOHNSON, SHERLAW (1932–)		✓																		✓			✓	✓		
JOLAS, BETSY (1926–)		✓															✓					✓	✓	✓	✓	✓
JOLIVET, ANDRÉ (1905–1974)	✓	✓															✓					✓	✓	✓	✓	✓
JOMMELLI, NICCOLÒ (1714–1774)										✓																
JONES, CHARLES (1910–)		✓			✓																					
JONES, KELSEY (1922–)													✓				✓									
JONGEN, JOSEPH (1873–1953)										✓	✓															
JOPLIN, SCOTT (1868–1917)			✓											✓												
JOSEPHS, WILFRED (1927–)	✓									✓																
JOUBERT, CLAUDE H. (?–)																	✓									
JULLIEN, RENÉ (?–)		✓																								
JUNG, HELGE (1943–)								✓																		
JUNGK, KLAUS (1916–)										✓																
KAGEL, MAURICIO (1931–)	✓	✓								✓											✓	✓	✓	✓	✓	✓
KAHN, ERICH I. (1905–1956)										✓								✓			✓					
KAHOWEZ, GÜNTER (1940–)		✓															✓						✓			
KALMAR, LASZLO (1931–)		✓																								
KALOMIRIS, MANOLIS (1883–1962)										✓																
KANITZ, ERNST (1894–1978)																	✓									
KAPLAN, ELLIOTT (?–)				✓																						
KAPR, JAN (1914–)											✓												✓			
KARCHIN, LOUIS S. (1951–)																		✓					✓		✓	
KARKOSCHKA, ERHARD (1923–)																										✓
KARLINS, M. W. (1932–)													✓				✓						✓	✓	✓	
KATZER, GEORG (1935–)		✓																			✓		✓	✓		✓
KAUER, FERDINAND (1751–1831)	✓																									
KAUFFMANN, GEORG F. (1679–1735)				✓																						
KAUFFMANN, JEAN (?–)																	✓									
KAUFMAN, FREDRICK (1936–)													✓								✓	✓		✓	✓	
KAUFMANN, ARMIN (1902–1980)	✓	✓								✓	✓						✓	✓								
KAUFMANN, SERGE (?–)				✓																						
KAUN, HUGO (1863–1932)												✓														
KEATS, DONALD (1929–)		✓																								
KELDORFER, ROBERT (1901–1980)				✓													✓								✓	
KELEMEN, MILKO (1924–)		✓							✓								✓				✓	✓	✓	✓	✓	✓
KELLER, HOMER (1915–)										✓								✓						✓		
KELLY, BRYAN G. (1934–)									✓												✓					
KELLY, ROBERT (1917–)										✓							✓					✓	✓	✓	✓	
KELTERBORN, RUDOLF (1931–)		✓								✓							✓	✓			✓	✓	✓	✓		✓
KENNAN, KENT W. (1913–)												✓														
KERNIS, AARON J. (1960–)		✓															✓	✓	✓				✓	✓	✓	✓
KESNAR, MAURITS (1900–1957)								✓																		
KESSLER, THOMAS (1937–)	✓	✓																								
KHACHATURIAN, ARAM (1903–1978)										✓								✓								
KHACHATURIAN, KARAN (1920–)		✓																								
KIEL, FRIEDRICH (1821–1885)		✓								✓																

	3 Strings	4 Strings	5 Strings	3 Winds	4 Winds	5 Winds	3 Brass	4 Brass	5 Brass	2 Strings & Keyboard	3 Strings & Keyboard	4 Strings & Keyboard	2 Winds & Keyboard	3 Winds & Keyboard	4 Winds & Keyboard	Brass & Keyboard	Misc. Ensembles (3 to 5)	Strings, Wind Keyboard Trio	Strings, Wind Keyboard Quartets	Strings, Wind Keyboard Quintets	Sextets & Larger Ensembles	Ensemble with Guitar/Harp	Ensembles with Keyboard	Ensembles with Percussion	Ensembles with Unusual Instruments	Ensemble with Voice
KIESEWETTER, TOMASZ (1911–)													✓													
KIEVMAN, CARSON (1949–)																	✓					✓	✓	✓	✓	✓
KING, JOHN L. (1953–)										✓									✓							
KINGMA, P (?–)																	✓									
KIRCHNER, LEON (1919–)		✓								✓													✓	✓	✓	✓
KIRCHNER, THEODOR (1823–1903)		✓																								
KITZKE, JEROME P. (1955–)																							✓	✓	✓	✓
KIVA, OLEH (1947–)																						✓	✓	✓	✓	✓
KLEBE, GISELHER (1925–)		✓								✓		✓									✓	✓	✓	✓	✓	
KLEINKNECHT, JACOB F. (1722–1794)													✓													
KLOSE, HYACINTHE (1808–1880)																							✓			
KLUSSMANN, ERNST G. (1901–)		✓																								
KNAB, ARMIN (1881–1951)													✓										✓			✓
KNAIFEL, ALEXANDER (1943–)																							✓	✓	✓	
KNIGHT, MORRIS (1933–)				✓			✓										✓									
KNUSSEN, OLIVER (1952–)																	✓				✓	✓	✓	✓	✓	✓
KOCH, JOHANNES H. (1918–)									✓															✓		
KOCHAN, GUNTER (1930–)		✓																								
KODALY, ZOLTAN (1882–1967)	✓	✓																								
KOECHLIN, CHARLES (1867–1950)		✓		✓								✓										✓	✓	✓	✓	
KOERING, RENÉ (1940–)		✓																					✓	✓	✓	
KÖHLER, SIEGFRIED (1927–1984)		✓																								
KOHOUTEK, CTIRAD (1929–)																	✓									
KOHS, ELLIS B. (1916–)											✓						✓							✓	✓	
KOKKONEN, JOONAS (1921–)		✓																					✓			
KOLB, BARBARA (1939–)																	✓					✓	✓	✓	✓	✓
KONDO, JO (1947–)																							✓	✓	✓	
KONINK, SERVAAS VAN (?–1718)	✓																									
KONT, PAUL (1920–)							✓	✓		✓							✓				✓	✓				
KOPELENT, MAREK (1932–)		✓							✓											✓			✓	✓		✓
KOPPRASCH, C. (?–)									✓																	
KORDA, VIKTOR (1900–)																	✓					✓		✓		
KORF, ANTHONY (1951–)																				✓						
KORN, PETER J. (1922–)									✓								✓									
KORNAUTH, EGON (1891–1959)		✓								✓	✓	✓					✓				✓					
KORNDORF, NIKOLAI (1947–)																								✓		
KORNGOLD, ERICH W. (1897–1957)		✓								✓	✓										✓					
KOTONSKI, WLODZIMIERZ (1925–)																						✓		✓		
KOUBA, JOSEF (1880–)		✓																								
KOVACH, F. (?–)																						✓				
KRAFT, LEO (1922–)																								✓		
KRAFT, WALTER (1905–1977)																							✓			✓
KRATOCHWIL, HEINZ (1933–)				✓					✓	✓							✓									
KRATZSCHMAR, WILFRIED (1944–)																	✓									
KRAUZE, ZYGMUNT (1938–)																			✓				✓		✓	
KREIGER, ARTHUR V. (1945–)																							✓	✓		
KREISLER, FRITZ (1875–1962)		✓																								
KREJCI, ISA (1904–1968)		✓																								
KREJCI, MIROSLAV (1891–1964)			✓																							
KREK, UROS (1922–)									✓																	
KREMEN, ISRAEL (?–1949)										✓													✓		✓	
KREMER, CLEMENS (1930–)								✓																		
ŘRENEK, ERNST (1900–)	✓	✓									✓						✓	✓				✓	✓	✓	✓	✓
KREUTZER, JOSEPH (1778–1832)																						✓				

	3 Strings	4 Strings	5 Strings	3 Winds	4 Winds	5 Winds	3 Brass	4 Brass	5 Brass	2 Strings & Keyboard	3 Strings & Keyboard	4 Strings & Keyboard	2 Winds & Keyboard	3 Winds & Keyboard	4 Winds & Keyboard	Brass & Keyboard	Misc. Ensembles (3 to 5)	Strings, Wind Keyboard Trio	Strings, Wind Keyboard Quartets	Strings, Wind Keyboard Quintets	Sextets & Larger Ensembles	Ensemble with Guitar/Harp	Ensembles with Keyboard	Ensembles with Percussion	Ensembles with Unusual Instruments	Ensemble with Voice
KREUTZER, KONRADIN (1780–1849)																	✓				✓					
KREUTZER, RODOLPHE (1766–1831)																	✓									
KRICKA, JAROSLAV (1882–1969)		✓																								
KRIEGER, JOHANN P. (1649–1725)										✓			✓													
KRIST, JOACHIM (1948–)											✓															
KROEGER, KARL (1932–)																	✓									
KROL, BERNHARD (1920–)									✓							✓		✓			✓		✓		✓	
KROLL, WILLIAM (1901–)																							✓		✓	✓
KROMMER, FRANTISEK V. (1759–1831)		✓		✓													✓									
KROPFREITER, AUGUSTINUS F. (1936–)																	✓						✓			
KRUL, ELI (1926–1970)		✓																								
KUBELIK, RAFAEL (1914–)		✓																								
KUBIK, GAIL (1914–)																							✓			
KUBIZEK, AUGUSTIN (1918–)																	✓	✓			✓	✓				
KUBO, MAYAKO (1947–)																							✓	✓		
KUHLAU, FRIEDRICH (1786–1832)																	✓	✓								
KUHN, MAX (1896–)																	✓									
KUNAD, RAINERN (1936–)		✓											✓				✓									✓
KUPFERMAN, MEYER (1926–)																					✓					
KURI-ALDANA, MARIO (1931–)													✓				✓									
KURKA, ROBERT (1921–1957)																	✓							✓	✓	
KURTAG, GYORGY (1926–)		✓															✓	✓				✓		✓	✓	✓
KVANDAL, JOHAN (1919–)																					✓					
LABEY, MARCEL (1875–1968)		✓									✓															
LABROCA, MARIO (1896–1973)		✓																								
LABURDA, JIRI (1931–)							✓																			
LACHENMANN, HELMUT (1935–)		✓																						✓		✓
LACHNER, FRANZ (1803–1890)																	✓						✓			✓
LACHNER, IGNAZ (1807–1895)		✓	✓							✓																
LACOUR, GUY (?–)																								✓		
LADERMAN, EZRA (1924–)		✓								✓		✓					✓				✓		✓			✓
LAJTHA, LASZLO (1892–1963)	✓	✓			✓																	✓				
LALO, EDOUARD (1823–1892)		✓								✓																
LAMPE, GÜNTER (1925–)																	✓									
LANCHBERY, JOHN (1923–)									✓																	
LANG, ISTVAN (1933–)		✓							✓								✓						✓	✓	✓	
LANGE, SAMUEL DE (1840–1911)		✓																								
LANNOY, EDUARD VON (1787–1853)																							✓			
LANTIER, PIERRE L. (1910–)		✓																								
LAUERMANN, HERBERT (1955–)		✓																								
LAWES, WILLIAM (1602–1645)			✓																		✓					
LAWSON, PETER (?–)																							✓	✓		
LAYTON, BILLY J. (1924–)																							✓	✓		
LAZAROF, HENRI (1932–)		✓		✓					✓												✓	✓	✓	✓	✓	
LEBARON, ANNE (1953–)																					✓	✓	✓	✓	✓	
LECHNER, KONRAD (1911–)																							✓	✓		✓
LECHTHALER, JOSEF (1891–1948)										✓																
LECLAIR, JEAN-MARIE (1697–1764)										✓		✓						✓		✓						
LEES, BENJAMIN (1924–)		✓								✓							✓						✓			
LEFEBVRE, CLAUDE (1931–)																					✓		✓			✓
LEFEVRE, JEAN X. (1763–1829)				✓																						✓
LEGE, GÜNTER (1935–)																										
LEGRENZI, GIOVANNI (1626–1690)										✓																
LEHMANN, HANS U. (1937–)																					✓					

	3 Strings	4 Strings	5 Strings	3 Winds	4 Winds	5 Winds	3 Brass	4 Brass	5 Brass	2 Strings & Keyboard	3 Strings & Keyboard	4 Strings & Keyboard	2 Winds & Keyboard	3 Winds & Keyboard	4 Winds & Keyboard	Brass & Keyboard	Misc. Ensembles (3 to 5)	Strings, Wind Keyboard Trio	Strings, Wind Keyboard Quartets	Strings, Wind Keyboard Quintets	Sextets & Larger Ensembles	Ensemble with Guitar/Harp	Ensembles with Keyboard	Ensembles with Percussion	Ensembles with Unusual Instruments	Ensemble with Voice
LEITERMEYER, FRITZ (1925–)	✓	✓															✓	✓			✓				✓	
LEITNER, E. L. (?–)																							✓			
LEKEU, GUILLAUME (1870–1894)										✓																
LEMAIRE, FELIX (?–)				✓																						
LEMELAND, AUBERT (1932–)	✓			✓													✓				✓					
LENNON, JOHN A. (1950–)		✓																								
LENOT, JACQUES (1945–)																		✓	✓		✓	✓	✓	✓	✓	✓
LEROUX, PHILIPPE (?–)																	✓									
LESSARD, JOHN (1920–)																	✓							✓	✓	
LEUKAUF, ROBERT (1902–)																	✓									
LEVI, PAUL A. (1941–)																	✓									
LEVINAS, MICHAEL (1949–)																					✓		✓	✓	✓	
LEWIN, FRANK (1925–)																					✓					
LEWIS, PETER T. (1932–)										✓												✓	✓	✓	✓	
LEWIS, ROBERT H. (1926–)																		✓			✓					
LEWKOVITCH, BERNHARD (1927–)																										✓
LEYENDECKER, ULRICH (1946–)		✓																				✓	✓	✓	✓	✓
LIADOFF, ANATOLE (1855–1914)		✓																								
LICKL, JOHANN G. (1769–1843)																	✓									
LIDHOLM, INGVAR (1921–)		✓																								
LIEBERMAN, GLENN (1947–)																	✓					✓	✓	✓	✓	
LIEBERSON, GODDARD (1911–1977)		✓																								
LIEBERSON, PETER (1946–)																			✓			✓	✓	✓	✓	✓
LIGETI, GYORGY (1923–)																						✓	✓	✓		✓
LINDBERG, MAGNUS (1958–)																							✓		✓	
LINDBERG, NILS (1933–)																								✓		
LINDBLAD, FREDRIK (1801–1878)			✓							✓																
LINDENFELD, HARRIS (1945–)										✓													✓	✓		
LINIKE, JOHANN G. (?–1737)																							✓			
LINKE, NORBERT (1933–)																					✓					
LIPP, CHARLES (?–1945)																	✓									
LIPTAK, DAVID (1949–)																	✓						✓	✓		
LISCHKA, RAINER (1942–)																								✓	✓	
LISZT, FRANZ (1811–1886)		✓																								
LIVIABELLA, LINO (1902–1964)		✓																								
LLOYD, JONATHAN (1948–)		✓	✓						✓								✓				✓	✓	✓	✓	✓	✓
LOCATELLI, PIETRO (1695–1764)										✓																
LOCKE, MATTHEW (1630–1677)	✓																									
LOCKWOOD, NORMAND (1906–)		✓															✓					✓				
LOEFFLER, CHARLES M. (1861–1935)		✓																				✓	✓			✓
LOEILLET, JEAN-BAPT. (1680–1730)													✓		✓											
LOGOTHETIS, ANESTIS (1921–)																										
LOHSE, FRED (?–)										✓							✓									
LOLINI, RUGGIERO (?–)	✓																									
LOMBARDO, ROBERT (1932–)																								✓		
LONDON, EDWIN (1929–)									✓													✓	✓	✓	✓	✓
LORA, ANTONIO (1899–1965)										✓																
LORENTZEN, BENT (1935–)		✓								✓								✓			✓	✓	✓	✓		✓
LORENZO, LEONARDO DE (1875–1962)				✓	✓																					
LOTHAR, FRIEDRICH W. (1885–)	✓																									
LOTHAR, MARK (1902–)																							✓	✓		✓
LOTTI, ANTONIO (1667–1740)													✓													
LOUCHEUR, RAYMOND (1899–1979)				✓																						
LOUIS FERDINAND, (PRINCE) (1772–1806)																							✓			

	3 Strings	4 Strings	5 Strings	3 Winds	4 Winds	5 Winds	3 Brass	4 Brass	5 Brass	2 Strings & Keyboard	3 Strings & Keyboard	4 Strings & Keyboard	2 Winds & Keyboard	3 Winds & Keyboard	4 Winds & Keyboard	Brass & Keyboard	Misc. Ensembles (3 to 5)	Strings, Wind Keyboard Trio	Strings, Wind Keyboard Quartets	Strings, Wind Keyboard Quintets	Sextets & Larger Ensembles	Ensemble with Guitar/Harp	Ensembles with Keyboard	Ensembles with Percussion	Ensembles with Unusual Instruments	Ensemble with Voice
LOUVIER, ALAIN (1945–)									✓								✓									
LOVENDUSKY, JAMES (1957–)										✓													✓	✓	✓	
LUDEWIG, WOLFGANG (1926–)													✓				✓	✓	✓			✓				
LUEDEKE, RAYMOND (1944–)																✓	✓	✓	✓			✓				
LUENING, OTTO (1900–)	✓	✓		✓	✓		✓		✓	✓			✓	✓			✓	✓			✓		✓	✓	✓	✓
LULLY, JEAN-BAPT. (1632–1687)										✓														✓		
LUMSDAINE, DAVID (1931–)																							✓		✓	✓
LUNDBORG, ERIK (1948–)																						✓	✓	✓	✓	
LUPPI, GIAN P. (?–)																	✓									
LUSTIG, MOSHE (1922–1958)																						✓				
LUTOSLAWSKI, WITOLD (1913–)		✓							✓												✓		✓	✓	✓	
LUZZASCHI, LUZZASCHO (1545–1607)								✓																		
LYBBERT, DONALD (1923–1981)																	✓				✓		✓	✓		✓
MAASZ, GERHARD (1906–)																	✓		✓							
MACBRIDE, DAVID H. (1951–)																							✓	✓	✓	
MACCOMBIE, BRUCE (1943–)																							✓	✓	✓	✓
MACDOWELL, EDWARD (1860–1908)								✓																		
MACERO, TEO (1925–)																							✓			
MACHE, FRANÇOIS B. (1935–)																						✓		✓	✓	✓
MACHOVER, TOD (1953–)		✓																								✓
MACKEY, STEVEN (1956–)											✓															
MACMILLAN, ERNEST (1893–1973)		✓																								
MACONCHY, ELIZABETH (1907–)		✓															✓					✓				
MADERNA, BRUNO (1920–1973)		✓																								
MADJERA, GOTTFRIED (1905–)		✓																								
MAHLER, GUSTAVE (1860–1911)											✓											✓	✓	✓	✓	✓
MAIGUASHCA, MESIAS (1938–)		✓																					✓		✓	
MAINARDI, ENRICO (1897–1976)		✓								✓																
MALEC, IVO (1925–)																					✓	✓		✓		✓
MALIPIERO, GIAN F. (1882–1973)		✓																		✓		✓	✓	✓	✓	
MALIPIERO, RICCARDO (1914–)		✓										✓					✓									
MAMANGAKIS, NIKOS (1929–)		✓																								
MAMLOK, URSULA (1928–)										✓							✓			✓		✓	✓	✓	✓	✓
MANNINO, FRANCO (1924–)		✓									✓												✓			
MANOURY, PHILIPPE (1952–)																							✓			
MANSURIAN, TIGRAN (1939–)																					✓		✓	✓	✓	✓
MANZIARLY, MARCELLE DE (1899–)																		✓								
MANZONI, GIACOMO (1932–)		✓															✓				✓					
MARCKHL, ERICH (1902–)		✓															✓									
MARCO, TOMÁS (1942–)		✓																								
MARCOS, MIKLOS (1943–)																							✓	✓		✓
MARENZIO, LUCA (1553–1599)			✓																							
MARINI, BIAGIO (1587–1665)										✓																
MARKEVITCH, IGOR (1912–1983)																	✓						✓	✓		
MARTEAU, HENRI (1874–1934)		✓																								
MARTELLI, HENRI (1895–1980)				✓																						
MARTI, HEINZ (1934–)	✓																									
MARTIN, FRANK (1890–1974)	✓	✓	✓							✓												✓	✓	✓	✓	✓
MARTINO, DONALD (1931–)		✓								✓							✓						✓	✓		
MARTINON, JEAN (1910–1976)	✓	✓		✓													✓									
MARTINS, MARIA (1926–)										✓																
MARTINŮ, BOHUSLAV (1890–1959)		✓	✓							✓	✓	✓					✓	✓			✓	✓	✓		✓	
MARTIRANO, SALVATORE (1927–)																					✓			✓	✓	
MARX, JOSEPH (1882–1964)		✓																								

	3 Strings	4 Strings	5 Strings	3 Winds	4 Winds	5 Winds	3 Brass	4 Brass	5 Brass	2 Strings & Keyboard	3 Strings & Keyboard	4 Strings & Keyboard	2 Winds & Keyboard	3 Winds & Keyboard	4 Winds & Keyboard	Brass & Keyboard	Misc. Ensembles (3 to 5)	Strings, Wind Keyboard Trio	Strings, Wind Keyboard Quartets	Strings, Wind Keyboard Quintets	Sextets & Larger Ensembles	Ensemble with Guitar/Harp	Ensembles with Keyboard	Ensembles with Percussion	Ensembles with Unusual Instruments	Ensemble with Voice
MARX, KARL (1897–1985)									✓											✓	✓		✓			✓
MASCHERA, FIORENZO (1540–1584)								✓																		
MASEK, VACLAV V. (1755–1831)																					✓					
MASELLI, GIANFRANCO (1929–)		✓																					✓			
MASON, BENEDICT (1954–)		✓							✓	✓												✓	✓	✓	✓	
MASON, DANIEL G. (1873–1953)		✓									✓						✓	✓				✓				
MASON, JOHN (?–)				✓																						
MASSEUS, JAN (1913–)																				✓						
MASSIAS, GÉRARD (1933–)																	✓									
MASSIS, AMABLE (1893–)																	✓									
MASSON, GÉRARD (1936–)		✓																				✓	✓		✓	
MASSONEAU, LOUIS (?–)																	✓									
MATHIAS, WILLIAM (1934–)		✓							✓	✓			✓	✓			✓					✓	✓	✓	✓	✓
MATSUDAIRA, YORI-AKI (1931–)										✓																
MATTHEWS, COLIN (1946–)		✓										✓					✓				✓	✓	✓	✓	✓	✓
MATTHEWS, WILLIAM (1950–)																			✓				✓	✓		
MATTHUS, SIEGFRIED (1934–)		✓																				✓				
MAURER, LUDWIG W. (1789–1878)									✓																	
MAVES, DAVID (1937–)																								✓		✓
MAW, NICHOLAS (1935–)		✓															✓					✓			✓	
MAXWELL DAVIES, PETER (1934–)		✓							✓								✓				✓	✓	✓	✓	✓	✓
MAYER, B (?–)								✓	✓																	
MAYER, WILLIAM (1925–)							✓																			
MAYR, GIOVANNI (1763–1845)																									✓	
MAYUZUMI, TOSHIRO (1929–)		✓																				✓	✓	✓	✓	✓
MAZZAFERRATA, GIOVANNI B. (?–1691)											✓															
MCBRIDE, ROBERT (1911–)											✓		✓				✓					✓			✓	
MCCABE, JOHN (1939–)									✓																	
MCEWEN, JOHN (1868–1948)		✓																								
MCGUIRE, JOHN (1942–)		✓																								
MCKAY, GEORGE F. (1899–1970)																	✓									
MCLEAN, EDWIN (1906–1951)																						✓	✓	✓	✓	✓
MCPHEE, COLIN (1901–1964)																							✓			
MEALE, RICHARD (1932–)																							✓	✓	✓	
MEFANO, PAUL (1937–)		✓																				✓	✓	✓	✓	✓
MEIER, JOST (1939–)								✓																		
MELBY, JOHN (1941–)																	✓									
MELLNÄS, ARNE (1933–)	✓						✓																✓	✓	✓	
MENDELSSOHN, FELIX (1809–1847)		✓	✓							✓	✓						✓	✓			✓		✓		✓	
MENEELY-KYDER, SARAH (1945–)																							✓			
MENNIN, PETER (1923–1983)																						✓	✓	✓	✓	✓
MENOTTI, GIAN C. (1911–)																						✓				✓
MENU, PIERRE (?–)		✓																								
MERILAEINEN, USKO (1930–)																							✓	✓		
MERSSON, BORIS (1921–)																	✓									
MERULO, CLAUDIO (1533–1604)								✓																		
MESSIAEN, OLIVIER (1908–1992)																			✓				✓	✓	✓	✓
METSK, JURO (1954–)																								✓		
METZLER, FRIEDRICH (1910–)																							✓	✓	✓	
MEYER, ERNST H. (1905–)		✓								✓							✓									
MEYER, JEAN (?–)				✓																	✓			✓		
MICA, JAN A. (1746–1811)		✓															✓									
MICHAEL, FRANK (1943–)										✓								✓								
MICHEELSEN, HANS F. (1902–1973)									✓														✓			✓
MICO, RICHARD (?–1665)			✓																							

	3 Strings	4 Strings	5 Strings	3 Winds	4 Winds	5 Winds	3 Brass	4 Brass	5 Brass	2 Strings & Keyboard	3 Strings & Keyboard	4 Strings & Keyboard	2 Winds & Keyboard	3 Winds & Keyboard	4 Winds & Keyboard	Brass & Keyboard	Misc. Ensembles (3 to 5)	Strings, Wind Keyboard Trio	Strings, Wind Keyboard Quartets	Strings, Wind Keyboard Quintets	Sextets & Larger Ensembles	Ensemble with Guitar/Harp	Ensembles with Keyboard	Ensembles with Percussion	Ensembles with Unusual Instruments	Ensemble with Voice
MIEG, PETER (1906–)																				✓						
MIEREANU, COSTIN (1943–)		✓																				✓	✓	✓	✓	✓
MIGOT, GEORGES (1891–1976)		✓		✓						✓							✓					✓				
MIHALOVICI, MARCEL (1898–1985)																							✓			
MILHAUD, DARIUS (1892–1974)	✓	✓	✓	✓			✓			✓	✓	✓		✓			✓	✓			✓	✓	✓	✓	✓	✓
MILLER, EDWARD (1930–)										✓											✓		✓	✓	✓	
MILLS, CHARLES (1914–)											✓						✓				✓		✓	✓		
MIROGLIO, FRANCIS (1924–)																					✓	✓	✓	✓	✓	
MITCHELL, DARLEEN C. (1942–)																							✓	✓	✓	
MITREA-CELARIAN, MIHAIL (1935–)																							✓	✓	✓	✓
MITTERGRADNEGGER, G (?–)						✓																				
MOENE, ALAIN (1942–)																										✓
MOESCHINGER, ALBERT (1897–)	✓			✓													✓									
MOLIQUE, BERNHARD (1802–1869)																	✓									
MOLLICONE, HENRY (1946–)																						✓	✓	✓	✓	
MOLTER, JOHANN M. (1695–1765)																	✓				✓					
MOMIGNY, JEROME DE J. (1762–1838)		✓																								
MONN, GEORG M. (1717–1750)											✓															
MONTEVERDI, CLAUDIO (1567–1643)			✓							✓	✓												✓			✓
MONTSALVATGE, XAVIER (1912–)																						✓	✓	✓	✓	
MOORE, DOROTHY R. (1940–)										✓																
MOORE, DOUGLAS S. (1893–1969)										✓																
MORERA, ENRIQUE (1865–1942)									✓																	
MORITZ, EDVARD (1891–)		✓															✓									
MORRICONE, ENNIO (1928–)																	✓									
MORRIS, HAROLD (1890–1964)		✓								✓		✓														
MORTARI, VIRGILIO (1902–)	✓											✓														
MORYL, RICHARD (1929–)																						✓				
MOSSOLOV, ALEXANDER (1900–1973)																						✓	✓	✓	✓	✓
MOTTE, DIETHER LA (1928–)																						✓	✓	✓	✓	✓
MOURANT, WALTER (1910–)																	✓									
MOURAVIEFF, LEON (1905–)		✓																								
MOYSE, LOUIS (1912–)																	✓									
MOZART, LEOPOLD (1719–1787)	✓		✓								✓						✓									
MOZART, WOLFGANG A. (1756–1791)	✓	✓	✓	✓						✓	✓						✓	✓			✓		✓	✓	✓	
MOZART, JR., WOLFGANG A. (1791–1844)											✓															
MUCZYNSKI, ROBERT (1929–)	✓									✓																
MUFFAT, GEORG (1653–1704)												✓														
MUFFAT, GOTTLIEB (1690–1770)											✓															
MÜLLER, IWAN (1786–1854)													✓										✓			
MULLER, PETER (1791–1877)																	✓									
MÜLLER-HERMANN, JOHANNE (1878–1941)		✓																								
MÜLLER-HORNBACH, GERHARD (1951–)		✓								✓															✓	
MÜLLER-WEINBERG, ACHIM (1933–)		✓															✓									
MÜLLER-ZÜRICH, PAUL (1898–)	✓	✓																							✓	
MUÑOZ MOLLEDA, JOSÉ (1905–)		✓																								
MUNTZING, A (?–)										✓																

	3 Strings	4 Strings	5 Strings	3 Winds	4 Winds	5 Winds	3 Brass	4 Brass	5 Brass	2 Strings & Keyboard	3 Strings & Keyboard	4 Strings & Keyboard	2 Winds & Keyboard	3 Winds & Keyboard	4 Winds & Keyboard	Brass & Keyboard	Misc. Ensembles (3 to 5)	Strings, Wind Keyboard Trio	Strings, Wind Keyboard Quartets	Strings, Wind Keyboard Quintets	Sextets & Larger Ensembles	Ensemble with Guitar/Harp	Ensembles with Keyboard	Ensembles with Percussion	Ensembles with Unusual Instruments	Ensemble with Voice
MURAIL, TRISTAN (1947–)																							✓	✓		
MUSGRAVE, THEA (1928–)		✓											✓								✓	✓	✓		✓	
MYSLIVECEK, JOSEF (1737–1781)			✓														✓				✓					
NARITA-YOSHIDA, KAZUKO (1957–)																							✓	✓	✓	
NAULAIS, JEROME (?–)									✓																	
NAUMANN, ERNST (1910–)		✓								✓											✓					
NAUMANN, JOHANN G. (1741–1801)	✓																									
NAWRATIL, KAREL (1867–1936)		✓																								
NEDBAL, MANFRED J. (1902–)	✓	✓															✓									
NEIKRUG, MARC (1946–)		✓																	✓				✓	✓		
NEJEDLY, VIT (1912–1945)		✓																								
NEMIROFF, ISAAC (1912–1977)				✓	✓												✓									
NEUBAUER, FRANZ C. (1760–1785)																	✓									
NEUBERT, GOTTFRIED (1926–)																✓										
NEUBERT, GÜNTER (1936–)																	✓					✓				✓
NEWELL, ROBERT M. (1940–)																							✓	✓	✓	
NEWLIN, DIKA (1923–)										✓		✓														
NICULESCU, STEFAN (1927–)																					✓	✓	✓	✓	✓	
NIELSEN, CARL (1865–1931)		✓	✓									✓					✓									
NIELSON, LEWIS J. (1950–)																							✓	✓	✓	
NIHASHI, (1ST NAME UNK.) (?–)																	✓									
NILSSON, BO (1937–)		✓															✓							✓	✓	✓
NONO, LUIGI (1924–)		✓																								✓
NORDEN, HUGO (1909–)										✓																
NORDENSTROM, GLADYS (1924–)																									✓	
NORDHEIM, ARNE (1931–)		✓																				✓	✓	✓	✓	
NORGARD, PER (1932–)		✓															✓	✓		✓		✓	✓	✓	✓	✓
NOSTRAND, BURR VAN (?–1945)																							✓		✓	
NOVAK, JIRI F. (1913–)																	✓									
NOVAK, VITESLAV (1870–1949)		✓										✓														
NOWAK, ALISON (1948–)										✓		✓					✓				✓	✓	✓			
NOWAK, LIONEL (1911–)										✓							✓	✓					✓	✓	✓	
NYSTEDT, KNUT (1915–)		✓							✓															✓	✓	✓
OEHRING, WOLFGANG (1941–)																										✓
OKUMURA, HAJIME (1925–)																		✓								
OLAH, TIBERIU (1928–)																					✓			✓	✓	
OLAN, DAVID (1948–)																	✓		✓				✓	✓	✓	
OLIVER, STEPHEN (1950–)									✓																	
OLLONE, MAX D' (1875–1959)										✓																
OLSEN, POUL R. (1922–1982)																						✓		✓		
OREFICE, GIACOMO (1865–1922)										✓																
ORR, BUXTON D. (1924–)									✓																	
ORTIZ, WILLIAM (1947–)										✓												✓	✓	✓	✓	
OSTENDORF, JENS-PETER (1944–)		✓																								
OTANO, NEMESIO (1880–1956)										✓											✓					
OTTERLOO, WILLEM VAN (1907–)	✓																									
OVERTON, HALL (1920–1972)		✓																				✓	✓	✓		
PABLO, LUIS DE (1930–)		✓																				✓	✓	✓	✓	✓
PACCIONE, PAUL (1952–)																						✓	✓	✓	✓	
PACHELBEL, JOHANN (1653–1704)										✓	✓															
PACKER, RANDALL (1933–)																						✓		✓		
PAGANINI, NICCOLÒ (1782–1840)		✓																								
PAISIELLO, GIOVANNI (1740–1816)		✓															✓									
PALESTER, ROMAN (1907–)	✓																									
PALLAVICINI, CARLO (?–1688)			✓																							

	3 Strings	4 Strings	5 Strings	3 Winds	4 Winds	5 Winds	3 Brass	4 Brass	5 Brass	2 Strings & Keyboard	3 Strings & Keyboard	4 Strings & Keyboard	2 Winds & Keyboard	3 Winds & Keyboard	4 Winds & Keyboard	Brass & Keyboard	Misc. Ensembles (3 to 5)	Strings, Wind Keyboard Trio	Strings, Wind Keyboard Quartets	Strings, Wind Keyboard Quintets	Sextets & Larger Ensembles	Ensemble with Guitar/Harp	Ensembles with Keyboard	Ensembles with Percussion	Ensembles with Unusual Instruments	Ensemble with Voice
PALMER, ROBERT (1915–)												✓														
PANIZZA, ETTORE (1875–1967)		✓																								
PANUFNIK, ANDRZEJ (1914–1991)		✓								✓											✓		✓			
PARK, JAMES (1942–)										✓												✓				
PARRIS, ROBERT (1924–)																✓	✓	✓			✓	✓	✓	✓	✓	
PÄRT, ARVO (1935–)																	✓									✓
PASCAL, ANDRÉ (1894–)		✓								✓																
PASCAL, CLAUDE (1921–)		✓																			✓					
PAUBON, PIERRE (1910–)				✓																						
PAUER, JIRI (1919–)																	✓									
PAVLYENKO, SERGEI (1952–)																						✓	✓	✓	✓	
PAYNE, ANTHONY (1936–)		✓							✓									✓				✓	✓	✓		
PEETERS, FLOR (1903–1986)				✓																						
PEIXINHO, JORGE R. (1940–)		✓																					✓			
PENDERECKI, KRZYSTOF (1933–)		✓																								
PENNISI, FRANCESCO (1934–)											✓							✓								
PEPUSCH, JOHANN C. (1667–1752)															✓			✓		✓						
PERAGALLO, MARIO (1910–)																					✓					
PERGOLESI, GIOVANNI B. (1710–1736)										✓	✓															
PERLE, GEORGE (1915–)		✓															✓									
PERLEA, JONEL (1900–1970)		✓																								
PERLONGO, DANIEL (1942–)																	✓					✓	✓	✓	✓	
PERRONI, GIOVANNI (1688–1748)																						✓				
PERRIN, JEAN-CHARLES (1920–)								✓																		
PERSICHETTI, VINCENT (1915–1987)		✓							✓	✓							✓				✓		✓	✓		
PETERKA, RUDOLF (?–)		✓																								
PETERS, RUDOLF (1902–1962)		✓																								
PETIT, JEAN-LOUIS (1937–)																					✓					
PETIT, PIERRE Y. (1922–)								✓																		
PETRASSI, GOFFREDO (1904–)	✓	✓																					✓	✓		
PETROVICS, EMIL (1930–)		✓							✓								✓									
PETTERSSON, ALLAN (1911–)			✓																							
PETYREK, FELIX (1892–1951)	✓																✓									
PEZ, JOHANN C. (1664–1716)											✓											✓				
PEZEL, JOHANN C. (1639–1694)									✓							✓		✓					✓			
PEZELIUS, JOHANN (1639–1694)																✓										
PFAUTSCH, LLOYD (1921–)									✓																	
PFISTER, HEIDI (1927–1978)													✓				✓									
PFITZNER, HANS (1869–1949)		✓																								
PFUNDT, REINHARD (1951–)		✓															✓									
PHALESE, PIERRE (1510–1573)					✓																					
PHILIPPOT, MICHEL (1925–)																					✓		✓	✓		
PHILLIPS, IVAN (?–)				✓																						
PHILLIPS, PETER (1930–)																							✓	✓	✓	
PICHA, FRANTISEK (1893–1964)		✓								✓																
PICHAUREAU, CLAUDE (1940–)																							✓			
PICHL, WENZL (1741–1805)		✓																								
PICHLER, ERNST (1908–)																					✓					
PICK, CARL-HEINZ (1929–)		✓																								
PICKER, TOBIAS (1954–)																							✓	✓	✓	
PICK-MANGIAGALLI, RICCARDO (1882–1949)		✓																								
PIER, GEORG (?–)																							✓	✓		
PIERNÉ, GABRIEL (1863–1937)	✓									✓							✓	✓			✓	✓	✓			
PIERNÉ, PAUL (1874–1952)				✓													✓									

	3 Strings	4 Strings	5 Strings	3 Winds	4 Winds	5 Winds	3 Brass	4 Brass	5 Brass	2 Strings & Keyboard	3 Strings & Keyboard	4 Strings & Keyboard	2 Winds & Keyboard	3 Winds & Keyboard	4 Winds & Keyboard	Brass & Keyboard	Misc. Ensembles (3 to 5)	Strings, Wind Keyboard Trio	Strings, Wind Keyboard Quartets	Strings, Wind Keyboard Quintets	Sextets & Larger Ensembles	Ensemble with Guitar/Harp	Ensembles with Keyboard	Ensembles with Percussion	Ensembles with Unusual Instruments	Ensemble with Voice
PIETRI, GIUSEPPE (1886–1946)										✓																
PIJPER, WILLEM (1894–1947)		✓															✓									
PILATI, MARIO (1903–1938)												✓														
PILLNEY, KARL H. (1896–1980)																							✓	✓	✓	
PILLOIS, JACQUES (1877–1935)																						✓				
PILSS, KARL (1902–)																	✓				✓					
PINKHAM, DANIEL (1923–)							✓		✓					✓			✓					✓	✓	✓	✓	
PIRCKMAYER, GEORG (1918–1977)										✓																
PISK, PAUL A. (1893–1990)				✓												✓		✓			✓					
PISTON, WALTER (1894–1976)	✓	✓		✓						✓	✓	✓					✓				✓	✓		✓		
PIZZETTI, ILDEBRANDO (1889–1968)		✓								✓																✓
PLACHETA, HUGO (1892–)																	✓									
PLANEL, ROBERT (1908–)		✓																								
PLATTI, GIOVANNI (1697–1763)													✓													
PLATZ, ROBERT (1951–)																						✓				
PLESKOW, RAOUL (1931–)																	✓	✓		✓	✓	✓	✓	✓	✓	
PLEYEL, IGNAZ J. (1757–1831)	✓	✓		✓													✓	✓			✓					
PODESVA, JAROMIR (1927–)		✓																								
POGLIETTI, ALESSANDRO (?–1683)																							✓			
POHLE, DAVID (1624–1695)																							✓			✓
POLIN, CLAIRE (1926–)									✓																	
POLZELLI, A (?–)																	✓									
PONCE, MANUEL (1886–1948)		✓																								
POOT, MARCEL (1901–)		✓															✓									
PORENA, BORIS (1927–)																								✓	✓	
PORPORA, NICOLA A. (1686–1768)											✓															
PORTER, QUINCY (1897–1966)		✓										✓					✓									
PORTER, WALTER (1595–1659)										✓																
POSER, HANS (1917–1970)		✓																								
POSSINGER, ALEXANDER (?–)																	✓									
POSSINGER, F A. (1767–1827)				✓																						
POULENC, FRANCIS (1899–1963)							✓						✓			✓		✓		✓			✓	✓	✓	✓
POUSSEUR, HENRI (1929–)																						✓	✓		✓	✓
POWELL, MEL (1923–)		✓								✓		✓					✓	✓				✓	✓	✓	✓	✓
POWERS, ANTHONY (1953–)		✓								✓		✓					✓		✓		✓	✓	✓	✓	✓	✓
POWNING, GRAHAM (?–)				✓																						
PRAETORIUS, MICHAEL (1571–1621)					✓												✓									
PREMRU, RAYMOND (1934–)																	✓									
PRESSER, WILLIAM (1916–)				✓				✓									✓									
PREVIN, ANDRÉ (1929–)									✓													✓	✓	✓		
PRIN, YVES (1933–)																							✓	✓	✓	
PRINZ, ALFRED (1930–)													✓				✓				✓					
PRIULI, GIOVANNI (1575–1629)																					✓					
PROBST, DOMINIQUE (?–)																						✓		✓		
PROCTER, LELAND H. (1914–)												✓														
PROKOFIEV, SERGE (1891–1953)		✓															✓						✓			
PROSPERI, CARLO (1921–)																						✓			✓	
PUCCINI, GIACOMO (1858–1924)		✓																								
PUGNANI, GAETANO (1731–1798)											✓															
PURCELL, DANIEL (1660–1717)													✓													
PURCELL, HENRY (1659–1695)		✓							✓		✓			✓									✓			✓
QUANTZ, JOHANN J. (1697–1773)													✓						✓							
QUARANTA, FELICE (1910–)																						✓	✓	✓		
QUERAT, MARCEL (?–)				✓													✓									
RABEY, R (?–)																							✓			✓
RACHMANINOFF, SERGEI (1873–1943)		✓								✓																

	3 Strings	4 Strings	5 Strings	3 Winds	4 Winds	5 Winds	3 Brass	4 Brass	5 Brass	2 Strings & Keyboard	3 Strings & Keyboard	4 Strings & Keyboard	2 Winds & Keyboard	3 Winds & Keyboard	4 Winds & Keyboard	Brass & Keyboard	Misc. Ensembles (3 to 5)	Strings, Wind Keyboard Trio	Strings, Wind Keyboard Quartets	Strings, Wind Keyboard Quintets	Sextets & Larger Ensembles	Ensemble with Guitar/Harp	Ensembles with Keyboard	Ensembles with Percussion	Ensembles with Unusual Instruments	Ensemble with Voice
RADAUER, IRMFRIED (1928–)																						✓		✓	✓	✓
RADULESCU, MICHAEL (1934–)	✓																✓									
RAFF, JOACHIM (1822–1882)																					✓					
RAGWITZ, ERHARD (1933–)		✓								✓																
RAKOWSKI, DAVID (?–)																							✓			
RAMEAU, JEAN P. (1683–1764)										✓							✓	✓			✓		✓			✓
RAMOUS, GIANNI (1930–)		✓																								
RAMOVS, PRIMOZ (1921–)		✓														✓	✓									
RANDS, BERNARD (1935–)																							✓	✓	✓	✓
RAPF, KURT (1922–)																	✓						✓	✓		
RAPHAEL, GÜNTHER (1903–1960)																		✓				✓	✓	✓		✓
RASMUSSEN, KARL A. (1947–)		✓															✓	✓			✓	✓	✓	✓	✓	✓
RATHAUS, KYRIL (1895–1954)		✓							✓								✓									
RATIU, HORIA (?–)																								✓		
RAUTAVAARA, EINOJUHANI (1928–)		✓																								
RAVEL, MAURICE (1875–1937)		✓			✓					✓							✓					✓	✓		✓	✓
RAVENOR, TERENCE (?–)								✓																		
RAWSTHORNE, ALAN (1905–1971)		✓								✓		✓					✓					✓	✓			✓
RAXACH, ENRIQUE (1932–)																						✓		✓		✓
RAYKI, GYÖRGY (1921–)																									✓	
RAZZI, FAUSTO (1932–)																									✓	
READ, GARDNER (1913–)																					✓		✓			
READ, THOMAS L. (1938–)				✓													✓				✓		✓	✓	✓	✓
RECK, DAVID (1935–)																						✓		✓		✓
REDEL, MARTIN C. (1947–)		✓								✓												✓	✓	✓	✓	✓
REGER, MAX (1873–1916)	✓	✓								✓	✓	✓					✓				✓		✓			✓
REICH, STEVE (1936–)		✓																					✓	✓	✓	✓
REICHA, ANTONIN J. (1770–1836)	✓																✓				✓					
REICHA, JOSEPH (1746–1795)	✓																									
REICHARD, JOHANN G. (1710–1782)											✓															
REIMANN, ARIBERT (1936–)																								✓	✓	
REINECKE, CARL (1824–1910)																		✓					✓			
REINER, HERBERT A. (?–)		✓																								✓
REINER, KAREL (1910–1979)																								✓	✓	
REINHART, FRANZ (?–?)																							✓			
REINHOLD, OTTO (1899–)										✓																
REISER, ALOIS (1887–1977)		✓										✓														
REITER, ALBERT (1905–)										✓							✓				✓				✓	
REIZENSTEIN, FRANZ (1911–1968)																	✓									
REMACHA, FERNANDO (1898–)		✓																								
RENIE, HENRIETTE (1875–1956)																						✓				
RENOSTO, PAOLO (1935–)	✓	✓																			✓					
RESPIGHI, OTTORINO (1879–1936)		✓																					✓			✓
REVERDY, MICHELE (1943–)																					✓			✓	✓	
REVUELTAS, SILVESTRE (1899–1940)		✓															✓						✓	✓	✓	
REYNOLDS, ROGER (1934–)		✓															✓	✓	✓				✓	✓	✓	✓
REZNICEK, EMIL (1860–1945)		✓																								
RHEINBERGER, JOSEF G. (1839–1901)										✓											✓					
RHENE-BATON, RENÉ (1879–1940)										✓											✓					
RHODES, PHILLIP (1940–)	✓																✓				✓	✓	✓			✓
RICCIO, TEODORO (1540–1595)																							✓			✓
RICCIOTTI, CARLO (1681–1756)																							✓			
RICHTER, FRANZ X. (1709–1789)		✓																								
RICHTER, MARGA (1926–)																						✓		✓		

	3 Strings	4 Strings	5 Strings	3 Winds	4 Winds	5 Winds	3 Brass	4 Brass	5 Brass	2 Strings & Keyboard	3 Strings & Keyboard	4 Strings & Keyboard	2 Winds & Keyboard	3 Winds & Keyboard	4 Winds & Keyboard	Brass & Keyboard	Misc. Ensembles (3 to 5)	Strings, Wind Keyboard Trio	Strings, Wind Keyboard Quartets	Strings, Wind Keyboard Quintets	Sextets & Larger Ensembles	Ensemble with Guitar/Harp	Ensembles with Keyboard	Ensembles with Percussion	Ensembles with Unusual Instruments	Ensemble with Voice
RIDIL, CHRISTIAN (?–)				✓																						
RIDKY, JAROSLAV (1897–1956)		✓								✓																
RIEGGER, WALLINGFORD (1885–1961)		✓		✓						✓		✓				✓	✓				✓	✓	✓	✓	✓	
RIES, FERDINAND (1784–1838)												✓						✓					✓			
RIESMAN, MICHAEL (1943–)																							✓	✓		
RIETI, VITTORIO (1898–)		✓															✓						✓			
RIGEL, ANTON (1745–1807)																	✓									
RIHM, WOLFGANG (1952–)	✓	✓								✓											✓		✓	✓	✓	
RIHOVSKY, VOJTECH (1870–1950)										✓																
RIISAGER, KNUDAGE (1897–1974)				✓						✓							✓									
RILEY, DENNIS (1943–)	✓																✓					✓	✓	✓	✓	✓
RIMSKY-KORSAKOV, NIKOLAI (1844–1908)		✓															✓				✓		✓			
RINEHART, JOHN M. (1937–)										✓																
RINGGER, ROLF U. (1935–)																										✓
RIVIER, JEAN (1896–1987)																	✓									
ROCCA, LODOVICO (1895–)																						✓	✓			
ROCHBERG, GEORGE (1918–)		✓	✓							✓	✓						✓		✓				✓			
RODGERS, LOU (?–)																	✓									
RODRIGUEZ, ALBERT (?–)																						✓				
ROGER-DUCASSE, JEAN J. (1873–1954)		✓									✓															
ROLAND-MANUEL, ALEXIS (1891–1966)																							✓			
ROLLA, ALESSANDRO (1757–1841)	✓	✓																								
ROMANOVSKY, ERICH M. (1929–)				✓																						
ROMBERG, ANDREAS (1767–1821)																	✓									
ROMBERG, BERNHARD (1767–1841)	✓																									
ROOSEVELT, JOSEPH W. (1918–)																	✓				✓					
ROPARTZ, GUY (1864–1955)	✓	✓								✓							✓				✓	✓				
ROREM, NED (1923–)		✓																✓		✓	✓		✓	✓	✓	✓
ROSEMAN, RONALD A. (1933–)													✓										✓			
ROSEN, JEROME (1921–)																	✓									
ROSENFELD, GERHARD (1931–)		✓																								
ROSENMAN, LEONARD (1924–)																							✓	✓	✓	
ROSENMÜLLER, JOHANN (1620–1684)																							✓			✓
ROSETTI, FRANTISEK A. (1746–1792)		✓				✓															✓				✓	
ROSIER, CARL (1640–1725)													✓													
RÖSLER, FRANZ A. (1746–1792)																										
ROSSE, FRANÇOIS (?–)																						✓				✓
ROSSI, SALOMONE (1587–1628)										✓																
ROSSINI, GIOACCHINO A. (1792–1868)		✓															✓								✓	
ROSZAVOLGYI, MARK R. (1790–1848)		✓																								
ROT, M (?–)									✓																	
ROTA, NINO (1911–1979)																	✓	✓								
RÖTSCHER, KONRAD (1910–)																	✓									
RÖTTGER, HEINZ (1909–1977)		✓																					✓	✓		
ROUSE, CHRISTOPHER (1949–)																								✓		
ROUSSAKIS, NICOLAS (1934–)																							✓	✓	✓	
ROUSSEL, ALBERT (1869–1937)	✓	✓								✓							✓					✓	✓			
ROVICS, HOWARD (1936–)										✓			✓	✓									✓	✓	✓	
ROWLEY, ALEC (1892–1958)										✓																

	3 Strings	4 Strings	5 Strings	3 Winds	4 Winds	5 Winds	3 Brass	4 Brass	5 Brass	2 Strings & Keyboard	3 Strings & Keyboard	4 Strings & Keyboard	2 Winds & Keyboard	3 Winds & Keyboard	4 Winds & Keyboard	Brass & Keyboard	Misc. Ensembles (3 to 5)	Strings, Wind Keyboard Trio	Strings, Wind Keyboard Quartets	Strings, Wind Keyboard Quintets	Sextets & Larger Ensembles	Ensemble with Guitar/Harp	Ensembles with Keyboard	Ensembles with Percussion	Ensembles with Unusual Instruments	Ensemble with Voice
ROY, KLAUS G. (1924–)					✓																					
ROZKOSNY, JOSEF (1833–1913)																					✓					
ROZSA, MIKLOS (1907–)	✓	✓								✓		✓														
RUBIN, MARCEL (1905–)	✓	✓								✓							✓							✓		
RUBINSTEIN, ANTON (1829–1894)		✓	✓																							
RUDERS, POUL (1949–)		✓																✓				✓	✓	✓	✓	✓
RUDHYAR, DANE (1895–1985)																							✓	✓		
RUDOLPH, JOHANN J. (1788–1831)																		✓								
RUEFF, JEANINE (1922–)		✓		✓																						
RUGGIERI, GIOVANNI M. (1690–1720)										✓																
RULON, C. B. (1954–)																	✓						✓	✓	✓	
RUTTER, JOHN (1943–)																								✓		
RUZICKA, PETER (1948–)		✓																								
SAARIAHO, KAIJA (1952–)																						✓	✓	✓	✓	
SABON, E. (?–)													✓													
SADLER, HELMUT (1921–)					✓																			✓	✓	
SAINT-MARTIN, LEONCE DE (1886–1954)																							✓			
SAINT-SAENS, CAMILLE (1835–1921)		✓								✓	✓	✓	✓	✓							✓		✓			
SAMAZEUILH, GUSTAVE (1877–1967)	✓	✓																			✓					
SAMMARTINI, GIOVANNI B. (1701–1775)																			✓							
SAMMONS, ALBERT E. (1886–1957)		✓																								
SAMUEL-ROUSSEAU, MARCEL (1882–1955)		✓																								
SAMYN, NOEL (?–)																	✓									
SANDER, PETER (1933–)		✓							✓								✓									
SAPIEYEVSKI, JERZY (1945–)		✓																						✓		
SAPP, ALLEN D. (1922–)										✓																
SARY, LASZLO (1940–)																									✓	✓
SATIE, ERIC (1866–1925)		✓							✓												✓	✓	✓	✓	✓	
SAUGUET, HENRI (1901–)		✓																								✓
SAUTEREAU, C. (?–)		✓																								
SAXTON, ROBERT (1953–)		✓										✓					✓			✓	✓	✓	✓	✓	✓	✓
SAYGUN, AHMED A. (1907–)		✓																								
SCARLATTI, ALESSANDRO (1660–1725)											✓												✓			✓
SCELSI, GIACINTO (1905–)		✓																			✓		✓	✓	✓	✓
SCHACHT, THEODOR (1748–1823)		✓																								
SCHAFER, R M. (1933–)		✓																				✓	✓	✓	✓	✓
SCHEDL, GERHARD (?–)										✓							✓						✓		✓	
SCHEIDT, SAMUEL (1587–1654)																✓										
SCHEIN, JOHANN H. (1586–1630)			✓					✓															✓			✓
SCHELB, JOSEF (1894–1977)																						✓	✓	✓		
SCHELLE, JOHANN (1648–1701)																							✓			✓
SCHELLE, MICHAEL (1950–)										✓													✓	✓	✓	
SCHENKER, FRIEDRICH (1942–)		✓		✓						✓			✓								✓					
SCHERCHEN, HERMANN (1891–1966)		✓																								
SCHERCHEN-HSIAO, TONA (1938–)																									✓	
SCHIBLER, ARMIN (1920–)			✓														✓									
SCHICKELE, PETER (1935–)	✓	✓		✓	✓				✓			✓	✓				✓	✓	✓	✓	✓		✓	✓	✓	
SCHICKHARDT, JOHANN C. (1680–1762)													✓	✓	✓				✓	✓		✓				

	3 Strings	4 Strings	5 Strings	3 Winds	4 Winds	5 Winds	3 Brass	4 Brass	5 Brass	2 Strings & Keyboard	3 Strings & Keyboard	4 Strings & Keyboard	2 Winds & Keyboard	3 Winds & Keyboard	4 Winds & Keyboard	Brass & Keyboard	Misc. Ensembles (3 to 5)	Strings, Wind Keyboard Trio	Strings, Wind Keyboard Quartets	Strings, Wind Keyboard Quintets	Sextets & Larger Ensembles	Ensemble with Guitar/Harp	Ensembles with Keyboard	Ensembles with Percussion	Ensembles with Unusual Instruments	Ensemble with Voice
SCHIDLOWSKY, LEON (1931–)																								✓		✓
SCHIEDERMAYER, JOHANN B. (1779–1840)																								✓		
SCHIFF, HELMUT (1893–)				✓																						
SCHIFRIN, LALO (1932–)																							✓	✓	✓	
SCHILDT, MELCHIOR (1592–1667)																							✓			✓
SCHILLINGS, MAX (1868–1933)		✓	✓																							
SCHISKE, KARL (1916–1969)	✓	✓								✓							✓				✓					
SCHLUMPF, MARTIN (1947–)		✓																								
SCHMELZER, JOHANN H. (1623–1680)																							✓		✓	
SCHMIDEK, KURT (1919–)	✓																✓									
SCHMIDT, CHRISTFRIED (1932–)		✓																					✓			
SCHMIDT, FRANZ (1874–1939)		✓										✓												✓		✓
SCHMIKERER, JOSEF A. (1660–1700)											✓															
SCHMITT, FLORENT (1870–1958)	✓	✓						✓		✓	✓	✓	✓	✓			✓		✓		✓	✓				
SCHMITT, MEINRAD (1935–)		✓																								
SCHNABEL, ARTHUR (1882–1951)	✓	✓																								
SCHNEIDER, GARU M. (1957–)																							✓	✓	✓	
SCHNITTKE, ALFRED (1934–)	✓	✓									✓	✓										✓	✓	✓	✓	✓
SCHOBER, BRIAN (1951–)																							✓	✓	✓	
SCHOECK, OTHMAR (1886–1957)		✓																			✓		✓	✓		✓
SCHOENBERG, ARNOLD (1874–1951)	✓	✓										✓					✓			✓	✓	✓	✓	✓	✓	✓
SCHOLLUM, ROBERT (1913–)		✓								✓			✓				✓				✓	✓	✓	✓		
SCHÖNBACH, DIETER (1931–)																							✓			✓
SCHOP, JOHANN (1590–1667)																							✓			
SCHROEDER, HERMANN (1904–)	✓																									
SCHRÖTER, HEINZ (1907–)										✓																
SCHUBERT, FRANZ (1797–1828)	✓	✓	✓							✓	✓	✓					✓				✓					
SCHUBERT, MANFRED (1937–)		✓															✓						✓			
SCHUBROW, MANUEL (1954–)		✓																								
SCHULLER, GUNTHER (1925–)		✓						✓	✓	✓	✓			✓		✓	✓	✓	✓	✓	✓	✓	✓	✓	✓	✓
SCHUMAN, WILLIAM (1910–1992)	✓	✓						✓	✓								✓					✓			✓	✓
SCHUMANN, CLARA (1819–1896)										✓																
SCHUMANN, ROBERT (1810–1856)	✓	✓								✓	✓	✓						✓					✓			
SCHÜRMANN, GEORG C. (1672–1751)																							✓			✓
SCHÜTZ, HEINRICH (1585–1672)																							✓		✓	✓
SCHWAEN, KURT (1909–)																					✓		✓		✓	
SCHWANTNER, JOSEPH (1943–)																	✓					✓	✓	✓	✓	✓
SCHWARTZ, ELLIOTT S. (1936–)																							✓	✓	✓	
SCHWARZ-SCHILLING, REINHARD (1904–1985)		✓																								
SCHWEINITZ, WOLFGANG VON (1953–)																					✓				✓	
SCHWEIZER, KLAUS (1939–)																				✓						
SCHWEIZER, ROLF (1936–)																										
SCHWERTBERGER, G. (?–)				✓																						
SCHWERTSIK, KURT (1935–)	✓	✓						✓	✓	✓							✓				✓	✓	✓	✓	✓	✓
SCIARRINO, SALVATORE (1947–)										✓							✓									
SCIORTINO, PATRICE (1922–)																					✓					
SCOTT, CYRIL (1879–1970)											✓															
SCRIABIN, ALEXANDER (1872–1915) AND OTHERS		✓																								
SCULTHORPE, PETER (1929–)		✓																						✓		✓
SEARCH, FREDERICK P. (1899–)																					✓					

	3 Strings	4 Strings	5 Strings	3 Winds	4 Winds	5 Winds	3 Brass	4 Brass	5 Brass	2 Strings & Keyboard	3 Strings & Keyboard	4 Strings & Keyboard	2 Winds & Keyboard	3 Winds & Keyboard	4 Winds & Keyboard	Brass & Keyboard	Misc. Ensembles (3 to 5)	Strings, Wind Keyboard Trio	Strings, Wind Keyboard Quartets	Strings, Wind Keyboard Quintets	Sextets & Larger Ensembles	Ensemble with Guitar/Harp	Ensembles with Keyboard	Ensembles with Percussion	Ensembles with Unusual Instruments	Ensemble with Voice
SEARLE, HUMPHREY (1915–1982)																					✓	✓	✓			✓
SECHTER, SIMON (1788–1867)		✓																								
SEGERSTAM, LEIF (1944–)																	✓									
SEIBER, MATYAS (1905–1960)		✓																			✓					✓
SEMEGEN, DARIA (1946–)																							✓			
SEMMLER-COLLERY, ARMAND (?–)								✓	✓																	
SEREBRIER, JOSÉ (1938–)		✓																								
SESSIONS, ROGER (1896–1985)		✓	✓																							
SETER, MORDECAI (1916–)																	✓									
SEYFRIT, MICHAEL E. (1947–)																	✓						✓	✓	✓	
SHATIN, JUDITH (1949–)																				✓				✓		
SHCHEDRIN, RODION (1922–)																							✓	✓	✓	
SHEINKMAN, MORDECHAI (1926–)																						✓				
SHEPHERD, ARTHUR (1880–1958)		✓																								✓
SHERIFF, NOAM (1935–)																							✓			
SHIFRIN, SEYMOUR (1926–1979)		✓																		✓			✓			✓
SHIMAZU, TAKEHITO (1949–)		✓											✓								✓					
SHIPLEY, EDWARD (?–)									✓																	
SHORT, DAVID (?–)									✓																	
SHOSTAKOVICH, DMITRI (1906–1975)		✓								✓		✓									✓		✓			✓
SHUT, VLADISLAV (1941–)																							✓	✓	✓	
SIBELIUS, JEAN (1865–1957)		✓																			✓					
SIEGL, OTTO (1896–1978)	✓	✓	✓							✓							✓				✓					
SIERRA, ROBERTO (1953–)																							✓			
SIGURBJORNSSON, THORKELL (1938–)																							✓	✓		
SILSBEE, ANN L. (1930–)																		✓	✓				✓	✓		
SILVESTROV, VALENTIN (1937–)		✓								✓		✓									✓	✓	✓	✓		✓
SIMONETTI, GIOVANNI P. (?–?)													✓					✓		✓						
SIMONS, NETTY (1913–)		✓																								
SIMPSON, ROBERT (1921–)		✓																								
SIMPSON, THOMAS (1582–1626)		✓																							✓	
SIMS, EZRA (1928–)																	✓				✓	✓		✓	✓	
SINDING, CHRISTIAN (1856–1941)		✓								✓		✓														
SITSKY, LARRY (1934–)					✓																					
SKOLNIK, WALTER (1934–)																	✓									
SKORZENY, FRITZ (1900–1965)	✓									✓							✓					✓				
SLAVENSKI, JOSIP S. (1896–1955)		✓																								
SLAVICKY, KLEMENT (1910–)																		✓								
SLONIMSKY, SERGEI (1932–)		✓															✓					✓		✓	✓	
SMALLEY, ROGER (1943–)																					✓		✓			
SMETANA, BEDRICH (1824–1884)		✓								✓																
SMIRNOV, DMITRI (1948–)		✓								✓												✓		✓	✓	✓
SMITH, DAVID S. (1877–1949)		✓										✓														
SMITH, HALE (1925–)																						✓	✓	✓	✓	✓
SMITH, JOHN S. (1750–1836)		✓																								
SMITH, JULIA (1911–)		✓								✓																
SMITH, LELAND (1925–)										✓							✓	✓					✓	✓	✓	
SMITH, LEO (1941–)																						✓	✓	✓	✓	
SMITH BRINDLE, REGINALD (1917–)																							✓	✓		✓
SMYTH, ETHEL (1858–1944)		✓																								
SOLLBERGER, HARVEY (1938–)																		✓		✓		✓	✓	✓		
SOMMER, VLADIMIR (1921–)		✓																								

	3 Strings	4 Strings	5 Strings	3 Winds	4 Winds	5 Winds	3 Brass	4 Brass	5 Brass	2 Strings & Keyboard	3 Strings & Keyboard	4 Strings & Keyboard	2 Winds & Keyboard	3 Winds & Keyboard	4 Winds & Keyboard	Brass & Keyboard	Misc. Ensembles (3 to 5)	Strings, Wind Keyboard Trio	Strings, Wind Keyboard Quartets	Strings, Wind Keyboard Quintets	Sextets & Larger Ensembles	Ensemble with Guitar/Harp	Ensembles with Keyboard	Ensembles with Percussion	Ensembles with Unusual Instruments	Ensemble with Voice
SONZOGNO, GIULIO C. (1906–1976)												✓														
SOPRONI, JOSZEF (1930–)		✓																	✓							
SORENSEN, BENT (1958–)		✓															✓				✓	✓		✓	✓	✓
SORESINA, ALBERTO (1911–)											✓															
SOURIS, ANDRÉ (1899–1970)								✓									✓						✓			✓
SOUSA, JOHN P. (1854–1932)		✓																								
SOWERBY, LEO (1895–1968)		✓																								
SPEER, DANIEL G. (1636–1707)									✓							✓							✓			
SPELMAN, TIMOTHY M. (1891–1970)		✓																								
SPERGER, JOHANN M. (1750–1812)																	✓									
SPEZZAFERRI, GIOVANNI (1888–1963)							✓																			
SPIES, CLAUDIO (1925–)																	✓									
SPINNER, LEOPOLD (1906–1980)		✓								✓							✓	✓				✓				
SPOHR, LOUIS (1784–1859)		✓								✓							✓				✓	✓	✓			✓
SPRONGL, NORBERT (1892–)																	✓									
SROM, KAREL (1904–)		✓																								
STADLMAIR, HANS (1929–)																					✓					
STAEPS, HANS U. (1909–)				✓	✓	✓																✓	✓			✓
STALLAERT, ALPHONSE (1920–)																	✓									
STALLCOP, GLENN (1950–)																		✓				✓	✓	✓	✓	
STALVEY, DORRANCE (1930–)																						✓		✓		
STAMITZ, CARL (1746–1801)																	✓									
STANKOVICH, YEVHEN (1942–)																					✓	✓	✓	✓	✓	
STANLEY, JOHN (1713–1786)																✓										
STARER, ROBERT (1924–)		✓						✓													✓	✓	✓			✓
STAUB, VOLKER (?–)																								✓		
STEARNS, PETER P. (1931–)																	✓		✓		✓	✓		✓	✓	
STEFFEN, WOLFGANG (1923–)																		✓					✓	✓		✓
STEIN, LEON (1910–)										✓											✓					
STETKA, FRANZ (?–)																	✓					✓				
STEVENS, HALSEY (1908–1989)																					✓					
STEWART, ROBERT (1918–)																	✓						✓	✓	✓	
STIBILJ, MILAN (1929–)																							✓	✓		
STILL, WILLIAM G. (1895–1978)		✓																								
STOCK, DAVID (1939–)																	✓				✓	✓	✓	✓	✓	
STOCKHAUSEN, KARLHEINZ (1928–)																	✓					✓	✓	✓	✓	
STOCKMEIER, WOLFGANG (1931–)																							✓			
STOJANTSCHEW, STOJAN (1931–)																						✓		✓		
STOLTZENBERG, CHRISTOPH (1690–1764)																							✓			✓
STÖLZEL, GOTTFRIED H. (1690–1749)										✓		✓														
STOUT, ALAN (1932–)																	✓					✓	✓	✓	✓	✓
STRANG, GERALD (1908–1983)																					✓		✓			
STRANZ, ULRICH (1946–)		✓		✓																						
STRAUSS, RICHARD (1864–1949)		✓									✓						✓				✓	✓	✓		✓	✓
STRAUSS, WOLFGANG (1927–)										✓																
STRAUSS, JR., JOHANN (1825–1899)																					✓		✓		✓	
STRAVINSKY, IGOR (1882–1971)		✓															✓	✓			✓	✓	✓	✓	✓	✓
STRAVINSKY, SOULIMA (1910–)		✓								✓																
STREET, TISON (1943–)		✓																				✓	✓			✓
STREIFF, PETER (1944–)																										
STRNISTE, JIRI (1914–)								✓													✓					
STROBL, L (?–)																	✓							✓		

	3 Strings	4 Strings	5 Strings	3 Winds	4 Winds	5 Winds	3 Brass	4 Brass	5 Brass	2 Strings & Keyboard	3 Strings & Keyboard	4 Strings & Keyboard	2 Winds & Keyboard	3 Winds & Keyboard	4 Winds & Keyboard	Brass & Keyboard	Misc. Ensembles (3 to 5)	Strings, Wind Keyboard Trio	Strings, Wind Keyboard Quartets	Strings, Wind Keyboard Quintets	Sextets & Larger Ensembles	Ensemble with Guitar/Harp	Ensembles with Keyboard	Ensembles with Percussion	Ensembles with Unusual Instruments	Ensemble with Voice
STROE, AUREL (1932–)																							✓	✓		
STROMHOLM, FOLKE (1941–)		✓				✓													✓					✓		
STRUTIUS, THOMAS (1621–1678)																							✓			✓
STUCKY, STEVEN E. (1949–)																			✓				✓	✓		
SUBEN, JOEL E. (1946–)																						✓	✓	✓	✓	
SUBOTNICK, MORTON (1933–)		✓																								
SUCHON, EUGEN (1908–)		✓																								
SUDER, JOSEPH (1892–1980)		✓															✓									
SUGAR, MIKLOS (1952–)																								✓		
SUGAR, REZSO (1919–)																							✓			
SURINACH, CARLOS (1915–)		✓																				✓	✓	✓	✓	
SÜSSMAYR, FRANZ X. (1766–1803)																	✓									
SUTER, HERMANN (1870–1926)		✓																								
SUTER, ROBERT (1919–)										✓			✓													
SWAN, ALFRED J. (1890–1970)													✓													
SWANSON, HOWARD (1907–1978)									✓												✓					
SYDEMAN, WILLIAM (1928–)																	✓					✓		✓	✓	
SYVERUD, STEPHEN L. (1938–)																	✓									
SZABO, XAVER F. (1902–1969)																					✓					
SZELL, GEORGE (1897–1970)												✓														
SZOKOLAY, SANDOR (1931–)		✓							✓																	
SZYMANOWSKI, KAROL (1882–1937)		✓																								
SZYMANSKI, PAWEL (1954–)		✓																✓					✓	✓		✓
TAFFANEL, PAUL (1844–1908)																	✓									
TAILLEFERRE, GERMAINE (1892–1983)		✓																								
TAIRA, YOSHIHISA (1938–)																					✓	✓	✓	✓	✓	✓
TAKACS, JENO (1902–)										✓							✓				✓					
TAKAHASHI, YUJI (1938–)																					✓		✓	✓	✓	
TAKEMITSU, TŌRU (1930–)		✓																	✓		✓	✓		✓	✓	
TALMA, LOUISE (1906–)		✓															✓	✓	✓				✓	✓	✓	✓
TAMBA, AKIRA (1932–)																					✓		✓	✓	✓	✓
TANENBAUM, ELIAS (1924–)										✓							✓	✓				✓	✓	✓	✓	
TANSMAN, ALEXANDRE (1897–1986)		✓								✓							✓						✓			
TANTZ, LUDWIG (?–1790)										✓																
TARANU, CORNEL (1934–)																						✓	✓	✓	✓	✓
TARTINI, GIUSEPPE (1692–1770)										✓	✓															
TATE, PHYLLIS (1911–1987)		✓															✓	✓				✓	✓	✓	✓	✓
TAUB, BRUCE J. (1948–)		✓															✓			✓		✓	✓	✓		✓
TAUBERT, ERNST E. (1838–1934)		✓																								
TAUSINGER, JAN (1921–)											✓										✓					
TAVENER, JOHN (1944–)									✓														✓	✓		✓
TAYLOR, CLIFFORD (1923–)										✓							✓	✓				✓		✓		
TCHAIKOVSKY, BORIS (1925–)																						✓	✓	✓	✓	
TCHAIKOWSKY, PETER I. (1840–1893)		✓			✓			✓	✓	✓							✓				✓		✓			
TCHEREPNIN, ALEXANDER (1899–1977)		✓							✓	✓							✓							✓	✓	
TELEMANN, GEORG P. (1681–1767)										✓			✓	✓			✓	✓	✓	✓			✓		✓	✓
TEMPLETON, ALEC (1909–1963)																					✓					
TERTERIAN, AVET (1929–)		✓																								
TERZAKIS, DIMITRI (1938–)		✓																			✓		✓	✓	✓	✓
TESSIER, ROBERT (1939–)																					✓	✓	✓	✓	✓	✓
TESTI, FLAVIO (1923–)																										✓
THÄRICHEN, WERNER (1921–)		✓																			✓	✓		✓	✓	

	3 Strings	4 Strings	5 Strings	3 Winds	4 Winds	5 Winds	3 Brass	4 Brass	5 Brass	2 Strings & Keyboard	3 Strings & Keyboard	4 Strings & Keyboard	2 Winds & Keyboard	3 Winds & Keyboard	4 Winds & Keyboard	Brass & Keyboard	Misc. Ensembles (3 to 5)	Strings, Wind Keyboard Trio	Strings, Wind Keyboard Quartets	Strings, Wind Keyboard Quintets	Sextets & Larger Ensembles	Ensemble with Guitar/Harp	Ensembles with Keyboard	Ensembles with Percussion	Ensembles with Unusual Instruments	Ensemble with Voice
THIELE, SIEGFRIED (1934–)		✓															✓	✓								
THILMAN, JOHANNES P. (1906–1973)		✓															✓					✓		✓	✓	
THOMAS, ANDREW (1929–)																	✓						✓	✓		
THOMAS-MIFUNE, WERNER (1941–)																	✓				✓					
THOMPSON, RANDALL (1899–1984)		✓															✓			✓			✓		✓	
THOMSON, VIRGIL (1896–)		✓				✓			✓								✓						✓	✓	✓	✓
THORNE, FRANCIS (1922–)																	✓	✓				✓	✓	✓	✓	
THORNE, NICHOLAS (1953–)													✓						✓				✓	✓		
TILLIS, FREDERICK C. (1930–)										✓												✓	✓			
TIPEI, SEVER (1943–)																										
TIPPETT, MICHAEL (1905–)		✓																					✓			
TIRCUIT, HEUWELL (1931–)		✓																					✓	✓	✓	✓
TISCHHAUSER, FRANZ (1921–)																					✓					
TISHCHENKO, BORIS (1939–)		✓																					✓	✓	✓	✓
TISNE, ANTOINE (1932–)		✓							✓	✓							✓			✓				✓		
TITTEL, ERNST (1910–)	✓																						✓			
TOCH, ERNEST (1887–1964)	✓											✓												✓		
TOGNI, CAMILLO (1922–)																						✓	✓	✓	✓	
TOLDRA, EDUARDO (1895–1962)		✓																								
TOMASI, HENRI (1901–1971)								✓									✓				✓	✓		✓		
TOMASINI, LUIGI (1741–1808)		✓																								
TOMKINS, THOMAS (1572–1656)	✓																									
TOOVEY, ANDREW (1962–)	✓	✓								✓												✓	✓	✓	✓	✓
TOPLIFF, ROGER (?–)				✓																						
TORELLI, GIUSEPPE (1658–1709)											✓												✓			
TORKE, MICHAEL (1961–)										✓										✓						
TOSI, DANIEL (1953–)																									✓	
TOUCHE, J. C. (?–)												✓														
TOURNIER, MARCEL L. (1879–1951)																						✓	✓			
TOVEY, DONALD F. (1875–1940)																							✓			
TOWER, JOAN (1938–)															✓		✓			✓	✓		✓	✓	✓	
TOWNSEND, DOUGLAS (1921–)														✓							✓		✓			
TRABACI, GIOVANNI M. (1575–1647)								✓																		
TREMBLAY, GILLES (1932–)																						✓	✓	✓	✓	✓
TRIEBENSEE, J. (1772–1846)				✓																						
TRIEBMANN, KARL O. (1936–)		✓																			✓		✓	✓		
TRIEDER, JAN (1957–)		✓																								
TRIMBLE, LESTER (1923–)		✓																			✓	✓	✓	✓	✓	✓
TROJAHN, MANFRED (1949–)		✓																						✓	✓	✓
TROMBLY, PRESTON A. (1945–)													✓					✓			✓	✓		✓		
TSONTAKIS, GEORGE (1951–)		✓							✓			✓					✓					✓	✓	✓		✓
TULL, FISHER (1934–)									✓														✓			
TUMA, FRANTISEK I. (1704–1774)											✓															
TUNDER, FRANZ (1614–1667)																							✓			✓
TURCHI, GUIDO (1916–)		✓															✓									
TURINA, JOAQUIN (1882–1949)		✓								✓	✓	✓									✓		✓			
TURNER, CHARLES (1921–)																								✓		
TUROK, PAUL (1929–)																										✓
UCCELLINI, MARCO (1603–1680)											✓															
UHL, ALFRED (1909–)		✓								✓								✓				✓				
ULLRICH, HERMANN (1888–)																							✓			
ULTAN, LLOYD (1929–)									✓													✓				
UNG, CHINARY (1942–)																						✓	✓	✓		✓
URAY, ERNST L. (1906–)								✓		✓							✓									
URBANNER, ERICH (1936–)		✓		✓						✓							✓				✓	✓	✓	✓	✓	

	3 Strings	4 Strings	5 Strings	3 Winds	4 Winds	5 Winds	3 Brass	4 Brass	5 Brass	2 Strings & Keyboard	3 Strings & Keyboard	4 Strings & Keyboard	2 Winds & Keyboard	3 Winds & Keyboard	4 Winds & Keyboard	Brass & Keyboard	Misc. Ensembles (3 to 5)	Strings, Wind Keyboard Trio	Strings, Wind Keyboard Quartets	Strings, Wind Keyboard Quintets	Sextets & Larger Ensembles	Ensemble with Guitar/Harp	Ensembles with Keyboard	Ensembles with Percussion	Ensembles with Unusual Instruments	Ensemble with Voice
USMANBAS, ILHAN (1921–)		✓																								
USTVOLSKAYA, GALINA (1919–)																		✓					✓	✓	✓	
VALEN, FARTEIN (1887–1952)		✓																								
VALENTINE, ROBERT (1680–1735)													✓													
VALERA, ROBERTO (?–)																								✓	✓	
VAN DE VATE, NANCY H. (1930–)																							✓	✓		
VANDOR, IVAN (1932–)		✓																				✓			✓	
VANHAL, JOHANN B. (1739–1813)																	✓									
VARÈSE, EDGAR (1883–1965)																					✓		✓	✓	✓	✓
VASKS, PETERIS (1946–)		✓								✓							✓									
VAUGHAN WILLIAMS, RALPH (1872–1958)		✓	✓					✓				✓									✓		✓			✓
VECCHI, ORAZIO (1550–1605)			✓																							
VEIGL, W (?–)																								✓	✓	
VEJVANOVSKY, PAVEL J. (1640–1693)																✓							✓			
VELLONES, PIERRE (1889–1939)																						✓				
VELTEN, KLAUS (1937–)					✓																					
VERACINI, ANTONIO (1659–1733)										✓																
VERDI, GIUSEPPE (1813–1901)		✓																								
VERESS, SANDOR (1907–)	✓	✓		✓						✓																
VERETTI, ANTONIO (1900–1978)															✓							✓				✓
VERRALL, JOHN (1908–)		✓		✓						✓		✓					✓			✓	✓					
VERRALL, PAMELA M. (1915–)				✓																						
VIADANA, LODOVICO (1560–1627)																					✓					
VIERDANCK, JOHANN (1605–1646)																							✓			✓
VIERNE, LOUIS (1870–1937)																							✓	✓	✓	
VIERU, ANATOLE (1926–)																						✓	✓	✓	✓	
VIEUXTEMPS, HENRI (1820–1881)										✓																
VILLA-LOBOS, HEITOR (1887–1959)	✓	✓		✓	✓	✓		✓		✓							✓				✓	✓	✓	✓	✓	✓
VINE, CARL (1954–)		✓																					✓	✓	✓	✓
VINTER, GILBERT (1909–1969)																	✓									
VIOLETTE, ANDREW (1953–)																				✓				✓	✓	
VIOTTI, GIOVANNI B. (1755–1824)	✓																✓									
VITALI, GIOVANNI B. (1632–1692)										✓	✓															
VIVALDI, ANTONIO (1678–1741)										✓	✓		✓	✓				✓	✓	✓		✓	✓		✓	✓
VIVIER, CLAUDE (1948–1983)																								✓		✓
VOGEL, ERNST (1926–)		✓								✓			✓								✓		✓	✓		
VOGEL, JOHANN C. (1758–1788)																	✓									
VOGEL, ROGER C. (1947–)										✓																
VOGEL, WLADIMIR (1896–1984)				✓													✓						✓			✓
VOGT, GUSTAV (1781–1870)				✓													✓									
VOGT, HANS (1911–)		✓								✓																
VOLANS, KEVIN (1949–)		✓																					✓	✓		
VOSS, FRIEDRICH (1930–)		✓				✓				✓												✓				
VRANICKY, ANTONIN (1761–1820)																									✓	
VRANICKY, PAVEL (1756–1808)		✓								✓																
VUSTIN, ALEXANDER (1943–)																						✓	✓	✓	✓	✓
WAGENSEIL, GEORG C. (1715–1777)		✓									✓							✓			✓	✓				
WAGGONER, ANDREW (1960–)																									✓	
WAGHALTER, IGNATZ (1882–1949)		✓																								
WAGNER, RICHARD (1813–1883)		✓																			✓					
WAHREN, KARL H. (1933–)																✓		✓					✓	✓	✓	
WALKER, JAMES (1929–)																	✓									
WALLACH, JOELLE (1929–)																	✓									
WALTER, JOHANNES (1964–)																								✓		

	3 Strings	4 Strings	5 Strings	3 Winds	4 Winds	5 Winds	3 Brass	4 Brass	5 Brass	2 Strings & Keyboard	3 Strings & Keyboard	4 Strings & Keyboard	2 Winds & Keyboard	3 Winds & Keyboard	4 Winds & Keyboard	Brass & Keyboard	Misc. Ensembles (3 to 5)	Strings, Wind Keyboard Trio	Strings, Wind Keyboard Quartets	Strings, Wind Keyboard Quintets	Sextets & Larger Ensembles	Ensemble with Guitar/Harp	Ensembles with Keyboard	Ensembles with Percussion	Ensembles with Unusual Instruments	Ensemble with Voice
WALTON, WILLIAM (1902–1983)		✓						✓			✓										✓			✓	✓	✓
WALZEL, LEOPOLD M. (1902–1970)	✓											✓					✓									
WANGENHEIM, VOLKER (1928–)																							✓	✓		
WANHAL, JOHANN B. (1739–1813)	✓																✓									
WARD, ROBERT (1917–)		✓																								
WARFIELD, GERALD A. (1940–)																				✓						
WARLOCK, PETER (1894–1930)																										✓
WASHBURN, ROBERT (1928–)		✓		✓					✓								✓				✓					
WEAIT, CHRISTOPHER (1939–)					✓																					
WEBER, ALAIN (1930–)									✓								✓						✓	✓		
WEBER, BEN (1916–1979)											✓						✓		✓			✓	✓		✓	
WEBER, CARL MARIA VON (1786–1826)										✓	✓						✓				✓		✓			✓
WEBERN, ANTON VON (1883–1945)	✓	✓										✓										✓	✓		✓	✓
WECKMANN, MATTHIAS (1621–1674)																							✓			
WEHRLI, WERNER (1892–1944)																							✓			
WEIGL, KARL (1881–1949)		✓								✓		✓			✓											
WEIGL, VALLY (1894–1982)																	✓	✓				✓	✓			✓
WEILAND, JULIUS J. (?–1663)																							✓			✓
WEILL, KURT (1900–1950)		✓																			✓	✓	✓	✓	✓	✓
WEINER, STANLEY (1925–)							✓		✓																	
WEINGARDEN, LOUIS (1943–)										✓													✓	✓		
WEINGARTNER, FELIX VON (1863–1942)		✓	✓														✓			✓			✓			
WEINSTEIN, MICHAEL H. (1960–)									✓	✓							✓						✓			✓
WEIR, JUDITH (1954–)		✓								✓												✓	✓	✓	✓	✓
WEISBERG, ARTHUR (1931–)										✓		✓					✓									
WEISGALL, HUGO (1912–)					✓												✓							✓		
WEISMANN, JULIUS (1879–1950)		✓																								
WEISS, MANFRED (1935–)		✓								✓													✓			✓
WELLESZ, EGON (1885–1974)	✓	✓	✓																		✓			✓	✓	✓
WELLMAN, SAMUEL (1951–)																						✓				
WENDLING, JEAN B. (1723–1797)																	✓									
WENTH, J (1745–1801)				✓	✓																					
WENZEL, EBERHARD (1896–1982)																✓							✓			
WENZEL, HANS J. (1939–)		✓																								
WERNER, FRITZ (1898–)																		✓								
WERNER, GREGOR J. (1693–1766)											✓							✓	✓							
WERNER, JEAN-JACQUES (1935–)				✓																						
WERNER, JOSEF (1837–1922)		✓																								
WERNERT, WOLFGANG (1936–)																								✓	✓	✓
WESTERGAARD, SVEND (1922–)		✓																								
WETZ, RICHARD (1875–1935)		✓																								
WETZLAR, HORST (1936–)								✓																		
WHITNEY, JOHN C. (1942–)		✓																								
WHITTENBERG, CHARLES (1927–)																					✓					
WIDMANN, ERASMUS (1572–1634)			✓																							
WIDOR, CHARLES M. (1844–1937)											✓															
WIENHORST, RICHARD W. (1920–)																					✓			✓		
WIGGLESWORTH, FRANK (1918–)																	✓					✓				
WILBY, PHILIP (1949–)									✓								✓				✓		✓			✓
WILDBERGER, JACQUES (1922–)																						✓	✓	✓	✓	✓
WILDGANS, FRIEDRICH (1913–1965)	✓			✓																	✓					
WILLIAMS, JOHN (1932–)																							✓	✓	✓	
WILLIAMS, WILLIAM (?–1701)													✓													

	3 Strings	4 Strings	5 Strings	3 Winds	4 Winds	5 Winds	3 Brass	4 Brass	5 Brass	2 Strings & Keyboard	3 Strings & Keyboard	4 Strings & Keyboard	2 Winds & Keyboard	3 Winds & Keyboard	4 Winds & Keyboard	Brass & Keyboard	Misc. Ensembles (3 to 5)	Strings, Wind Keyboard Trio	Strings, Wind Keyboard Quartets	Strings, Wind Keyboard Quintets	Sextets & Larger Ensembles	Ensemble with Guitar/Harp	Ensembles with Keyboard	Ensembles with Percussion	Ensembles with Unusual Instruments	Ensemble with Voice
WILLIS, RICHARD (1819–1900)		✓																								
WILSON, DONALD (1937–)																	✓	✓								✓
WIMBERGER, GERHARD (1923–)		✓																			✓		✓	✓		✓
WINBECK, HEINZ (1946–)		✓	✓								✓															
WINSLOW, WALTER K. (1947–)																			✓			✓	✓	✓	✓	
WINTER, PETER (1754–1825)		✓																						✓	✓	
WIREN, DAG (1905–)		✓																								
WITKOWSKI, GEORGES M. (1867–1943)		✓																								
WITT, CHRISTIAN F. (1660–1716)														✓												
WITTINGER, ROBERT (1945–)		✓															✓				✓	✓	✓	✓	✓	
WOHLGEMUTH, GERARD (1920–)		✓																								
WOLF, HUGO (1860–1903)		✓																								
WOLFF, CHRISTIAN (1934–)		✓								✓							✓					✓	✓	✓	✓	✓
WOLF-FERRARI, ERMANNO (1876–1948)		✓								✓													✓			
WÖLFL, JOSEPH (1773–1812)				✓																						
WOLPE, STEFAN (1902–1972)																					✓					
WOLPERT, FRANZ A. (1917–1978)		✓																								
WOLSCHINA, REINHARD (1952–)										✓							✓									
WOOD, CHARLES (1866–1926)																	✓									
WOOD, HUGH (1932–)		✓								✓													✓			
WOOD, JOSEPH (1915–)												✓														
WOOLLEN, RUSSELL (1923–)										✓	✓						✓				✓					
WOYRSCH, FELIX VON (1860–1944)		✓																								
WRANITZKY, ANTON (1761–1820)				✓																						
WRIGHT, MAURICE (1949–)																					✓		✓	✓	✓	
WUORINEN, CHARLES (1938–)	✓	✓								✓							✓	✓	✓	✓	✓	✓	✓	✓	✓	✓
WÜRDINGER, E (?–)																	✓									
WYNER, YEHUDI (1929–)												✓							✓				✓			
XENAKIS, IANNIS (1922–)		✓								✓											✓	✓	✓	✓	✓	✓
YANNATOS, JAMES (1929–)		✓																								
YAVELOW, CHRISTOPHER J. (1950–)		✓								✓									✓		✓		✓	✓		
YSAŸE, THÉOPHILE (1865–1918)												✓														
YTTREHUS, ROLV (1926–)																							✓	✓	✓	
YUN, ISANG (1917–)		✓								✓							✓				✓	✓	✓	✓	✓	✓
ZACH, JOHANN (1699–1773)	✓									✓																
ZACHOW, FRIEDRICH W. (1663–1712)	✓																									
ZADOR, EUGEN (1894–1977)																					✓					
ZAFRED, MARIO (1922–)										✓							✓				✓					
ZAGORTSEV, VASILY (?–)																							✓			
ZAHLER, NOEL B. (1951–)										✓																
ZBAR, MICHEL (1942–)																					✓			✓	✓	✓
ZECHLIN, RUTH (1926–)		✓															✓							✓		
ZELENKA, ISTVAN (1936–)																									✓	
ZELENKA, JAN D. (1679–1745)														✓				✓					✓			✓
ZELJENKA, ILJA (1932–)		✓																								
ZEMLINSKY, ALEXANDER VON (1871–1942)		✓															✓	✓								
ZENDER, HANS (1936–)																	✓	✓					✓	✓	✓	✓
ZIKA, RICHARD (1897–1947)		✓																								
ZILLIG, WINFRIED (1905–1963)		✓															✓					✓	✓	✓	✓	
ZIMMERMANN, BERND-ALOIS (1918–1970)																						✓			✓	

	3 Strings	4 Strings	5 Strings	3 Winds	4 Winds	5 Winds	3 Brass	4 Brass	5 Brass	2 Strings & Keyboard	3 Strings & Keyboard	4 Strings & Keyboard	2 Winds & Keyboard	3 Winds & Keyboard	4 Winds & Keyboard	Brass & Keyboard	Misc. Ensembles (3 to 5)	Strings, Wind Keyboard Trio	Strings, Wind Keyboard Quartets	Strings, Wind Keyboard Quintets	Sextets & Larger Ensembles	Ensemble with Guitar/Harp	Ensembles with Keyboard	Ensembles with Percussion	Ensembles with Unusual Instruments	Ensemble with Voice
ZIMMERMANN, UDO (1943–)																							✓			✓
ZINN, WILLIAM (?–)		✓																								
ZINZADSE, SULCHAN F. (1925–)		✓																								
ZIPP, FRIEDRICH (1914–)			✓					✓													✓		✓			✓
ZOEPHEL, KLAUS (1929–)																	✓									
ZONN, PAUL (1938–)										✓	✓						✓					✓	✓	✓	✓	
ZUPKO, RAMON (1932–)									✓	✓							✓									
ZWILICH, ELLEN T. (1939–)	✓																				✓					

PUBLISHERS' CODES

Adler	Edition Adler, Berlin
Affil	Affiliated Musicians, Los Angeles
Ahn&S	Ahn & Simrock, Berlin
AiblV	Josef Aibl Verlag, Munich
Amade	Amadeus Verlag, Winterthur, Switzerland
AmCom	American Composers Alliance, New York
AMP	Associated Music Publishers, Inc., New York
APSch	Arthur P. Schmidt, Boston
Aquar	Aquarius Music, Long Eddy, New York
Arrow	Arrow Music Press, Inc., New York
Artia	Artia Edition, Prague
Assma	Musikverlag Hermann Assmann, Frankfurt
Augen	Augener Ltd., London
Bardi	Bardic Edition, Aylesbury, Bucks., U.K.
Bären	Bärenreiter Verlag, Kassel-Wilhelmshohe, Germany
Barry	Barry & Cie., Buenos Aires
Belai	M.P. Belaieff, Bonn
Benja	Musikverlag Anton J. Benjamin, Hamburg
Billa	Editions Billaudot, Paris
Birnb	Musikverlag Richard Birnbach, Berlin
Blake	Whitney Blake, New York
Bocca	Boccaccini e Spada Editori, Rome
Boelk	Boelke-Bomart, New York
Bomar	Bomart Music Publications, New York
Boose	Boosey & Hawkes, Inc., London/New York
Bosse	Gustav-Bosse-Verlag, Regensburg, Germany
BoteB	Bote & Bock Musikverlag, Berlin/Wiesbaden
Breit	Breitkopf & Hartel, Wiesbaden/Leipzig
BrLib	Manuscript in the British Library, London
Broud	Broude Brothers, New York
BScho	B. Schott's Söhne, Mainz, Germany
Caris	Carisch S.P.A. Editori, Milan
CarlF	Carl Fischer, Inc., New York
Cefes	C. F. Schmidt, Heilbronn, Germany
Chant	Editions Chanterelle S.A., Monte Carlo
Chapp	Chappell & Co., London
CheHa	Edition Wilhelm Hansen/Chester Music, New York, Inc., New York
Chest	J. & W. Chester Ltd., London
Choud	Editions Choudens, Paris
CMC	Carlanita Music Co., New York
Colom	Franco Colombo, New York
ComPr	Composers Press, Inc., New York
CosCb	Cos Cob Press, Inc., New York
Costa	Editions Costallat, Paris
Curti	Martin Curtius Verlag, Berlin
Curwn	J. Curwen & Sons, Ltd., London
DeutV	Deutscher Verlag für Musik, Leipzig
Dobli	Ludwig Doblinger Verlag, Vienna
Donem	Donemus, Amsterdam
Duran	Editeurs Durand & Cie., Paris
EBMar	Edward B. Marks, New York
ECSch	E.C. Schirmer, Boston
EdMod	Edition Modern, Munich
EdMus	Edition Musicus N.Y., Inc., New York
EdSoc	Editions Sociales Internationales, Paris
Elkan	Elkan-Vogel Company, Inc., Philadelphia
EMBud	Editio Musica, Budapest
EMTra	Editions Musicales Transatlantique, Paris
Engst	Engstrom & Sodring, Copenhagen
Enoch	Editeurs Enoch & Cie., Paris
Eschi	Editions Max Eschig, Paris
ESPLA	Editura de Stat pentru Literatura si Arta, Bucharest
Faber	Faber Music, London
Fazer	AB Fazers Musikhandel, Helsinki
Feedb	Feedback Studio Verlag, Cologne
Foeti	Edition Foetisch Frères, Lausanne
Forbe	Robert Forberg Musikverlag, Bad Godesberg, Germany
Galax	Galaxy Music Corporation, New York
GenMu	General Music Publishers, New York
Gerig	Musikverlage Hans Gerig, Cologne

Graph	Music Graphics Press, San Diego
Gulbe	Fundaçaõ C. Gulbenkian, Lisbon
HalsC	Halsco Music Publishers, Freeport, N.Y.
Hamel	Hamelle & Cie., Paris
HanCh	Edition Wilhelm Hansen/Chester Music New York, Inc., New York
Hanse	Wilhelm Hansen Musik-Forlag, Copenhagen
Harmo	Harmonia Uitgave, Hilversum, Netherlands
Hendo	Hendon Music, Inc., New York
Henle	G. Henle Verlag, Munich
Heuge	Heugel & Cie., Paris
Highg	Highgate Press, Boston
Hinri	Hinrichsen Edition Ltd., London
Hofme	Musikverlag Friedrich Hofmeister, Leipzig
Hudeb	Hudebni Matice Umelecke Besedy, Prague
Hug	Hug & Co., Zurich
IIMus	Instituto Interamericano de Musicologia, Montevideo
IMBib	Internationale Musik Bibliothek, Hamburg
Inter	International Music Company, New York
IoneP	Ione Press, Boston
IsrMI	Israel Music Institute, Tel Aviv
IsrMP	Israeli Music Publications, Tel Aviv
Jatho	Carl Hermann Jatho-Verlag, Berlin
JFisc	J. Fischer, New York
JosWi	Joseph Williams, Ltd., London
Juill	Juilliard Repertory Library, Cincinnati
Jurge	P. Jurgensen, Moscow/Leipzig
Kalmu	Edwin F. Kalmus, New York
Kerby	E.C. Kerby, Toronto
Kistn	Kistner & Siegel & Co., Leipzig
Kneus	F. Kneusslin, Basel
Krono	Kronos-Musik-Verlag, Dinkelsbuhl, Germany
Kunze	Edition Kunzelmann, Lottstetten/Waldshut, Germany
LautK	Lauterbach & Kuhn, Leipzig
Leduc	Alphonse Leduc & Cie., Paris
Lengn	Alfred Lengnick & Co., Ltd., London
Leuck	Musikverlag F.E.C. Leuckart, Munich/Leipzig
Liena	Robert Lienau Musikverlag, Berlin
Litol	Henry Litolff's Verlag, Frankfurt
MABoh	Musica Antiqua Bohemica, (Artia) Prague
Malco	Malcolm Music, Delaware Water Gap, New Jersey
Manus	Composer's unpublished manuscript
Margu	Margun Music Inc., Newton Centre, Massachusetts
Matho	Collection A.Z. Mathot, Paris
Maure	Maurer, Brussels
MCA	Music Corporation of America, New York
McGMa	McGinnis & Marx, New York
Mento	Mentor Music, Albuquerque, New Mexico
Mercu	Mercury Music Corp., New York
Merio	Merion Music, New York
Merry	Merrymount Music, Bryn Mawr, Pennsylvania
Merse	Merseburger Verlag GmbH, Berlin
Micha	Micha Music, Boston
Mills	Mills Music, Inc., New York
Mitte	Mitteldeutscher Verlag, Halle, Germany
ModJQ	Modern Jazz Quartet, New York
Moeck	Hermann Moeck Verlag, Celle, Germany
Monde	Le Chant du Monde, Paris
Ms/Dn	Music Sales/Dunvagen, New York
Murdo	John G. Murdoch & Co., London
MusRa	Musica Rara, Monteux, France
Nagel	Nagels Verlag, Kassel-Wilhelmshohe, Germany
NeueM	Verlag Neue Musik, Berlin
NewMu	New Music Editions, Bryn Mawr, Pa.
Noetz	Otto Heinrich Noetzel Verlag, Wilhelmshaven, Germany
Nordi	AB Nordiska Musikforlaget, Stockholm
Novel	Novello & Company, Ltd., London
OBV	Osterreichischer Bundesverlag, Vienna
Oisea	Editions L'Oiseau Lyre, Paris/Monaco
Omega	Omega Music Company, New York
Ongak	Ongaku-no-Tomo Sha, Inc., Tokyo
Oxfor	Oxford University Press, Inc., London/New York
Peer	Peer International Corporation, New York
Pembr	Pembroke Music, New York
Peter	C.F. Peters, New York/Frankfurt/Leipzig
Phant	Phantom Press, Rhinebeck, New York
Press	Theodore Presser Company, Bryn Mawr, Pennsylvania
PWP	Polskie Wydawnictwo Muzyczne, Warsaw
Raabe	Raabe & Plothow, Berlin
Rahte	D. Rahter Musikverlag, Hamburg
Ricor	G. Ricordi & Company, Milan
Ridea	Editions Rideau Rouge, Paris
RKing	Robert King Music Co., North Easton, Mass.
Rongw	Rongwen Music Inc., New York
Rouar	Rouart, Lerolle & Cie., Paris
Rozsa	Rozsavolgyi & Co., Budapest
RusMV	Russische Musikverein, Berlin
Russi	Russischer Staatsvelag, Moscow
Salab	Editions Salabert, Paris
Samfu	Samfundet til Udgivelse af Dansk Musik, Copenhagen
SchFr	Schott Frères, Brussels
Schir	G. Schirmer, Inc., New York
Schot	Schott & Co., Ltd., London
Schro	Musikverlag Andreas Schroth, Berlin/London
Scree	Screen Gems-EMI Music Inc., New York
Senar	Maurice Senart & Cie., Paris
Senff	Bartholf Senff, Leipzig

Shawn	Shawnee Press, Inc., Delaware Water Gap, Pennsylvania
Sikor	Hans Sikorski Musikverlag, Hamburg
Simro	N. Simrock, Hamburg
Siren	La Sirène Musicale, Paris
SKABO	Skandinavisk og Borups Musikforlag, Copenhagen
South	Southern Music Publishing Company, New York
SPAM	Society for the Publication of American Music, Inc., New York
Stain	Stainer & Bell Ltd., London
Stein	Steingräber-Verlag, Offenbach
Styri	Styria Musikverlag, Vienna
SudDM	Suddeutscher Musikverlag, Strassburg
Suvin	Edizioni Suvini Zerboni, Milan
Tisch	Musikverlag Tischer & Jagenberg, Starnberg, Germany
Tonos	Tonos-Musikverlag, Darmstadt, Germany
UMEsp	Union Musical Española, Madrid
Unive	Universal Edition, Vienna
UnWas	University of Washington Press, Seattle
Urban	Fr. A. Urbanek, Prague
VAAP	Copyright agency of the former Soviet Union
Valle	Valley Music Press, Northampton, Massachusetts
VarPb	Various publishers
Viewe	Musikverlag Chr. Friedrich Vieweg, Berlin
VNMus	Verlag Neue Musik, Berlin
Weinb	Josef Weinberger, Frankfurt
Weint	Eugene Weintraub, Inc., New York
Withd	Withdrawn by the composer
WrnBr	Warner Brothers, Secaucus, New Jersey
Wunde	Wunderhorn Verlag, Munich
Zanib	Edizioni Guglielmo Zanibon, Padua, Italy
Zenem	Zenemukiado Vallalat, Budapest